Europe For Dummies
1st Edition

D0204694

A List of Handy Foreign-Language Words and Phrases

English	French	Italian	German	Spanish
My name is...	Je m'appelle... (zhuh mah-*pell*)	Mi chiamo... (me key-*ah*-mo)	Ich heisse... (eek *high*-suh)	Me llamo... (male)/ Me llama... (female) (may *yah*-moe/*yah*-mah)
Thank you	Merci (mair-*see*)	Grazie (*grat*-tzee- yay)	Danke (*dahn*-kah)	Gracias (*grah*-thee-yahs)
Please	S'il vous plaît (seel-vou-*play*)	Per favore (pair fa-*vohr*-ray)	Bitte (*bih*-tuh)	Por favor (por fah-*bohr*)
Yes/No	Oui/Non (wee/no)	Sì/No (see/no)	Ja/Nein (yah/nine)	Sí/No (see/no)
Do you speak English?	Parlez-vous anglais? (par-lay-*vou* on-glay)	Parla Inglese? (par-la een-glay-zay)	Sprechen Sie Englisch? (zprek-can zee een-glish)	Habla usted inglés? (ah-blah oo-sted een-glais)
Good day	Bonjour (bohn-*szourh*)	Buon giorno (bwohn *jour*-noh)	Guten tag (*goo*-tehn tahg)	Buenos días (*bway*-nohs *dee*-hs)
Goodbye	Au revoir (oh-ruh-*vwah*)	Arrivederci (ah-ree-vah-*dair*-chee)	Auf wiedersehen (owf *vee*-dair-zay-yen)	Adiós (ah-dee-yohs)
Excuse me	Pardon (pah-*rdohn*)	Scusi (*skoo*-zee)	Entschuldigung, bitte (ent-*shool*-dee-gung *bih*-tuh)	Perdóneme (pair-*dohn*-eh-meh)
I'm sorry	Je suis desolée (zhuh swee day-zoh-*lay*)	Mi dispiace (mee dees-pee-*yat*-chay)	Es tut mir leid (ehs toot meer lyd)	Lo siento (lo see-*yen*-toh)
How much is it?	Combien coûte? (coam-bee-*yehn* koot)	Quanto costa? (*kwan*-toh coast-ah)	Wieviel kostet es? (*vee*-feel *koh*-steht es)	Cuánto cuesta? (*kwan*-toh *kway*-stah)
1/2/3	un (uhn)/ deux (douh)/ trois (twah)	uno (*oo*-no)/ due (*doo*-way)/ tre (tray)	eins (eye'nz)/ zwei (zv eye)/ drei (dr'eye)	uno (*oo*-noh)/ dos (dohs)/ tres (trays)

Europe For Dummies,® 1st Edition

Cheat Sheet

A List of Handy Foreign-Language Words and Phrases

English	French	Italian	German	Spanish
Where is the bathroom?	Où est la toilette? (ou *eh* lah twah-*let*)	Dov'é il bagno? (doh-*vay* eel bahn-yoh)	Wo ist die toilette? (voh eest dee toy-*leht*-tah)	Dónde está el servicio/el baño? (*dohn*-day eh-*stah* el sair-*bee*-thee-yo/ el *bahn*-yoh)
I would like this/that	Je voudrais ce/ça (zhuh vou-*dray* suh/sah)	Vorrei questo/quello (voar-*ray* kway-sto/ kwel-loh)	Ich möchte dieses/das (eek mowk-tah dee-zes/dahs)	Quisiera éste/ése (kee-see-*yair*-ah eh-stay/eh-seh)
...a double room for X nights	une chambre pour deux pour X soirs (oou-n *shaum*-bra pour douh pour X swa)	una doppia per X notte (ooh-nah *dope*-pee-ya pair X noh-tay)	ein Doppelzimmer für X nachts (eye'n *doh*-pel-tzim-merr fear X nahkts)	una habitación doble por X noches (*oo*-nah ah-bee-ta-thee-*yon* doh-blay poar X noh-chays)
with/without bath	avec (ah-*vek*/ sans (sahn) bain (baahn)	con/(coan)/ senza (*sen*-zah) bagno (*bahn*-yoh)	mit (miht)/ ohne (oh-nuh) Bad (baad)	con (cohn)/ sin (seen) baño (*bah*-nyoh)
Check, please	La conte, s'il vous plaît (lah kohnt-ah seel-vou-play)	Il conto, per favore (eel *coan*-toh, pair fah-voar-ay)	Die Rechnung, bitte (dee rek-noong bit-tuh)	La cuenta, por favor (lah kwain-tah por fah-bohr)
Is service included?	Le service est-il compris? (luh sair-*vees* eh-teal coam-pree)	É incluso il servizio? (ey een-clou-so eel sair-veet-zee-yo)	Ist die Bedienung inbegriffen? (ihst dee beh-dee-nung in-beh-grih-fen)	Está el servicio incluido? (eh-stah el sair-bee-thee-yo een-clu-*wee*-doh)

The IDG Books Worldwide logo is a registered trademark under exclusive license to IDG Books Worldwide, Inc., from International Data Group, Inc.
The ...For Dummies logo and For Dummies are trademarks of IDG Books Worldwide, Inc. All other trademarks are the property of their respective owners.

For Dummies™: Bestselling Book Series for Beginners

™

References for the Rest of Us!™

BESTSELLING BOOK SERIES

Do you find that traditional reference books are overloaded with technical details and advice you'll never use? Do you postpone important life decisions because you just don't want to deal with them? Then our *...For Dummies*® business and general reference book series is for you.

...For Dummies business and general reference books are written for those frustrated and hard-working souls who know they aren't dumb, but find that the myriad of personal and business issues and the accompanying horror stories make them feel helpless. *...For Dummies* books use a lighthearted approach, a down-to-earth style, and even cartoons and humorous icons to dispel fears and build confidence. Lighthearted but not lightweight, these books are perfect survival guides to solve your everyday personal and business problems.

> *"More than a publishing phenomenon, 'Dummies' is a sign of the times."*
>
> — *The New York Times*

> *"...you won't go wrong buying them."*
>
> — *Walter Mossberg, Wall Street Journal, on IDG Books' ...For Dummies books*

> *"A world of detailed and authoritative information is packed into them..."*
>
> — *U.S. News and World Report*

Already, millions of satisfied readers agree. They have made *...For Dummies* the #1 introductory level computer book series and a best-selling business book series. They have written asking for more. So, if you're looking for the best and easiest way to learn about business and other general reference topics, look to *...For Dummies* to give you a helping hand.

IDG
BOOKS
WORLDWIDE

EUROPE FOR DUMMIES®

1ST EDITION

by Steven Richards

IDG Books Worldwide, Inc.
An International Data Group Company

Foster City, CA ✦ Chicago, IL ✦ Indianapolis, IN ✦ New York, NY

Europe For Dummies,® 1st Edition

Published by
IDG Books Worldwide, Inc.
An International Data Group Company
919 E. Hillsdale Blvd.
Suite 400
Foster City, CA 94404
www.idgbooks.com (IDG Books Worldwide Web Site)
www.dummies.com (Dummies Press Web Site)

Library of Congress Control Number: 00-103383

ISBN: 0-7645-6190-1

ISSN: 1531-1473

Printed in the United States of America

10 9 8 7 6 5 4 3 2 1

1B/QV/QZ/QQ/IN

Distributed in the United States by IDG Books Worldwide, Inc.

Distributed by CDG Books Canada Inc. for Canada; by Transworld Publishers Limited in the United Kingdom; by IDG Norge Books for Norway; by IDG Sweden Books for Sweden; by IDG Books Australia Publishing Corporation Pty. Ltd. for Australia and New Zealand; by TransQuest Publishers Pte Ltd. for Singapore, Malaysia, Thailand, Indonesia, and Hong Kong; by Gotop Information Inc. for Taiwan; by ICG Muse, Inc. for Japan; by Intersoft for South Africa; by Eyrolles for France; by International Thomson Publishing for Germany, Austria and Switzerland; by Distribuidora Cuspide for Argentina; by LR International for Brazil; by Galileo Libros for Chile; by Ediciones ZETA S.C.R. Ltda. for Peru; by WS Computer Publishing Corporation, Inc., for the Philippines; by Contemporanea de Ediciones for Venezuela; by Express Computer Distributors for the Caribbean and West Indies; by Micronesia Media Distributor, Inc. for Micronesia; by Chips Computadoras S.A. de C.V. for Mexico; by Editorial Norma de Panama S.A. for Panama; by American Bookshops for Finland.

For general information on IDG Books Worldwide's books in the U.S., please call our Consumer Customer Service department at 800-762-2974. For reseller information, including discounts and premium sales, please call our Reseller Customer Service department at 800-434-3422.

For information on where to purchase IDG Books Worldwide's books outside the U.S., please contact our International Sales department at 317-572-3993 or fax 317-572-4002.

For consumer information on foreign language translations, please contact our Customer Service department at 1-800-434-3422, fax 317-572-4002, or e-mail rights@idgbooks.com.

For information on licensing foreign or domestic rights, please phone +1-650-653-7098.

For sales inquiries and special prices for bulk quantities, please contact our Order Services department at 800-434-4322 or write to the address above.

For information on using IDG Books Worldwide's books in the classroom or for ordering examination copies, please contact our Educational Sales department at 800-434-2086 or fax 317-572-4005.

For press review copies, author interviews, or other publicity information, please contact our Public Relations department at 650-653-7000 or fax 650-653-7500.

For authorization to photocopy items for corporate, personal, or educational use, please contact Copyright Clearance Center, 222 Rosewood Drive, Danvers, MA 01923, or fax 978-750-4470.

About the Author

Steven Richards has traveled widely throughout Europe. He is the author of numerous travel guides for Frommer's.

ABOUT IDG BOOKS WORLDWIDE

Welcome to the world of IDG Books Worldwide.

IDG Books Worldwide, Inc., is a subsidiary of International Data Group, the world's largest publisher of computer-related information and the leading global provider of information services on information technology. IDG was founded more than 30 years ago by Patrick J. McGovern and now employs more than 9,000 people worldwide. IDG publishes more than 290 computer publications in over 75 countries. More than 90 million people read one or more IDG publications each month.

Launched in 1990, IDG Books Worldwide is today the #1 publisher of best-selling computer books in the United States. We are proud to have received eight awards from the Computer Press Association in recognition of editorial excellence and three from Computer Currents' First Annual Readers' Choice Awards. Our best-selling ...For Dummies® series has more than 50 million copies in print with translations in 31 languages. IDG Books Worldwide, through a joint venture with IDG's Hi-Tech Beijing, became the first U.S. publisher to publish a computer book in the People's Republic of China. In record time, IDG Books Worldwide has become the first choice for millions of readers around the world who want to learn how to better manage their businesses.

Our mission is simple: Every one of our books is designed to bring extra value and skill-building instructions to the reader. Our books are written by experts who understand and care about our readers. The knowledge base of our editorial staff comes from years of experience in publishing, education, and journalism — experience we use to produce books to carry us into the new millennium. In short, we care about books, so we attract the best people. We devote special attention to details such as audience, interior design, use of icons, and illustrations. And because we use an efficient process of authoring, editing, and desktop publishing our books electronically, we can spend more time ensuring superior content and less time on the technicalities of making books.

You can count on our commitment to deliver high-quality books at competitive prices on topics you want to read about. At IDG Books Worldwide, we continue in the IDG tradition of delivering quality for more than 30 years. You'll find no better book on a subject than one from IDG Books Worldwide.

John Kilcullen
Chairman and CEO
IDG Books Worldwide, Inc.

VIII WINNER
Eighth Annual Computer Press Awards ≥1992

IX WINNER
Ninth Annual Computer Press Awards ≥1993

X WINNER
Tenth Annual Computer Press Awards ≥1994

XI WINNER
Eleventh Annual Computer Press Awards ≥1995

IDG is the world's leading IT media, research and exposition company. Founded in 1964, IDG had 1997 revenues of $2.05 billion and has more than 9,000 employees worldwide. IDG offers the widest range of media options that reach IT buyers in 75 countries representing 95% of worldwide IT spending. IDG's diverse product and services portfolio spans six key areas including print publishing, online publishing, expositions and conferences, market research, education and training, and global marketing services. More than 90 million people read one or more of IDG's 290 magazines and newspapers, including IDG's leading global brands — Computerworld, PC World, Network World, Macworld and the Channel World family of publications. IDG Books Worldwide is one of the fastest-growing computer book publishers in the world, with more than 700 titles in 36 languages. The "...For Dummies®" series alone has more than 50 million copies in print. IDG offers online users the largest network of technology-specific Web sites around the world through IDG.net (http://www.idg.net), which comprises more than 225 targeted Web sites in 55 countries worldwide. International Data Corporation (IDC) is the world's largest provider of information technology data, analysis and consulting, with research centers in over 41 countries and more than 400 research analysts worldwide. IDG World Expo is a leading producer of more than 168 globally branded conferences and expositions in 35 countries including E3 (Electronic Entertainment Expo), Macworld Expo, ComNet, Windows World Expo, ICE (Internet Commerce Expo), Agenda, DEMO, and Spotlight. IDG's training subsidiary, ExecuTrain, is the world's largest computer training company, with more than 230 locations worldwide and 785 training courses. IDG Marketing Services helps industry-leading IT companies build international brand recognition by developing global integrated marketing programs via IDG's print, online and exposition products worldwide. Further information about the company can be found at www.idg.com.   1/26/00

Author's Acknowledgments

First off, no thanks are enough for my editor Kelly Regan, who shared with me the Herculean task of squeezing so much of Europe into so few pages.

My research assistant Jay Sayers did a bang-up job on Scotland, Ireland, and the Netherlands. But he really went beyond the call of duty to test those hospital emergency numbers in the Paris chapter; Jay took a French knuckle sandwich in the face after glancing the wrong way at a car crash involving what turned out to be one very irate Parisian.

I am grateful for the continued support and encouragement from my parents, who taught me how to travel. And finally, I thank Frances Sayers for her invaluable help at every step of the way — from planning the research trip and fielding the faxes to pre-editing the manuscript, unearthing all those fast facts, and putting up with my long hours at the computer.

Publisher's Acknowledgments

We're proud of this book; please register your comments through our IDG Books Worldwide Online Registration Form located at `http://my2cents.dummies.com`.

Some of the people who helped bring this book to market include the following:

Editorial and Media Development

Editors: Alissa Cayton, Kelly Regan

Cartographer: Elizabeth Puhl

Editorial Managers: Christine Beck, Jennifer Ehrlich

Editorial Assistants: Carol Strickland and Jennifer Young

Production

Project Coordinator: Amanda Foxworth

Layout and Graphics: Joe Bucki, Jason Guy, Barry Offringa, Tracy K. Oliver, Rashell Smith, Erin Zeltner

Proofreaders: Laura Albert, Melissa D. Buddendeck, Linda Quigley, Charles Spencer

Indexer: Steve Rath

Special Help
Sherri Fugit, Gregg Summers, Seta Frantz, Brian Kramer, Gwenette Gaddis, Billie Williams, Corey Dalton, Esmeralda St. Clair

---

General and Administrative

IDG Books Worldwide, Inc.: John Kilcullen, CEO; Bill Barry, President and COO

IDG Books Consumer Reference Group

Business: Kathleen A. Welton, Vice President and Publisher; Kevin Thornton, Acquisitions Manager

Cooking/Gardening: Jennifer Feldman, Associate Vice President and Publisher

Education/Reference: Diane Graves Steele, Vice President and Publisher; Greg Tubach, Publishing Director

Lifestyles: Kathleen Nebenhaus, Vice President and Publisher; Tracy Boggier, Managing Editor

Pets: Dominique De Vito, Associate Vice President and Publisher; Tracy Boggier, Managing Editor

Travel: Michael Spring, Vice President and Publisher; Suzanne Jannetta, Editorial Director; Brice Gosnell, Managing Editor

IDG Books Consumer Editorial Services: Kathleen Nebenhaus, Vice President and Publisher; Kristin A. Cocks, Editorial Director; Cindy Kitchel, Editorial Director

IDG Books Consumer Production: Debbie Stailey, Production Director

IDG Books Packaging: Marc J. Mikulich, Vice President, Brand Strategy and Research

◆

The publisher would like to give special thanks to Patrick J. McGovern, without whom this book would not have been possible.

◆

Contents at a Glance

Cartoons at a Glance

By Rich Tennant

page 547

page 127

page 215

page 57

page 7

page 379

Fax: 978-546-7747
E-mail: richtennant@the5thwave.com
World Wide Web: www.the5thwave.com

Maps at a Glance

Table of Contents

Chapter 23: Madrid and the Best of Castile 473

Introduction

● ●

*F*inally, you've decided to take that long-awaited trip to Europe. First, I'd like to congratulate you on your decision. Second, I'd like to assure you that there is no reason to feel overwhelmed. Yes, you have lots of plans to make: where to stay, where to dine, how long to wander in different areas, and how to choose the best activities — but I will help you every step of the way. You've taken the first step in the right direction by buying *Europe For Dummies,* 1st Edition.

About This Book

You have in your possession a reference book, not a history or hand-holding guided tour disguised as a guidebook. Open up this book to any chapter and start figuring out how to make your European travel dreams come true. Or, you may read *Europe For Dummies,* 1st Edition, all in order, too (and I do recommend that, at some point, you get to each of the first ten chapters).

You may also skip right to the passports section if you want to get started on the paperwork or peruse the suggested itineraries if you're feeling at a loss for how to make the best use of your two-week vacation. And maybe you are keen to go to Rome; turn right to the chapter on your most anticipated dream destination and get started on the details.

Please be advised that travel information is subject to change at any time — and this is especially true of prices. I therefore suggest that you write or call ahead for confirmation when making your travel plans. The authors, editors, and publisher cannot be held responsible for the experiences of readers while traveling. Your safety is important to us, however, so we encourage you to stay alert and be aware of your surroundings. Keep a close eye on cameras, purses, and wallets, all favorite targets of thieves and pickpockets.

Conventions Used in This Book

Again, *Europe For Dummies,* 1st Edition, is a reference book, meaning you may read the chapters in any order you wish. I'll be using some standard listings for hotels, restaurants, and sights. These listings allow you to open the book to any chapter and access the information you need quickly and easily.

Other conventions used in this book include the following:

- The abbreviations for credit cards: AE (American Express), DC (Diner's Club), MC (MasterCard), and V (Visa).

- Two prices for everything are provided — first in the local currency and second in the dollar equivalent. These dollar conversions were calculated using the exchange rate listed in each destination chapter and were accurate, well, at the time I was writing that chapter (when the dollar was high).

  Exchange rates can and will fluctuate, and the rate probably will not be the same when you visit. However, because the fluctuations tend to stay within around 10 to 20 percent, these conversions will give you a fair idea about how much you'll be paying (assuming the price itself doesn't go up, of course).

- All hotels and restaurants in this book are rated with dollar signs to indicate the range of costs for one night in a double-occupancy hotel room or a meal at a restaurant, from $ (budget) to $$$$ (splurge). Because of the number of countries covered in this book, these ratings are relative, applied on a city-by-city basis. So a "$" hotel in pricey London may be a quirky bed-and-breakfast (B&B) with mismatched furniture and shared baths; but a "$" hotel in the far-cheaper Prague could well be a centrally located but extremely spartan former convent. The same goes for restaurants: at a rustic "$$$$" joint in Madrid you'll get a delicious, stick-to-your ribs stew for about $22; but a "$$$$" restaurant in Paris dishes up fancy, haute-cuisine dishes that can cost as much as $85 per course. For more specific guidelines, consult the hotel and restaurant sections in each destination chapter.

I've divided the hotels and restaurants into two categories — my personal favorites and those that don't quite make my preferred list but still get my hearty seal of approval. Don't be shy about considering these "runners-up" if you're unable to get a room or a table at one of my favorites or if your preferences differ from mine. The amenities that the runner-up hotels offer and the services that each provides make all of the accommodations good choices to consider as you determine where to rest your head at night. The runner-up restaurants are all enjoyable standbys that are sure to serve up a favorite meal.

Foolish Assumptions

As I wrote this book, I made some assumptions about you and what your needs might be as a traveler. Here's what I assumed about you:

- You may be an inexperienced traveler looking for guidance when determining whether to take a trip to Europe and how to plan for it.

- You may be an experienced traveler, but you don't have a lot of time to devote to trip planning or you don't have a lot of time to spend in Europe once you get there. You want expert advice on how to maximize your time and enjoy a hassle-free trip.

✔ You're not looking for a book that provides all the information available about Europe or that lists every hotel, restaurant, or attraction available to you. Instead, you're looking for a book that focuses on the places that will give you the best or most unique experience in Europe.

If you fit any of this criteria, then *Europe For Dummies,* 1st Edition, gives you the information you're looking for!

How This Book Is Organized

Europe For Dummies, 1st Edition, is divided into six parts. The first two parts cover planning and travel skills you'll want on the road. The next three parts divide Europe into three regions; you'll get the lowdown on 15 of Europe's most popular destinations, and all destinations read as mini-guidebooks. You'll find all the scoop you'll need to conquer each city: historical background, local customs, the best hotels and restaurants for every budget, out-of-the-way gems, and more. I'll even recommend how much time to spend at each major attraction. The last part includes the famous Part of Tens chapters as well as two appendixes packed with helpful travel info you can use on the go.

Part I: Getting Started

This part covers where to go, how to link it all together, and how to figure out how much your dream trip will cost. I'll give you my picks of the best destinations and sights, the most fun-packed itineraries to fit your interests and vacation schedule, and specialized tips. These tips are for students, seniors, families, the physically challenged, and gay and lesbian travelers.

Part II: Ironing Out the Details

If you're looking for a deal (and isn't everybody?), in this part I'll teach you the tricks of the trade for finding the best prices on plane tickets, rail passes, and car rentals. I'll help you find the best hotel at any price range and reveal all the best budgeting tricks so you may travel Europe without breaking the bank. You'll apply for passports, make reservations, buy trip insurance and talk about health issues, deal with customs, and find out how to keep in touch while traveling. I'll do everything but help you pack!

Part III: The British Isles

First, this part tackles London and side trips in England to Bath, Salisbury and Stonehenge, and Oxford. Then you'll head north to Edinburgh and other Scottish highlights such as Loch Ness, Inverness, and Glasgow. Finally, you will cross the waters to Dublin and the best of Ireland's countryside, from the Wicklow Mountains to the Ring of Kerry.

Part IV: Central Europe

From the much-loved and often-visited city of Paris, you'll pop by the palaces at Versailles and the Gothic cathedral at Chartres. After cruising Amsterdam's canals and Red Light district, you'll explore the Dutch tulip fields, Haarlem, and Hoge Veluwe Park with its Kröller-Müller Museum. You'll hit the most German region in Germany, Munich and Bavaria, where you'll drink beer with oompah bands and explore Neuschwanstein, the ultimate Romantic castle.

You'll raise a glass (of coffee) to the Hapsburgs in genteel Vienna before heading to Innsbruck in the Austrian Alps. And the magical baroque cityscape of Prague rarely disappoints (nor do the Czech Republic's cheap prices).

Part V: Mediterranean Europe

The bright Mediterranean basin has been home to Europe's great Empires. From the multilayered city of Rome, you'll day-trip to the ancient Roman town of Ostia Antica. Florence is the city of the Renaissance, while the nearby Tuscan towns of Pisa, Siena, and San Gimignano help bring the Middle Ages back to life. Venice and her canals remain one of the most beautiful and unique cities on Earth.

Madrid houses great museums and tapas bars, while nearby towns Toledo and Segovia provide medieval respites from city sightseeing. Barcelona, with its *modernisme* architecture and Gothic quarter, is the other great city in Spain you'll visit.

Part VI: The Part of Tens

I have filled the Part of Tens chapters with ten of Europe's must-see sights (and ten overrated ones) as well as ten affordable European souvenirs for $10 or less.

I've also included two helpful appendices in the back of this book that contain lots of handy information you may need when traveling in Europe.

You'll also find a bunch of worksheets to make your travel planning easier — among other things, you can determine your travel budget, create specific itineraries, and keep a log of your favorite restaurants so you can hit them again next time you're in town. You can find these worksheets easily because they're printed on yellow paper.

Icons Used in This Book

Throughout this book, helpful little icons highlight particularly useful information. Here's what each symbol means.

This icon is a catchall for any special hint, tip, or bit of insider's advice that'll help make your trip run more smoothly. Really, the point of a travel guide is to serve as one gigantic "tip," but this icon singles out the nuggets o' knowledge you may not have run across before.

This icon pegs the best bargains and juiciest money-saving tips. You may find a particularly value-conscious choice of hotel or restaurant, a discount museum or transportation pass, or simply a way to avoid spending more than you have to.

When you need to be aware of a rip-off, an overrated sight, a dubious deal, or any other trap set for an unsuspecting traveler, this icon will alert you. These hints also offer the lowdown on the quirks, etiquette, and unwritten rules of the area so you may avoid looking like a tourist and instead, be treated like a local.

This icon, in addition to flagging tips and resources of special interest to families, points out the most child-friendly hotels, restaurants, and attractions. If you need a baby-sitter at your hotel, a welcoming, relaxed atmosphere at a restaurant, or a dazzling site that will delight, instead of bore, your child, look for this icon. I will include information regarding larger, family-sized rooms at hotels and restaurants that serve meals that go easy on your little one's tummy.

Sometimes a great hotel, restaurant, or sight may be a bit out of the center or require a bit of effort to get to. I'll let you in on these secret little finds, and you can rest assured, I won't include any spots that aren't truly worth the energy. I'll also use this to peg any resource that's particularly useful and worth the time to seek out.

Where to Go from Here

Europe For Dummies is different from other travel guides, because it explains anything you may need to know and only assumes the "foolish assumptions" previously mentioned. I don't overwhelm you with more choices than you could ever use or bury you under a ton of information.

I offer to you the best choices in each country, whether you're on a tight budget or a generous expense account. What I don't give you are a lot of marginal choices that you have to read through and reject. I've already done that work for you.

In fact, think of me as your advance scout. These pages are chock-full of insider tips, hints, advice, secrets, and strategies I've collected while crisscrossing the continent. I've explored. I've taken notes. And I've made mistakes — and learned from them — so that you don't have to make the same errors, even if you are a first-time traveler.

I'd like you to keep in mind that Europe is not just a giant museum from the past. Remember that a living and vital culture surrounds you. Open yourself to all the possibilities: new friends, experiences, sights, and sounds. I'll get you to Europe and back, but the rest is up to you!

Bon Voyage.

Part I
Getting Started

The 5th Wave   By Rich Tennant

"And how shall I book your flight to Europe – First Class, Coach, or Medieval?"

In this part . . .

You get out the map again and look at Europe — so many beautiful countries, so many glamorous cities, and so many possible itineraries. Before you jump on that plane, you need a travel plan. Your plan should allow you to visit all the places on your wish list without having to second mortgage your home. This part guides you through all the necessary steps that you need to take in order to build your ideal travel plan. For example, you get insider advice on how to avoid common pitfalls. In addition, the following chapters introduce you to Europe, help you draw up your dream itinerary, prepare a budget, and find the resources that cater to every sort of traveler — from students to seniors and everyone in between.

Chapter 1

Discovering the Best of Europe

· ·

In This Chapter

▶ Checking out the must-see sights

▶ Learning the misconceptions before you go

▶ Locating the most popular sights to see in Europe

▶ Enjoying good food and drink along the way

▶ Noting every city, town, and village this book covers

· ·

*Y*ou need to get started on plenty of details a few months before you leave — things such as passports (Chapter 10), rail passes (Chapter 7), plane tickets (Chapter 6), and traveler's checks (Chapter 9). But for now, just sit back and dream of the possibilities.

Going to Europe: The Cultural Attractions

Europe has some of the world's greatest museums, such as the **Louvre** in Paris, the **Vatican** in Rome, the **Prado** in Madrid, the **British Museum** in London, and the **Uffizi** in Florence. European museums cover the history of art from classical busts to Renaissance frescoes to impressionist landscapes and post-modern sculpture.

Hand in hand with the museums go the great cathedrals and churches of Europe, from marveling at the diversity of gargoyles of Paris's **Notre Dame** to gaping at Michelangelo's *Pietà* in Rome's **St. Peter's** and everything in between (Chartres' **Cathedral,** Venice's **St. Mark's, Salisbury,** Barcleona's **Sagrada Famiglia,** Florence's **Duomo,** and so on).

Europe is the wellspring of Western culture. People think in terms of centuries and millennia here, not decades. You can dip into history at just about any point. From 3,000 to 1,500 years ago, you can see remnants of the ancient Greek and Roman empires, with half-ruined temples at **Acropolis** and **Agora** in Athens, **Delphi** in inland Greece, and the **Roman and Imperial Forums** in Rome. I haven't even mentioned the ultimate sports arena, Rome's **Coloseum,** the Roman ghost town of **Ostia Antica,** and other prehistoric sites such as **Stonehenge** in England and **Akrotiri** on the Greek island of Santorini, and **Celtic ruins** in Ireland and even under the square in front of Notre-Dame in Paris.

Europe

The Dark Ages and Middle Ages from a.d. 500 to 1500 have left castles strewn from the **Tower of London** to the papal stronghold to **Castel Sant'Angelo** in Rome. Also in this era, the major cities of today really developed, leaving us with cobblestone medieval quarters to explore, such as the **Altstadt** of Bern, the **Staré Město** in Prague, **Trastevere** in Rome, and the **Barri Gòtic** in Barcelona. Tiny hilltowns and hamlets also sprung up in this period, and this book describes the best of them, from **Chartres** in France to Austria's **Innsbruck,** the Tuscan hill towns of **Siena** and **San Gimignano,** and Spain's time capsules such as **Toledo** and **Segovia.**

Then of course, came the Renaissance and baroque eras, filling the great museums described previously with works by the likes of Giotto, Leonardo da Vinci, Michelangelo, Botticelli, Raphael, Rembrandt, Dürer, Titian, and Caravaggio.

As often as a European itinerary seems like a laundry list of historic and artistic sightseeing, some people just head over to sample the culture. These travelers take the pulse of a different sort of lifestyle, immerse themselves in Old World atmosphere, and sip *café au lait* at a sidewalk cafe in Paris while watching the street parade of life go by and writing postcards to jealous friends back home.

A cultural exploration of this type may include sipping a liter of Munich's tastiest brew in a Bavarian bierhalle, a basket of warm pretzels in front of you, and an oompah band in the background. Or you can visit Barcelona for a tapas bar crawl, seizing the opportunity to stroll the crowded parks and sample tasty tidbits all evening.

Attending one of London's West End theaters is a great way to spend an evening. Alternatively, you can view an opera in Vienna's extravagant **Staatsoper** (or visit the church on the grounds of the lavish **Hofburg Palace** to hear a performance by the famed Boys Choir), a church chamber orchestra in Prague, or the ruins of an ancient Roman theater above Florence for some classical music beneath the open sky. Hit the latest, hottest clubs in London, and make a round of the Prague beer halls.

And while the words "road trip" in the United States summon images of Route 66, theme parks, and the biggest balls of twine in Minnesota, Europe has its share of spectacular scenic drives as well. Flit from hill town to medieval hill town through the wine-soaked arcadia of **Tuscany**'s Chianti region. Wind your way slowly up the skyscraping highways and over the dramatic mountain passes of the **Swiss Alps.** If you want to view a stunning coastline, colorful fishing villages, and prehistoric Celtic sites, take a drive around the **Ring of Kerry** on the southwest coast of Ireland.

A trip to Europe is staring at Michelangelo's **Sistine Chapel** ceiling in Rome. It's sitting atop the **Schilthorn,** surrounded by peaks covered with snow and glacier-filled valleys, while eating your breakfast. It's eating lunch on the Greek island of Santoríni hundreds of feet above the Mediterranean amidst the ruins of a Mycenean city.

It's sailing past decaying palaces and sinking churches on Venice's Grand Canal for the price of a bus ticket. It's draining creamy mugs of Guinness and clapping along to traditional Celtic music while on a pub-crawl through Dublin. It's guiltlessly splurging on that five-star meal in the mecca of haute cuisine, Paris. Europe is yours to discover. This book opens the doors.

Understanding Some Misconceptions

Don't allow common misconceptions to change or restrict your itinerary or to color your impressions before you even set foot in Europe. Anticipate little, assume even less, and go into the experience anticipating a wonderful time. Some of the things you won't find in Europe, but you may think you will, include:

- ✔ **Overly rude Parisians.** Parisians may not welcome you as warmly as, say, a Sicilian trattoria owner might. However, they won't treat you like a used handkerchief, either. As long as you make the attempt to get the accent right, they will eventually warm up to you.

- ✔ **Italian spaghetti and meatballs.** Many American versions of European foods differ drastically from the cuisines that inspired them, and this dish is the perfect example. It's an American invention, plain and simple. Luckily, the original European dishes almost always outshine their Americanized counterparts.

- ✔ **Germans in lederhosen.** Europeans don't often wear "traditional costumes," except at festival times — or in folk villages set up for the tourists, such as Colonial Williamsburg on this side of the pond. Sure, you will encounter little old ladies all bundled in black and farmers sporting wool caps and slacks, but don't expect everything and everyone in Europe to be quaint or behind the times. Remember, aside from a few New York designers, Paris and Milan set the pace for cutting-edge fashion.

- ✔ **Terrorist attacks.** Your chances of getting killed by a terrorist, either in the air or anywhere abroad, are virtually nil. Statistically, you are more likely to get hit by lightning at home (honest). As long as you steer clear of danger areas such as Bosnia, you shouldn't have any trouble.

- ✔ **An insurmountable language barrier.** If you know just a few key words and can pantomime, you'll make yourself understood just about anywhere.

Everywhere You Want to Be: What This Book Covers and Why

Europe is huge and rich with possible destinations. Choosing the 15 top cities to cover was tough, but a guidebook only contains so much room, and you only have so much time in your vacation schedule!

As I said in the introduction's "Foolish Assumptions," most of you are first-time travelers to Europe — or this is the first time you're going it alone without a tour. So, I've settled on the 15 must-see cities and the best of all possible side-trips from each to try and give you the true, wide-ranging flavor of all that Europe has to offer.

As you're about to see, however, even the fraction of Europe that made the cut will provide a phenomenal amount of sightseeing and experiences to last a lifetime.

The splendors of the British Isles

The best place to start is **London,** capital of the old British Empire (a colonial power mightier even than Ancient Rome, which has provided the British Museum with the single richest collection of cultural artifacts in the world). From the medieval Tower of London where Henry VIII's wives lost their heads to the neo-Gothic halls of Westminster, where you can watch Parliament in heated debate, London offers a wealth of sightseeing possibilities.

It vies with New York as the hotbed of English-language theater, and its museums cover everything from Old Masters (National Gallery) and decorative arts (the Victoria & Albert Museum) to naval history (Greenwich's Maritime Museum) and World War II (the War Cabinet Rooms). It contains the pomp and circumstance of the royal family and the bump and grind of the trendiest nightclubs. You can dine on everything from pub grub to Indian fare to modern British fusion cuisine.

Easy daytrips from London include the Georgian splendors and Roman ruins of **Bath,** the mysterious prehistoric stone circles of **Stonehenge** and **Avebury,** the Gothic cathedral of **Salisbury,** and the *sine qua non* of world academia, the hallowed halls of **Oxford** University (see Chapter 11).

Edinburgh, the capital of Scotland, is a vibrant university town whose old city is presided over by one of the best glowering castles in Europe, and whose Georgian new city is a genteel grid of streets for shopping and finding cheap townhouse accommodations. You can haunt the pubs once frequented by local son Robert Louis Stevenson, learn about Scottish impressionism at the National Gallery, and stroll the Royal Mile in search of tartan scarves and memorable sights (from the hokey whisky tour to the royal Holyrood Palace).

You can also day-trip to **Inverness** and search for the **Loch Ness Monster** from the ruins of Urquart Castle, or head down to happening **Glasgow,** an industrial city revitalizing itself as a cultural center (see Chapter 12).

While the Irish capital of **Dublin** has its charms, such as admiring the *Book of Kells* at Trinity College, exploring Celtic history at the Archaeological Museum, following in the footsteps of James Joyce and other Irish scribes, and pub crawling through Temple Bar — the best way to enjoy Ireland is to rent a car and drive through the Irish countryside.

To that end, I have left plenty of room for the passage tombs at **Newgrange,** the Celtic crosses and windswept heaths of the **Wicklow Mountains** and **Glandalough,** and the fishing villages and ancient sites of the **Ring of Kerry** and **Dingle Peninsula** (see Chapter 13).

The heart of the continent: Central Europe and the Alps

Many people consider **Paris** the capital of European sightseeing. From the masterpieces in the Louvre (quite possibly the world's greatest art museum) and the impressionists collection of the Musée d'Orsay to climbing the Eiffel Tower, cruising the Seine, or simply whiling the day away at the sidewalk tables of a cafe in the St-Germain-de-Pres or Marais neighborhoods, Paris has enough to keep you busy for a lifetime. And I haven't even mentioned the bistros, brasseries, and boîtes of the city, where you can sample everything from the finest five-star kitchens in town to cheap fixed-price menus with local workers.

But do take the time to day-trip out to one of Paris's fantastic palaces from the age of Divine Monarchs: over-the-top **Versailles,** the greatest royal residence in Europe. Also don't miss one of the world's great Gothic cathedrals at **Chartres,** a holy spot since ancient Druid days (see Chapter 14).

Amsterdam is as famed for its examples of Dutch tolerance (from the libidinous — the Red Light district and "smoking" cafes — to the serious — the Dutch house that hid Anne Frank and her family during the Nazi occupation) as it is for its canals lined by genteel seventeenth-century town houses and artistic giants such as Rembrandt and van Gogh. And don't forget the Indonesian feasts in the Leidesplein district, rib-sticking dinner pancakes, and local brews Heiniken, Amstel, and gin.

Nearby, you can sample a less hectic Dutch way of life in the smaller city of **Haarlem,** tour tulips, windmills, and re-created villages in the countryside. You can also ride bikes for free in **Hoge Veluwe National Park** with its **Kroller-Müller Museum** dedicated to van Gogh and other modern-era artists (see Chapter 15).

The pulsing heart of life-loving, beer-happy Bavaria is **Munich,** an industrial powerhouse packed with a bevy of fine museums and two outstanding baroque palaces — and host to the biggest fraternity party in the world, the annual September Oktoberfest. You can munch on bratwurst and pretzels in beer halls and stroll the pedestrianized old center and expansive Englisher Garten city park.

Half the fun of Munich is traveling out of town to visit **Neuschwanstein,** the ornate fairy-tale castle (and model for Cinderella's Castle at Disney World) built by Mad King Ludwig. The darker side of history is here too, of course. Just outside Munich, the town where the Nazi party got its start, you can tour the sobering concentration camp of **Dachau** (see Chapter 16).

Over the Alps in Austria, you can sip from the cup that was the Austro-Hungarian Empire in **Vienna,** a city that retains its refined nineteenth-century air such as no other in Europe. Steep yourself in this heritage by climbing the cathedral towers, touring the sprawling complex of Hapsburg palaces at the city's heart, sipping coffee at a famous cafe, exhausting yourself on the masterpieces of the Kunsthistoriches Museum, or waiting in line for standing-room tickets ($3) at the renowned State Opera house. Another popular Austrian destination is **Innsbruck,** a great little town tucked away in the heart of the Austrian Alps (see Chapter 17).

After a quick visit to the Swiss capital of **Bern** to admire hometown boy Paul Klee's masterpieces, see where Einstein came up with $E=MC^2$, feed the town mascots at the Bear Pits, and float down the river with the locals, you can delve into the heart of the **Swiss Alps,** the Berner Oberland region around the towering **Jungfrau** peak. Here, small resort towns and Alpine villages cling to the lips of the mighty Lauterbrunnen and Grindlewald Valleys, surrounded by glaciers and ribbon-thin water-falls accessible by miles of hiking and skiing trails, scenic cog railway runs, and gravity-defying cable cars (see Chapter 18).

Finally, take a foray into Eastern Europe to see how the medieval and baroque masterpiece city of **Prague** has come roaring out from behind the defunct Iron Curtain to become one of Europe's greatest destinations. This dreamy city of fairy-tale spires, castles, and churches is one of the world's top centers for sampling beer (Pilsner and Budweiser both descend from Czech origins) and classical music. You'll find a plethora of cheap concerts every night and in every venue imaginable — from symphonies playing in grand halls to street trios playing under an acoustically sound medieval bridge abutment (see Chapter 19).

Mediterranean charms and ancient history

Rome has both ancient sites — the Forum, Colosseum, and Pantheon are but the beginning — and over 900 churches, starting with St. Peter's and working its way on down through massive basilicas to tiny medieval chapels. It's the city's dozens of museums that house everything from ancient Roman statues, frescoes, and mosaics to Renaissance masterpieces such as Michelangelo's Sistine Chapel ceiling at the Vatican. The cityscape itself is a joy to wander, a tangle of medieval streets and Renaissance-era boulevards punctuated by public squares sporting baroque fountains and Egyptian obelisks, including Piazza Navona, Piazza del Popolo, and the Trevi Fountain.

Whether you want to explore the Paleochristian Catacombs of the Via Appia or window-shop around the Spanish Steps, this book will take you there. It will also direct you in taking day trips out to **Tivoli** (home to the ruins of Hadrian's villa and some palatial gardens) and **Ostia Antica,** a half-decayed ghost town preserved from ancient Roman times. (See Chapter 20.)

Florence is the birthplace of the Renaissance, with more world-class museums and frescoed churches than you can shake a Michelangelo at. This is where you'll find his *David,* Botticelli's *Birth of Venus,* Leonardo's *Annunciation,* and other artistic icons. It also makes a great place to chow down on succulent steaks, sample fine Italian wines, and wander Dante's old neighborhood.

Florence is the capital of **Tuscany,** one of Europe's most (deservedly) popular regions. This is where the tower of **Pisa** leans, where the grape vines terraced up hillsides will be squashed into Brunello or **Chianti** wines, where hilltowns such as **Siena** and **San Gimignano** still bring the Middle Ages to life with tall stone towers, friendly atmospheres, and beautifully decorated churches (see Chapter 21).

Venice seems to float like a dream city on its lagoon, a fantasy world of ornate palaces and tiny footbridges springing over a network of canals. Cars can't even penetrate Venice; the only modes of transportation are boats or your own two legs. The interior of St. Mark's Cathedral glitters with more mosaics than you would think possible, and the works of great Venetian artists such as Titian, Tintoretto, and Veronese cover the walls of both the Accademia Gallery and of the Doge's Palace.

After feasting on Venice's seafood delicacies, take the public ferry to explore the outlying islands of **Murano** (where Venetian glassblowing was invented), **Burano** (a colorful fishing village), and **Torcello** (a desolate, undeveloped island hiding another gorgeously mosaicked church) in the Ventian Lagoon. And don't forget to set aside a day on the Veneto mainland to see the Giotto frescoes in **Padova (Padua)** (see Chapter 22).

The Spanish capital of **Madrid** also grabs you with its museums, from the Velázquez, El Greco, and Goya masterworks in the Prado to Picasso's *Guernica* in the Reina Sofia. Tour the Royal Palace, take in a professional bullfight, and do a tapas crawl in the old center of town. A tapas crawl involves moving from bar to bar sampling appetizer-sized tapas before indulging in a hearty 10:00 p.m. dinner and resting up to party in the clubs until dawn.

If you still have the energy, take a few days to explore the medieval capital of **Toledo,** the kingly monastery at **El Escorial** (both boasting many El Greco paintings), and the impressive Roman aqueduct and Gothic cathedral of **Segovia** (see Chapter 23).

Barcelona, the capital of Spain's Catalonia region, boasts a great Gothic quarter to explore, *Las Ramblas* (one of Europe's most fun pedestrian promenades), and the work of local early twentieth-century greats. You'll find the work of Picasso, Joan Miró, and especially Gaudí, whose *modernisme* take on art nouveau architecture pops up in everything from private town houses to a city park to the only great European cathedral still (slowly) being built, his Sagrada Familgia (see Chapter 24).

Last, but certainly not least, head off to the heart of the Mediterranean, the ancient Greek capital of **Athens,** a sprawling modern city still overseen by the ruins of the 2,500-year-old Parthenon atop the Acropolis Hill. In between contemporary buildings and souk-like neighborhoods (packed with inexpensive *tavernas* and bargain-friendly shops) lie more crumbling reminders of the Greek Golden Age such as the ancient Agora marketplace, Temple of the Olympian Zeus, and Temple of the Winds. The city's archaeological museums highlight not only Classical Age remains but also statues from the Cycladic era and *Kouros* from the earlier age when ancient Egypt was the arbiter of artistic taste.

The sidetrips from Athens are phenomenal. First visit the romantic ruins of **Delphi,** where the ancient world's premier oracles advised kings and commoners alike. (The riches from this profitable soothsaying business flowed into the creation of a complex of temples, buildings, and theaters, which still sit halfway up the mountainside, overlooking a lush green valley.)

Then we take off for the highlight of the hundreds of islands that pepper the azure waters of the Mediterranean Sea, **Santoríni.** This volcanic crescent of an island sits at the end of the Cyclades, and offers its beaches, white wine, summer nightlife, and Minoan and Mycenean ruins to sun-worshippers from around the world (see Chapter 25).

Chapter 2

Planning When and Where to Travel

· ·

· ·

So when will this trip take place? The usual answer is whenever you can schedule vacation time — when the kids are on summer break or when your workload eases up a bit. This chapter will take you through the pros and cons of traveling to Europe at different times of the year. You'll also find a rundown of the most popular festivals, as well as some strategies for staving off sightseeing sensory overload.

Discovering the Secret of the Seasons

Europe brings few seasonal surprises, for the most part, with the weather being similar to that of the northeastern United States, although you may run into a warm, breezy day in December in Sicily, or a cold snap in summer in Scotland.

Europe tends to be slightly wetter than the United States (not including the Pacific Northwest) in autumn, winter, and spring; and drier in summer (not including Arizona and New Mexico). It does seem to rain an awful lot (or at least more constantly) in England, and the peaks of the Alps never lose their snow entirely.

You should be prepared for all varieties of weather and pack clothes to layer and long underwear, a folding pocket umbrella, and lightweight clothes for the warmer days.

Spring is great because . . .

- ✔ This is the shoulder season, when the weather tends to be pleasantly mild, even if it's sometimes temperamental. It might be cool enough to go skiing in the Alps, and at the same time warm enough to go for a dip in the North Sea off Ireland. Be prepared for rain, cold spells, and/or sudden heat waves.

- ✔ Airlines offer reasonable rates, most of the sights, restaurants, and hotels, are open, and Europe is neither too crowded nor too solitary in shoulder season.

- ✔ The tulips in Holland (and elsewhere) are blooming.

But keep in mind. . .

- ✔ Shoulder season is becoming ever more popular (and crowded) as frequent travelers tire of the summer hordes.

- ✔ The off-season often runs October to Easter, so in early spring, many things may still be closed — from hotels to some sights to "rural tourism," like vineyard visits or farm stays.

Summer is great because. . .

- ✔ Early summer is the most popular time to visit Europe, especially June and July. All the services that cater to tourists open their welcoming arms — this is the top of the season, with the exception of ski resorts.

- ✔ Early summer is when the colorful folk festivals, open-air music, and theatrical performances abound.

- ✔ Lots of other Americans are around to keep you company. The crowds can also be one of the biggest drawbacks.

But keep in mind. . .

- ✔ In summertime, Europe can feel like one giant bus tour. It seems like there are more foreigners than natives around.

- ✔ The prices are highest of the year — especially for airfares and hotels, and the hotels book up quickly.

- ✔ You are going to stand in long lines, sometimes for hours, for the popular museums.

- ✔ Europe in August, especially August 15 through 31, is when you really suffer with the hot weather. Europeans go to the beaches, leaving the cities to the tourists to do with as they will.

- ✔ The sweltering temperature is often unbearable, especially in southern climates.

Fall is great because. . .

- ✔ The bulk of tourists have left, and the crops are in. This is the season for wine and harvest festivals.

- ✔ Fall is the other shoulder season, and you get to enjoy many of the same benefits described for the shoulder season in Spring, earlier in this chapter.

- ✔ The opera and concert seasons for the best companies and grand performance halls in European cities both tend to begin in mid- to late Fall.

But keep in mind. . .

- ✔ The weather can turn on you suddenly, with lots of drizzle, and the occasional downright wintery cold snap.

- ✔ Some tourist facilities — hotels, restaurants, and even some sights — begin closing up for the season in October and November.

Winter is great because. . .

- ✔ Low season in most places occurs from mid- or late November through Easter (excluding Christmas week). Hotel and travel expenses drop and you often have entire churches, museums, or even small towns to yourself.

- ✔ Christmas in Paris — or Rome, or Madrid, or Venice — can be beautiful, and an experience to remember.

- ✔ You haven't really skied until you've been to the Swiss Alps and gone downhill for over an hour without ever having to catch a lift.

But keep in mind. . .

- ✔ You *are* facing winter and you may not want to spend your vacations bundling up, shielding yourself from the cold.

- ✔ The local tourist industries tend to freshen up during this period of calm. You'll find that restaurants and hotels close up for a week or even a month. Museums review and reorganize their exhibits. Churches and monuments are slated for restoration or cleaning. And local transportation, tourist offices, and shops shorten their hours for winter.

- ✔ In winter, some of the most popular destinations close up almost entirely, such as islands, sun-drenched destinations south of the cities, smaller cities, and spas. You shouldn't have this problem in larger, more cosmopolitan cities, such as London, Paris, or Rome.

Partaking in Festivals and Holidays: Keg Parties and Pagan Feasts

A great way to tour is to plan an entire vacation around a single large festival. Even though the traditional sights of the location may be closed, especially in smaller towns, this visit may become your most memorable trip. You can witness a slice of European life most tourists never get to see. Celebrate the festival with the locals, take tons of pictures, and make some unforgettable memories.

Book your accommodations as soon as you can if your plans include traveling to a location where a major festival or other cultural event is taking place. Accommodations are snatched up quickly at festival time, sometimes months in advance. For big festivals in smaller places, such as the Palio in Siena, Italy, all the hotels within the town walls may be sold out over a year beforehand. Instead, you can book a room in a neighboring town.

In case you do want to go to one of these great festivals, here are the top ten festivals in Europe. Country guidebooks, such as *Frommer's,* list many, many more of these festivals. For specific dates or more information, contact the local tourist offices.

- **Carnevale,** Venice, Italy (and just about everywhere else). Carnevale is a feast of food and wine and a raucous celebration of spring — a true pagan holdover grafted onto the Christian pre-Lenten period. The world is turned upside down at Carnevale, where the lowly hobnob with the elite, and everyone has a roaring good time. The whole Christian world celebrates Carnevale (called "Carnival" in Rio and "Mardi Gras" in New Orleans). The most famous in Europe, however, is Carnevale, which is a series of elegant-yet-drunken masked balls held in Venice, which remind one of the old days of Casanova's eighteenth century. But anywhere that you see Carnevale is an experience in itself. You could see chariot parades and wild bacchanal in the Greek city of Pátras; the solemn burial of a sardine in Madrid, Spain; satiric political floats in the port of Livorno, Italy; and flower battles and bonfires in Nice, France. Carnevale starts two or three weeks before Ash Wednesday (usually in late February) and culminates on the final Tuesday, called "Fat Tuesday" (*Mardi Gras* in French). Fat Tuesday immediately precedes the sober period of Lent.

- **Shakespeare season,** Stratford-upon-Avon, England. Fans of great theater will relish this experience. The Royal Shakespeare Company performs its season here, where Shakespeare was born and where he also retired. The Shakespeare trade provides the community with a profitable business, thus they wouldn't want to see this theatre company make its home anywhere else. You can purchase tickets through an agent like Keith Prowse (☎ **800-669-8687** in the United States). The season runs from April through January.

✔ **Easter,** is celebrated across Europe. In London, you can see multi-colored floats parade around Battersea Park. You can hear hooded processioners sing love songs to the Virgin Mary in Seville, Spain. In Florence, you can watch an ox-drawn cart stuffed with fireworks explode in front of the cathedral. Celebrations vary widely between Good Friday and Easter Monday; Easter falls approximately in late March or early April.

✔ **Palio,** Siena, Italy. One of the highlights of the Italian summer is this breakneck, bareback, anything-goes horse race that goes around the sloping, dirt-covered main piazza of medieval Siena. Even a horse who's thrown its rider, which is not uncommon, can take the prize, and whips are used as much on the other riders as on the horses. The parties held before and after the horse race are street feasts to behold, no matter who wins, so take part in them. The horse race occurs twice each summer, July 2 and August 16.

✔ **Running of the Bulls,** Pamplona, Spain. One of the more dangerous festivals you can see is this one where courageous fools dress in white with red kerchiefs and run while enraged bulls chase them through the narrow streets of Pamplona. The wild chase ends when the bulls chase the last few of the fools out into the harbor's waters, after forcing most of the runners to jump the fences for safety. After that, all involved drink much wine, set off fireworks, and, of course, attend the many bullfights. You can enjoy it vicariously via Hemingway's *The Sun Also Rises* or see it yourself from July 6 to 14.

✔ **Bastille Day,** Paris, France. France celebrates its nation's birthday with street fairs, parades, feasts, and pageants, starting with a procession along the Champs-Elysées and ending with fireworks over Montmartre. Bastille Day is July 14.

✔ **Edinburgh Festival,** Edinburgh, Scotland. This festival features the art, dance, film, plays, and music of some of the world's top creative talents and performers for three weeks every August. As one of Europe's premier cultural extravaganzas, it has spawned a **Fringe Festival,** which makes use of even more venues in the town for smaller, more experimental performances. The traditional bagpipes-and-kilt Military Tattoo at the castle is the highlight of this festival. See Chapter 12 for more details.

✔ **Bloemencorso,** Amsterdam, the Netherlands. In a country obsessed with blooms, you can experience one of the major flower festivals with this festival. The event begins with a colorful parade of floral floats in the nearby flower market town of Aalmeer and ends in Amsterdam on the Dam Square. (You won't believe it, but there are no tulips.) The festival takes place on the first Saturday in September.

✓ **Oktoberfest,** Munich, Germany. Welcome to the world's biggest keg party! This festival attracts tens of thousands of people who listen to brass bands oompah, watch as a whole oxen roasts on a spit, and sit under giant tents drinking liter-sized mugs of beer. (I'm told that five million liters of beer are consumed here nearly every year.) Oktoberfest actually begins in mid-September. The first weekend in October is the final flourish. See Chapter 18 for details.

✓ **Christmas,** is celebrated all over Europe. You can enjoy the Christmas fun and festivities anywhere in Europe from a few weeks before the holiday until January 6 (the Epiphany). Christmas is not completely commercialized yet in Europe, luckily. Look carefully and you can see crèches (Nativity scenes) in public squares and church chapels across the continent. Some of these crèches are live, some ultratraditional, and others are post-modern. I love one in Naples where the holy manger seems an insignificant detail in a very Italian Bethlehem, complete with pizza parlors. On Christmas Eve, you can go to Oberndorf, north of Salzburg, Austria, to sing *Silent Night* in the town where it was written, or receive a blessing from the Pope on Christmas Day when he leans out his window in Rome at noon to give a mass blessing that is broadcast around the world.

Adopting Easy Trip-Planning Tips

When planning your trip, both the whole trip and the daily schedule, add some spontaneity to your itinerary. Leave some elbow room in the agenda, allowing both for relaxation en route and for changes in your plans. Plan at least two days for doing little or nothing for every 10 to 15 days of rigorous sightseeing. You never know when you'll want to take advantage of unexpected opportunities like a day trip or a festival, or when you may want to spend more or less time in a place once you get to know it.

Often, travelers returning to Europe for the second or third time discover that they can see so many sights outside of the major cities that they aren't taking trains and staying in hotels on their subsequent visits, but rather are renting cars and staying in villas. They go hill-town-hopping and explore one tiny corner of Europe at a time, which enables them to travel at a leisurely pace away from the crowds and pressures of a rigorous sightseeing schedule in the big city. But on your first visit, you probably want to visit as many major cities and sights as possible, and there's nothing wrong with that.

The whirlwind tour is still the best way to plan your first-time visit because you get a sampling of everything, so you know which parts of Europe to return to and explore in more depth. The whirlwind tour also lets you get all the "required" sights out of the way, so when you come back (and you *will* return), you can concentrate on checking out

Europe's lesser-known sights on your own. When you realize how enjoyable and effortless travel here is, it will be so easy to come back; you can't exhaust Europe in one trip. I've been returning for 15 years and haven't even come close to seeing all I want to see.

Seeing it all without going nuts

The idea of planning a large-scale trip can seem overwhelming — so much history and culture, so little time! Here are six ways to maximize your time and still see as much as you'd hoped.

- ✔ **Don't duplicate types of sights.** You know that every sight in Europe is unique and worth seeing in its own right. But let's face it: Visit some royal palaces or Gothic cathedrals, and they all start to look the same. Pick one and move on.

- ✔ **Stay centrally located.** Use your limited time to see as much of Europe as you can, rather than taking days to travel to a peripheral corner, especially on your first trip. Think about skipping some of the more geographically remote countries, such as Scandinavia, Portugal, Spain, and especially Greece, because it takes forever to travel to them. See Parts III through V to help you choose destinations that keep this idea in mind.

- ✔ **Select side trips prudently.** I highly recommend daytrips ordinarily because they add variety. But pick your excursions wisely, and make sure these trips do not take time away from the major city you're visiting. If you're in Florence for just one day, don't plan to see Pisa because you'll end up seeing neither. Reserve a full day to see any destination that's more than a city bus ride away.

- ✔ **Go your separate ways.** If you plan six days in London to accommodate the sightseeing wishes of each member of the family, you're wasting time unnecessarily. You don't have to tour Europe as Siamese triplets. Your partner can spend a few more hours in the British Museum and your kids can take a tour out to Windsor Castle while you check out Shakespeare's Globe Theatre. That way you all spend a single afternoon doing what would have taken a whole day and a half otherwise.

- ✔ **Practice extreme time-saving techniques.** No matter how pretty the countryside en route is, you can save a lot of precious vacation time by taking night trains between major cities so as not to use a whole day just getting from point A to point B, even though this may not be the most comfortable way to spend the night. But this way you can be up early to get into a museum before the crowds, and then take a siesta later with the locals.

- ✔ **Know that you will probably come back.** Go ahead and assume that you'll be back. Europe still has a lot left to see, no matter how much you pack in. Europe will wait for you.

Doing museums: Nine ways to make it more enjoyable

Europe has generated quite an output of history and art over the past millennium, and you'll feel like you've seen it all by the time your vacation's over. These hints can help you get the most out of your visits to the great museums without overloading your brain.

- ✓ **Plan to go to big museums twice.** Spread the visit over several days, if you have the time and inclination, because some museums are just too big to get through in one day. Consider this strategy for the Louvre, Prado, Vatican, British Museum, Uffizi, and the National Gallery (London).

- ✓ **Go your separate ways.** You and your companions don't have to stick together in museums and spend all your time looking at the same paintings because nothing is as subjective as taste in art. You can each go through at your own pace and peruse what pleases each of you if you part ways at the front door and set a time to meet. This strategy also gives you and your companions some time apart. (Even the closest of friends and family get on each other's nerves after a while.)

- ✓ **Try out the audio tour.** Audio tours in museums are much improved since the early 1990s. Visitors no longer have to deal with those barely understandable cassette audio guides that make everyone go in a big group from one masterpiece to the next. Now, most audio tours are digital contraptions that look like elongated cellular phones. The exhibited works have numbers next to them, which you just punch into the wand's keypad, and it then gives you the facts and background of the work, artist, era, and so on. You can just press stop when you want to and continue on to the next painting. That way, you get the lowdown on the works that intrigue you, and you tour the museum at your own pace.

- ✓ **Do the guided tour thing.** You can learn from a certified expert a lot more information than you would learn on your own. These experts explain the background and significance of the most important works and can answer all of your questions.

- ✓ **Do your homework.** When you have informed yourself as to what you're looking at, the art can be much more engaging and interesting. Whether you skim your guidebook for the information or take a class in art history before your trip, a little brushing up on European artists and movements can enrich any museum-going experience.

- ✓ **Make it fun with cartoon balloons.** Look for humorous details the artist included, and try putting dialogue next to the figures on the canvas (on your own piece of paper, that is!). Any large canvas of a courtly scene or a banquet usually features details like two servants getting frisky with each other in the background, or a monkey and dog eyeing each other warily under the table. Most of us get a little punchy after too many hours spent soberly contemplating creative genius. Feel free to make up stories to go with the scenes.

✔ **Keep the museum hours in mind.** In the later hours, museums empty out, especially the big museums that may stay open until 7:00 or 8:00 p.m. In a recent summer trend, some museums may stay open as late as 10:00 p.m. or even midnight. If you are a fan of museum books and postcards and plan to stay until closing, check to see when the gift shop closes. Gift shops often close 30 minutes before the museum itself closes.

✔ **Spend your time on the masterpieces.** Even a moderate-sized museum can overwhelm you if you don't pace yourself. You don't have to feel obligated to see it all. Just concentrate your energies on select paintings on your first visit, or if you only have limited time. Many museums include a list of the masterpieces on their floor plans and you can skip whole wings that you don't feel like going through.

✔ **See the pieces that you want to see.** Art is not supposed to be a chore — it's supposed to be enjoyable. It's just as nice to go through a museum and just look at the paintings, pause at the ones you are most interested in and study them, and continue on without even reading the placard that informs of the title, artist, and background information.

Dealing with cultural overload: The Stendhal syndrome

The French writer Stendhal, while once visiting Florence, was so over-whelmed by the aesthetic beauty of the Renaissance and exhausted by trying to see absolutely everything that he collapsed. Stendhal's case is an extreme one, perhaps, but he's not the last one to break down from too much Europe.

Even if you don't faint in the piazza, you may become irritable and tired, catch a cold, or just stop caring whether you see another Giotto fresco in that church. You can really start wearing down after a few days or weeks of full-steam-ahead sightseeing, believe me. It's time to recharge your mental batteries when the idea of visiting the Louvre makes you merely groan and want to take a nap.

Check out these hints for remedying traveler's burnout:

✔ **Just because something's famous, don't feel obligated to do or see it.** If you're going to wear yourself out, do it on the stuff you like. Feel free to skip what doesn't interest you and go see what really floats your boat.

✔ **Pace yourself.** Go a little bit at a time in soaking up the variety of Europe's cultural offerings. Schedule in rest periods. I say again what is worth repeating: Leave room to picnic, to breathe, and to stop and smell the cappuccino. Do not pack too much into either your trip itinerary or your daily sightseeing agenda.

✔ **Put variety into your sightseeing.** Visit a church, ruin, park, or relax in a cafe in between sights. Don't hit one big museum after another. Give other areas of your brain a workout for a while. Your whole trip doesn't then blur into one large, colorful mirage of Gothic cathedrals and old masters from which your memory can't distinguish where Prague left off and Paris began.

✔ **Do the siesta thing.** In Mediterranean countries, almost all businesses are closed in the early afternoon anyway, so why not do as the Europeans do: Take a nap! A nap in the middle of the day can do you a world of good, both physically and mentally. You can learn to take a *riposo* along with the Italians, and you'll not only appreciate the culture more, but also be able to finish the sightseeing in Florence that Stendhal started.

✔ **Take a break when the sightseeing starts getting to you.** Whatever it takes to bring your cultural appreciation back from the brink, do it. Take a day to get off the beaten path. Go shopping. Go to a soccer match. But stop trying to rack up sightseeing points. Sit down and write out all those postcards you mean to send. Chances are you'll get psyched to get back on the sightseeing wagon after describing the once-in-a-lifetime experiences you've had and the wonders you've seen to your friends back home.

Knowing How Much Time to Spend in Each City

Table 2-1 gives you an idea of the minimum amount of time that it's reasonable to take to "see" Europe's major cities. "Seeing" a city includes settling in, seeing the major sights, getting a taste for the place, and maybe going on one daytrip. You'll definitely miss important sights if you spend less time than recommended here. Also remember to add on at least an extra day for each side trip or major excursion you want to take.

Remember that it's not possible to run out of things to do if you stay longer in any city. I highly recommend more days than this minimum for some cities in particular, such as London, Paris, or Rome. You couldn't exhaust most of these cities in a lifetime of diligent sightseeing.

Table 2-1	Allocating Time for Each City on Your List
City	*Time That Needs to be Spent*
Amsterdam	2 to 3 days
Athens	1 to 2 days
Barcelona	2 to 3 days
Bern/Alps	1 to 3 days
Florence	2 to 3 days
Edinburgh	1 to 2 days
Dublin	1 to 2 days
London	3 to 4 days
Madrid	2 to 3 days
Munich	1 to 2 days
Paris	3 to 4 days
Prague	2 to 3 days
Rome	3 to 4 days
Venice	2 to 3 days
Vienna	1 to 3 days

Chapter 3

Five Great European Itineraries

● ●

In This Chapter

▶ Seeing the best of Europe in two weeks

▶ Experiencing Europe: The three-week Grand Tour

▶ Taking in two weeks of the best art and architecture

▶ Spending a romantic week with your lover

▶ Bringing the kids: A week of fun for ages 5 to 105

● ●

*B*efore you start gathering information on specific destinations or looking for airfares, you'd probably like to know a bit more about the trip as a whole. What can you reasonably expect to do in a given amount of time? How long will it take you to see these famous cities you've always heard so much about? How can you link it all together?

Once you know this information, you can approach your travel agent or look into package tours with an idea of what to expect. Then, you'll be able to hammer out the skeleton of the trip: your very own European itinerary.

All of the nitty-gritty details on just how to arrange the trip will be explained in the following chapters, but for now, just keep reading and see how easy it is to plan and take a vacation to Europe. Choosing all the places you want to visit is the easy part. Figuring out which of them you have time to see, how long to spend in each city, and how to coordinate it all is what takes some work.

Because most Americans get just one or two precious weeks of vacation, I've crafted most of these tours to fit those schedules. I've also included a three-week whirlwind extravaganza if you can carve out that much time for your trip.

You'll notice that these itineraries include the two extra "freebie" days that the weekends snag for you when planning a vacation. Most flights from the United States to Europe leave in the evening, so if you can get off work a little early on Friday to get to your closest gateway city, you get all Saturday in Europe as well. And forget about taking a day to rest when you get home before going back to the office — life's too short; don't bother coming home until the last Sunday. All of a sudden, your "week" is nine days long! Sure, you'll be exhausted at work on Monday, but will you have stories!

Keep in mind that open hours vary from season to season. Because summer is the most popular travel time, I arranged these itineraries assuming summer schedules. You may have to tweak them if you're visiting in the off-season or if one of the days you happen to be in town falls on a Monday, Sunday, or another day when some sights may be closed.

Occasionally, I'll include specific train times and schedules, but remember that this is just to get you thinking about how early to catch a train. Rail timetables can and will change regularly, so always check the train times listed here against more current schedules (Chapter 7 shows you how to do just that).

The "Everything but the Kitchen Sink in Two Weeks" Tour

If you're determined to see as much as you can on your trip to the continent, here's the way to do it. But rest up — you'll be on the go non-stop.

- ✔ **Day 1–4:** Your overnight plane lands in **London** (Chapter 11) early. Spend these fours days as outlined in Chapter 11 — taking one day to side-trip out to **Oxford, Bath,** or **Stonehenge**. This'll get in all the greatest sights and experiences of London, from the National Gallery and British Museum to the Tower of London and Westminster Abbey; from shopping at Harrods and peeking at a session of Parliament to joining a London Walks tour and taking in a Shakespearean play at the Globe.

- ✔ **Day 5–8:** On Day 5, take the earliest Eurostar train through the Channel Tunnel to **Paris** (Chapter 14). Get settled in your hotel, have lunch, and head to the Rodin Museum. Then, leave the sightseeing until tomorrow and instead spend the late afternoon in a classic French cafe, ambling down to the river to take a sunset cruise on the Seine.

  Spend Days 6 through 8 as outlined in Chapter 14 (the "If you have three days" suggested itinerary), marveling at Notre-Dame and Sainte-Chapelle, indulging yourself with the art treasures of the Louvre and Musée d'Orsay, and climbing the Eiffel Tower.

  Leave plenty of strolling time: through the genteel Marais, along the banks of the Seine River, around the bohemian-turned-touristy (but still fun) Montmartre. Day trip to the extravagant Versailles, the palace to end all palaces. Treat yourself to at least one first-class dinner to celebrate your arrival in one of the world capitals of cuisine.

  On the morning of Day 8, be sure to get up early and head to the Gare de Lyon train station to leave your bags and reserve a couchette for tonight's train to Venice (it leaves around 7:00 or 8:00 p.m.).

✔ **Day 9:** When you arrive in **Venice** (Chapter 22), check out the next morning's schedule for trains on to Florence and leave your bag in the lockers; you can live out of your daypack for one day and night, and this trick lets you check into your hotel later in the day.

Then dive into the city of canals (well, not literally). Cruise the Grand Canal on the *vaporetto* (public ferry) to one of Europe's prettiest squares, Piazza San Marco. Tour the glittering mosaic-filled St. Mark's cathedral and ride the elevator to the bell tower for sweeping views across the city and its canals.

Take the "Secret Itineraries" tour of the Doge's Palace at 10:30 a.m. for a behind-the-scenes look at Venetian history and intrigue. Have a snack on your way to check into your hotel in the early afternoon, and then see the masterpieces of the Accademia in the midafternoon. Take a gondola ride before dinner and wander the quiet, romantic streets a while after your meal. Try to get to bed at a reasonable hour, because you'll have to get up early.

✔ **Day 10:** Head to the train station at least 90 minutes before your train (this gives the slow public ferry time to get there). Take the first morning train you can to **Florence** (Chapter 21), call around for a room, and then drop your bags by the hotel.

Have a lunch on the go so you don't waste time that's better spent seeing the Duomo (cathedral), climbing its ingenious and noble dome to get a city panorama, and marveling at the mosaics inside the adjacent baptistery. By 3:00 p.m., start heading a few blocks down to the world's premier museum of the Renaissance, the Uffizi Galleries. Have a Tuscan feast at Il Latini before bed.

✔ **Day 11:** Be in line at the Accademia when it opens so you can see Michelangelo's *David* before the crowds arrive. If you don't linger too long, you can swing by Santa Maria Novella church before lunch for a look at its Renaissance frescoes (a young apprentice named Michelangelo helped out on the Ghirlandaio fresco cycle).

After lunch, while the city is shut down for the midday *riposo* (nap), make your way over to the Giotto frescoes in Santa Croce church, Florence's version of Westminster Abbey and the final resting place of Michelangelo, Galileo, and Machiavelli. On your way back to the heart of town, stop by Vivoli for the best *gelato* (ice cream) you'll probably ever have.

Cross the jewelry shop-lined medieval bridge called Ponte Vecchio to get to Oltrarno, the artisan's quarter, and the Medicis' grand Pitti Palace, whose painting galleries will keep you occupied until closing time at 7:00 p.m. Oltrarno is full of good, homey restaurants where you can kick back, toast your 36 hours in Florence, and vow a return.

✔ **Days 12–14:** Get up extra early to catch the 7:30 a.m. train to **Rome** (Chapter 20), which pulls in around 9:15 a.m. Spend the next three days as outlined in Chapter 20 under "If you have three days." See the glories of ancient Rome at the Forum, Colosseum, and Pantheon, and the riches of the capital of Christendom at St. Peter's and the Vatican Museums.

Rome's world-class museums include both the well known — Capitoline Museums, Galleria Borghese (which you should book before you leave home), Galleria Doria Pamphilij — and the brand new, such as Palazzo Altemps and Palazzo Massimo alle Terme.

✔ **Day 15:** Spend your last full day in Europe outside the big city at **Tivoli,** a nearby hill town full of palaces, gardens, and the ruins of Emperor Hadrian's wildly eclectic villa. Return to Rome in time for dinner and then make your way to the famous Trevi Fountain. It's tradition to toss a few coins in the water to ensure that one day, you'll return to the Eternal City.

✔ **Day 16:** Most flights from Rome back to the United States leave either in the morning or early afternoon. Either way, the day's a wash; you'll spend the morning getting to the airport and the day in the air.

The Three-Week Grand Tour of Europe

Slightly less intense than the two-week tour outlined in the previous section, this itinerary allows a little leisure time to get out and enjoy the countryside, with a few scenic drives and mountain hikes thrown in for good measure.

✔ **Days 1–4:** The first four days of this trip is the same as those under the "Everything but the Kitchen Sink in Two Weeks" trip preceding — **London.**

✔ **Day 5–6:** On Day 5, take an early no-frills flight to **Amsterdam** (Easyjet currently offers several). After you settle in, start your sightseeing as described in the "If you have two days" itinerary of Chapter 15 — relaxing with a canal cruise, ogling all those skinny, gabled seventeenth-century town houses.

Continue with that two-day itinerary, enjoying the masterpieces in the Rijksmuseum and van Gogh Museum, a Dutch-style tool around town on two wheels, titillation in the Red Light District, an Indonesian feast in the hopping Leidseplein neighborhood, and a sobering tour of the Anne Frank House. Dine early on the evening of Day 6, because you need to grab the overnight train to Munich, which leaves around 7:30pm.

✔ **Days 7–8:** First thing to do when you arrive in **Munich** (Chapter 16) is pause at the train station to book an overnight couchette to Venice for tomorrow evening. Spend your pair of days in Munich as recommended in Chapter 16. For the evening of Day 8, know that the overnight train to **Venice** leaves very late (around 11:30 p.m.), so after a rib-sticking dinner, bide your remaining time in **Munich** in true Bavarian style at the Augustinerkeller beer hall, five long blocks past the train station.

✔ **Days 9–11:** When you get to **Venice** (Chapter 22), check into your hotel then head to the center of town. Spend your first day as described as Day One under "If you have two days" in Chapter 22, drinking in the big three sights: St. Mark's Cathedral, the Doge's Palace, and the Accademia Gallery. Spend Day 10 visiting the outlying islands of the Venetian lagoon with their glass and lace making traditions, fishing villages, and glittering church mosaics.

Then, for Day 11, flip-flop the second day described in the chapter's "If you have two days" itinerary — spend the morning in the museums such as the Peggy Guggenheim and Ca' Rezzonico, then the early afternoon simply lost in Venice's enchanting back alleys. Be sure to find yourself in plenty of time to hop on a late-afternoon train to **Florence** (Chapter 21), arriving in time to check into your hotel and grab a late dinner.

✔ **Days 12–14:** As usual, I've already outlined the perfect two Florentine days in Chapter 20: Michelangelo's *David,* the Uffizi Galleries, the Pitti Palace museums, Fra' Angelico's frescoes in San Marco monastery, the Medici Tombs, the cathedral and its dome, Bargello sculpture gallery, and the shop-lined Ponte Vecchio spanning the Arno River.

✔ **Days 15–18:** Starting with an early-morning train to **Rome** (Chapter 20), spend days 15 through 18 exactly as days 12 through 15 on the "Everthing but the Kitchen Sink . . ." itinerary preceding, though be sure to fit in the Trevi Fountain on Day 16.

On the morning of Day 18, take your bags to the train station to check them at the left-luggage office and to book a couchette for the overnight train to Paris before heading out to **Tivoli** for the day. Leave Tivoli by 4:00 p.m. to get back to Rome by 5:00 p.m. to pick up some picnic supplies for dinner on the train. The Paris train leaves around 7:30 p.m.

✔ **Days 19–22:** Spend your four days in **Paris** (Chapter 14) just as in Days 5-8 under the two week itinerary above.

✔ **Day 23:** As in the two-week tour, most flights from Paris back to the United States leave in the morning or early afternoon, so you'll spend the morning getting to the airport and the day flying home.

Two Weeks in Europe for Lovers of Art

For this trip, you can work out the daily sightseeing schedules on your own, depending on what most floats your artistic boat. Most cities have 2½ days of sightseeing time budgeted, which should be enough to give the major museums a good once-over.

We're going to diverge from the "If you have two days" itineraries described in the destination chapters to concentrate on artistic sights in each city.

✔ **Days 1–3: London** (Chapter 11) — Your first order of business should definitely be the medieval, Renaissance, and baroque masterpieces of the National Gallery. The other great art collection is the Tate Gallery, now divided between two buildings on both sides of the Thames; the original neoclassical gallery covers the British greats and the vast new space concentrates on international art in the nineteenth and twentieth centuries (from impressionism to contemporary works).

You may also want to stop by the National Portrait Gallery; it exists more for the historical interest of the subjects, but it has some artistically fine portraits as well (especially by Holbein, Reynolds, and Warhol).

No museum buff should miss the Victoria & Albert Museum, which has London's best sculpture collection (Donatello, Giambologna, Bernini) and a fascinating exhibit on artistic fakes and forgeries, in addition to miles of decorative arts.

If you're into Christopher Wren's brand of Renaissance architecture, the city's full of it; his greatest hit is St. Paul's Cathedral. I can't imagine a trip to London without calling on the British Museum, at least briefly, where you can get the best overview of the ancient world's art forms (Greek, Roman, Egyptian, Assyrian, Asian, Indian, and Islamic).

On the morning of Day 4, catch an early Eurostar train to Paris.

✔ **Days 4–6: Paris** (Chapter 14) — You'll want to explore the treasures of the Louvre over a full day at least. Fans of impressionism and French art in general should devote at least two-thirds of a day to the Musée d'Orsay.

Paris has so many smaller art museums it's hard to choose from among them and nearly impossible to squeeze them all in. Whole museums are devoted to single artists (Rodin, Picasso, Delacroix, Le Corbusier, Dalí), and others are devoted to eras — the medieval at Thermes de Cluny, the modern in the Pompidou.

Two of my favorite, slightly lesser-known art treasures are the Delacroix murals in the church of St-Suplice and Monet's 360° *Waterlilies* in specially built basement rooms of the Orangerie, off Place de la Concorde. At the end of Day 6, hop on the overnight train to Florence.

✔ **Days 7–9: Florence** (Chapter 21) — Reserve one entire day for the Uffizi galleries, a living textbook of Renaissance development. The Pitti Palace's Galleria Palantina covers the High Renaissance and baroque eras thoroughly. Michelangelo's *David* and his unfinished *Slaves* in the Accademia are a must, and Donatello reigns supreme at the Bargello sculpture museum.

Fra' Angelico frescoed his brothers' cells at his monastery of San Marco, and they've set up a fine museum to him there. Florence's churches are so richly decorated I scarcely know where to begin: Giotto in Santa Croce; Ghirlandaio in Santa Maria Novella and Stana Trìnita; Donatello and Michelangelo at San Lorenzo and again in the Museo dell'Opera dell Duomo; and Masaccio in Santa Maria della Carmine (the restored St. Peter's frescoes by him and teacher Masolino); and Santa Maria Novella (his *Trinità* fresco is the first work using true linear perspective in history).

Then there's Brunelleschi's architecture, from the Duomo's dome to Santo Spirito to the Pazzi chapel at Santa Croce. Florence is one place where you'll run out of time long before you run out of art.

✔ **Days 10–12: Rome** (Chapter 20) — Take the morning train here from Florence on Day 10 and start in on the baroque period with Bernini's sculpture in Piazza Navona, Piazza Barberini, and the Galleria Borghese.

The Vatican Museums (home to the Raphael Rooms, the Pinacoteca, and Michelangelo's Sistine Chapel) will take two-thirds of a day. The Capitoline Museums split their collections between ancient sculpture and mosaics and Renaissance and baroque painting. Some smaller museums include the Doria Pamphilij collections and the Galleria Nazionale d'Arte Antica, split between the Palazzo Barberini (near Via Veneto) and Palazzo Corsini (in Trastevere).

Rome's churches are blanketed with art, from Filippino Lippi's frescoes in Santa Maria Sopra Minerva (where you'll also find Michelangelo's *Risen Christ*) to the Caravaggios in Santa Maria del Popolo and Michelangelo's *Moses* in San Pietro in Vincoli. Again, you're unlikely to run out of art to ogle in just three days here.

On the evening of Day 12, get on the overnight train for the long haul to Barcelona.

✔ **Day 13: Barcelona** (Chapter 24) — You should definitely take in the intriguing early Picasso works at the museum dedicated to this hometown hero and make a survey of Gaudí's whimsical architecture in this Catalonian capital.

On this tour, however, Barcelona's more of a way station and a one-day breather before we press on. At the end of the day, hop the overnight train to Madrid, where we'll plunge into its myriad museums.

✔ **Days 14–16: Madrid** (Chapter 23) — Spain is the land of Picasso, Velázquez, Goya, El Greco (by adoption), Murillo, and Ribera. You have a day to devote to the Prado and another day to split between the Reina Sofía museum (home of Picasso's *Guernica*), the Thyssen-Bornemisza Museum, and — if you can stand any more art at this point — the Museo Làzaro Galdiano. Day 16 is spent getting back home.

A Week of Romance, European Style

As with the art tour, I'll leave much of the daily scheduling up to you in this tour — nothing kills a romantic mood more than being hurriedly shuttled from place to place.

✔ **Days 1–3: Paris** — The mere mention of the City of Light conjures up romantic images, so it's a great place to start. See your fair share of Paris's famed museums — the Musée d'Orsay has both French Romantic-era painters and scads of those lovable impressionists, but take time to enjoy the finer points of Parisian life.

Linger at cafe tables for hours, spend an evening strolling Montemartre, have long meals at fine restaurants and cozy bistros, explore Paris's gorgeous parks, take a dinner cruise along the Seine river, and ascend the Eiffel Tower one evening for a panorama of Paris that lives up to its nickname, City of Light.

To indulge in the romance of yesteryear, make a palatial day trip to Versailles, the palace to end all palaces. On the evening of Day 3, board the overnight train to Prague.

✔ **Days 4–5: Prague** — Prague is a city of baroque palaces and mighty fortresses, church concerts and powerful beers, hidden gardens and classical street musicians who play a mean Dvorak. Pass an afternoon delving into Prague's rich Jewish heritage at its synagogues and museums; take a sunset stroll across the statue-lined Charles Bridge.

Spend a day (or at least a morning) exploring Prague Castle, both for its soaring Gothic cathedral and to see how a fortress-city of the Middle Ages looked and worked.

Whatever else you do, try to fit in as many of Prague's delightful evening concerts as you can. At the end of Day 5, hop an over-night train to Venice.

✔ **Days 6–8: Venice** — *La Serenissima*, "The Most Serene" city of canals, palaces, Byzantine mosaics, and delicate blown glass, has made a romantic out of everyone, from Shakespeare and Thomas Mann to Casanova and Woody Allen. Venice has always been a haven of secrets, so I'll leave you to your own devices in exploring.

Don't pass up a spin in a traditional gondola (despite the out-rageous prices). Make sure you have a couple of long, drawn-out Italian feasts by candlelight, a cruise down the majestic sweep of the Grand Canal, and some moonlit strolls through the narrow, winding alleys and over countless tiny canals.

I will suggest one personal favorite among romantic Venetian experiences: set aside one full day to explore the smaller fishing, glassblowing, and lace-making islands in the Venetian lagoon.

✔ **Day 9:** You'll most likely have to fly home from (or at least connect through) Milan, so leave this entire day free for the return trip. Remember in Venice, with its languid pace, to allow at least an hour from the time you leave the hotel until you get to the train station (either to train it to Milan in 2½ to 3½ hours, or catch the shuttle to the Venice airport in 20 minutes).

A Week in Europe the Kids Will Love

For this trip, fly open-jaws into London and out of Rome. Leave plenty of time for the kids to rest, and remember that kids' constitutions and ability to appreciate even the finest art and coolest palace wears out quickly. You may want to spend five hours in the Louvre; the tykes'll be lucky to last two. Take Europe at their pace so you can all get something out of it and have a fantastic, rewarding, and (shh! don't tell) educational time of it.

✔ **Day 1:** Your overnight plane lands in **London** (Chapter 11) early. Check into your hotel, and then head for the Tower of London, London's bastion of the Middle Ages, where knights were knighted, and where even the famous could be held prisoner. The Crown Jewels glitter as brightly as the armor and battleaxe blades on display in the armory-and-torture-device museum, and Henry VIII did away with a couple of his wives there too.

The Yeoman Warders (or Beefeater Guards) give some of the most entertaining tours in all of Europe, turning a millennium of dry history into the most fantastic tales of intrigue and swordplay, kings, and fair damsels alike in distress.

After lunch, head to Westminster Abbey to see the tombs of great poets, scientists, explorers, and kings and queens. In the cloisters, the kids can grab giant sheets of black paper, fat gold and silver crayons, and engage in brass rubbing, a fun pastime (from the nineteenth century) of making imprints from floor tomb slabs featuring knights lying in repose and coats of arms.

From Westminster, you can walk past the houses of Parliament, lorded over by the Clock Tower, in which tolls a bell named Big Ben. You may have time to pop into the War Cabinet Rooms where Churchill's best and brightest kept track of troop movement and planned daring World War II offensives. You can also cross St. James's Park to peer through the gates at the Queen's home, Buckingham Palace (though the changing of the guard is, in all honesty, rather overrated; I didn't particularly enjoy it at age 11, and still find it a big yawn).

✔ **Day 2:** Start off with a cruise down the Thames to **Greenwich,** which still retains a bit of its village ambiance and is home to a bevy of exciting sights. Start off learning about the famed Royal British Navy in the days when the sun never set on the British Empire at the Maritime Museum. Moored nearby is the most famous of the multi-sailed Clipper Ships — and liquor icon — the *Cutty Sark.*

Greenwich is a town of world standards. You can tight-rope walk down the Prime Meridian (the line which separates the Earth's two hemispheres), and set your watch at the source from which all the world's clocks get their reading: by Greenwich mean time.

For a dose of the modern (and a theme park experience that hopefully, will fend off any begging to visit Disneyland Paris once you're in Paris), check out London's newest big sight, the Millennium Dome, whose interactive stations are a cross between a digital-age Epcot and those futuristic exhibits from the old World's Fairs.

Take the late afternoon to relax back in London proper, and this evening get cultural. It doesn't matter if it's a big production musical such as *Phantom,* a cutting-edge play in the West End, Shakespeare performed in the Globe Theatre or under the stars in Regent's Park. Take in whatever you're in the mood for and think the kiddies will enjoy (or at least tolerate). Get to bed early to finish off that jet lag and be ready for a day trip tomorrow.

✔ **Day 3:** Take this day to sidetrip out to **Salisbury,** with its towering Gothic cathedral, and evocative **Stonehenge** where your imagination can run wild over ancient tales of druids and star-worshipers.

✔ **Day 4:** Take the earliest Eurostar train through the Channel Tunnel to **Paris** (Chapter 14). Get settled in your hotel, have lunch, and head to Notre-Dame Cathedral, which you can make even more interesting if you take the time to clamber up the North Tower so the kids can examine those famed gargoyles up close (though Quasimodo — animated or otherwise — is a no-show). On a sunny day, even the most jaded of teenagers can't fail to be impressed by the delicate spectacle of light and color courtesy of Saint-Chapelle's stained-glass windows.

After a quick lunch, spend the obligatory two hours in the Louvre to see the *Mona Lisa* and other artistic treasures. Try to get to quai d'Orsay by 4:00 p.m. (3:00 p.m. in winter) so you can tour one of the oddest sights in Paris, *Les Egouts,* the sewers — as much to see a marvel of nineteenth-century metropolitan engineering as to conjure up images of *Les Misérables* and partisans hiding from the Nazis and Vichy during World War II.

From here, it's just a short stroll to the ultimate Parisian sight, the Eiffel Tower. If your kids are anything like I was at age 12, you won't get away without climbing to, and pausing at, every level up to the top. Here's something fun: have them call relatives from the pay phones halfway up ("Hey, Grandma, guess where I am?").

✔ **Day 5:** In the morning, take your bags to Gare de Lyon train station and leave them in lockers so you can catch the overnight train to Rome tonight (it leaves around 7:30 p.m.).

Then grab the RER out to **Versailles,** the biggest, most impressive palace in all of Europe. Even all this lavishness gets pretty boring pretty quickly, so just take a quick tour of the highlights (a guided tour that reveals the daily life of Louis XIV or something of that nature might hold the children's attention a little longer), and then head out to enjoy the vast gardens. Visit Marie Antoinette's *Hameau* in the gardens' far corner, a fake thatched village she had built so she could sort of slum it as a peasant girl, shepherdess-ing perfumed lambs and feeding ducks on the pond.

Be back in Paris in plenty of time to grab supplies for a picnic dinner on the train and be back at the station by 7:00 p.m.

✔ **Day 6:** Your train pulls into **Rome** (Chapter 20) around 9:56 a.m. Check into your hotel, splash some water on your faces, and head off to the Markets of Trajan, where the kids can wander down a block of an ancient Roman street and explore the empty shops pigeonholing the remarkably intact ruins of the world's first multi-level shopping mall.

Truth be told, this section of the Imperial Fori is a bit more impressively intact than the far more famous Roman Forum across the street, but you'll still want to wander through that seat of Roman Imperial power — if only to pose as Vestal Virgins on the few empty pedestals in between the remaining statues in the Vestal's ancient home.

In the middle of touring the Forum, detour out the back door to pop into the portico of Santa Maria in Cosmedin church and test your children's veracity with the help of the Mouth of Truth à la Gregory Peck and Audrey Hepburn (there are also two midget temples here to admire, and just around the corner, the Circus Maximus, where chariot races were once held).

Return to the Roman Forum to finish seeing its sights, and then show the kids the original model for sports stadiums the world over. The massive Colloseum has recently reopened much more of its interior to visitors so the kids can clamber around and imagine tournaments of wild beasts and gladiator fights featuring Russell Crowe (or, if they're a bit older, Charlton Heston).

If you finish with the Forum and Colloseum by 2:00 p.m. — and I suggest you try to — you have enough time to get in a visit to one or two of the Catacombs along the Appian Way. The littlest kids might be afraid, but most will get a thrill out of wandering miles of spooky underground tunnels lined with the niched tombs of ancient Christians. The best catacomb to visit if you only have time for one: the Catacombe di San Domitilla.

✔ **Day 7:** Today, head across the Tiber to the holiest side of **Rome,** St. Peter's Basilica and the Vatican Museums. St. Peter's may yet be another church to drag the kids into, but its sheer size is impressive to anyone — especially if you make sure to tour the subcrypt of papal tombs and climb the dome. Inspire the kids by pointing out that Michelangelo carved his moving *Pietà* sculpture when he was just 19 years old.

Then walk around the wall to plunge into the Vatican Museums, home to loads of ancient sculpture, the Raphael Rooms, and of course, the Sistine Chapel frescoed by Michelangelo.

Just a few blocks away on the riverbanks squats the massive Castel Sant'Angelo, the papal stronghold for centuries and a great medieval fortress to explore.

If you can get there before 5:30 p.m., pop into the Capuchin crypt where generations of silent monks — after whose dun-colored robes cappuccino was named — used their dead brothers' bones to craft mosaics, make chandeliers, or simply stack skulls in a series of cryptlike chapels under the church. Mosey from here to the Spanish Steps in time for the passeggiata see-and-be-seen stroll in the surrounding streets. Be sure before you head to bed for the night that you all stop by the Trevi Fountain (best after dark) to toss in a few coins and ensure your return to the Eternal City.

✔ **Day 8:** It's day trip time again, this time out to **Ostia Antica,** ancient Rome's port. It's an Imperial-era ghost town of crumbling temples, weed-filled shops, mosaic-floored houses, dusty squares, cavernous baths, and paved streets deeply rutted by cart wheels — on a par with Pompeii, but without the hordes of tourists and just a Metro ride away from downtown Rome. Great fun to explore. Picnic amid the grasses in the shade of an armless statue of a forgotten goddess.

✔ **Day 9:** Most flights from Rome leave in the early afternoon, so plan on spending today just getting packed and to the airport two hours before your flight.

Chapter 4

Planning Your Budget

● ●

In This Chapter

▶ Getting a general idea of your trip's total cost

▶ Working out a budget

▶ Avoiding hidden costs

▶ Finding out what things cost in Europe

▶ Discovering hints and tips to save you money

● ●

*E*ven though other guides may gloss over the money issue, this chapter addresses such questions as, "Can I afford this?" and "What are the real expenses involved?" Let's face it, overcoming the expense of a trip to Europe usually makes for the biggest hurdle.

This chapter tells you straight-out how much you should budget for every major aspect of your trip and how to keep the total to a reasonable amount. But that's not all! It also gives you 28 hints, tips, and secrets on how you can trim your budget down to a price that you can actually afford.

Vacationing frugally does *not* mean you must cut out the fun. One of my rules of travel states that the less money you spend while traveling, the closer you get to experiencing the real people and culture. While you can't realistically manage a trip to Europe on just $5 a day anymore, you can go for $60 to $90 a day, plus transportation costs, which is still a great value.

Luxurious extras and greater creature comforts may come with more money, but greater extravagance will also keep you at an arm's length from truly experiencing Europe. Traveling in second class, sleeping in budget pensions and hotels with European families, and eating heartily at local bistros not only saves you money, but doing so also grants you a window into the European lifestyle.

Adding Up the Trip Components

You could make two different trips to the same city for the same amount of time and see all the same sights, but come out with a total bill that differs by thousands of dollars. This book shows you how to maintain the quality of your trip while stretching every dollar along the way.

Traveling frugally means looking for clean, comfortable, central, and safe hotels rather than those with minibars and massage services; knowing when to splurge, when to skimp, and how to spot rip-offs; buying rail passes and museum cards instead of individual tickets; and chowing down on authentic meals in local *trattorie* (family-run restaurants) rather than on continental slop at overpriced tourist-oriented restaurants.

Before you delve into the specific tips on saving money, plan out a rough trip budget. Your total cost will depend greatly on your means and taste. If you look through the listings in the destination chapters of this book, you can easily figure out what price level of hotel and restaurant appeals to you. Just plug the average cost for these accommodations into your expected daily expenses.

- **Lodging.** Hotels range in price from around $60 per double for a budget hotel to $100 and up (into the thousands!) for a luxury room.

- **Dining.** To me, sampling an area's local cuisine plays as large a role in my vacation as sightseeing does. So I allow a generous budget for my meals. I plan to spend $12 on an average lunch — I may spend more on one day for a restaurant meal, and considerably less the next day for a picnic. For dinner, I assume I'll indulge in a big meal every night (appetizer, two courses, table wine or beer, dessert, and coffee) and budget around $22 per dinner (per person, based on dinner for two).

  I don't allow myself any money for breakfast because most hotels offer a roll and coffee along with a room. If not, buying a small breakfast at a cafe costs $2 to $3, which can come out of the lunch allowance.

- **Attractions/Shopping.** Museum hounds and sightseeing fanatics should figure enough cash into their budgets to cover the rising costs of admission. Don't be chintzy here. I usually estimate an average of $5 per sight ($7 to $10 for biggies and $2 to $3 for smaller sights). Therefore, stopping at four major sights per day adds up to $20. Budget at least $5 a day for postcards and other minor souvenirs, more if you're an inveterate shopper.

- **Transportation.** The numbers in Table 4-1 reflect the per-person cost of two people traveling together. Buying the Eurodrive pass with an extra rail day makes sense for this trip. Ride the trains only for long overnight hauls — but validate the pass in time to get a discount on Eurostar — and pay individually for a few short Italian rail hops and the uncovered train ride from the Netherlands/Germany border to Amsterdam.

Use your personal estimates to create something such as Table 4-1. Using the three-week grand tour from Chapter 3 as a sample, I worked out a cost-per-person budget for two adults traveling together. I used only the information and suggested hotels contained in this book (plus 20 minutes online: a quick stop at www.Easyjet.com and a search of the top half-dozen Web travel agents to get airfares and www.raileurope.com for the price of a train ticket from Amsterdam to the Netherlands/Germany border).

As long as you round all dollar amounts up to allow for some padding, you should get a good idea of your costs. As always, overestimating is wise. End your trip with some surprise leftover cash, rather than a disastrous shortfall.

Table 4-1	Expenses for a Sample Trip to Europe
Expense	**Cost**
Airfares (open-jaw NYC–London and Paris–NYC $387; London–Amsterdam $44)	$431
Europass	$296
Individual rail ticket to cover Amsterdam–German border	$25
Three nights in train couchettes ($20 each, because you can reserve a second-class couchette even on a first-class pass)	$60
19 nights in hotels ($30 per person per night, averaged from hotel prices in this book)	$570
44 meals (22 lunches at $12, plus 22 dinners at $22. Breakfast comes with hotel room; if not, grab a quick cafe breakfast and picnic for lunch to offset the cost)	$748
Sightseeing admissions ($20 a day for 18 days, leaving out Paris. For Paris, $36 covers the museums pass plus Eiffel tower admission)	$396
18 days of city transportation ($4 a day)	$72
Souvenirs, postcards, gelato, and miscellaneous stuff ($10 a day)	$220
TOTAL	$2,818

Worrying about the Cost

You *can* afford a trip to Europe. No one should deny themselves the gift of such an experience. As you can see in Table 4-1, you can finance a thrilling three-week trip, which hits most of Europe's must-see sights, for around $2,818 per person. If that amount is still too rich for your blood, don't give up hope — the budget has some leeway.

To trim more money from your budget, for example, you could cut out $60 by sleeping in unreserved compartments on overnight trains (the pull-out seat kind) instead of couchettes. Pack picnic lunches (around $7 a person) and keep your dinner costs down to $18 a piece — plenty for a full, hearty meal — and your dining total magically shrinks from $748 to $550. Reduce your miscellaneous expenses to $4 a day by making your photos your postcards and skipping the souvenirs.

Factoring in these adjustments, the new grand total comes to around $2,428 — certainly not peanuts, but still a great value for everything that you're getting. You could even manage a two-week trip to Europe for as little as $1,000, if you travel smart and keep your budget in mind. The next section presents some tips to help you do just that.

Keeping a Lid on Hidden Expenses

No matter how carefully you plan out a budget, it seems like you always end up shelling out for expenses that you didn't bargain for. The following is a list of common (yet completely avoidable) travel expenses, and ways to keep them from putting a dent in your vacation fund.

✔ **Find out what your rental covers.** When shopping for car rentals, always make sure you know what the quoted rate. Some charges the rental agent may or may not mention to you are: airport pickup/drop-off surcharge, drop-off fee for renting in one city and dropping off in another, CDW (collision damage waiver), local taxes, mileage (limited or unlimited?), and a tank of gas. See Chapter 7 for more information.

✔ **Find out if taxes are included.** In most of Europe, any hotel or tourist taxes are automatically included in the hotel rates. In some countries, however, hotels may quote you the prices before tax — usually in Spain (7 percent), often in France (3–7F/50 cents –$1.15 per person per day, depending on the hotel's star rating), sometimes in England (17.5 percent), and occasionally at expensive hotels in the Czech Republic (22 percent). Always ask to be sure.

✔ **Never place a phone call from a hotel.** On long-distance calls, the markup is often 200 percent. They even charge for what should be free calls to the local AT&T, MCI, or Sprint calling card number. Always use a pay phone (see Chapter 10).

✔ **Look before you tip.** Many restaurants include a service charge in your bill, so tipping another 15 percent is tossing your money out the window. Always ask if service is included. If not, tip 10 to 15 percent just like at home. If service is included, and you felt that your server did a good job, leave a bit extra on the table anyway (one of the currency's smallest bills per person — or in England, a pound coin each).

✔ **Is that great exchange rate for real?** Find out the bank's commission fee or percentage before exchanging traveler's checks or you could end up leaking a little extra cash each time you change money.

Cost-Cutting Tips

No doubt you'll encounter more ways to stretch your travel dollar than I could possibly list in this section. The following list just gives you a taste of all the budget strategies that exist. This book offers lots more advice, hints, and tips on saving money. Some of the following tips highlight the best pointers that you can find elsewhere in this book, but most are new.

✔ **Go in the off-season.** During nonpeak times (October to May, for most major cities and tourist centers), hotels slash their prices by as much as half. Obviously, if you can travel at nonpeak times, do so!

✔ **Travel midweek.** If you can travel on a Tuesday, Wednesday, or Thursday, you may find cheaper flights to your destination. When you inquire about airfares, ask if you can obtain a cheaper rate by flying on a different day.

✔ **Try a package tour.** By making one simple call to a packager or travel agent, you can often book airfare, hotel reservations, ground transportation, and even some sightseeing for many destinations for a lot less moolah than if you tried to put the trip together yourself. (For more information, including specific companies you can call, see "Running through Package Tour Possibilities," in Chapter 6.)

✔ **Reserve your rental car before you leave.** If you know you want to have a car for some or all of your trip, rent it before you leave through a major United States company to save big bucks over the cost of renting on the spot in Europe (see Chapter 7 for details).

✔ **Invest in a rail pass.** Europe's extensive train system constitutes its greatest transportation asset. The train system's best value is its family of Eurorail passes (see Chapter 7).

✔ **Catch twenty winks on an overnight train for $0 to $20.** Armed with your trusty rail pass, you can jump on an overnight train and fork out just $20 for a reserved bunk in a sleeping couchette. Or if you're feeling lucky, take your chances on finding an empty sitting couchette, slide down the seat back, and voilà, you have a bed for free! In the morning, you'll have reached your destination plus saved yourself a night's hotel charge (see Chapters 7 and 8).

✔ **Leave the private plumbing at home; take a room without a bathroom.** You can get a hotel room that shares a bathroom down the hall for about two-thirds as much as you'll pay for a virtually identical room with its own plumbing (see Chapter 8).

✔ **If you have kids, get a triple or cots, not two rooms.** At most European hotels, kids stay for free in their parents' room. At the worst, a hotel may charge a nominal fee ($5 to $15) for the extra bed.

✔ **Rent a room instead of staying at a hotel.** At $15 to $40 a night, private room-for-rent beats out even the cheapest B&Bs or pensions. You also often get the experience of staying in a real European's home, which no five-star hotel can give you for any price (see Chapter 8).

✔ **Give the ultra-cheap accommodations a try.** If sleeping near 150 roommates (mostly students) on a wooden floor under a big tent sounds appealing, you can spend a night in Munich for $7. Budget options abound in Europe, from hostels (dorm bunks cost between $8 and $20) to campgrounds (for as little as $4 to $15) to crash-ins like Munich's aforementioned mega tent (see Chapter 8).

✔ **Opt for a double bed instead of two singles.** Fewer sheets for the hotel to wash equals savings for you. Even noncouple buddies can travel this way — although if your traveling partner is of the opposite sex, pretend you're married just to put traditionalist Europeans more at ease (see Chapter 8).

✔ **Do your own laundry.** To avoid Laundromat fees, wash a few pieces of clothes in the sink each night, roll them in towels to sop up the dampness, and hang them on the radiator to dry — or even better, on the heated towel racks (a silly amenity even cheap places are installing). Never allow the hotel to handle your laundry unless you enjoy being taken to the cleaners, so to speak.

✔ **If your room rate includes breakfast, stuff yourself.** Don't be shy about loading up on the food that comes with your room. Have three rolls and a big bowl of cereal or as much meat and cheese as you can eat. Trust me; you're paying for the food. To avoid an expensive lunch, stick an orange and an extra roll in your pocket for later.

✔ **If you can find a room without breakfast for less money, take it.** You can get the same food for which the hotel charges around $10 for about $3 at any cafe on your way out the door.

✔ **Reserve a room with a kitchenette.** Doing your own cooking and dishes may not be your idea of a vacation, but you'll save a lot of money by not eating in restaurants three times a day. Even if you only make breakfast or cook the occasional dinner, you'll save in the long run.

✔ **Get out of town.** In many places, big savings are just a short drive or taxi ride away. Hotels outside the historic center, in the next town over, or otherwise less-conveniently located are great bargains. See Chapter 8 for more information.

✔ **Eat at the expensive restaurants at lunch instead of dinner.** Lunch menus often boast many of the same specialties, but at a fraction of the dinnertime cost.

✔ **In Britain and Ireland, lunch on pub grub.** An authentic, yet cheap, meal in a British pub includes a sandwich and a sturdy pint of ale. You can find options for sandwiches and snacking in every country.

✔ **Order from fixed-price and tourist menus.** Fixed-price meals can be up to 30 percent cheaper than ordering the same dishes à la carte. While the options on a fixed-price menu are limited, you can't beat the price.

✔ **Picnic often.** For well under $10 you can dine like a king wherever you want — on a grassy patch in the city park, in your hotel room, or on the train.

✔ **Purchase a Paris Museum Pass.** This pass represents the single best example of a city doing right by its tourists. The Paris Museum Pass gives you unlimited entry for three full days to virtually all Parisian museums and sights (the Eiffel Tower is the only major one not on the list) for only $27. As an added bonus, it will save you the hassle of waiting in ticket lines! You can find similar passes in other cities (Austrian and Scandinavian ones are particularly great on this) that also grant you free travel on city buses and subways and other benefits.

✔ **Visit the free or near-free sights.** You can, for example, witness first-hand Paris cafe culture for the price of a cup of coffee ($2) or cruise the Grand Canal in Venice for under $4 on the public *vaporetto*. Other free sights and experiences include London's British Museum, the Tate and National Gallery, Rome's Pantheon, most churches and cathedrals, lively piazzas, church services where choirs sing, medieval quarters, sidewalk performers and buskers, baroque fountains, city parks, and street markets across Europe.

✔ **Take advantage of free or reduced-price museum days.** See the Vatican for free on the last Sunday of every month. You can uncover such policies at many other museums as well. The Louvre, for example, waives admission on the first Sunday of the month and is also almost half price after 3:00 p.m. Read your guidebooks carefully and take advantage of the free days and hours of reduced admission, but remember that other people have the same idea — the museums will be most crowded during these free times.

✔ **Walk as much as possible.** You can save lots of taxi money by strapping on a comfortable pair of walking shoes. Exploring on foot at a slower pace also grants you the opportunity to know your destination more intimately.

✔ **Pass over the souvenirs.** Ten years down the road, you won't care about the T-shirts, key chains, cuckoo clocks, Biersteins, and the like. Your photographs and memories serve as the best mementos of your trip.

✔ **Never pay in traveler's checks.** Trade traveler's checks at the bank for local currency or you'll get a bad exchange rate. Also, exchange booths at major tourist attractions give the most miserable rates.

✔ **Always check for discounts.** You may be pleasantly surprised to discover that you're eligible for discounts on sights, transportation, hotels, you name it. Members of AAA, trade unions, or AARP; frequent flyers; teachers; and members of other groups sometimes get discounted rates on car rentals, plane tickets, and some chain hotel rooms. Ask your company if employees can use the corporate travel agent and corporate rates even for private vacations. You never know until you ask.

If your family immigrated from Europe, you may get another discount. Many ethnic travel agencies specialize in getting forgotten sons and daughters rock-bottom rates when returning to the Old Country. Check out the nearest ethnic neighborhood that fits your background for details. When you're traveling, always ask about discounts for any demographic group to which you might belong. Are you over 60? Under 26? A student? A teacher or professor? A professional? How about a family discount, or at least one for just the kids? Work every angle to get the best price.

Chapter 5

Tips for Travelers with Special Interests or Needs

In This Chapter

▶ Taking the family to Europe

▶ Traveling discounts for the senior set

▶ Accessing Europe for travelers with disabilities

▶ Getting out and about in Europe for gays and lesbians

▶ Traveling with a particular hobby or interest in mind

*I*f you're headed to Europe with a particular interest or concern in mind, here is the place to look for information. This chapter has resource information and travel tips for families, senior citizens, gay men and lesbians, and travelers with disabilities.

Advice for Families

By all means, take the kids! Going to Europe often opens their impressionable young eyes and minds to the diversity of the world's cultures and peoples, impacting them profoundly. Every once in a while you may want the hotel to find you a baby-sitter so you can go out for a romantic dinner, but on the whole, traveling as a family is far from impossible. Prepare yourself to take things more slowly with the little ones along, however. Intersperse the heavy-duty cultural sights with some fun activities (which can be a welcome respite for everyone).

Europeans expect to encounter traveling families, because that's how they travel. You'll likely run into caravanning European clans, including grandparents and babes in arms. Locals tend to love kids, especially in Mediterranean countries. You'll often find that hotels and restaurants give you an even warmer reception if you have a child in tow.

Most Europeans will offer loads of encouragement and attention to a teenager struggling to order a meal in the local lingo, not to mention how they'll coo over an infant or toddler. Ask for a half portion to fit Junior's appetite. Three-star and four-star hotels may be your best bet for help with small children. The baby-sitters on call and a better infrastructure for helping visitors access the city and its services will more than offset the higher cost. Still, even cheaper hotels can usually find you a sitter.

When you travel with a child, you can usually expect lower rates. Most museums and sights offer reduced-price or free admission for children under a certain age (which can range from 6 to 18) and getting a cot in your hotel room won't cost you more than 30 percent extra, if that. Always ask about discounts on plane and train tickets for kids, too.

A number of books that offer hints and tips on traveling with kids are available. *Take Your Kids to Europe, How to Travel Safely (and Sanely) in Europe with Your Children* (Globe Pequot) offers practical advice based on the author's four-month trip with her hubby and two kids, along with tips from other familial travelers. Two other books, *Family Travel* (Lanier Publishing International) and *How to Take Great Trips with Your Kids* (The Harvard Common Press), give some good general advice that you can apply to travel in the United States, Europe, and elsewhere. You also may want to check out two reliable guides that present a worldwide focus, *Adventuring with Children* (Foghorn Press) and Lonely Planet's *Travel with Children*. You'll find specific advice on dealing with everyday family situations, especially those involving infants, which become Herculean labors when you encounter them on the road.

Families Welcome!, 92 N. Main St., Ashland, OR 97520 (☎ **800-326-0724** or 541-482-6121), a travel company specializing in worry-free vacations for families, offers "City Kids" packages to certain European cities.

If you're the adventurous type, look into **Familyhostel** (☎ **800-733-9753;** Internet: www.learn.unh.edu), an educational and intergenerational alternative to standard guided tours run by the University of New Hampshire. In this two- or three-week program, you live on a European college campus, attend lectures and seminars, go on lots of field trips, and sightsee with a team of experts and academics. The program caters to children (age 8 to 15), parents, and grandparents.

The highly regarded (albeit expensive) **Smithsonian Study Tours** have inaugurated a "Family Adventures" division (☎ **877-338-8687** or 202-357-4700; Internet: www.si.edu/tsa/sst) that runs escorted educational and adventure trips specifically designed for the whole clan.

Advice for Seniors

People over the age of 60 are traveling more than ever before. If you're a senior citizen, you can discover some terrific travel bargains. You can get discounts on some car rentals and chain hotels if you're a part of the **AARP (American Association of Retired Persons),** 601 E St. NW, Washington, DC 20049 (☎ **800-424-3410;** Internet: www.aarp.org). Membership has its privileges.

Don't look for discounts from the big car rental agencies while in Europe, however. Only National currently gives an AARP discount (10 percent). On the other hand, the many rental dealers that specialize in Europe — Auto-Europe, Kemwell, Europe by Car, and so forth — offer rates 5 percent lower to seniors. Take a look in Appendix A for contact information.

Make sure to ask about senior discounts whenever you book your flight. People over 60 or 65 also get reduced admission at theaters, museums, and other attractions in most European cities. Additionally, they can often get discount fares or cards on public transportation and national rail systems. Make sure to carry identification that proves your age.

Besides publishing the free booklet *101 Tips for the Mature Traveler,* **Grand Circle Travel,** 347 Congress St., Boston, MA 02210 (☎ **800-221-2610** or 800-597-3644; Internet: www.gct.com), specializes in vacations for seniors (as do hundreds of travel agencies). Beware of the tour-bus style of most of these packages, however. If you're a senior who wants a more independent trip, you should probably consult a regular travel agent. **SAGA International Holidays,** 222 Berkeley St., Boston, MA 02116 (☎ **800-343-0273;** Internet: www.sagaholidays.com), has 40 years' experience running all-inclusive tours and cruises for those 50 and older. It also sponsors the more substantial "Road Scholar Tours" (☎ **800-621-2151**) — fun-loving tours with an educational bent.

Give **Interhostel** (☎ **800-733-9753;** Internet: www.learn.unh.edu) or **Elderhostel** (☎ **877-426-8056** or 617-426-8056; Internet: www.elderhostel.org) a ring if you want to try something more than the average guided tour or vacation. Foreign universities host these trips, which cost around $2,000 to $3,500. Interhostel and Elderhostel fill your days with seminars, lectures, field trips, and sightseeing tours, all led by academic experts. You must be over 55 to participate in Elderhostel (a spouse or companion of any age can accompany you), and the programs range from one to four weeks. Interhostel requires its participants to be over 50 (any companion must be over 40), and offers two- and three-week programs.

Unfortunately, all specialty books on senior travel focus on the United States. Nevertheless, three do provide good general advice and contacts: *The 50+ Traveler's Guidebook* (St. Martin's Press), *The Seasoned Traveler* (Country Roads Press), and *Unbelievably Good Deals and Great Adventures That You Absolutely Can't Get Unless You're Over 50* (Contemporary Books). *Travel 50 & Beyond,* a quarterly magazine, also offers sound advice.

If you'd like an extended stay abroad during the off-season at huge discounts, consult **Sun Holidays,** 2777 Summer St., Suite 505A, Stamford, CT 06905 (☎ **800-422-8000** or 561-367-0105; Internet: www.sun-holidays.com).

Advice for Travelers with Disabilities

A disability shouldn't stop anybody from traveling to Europe, even though the continent has never won any medals for handicapped accessibility. After all, the big cities have made an effort to accommodate people with disabilities in the past few years. The list of organizations to help you plan your trip and to provide specific advice before you go never ends.

For years, the **Moss Rehab Hospital** (☎ **215-456-9600** or 215-456-9602 TTY) has provided phone advice and referrals to travelers with disabilities. The **American Foundation for the Blind,** 11 Penn Plaza, Suite 300, New York, NY 10001 (☎ **800-232-5463** or 212-502-7600), can fill you in on travel in general and how to facilitate passage of your Seeing-Eye dog into Europe. Travelers with a hearing impairment should contact the **American Academy of Otolaryngology,** 1 Prince St., Alexandria, VA 22314 (☎ **703-836-4444** or 703-519-1585 TTY; Internet: www.entnet.org).

To gain access to a vast network of connections in the travel industry, join **The Society for the Advancement of Travel for the Handicapped (SATH),** 347 Fifth Ave., Suite 610, New York, NY 10016 (☎ **212-447-7284,** fax: 212-725-8253), for $45 annually. The organization provides referrals to tour operators that specialize in travelers with disabilities and as well as information sheets on travel destinations. For $13 a year ($21 outside the United States), its quarterly magazine *Open World* provides you with good information and resources.

The worldwide organization known as **Mobility International,** P.O. Box 10767, Eugene, OR 97440 (☎ **541-343-1284** V/TDD, fax: 541-343-6812; Internet: www.miusa.org), promotes international disability rights, provides reference sheets on travel destinations, and hosts international exchanges for people with disabilities. Its *A World of Options* book lists information on everything from biking trips to scuba outfitters. Annual membership is $35, which includes the quarterly *Over the Rainbow* newsletter.

The 500-page *Travelin' Talk Directory,* P.O. Box 3534, Clarksville, TN 37043 (☎ **931-552-6670,** fax: 931-552-1182), lists outfits and people who help travelers with disabilities. It sells for $35.

Some guided tours cater specifically to travelers with disabilities. **Flying Wheels Travel** (☎ **800-535-6790,** Internet: www.travelexplorer.com/f/flying) is one of the best. It offers various escorted tours and cruises, as well as private tours in minivans with lifts. Other reputable specialized tour operators include **Access Adventures** (☎ 716-889- 9096), **Accessible Journeys** (☎ 800-846-4537, Internet: www.disabiliytravel.com), **Directions Unlimited** (☎ 800-533-5343), and **Wheelchair Journeys** (☎ 206-885-2210). In addition, you can obtain lists of travel agents who specialize in tours for disabled travelers from the **Information Center for Individuals with Disabilities** (☎ 800-462-5015).

Advice for Gay and Lesbian Travelers

Much of Europe now accepts same-sex couples, and homosexual sex acts are legal in most countries. Do some research on the city or area you're planning to visit, however, to ensure your safety. Many European cities have blossomed into centers for gay lifestyles, including parts of London, Paris, Berlin, Milan, and Greece. As is usually the case, smaller, more traditional towns are often not as accepting.

Your best all-around resource is the **International Gay Travel Association** (IGTA), P.O. Box 4974, Key West, FL 33041 (☎ **800-448-8550** or 305-292-0217; Internet: www.iglta.org). The cost to join is $100, plus $150 a year. For the price of membership you get a newsletter, advice on specialist travel agencies (you can search for local ones on the Web site), and a membership directory. Some gay and lesbian travel agencies include **Our Family Abroad** (☎ **800-999-5500**; Internet: www.familyabroad.com; gay and lesbian); **Yellowbrick Road** (☎ **800-642-2488**; gay and lesbian); and **Islanders/Kennedy Travels** (☎ **800-988-1181**; gay and lesbian).

IDG Books Worldwide is now proud to publish *Frommer's Gay & Lesbian Europe,* one of the first guidebooks focusing on gay-friendly hotels, restaurants, and nightlife. *Spartacus International Gay Guide* and *Odysseus* are two other biannual English-language gay guides, both focused on gay men but including information for lesbians as well, that cover the whole world in a sort of database style. Another very good series of books covering gay and lesbian travel is the Ferrari Guides (Internet: www.q-net.com).

Most gay and lesbian bookstores offer these titles. Although general-interest bookstores carry the well-known brands, such as Frommer's, you may need to order some of the other titles from services such as **Giovanni's Room** (☎ **215-923-2960**; Internet: giophilp@netaxs.com) or **A Different Light Bookstore** (☎ **800-343-4002** or 212-989-4850; Internet: www.adlbooks.com).

The newsletter ***Out and About,*** 8 W. 19th St., #401, New York, NY 10011 (☎ **800-929-2268** or 212-645-6922) offers good information on the global gay and lesbian scene. The cost is $49 for a one-year/ten-issue subscription. ***Our World,*** 1104 North Nova Rd., Suite 251, Daytona Beach, FL 32117 (☎ **904-441-5367**), a slicker monthly magazine, highlights and promotes travel bargains and opportunities. The annual subscription rate for this magazine is $35 in the United States and $45 outside the United States.

Part II
Ironing Out the Details

The 5th Wave   By Rich Tennant

WHILE ON VACATION IN EUROPE, SYLVIA FINDS
HERSELF MYSTERIOUSLY DRAWN TO A FELLOW
TRAVELER ON THE TRAIN.

In this part . . .

Now I get down to the nitty-gritty of trip planning, from shopping for plane tickets to choosing a tour operator to reserving a room at a hotel. You get the bottom line on how to pack, get your passport, and get the most miles out of your rental cars and rail passes. I clear up whether or not you should use traveler's checks or your ATM card. Soon you will be winging your way across the Atlantic with all the information you need to fulfill all your European vacation dreams.

Chapter 6

Getting to Europe

● ●

In This Chapter

▶ Partnering with a travel agent

▶ Considering package tours

▶ Choosing an escorted tour

▶ Arranging your own flights

● ●

*Y*our destination rolls through your thoughts like a richly colored banner. You know where you're headed, and your mind is reeling with all the sights, scenes, and excitement you expect to experience. You have just one more fine point to figure out before you connect with those places you're imagining: how to get there.

Airline options are far from limited. To check out the offerings, you can tap a travel agent for assistance, call flight reservation desks on your own, or cruise the Internet for the best deals. Also, you can choose to set out on your European explorations with or without a professional guide.

Before you get down to the business of booking a flight, take time to wing your way through this chapter. You've landed on a great resource for suiting your travel to your tastes and your budget.

Seeking a Travel Agent's Advice

Word of mouth goes a long way toward finding a qualified, reliable travel agent. If the brother of the friend of your Aunt Tillie's dog groomer speaks highly of his travel expert's treatment, stay tuned to clues about level of service. Finding a cheap deal on airfare, accommodations, and a rental car is the least an agent can — and sometimes does — do. A more helpful agent will go the extra mile to give you vacation value by weighing comfort with expense, so you don't end up having the worst time of your life.

A great agent can give advice on several travel issues, including how much time to spend in a particular destination and how to choose an economical and practical flight plan. They can also make reservations for competitively priced rental cars and find deals at some of the better hotels.

To help your travel agent help you, do a little research before you sit down to talk accommodations and attractions; picking up this book is a great start on your homework! Have a general idea of where you want to stay and what you want to do by reading up on locations. If you have access to the Internet, check prices on the Web to get a ballpark feel for prices (see "Buying your ticket online" later in this chapter for shopping ideas).

When you have enough information in hand — and in your head — pack up your notes and trot off to the travel agency. Agents rely on a variety of resources, so your arrangements are likely to cost less than if you sealed the deal by yourself. Plus, your agent can suggest alternatives if your first choice of hotels is unavailable and issue airline tickets and hotel vouchers right then and there.

The travel industry is built on commissions. When you book a vacation, your agent earns a paycheck from the airline, hotel, or tour company with which you're doing business. Be on the lookout for unscrupulous travel agents who are bent on coaxing you to go for the plan that brings them the most bucks in commissions.

Some airlines and resorts started waving good-bye to agents' commissions several years ago. Customers now have to make specific mention of certain hotels or airlines if they're interested in booking; otherwise, the agent may not bring them up as options.

Exploring Package Tour Possibilities

Package tours and escorted tours are different critters. So, if you're imagining a tour guide standing at the front of a busload of fellow travelers, pointing out don't-miss sights and unveiling the inside scoop on Europe, put on your mental brakes. Package deals won't take you by the hand after you plunk down your reservation dollars, but you will save money. You can look into package and escorted tours on your own, or enlist the help of a travel agent. This section helps you figure out where to look to book your tour.

Honing in on definitions

Packages wrap up airfare and accommodations into a neat little parcel — plain and simple.

By combining airfare, hotel, and airport transportation into a single arrangement, a package deal can reduce your overall costs. You may actually pay less for the entire package than you would have for the hotel stay alone if you booked each element separately.

Packages come from, well, packagers. Tour operators fit the category, as do airlines, which sometimes offer flights paired with accommodations for one price.

When dealing with packagers, keep in mind that differences exist among the available options — differences that may significantly affect your travel experience. Set side by side, one combo may top another in any of the following ways:

✔ Better class of hotels.

✔ Same hotels for lower prices.

✔ Accommodations and travel days (days of departure and return) — limited or not?

✔ Escorted and independent packages available — not one or the other only.

✔ Option to add on just a few excursions or escorted day trips (also at discounted prices) without booking an entirely escorted tour.

Some packagers specialize in overpriced, international chain hotels, which means that you could book a cut-rate airfare and stay in modest B&Bs or small hotels in the heart of town for even less. Spending time shopping around can yield rewards; don't hesitate to compare deals and details before you fork over your funds.

Hunting down the deals

You can find a tour package on your own, without the assistance of a travel agent. In fact, the information is right under your nose for news: Start by looking for packagers' advertisements in the travel section of your local Sunday paper. Also check the back of national travel magazines such as *Travel & Leisure, National Geographic Traveler,* and *Condé Nast Traveler.*

Reputable packers include these standouts:

✔ **Central Holidays** (☎ **800-111-1139;** Internet: www.centralholidays.com)

✔ **American Express Vacations** (☎ **800-346-3607;** Internet: www.americanexpress.com/travel)

✔ **Liberty Travel** (☎ **888-271-1584;** Internet: www.libertytravel.com)

Airlines themselves often package their flights together with accommodations. When you check out the airline choices, look for one that offers both frequent service to your hometown and frequent-flyer miles. By buying your package through the airline rather than a tour operator — some of whom, sadly, do not operate in your best interest — you can be pretty sure that the company will still be around when your departure date arrives.

The following airlines offer tour packages:

- **American Airlines Vacations** (☎ **800-321-2121;** Internet: www.aavacations.com)

- **Continental Airlines Vacations** (☎ **888-898-9255;** Internet: www.coolvacations.com)

- **Delta Vacations** (☎ **800-872-7786;** Internet: www.deltavacations.com)

- **U.S. Airways Vacations** (☎ **800-455-0123;** Internet: www.usairwaysvacations.com)

Most European airlines offer competitive packages as well (see Appendix A for their Web sites and toll-free numbers).

The biggest hotel chains and resorts also offer packages. If you already know where you want to stay, call the hotel or resort and ask about land/air packages.

Joining an Escorted Tour

If getting away from everyday routine and responsibilities means letting someone else worry about traffic and the details of travel, then an escorted tour is the way to go. Sit back in comfort and rely on a tour guide's mastery of the roadways and explanation of the scenery. The tour company takes care of all the particulars and tells you what to expect at each attraction. Escorted tours can take you to the maximum number of sights in the minimum amount of time with the least amount of hassle.

If you decide you want an escorted tour, think strongly about purchasing trip-cancellation insurance, especially if the tour operator asks you to pay up front for the tour. But don't buy this insurance from the tour operator! If they cancel the trip, there's no reason to think that they'll fulfill their obligations for the insurance payout. Buy trip-cancellation insurance through an independent agency. See "Buying Travel and Medical Insurance" in Chapter 10.

When choosing an escorted tour, ask a few simple questions before you plunk down the dollars:

- **What does the tour include?** Some tours provide transportation to and from the airport; others don't. If box lunches are part of the deal, drinks, including alcoholic beverages, may cost extra. Can you select from a menu that offers several options, or are you and your fellow travelers going to face the same bill of fare?

- **How much does each tour compact into one trip?** Packing 11 hours of travel and touring into excursions day after day may leave you exhausted — sort of like being at work. If early rising and late returns sound like a grind, certain escorted tours may not be for you.

✔ **Can you opt out of certain activities?** Does the tour allow picking and choosing activities; or does the bus leave once a day, and you're out of luck if you're not onboard?

✔ **How big is the group?** Because some tours accept additional people up to the last moment, your tour operator may be hard-pressed to give you any more than a rough estimate based on reservations. Keep in mind that larger groups take more time to get on and off the bus. Some tours have a minimum group size, and the trip may not get off the ground if they don't book enough people.

✔ **What is the cancellation policy?** Is a deposit required to reserve your place on the tour? How far ahead do you pay in full? If you have to cancel, what's the latest date that you can notify the tour operator and still expect a refund? And what happens if not enough people sign up for a given tour? If the tour doesn't go out, do you receive early notice and a refund?

Making Your Own Arrangements

So you want to plan the trip on your own? This section tells you all you need to know to research and book the perfect flight.

Booking your flight

With the introduction of codesharing — one carrier selling flights as its own on another carrier — customers now enjoy more travel options and an easier time making flight arrangements. Chances are, you can call your favorite airline and come up with a plan that flies you from just about anywhere in the United States to just about anywhere in Europe.

Finding out who flies where

Listed below are those airlines that offer direct flights from North America to major European cities. To reach smaller European cities, you may have to travel first to a U.S. hub, such as New York, in order to pick up a direct flight to your destination. The phone numbers and Web sites for all these airlines are in Appendix A. (Note that references on this list to New York include all the major NYC airports, as well as Newark.)

Major North American carriers

✔ **Air Canada** flies from Halifax, Montreal, Toronto, and Vancouver to Amsterdam, Copenhagen, Glasgow, Frankfurt, London, Manchester, Milan, Munich, Paris, and Zurich.

✔ **American Airlines** flies from Boston, Chicago, Dallas, Los Angeles, Miami, New York, Raleigh/Durham, San Jose, and Seattle to Birmingham, Brussels, Frankfurt, London, Manchester, Madrid, Milan, Paris, Stockholm, and Zurich.

✔ **Canadian Airlines** flies from Calgary, Montreal, Ottawa, St. Johns, Toronto, and Vancouver to London, Milan, and Rome.

✔ **Continental** flies from Boston, Cleveland, Houston, Los Angeles, Miami, Newark, Orlando, San Francisco, and Washington, D.C. to Birmingham, Brussels, Dublin, Düsseldorf, Frankfurt, Glasgow, Lisbon, London, Madrid, Manchester, Milan, Paris, Prague, Rome, Shannon, and Zurich.

✔ **Delta** flies from Atlanta, Cincinnati, Los Angeles, New York, and San Francisco to Amsterdam, Athens, Barcelona, Brussels, Budapest, Dublin, Frankfurt, Istanbul, London, Lyon, Madrid, Manchester, Milan, Moscow, Munich, Paris, Rome, Stockholm, Shannon, Venice, and Zurich.

✔ **Northwest** flies from Detroit, Memphis, Minneapolis/St. Paul, and Washington, D.C. to Amsterdam, Frankfurt, London, Milan, Paris, and Rome.

✔ **TWA** flies from New York to Amsterdam, Barcelona, Lisbon, London, Paris, Madrid, Milan, and Rome.

✔ **United** flies from Boston, Chicago, Los Angeles, New York, San Francisco, and Washington, D.C. to Brussels, Düsseldorf, Frankfurt, London, Milan, Munich, and Paris.

✔ **US Airways** flies from Charlotte, Philadelphia, and Pittsburgh to Amsterdam, Frankfurt, London, Madrid, Munich, Paris, and Rome.

Major European Carriers

✔ **Aer Lingus** flies from Boston, Chicago, New York, and Los Angeles to Belfast, Dublin, and Shannon.

✔ **Air France** flies from Atlanta, Boston, Houston, Chicago, Los Angeles, Miami, New York, Philadelphia, San Francisco, and Washington, D.C. to Paris (also New York to Lyon).

✔ **Alitalia** flies from Boston, Chicago, Detroit, Los Angeles, Miami, New York, San Francisco, and Toronto to Milan and Rome.

✔ **Austrian Airlines** flies from Chicago, New York, and Washington, D.C. to Vienna.

✔ **British Airways** flies from Atlanta, Baltimore, Boston, Charlotte, Chicago, Dallas, Denver, Detroit, Houston, Los Angeles, Miami, New York, Orlando, Philadelphia, Phoenix, San Diego, San Francisco, Seattle, Tampa, and Washington, D.C. to London (also New York to Manchester).

✔ **CSA Czech Airlines** flies from New York to Prague.

✔ **Iberia** flies from Chicago, Miami, and New York to Madrid (also New York to Barcelona).

✔ **IcelandAir** flies from Baltimore/Washington, Boston, Halifax, New York, Minneapolis/St. Paul, and Orlando to Reykjavík. You can choose to take a layover in Reykjavík for up to three days at no extra charge, and then continue on to Amsterdam, Copenhagen, Edinburgh, Frankfurt, Glasgow, Hamburg, Helsinki, London, Oslo, Paris, or Stockholm.

- ✔ **KLM Royal Dutch Airlines** flies from Atlanta, Boston, Chicago, Detroit, Houston, Los Angeles, Memphis, Minneapolis/St. Paul, Montreal, New York, San Francisco, Toronto, and Vancouver to Amsterdam.

- ✔ **Lufthansa** flies from Atlanta, Boston, Chicago, Dallas, Detroit, Houston, Los Angeles, Miami, New York, Philadelphia, San Francisco, Toronto, and Vancouver to Frankfurt (also New York to Düsseldorf and Munich).

- ✔ **Swissair** flies from Atlanta, Boston, Chicago, Los Angeles, Miami, Montreal, New York, San Francisco, and Washington, D.C. to Zurich (also New York to Geneva).

- ✔ **Virgin Atlantic** flies from Boston, Chicago, Las Vegas, Los Angeles, Miami, New York, Orlando, San Francisco, and Washington D.C. to London.

Shopping for the best airfare

Competition among the major U.S. airlines is unlike that of any other industry. A coach seat is virtually the same from one carrier to another, yet the difference in price may run as high as $1,000 for a product with the same intrinsic value.

The great difference among fares boils down to meeting customers' individual needs and urgencies. Here's a rundown of how traveler profiles play into pricing:

- ✔ Business travelers may want a flight out at a moment's notice, and they're likely to adjust their itineraries often and late in the game. They're going to pay top price — otherwise known as full fare — for either privilege, just as they will for the pleasure of flying home before the weekend.

- ✔ Travelers who book early and accept an overnight stay on Saturday, or who are willing to travel on a Tuesday, Wednesday, or Thursday, pay the least, usually a fraction of the full fare.

By buying your tickets a week or two in advance, you can cut your purchase price in half — or more. Planning pays off!

Even airlines stage sales now and then — usually in seasons when travel volume is low. These fare reductions apply to popular routes and carry certain requirements, such as advance purchase and travel on particular days of the week only. Don't expect a bargain between mid-June to mid-September or around Christmas, when summer vacations and holiday travel command top dollar.

Often, flying into Europe's major cities (usually London and Paris) will bring the price of a ticket down. Also, look into purchasing an "open-jaw" plane ticket. This is when you fly into one European city and then depart from another — say, flying into London but then out of Madrid

on your way home. It can sometimes be a more expensive option —
though usually no more than half the price of a round-trip ticket to
London plus half the round-trip Madrid fare — but it's a wonderful way
to keep your itinerary flexible, and you don't have to backtrack to the
first city on your trip.

Low-as-they-go fares reside with consolidators, often called bucket
shops, which offer discounted tickets to a retail market. These are
often better fares than you can find by calling the airlines directly —
or by working in tandem with a travel agent. You'll find display ads for
these outlets in small boxes at the bottom of the page in your Sunday
travel section.

Some reliable consolidators include the following:

- ✔ Cheap Tickets (☎ 800-377-1000; Internet:
  www.cheaptickets.com).
- ✔ **1-800-FLY-CHEAP** (Internet: www.flycheap.com).
- ✔ Travac Tours & Charters (☎ 877-872-8221; Internet:
  www.thetravelsite.com).
- ✔ **Council Travel** (☎ 800-226-8624; Internet: www.counciltravel.
  com), caters especially to young travelers, but their bargain-
  basement prices are available to people of all ages.

Buying your ticket online

Another way to find a cheap fare is to scour the Internet, relying on
your computer to connect with millions of pieces of data that your
search engine can return in rank order. Online virtual travel agents
abound these days, and their numbers are ever-increasing on the
Internet.

Travel-booking sites are so plentiful that space permits mention of just
a few of the better-respected (and more comprehensive) resources:
www.LowestFare.com, www.travelocity.com, and Microsoft's
www.expedia.com. Each has its own little quirks, but all provide varia-
tions of the same service. Just enter the dates you want to fly and the
cities you want to visit, and the computer looks for the lowest fares.

Several other features are now standard to these sites: the ability to
compare flights at different times and dates to locate a cheaper fare;
e-mail alerts when fares drop on a route you have specified; and a database of last-minute deals that advertises super-cheap vacation packages, or airfares for those who can get away at a moment's notice.

Through free e-mail services called **E-savers,** airlines can keep you up
to date on their great last-minute deals. Each of the major airlines individually sends out a weekly electronic communication at your request
listing discounted flights, usually leaving the upcoming Friday or

Saturday, and returning the following Monday or Tuesday. You can sign up to receive information from all the major airlines at once by logging on to **Smarter Living** (www.smarterliving.com), or you can go to each airline's individual Web site for schedules, flight booking, and information on late-breaking bargains. Web addresses appear in Appendix A.

Chapter 7

Getting Around Europe After You Arrive

*E*urope is a very interconnected place. Between planes, buses, rental cars, and especially trains, moving from country to country using public transportation in Europe is easier than getting from state to state in the United States.

Choosing the right rail pass, knowing the ground rules for figuring out schedules, and having a pocketful of helpful hints on getting the best deal out of airlines, train stations, and rental car agencies can slash your travel time and budget in half.

Flying Around Europe

Air travel within Europe makes sense only if you need to cover very large distances in a limited amount of time, such as getting out of Scandinavia, Spain, Portugal, Greece, or Sicily. And with the advent of no-frills airlines, air travel in Europe is now open even to the strictest budgeteer.

When is it worthwhile to fly instead of taking the train? Compare the extra money you spend on a plane ticket with the time that you waste traveling by train. If you find that you have to spend close to a full day on the train — or if a plane ride is actually cheaper — fly.

You have four choices for air travel within Europe:

- ✔ **Regular flights on major European carriers.** Although this is your best bet, it's also the most expensive option. You can call the airlines' 800 numbers before you leave for Europe to arrange these flights (see Appendix A), or you can contact a travel agent or the airline's office in any European city.

- ✔ **Consolidator tickets.** Often the cheapest way to fly, you can find these tickets from consolidators (also known as bucket shops) and budget travel agencies across Europe, especially in London and Athens. Although consolidator tickets aren't totally unreliable, using them is the least safe way to fly. Shady consolidators can go out of business overnight (make sure you pay by credit card for insurance), they have a higher rate of cancellation, and many of the airlines (often Middle Eastern and Asian carriers) follow lower safety standards than major U.S. and European carriers.

- ✔ **Small, no-frills airlines.** A recent option for travelers, smaller carriers offer bargain-basement rates — usually $50 to $250 — for a limited set of routes. These airlines use secondary airports in major cities as hubs, and they cut ticket costs as well as in-flight frills (no free drinks, for example). These airline tickets are your best bet for getting dirt-cheap, reliable tickets in Europe. For example, you can often find a 3-hour London-to-Venice flight for $48 (versus a 15-hour, $246 train ride). Some of the companies offering these great deals are independent start-ups, while others are baby branches of major airlines.

  The small, no-frills airline system is still evolving, but a few outfits that have emerged as dependable choices include **Air Europa** (out of Spain; ☎ **34-902-401-501;** Internet: www.air-europa.com), **Easyjet** (out of London ☎ **44-870-600-0000;** Internet: www.easyjet. com), **Ryanair** (in Dublin ☎ **353-1-609-7889;** Internet: www. ryanair.ie), **British Midland** (in London ☎ **800-788-0555** in the United States, **01332-854-274** in the U.K.; Internet: www. iflybritishmidland.com), British Airways' **Go** (in London ☎ **44-1279-666-388;** Internet: www.go-fly.com), **PGA** (out of Lisbon and Porto; ☎ **351-21-842- 5500** in Lisbon, **44-161-489-5040** in the U.K.; Internet: www.pga.pt), **VLM** (out of Antwerp and London; ☎ **32-3-285-6868** in Antwerp, **44-20-7476-6677** in London; Internet: www.vlm-air.com), and **Virgin Express** (in Belgium ☎ **32-2-752-0505;** Internet: www.virgin-express.com).

- ✔ **Europe-By-Air Pass** (☎ **888-387-2479;** Internet: www.europebyair. com). This is a handy booklet of coupons, each coupon costing $99, that you can redeem for a one-way flight between more than 100 cities on any of the 14-and-growing participating European airlines — from tiny no-frills start-ups to high-profile outfits like Virgin Express.

You must buy at least three coupons at once, and then book each of your flights with the respective airline. The coupon doesn't cover airport taxes, which run about $10 to $30. The best idea is to figure out how many flights you may take and check out the no-frills airline Web sites that I mention earlier in this section to compare prices; if three or more planned flights cost more than $99, get the pass (and buy any cheaper tickets individually).

Taking the Train

Fast, efficient, relatively cheap, and incredibly well interconnected, the train is king of European travel. As a rule, European trains run on time, are clean and comfortable, and have a vast network that covers almost every major and minor city.

Rail details

In Europe, the shortest — and cheapest — distance between two points is lined with railroad tracks. But before you ride the rails, there are a few things you should know.

Train classifications

Europe offers many train classifications that range from local runs that stop at every tiny station to high-speed bullet trains (France's TGV, Italy's ETR/Pendolino, Spain's AVE), new international high-speed runs (Thalys from Paris to Brussels; Artesia from Paris to Torino and Milan in Italy), and the **Eurostar** Channel Tunnel train. Beyond these, the fastest trains you'll probably take are the popular **EC** (Eurocity), **IC** (Intercity), or **EN** (Euronight).

Layout of the train

Many European trains have the old-fashioned couchette configuration. Each car has a corridor along one side, off of which ten small couchettes, or compartments, reside. Each couchette seats six to eight people each, or, in first-class compartments, four to six people in slightly plushier chairs. (First class isn't worth the added expense).

However, most short-run trains are switching to modern, straight-through cars with seats running down both sides of an open aisle.

Europe's Primary Train Routes

The **Eurostar** train (☎ **0990-300-003** in London, 01-44-51-06-02 in Paris, and 800-EUROSTAR in the United States; Internet: www.eurostar.com) runs through the Channel Tunnel and connects London's Waterloo Station both with the Gare du Nord in Paris and Central Station in Brussels. Both trips take about three hours (you arrive four hours later with the time change). Because the old train-ferry-train route (through Dover and Calais) takes all day and costs almost the same, the Eurostar option is a great deal.

Many high-speed trains throughout Europe require that you pay a supplement of around $5 to $15 in addition to your regular ticket price. However, if you buy point-to-point tickets, this supplement is included in the full price (though sometimes printed on a second ticket — validate both). With a pass such as Eurail, you may have to purchase a supplement separately (only with some specialty trains). You can buy a supplement from the train conductor, but he or she will also charge you a small penalty fee. Always check at the ticket office and pay for it in advance.

Contact **Rail Europe** (☎ **800-4-EURAIL;** Internet: www.raileurope.com) to receive more information about train travel in Europe, as well as automated schedule information online or by fax.

Until becoming a travel writer, I never needed to buy the rail schedule bible, the **Thomas Cook European Timetable** (available at travel specialty stores or by calling ☎ **800-FORSYTH**). However, now that I use this handy tool, I can't imagine traveling without it. The book's 500 pages — updated monthly, but rumored to go quarterly soon — contain the daily schedules of all major European train and ferry routes.

If you have Internet access, visit **Mercurio** at mercurio.iet.unipi.it/misc/timetabl.html. At this site, you can find each country's national railway Web site, which include schedules and fare information, occasionally in English.

Most train schedules and signs use native names for cities, not the English equivalent. For example, Athens is Athinai, Cologne is Köln, Copenhagen is København, Florence is Firenze, Lisbon is Lisboa, Munich is München, Naples is Napoli, Pamplona is often Iruñea, Prague is Praha, Vienna is Wien, Venice is Venezia, and so on.

Make sure that you get on the right car, and not just the right train. Individual train cars may split from the rest of the train down the line and join a different train headed to a different destination. Making sure that you're on the right car is especially important when taking a night train (if you have a reserved spot, you needn't worry). Each car has its own destination placard, which may also list major stops en route, and always check with the conductor.

To reserve or not to reserve

In addition to supplements, some of the speediest high-speed trains, including Eurostar (the Channel Tunnel train), TGV in France, Pendolino in Italy, and long-distance trains in Spain, require reservations.

You must reserve any train marked with an R on its schedule ahead of time for a fee — usually around $10, but the price can reach beyond $50 if you include a meal. You can almost always reserve a seat within a few hours of the train's departure, but booking a few days in advance at the station assures that you have a seat. You must also reserve any sleeping couchettes or sleeping berths.

However, you don't need to buy or reserve individual train tickets through your travel agent before leaving the United States. Doing so only locks you into a schedule that you may want to change after you've hit the road, and the travel agent will charge you a few extra dollars for his or her assistance. (Remember, though, you do need to buy your rail pass before leaving the United States; see information on these later in this chapter.)

I make only two exceptions to this rule:

✔ The high-speed Artesia train requires a supplement. If you have a rail pass, you can receive a substantial discount, but only if you buy the supplement in the United States at the same time that you purchase your rail pass.

✔ Reserving a seat on the Eurostar is always a good idea. Tour groups and England's frequent bank holidays (three- or four-day weekends) book the train solid, because many Londoners take short vacations to Paris.

Traveling without a reserved seat on a regular train is rarely a problem (unless you happen to catch a train toward the beach on a holiday weekend).

Outside each couchette, you find a little plastic window where bits of cardboard are inserted if someone at this stop or at a stop down the line has reserved a seat. Check to make sure that you're occupying an unreserved seat before you claim the couchette to save yourself the trouble of getting booted out later in your trip.

Overnight trains

Go to bed in Paris; wake up in Rome. Convenience doesn't get any easier. Why waste an entire day watching the countryside (no matter how pretty it is) pass you by when you traveled to see the cities? On an overnight train, you not only get a cheap (if uncomfortable) bed for the night, but you also eliminate wasted travel time. To maximize your time and money in Europe, make any trip over six hours an overnight ride.

Don't drink the water on the trains, not even to rinse your mouth. Use this water for handwashing only. Trains, especially overnight trains, dehydrate you quickly, so make sure that you bring bottled water to sip throughout the night as well as to rinse your mouth and toothbrush the next morning.

On an overnight train, you have four sleeping choices:

- ✔ **Sitting up.** Use this as a last resort, because you won't get much sleep.

- ✔ **Fold-out seats.** In regular couchettes, you can often pull facing seat bottoms out toward each other, collapsing the seat backs. If you collapse all the seat backs on the couchette, you have a little padded romper room in which to nap, but usually no doors lock. Your privacy isn't guaranteed, so as soon as you find an unoccupied couchette, pull out all the seats, close all the curtains, turn out the lights, and lie down like you're asleep — even if it's only 5:00 p.m. Hopefully, potential roomies will pass by your couchette in search of a more inviting one.

- ✔ **Flip-down bunks.** These are always my first choice. Sleeping couchettes can sleep six in minor discomfort on narrow, flip-down, shelflike bunks. Doors lock (make sure they're locked before you go to bed) and the conductor watches over your car (and your passport; he holds it overnight for border crossings). For around $20 a reservation, this option is one of the cheapest sleeping deals that you can find in Europe. Unless you reserve an entire couchette, prepare to share your room with strangers. (Don't flash anything valuable, and sleep with your moneybelt on.)

- ✔ **A sleeping car berth.** Usually, sleeping car berths are only a first-class option, in which for a bit more money you get a tiny room with two to three bunks and a private sink. Berths are a smidgen comfier than a couchette, but strangers may populate the other bunk if you're alone.

The rail pass: Will I need one?

The rail pass, a single ticket that allows you unlimited travel or a certain number of days within a set period of time, has always been the greatest value in European travel. If your trip will cover countless kilometers on the rails, a pass ends up costing you considerably less than buying individual train tickets. And, a rail pass gives you the freedom to hop on a train whenever you feel like it, making a day trip out of town cheap and easy. An extra bonus of the rail pass is that you don't have to wait in ticket lines.

A rail pass primer

The granddaddy of passes is the **Eurail** pass, which covers 17 countries (not including England). If you're taking a whirlwind, pan-European tour, this is your single best investment. The **Europass,** which covers five countries, excluding England (though you can add more), is a recent addition to your list of rail passes. If you're staying within the heart of western Europe, the Europass will work well for you. Both Eurail and Europass offer various rail-and-drive and partner-pass subsidiaries (see later in this section for details).

These rail passes also often make you eligible for discounts on private rail lines (such as those in the Alps), the Eurostar between London and Paris or Brussels, as well as give you discounts or free travel for ferry crossings (Italy to Greece) and some boat rides on rivers (Rhine, Mosel) and lakes (especially Swiss lakes). These bonuses can change from year to year, so check with the agency that issues your pass and read the literature that they send with your pass to find out about any extra goodies you may receive.

Rail passes are valid all the way to the borders of the countries they cover. For example, if you're traveling from a Eurail country to a non-Eurail country — say Vienna, Austria to Prague, Czech Republic — you can visit the ticket window in Vienna and purchase a ticket for the stretch of your trip from the Austrian/Czech border to Prague. Your pass covers the Vienna-to-the-border segment.

The mechanics of rail passes

From the date that you buy your rail pass, you have six months to begin using it. You have to validate your pass at a European train station the day you want to start using the pass. Aside from reserving couchettes or buying supplements, validating your rail pass is the only time that you'll have to wait in a ticket line. With consecutive-day, unlimited-use Eurail passes, you can just hop on trains at whim.

Consecutive-day passes work best if you take the train very frequently (every few days), cover a lot of ground, and make many short train hops. However, if you want to range far and wide, but you plan to take your time over a long trip, intending to stay in each city for a while, a **flexipass** is the smartest option for you.

Both the Europass and Eurail flexipass give you a certain number of days (5 to 15) to travel within a two month window. Printed on your flexipass are a number of little boxes that correspond with the number of travel days you bought. Write the date in the next free box (in ink) every time you board a train. The conductor comes around, checking your ticket to make sure that you've put down the right date.

What date do I write down for overnight trains, you say? A Eurail day begins at 7:00 p.m. and runs 29 hours until the following midnight. In other words, when you board an overnight train after 7:00 p.m., write the next day's date in the box. Doing so clears you for that night and any traveling that you do the next day.

Here is a list of the countries that Eurail and Europass cover (I explain add-on zones later in the chapter):

   ✔ **Eurail countries:** Austria, Belgium, Denmark, Finland, France, Germany, Greece, Hungary, Ireland, Italy, Luxembourg, the Netherlands, Norway, Portugal, Spain, Sweden, and Switzerland.

   ✔ **Europass countries:** France, Germany, Switzerland, Italy, and Spain.

✔ **Europass add-on zones:** Austria/Hungary, Belgium/Netherlands/ Luxembourg, Greece (including the ferry from Brindisi, Italy), and Portugal.

None of these passes include Great Britain.

Different Types of Rail Passes

If you're under 26, you can buy a regular first-class pass or a second-class **youth pass;** if you're 26 or over, you must buy a first-class pass (except for sleeping cars, because the class difference is negligible). Children under 4 travel free and passes for kids 4 to 11 are half price. The following prices that I list for the various rail passes are for 2000, but keep in mind they rise each year:

✔ **Eurailpass:** Consecutive-day Eurail passes cost $554 for 15 days, $718 for 21 days, $890 for 1 month, $1,260 for 2 months, or $1,558 for 3 months.

✔ **Eurail Flexipass:** Good for 2 months of travel, within which you can travel by train for 10 days (consecutive or not) for $654, or 15 days for $862.

✔ **Eurail Saverpass:** A Saverpass is good for 2 to 5 people traveling together. The Saverpass costs $470 per person for 15 days, $610 for 21 days, $756 for 1 month, $1,072 for 2 months, or $1,324 for 3 months.

✔ **Eurail Saver Flexipass:** This is the flexipass for 2 to 5 people traveling together. The Saver Flexipass costs $556 per person for 10 days within 2 months, or $732 per person for 15 days within 2 months.

✔ **Eurail Youthpass:** This second-class railpass for travelers under 26 costs $388 for 15 days, $499 for 21 days, $623 for 1 month, $882 for 2 months, or $1,089 for 3 months.

✔ **Eurail Youth Flexipass:** Only for travelers under 26, this pass allows for 10 days of travel within 2 months for $458, or 15 days in 2 months for $599.

✔ **Europass:** If your trip focuses on the core of western Europe — specifically France, Germany, Switzerland, Italy, and Spain — Eurail is wasteful spending. Opt for the Europass, which gives you 5 days of train travel in these 5 countries for 2 months.

Purchase 1 or 2 of the 4 possible add-on zones — Austria/ Hungary; Greece (including the ferry from Brindisi, Italy); Belgium/ Netherlands/Luxembourg; and Portugal — to expand the scope of your pass. The base rail pass costs $348, $408 with 1 zone added, and $448 with two zones. You can also add up to 10 extra days (for 15 days total), at $20 to $38 per day, figured on an inverse sliding scale. (The more days you add, the more expensive each day becomes.)

✔ **Europass Saverpass:** For 2 or more people traveling together; the prices are the same as the previous bullet, but with a 15 percent discount per person.

✔ **Europass Youth:** The Europass Youth is valid in second-class only and is for travelers under 26. The base pass costs $233, $278 with one zone added, $311 with two zones, and $20 to $28 (on an inverse sliding scale) for each additional day.

✔ **EurailDrive Pass:** This pass offers the best of both worlds, mixing train travel and car rentals (through Hertz or Avis) for less money than it costs to do so separately. (It's also one of the only ways to avoid the high daily car-rental rates in Europe when you rent for less than a week.) You receive 4 first-class rail days and 2 car days within a 2-month period.

Prices (per person for 1 adult/2 adults) vary with the class of the car: $439/$385 economy class, $475/$402 compact, $495/$410 midsize. You can also add up to 5 extra rail days ($45 each) and unlimited extra car days ($59 each for economy class, $75 for compact, and $85 for midsize).

You must reserve your first car day a week before leaving the States, but you can make your other reservations as you go (always subject to availability). If you're traveling with more than 2 adults, extra passengers receive the car portion free but they must buy the 4-day railpass for $329.

✔ **Eurodrive Pass:** This deal is similar to the EurailDrive Pass, but it's valid only for Europass countries (no add-on zones) and shorter trips. The pass is good for 3 rail days and 2 car days within a 2-month period. Prices (per person for 1 adult/2 adults) are $355/$299 economy class, $385/$315 compact, and $409/$325 midsize. You can add up to 7 extra rail days at $39 each, and unlimited extra car days for $55 to $80 each, depending on the class of car.

Other rail passes

As if all the Eurail options weren't confusing enough, you can also buy **national passes** of various kinds: flexi, consecutive-day, rail-and-drive, rail-and-fly, kilometric (you buy a certain number of kilometers on the national rail system), and others.

You can also choose from **regional passes** such as **ScanRail** (for Scandinavian countries), **BritRail** (covering Great Britain, which is not a part of the Eurail gang), and the **European East Pass** (valid for travel in Austria, Czech Republic, Slovakia, Hungary, and Poland).

You must buy some types of national passes in the United States, while others you can get on either side of the Atlantic, and still others you can only purchase in Europe. In some countries, seniors, students, and youths can usually get discounts on European trains by simply asking for a discount, while in others, they can buy a discount card good for a fixed period. Rail Europe (see the following section) or your travel agent can give you all the details.

Purchasing your rail pass

You must buy passes for Eurail and its offshoots in the United States before you leave. (You can purchase them in some major European train stations, but you'll pay up to 50 percent more.) You can buy rail passes from most travel agents, but the largest supplier is **Rail Europe** (☎ 800-438-7245; Internet: www.raileurope.com), which also sells most national passes, except German passes.

I recommend contacting Rick Steve's **Europe Through the Back Door** (☎ 425-771-8303; Internet: www.ricksteves.com). Rick sells all Europewide and all national rail passes and sends you a free video and guide on using rail passes with every order. Plus, he doesn't tack on the $10 handling fee like other agencies.

BritRail (☎ 800-4-EURAIL; Internet: www.britrail.co.uk) specializes in Great Britain's rail passes. **DER Tours** (☎ 800-782-2424; Internet: www.dertravel.com) is a Germany specialist that also sells other national passes (except French and British).

When don't I need a rail pass?

Nifty as they are, rail passes aren't the wisest investment for every trip. If you're on an extended tour of Europe, Eurail is for people like you. However, if you're taking shorter, more focused trips, Europass is handier, but it may be overkill if you plan to only take a few train rides over the course of your visit.

Is any pass right for you? The answer is different for every trip, so prepare to do some math. For example, you have to travel at least 22 days (24 days with the youth pass) with a 2-month consecutive-day pass before your costs per trip drop to the 15-days-within-2-months flexipass. You have to decide if the extra days are worth it, depending on your travel plans and how much freedom you want to jump trains on a whim.

After you create an itinerary, estimate how much you think you'll spend on individual tickets, decide if a rail pass will save you dough and still do the job, and then go for it. To find individual ticket prices, contact **Rail Europe** (☎ 800-438-7245; Internet: www.raileurope.com).

Navigating the European Train Station

Like the trains themselves, European train stations are generally clean and user-friendly. They also offer better snack bars than you'd expect (in case you forget to pick up train picnic supplies in town). If you know your way around the train station, you can spend 20 minutes there when you first arrive in a city and arrive well oriented and fully armed for your visit.

Here's a helpful battle plan that you can use upon your arrival at a train station:

1. Stop by the station's ATM or bank for a bit of local cash (not too much, however — a downtown branch may offer better rates).

2. Find the tourist board kiosk or desk and pick up all the free info, maps, and brochures you can get.

 3. Visit a newsstand and decide whether the city maps for sale are better than the free one that you picked up from the tourist office. (Newsstand maps are usually better, so make the investment. You won't regret doing so later.) Pick up a phone card (if you'll be in the country long enough to use it), grab a few city bus or metro tickets to get you on your way, and buy the local English-language information/events magazine.

4. Now that you have some pocket change and a map that you can use to discover your destination, you may want to dump your main bag in a locker or left-luggage office for $2 to $10 a day, keeping only your daypack. If you'll only be in town for a half-day visit, keep your bags at the locker or luggage office. Even if you're spending the night, go hotel hunting *without* your luggage, and you'll have more stamina and bargaining leverage to find the best deal.

5. Find a phone and call around for a hotel, or use the station's hotel booking service. (See Chapter 8 for more hotel advice.)

In smaller towns, the tiny station bar may double as the ticket office. Most stations, however, have banks of ticket windows. Try to figure out which window you need before getting in the invariably long lines. The bulk of windows are for purchasing regular tickets, and a few windows are for people who need reservations only (if, for example, you have a Eurail pass but plan to take a reservations-required train or want to reserve a sleeping couchette). You may find a few windows for international or special high-speed trains only.

 Before you exit the train station, check your train options for when you leave town, as well as for any day trips that you plan to make. You can then swing by the train station a day or two before you leave to buy your tickets and reserve seats or couchettes rather than wait until the last minute when the lengthy ticket lines may thwart your precision-timed plans.

The rail information desk — not to be confused with the city tourist board's desk (the two won't answer each other's questions) — usually has a long line and a harried staff. Use the do-it-yourself information sources as much as possible. Modern stations in big cities often have computerized rail information kiosks and automatic ticketing machines, but both are often not working.

Luckily, you can still access the information you need the old-fashioned way. Almost all stations (except some in Paris) have schedule posters that list the full timetables and regular track numbers for all trains that pass through the station. Usually, but not always, arrivals are on a white poster and departures are on a yellow one. These posters show you the amount of trains per day that go where you want to go, their departure times, whether you need a reservation (often marked by a prominent **R**), and the ultimate destination for that train. For example, you may want to travel from Paris to Pisa, but the train's destination is marked Rome.

Keep in mind that track assignments may change on a daily basis. In larger stations, check the big, electronically updated departure boards. You can then seek out a conductor on the indicated platform and blurt out your destination in a questioning voice while pointing at the train-in-waiting for reconfirmation before boarding. Once on board, you may also want to triple-check with one of the other passengers.

Most train stations are fairly safe, but because they are central clearinghouses for bewildered tourists who are overwhelmed by a new city and probably not paying close attention to what's going on around them, pickpockets flourish. Never abandon your bags, take caution, and don't become distracted by the many hotel touts who will swarm you offering rooms.

In many countries now, you *must* stamp your ticket in a little box — usually attached to a column at the beginning of each track — in order to validate it before boarding the train. Conductors are increasingly issuing fines for not validating the ticket, even to unknowing tourists who plead ignorance.

Ticketing tips for public transport

Although metros (subways) have turnstiles, most public transportation (buses, trams, cable cars) in European cities operate on the honor system. As soon as you board, you're expected to punch your ticket in a little box on the bus. Make sure that you hold on to all tickets (metro, bus, or otherwise) for the duration of your ride, because spot inspectors board regularly or stop you in the metro tunnels. If they discover that you don't have a valid ticket, they will fine you on the spot, ranging from $20 to $300. And, on the London subway, you'll need your ticket to get back out at the end of your journey!

Floating to Your Destination by Ferry

Throughout the length of your stay, you may occasionally cross the waters in Europe, whether you do so over the traditional (pre-Channel Tunnel) English Channel crossing from Dover, England, to Calais, France; en route to Greece from Italy; around Scandinavia; or just off to an island somewhere. Ferry travel is often scenic, and can be cheap, but it's also invariably slow. Don't think of it as a cut-rate cruise or you'll be disappointed. Ferry rides are strictly a mode of public transportation.

For approximately double the money of a ferry, you can often take a *hydrofoil* (a sort of a ferry on steroids). A hydrofoil travels about twice as fast as the ferry, but you're stuck below deck for the entire trip. I advise taking the Eurostar train through the Channel Tunnel to get from England to France or Belgium. The time that you save and the aggravation and seasickness that you avoid more than offsets the difference in fare.

Getting Around by Bus

Regional and long-haul bus service in Europe mirrors the trains in its efficiency and remarkable network density. If a train in Europe can't take you where you want to go, a bus can almost certainly get you there.

Although prices are comparable to train prices, riding a bus takes two to four times as long, and they're five to ten times more uncomfortable. Avoid uncomfortable overnight bus trips at all costs.

I only take buses when a train isn't running to my destination point (as is often the case in rural areas), or if the bus makes a better connection (Florence to Siena, for example). In some countries — especially Ireland, Greece, Turkey, Portugal, and parts of Spain and Scandinavia — the bus network is more vast and better connected than the train service.

Driving in Europe

Although trains are great, a car is sometimes the best way to visit Europe — the wind in your hair, the freedom to turn down any road and visit vineyards, medieval hamlets, and crumbling castles. With a car, you can make your own schedule and get away from the set time structures of trains. Using a car is the only way to explore any small region in depth.

Of course, driving a car also has its downfalls. For example, you have to deal with aggressive drivers, navigate nerve-racking and confusing city traffic on occasion, and find and pay for parking whenever you stop. Likewise, you can't relax and do research on the trip between towns (you're driving, after all), and the gasoline prices will make your eyes look huge. Regardless, unless you walk or bike through Europe, you can't get any closer to the land and have the true freedom to go where you want than you can renting a car.

Obtaining an International Driver's Permit

If you plan to drive in Europe, you may want to bring along and carry (although it's not required), in addition to your regular driver's license, an *International Driver's Permit.* (This permit merely translates your data into several languages.) The permit costs $10 from AAA (you don't have to be a member; call ☎ 407-444-7000 to find the office nearest you). However, if you are an AAA member, ask for any free info and maps that they can send you to cover the countries in which you'll drive.

Knowing when to rent a car

If you want to cover lots of ground, concentrate on the cities, or go solo, taking the train is better than renting a car. However, if you're exploring a single country or region, planning to visit many small towns and you're traveling in a party of three or more, rent a car. Splitting one car rental is cheaper than train tickets when traveling in groups, and renting a car allows you more flexibility if you're traveling with kids. Tuscany, Provence, southern Spain, and Ireland are among the most scenic and rewarding areas in Europe to explore by car.

Avoid renting and having a car in cities at all costs. I can think of no aspect of European travel less exciting or more stressful. Plus, parking fees gobble at your travel budget. Between hotel charges and garages and lots, you can expect to pay anywhere from $10 to $60 a day just to park your rental. Save renting the car for exploring the countryside. Arrange to pick up your rental car the morning you leave the first city on your driving itinerary, and to drop it off as soon as you pull into your final destination.

The best trips mix and match modes of transportation. For example, you can take the train to Florence, and then drive through the vineyards and hill towns of Tuscany to Rome. Rail-and-drive passes (see "Different Types of Rail Passes," earlier in this chapter) can sometimes offer you bargain rates. I recommend breaking up your metropolis itinerary with some jaunts through the countryside to smaller towns to ensure that you don't miss out on a big part of the continent in your travels.

Saving time and money with rental car tips

Follow these tips to get the best deal on a rental car:

- **Rent in the United States.** You can get the best rates on car rental if you rent ahead of time directly through a U.S. company. If you're on the road and decide that you want a car, contact a friend or relative back home and ask them to cut the deal, faxing the confirmation directly to your hotel — the money you'll save is worth it. I list the numbers for the major rental companies, plus those that specialize in European travel, in Appendix A.

- **Shop around.** You may think that the rental car companies offer similar rates, but nothing is further from the truth. For the same four-day weekend, you may hear $49.95 from one company and $129.99 from another. I've found that the Europe specialists, Auto-Europe (☎ **800-223-5555**; Internet: www.autoeurope.com) and Europe By Car (☎ **800-223-1516**; Internet: www.europebycar.com), invariably offer the best rates. Make sure when you ask about what part of the quoted rate is the base rate that you also ask what else is included, such as a collision-damage waiver (CDW) and taxes, whether you get unlimited mileage, which you definitely want, and any other restrictions that may apply.

- **Be flexible.** Sometimes, picking up the car Thursday instead of Friday or at the downtown office instead of the airport or keeping the car over the weekend will save you big bucks. When giving the rental company your dates for pick up and delivery, inform them that you're also open to other dates as well if changing your dates means saving money. You may also save money if you rent for a full week rather than two days.

- **Know your restrictions.** Most rental companies restrict where you can drive. With some companies, you must stay in the country of rental (usually only smaller, national outfits mandate this rule). Likewise, most don't allow you to take a car that you rented in England to Ireland or the continent. Few let you drive from any Western European country into Eastern Europe, so if you're planning to drive to Prague, make sure that you make arrangements with the rental agency before you leave.

- **Lease for longer periods of time.** Companies don't always remind you of the leasing option, but if you want a car for more than 17 days (up to 6 months), tell them that you want to short-term lease the car (Auto-Europe and Europe By Car both offer this option). Leasing a car gives you a brand-new car and *full* insurance coverage with no deductible. You can also get around a technical loophole for those too young to rent under official company policy if you lease. The minimum age for renting a car ranges from 18 to 27, but it's usually 21 to 25. Anyone over 18, however, can usually lease a car.

✔ **Stick shifts are cheaper than automatics.** You can save up to 40 percent on the price of car rental if you rent a stick shift car instead of an automatic. As an added bonus to renting a manual shift, they often give you better control on Europe's many narrow, windy, hilly roads and tight streets in ancient cities.

✔ **Look into coverage you may already have.** The *collision damage waiver,* or CDW, basically allows you to total the car and not be held liable. Your credit card may cover the CDW if you use it to pay for the rental, so make sure that you check the terms of your credit card before purchasing CDW. However, keep in mind that some rental agencies in Italy won't accept credit-card CDW for rentals. You must purchase it separately instead. Travel Guard (☎ 800-826-1300) sells independent CDW coverage for a mere $6 a day.

✔ **Remind the company that you've already paid.** Make sure that you know exactly what you paid for when you arranged your car rental. Many times, the car pick up offices in Europe often over-look the fact that your credit card was already charged for the rental cost, and they try to double-charge you. Usually, you end up with one charge on your card from the European office for the first full tank of gas that it provides (which is almost never included in the original rental price).

✔ **Inspect the car before driving away.** If the rental agency doesn't know that something is wrong with the car you rented when you drive it off, it'll assume that you broke the car and charge you accordingly. If the car's condition doesn't match the inspection form that they want you to sign, point out the discrepancy. Otherwise, you're legally liable for the condition after you drive away. Make sure that all locks and doors work, check the various lights, and quickly scan the entire car for dents, scratches, and fabric rips.

✔ **Check for repair and safety equipment.** Check the trunk to make sure that your rental car is equipped with a jack, inflated spare, snow chains (for winter driving), and a hazard triangle (most countries require that you hang this on your trunk if you're broken down on the side of the road). Likewise, check the glove compartment for a parking disc. (Ask the rental agency about the parking disc; they'll explain the country's honor-system parking lots, if the system applies.)

✔ **Gas up before you return the car.** When leaving the rental com-pany, make sure the the car has a full tank of gas so you don't have to worry about dealing with local gas stations immediately. However, make sure that you return the car with a full tank of gas. Similar to rental company practices in the United States, if you forget to fill up the car before you return it, the company will kindly fill it for you at obscenely jacked-up prices. Before you return the car, find a gas station and top off the tank.

Understanding European road rules

Except for driving on the left in Great Britain and Ireland, European road rules are similar enough to American ones that you can drive without further instruction. However, the following important differences do exist:

- ✔ Most European drivers are much more aggressive than American drivers.

- ✔ *Do not ride* in the left lane on a four-lane highway; it is truly for passing only. (Or for Mercedes with the pedal down and their hazards blinking to let you know they don't intend to use the brake pedal.)

- ✔ If a vehicle comes up from behind and flashes its lights at you, it's signaling for you to slow down and drive more on the shoulder of the road, so they can pass you more easily. (Two-lane roads in Europe routinely become three cars wide.)

- ✔ Except for parts of the German Autobahn, most highways list speed limits of approximately 60 to 80 miles per hour (100 to 135 kilometers per hour).

- ✔ European measurements relating to vehicles, are in kilometers (mileage and speed limits). For a rough conversion, remember that one kilometer equals about 0.6 miles.

- ✔ Gas may look reasonably priced, but remember that the price is per liter (3.8 liters equals one gallon, so multiply by four to guestimate the equivalent per-gallon price).

- ✔ Some countries, such as Austria and Switzerland, require highway stickers in lieu of paying tolls (or as a supplement to cheap tolls). If you rent a car within such a country, your car already has a sticker. But, if you're crossing a border, check at the crossing station to see whether you need to purchase a sticker on the spot for a nominal fee.

- ✔ Drive defensively and carefully, assume that other drivers have a better idea of what they're doing than you do, and take your hints from them.

Chapter 8

A Room with or without a View: Finding Lodging

*L*odging is the second-biggest expense of most any European trip — only transportation will cost you more. But because you usually have so many options when deciding where to stay, lodging is also an area in which you can save a lot of money. In Paris, for example, you can spend several hundred dollars on a lavish palace, stay in a middle-of-the-road hotel down the street for $60, or check into a hostel for just $18 a night.

During your travels, you will encounter an astounding number of accommodation options. If you do a little bit of legwork, note the hotel recommendations in this book, and follow the hotel-hunting tips in this chapter, you'll never get stuck spending more than $80 to $100 a night for a neat, clean, centrally located double room — unless, of course, splurging is in your budget.

Understanding European Hotels

Hotels in Europe tend to have fewer frills and features than Americans are used to in their hotels. For example, free cable television is standard at even the cheapest American motel chains. In Europe, however, few moderately priced and inexpensive hotel rooms even contain televisions.

Amenities are not nearly as important to European hotel operators as cleanliness and friendliness. Sure, most midrange European hotels can be somewhat worn around the edges, with functional furnishings that are either mismatched or aging, but they're great deals.

Europe's cheaper, more traditional hotels and *pensions* (smaller, family-run establishments) typically differ from American hotels in the following ways:

✔ **The appearance of the lobby rarely matches the appearance of the rooms.** Never judge a European hotel by the front entry; expensive hotels sometimes invest heavily in the lobby but cut corners on the rooms, and cheaper hotels often have just a dingy desk in a hallway but spotless, fine accommodations upstairs.

✔ **"Double" beds are often two side-by-side twin beds made with a single sheet and blanket** (or overlapping twin sheets). If you are worried about suffering from separation anxiety (or slipping through the crack) during the night, turn the twin mattresses perpendicular to the springs. Also, watch out for lazy springs and mattresses that sag in the middle.

✔ **Hotels in old European buildings often don't have elevators.** If they do, the few elevators that are available are likely to be so rickety and slow that they belong in a museum.

✔ **Floors are often covered with tile or linoleum instead of carpet.**

✔ **Bathrooms are vastly and surprisingly different from the American norm** (see the next section, "Cleanliness is next to friendliness: Sharing bathrooms").

✔ **Even though you may be tempted by the convenience of having the hotel do your laundry, it will cost you a pretty *peseta*** and is usually an option only at middle-range hotels and up. The obvious alternative is to go to a laundromat, but it seems like such a waste to watch your clothes swirl around when you're a quarter of a mile from one of the world's most beautiful monuments. Instead, look for a laundry shop that will wash and dry your clothes based on weight (an average load costs $7). Most European cities have them; start looking near the local university.

✔ **You can trust hotel staff to provide you with general information and pamphlets about sightseeing and attractions, but be wary of anything beyond that.** A restaurant recommended by an employee may be one owned by a relative or someone who has agreed to give the hotel a kickback. Usually the place is fine, but never count on a hotel to direct you to the best food in town. Hotel staff members sometimes also offer to get you tickets for local theater or cultural shows, but these tickets are usually cheaper from the box office or local tourism office.

In short, think of the hotel simply as a place with a room where you can rest your body between long days of sightseeing. Don't expect to see chocolates on your pillow or little bottles of shampoo and conditioner. If your sole reason for being there is to rest or sleep, the room just needs to be safe, clean, and reasonably close to the sights. With the money you save on lodging, you can treat yourself to the occasional fancy meal, souvenirs, extra museum admissions, or a day trip out of town.

Cleanliness is next to friendliness: Sharing bathrooms

People who haven't traveled in Europe think that language, architecture, and food best illustrate the cultural differences between America and the Continent. Sorry, guess again. Americans traveling in Europe experience the greatest culture shock in the bathroom. It all starts in your first cheap pension, when you find out that, just like when you were growing up, the only bathroom is down the hall and shared by everyone on the floor — of *both* sexes.

European hoteliers have trouble understanding why so many American travelers don't want to share a bathroom. Although more European hotels are installing bathrooms in every room, this is far from the norm. If you simply can't bear the thought of sharing a bathroom, you'll have to pay extra for a private bathroom in your room.

Important safety tip: See the section on electricity in Chapter 10 for information on what isn't safe to plug into European bathroom outlets. (Here's a hint: everything.)

The adventure of showering

In many European hotels, the concept of a shower is something like this: A nozzle stuck in the bathroom wall and a drain in the floor, curtains optional. In some cramped private baths, you have to remove the toilet paper from the bathroom to keep it dry while you drench the whole room with your shower.

Bath-takers are not home free, either. Some European hotels still have half-tubs, in which you can only sit, not stretch out. The half-tub usually also sports a shower nozzle that has nowhere to hang — so while your knees get very clean, the floor gets very wet.

Hot water may be available only once a day — and not when you want it. This is especially true in hotels with shared baths. Because heating water is costly, many smaller hotels only do it once a day, in the morning; after the hot water is used up, you won't be able to get any more until the next day. So when you check in, ask "When is the water hot?" Try to be the first in line, take your shower quickly, and soap up with the water off. In some countries, especially Britain, you may have to turn on the hot water yourself at a small hot water heater either inside or just outside the stall.

Before you take your shower or bath, remember that traditional European towels are annoyingly unabsorbent. Carry your own towel for just such an emergency (a terry-cloth hand towel is less bulky than a full-sized; camping towels work great).

No, it's not an extra toilet

The extra porcelain fixture that looks like another toilet is called a *bidet* (bi-DAY). *Do not use the bidet as a second toilet.* The water that jets up and out is supposed to clean your private parts more thoroughly than toilet paper. Some non-European travelers wash clothes or store fruit or beverages in the bidet. (If you think about what the bidet is supposed to be used for, the sink looks like a great place to do your laundry.)

Finding the Right Hotel

One of the biggest disappointments of any trip is getting to your hotel room and realizing that it's too small, too dirty, or too expensive. This section offers information and advice that will help you find the accommodations that meet your needs — and your budget.

Comparing room rates and ratings

The hotels listed in this book are rated from $ to $$$$. These ratings are not an official ranking system; they do not reflect the overall quality of a hotel; rather, they reflect the approximate price range of the hotels that I recommend because of their overall *value*. A ranking of $ indicates a budget gem, $$ means a moderate hotel, $$$ is applied to more upscale accommodations, and $$$$ is for a recommended splurge. These ratings are comparable only within the same city, meaning that a $ joint in an expensive place like London may cost about the same as a $$$$ hotel in a cheaper area like Athens.

I include the hotel's actual rates so you can find your price range easily. Of course, rates can and will go up regularly (and probably will during the shelf life of any travel book), but barring massive renovations, a budget gem or moderate choice this year will fall in the same category next year, even if the price tags are $10 higher.

Settle all hotel charges when you check in. You don't need to pay in advance, but make sure that you and the hotel clerk agree on the rate; whether it includes breakfast, taxes, and showers; the phone rates (never make long-distance calls from the hotel); and so on. Also be sure that the price you were quoted is per room, *not per person,* as it often is in resort-type coastal towns and islands.

In most European destinations, taxes are automatically included in the rates quoted you. However, in some countries (often in Spain, where it's 7 percent, and sometimes in England, where it's 19 percent) these local taxes are not included in the price you get over the phone. Always ask, "Does that price include all taxes?"

When you check in, always take one of the hotel's business cards. You'd be surprised by how many people forget their hotel's name or location after a long day of sightseeing. Most cards have a little map on the back. If you're clueless where your hotel is, hop in a cab and show the driver the card. He'll get you home.

Making reservations

I always reserve at least the first night's stay before leaving home, especially if I will be arriving on a weekend. Having somewhere to base yourself right away minimizes the stress and uncertainty when you arrive — tired and in a strange place. But don't book the room for more than a few days; it's nice to have the option of looking for other accommodations if your choice isn't what you expected.

Reserving every night of a vacation in advance can strangle your trip's spontaneity and limit you to your first (and potentially bad) choice. Calling ahead to reserve at least the first night in a new town usually works well. I often book my first night's stay in a new city simply by phoning from the train station when I arrive.

You should be aware that making last-minute arrangements this way can cause headaches. If you're traveling with young children, you don't want to be fumbling for coins in the train station as you try to simultaneously reserve a room and keep the kids from running off for parts unknown.

You should also find out whether you will be arriving in town during a festival. If you are, the gala may be the highlight of your trip, but you could end up sleeping under the stars if you haven't booked a room well in advance (from the States).

If you reserve a room before leaving home for your vacation, *always confirm the reservation with a follow-up fax*. Most hotels prefer this, and it gives you printed proof that you've booked a room. Faxes to hotels should use simple language and include the following:

- ✔ Your name.
- ✔ The number of people in your party.
- ✔ What kind of room you want (make sure you say "double with one bed" or "double with two beds," and specify "two adults, one child, in same room").
- ✔ The number of nights you want to stay.
- ✔ The date of the first night.

To avoid confusion, *always* spell out the full name of the month — Europeans numerically abbreviate dates day/month/year, not month/day/year as we do (so "5/6/2002" would be read May 6 in America, June 5 in Europe).

Smaller, less-expensive hotels often won't take reservations far in advance for short stays (fewer than three nights). This policy protects them from cancellations, which can be particularly damaging to smaller hotels' bottom lines, and no assurance you offer will convince the hotelier that you will show up. Even when you have a reservation, these hotels will hold your room only if you call from the station to say you're on the way.

Using a hotel booking service

Either the train station or the local tourism office in most European towns will have a desk that serves as a central reservation service for the city. To use the service, tell the people working there your price range, the part of the city you'd like to stay in, and sometimes even the type of hotel, and they'll use a computer to find you a room. In each city chapter in this book, I list booking services at the start of the "Runner-up accommodations" section.

Here are the advantages of booking services:

✔ They do all the legwork for you. Staff members speak English, while many individual hoteliers may not, so they can act as interpreters while calling around for you.

✔ If everything's booked up — during a convention or festival, or maybe just in high season — they can often find rooms in hotels that aren't listed in the guidebooks or other popular sources.

✔ The best ones can find accommodations that perfectly match your needs and price range.

Of course, booking services do have their drawbacks:

✔ They usually charge a fee — a nominal one (say, $3 to $10), but a fee nonetheless. And in many countries, hotels often charge higher rates for bookings they receive through services. It's cheapest to contact hotels directly.

✔ A tourism office booking desk clerk will offer no opinion about the hotels; he or she will just provide you a list to choose from that may include amenities and prices, but little else.

 ✔ A booking agency, especially a private one (which is probably run by a group of local hotels), will try to steer you to places on its "push list." Rather than an honest evaluation, its "advice" is frequently a biased sales pitch dictated by the hotel itself.

You can get mixed results from the information that booking services provide. I've found wonderful little bed-and-breakfasts in Ireland through the glossy promotional catalog the tourist office sent me. I've also had a Prague hotel agency stick me in what appeared to be an old high school almost an hour from the city center; the room made me long for my college dorm. The only way to protect yourself is to read promotional fluff with a skeptical eye and ask tough questions when you call around.

In most cities — Prague and Rome come to mind — and on popular islands, hotel *touts* will swarm you as you step off the train or boat. Some are honestly drumming up business, but others are out to fleece you. If an offer interests you, make sure the tout pinpoints the exact location of the hotel on a map and get the price in writing before you go off with him. Pay close attention to any photos he shows you, but remember that a little photo retouching and some strategic furniture rearrangement can make a dismal cell look more like a palatial suite.

Surfing the Web for hotel deals

Although the major travel Web sites (Travelocity, Expedia, Yahoo! Travel, and Cheap Tickets; see Chapter 6 for details) offer hotel booking, you may be better off using a site devoted primarily to lodging because it may have properties that aren't listed on more general travel sites.

One of the pluses of Web sites is that they often include virtual brochures, so you can see pictures of the rooms ahead of time. You can also usually get the latest hotel rates, plus any discounts the booking service might be able to secure (especially at pricier inns).

But these sites also have some big minuses. Because most of them charge a fee to the hotels they list and the hotels themselves provide the write-ups and other info, you must take any descriptions or recommendations with a grain of salt. Travel guidebooks like this one provide unbiased recommendations, but most hotel booking Web sites are just a new form of promotional material. Also, the bulk of the hotels that choose to be listed on these sites are high-end, business-oriented, owned by chains, or all of the above. The best small hotels in the historic city centers, mom-and-pop pensions, and outright cheap places are glaringly absent from most of these sites.

Some lodging sites specialize in a particular type of accommodations, such as B&Bs, which you won't find on the more mainstream booking services. Others such as TravelWeb offer weekend deals on major chain properties, which cater to business travelers and have more empty rooms on weekends.

Following is information on some of the top lodging sites on the Web:

- ✔ **All Hotels on the Web** (www.all-hotels.com). Although the name is something of an exaggeration, this site *does* have tens of thousands of listings throughout the world and is one of the most complete out there. Bear in mind that each hotel has paid a small fee ($25 and up) to be listed, so it's less an objective list and more like a book of online brochures.

- ✔ **Hoteldiscount!com** (www.180096hotel.com). This site books blocks of rooms in advance, so sometimes it has rooms — at discount rates — at hotels that are "sold out." The downside: Other than London and Paris, which have 40 to 50 listings each, most European cities are represented by only 6 to 25 hotels. Select a city, input your dates, and you'll get a list of best prices for a selection of hotels. This site is notable for delivering deep discounts in cities where hotel rooms are expensive. The toll-free number is printed all over the site (☎ **800-96-HOTEL**); call it if you want more options than are listed online. Also, half the time the site's search engine just reroutes you into the Places to Stay site, described later.

✔ **InnSite** (www.innsite.com). This site is less slick but much less commercial than the other sites here — more of a community-run, Yahoo!-like list portal for inns, B&Bs, and rental rooms. Find an inn at your destination, see pictures of the rooms, and check prices and availability. This extensive directory of B&Bs only includes listings submitted by proprietors (it's free to get an inn listed), so it's spotty in some destinations, exhaustive in others. The innkeepers write the descriptions, and many listings link to the inn's own Web sites. It also lets you do a mini-search across several key Web sites to come up with recommendations outside its own guide. Also try the **Bed and Breakfast Channel** (www.bedandbreakfast.com).

✔ **Places to Stay** (www.placestostay.com). All-inclusive business hotels and resort accommodations are the focus of this site. Again, listing is selective — this isn't a comprehensive directory — but it can give you a sense of what's available at different destinations.

✔ **TravelWeb** (www.travelweb.com). Focusing on chains such as Hyatt and Hilton, this site lists more than 26,000 hotels in 170 countries — and you can book almost 90 percent of these online. TravelWeb's Click-It Weekends, updated each Monday, offers weekend deals at many leading hotel chains.

✔ **Barclay International Group** (www.barclayweb.com). Families that are home-basing and day-tripping rather than flitting from town to town will find this site useful. It's a great resource for apartment rentals across Europe — usually with a minimum stay of five to seven days.

Remember that I include the Web address for any hotel recommended in this guidebook that has its own site. And most city chapters list the official tourist info Web site for the city near the beginning of the chapter. These sites vary in the amount of information they provide; some merely list phone numbers and addresses (and, if you're lucky, prices) of area hotels, some link you to a private Web site run either by a consortium of local hotels or by a private agency that charges a fee for local hotels to join.

Getting the best deals, even at the last minute

If you pull into your destination with no hotel reservation, a guidebook like this can come in very handy. Before you arrive in town (perhaps on the train ride in), study the hotel reviews and figure out which ones best fit your taste and budget. Then rank your top choices by writing 1, 2, 3, and so on in the guide's margin. Prioritizing the hotels prepares you to move quickly to the next best option if your first choice is full.

Once you pull into the station, get some change or buy a phone card at a newsstand and immediately start calling hotels to check for vacancies. This gives you a head start on the many people who look for a room by marching out of the station with their bags and walking to the nearest hotel. If you're uncomfortable making the calls yourself, the train station or tourism office usually runs a reservation service (see "Using a hotel booking service" earlier in this chapter).

If you can't find a room this way, you can try wandering the streets checking each hotel you pass. But the areas around city train stations usually are full of cheap hotels, and they often are bland — sometimes seedy — neighborhoods and not centrally located.

Also try expanding the scope of your search. Hotels outside the center of town often have more rooms available and are cheaper than centrally located hotels. You may be able to get an even better deal in the next town over, but it won't be worth the trouble if it's more than a 30-minute train ride away. Venture out of the city only as a last resort.

To get the best price on a room, follow these tips:

✔ **Ask to see different rooms.** When you get to the hotel, don't take the first room you're shown. Ask to see some other ones. Open and close windows to see how well they block out noise. Check the rates posted on the room door (usually there by law) to make sure they match the rate you were quoted and the rate that's posted in the lobby. Ask about heating. Ask whether some rooms are less expensive than others.

✔ **Bargain.** Room prices are rarely set in stone, especially in pensions and mom-and-pop joints. The more empty rooms a hotel has to fill for the night, the lower it'll go with the price. If you're going to be there a single night during the height of the tourism season, you'll have to pay the going rate. But for off-season stays and for longer than three nights, ask for a discount. Many places have weekend discounts. Keep in mind that double rooms are sometimes cheaper if they have one large bed instead of two single beds. A triple with an additional cot for a family of four is much cheaper than two double rooms.

✔ **Remember, rooms cost less without bathrooms.** If you don't mind walking down the hall and sharing a bathroom, your savings will be nothing to sneeze at.

✔ **Compare different hotels.** Many people don't want to run from place to place, but if you have some time and are counting the pennies, it's probably worth a try. Don't assume that the first hotel you visit is the best. If you've called around and lodging seems in short supply around town, take a room where you can get it. But if rooms seem plentiful, tell the first hotel you stop in that you'll think about it and head to another one nearby. You'll feel and appear better prepared to search and bargain effectively if you leave your luggage in a train station locker while you look for a hotel. When you decide which hotel you like best, return there and ask the clerk for the best price he or she can offer. (The price will often lower if it appears you have another option waiting nearby.)

✔ **Ask for rates without breakfast.** A room can be $5 to $10 cheaper without breakfast included. Hotel breakfasts are always overpriced; they're usually just a roll and coffee or tea. Any corner cafe can sell you the same thing much cheaper. The only hotel breakfasts worth keeping are the feasts served in the B&Bs of Great Britain.

Discovering Other Types of Accommodations

The reviews in this book concentrate on standard hotels (along with a few traditional and charming family-run pensions) because hotels generally are larger and thus are more likely to have rooms available.

But hotels aren't your only lodging option. In fact, compared to the other options available, they're usually among the most expensive and are rarely the most fun or memorable. Even if your room truly is just a place to rest your weary body, if you can get a bed that's both cheaper and in unique surroundings, why not do it?

The most popular alternatives

Each country seems to have its own hotel alternatives, from Alpine hiker's shacks to rental villas in Tuscany. Far too many different options exist — some 36 in Europe by my last count — to do justice to each of them here. However, here's a quick rundown on the most popular substitutes for the traditional hotel (for more information on each of these, check with the local tourism office):

✔ **B&Bs or pensions.** When Europeans go on vacation, these small, family-run versions of hotels are where they stay. If the hotels in town charge $100 for a double, a pension will usually cost only $40 to $60. Upscale B&Bs — often offering what amounts to a chic apartment — are becoming popular in cities like London and Paris as well.

Some B&Bs require you to pay for breakfast or half or full board (meals included); private baths are still rare (though that's starting to change); and the service is almost always genial and personable. Don't accept the meal options unless you have no other choice, as is often the case in resort locations like spas and beaches, especially during the tourism season. You usually get better food and more variety in a local restaurant.

International chains: Hotels, but not in a European sense

International chain hotels, which you can usually reserve from the United States, are often located on the edge of town in the business or industrial district. They're huge, impersonal, and expensive, but you can count on a certain level of amenities and services.

Unlike most international chains, whose hotels suffer from a bland sameness (and often a perimeter location) no matter what country they're in, Best Western has followed a commendable strategy of partnering with existing downtown hotels. Often a European Best Western is really a local bastion of a hotel that's been a solid low-end-of-luxury choice in that city for decades, if not a century or more.

✔ **Private room rentals.** Even the cheapest B&B can't beat the price of renting a room in a private home, which can run as low as $15 to $40 for a double. This is a great option for single travelers because you don't pay the outrageous single-occupancy rate that most hotels charge.

The quality of the accommodations in rental rooms is less consistent than at standard hotels, but at worst you'll be stuck in a tiny, plain room. At best, you get comfortable furniture, a homey atmosphere, a home-cooked breakfast, and a feel for what it's like to be part of a real European family.

✔ **Motels.** Europe has adopted this American form of modular innkeeping, but most travelers don't know this because — as in the United States — motels cluster around city outskirts at highway access points. If you're doing your travel by car and are arriving late, these places are a great, cheap lodging option. They are completely devoid of character, but they are often real bargains. Some are even fully automated so you check yourself in and out.

✔ **Converted castles and other historic buildings.** These usually high-quality lodgings can be outrageously expensive, or they can be surprisingly cheap state-run operations. (Spain's *paradores* are the best example of the latter.)

✔ **Rental apartments or villas.** If you're planning a long stay in one location and want to feel like a temporary European, or if you have a large traveling party (a big family or two families traveling together), these options are the best.

Newspaper travel sections and magazines contain many ads for apartment and villa rentals. They're easiest to book through a travel agent or villa rental consortium, but you can sometimes get better rates by contacting people at the destination directly (with addresses or phone numbers from local papers, English-language magazines, and the tourism board).

Before you reserve an apartment or villa, shop around a lot, ask many questions, and look at pictures — both of the rooms and of the views in every direction so you'll be familiar with the setting. For particularly long stays, it may pay for one member of the party to make a quick trip to the country in question to tour the top options before you settle on one.

Hostels and other money-saving options

If you're on a severely limited budget, or if you like hanging out with primarily youthful backpackers, you might want to stay in a hostel. They used to be called *youth* hostels, but the only ones that still follow the under-26-only rule are in southern Germany. Most hostels are now open as cheap digs for travelers of all ages, with nightly rates ranging from $10 to $30 per person.

Some are affiliated with the official hostel organization, Hostelling International (or IYH, as it's known abroad), which means they have to live up to a certain set of standards. Increasingly, private, unaffiliated hostels are opening up (often closer to the center of town than the official hostel), and while they may not have the IYH stamp of approval, in some cases they're actually nicer joints than the town's IYH hostel (by the same token, they may also be squalid dumps). In a hostel, you stay in bunks in shared, dormlike rooms. Hostels will have anywhere from a few beds per room to as many as 100 beds in one big gymnasium-like space; most hostels have a mix of different-sized rooms at varying prices. Families can often find hostels with four-bunk rooms for semi-private housing. Many hostels separate the sexes into different rooms or floors. There are lockers for safe bag storage. Bathrooms are always shared, breakfast is often included, and other meals may be available.

Hostels (especially the official IYH ones) are often far from the city center, occasionally on the outskirts of town, and they fill up with high school students in the summer. Year-round, many seem to be little more than giant backpacker singles' bars — great for meeting your fellow travelers, but terrible for getting to know the city and culture you're visiting.

Almost all hostels impose evening curfews (usually between 10:00 p.m. and midnight), midday lockout periods, and length-of-stay limits (often a maximum of three days). You may only be able to make reservations one day ahead of time, or not at all, so be sure to show up early.

To stay in many "official" IYH hostels — or at least to get a discount — you must be a card-carrying member of **Hostelling International,** 733 15th Street NW, Suite 840, Washington, DC 20005 (☎ **202-783-6161;** Internet: www.hiayh.org). Membership is free for people under 17; the cost is $25 per year for people 18 to 54, and $15 for those 55 and older. You can also buy the card at many hostels abroad.

Hostelling International sells *Hostelling International Budget Accom-modations You Can Trust, Vol. I: Europe and the Mediterranean* for $13.95. Also check out *Frommer's Complete Hostel Vacation Guide to England, Wales and Scotland* ($14.95), the first guide to the 300-plus hostels in those countries. For an independent Internet hostelling guide, try www.hostels.com.

Most hostels furnish a blanket but require you to have your own *sleep-sack,* which is basically a sleeping bag made out of a sheet. If you plan to stay in hostels on your trip, before you leave you should buy (from Hostelling International) or make one (fold a sheet in half and sew it closed across the bottom and halfway up the side). Some hostels will sell you a sleep-sack, and a few will insist that you rent one of theirs.

In addition to hostels, several other options exist for low-budget lodging in Europe:

✔ **Convents.** Especially in predominantly Catholic countries (Italy, Spain, and France), convents and other religious buildings enable you to save a lot of money and get an immaculate and safe room, no matter what your religious affiliation. Rooms in convents, avail-able in many major cities and pilgrimage sites, cost as little as $5 to as much as $50 per night. Your room probably won't be any fancier than the cells the nuns or monks occupy, but a few are quite posh. Many convents do give preference to visitors of their own denomination or from that religious order's country of origin.

✔ **University housing.** During the summer when school is not in ses-sion, it is worth your while to check with local universities or the tourism office to see whether any unused dorms rooms are for rent (at rates comparable to hostels).

✔ **Crash-ins.** Some cities (Munich, London, Paris, Venice, and Copenhagen) have what I call "crash-ins," hangarlike rooms or large tents open at the height of the summer season for travelers on an extremely tight budget. For anywhere from $7 to $20, you'll get a floor mat and a blanket, more than 100 roommates, and a cup of tea in the morning. Most of the people at these giant slumber parties are students, but they are open to everyone. Essentially, this is one step above sleeping on a park bench (which, by the way, is dangerous, not recommended, and usually illegal).

✔ **Overnight trains.** This is one the best sleeping and travel bargains in Europe. For just $20 — free if you take a chance on finding an empty couchette — plus the cost of your ticket or rail pass, you get a bunk in a couchette, and you wake up in your next destina-tion without having wasted a day getting there. The main thing you sacrifice is a sound night's sleep. (See Chapter 7 for more details.)

If you use any type of shared-space lodging — hostels, crash-ins, and, to a lesser extent, camping — be very careful with your belongings. Always play it safe; leave your pack in the lockers if you are staying in a hostel, or at the train station if you are staying in another type of communal lodging.

Chapter 9

Money Matters and Safety Issues

In This Chapter

▶ Deciding which is best: ATMs, credit cards, and traveler's checks

▶ Beating the exchange rate game

▶ Avoiding theft

▶ Understanding the VAT tax and getting it back

*O*nce you've planned your trip and created a budget (see Chapter 4), you need to decide how to carry and access your money: traveler's checks, ATM cards, credit cards, local currency, U.S. dollars, and so on. This chapter weighs the benefits and annoyances of each method and shows you how to get the most out of your dough. I also enter the sometimes confusing realm of exchange rates, where one day you're thinking in terms of a few British pounds and the next you're calculating tens of thousands of Italian lire. Likewise, I give you some advice about how to shop around for and secure the best exchange rate.

Traveler's Checks, Credit Cards, ATMs, or Cash

A traveler's check and the local American Express or Thomas Cooke office used to be your only means of obtaining local currency abroad. Nowadays, however, traveler's checks are the dinosaurs of European travel. ATM cards and credit card cash advances are much cheaper and easier. The inconvenience of waiting in line at banks or exchange booths, digging your passport out of your money belt, and getting charged sometimes high commissions has led most frequent travelers to abandon traveler's checks in favor of a trip to a street-corner ATM.

Using your ATM card

In Europe, your bank card was useless plastic about a decade ago. These days, however, you can saunter up to an ATM in virtually any city and most small towns, and retrieve local cash the same as you would in the United States. Using the ATM machine is the fastest, easiest, and least expensive way to exchange money. When you use an ATM, you take advantage of the bank's bulk exchange rate (better than any rate you can find on the street) and, unless your home bank charges you for using a nonproprietary ATM (usually $2 tops), your transaction is commission free.

Both the **Cirrus** (☎ 800-424-7787; Internet: www.mastercard.com/atm) and **Plus** (☎ 800-843-7587; Internet: www.visa.com/atms) networks offer automated ATM locators that list the banks in each country that will accept your card. Or, as an alternative, you can search for any machine that carries your network's symbol. Increasingly, Europe is like the United States in that there's a bank on virtually every corner, and most are globally networked. In fact, I've rarely run across a European ATM that wouldn't honor my U.S. bank card.

Increased internationalism has essentially eliminated the worry that your card's PIN needs special treatment to work abroad, but you should still check with the issuing bank before you leave. Most European systems use four-digit PINs; six-digit ones often won't work.

If you get a strange message at the ATM that says your card isn't valid for international transactions, most likely the bank isn't able to make the phone connection to check your PIN (occasionally this epidemic occurs citywide). Don't panic. Try another ATM, cash a traveler's check, or wait until tomorrow or the next town that you visit.

Europe takes plastic: Pulling out your credit card

Visa and **MasterCard** are now almost universally accepted — and in many places preferred — at most European hotels, restaurants, and shops. The majority of these places also accept **American Express,** though its high commissions and unhurried reimbursement process is leading more and more small businesses to deny acceptance. The **Diner's Club** card continues to gain ground, however, especially in the cities and more expensive establishments.

Except in the most exclusive restaurants and hotels, most Europeans have never heard of **Carte Blanche, Discover** has yet to provoke a reaction from anybody, and gas station and department store credit cards are worthless overseas. Likewise, when visiting smaller, cheaper family-run businesses, such as some inexpensive hotels and cheap restaurants, most rental rooms, and some neighborhood shops, you may find that your plastic is useless. Therefore, never rely solely on credit cards.

You can also use your credit card to get a *cash advance* through Visa or MasterCard (contact the issuing bank to get a PIN), but these days this can prove to be an expensive option. Until recently, you could take advantage of the bulk bank exchange rate (4 percent better than what you get on your own) on credit card cash advances, just as with an ATM card. However, the credit card companies started charging a 1- percent commission for the cost of foreign conversion. (The conversion doesn't cost the issuing banks anything. They just use the excuse as another opportunity to nickel-and-dime you to death.) Most issuing banks thought that this was a great idea and have started tacking on 1 to 3 percent themselves, shrinking your total savings to 2 percent at best and nothing at worst.

Adding insult to injury, when you use your credit cards overseas, you pay the premium interest rate (usually around 19 percent) on cash advances, not the low introductory rate that many credit cards offer. Likewise, with most cards, you start to accrue interest immediately when you make a cash advance (rather than at the end of the month and only if you don't pay up, as with purchases). If you use American Express, you can usually only obtain a cash advance from an American Express office.

Consider informing your card's issuing bank that you're taking a trip. Most companies use computerized watchdogs, which look for radical changes in the frequency or location of charges, to monitor your card's use. When the watchdog finds these types of changes, it automatically freezes your account. Ideally, this system alerts issuing companies if someone steals your card and goes on a shopping spree, but it also has the unfortunate side effect of leaving travelers without access to their cash, because on a typical vacation, you charge more than usual and you charge from strange places. However, if you are the victim of real theft, see "Coping with a Stolen Wallet" later in this chapter.

Cashing traveler's checks

A *traveler's check* is a prepaid slip of paper worth $20, $50, or $100 (larger denominations are unwieldy to exchange and so not useful for European travel). You sign traveler's checks once at the bank or issuing office when you buy them and again in the presence of the person who accepts or cashes the check. You can take them (along with your passport for I.D.) to any bank, American Express office, or exchange booth in Europe, and they'll change the checks for the equivalent amount of local currency, minus exchange rate fees (more on shopping for exchange rates later in the chapter).

However, unlike an ATM card, when you cash in your traveler's checks, you only get the street exchange rate (about 4 percent below prime), and you have to wait in long bank lines, as well as wait for them to check and photocopy your passport. If you're comfortable doing so, using the ATM is the better, all-around choice.

So why do so many people still use traveler's checks? Insurance. Traveler's checks are theft- and computer-proof. Unlike regular currency, if you lose your traveler's checks, you haven't lost your money. As long as you keep a list of the check numbers in a safe place, separate from the checks themselves, and cross each number out as you exchange it, you can get replacements at no charge. (You can't get reimbursed if you can't cite the numbers of the checks that you haven't yet cashed.)

Traveler's checks also remain popular because you can sometimes find the ATMs of an entire town evilly disposed to your bank card or Visa (perhaps there's a computer glitch or the phone connections to check your PIN are down). A handful of traveler's checks in your money belt can save your day, and they remain the safest way to carry your dollars.

American Express (☎ 800-221-7282; Internet: www.americanexpress. com) is one of the largest issuers of traveler's checks, and its are the most commonly accepted. American Express will also sell checks to holders of certain types of American Express cards at no commission. **Thomas Cook** (☎ 800-223-7373 in the United States and Canada, 0171-480-7226 in London, or 609-987-7300 collect from other parts of the world; Internet: www.thomascook.com) issues MasterCard traveler's checks. **Citicorp** (☎ 800-645-6556 in the United States and Canada, or 813-623-1709 collect from anywhere else in the world; Internet: www.citicorp. com) and many other banks issue checks under their own name or under MasterCard or Visa.

Buy your traveler's checks in U.S. dollar amounts, (as opposed to, say, French francs) because they're more widely accepted abroad. You should also buy your traveler's checks in different denominations. For example, you can cash $100 checks when you're visiting a town for a while and $50 checks closer the end of your visit to ensure that you don't end up with currency that you'll never use. Likewise, if you're just passing through a country, $20 checks are good to use.

Most places charge you a 1 to 4 percent fee when you buy traveler's checks. If you're a AAA member, you can buy American Express checks free of charge. Some banks also sell no-fee checks to their account holders.

Most places in Europe (excluding the town barber or the elderly couple with the five-table bistro perhaps) accept traveler's checks, especially American Express traveler's checks. However, paying for a hotel room, purchase, or meal directly with a traveler's check virtually ensures that you get the worst possible exchange rate. Exchange your traveler's checks for local cash at a bank or the American Express office.

Exchanging Money at the Best Rate

Make sure that you do some research before you change your money, or you risk getting ripped off. Exchange rates are the best and easiest way small-time financiers can take advantage of inattentive tourists. Avoid exchanging your money in the branch offices of banks you'll see in airports (and, to a lesser extent, train stations). Instead, exchange your money in a bank or at one of its ATMs if at all possible. Bank branches located in airports and train stations often offer a rate inferior to that of the same bank's downtown office.

Shop around for the best exchange rate. If you do, you often notice that exchange rates at banks right next door to each other can differ by 40 percent. The business section of major newspapers (and Europe's main English-language paper, the *International Herald Tribune*) lists the current rates for European currencies. The figures published are prime rates, so although you won't find a street price that's as attractive, they're a good guide to follow when shopping for rates.

At the beginning of each destination chapter in this book, I give you a ballpark estimate of the local exchange rates, current to mid-2000. (Keep in mind that during mid-2000, the dollar was strong, which means you could buy more foreign currency for your money.) Likewise, I use that mid-2000 figure to calculate all the dollar amounts that I give you in each chapter. Rates, however, can fluctuate wildly over even brief periods of time, although they're more likely to rise or fall slowly over the course of months. You can't control rate fluctuations, but they affect your trip. For up-to-date rates, look in the business pages or travel section of any major U.S. newspaper, or check online at the **Universal Currency Converter** (www.xe.net/currency) or **Oanda** (www.oanda.com/converter/classic).

Most banks display a chart of the current exchange rates that they offer, usually in either an outside window or inside at the international teller's window. Make sure that you look at the rate the bank *buys,* not sells, U.S. dollars. When you compare the rates at different banks, look for the chart with the highest number in the buying dollars column to find the best rate.

Remember to factor in the commission, if any, when comparing rates. The *commission* is a fee that's tacked on to your transaction, which is sometimes a flat fee that equals a few dollars, while other times it constitutes 2 to 10 percent of however much you exchange. (Banks display commission costs in the fine print at the bottom of the daily rate chart.) Occasionally, a slightly less attractive exchange rate coupled with low or flat fee commission can cost you less in the long run (depending on how much you change) than a great-looking rate with a whopping commission.

Before you shop for an exchange rate, decide the amount that you're going to exchange. Doing so will help you figure out which rate-and-commission combo best suits your needs. I usually exchange enough money to last a few days, because I save myself the hassle of visiting the bank every day and I can save money using a flat-fee commission. However, remember to stow most of this cash in your money belt — carry only enough for the day in your wallet.

You can also exchange money at commercial exchange booths (multi-lingually labeled as *change/cambio/wechsel*). However, the rates here are generally lousy and the commissions high, but they do keep longer hours than banks. Only use commercial exchange booths as a last resort if all the banks are closed and you can't access an ATM. Hotels and shops also offer terrible rates, but multinational travel agencies such as American Express and Thomas Cook usually give good rates and will exchange their own traveler's checks for no commission.

Buying Currency Before You Leave

Before you leave home, purchase about $50 worth of local currency for each country that you'll visit. Doing so gets you from the airport or train station to the better exchange rates of a downtown bank. Likewise, this money can tide you over until you get your hands on some more, if you arrive in town late at night or on a bank holiday.

AAA offices in the United States sell ready-to-go packs of several currencies at relatively reasonable rates, though you can get better ones at any bank (call ahead — usually only banks' main, downtown branches carry foreign cash). Shop around for the best rate, and ask the teller to give you small bills (close to $10 denominations) because you need the cash primarily to buy inexpensive items like maps, bus tickets, and maybe food.

One continent, one currency? The future of the euro

The adoption of the *euro,* a single European currency, is a controversial move within Europe. Although most of Western Europe has been closely interconnected as an economic and trade unit for years, the official merger of its national currencies and economies is another matter. Up until the last minute of the merger, all the countries involved jockeyed for the best deal for their own nation before signing the final papers. And, even now that the euro is an official currency, countries are still fighting over the details of how they will phase in the currency.

In January 1999, the 11 countries that adopted the euro — Austria, Belgium, Finland, France, Germany, Ireland, Italy, Luxembourg, the Netherlands, Portugal, and Spain (later joined by Greece) — officially locked their exchange rates together and switched most business transactions and computer and credit card banking over to the new, single currency. Several countries have opted out of using the euro for now, including Britain, Denmark, and Sweden.

Things changed immediately for the 12 countries that switched to the euro. For example, everything from stocks and bonds to hotel rooms and canned peas were marked with two prices: the rate in local currency and the rate in euros. Not every little shopkeeper and greengrocer has started double pricing yet, but the euro is gradually seeping into every nook and cranny of Europe. In many establishments, you can even choose to charge items on your credit card at the euro price rather than, say, the price in Italian lire. Both prices translate to the exact same dollar amount, of course, but you can better comparison shop without juggling any complicated conversions in your head because you can now see the flat euro price for hotel rooms in Paris, Berlin, and Rome.

But don't get too excited. The euro as a physical banknote and coin currency won't be issued until January 1, 2002, and the various national currencies won't fully withdraw until March 1, 2002 (originally, the date was July 1, but country leaders decided to cut the length of the confusing, overlapping double-currency period). Because you'll still be juggling marks, lire, francs, and pesetas until these dates, I quote the prices in this book in the local national currencies.

Street Smarts: Avoiding Theft

Random, violent crime rates are much lower in Europe than in the United States. Murder is rare, and terrorism is more a scary bluff than harsh reality. On the whole, Europe's big cities are safer than U.S. cities. Therefore, the two biggest things you need to worry about are pickpockets and the crazy traffic.

Be smart, safe, and enjoy yourself. Stick to populated streets after dark, and know the locations of bad neighborhoods. Each destination chapter in this book offers "What You Need to Know" and "Neighborhood" sections on safety, which also list the less savory parts of town.

Usually, if your wallet is missing and you didn't leave it in a restaurant or hotel, it's gone for good. If you heed my advice in Chapter 10 and keep all your important stuff in your money belt, all you've lost is a day's spending money (and a wallet).

Make two copies each of your itinerary, plane tickets, and your vital information, the latter featuring the information page of your passport, your driver's license, and your student or teacher's identity card. Also, include your traveler's check numbers, your credit card numbers (write the numbers backward to "code" them), and the phone numbers that I list later in this chapter for the issuers of your bank cards, credit cards, and traveler's checks. (If you lose any of these items on the road, call those numbers collect to report your loss immediately.) Leave one copy of each of these items with a neighbor or friend at home and carry the second copy with you in a safe place (separate from the originals) while you travel.

Pick-pocket pickers

Pickpockets target tourists, especially American tourists. Pickpockets know that the United States is a wealthy country, and they also know that American tourists carry more money and better cameras. Make sure you're especially careful in crowded areas (buses, subways, train stations, street markets) as well as most touristy areas (the Eiffel Tower, Colloseum, and so on).

Don't tempt thieves. Leave your jewelry at home and don't flaunt your wallet or valuables. Follow these tips to theft-proof yourself:

- ✔ Keep all valuables (plane tickets, rail passes, traveler's checks, passport, credit cards, driver's license, and so on) in your money belt and wear it at all times (see Chapter 10 for more information). Keep only a day's spending money in your wallet.

- ✔ Carry your wallet in a secure place, such as a back pocket that buttons or in the front pocket of your jeans. When riding buses, casually keep one hand in your front pocket with your wallet.

✔ Don't hang your purse strap off one shoulder where a thief can easily grab it. Instead, hang your purse across your chest. If your purse has a flap, keep the flap and latch side against your body, not facing out where nimble fingers have easy access. When on the sidewalk, walk against the wall instead of close to the curb, and keep your purse toward the wall. Also, beware of thieves who zip up on their scooters and snatch away purses.

✔ Don't leave your camera bouncing around on your belly when you aren't using it. Instead, stow your camera in a plain bag (a camera bag announces "steal my camera" to thieves).

✔ Travel in a trench coat (good for warmth, rain, a makeshift blanket, and fitting into European crowds). You can fit all your valuables inside your coat or pants pockets, and with the trench coat wrapped around you, you can feel pickpocket-proof. Remember: Always button up your coat before stepping on a bus, metro, or train.

Beware of thieves young and old

As you make your way around Europe, be aware that you may encounter masterful thieves and pickpockets (though you won't realize it until you reach for your wallet and find it missing). These thieves often wear colorful but dirty, ragged clothes, so they are easy to spot. Although you may find them anywhere — especially around major tourist attractions — they're most prevalent in southern Europe.

The adults mainly beg for money and can be very pushy doing so. The ones you really need to watch out for, however, are the children. They will swarm you while babbling and sometimes holding up bits of cardboard with messages scrawled on them to distract you, during which time they rifle your pockets faster than you can say "Stop. . . ." If you're standing near a wall or in a metro tunnel, they'll even be so bold as to pin you against the wall with the cardboard message so as to fleece you more easily.

Although not physically dangerous, they are very adept at taking your stuff, and they're hard to catch. Keeping on the lookout is your best defense. If a group of scruffy-looking children approaches, yell "No!" forcefully, glare, and keep walking; if they persist, yell "Politz!" (which sounds close enough to "police" in any language). If they get near enough to touch you, push them violently away — don't hold back just because they're children.

Avoiding scams

 Each con artist uses his or her own specific tactics to rip you off. I list specific swindles that you should look out for in each destination chapter's "Where to go in a pinch" section. Here, however, is a list of a few common swindles:

✔ Watch out for dishonest types in countries that count pocket change in increments of hundreds, who confuse new arrivals with all those zeros. For example, some people will give you change for 5,000 lire when you paid with a 50,000 bill, unless you catch them. Until you're used to the money system, examine each bill carefully before you hand it over and make sure you show the receiver that you know what you're doing.

✔ Waiters sometimes add unordered items to your tab, "double" the tax (allocating 15 percent for the state and 15 percent for the waiter), or simply shortchange you.

✔ A stranger may offer to help you exchange money, make friends with you, and walk off with your wallet after hugging you good-bye. Decline their offer for assistance and continue on your way.

✔ Hotels may sneak in minibar, phone, or other charges. So, if your bill is any higher than the rate (plus tax) you agreed upon times the nights that you stayed, ask a manager to explain your bill.

✔ Hotels charge obscenely high telephone rates, with markups any-where from 150 to 400 percent — especially on long-distance calls, and their scam is perfectly legal. In fact, hotels often charge you for the free local call to your calling card company! Do your wallet a favor and pretend that the hotel phone doesn't exist. Use pay phones or the post office instead.

✔ If your escort on a guided bus tour recommends a best shop for buying local crafts or souvenirs, she's maybe getting a kickback from that store. In return, the store charges heavily inflated prices for items. (In defense of tour guides, however, this kickback system is one of the only ways they can make a living, because they're notoriously underpaid — in part because companies unofficially expect them to take advantage of this option as an unlisted perk.)

Keeping Valuables Safe on Trains

Here are some tips for keeping your stuff safe and secure on an overnight train (see Chapter 7 for more tips):

✔ **Don't flaunt your valuables.**

✔ **Lock your door and make sure that everyone in the couchette understands the importance of keeping your door locked.** (Conductors usually emphasize this point, but doing it yourself doesn't hurt either).

- ✔ **Reserve the top bunk.** Although the top bunk is hotter, it puts your goods above the easy reach of most thieves, and you can sleep with your head next to your bags.

- ✔ **Stow your bags in the luggage niche above the door.** If you strap or lock your bags to this railing, a thief can't easily tug them down and run off with them.

- ✔ **Wear your money belt while you sleep.** After you take care of your tickets and passports with the conductor, excuse yourself to the bathroom and strap your waistbelt around your upper thigh. Doing so may sound creepy, but thieves with light touches sometimes unzip your pants and deftly empty your money belt while you sleep. But, if you strap your money belt around your thigh, they can't get away with your goods without you noticing.

- ✔ **Turn your valuables into a pillow.** You may not experience the most comfortable sleep, but if you wrap your valuables in your clothes and put it in a stuff sack, the discomfort is worth the reward.

- ✔ **Take special precautions when sleeping in unreserved sitting couchettes.**

Coping with a Stolen Wallet

In this section, I list the numbers for some of the biggest companies to call if you lose your credit and ATM cards or checks (after, of course, you quickly check the last place you had your wallet, in case you simply left it in a restaurant or shop).

If you lose your credit cards, most issuers delete your old account number and transfer your account to a new one, which means you get new cards. However, getting new cards takes time. In situations such as these, carrying traveler's checks can save your entire vacation, as American Express commercials waste no time trumpeting.

If you lose your traveler's checks and you remembered the all-important rule of writing down the check numbers in a safe place, you can easily replace them in any big European city. Or, you can have a friend wire you money. Most city and country guides list local Western Union representatives.

Some major credit cards offer a service (usually for a small fee) in which you can register the numbers of all your major cards (credit, bank, and calling card), and they'll cancel them for you with one phone call, as well as provide you with emergency cash or traveler's checks. (You can pick up the traveler's checks at a local American Express, Thomas Cook, or Western Union office.)

Note that these services are special U.S. numbers set up explicitly for emergencies abroad. Go to any pay phone in Europe and dial an international operator to connect your collect call. You can choose from

AT&T, MCI, or Sprint. (You can find a list of their local numbers under "Telephones" in the "Staying in touch" section of each destination chapter).

Ask your bank for their emergency, call-collect number for your ATM card. Likewise, get the numbers for any company whose products you plan to use and take with you. Keep your list in a safe place separate from your cards and checks — not in your wallet or moneybelt! Here is a list of the most common credit card collect numbers:

- ✔ American Express (credit cards or traveler's checks):
  ☎ 336-393-1111

- ✔ Thomas Cook MasterCard (checks): ☎ 609-987-7300

- ✔ Citicorp Visa (checks): ☎ 813-623-1709

- ✔ MasterCard: ☎ 314-542-7111

- ✔ Visa Cards

  - •Bank of America: ☎ 757-677-4701
  - •Bank One: ☎ 410-581-3836
  - •Capital One: ☎ 804-747-7200
  - •Chase Visa: ☎ 813-884-5633
  - •Citibank: ☎ 605-335-2222
  - •First Union: ☎ 540-561-9300
  - •First USA: ☎ 302-594-8200
  - •MBNA: ☎ 302-457-2165

When traveling abroad, you're a nonentity without your passport. If you lose your passport, go immediately to the nearest U.S. consulate. Make sure that you bring a photocopy of the information pages (the two pages facing each other with your picture and vital information) of your missing passport, passport-sized photos that you brought with you, and any other form of identification that wasn't lost.

Understanding Value Added Tax (VAT) and Getting It Back

Most purchases that you make in Europe have a built-in **value-added tax (VAT)** of approximately 17 to 33 percent, depending on the country (Switzerland doesn't participate). Theoretically, most EU countries are supposed to adopt the same VAT tax across the board (especially the euro countries, because technically, they share a single economic system), but that's a convention still being worked out.

The VAT tax is the European version of a state sales tax, only it's already embedded in the price instead of tacked on at the register. The price tag on merchandise is the price you pay.

If non-European Union (EU) citizens spend more than a certain amount at any one store (always *before* tax), they're entitled to some or all the VAT via refund. This amount ranges from as low as $80 in England (although some stores, like Harrods, require as much as $150) to $200 in France or Italy. You can also avoid the VAT if you have your purchases shipped directly from the store, but this can get expensive quickly.

To receive a VAT refund, request a VAT refund invoice from the cashier when you make your purchases and take this invoice to the customs office at the airport of the last EU country that you visit. Have the VAT refund invoice stamped before you leave Europe. In other words, if you fly home from London, bring all your slips from Italy, Germany, Ireland, and so on to the airport in London. After you've returned to the United States, and within 90 days of your purchase, mail all your stamped invoices back to the stores, and they'll send you a refund check. This process usually takes a few weeks or months. However, I've waited as long as 18 months.

Many shops now participate in the **Tax Free for Tourists** network (look for a sticker in the store window). Shops in this network issue a check along with your invoice. After customs stamps the invoice, you can redeem it for cash directly at the Tax Free booth in the airport (usually near customs or the duty-free shop), or you can mail it back to the store in the envelope provided within 60 days for your refund.

Chapter 10

Last-Minute Details and Other Things to Keep in Mind

● ●

In This Chapter

▶ Obtaining passports and travel insurance

▶ Keeping illness from ruining your trip

▶ Booking plays, restaurants, and sights before you leave

▶ Packing light and loving it

▶ Saving money on phone bills

▶ Going through customs

● ●

So you've chosen your destinations and you've made your plans. What else will you need to do? This chapter helps you answer that question — from getting a passport (or renewing the one you have) to deciding whether to purchase additional insurance, to offering tips on packing and staying in touch while you're away from home.

Getting a Passport

When you travel throughout the United States, you rely on your driver's license to prove that you are who you profess to be (give or take a few pounds). If you journey beyond international borders, a valid passport is the only legal evidence that can attest to your identity.

You need to have your passport in hand whenever you set foot on European terrain. Although you may not be required to show an ID when crossing land borders — often, no one asks for formal documentation — you definitely need to have your trusty passport ready for a look if you arrive by plane or ferry.

Securing a passport isn't difficult, but the start-to-finish mechanics of the process do take time. First-time applicants have to appear in person at one of 13 passport offices throughout the United States; federal, state, and probate courts and some major post offices also accept applications (check out the Web site at travel.state.gov for local post offices where you can take care of passport business).

Plan to bring a certified birth certificate (one with a raised seal; not a copy), plus an ID that shows your picture — a driver's license or state or military ID works fine. Your passport also requires two *identical* 2-x-2-inch photos taken within the last six months. You can rely on the services of just about any corner photo shop for your pictures; they use a special camera to duplicate the image. The strip photos from a photo vending machine are not acceptable for your passport.

Request four to six extra copies of your passport photo. Tote the extras with you; they may come in handy in such situations as purchasing a London Travelcard (see Chapter 11) or replacing a lost passport — heaven forbid!

The following list is the rundown on passport prices and particulars:

- ✔ First-time applicants age 16 and over pay $45 plus a $15 handling fee. The passport is valid for ten years.

- ✔ If you're 16 or older and have a valid passport issued less than 12 years ago, you can renew it by mail for $40 by filling out the application available at the places described earlier or at the State Department Web site (travel.state.gov).

- ✔ First-time applicants who are age 15 and under fork over $25 plus a $15 handling fee. Their passports are valid for five years.

Allow plenty of time — at least two months, preferably longer — before your trip to apply. The processing generally takes about four weeks, sometimes longer during heavy travel seasons (especially spring). To speed up the process, you may want to indicate on the application form a departure date within the next three weeks.

If you are traveling very soon and need your passport in a hurry, expedited processing is available for an additional $35. You must appear in person before a regional passport agency (or if you aren't near one, submit your application to a court or post office and have them overnight it to an agency). You can expect your passport in five business days. To locate your regional passport office, go to the State Department Web site (travel.state.gov) or contact the National Passport Information Center ☎ **900-225-7778** (35 cents a minute for automated service; $1.05 a minute to speak with an operator).

Always carry your passport with you — safely tucked away in your money belt. Take it out only on necessary occasions: at the bank while changing traveler's checks (it needs a photocopy); for the guards to verify when crossing borders and to the train conductor on overnight rides; if any police or military personnel request it; and *briefly* to the concierge while checking into your hotel.

European hotels customarily register all guests with police. When checking into your hotel (particularly in southern Europe), the concierge may ask to hold on to your passport for the night (to fill out the paperwork when business is slow), in which case it is dumped into a drawer with everyone else's. To avoid having your passport lost in the shuffle, ask the concierge to fill out your paperwork while you wait, or arrange to pick it up in a few hours.

As an American, the only identification you need to cross European borders is your trusty passport. Wherever you enter Europe, an official stamps your passport (in the blank pages) with a visa that is valid for 90 days within the same country. If you plan to visit longer in any one country, you can get a specific visa by contacting any of the country's consulates in the United States before you leave, or any U.S. consulate once you are abroad.

If you lose your passport while traveling, don't panic — yet. Immediately find the nearest U.S. embassy or consulate. Bring any forms of identification (hopefully you haven't lost these, too), so they can process a new passport for you.

Buying Travel and Medical Insurance

The three major kinds of travel coverage are trip cancellation insurance, medical insurance, and lost luggage insurance.

Purchasing trip cancellation insurance is a good idea if you pay a large portion of your vacation expenses up front. But the other two types of insurance — medical and lost luggage — don't make sense for most travelers. Some health insurance plans cover you abroad (see the "Dealing with European Pharmacies, Physicians, and Hospitals" section later in this chapter). Most homeowner's insurance covers stolen luggage for off-premises theft. Check your existing policies before you buy any additional coverage.

If your luggage is lost, the airline is liable for up to $2,500 on domestic flights and up to $640 ($9.07 per pound) on international flights. Pack your more valuable items in your carry-on bag.

Some credit cards (American Express and certain gold and platinum Visa and MasterCards, for example) offer automatic flight insurance against death or dismemberment in case of an airplane crash. If you feel that you still need more insurance, try one of the companies in the following list.

Don't pay for more insurance than is necessary. For example, if you need only trip cancellation insurance, don't purchase coverage for lost or stolen property. Trip cancellation insurance costs approximately 6-8 percent of the total value of your vacation. For more information, contact one of the following reputable issuers of travel insurance:

- ✔ **Access America**, 6600 W. Broad St., Richmond, VA 23230. ☎ **800-284-8300** and fax: 800/346-9265; Internet: www. accessamerica.com.

- ✔ **Travelex Insurance Services**, 11717 Burt St., Ste. 202, Omaha, NE 68154. ☎ **800-228-9792**; Internet: www.travelex-insurance.com.

✔ **Travel Guard International,** 1145 Clark St., Stevens Point, WI 54481. ☎ **800-826-1300;** Internet: www.travel-guard.com.

✔ **Travel Insured International, Inc.,** P.O. Box 280568, 52-S Oakland Ave., East Hartford, CT 06128-0568. ☎ **800-243-3174;** Internet: www.travelinsured.com.

Treating sickness away from home

Apart from how getting sick can ruin your vacation, finding a trustworthy doctor can make you feel worse. Bring all your medications with you, as well as an extra prescription lest you run out. (Ask your doctor to write out the generic, chemical form rather than a brand name to avoid any confusion at foreign pharmacies.) Pack an extra pair of contact lenses in case you lose one. And don't forget the medicine for common travelers' ailments like upset stomach or diarrhea.

If you have health insurance, check with your provider to find out the extent of your coverage outside your home area. Be sure to carry your identification card in your wallet. And if you worry that your existing policy is insufficient, purchase medical insurance for more comprehensive coverage (see the "Buying Travel and Medical Insurance" section earlier in this chapter).

If you have a chronic illness, talk to your doctor before taking the trip. For such conditions as epilepsy, diabetes, or a heart condition, wear a Medic Alert identification tag, which immediately alerts doctors to your condition and gives them access to your records through Medic Alert's 24-hour hotline. For more information on how to obtain one of these tags, call ☎ **800-825-3785** or visit the Web site at www.medicalert.org. Membership is $35, plus $15 annually.

If you do get sick, ask the concierge at your hotel to recommend a local doctor — even his or her own doctor if necessary — or contact the local U.S. embassy for a list of English-speaking doctors.

Dealing with European Pharmacies, Physicians, and Hospitals

The one good thing about getting sick in Europe is not waiting at the doctor's office. Europeans rely on their local pharmacist to treat their ailments. So even if you don't speak the language, just walk (or crawl, depending on how badly you feel) up to the counter, groan, and point to whatever hurts.

If your condition requires further medical attention, you can visit any European hospital. (Don't worry: Most hospitals have English-speaking doctors.) Many European countries practice semi- or fully socialized medicine, so they may send you on your way with a generous prescription and a small medical bill (sometimes the visit is free or costs no more than $35 or $40).

If you aren't comfortable visiting a public European hospital, you can find private hospitals with native English speakers in bigger cities. Each destination chapter in this book lists the most convenient central hospital in town along with any hospitals that staff English-speaking physicians.

If you must pay for health care, especially overnight care or other costly procedures, most health insurance plans and HMOs foot some of the bill. Many plans require you to pay the expenses up front but reimburse you when you get back. (Save your hospital receipt; you need it to fill out claim forms.) Members of **Blue Cross/Blue Shield** can use their cards at certain hospitals in most major cities worldwide, which means lower out-of-pocket costs. For more information, call ☎ **800-810-BLUE** or visit the Web site at www.bluecares.com/blue/bluecard/wwn for a list of participating hospitals.

To find out the latest tips on travel and health concerns in the countries you plan to visit, and for lists of local English-speaking doctors, contact the **International Association for Medical Assistance to Travelers (IAMAT),** 417 Center Street, Lewiston, NY 14092. ☎ **716-754-4883;** or check out IAMAT's Web site at www.sentex.net/~iamat.

For current information on required vaccines and health hazards by country, contact the **United States Centers for Disease Control and Prevention,** 1600 Clifton Rd. NE, Atlanta, GA 30333. ☎ **404-639-3311;** or go to the Web site at www.cdc.gov/travel (requesting a booklet by mail costs $20; visiting the Web site is free).

Reserving in Advance for Popular Restaurants, Events, and Sights

Planning ahead not only takes the fun out of spur-of-the-moment activities but can shackle your trip to a schedule that may not work out once you get there. But to avoid missing out on the opera, dinner, or museum of your dreams, you want to book these activities before you leave (or at least a few days ahead while on the road).

Top restaurants in Paris and London (and, to a much lesser extent, other major cities) can have waiting lists up to two or three weeks long for tables. More than likely, you can call the day before (or the day of) your planned dinner and get a spot with no problem, but you may want to call further ahead to ensure a table at Gordon Ramsey, Alain Ducasse, or some other restaurant of stratospheric reputation (and price!).

Increase your chances of landing a coveted eatery by reserving for lunch rather than the more popular dinner hour. Also, while traveling, you may want to reserve dinners a day or so ahead of time even at undistinguished restaurants if missing a meal there would break your trip.

If you want to avoid missing a single performance — a musical or play in the West End, the Vienna Boys Choir, an opera at the ancient Roman amphitheater in Verona, or standing-room Shakespeare at the Globe — reserve your tickets several weeks before you leave. Call the box office direct, book at the theater's Web site (which allows you to peruse the schedule and pick your performance), or contact the local tourist office.

You can also contact a centralized ticketing agency like **Edwards & Edwards/Global Tickets** (all of Europe; ☎ **800-223-6108;** Internet: www.globaltickets.com), **tickets.com** (the U.K., Netherlands, Germany, and Belgium), or **Ticket Select** (London; ☎ **44-020-7494-5399;** Internet: www.stoll-moss.com).

If you don't have time before you leave, try to reserve tickets when you first arrive in town. To find out what is playing, pick up the local events magazine — like *Time Out* in London or *Pariscope* in Paris — at a newsstand. I recommend the best ones under the "Visitor Information" section in each destination chapter.

At several museums and sights across Europe (especially in Italy), you can call ahead and reserve an entry time. This feature can save you virtually hours of standing in line at popular places like Florence's Uffizi and Rome's Galleria Borghese (where reservations are mandatory and sell out weeks ahead of time).

Of course, you don't need to book in advance at all museums or sights that allow you to do so. The sights worth reserving are the Lippizaner Horse Show in Vienna, the Galleria Borghese and Papal Audiences in Rome, the Uffizi Galleries and the Accademia (Michelangelo's *David*) in Florence, and the "Secret Itineraries" tour of the Doge's Palace in Venice. (See the separate sights in the destination chapters for phone numbers and Web sites.)

Packing Tips

Start packing: Take everything you think you need and lay it out on the bed. Now get rid of half!

Airlines certainly allow you to take everything — within reason — but why do you want to get a hernia from lugging half your house around with you? Suitcase straps can be particularly painful to sunburned shoulders.

So what are the bare essentials? Comfortable walking shoes, a camera, a versatile sweater and/or jacket, a belt, toiletries, and medications (pack these in your carry-on bag in case the airline loses your luggage), and something to sleep in. Unless you attend a board meeting, a funeral, or one of the city's finest restaurants, you don't need a suit or a fancy dress. You can rely on a pair of jeans or khakis and a comfortable sweater.

Mastering the rules of travel bags and carry-ons

When choosing your travel bag, think about the kinds of traveling you have planned. If you intend to walk with your luggage on hard floors, then a bag with wheels makes sense. If you plan on carrying your luggage over the uneven, cobblestoned streets of Europe or up and down stairs, wheels don't help much.

A foldover garment bag helps keep dressy clothes wrinkle-free, but can be a nuisance if you frequently pack and unpack. Hard-sided luggage protects breakable items better but weighs more than soft-sided bags. I use a soft-sided travel suitcase that converts into a backpack (the shoulder straps and hip-belt tuck and zip away for respectability).

When packing, start with the biggest pieces and then fit smaller items in and around them. Pack breakable items in between several layers of clothes, or keep them in your carry-on bag.

Put things that may leak, like shampoo and suntan lotion, in zippered plastic bags. Lock your suitcase's zippers with small combination padlocks (available at most luggage stores, if your bag doesn't already have them; locks with keys just means you have to keep track of tiny keys), and put a distinctive identification tag on the outside so your bag is easy to spot on the carousel.

On the plane, you're allowed two pieces of carry-on luggage, measuring less than 42" total dimensions (length plus width plus height; regulations vary airline to airline, but 42" is the most stringent). Many airlines seriously crack down on carry-ons and allow only one bag of the larger dimensions; the other can be a purse or tiny daypack. However, both bags must measure small enough to fit in the overhead compartment or under the seat in front of you.

Sensible carry-on items include a book, any breakable items you don't want to put in your suitcase, a personal headphone stereo, a snack in case you don't like the airline food, any vital documents you don't want to lose in your luggage (like your return tickets, passport, and wallet), and some empty space to stuff a sweater or jacket while waiting for your luggage in an overheated terminal.

Dressing like the locals

Clothed in bargains or brand names, most urban Europeans are known for their savvy fashion sense. But what most Americans wear for an expensive meal out or a night on the town, many Europeans throw on for an evening walk before dinner.

Of course, comfort is essential, but you may feel more at ease looking less like a tourist. Leave the silly garments at home (you know what they are), pack a sensible, sporty outfit, and mingle with the locals on the town's main drag.

If your travel plans include visiting churches and cathedrals, keep in mind that some adhere to strict dress codes. St. Peter's Basilica in Rome turns people away who are showing too much skin. Plan ahead: Wear shorts or skirts that fall past the knee and cover your shoulders. During warmer seasons, layer a shirt under a sleeveless jumper, and in cooler temperatures, an oversized scarf (check out nearby souvenir stands for a good bargain) can substitute for a wrap — a very chic look! Men may not want the same fashion statements as women, but if necessary, they can drape one of these handy scarves over the bare parts as well.

Sporting money belts

Tote your most important documents, such as your plane tickets, rail passes, traveler's checks, credit cards, driver's license, and passport, in a money belt.

Money belts are flat pouches worn under clothing. You can choose from three kinds: one that dangles from your neck; one that fastens around your waist, over your shirt tails but under your pants (larger and more safely concealed, but less comfortable); and one that sways by your pants leg, attached to your belt by a loop.

Don't take any keys except your house key and leave behind any unnecessary wallet items (department store and gas station credit cards, library cards, and so on).

Traveling without electronics

When traveling, electronics take up valuable luggage space, waste too much time, and blow hotel fuses. In other words, leave them at home. Take a small battery-operated alarm clock and one of those tiny flash-lights for poking around ancient ruins and finding stuff in the dark. Otherwise, travel without electronics.

Still determined to lug around half of an electronics store? Then you need to know the following: American current runs on 110V and 60 cycles, and European current runs on 210V to 220V and 50 cycles. Don't expect to plug an American appliance into a European outlet without harming your appliance or blowing a fuse. You need a currency converter or transformer to decrease the voltage and increase the cycles.

Travel-sized versions of popular items such as irons, hair dryers, shavers, and so on come with dual-voltage, which means they have built-in converters (usually you must turn a switch to go back and forth). Most contemporary camcorders and laptop computers auto-matically sense the current and adapt accordingly (first check either the manuals on the bottom of the machine or with the manufacturer to make sure you don't fry your appliance).

You can find plug adapters and converters at most travel, luggage, electronics, and hardware stores. For more information, call the **Franzus Corporation ☎ 203-723-6664** for a copy of the pamphlet "Foreign Electricity Is No Deep Dark Secret" (complete with a convenient order form for adapters and converters). **Magellans** travel supply catalogue (**☎ 800-962-4943;** Internet: www.magellans.com) also sells international electronic devices and adapters.

A hair dryer, even the teeny, portable kind, is just another burden. The majority of European hotels (from the moderate range up) provide built-in hair dryers in the baths. If you insist on lugging your own hot air, bring either a dual-voltage hair dryer or carry along a converter.

For shaving, stick with regular razors unless you have a battery-operated electric shaver — which eliminates voltage problems. If you must bring an electric shaver, however, most hotels supply special plugs for only low-wattage shavers. Before packing any electronic device, ask yourself whether you really need it (the answer is probably *no*). One exception I find useful is a personal tape deck, but not to listen to tunes — why shut your ears off from the audio portion of your vacation? I take one with a record button to capture the sounds and conversations of Europe and the occasional snippet of an audio journal.

Mastering Communication

This section will help you figure out how to call another country — if you need to make advance reservations or book a hotel before you leave — as well as how to stay in touch while you're away from home.

Calling Europe from the United States

When calling Europe from the United States, you must dial the international access code (011), and then dial the country code (a number of one to three digits; each destination chapter in this book lists the country code under the section "Staying in touch").

Before the number itself, you may need to dial a city code, which is like an area code in North America. Most of these codes begin with a zero (in Spain, with a 9), which you dial only if you're calling a city from another area within the same country. To call a city from outside the country's borders (for example, from the United States), you drop the zero.

However, as in some areas of America, many countries (France, Italy, and Spain, among others) are incorporating the separate city codes into the numbers themselves. In some cases you still drop the initial zero; in others you do not. If all this seems confusing, don't worry: The rules for dialing each city are included in the chapters themselves.

Calling home from Europe and using calling cards

No matter which calling method you choose, overseas phone rates are costly. But some money pits are avoidable. For example, *never* make a transatlantic call from your hotel room, unless you can spare considerable cash.

As I point out elsewhere in Chapter 9, phone charges are one of hotels' greatest legal scams. Surcharges tacked on to your hotel bill can amount to a whopping 400 percent over what you pay if you make the call from a public pay phone. They even overcharge for local calls. Just ignore your hotel room phone; look for one in a nearby bar or cafe instead.

Using a calling card— like a credit card for phone bills — is the simplest and most inexpensive way to call home from overseas. (Even some credit cards double as calling cards.) You just dial a local number — which is usually free — and then punch in the number you're calling plus the calling-card number (usually your home phone number plus a four-digit PIN). The card comes with a wallet-sized list of local access numbers in each country (I list these numbers in the "Staying in touch" section of each destination chapter). Before leaving home, set up a card account with MCI, AT&T, or Sprint.

If you're calling from a nontouch-tone country like Italy, just wait for an American operator, who will put your call through, or for the automated system in which you speak your card's numbers out loud.

To make a collect call, dial a phone company's number, and then wait for the operator.

Phone companies offer a range of calling card programs. When you set up an account, tell the representative that you want the program and card most appropriate for making multiple calls from Europe to the United States.

When dialing directly, calling from the United States to Europe is much cheaper than the other way around, so whenever possible, ask friends and family to call you at your hotel rather than you calling them. If you must dial direct from Europe to the United States, first dial the international access code (often, but not always, 00), then the country code for the United States (which is 1). After 001, just punch in the area code and number as usual.

Using European pay phones and phone cards

European and American pay phones operate similarly, but the major difference is that European ones accept phone cards. You may find three types of phones in Europe: coin-operated, phone card-only, and a hybrid of the two. Phone card units are quickly replacing coin-operated phones all over the continent (the old phone tokens are a relic of the past).

Slide phone cards into the phone like an ATM card at a cash machine. You can buy prepaid cards in increments equivalent to $5, $8, $12, or $17. (Phone cards are legitimate in Europe; in America, they are often thinly disguised scams.) Phone cards come in handy only if you plan on staying for a while or if you want to make direct long-distance calls. If you are visiting for only a few days and expect to make mainly local calls, just use pocket change.

Calling cards have made phoning the United States from Europe cheap and easy from any pay phone, but some traditionalists still prefer heading to the post office or international phone office where you make your call on a phone with a meter and then pay when you're done. This method is no cheaper than direct dialing from a pay phone, but at least you don't need a bag full of change (once phone cards caught on at public pay phones, phone offices lost business).

Bringing It Home: Getting through Customs

You _can_ take your goodies with you — up to a point. You aren't limited to how much stuff you can lug back from your trip, but you are restricted to how much you can bring back into the U.S. for free. If you go over a certain amount, the customs officials impose taxes on your goods.

You may bring home $400 worth of goods duty-free, providing you've been out of the country at least 48 hours and haven't used the exemption in the past 30 days. This regulation includes one liter of an alcoholic beverage (you must, of course, be over 21), 200 cigarettes, and 100 cigars. Anything you mail home from abroad is exempt from the $400 limit.

 You may mail up to $200 worth of goods to yourself (marked "for personal use") and up to $100 to others (marked "unsolicited gift") once each day, so long as the package does not include alcohol or tobacco products. Anything over these limits, you must pay an import duty.

 Items bought at a duty-free shop before returning to the U.S. still count toward your U.S. customs limit. The "duty" that you're avoiding in these shops is the local tax on the item (like state sales tax in the United States), not any import duty that may be levied by the U.S. Customs office.

If you need more information, or for a list of specific items you can't bring into the United States, look in your phone book (under U.S. Government, Department of the Treasury, U.S. Customs Service) to find the nearest customs office, or check out the Web site at www.customs. ustreas.gov.

Part III
The British Isles

The 5th Wave   By Rich Tennant

"We're a modern European community, but we also enjoy our ties to the past. That's why most homes around here come with in-deck catapults."

In this part . . .

You may wish to begin your journey with a stop in the British Isles. Why? Because the folks speak English. You may find Britain more familiar than other parts of Europe. After spending time in Bavaria, Sicily, or Budapest, London may seem tame and ordinary. But, remember that you *will* drive on the wrong side of the road.

Beginning your visit with stops in Great Britain and Ireland means finding plenty of adventures. From enjoying high tea in Bath to hiking the highlands of Scotland, a visit to the British Isles makes for a memorable stop on any European vacation.

Chapter 11

London and the Best of England

. . . .

In This Chapter

▶ Getting to London

▶ Finding what you need once you're in London

▶ Exploring London by neighborhood or by passion

▶ Discovering London's best places to sleep and eat

▶ Planning London itineraries and side trips

. . . .

*T*he wondrous city of London — home to Buckingham Palace and Big Ben, Sherlock Holmes and Scotland Yard, Prince William and a stiff upper lip, pubs and pints, giant black taxicabs and St. Paul's Cathedral, tea time and scones, Harrods and the British Museum. You can spend the evening at the latest West End production, dance until dawn at the hippest clubs, and have a pint in the same pubs where Shakespeare hung out. And if that's not enough, you have the Tower of London, the River Thames, and the Crown Jewels. London also has some of the world's foremost museums, including exhaustive collections of historical artifacts, paintings, antiquities, wax figures, and film memorabilia.

Spending less than three days in London is simply not enough time to appreciate more than a smidgen of what the city has to offer; four or five days are more reasonable. I know this philosophy is tough on a tight schedule, but if London is your first stop in Europe, you want to plan one day of officially doing nothing to recover from jet lag anyway — giving London five days in your itinerary is worth it.

Making Your Way to and around London

Air travel is the most convenient option for getting to London, though if you're coming from the Continent you can always hop a ferry or take the train through the Channel Tunnel (Chunnel for short). When you arrive, your choices are a bit more diverse, from subway (called the Underground here) to bus to taxi to foot, of course.

Getting to London by air

Transatlantic flights usually land west of the city at **Heathrow Airport** (☎ 020-8759-4321), from which you can take either a 15-minute ride on the Heathrow Express bullet train (departures every 15 minutes) to London's Paddington Station or a leisurely 50-minute Underground ride on the Piccadilly Line, which runs through the center of town and may more conveniently drop you off right at your hotel.

Some flights (especially from the Continent) and charter planes land at **Gatwick Airport** (☎ 01293-535-353), 30 miles south of London and a 30- to 35-minute ride on the Gatwick Express from London's Victoria Station; or at **London Stansted Airport** (☎ 01279-680-500), 35 miles northeast of town with the Skytrain, which gets you to London's Liverpool Street Station in 45 minutes.

Some flights from Britain and northern Europe land at **London City Airport** (☎ 020-7646-0000), nine miles east of the center, where a shuttle bus whisks you to the nearby Liverpool Street Station in 25 minutes. Easyjet and some other of the new no-frills/low-cost European airlines are making little **London Luton Airport** (☎ 01582-405-100), 30 miles northwest of the city, into a busy hub for their budget flights from other parts of Britain and the Continent. From Luton Airport, you have hourly coaches (a 90-minute trip) to a bus shelter on Buckingham Palace Road near the corner with Eccleston Bridge (a block from Victoria Rail and Victoria Coach stations); or you can take a bus (eight minutes) to Luton's rail station and connect to a train (30 minutes) to London's King's Cross Station or next-door neighbor St. Pancras Station.

Getting to London by rail

Trains coming from Dover (where ferries from the Continent land) arrive at either **Victoria Station** or **Charing Cross Station,** both in the center of town (10½ hours total travel time from Paris via the ferry route).

The direct Eurostar trains that arrive from Paris and Brussels (a trip of three hours — two after you factor in the time change) via the Channel Tunnel, pull into **Waterloo Station** in Southbank. If you're coming from Edinburgh, you arrive at **King's Cross Station** in the northern part of London.

Getting around once you're in London

Pick up a copy of the *Travelling in London* pamphlet, which outlines the major bus routes and includes a copy of the widespread Tube map, at any Tube stop or tourist center.

The Travelcard convenience

You can hop aboard London's buses, Tube, and light rail systems with the **Travelcard** (valid only after 9:30 a.m. but not on night buses or airport lines). For all but the one-day version, you need a passport-sized photo. You can find instant-photo booths in most major underground stations near the ticket offices where you can buy the pass. One-day Travelcards are valid in zones 1 and 2 and cost £3.80 ($6.35). Weekly Travelcards covering zone 1 cost £14.30 ($23.85), £17.60 ($29.35) for zones 1 and 2. Zone 1 covers all of central London — plenty for the average visit; zone 2 is the next concentric ring out, getting in most of the outlying attractions.

For longer trips or single tickets, you can find machines in Tube stations (they take coins only) and manned booths; a single ticket in zone 1 costs £1.40 ($2.35), or you can buy a package of ten tickets for £10 ($16.65). Charts posted by the machines help you figure out how many zones away your destination is. **Weekend** and **Family Travelcards** are also available, as well as the **One-Day LT Cards** that get you unlimited rides (and no after 9:30 a.m. rule) on the Tube, buses, and the Docklands Light Railway system for £4.80 ($8) in zones 1 and 2. Kids ages 5 to 15 usually get discounts of up to 40 or 50 percent on most cards, and 16- to 17-year-olds can get discounted student versions. On a bus, you just pay the conductor cash; 70p ($1.15) for a short hop, or £1 ($1.65) for a longer ride in zone 1 (riding in more remote zones costs less). The **One-Day Bus Pass** covers zones 1-4 for £2.80 ($21.35).

By Tube (subway)

The city of London is too spread out for you to rely on your feet to get from here to there. The quickest and most popular way to get around town is London's subway system, though in British the word "subway" means "pedestrian underpass." Known locally as the Tube, the Underground is a complex network of lines and interchanges that make getting anywhere in London easy. For travel time, count on an average of five minutes between Tube stops.

By bus

The city has an extensive network of those famous red double-decker buses, which are slowly disappearing in favor of new buses that look more modern. Though you can use the Tube and its many transfer stations to tunnel your way just about anywhere in London, I suggest you ride the bus a few times — but not during rush hour — because you can see where you're going. Riding the bus gives you a much better feel for the city layout than when you travel underground. Bus stop signs with a red slashed circle on white are compulsory stops, so you just wait and the bus will stop for you; if the slashed circle is white on red, you're at a request stop, and you have to wave down the bus.

By taxi

London's Tube and buses can get you around town nicely, but for longer distances, more convenient travel, travel at night, or just the novelty of riding in one of those fabled London black cabs, you may opt for a taxi instead. The drivers are highly trained and experienced drivers while also being incredibly knowledgeable of London information. The drivers know every thoroughfare of this city and a lot of London's history. In fact, many people use these drivers as auxiliary city guides, asking them for information as they ride. Prices, however, are far from a bargain.

Hail a taxi on the street or find one at a taxi rank (stand). Keep in mind that you pay for your fun; London's taxi fares are steep. The initial charge for a lone passenger is £1.40 ($2.35), and then 20p (33 cents) for every third of a mile (or 48 seconds) thereafter. Additional passengers raise the fare 40p (65 cents) each, and each piece of luggage adds 10p (15 cents). Expect to pay surcharges for travel after 8:00 p.m., on the weekend, and on holidays. To call for a taxi, dial ☎ 020-7272-0272 or 020-7253-5000. Take note, though: The meter begins running after the driver picks up the call.

Minicabs are meterless taxis that operate out of offices rather than drive the streets for fares. These taxis are more useful at night when the Tube stops running and few regular taxis are available. Negotiate the fare before you get into the minicab. You can find minicab stands in popular spots such as Leicester Square; or try Abbey Cars (☎ 020-7727-2637) in west London; Greater London Hire (☎ 020-8340-2450) in north London; London Cabs Ltd. (☎ 020-8778-3000) in east London; or Newname Minicars (☎ 020-8472-0400) in south London. Women may prefer Lady Cabs, with only women drivers (☎ 020-7254-3501).

Discovering London: What You Need to Know

This section provides information that you'll need for the basic necessities of getting the most out of your money, as well as what you'll need in an emergency or if you get stuck.

The local dough

The British unit of currency is the pound sterling (£), which is divided into 100 pence, called *pee* (p). Roughly, $1 equals 60p; or £1 equals $1.65. British coins include 1p, 2p, 5p, 10p, 20p, 50p, and £1. Bills come in denominations of £5, £10, £20, and £50.

Where to get info after you arrive

The **Tourist Information Centre** in Victoria Station is always busy, but the folks who work there are amazingly helpful. Much better is the **British Travel Centre,** at 1 Lower Regent Street, three blocks down from Piccadilly Circus. The British Travel Centre has plenty of information on all of Britain, plus a convenient travel bookshop, BritRail ticket window, and both travel and theatre ticket agencies. The British Travel Centre is open Monday, 9:30 a.m. to 6:30 p.m.; Tuesday to Friday, 9:00 a.m. to 6:30 p.m.; and Saturday and Sunday, 10:00 a.m. to 4:00 p.m. (late June to late September, Saturday hours are 9:00 a.m. to 5:00 p.m.).

Heathrow Airport and Liverpool Street station also have information desks, but unfortunately no office answers phone inquiries. To find other tourist office locations and their open hours, call ☎ **020-7932-2000.** For recorded tourist information call ☎ **09064-123-456** or 0839-123-456 (cost is 42p per minute).

Because the Web isn't charged for (yet), you can get free information from the national BTA site (www.visitbritain.org) and London's www.londontown.com. The best way to find out what's going on around town, from shows to restaurants to events, is to buy a copy of *Time Out* magazine, published every Tuesday and available at newsstands. You can also get listings from *Time Out* magazine's competitor, *What's On,* as well as from the *Evening Standard.*

Where to go in a pinch

London is a friendly city to its visitors, and in heavily touristy areas, you may feel safer than you do in your own hometown. Areas where you may be a bit uneasy — Tottenham, South London, and Hackney — lie far beyond central London. Even so, London is a very large city, so you are wise to take general precautions to prevent being targeted by thieves or pickpockets. Another borough to be wary of is Soho; it has a few borderline secure areas.

But if you find yourself in a bit of a pickle, here are a few handy references to help you get unstuck:

- **Embassy:** The U.S. Embassy (☎ **020-7499-9000**) is located at 24 Grosvenor Sq., W1A 1AE. For passport and visa information, contact the U.S. Passport and Citizenship Unit, 55-56 Upper Brook Street, W1 (☎ **020-7499-9000,** extension 2563 or 2564).

- **Emergency:** Dial ☎ **999** to call the police, report a fire, or call for an ambulance.

- **Transit information:** Call ☎ 020-7922-1234.

- **Doctors/hospitals:** Ask the concierge if your hotel keeps a doctor on call. Otherwise, try **Doctor's Call** (☎ **0700-037-2255**). **Medical Express** (☎ **020-7499-1991**) at 117A Harley St., W1, is a privately run clinic. The clinic is open Monday to Friday, 9:00 a.m. to 6:00 p.m., and Saturday, 9:30 a.m. to 2:30 p.m. For 24-hour emergency care, go to the **Royal Free Hospital**, Pond Street, NW3 (☎ **020-7794-0500**) or the **University College Hospital**, Grafton Way, WC1 (☎ **020-7387-9300**).

✔ **Pharmacies:** London has only one 24-hour chemist (British for drugstore): **Zafash Pharmacy,** 233-235 Old Brompton Road (☎ **020-7373-2798**). Also try **Bliss the Chemist,** 5 Marble Arch, W1 (☎ **020-7723-6116**), open daily 9:00 a.m. to midnight, or **Boots,** Piccadilly Circus, W1 (☎ **020-7734-6126**), open Monday to Saturday 9:00 a.m. to 10:00 p.m. and Sunday noon to 6:00 p.m. Police stations keep a list of chemists (pharmacies) open late hours. Just dial ☎ **192** and ask for the local police.

Staying in touch

Whether you need to wire home for money or e-mail your boss to say you're not coming back, London offers a variety of ways to keep in touch. Following is a list of a few essential facts and locations for handling your communications needs:

✔ **American Express:** The main American Express office, 6 Haymarket, SW1 Y4BS (☎ **020-7930-4411**), near Piccadilly Circus, is open Monday to Friday, 9:00 a.m. to 5:30 p.m., and Saturday, 9:00 a.m. to 4:00 p.m. The currency exchange desk is open Monday to Saturday, 9:00 a.m. to 5:30 p.m., and Sunday, 10:00 a.m. to 4:00 p.m.

✔ **Internet Access and Cyber Cafes:** The best cyber cafes in London are the **easyEverything** shops (www.easyeverything.com), open 24 hours a day, 7 days a week and offering from 400 to 550 terminals and the best rates in town — £1 ($1.65) per hour. Locations are at 456-459 The Strand, across from Charing Cross station (☎ **020-7482-9506;** Tube: Charing Cross); 12 Wilton Road, opposite Victoria Station (☎ **020-7482-9502;** Tube: Victoria), and on Tottenham Court Road (☎ **020-7482-9514;** Tube: Tottenham Court Road or Goodge).

In Bayswater, just off the northwest end of Hyde Park, the **Internet Exchange** (www.internet-exchange.co.uk) has two locations serving Starbucks coffee and 10p per minute rates: 47/49 Queensway (☎ **020-7792-5790;** Tube: Bayswater or Queensway), open 7:00 a.m. to 10:30 p.m.; and the 2nd Floor of Whiteleys Shopping Centre on Queensway (☎ **020-7792-0619;** Tube: Bayswater or Queensway), open 9:00 a.m. to 11:00 p.m. They have a third location in the Trocadero Centre at Piccadilly Circus (☎ **020-7437-3704;** Tube: Piccadilly Circus), open 10:00 a.m. to 1:00 a.m.

✔ **Mail:** The most central post office is the Trafalgar Square branch at 24-28 William IV Street (☎ **020-7930-9580**), open Monday to Thursday and Saturday, 8:00 a.m. to 8:00 p.m., and Friday, 8:30 a.m. to 8:00 p.m.

✔ **Telephone:** London has three kinds of pay phones — one that accepts only coins; the Cardphone, which takes only phonecards; and one that accepts both phonecards and credit cards. The minimum charge for a local call is 10p (15 cents) for the first two minutes. Stick to small coins at coin-operated phones because they don't make change. **Phonecards** are sold at newsstands and post offices for £2 ($3.35), £4 ($6.65), £10 ($16.65), or £20 ($33.35). **Credit card** pay phones accept the usual credit cards — Visa, MasterCard, American Express. These phones can be found grouped together in airports and train stations. For directory assistance, dial **192** for the U.K. or **153** for international; for operator assisted calls, dial **100** for the U.K. or **155** for international.

The country code for the United Kingdom is **44.** London used to have two city codes (0171 and 0181), but as of late 1999 these codes were done away with, and a new, single code for the city was established: **020.** If you run across an old prefix, though, the conversion is simple to perform: All numbers are now prefixed with 020, with the 7 (from 0171) or 8 (if an 0181) surviving by being added to the beginning of the number itself, which otherwise remains the same. For example, 0171-123-4567 became 020-7123-4567, and 0181-123-4567 became 020-8123-4567.

If you're calling from outside the U.K., drop the initial zero. To call London from the United States, dial **011-44-20,** and then the local number. To call the United States direct from London, dial **001** followed by the area code and phone number. To charge a call to your calling card or make a collect call home, dial **AT&T** (☎ **0800-890-011**), **MCI** (☎ **0800-890-222**), or **Sprint** (☎ **0800-890-877** or 0500-890-877).

Touring London by Neighborhood

London is a large and sprawling city. Urban expansion has been going on around London for centuries, and the 625 square miles of London consist of many small towns and villages that slowly have been incorporated over time. Officially, 33 boroughs divide London, but most of its 7 million residents still use traditional neighborhood names, which I do as well.

This section sketches out the character of London's primary neighborhoods. The following map can help you locate these neighborhoods as well as the city's main districts and thoroughfares.

Most of central London lies north of the Thames River (west of it when the river turns southward) and is more or less bounded by the two loops of the District and Circle Tube (subway) lines. Central London can be divided into **The City** and the **West End.**

Located on what now is the eastern edge of London's center, **The City** is the ancient square mile where the Romans founded the original *Londinium*. This area is now home to St. Paul's Cathedral, the Tower of London, world financial institutions, and the one-time center of newspaper publishing, Fleet Street.

The **West End** is much larger and harder to classify. This lively center of London's shopping, restaurant, nightlife, and museum scene includes many neighborhoods.

One old district West End neighborhood, **Holborn,** abuts The City and today is filled with the offices of lawyers and other professionals. North of this district, the British Museum and the University of London lend a literary, academic feel to **Bloomsbury.** West of Bloomsbury, **Fitzrovia** is an old writer's hangout with shops and pubs that fade into Soho to the south. Farther to the west, the bland residential grid of **Marylebone**'s streets attracts visitors to Madame Tussaud's Wax Museum and the stomping grounds of the fictional Sherlock Holmes.

The area below Bloomsbury gets livelier. **Covent Garden** and **the Strand** comprise an upscale restaurant, entertainment, and funky shopping quarter. To the west, **Soho,** once a seedy red-light district, is cleaned up and contains numerous budget eateries and London's Chinatown. To the south is **Piccadilly Circus/Leicester Square,** party central with the bulk of London's theatres; lots of crowded pubs, bars, and commercial clubs; the biggest movie houses; and Piccadilly Circus, which is a bustling square of traffic and tacky neon.

Southwest of Piccadilly Circus are the exclusive, old residential streets of **St. James** (imagine a gentlemen's club and expand it several blocks in each direction). Northwest of this (west of Soho) neighborhood is fashionable and tony **Mayfair,** which is full of pricey hotels. **Westminster,** running along the western bank of the Thames' north-south stretch, is the heart and soul of political Britain, home to Parliament and the royal family's Buckingham Palace. Westminster flows into **Victoria** to the south. Centered upon Victoria train station, this neighborhood remains genteel and residential, not rundown as some station neighborhoods in most cities. Northwest of Victoria and west of Westminster is **Belgravia,** an old aristocratic zone full of stylish townhouses that's just beyond the West End.

West of the West End, the neighborhoods are divided north-south by enormous **Hyde Park.** South of Hyde Park stretch the uniformly fashionable residential zones of **Knightsbridge, Kensington,** and **South Kensington,** which are also home to London's grandest shopping streets. (Harrods is in Knightsbridge.) South of Belgravia and South Kensington is the artists' and writers' quarter of **Chelsea,** which manages to keep hip with the changing times (Chelsea announced miniskirts in the 1960s and punk in the 1970s).

North of Hyde Park are the more middle-income residential neighborhoods of **Paddington, Bayswater,** and **Notting Hill,** popular among budget travelers for their abundance of B&Bs and inexpensive hotels. Nearby **Notting Hill Gate** is similar and is becoming a rather hip fashion and dining center in its own right.

On a first-time or quick visit, you probably won't venture too far beyond this huge area of central London. But just in case, here are descriptions of a few of the outlying districts. East of The City, you run into the revitalized **Docklands,** home to many businesses and grand, upscale housing developments of the 1980s. Also, near this area of the city is the **East End,** ever an economically depressed area — part of the real, working class of London and many recent immigrants. On the other side of the Thames are **Southbank** and, just across the river from The City, **Southwark.** Both boroughs are arts and cultural centers, especially the former, which contains London's premiere performance halls as well as the National Theatre.

If you are exploring London to any extent, one of your most useful purchases will be **London A to Z,** one of the world's greatest street-by-street maps. This publication is the only one that lists every tiny alley and dead-end lane of the maze that is London's infrastructure. You can buy one at any bookstore and most newsstands.

Staying in London

Hotel rates in London come at premium prices, especially when compared to other large European cities, such as Paris. To avoid exorbitant room rates, your best bet is to find a B&B, pension, or small hotel offering low rates. You may not sleep in luxury, but you can afford the rest of your trip. Many hotels — especially those owned by chains, such as Forte, which runs the Regent Palace (see review) — offer **Weekend Breaks** that can get you 20 percent to 50 percent off a room rented for two or three weekend nights.

The best **hotel booking service** is the tourist board's **Hotel Booking Hotline** (☎ 020-7932-2020); it also has desks in each tourist information center and in Victoria Station. You have a ₤5 ($8.35) booking fee.

Britain sports two types of **Bed-and-Breakfasts** these days: the old pension-type inn — cheap, worn about the edges, and pretty hit or miss, but costing from only ₤35 ($58.35) — and the upscale private home type of B&Bs that burgeoned in the 1990s (at rates from ₤65/$103.35 on up). The place to find the crème of the crop among the latter type is **The Bulldog Club** (☎ 877-727-3004 in the United States, 020-7371-3202 in the U.K., fax 020-7371-2015; Internet: www.bulldogclub.com), but the club charges a ₤25 ($41.65) membership fee.

Not quite as exclusive, but still representing tony joints, is **Uptown Reservations** (☎ 020-7351-3445, fax 020-7351-9383). Solid midrange agencies include **London Homestead Services** (☎ 020-8949-4455, fax 020-8549-5492; e-mail: lhs@netcomuk.co.uk), **London Bed & Breakfast Agency** (☎ 020-7586-2768, fax 020-7586-6567; Internet: www.londonbb.com), **London B and B** (☎ 800-872-2632 in the United States; Internet: www.londonbandb.com) and **At Home in London** (☎ 020-8748-1943, fax 020-8748-2701; Internet: www.athomeinlondon.co.uk).

Accommodations, Dining & Attractions in Central London

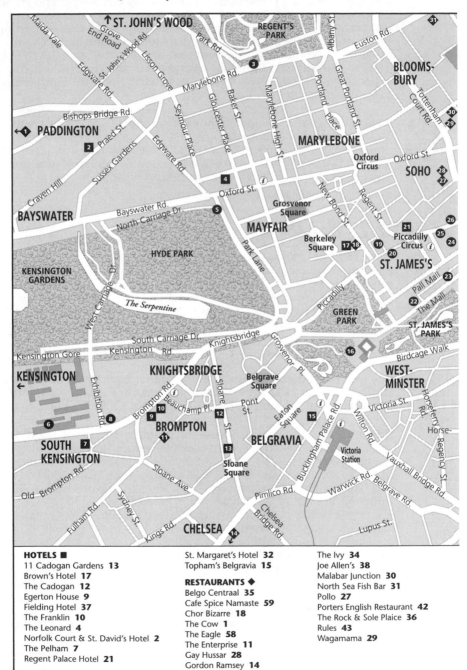

HOTELS ■
11 Cadogan Gardens **13**
Brown's Hotel **17**
The Cadogan **12**
Egerton House **9**
Fielding Hotel **37**
The Franklin **10**
The Leonard **4**
Norfolk Court & St. David's Hotel **2**
The Pelham **7**
Regent Palace Hotel **21**

St. Margaret's Hotel **32**
Topham's Belgravia **15**

RESTAURANTS ◆
Belgo Centraal **35**
Cafe Spice Namaste **59**
Chor Bizarre **18**
The Cow **1**
The Eagle **58**
The Enterprise **11**
Gay Hussar **28**
Gordon Ramsey **14**

The Ivy **34**
Joe Allen's **38**
Malabar Junction **30**
North Sea Fish Bar **31**
Pollo **27**
Porters English Restaurant **42**
The Rock & Sole Plaice **36**
Rules **43**
Wagamama **29**

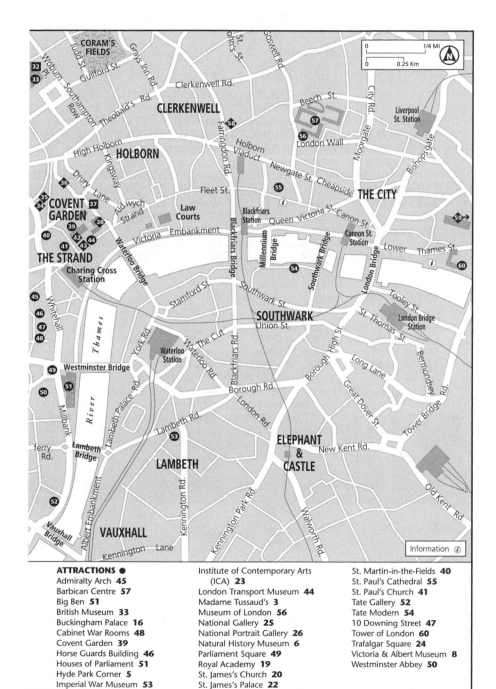

ATTRACTIONS ●

Admiralty Arch **45**
Barbican Centre **57**
Big Ben **51**
British Museum **33**
Buckingham Palace **16**
Cabinet War Rooms **48**
Covent Garden **39**
Horse Guards Building **46**
Houses of Parliament **51**
Hyde Park Corner **5**
Imperial War Museum **53**

Institute of Contemporary Arts
  (ICA) **23**
London Transport Museum **44**
Madame Tussaud's **3**
Museum of London **56**
National Gallery **25**
National Portrait Gallery **26**
Natural History Museum **6**
Parliament Square **49**
Royal Academy **19**
St. James's Church **20**
St. James's Palace **22**

St. Martin-in-the-Fields **40**
St. Paul's Cathedral **55**
St. Paul's Church **41**
Tate Gallery **52**
Tate Modern **54**
10 Downing Street **47**
Tower of London **60**
Trafalgar Square **24**
Victoria & Albert Museum **8**
Westminster Abbey **50**

London's top hotels and B&Bs

11 Cadogan Gardens
$$$$ Chelsea

Of all London's boutique inns, this one succeeds the best at creating a cozy private-home feel — with discreet hotel comforts — in a building from the 1800s. Victorian antiques and artwork abound, and the choicest room overlooks a private garden. The inn has a restaurant, a small gym and sauna, and you can treat yourself to in-room massages.

11 Cadogan Gardens (just off Sloane Square). ☎ **020-7730-7000.** *Fax: 020-7730-5217. Internet:* www.number-eleven.co.uk. *Tube: Sloane Square; from the Tube stop, walk the long way across the square, and turn right (north) out the far corner onto Pavilion Road.; take an immediate left onto Cadogan Gardens, and then your first right onto another Cadogan Gardens (you find four "Cadogan Gardens" streets that all intersect). The unheralded hotel is on the right. Rates: £198–£258 ($327–$430) double; £288–£398 ($480–$663.35) suite. AE, DC, MC, V.*

The Cadogan
$$$ Chelsea

This boutique inn on tony, boutique-lined Sloane Street still gives you the feeling of living in one of the posh nineteenth-century homes that were linked together over a century ago to make a hotel. The antiques-stuffed rooms unfold above a series of genteel lounges and bars. Suites have much larger sitting rooms than do junior suites — plus marble-finished baths and nonworking fireplaces — but all the rooms are huge, quiet, and absolutely lovely. No. 118 is a smallish corner suite furnished, with a half-tester bed and fin-de-siècle decor, just as it was the day in 1895 when guest Oscar Wilde was arrested here for "offenses against young men" and carried off to two years of hard labor.

75 Sloane Street (at Pont Street). ☎ **800-637-7200** *in the United States, 020-7235-7141 in the U.K. Fax: 020-7245-0994. Internet:* info@thecadogan.u-net.com. *Tube: Knightsbridge or Sloane Square. Rates: £190–£225 ($313.50–$371.25) doubles; suites £290–£330 ($478.50–$544.50). AE, DC, MC, V.*

The Leonard
$$$ Marylebone

The Leonard links four eighteenth-century townhouses for a British atmosphere with an Imperial touch — the furnishings in public areas are often of Indian origin or inspiration and the air is lightly scented with exotic spices. The enormous Grand Suites have high stuccoed ceilings and tall windows opening onto balconies. Two-bedroom suites are like renting your own posh little London pad, fitted with marble fireplaces, oil paintings, and old fashioned settees. Even the simple doubles are elegant (though some can verge on cramped), and all come with a CD stereo. A tiny exercise room is available.

15 Seymour Street (between Old Quebec Street and Park Street). ☎ *020-7935-2010. Fax: 020-7935-6700. Internet:* www.theleonard.com. *Tube: Marble Arch. Rates: £200 ($330) doubles, £250–£410 ($412.50–$676.50) suite, £450–£500 ($742.50–$825.00) two-bedroom suite. AE, DC, MC, V.*

The Pelham
$$$ South Kensington

The Pelham is an oasis of tranquility in a busy road hub, mere steps from a Tube stop and blocks from the shopping of Brompton Road. Tom and Kit Kemp, the owners, love antiques, and she is an interior decorator who has given each room its individual style, the beds piled high with pillows, the walls sheathed in carefully chosen rich fabrics, and the TVs hooked to VCRs. The suites feel nothing like a hotel and feel very much as if you're in your own London flat. The Pelham has an Olde English front lounge for afternoon tea and modern British cuisine in the downstairs restaurant.

15 Cromwell Place (between South Kensington Tube station and Cromwell Road). ☎ *020-7589-8288. Fax: 020-7584-8444. Internet:* www.firmdale.com. *Tube: South Kensington. Rates: £175–£235 ($291.65–$387.75) doubles or mews studio, £295–£595 ($486.75–$981.75) suite. AE, MC, V.*

Norfolk Court & St. David's Hotel
$ Paddington

Accomodations aren't fancy at this comfortable old B&B (only six rooms have showers), but the clients who sing this hotel's praises stretch all the way back to the nineteenth century. The furniture is mismatched, which is the decorative flair of late, the atmosphere is welcoming, and the price can't be beat for a B&B in a neighborhood full of them. Rates include a full English breakfast, and they offer lower rates for longer stays.

16-20 Norfolk Sq. ☎ *020-7723-4963 or 020-7723-3856. Fax: 020-7402-9061. Tube: Paddington, and then exit onto Praed Street; catercorner to Paddington Station is Norfolk Square. Rates: £59 ($97) doubles without bath, £69 ($114) doubles with bath. MC, V.*

Regent Palace Hotel
$ Piccadilly Circus

This huge (908 rooms), institutional hotel operates much like a small city, with restaurants, bars, boutiques, and an after-hours pub. Rooms are rather nondescript, but the location is wonderful. Your first impression may be that it looks like a dorm or hostel, but the clientele is a mix of students, businesspeople, families looking for value, and seniors in town for two weeks of theater. Longer stays come with lower rates.

Piccadilly Circus (between Glasshouse and Sherwood Streets); take exit 1 from the Tube station, and the hotel is opposite where you emerge. ☎ *0870-400-8703 or 020-7734-7000. Fax: 020-7734-6435. Internet:* www.forte-hotels.com *or* www.london.hotels.co.uk. *Tube: Piccadilly Circus. Rates: £59–£84 ($97–$139) doubles without bath, £99–£109 ($163–$180) doubles with bath. AE, DC, MC, V.*

St. Margaret's Hotel

$ Bloomsbury

This clean and comfortable old hotel is the best of a cluster of inexpensive accommodations that line a quiet street. The Marazzi family has offered kind, homey service for over 50 years. Rooms are carpeted and the furniture is worn but cared-for. Ask for a room in the the rear of the hotel; those are the nicest. The breakfast is large and included in the low rates. The British Museum is just around the corner — a huge plus.

26 Bedford Place (near the Russell Square end of the street, two blocks west of the British Museum). ☎ *020-7636-4277. Fax: 020-7323-3066. Tube: Russell Square; turn left out of the Tube station for the half-block to the square; turn left down the square, and then right across the south end of it to Bedford Place, where you turn left; the hotel is on the right. Rates: £58.50–£60.50 ($97.50–$99.80) doubles without bath, £85–£90 ($140.25–$148.50) doubles with bath. No credit cards.*

Topham's Belgravia (Ebury Court Hotel)

$$ Belgravia

This excellent choice is in a fine residential area near the station (Margaret Thatcher is a neighbor). The smaller rooms are quite cozy. The owner — part of a third generation of family management — is an interior decorator and has decorated the rooms in an English country inn style. The rooms are Laura Ashley-like without being too floral and feminine. Rates vary with bathroom status and room size.

28 Ebury St. (one block east of, and parallel to, Buckingham Palace Road). ☎ *020-7730-8147. Fax: 020-7823-5966. Internet:* www.btinternet.com/ ~tophams_belgravia. *Tube: Victoria; from Victoria Station walk one block west on Eccleston Street (which dead-ends at the station) and turn right on Ebury Street. Rates: £130–£150 ($216.65–$250) doubles. AE, DC, MC, V.*

London's runner-up accommodations

Brown's Hotel

$$$$ Brown's Hotel and its vaguely belle époque decor have since 1837 hosted the likes of Agatha Christie (*At Bertram's Hotel* is set here), Rudyard Kipling (he finished *The Jungle Book* while a guest), Napoleon III, and Teddy Roosevelt. The hotel still serves one of London's best afternoon teas in the genteel Drawing Room. *Albemarle Steet, two blocks off Picadilly (*☎ *800-323-7500 in the United States, 800-893-391 toll free in the U.K., or 020-7493-6020 direct in the U.K.; Fax: 020-7493-9381; Internet:* www.brownshotel. com; *Tube: Green Park).*

Egerton House

$$$ Egerton House offers Victorian comfort (if smallish rooms) with a modern touch overlooking grassy Egerton Gardens. The location puts you near the chicest boutiques, Harrods, and the Victoria and Albert Museum. Go for the "deluxe" rooms half-tester beds. *17 Egerton Terrace, off Brompton Road (☎ 800-473-9492 in the United States, 020-7589-2412 in the U.K.. Fax: 415-788-0150 in the U.S., 020-7584-6540 in the U.K. Internet:* www.egertonhousehotel.co.uk; *Tube: Knightsbridge or South Kensington).*

Fielding Hotel

$$ Fielding Hotel is an old-fashioned hotel with small, worn, but comfortable rooms and traditional charms. The hotel is located in one of the best parts of town, on a gas lamp-lit pedestrian street across from the Royal Opera House and near the busy Covent Garden. *4 Broad Court, Bow Street (☎ 020-7836-8305; Fax: 020-7497-0064. Tube: Covent Garden).*

The Franklin

$$$ The Franklin is the slightly more expensive sister hotel to Egerton House, with elegantly posh suites, high ceilings, and garden-view rooms. *28 Egerton Gardens (☎ 020-7584-5533; Fax: 020-7584-5449. Tube: Knightsbrige or South Kensington).*

Dining in London

Granted, the British have long been mocked for the drab quality of their national cuisine (mushy peas, anyone?). And certainly you can still go to a corner pub in London and get food lousy enough to curl your toenails. But over the past decade, London's top chefs have started paying attention to the quality of old-fashioned dishes, while adopting new culinary techniques and using more international ingredients. This fusion of old-world tradition with new-world foodstuffs has led to the rise of Modern British cuisine. Add to this London's variety of ethnic restaurants — locals go out for Indian the way Americans go out for Chinese — and you won't ever have to touch steak and kidney pie unless you want to.

When you're not dining high on modern innovations, Britain still has a formidable array of time-tested dishes for you to try. The ploughman's lunch is a hunk of bread, a chunk of cheese, butter, pickle (relish), and chutney. The two most familiar of the many meat pies you find are Cornish pasty (beef, potatoes, onions, and carrots baked in a pastry shell) and shepherd's pie (lamb and onions stewed under a lid of mashed potatoes — if they use beef, it's called cottage pie). The English are masters of roast beef, which is often served with Yorkshire pudding (a popover-like concoction cooked under the meat joint so the juices drip into it).

Then you can partake in the truly oddly named British dishes, such as bangers and mash (sausages, of which the best are Cumberland, and mashed potatoes), bubble-and-squeak (fried cabbage and potatoes), or toad in the hole (what Americans call pigs-in-a-blanket). Fish 'n' chips (fried fish with french fries) is a greasy delight, and oysters from Colchester can also be fabulous.

Traditional English breakfasts — scarce in these days of the continental croissant-and-coffee — are tasty, but really high on cholesterol: ham and/or sausage, fried eggs, fried tomatoes, and toast or scones with butter and jam. Even better is the tea ritual, detailed under "More cool things to see and do in London," later in the chapter.

If the British are masters of anything culinary, it's their cheeses and desserts. Of the former, blue-veined Stilton is the king, which is best enjoyed with a glass of port wine. Regional delicacies pop up on the cheese board as well, one of the most famous being cheddar. If you prefer your meal to end with something sweet, English puddings are some of the best desserts around. Trifle is sponge cake soaked with brandy, smothered in fruit or jam, and topped with custard. Light cream whipped with fresh fruit is called a fool, and a treacle pudding is a steamed trifle without the sherry and with syrup instead of fruit.

Wash down your meal with a pint of bitter — but make sure it's a proper English ale and not a wimpy import or lager. A few of the most widely available are listed under the pub section of "More cool things to see and do in London."

London's top restaurants

Belgo Centraal
$ Covent Garden BELGIAN

This bastion of Belgian beer and bangers (sausages) is one of the best dining deals in London. You take a fright elevator down to the basement eatery, where rows of communal bench-lined tables fill room after room, the waiters dress as monks, the Belgian grub (pots of mussels, wild boar sausages, roast chickens) is excellently prepared, and the beer flows freely. The restaurant offers several bargain meals, including the Fiver Lunch — noon to 5:00 p.m., just £5 ($8.35) buys you a basic dish plus beer (from 5:00 to 6:30 p.m., you pay whatever the clock shows at the time you order).

50 Earlham Street (three blocks north of the Covent Garden Piazza, off Shaftesbury Avenue). ☎ *020-7813-2233. Reservations not necessary. Tube: Covent Garden. Main courses: £7.95–£19.95 ($13.25–$33.25); fixed-price menus from £5 ($8.35). AE, DC, MC, V. Open: Lunch and dinner daily.*

Cafe Spice Namaste

$ The City INDIAN/EASTERN

Don't let the atmosphere fool you. The restaurant is a large, Victorian Hall without any style or character, but the Indian cuisine is some of the best in London. The owner, who hails from the Indian island of Goa, has added specialties from his own land (try the three-alarm sorpotel pork), but you also taste Thai, Malay, Sri Lankan, and Singaporian influences. The daily specials are usually a sure thing, or try the complex chicken curry dish of *galinha xacutti*.

16 Prescott Street (between Mansell Street and Leman Street). ☎ *020-7488-9242. Reservations recommended. Tube: Tower Hill or Aldgate. Main courses: £5.50–£10.50 ($9.15–$17.50). AE, DC, MC, V. Open: Lunch Mon–Fri, dinner Mon–Sat.*

Gay Hussar

$$$$ Soho HUNGARIAN

This Soho standby is a perennial favorite of left-wing politicians and paprika lovers. The Hungarian grub is outstanding, and the wood-paneled interior with deep red velvet-cushioned benches and bow-tied service a comfortable throwback to an earlier era. Try the veal goulash with thimble egg dumplings after a bowl of the soup of the day, perhaps cold wild cherry or a light lemon and chicken.

2 Greek Street (a block off Soho Square, one block west of Charing Cross Road). ☎ *020-7437-0973. Reservations recommended. Tube: Tottenham Court Road. Main courses: £12–£16.50 ($20–$27.50); fixed-price lunch menus £15–£18 ($25–$30). AE, MC, V. Open: Lunch and dinner Mon–Sat.*

Gordon Ramsey

$$$$ Chelsea MODERN BRITISH

Book well ahead (at least several days) for the popular dining room of soccer-player-turned-über-trendy-chef Gordon Ramsey, who in 1998 huffed his entire staff out of the kitchens of famed restaurants Aubergine and L'Oranger to open this eponymous eatery where his flavorful yet light, inventive cooking needs answer to no one save the palates of an appreciative and fashionable clientele who reserve months in advance. The set lunches are a steal at £25 ($41).

68-69 Royal Hospital Road (a block off the Thames). ☎ *020-7352-4441. Reservations required. Tube: Sloane Square. Fixed-price menus: £25 ($41.65) at lunch, £50–£65 ($83.35–$108.35) at dinner. AE, DC, MC, V. Open: Lunch daily, dinner Mon–Fri.*

Malabar Junction

$ Bloomsbury INDIAN

The owner comes from the southern Indian province of Kerala, spice capital of the subcontinent and a region renowned for its cuisine. The subdued decor may not be as funky as Chor Bizarre, but the cooking is perhaps a notch or two better and is surprisingly well-priced.

107 Great Russell Street (a block off New Oxford Street, near the British Museum). ☎ *020-7580-5230. Reservations recommended. Tube: Tottenham Court Road. Main courses: £3–£9 ($5–$15). AE, MC, V. Open: Lunch and dinner daily.*

Porters English Restaurant
$$ Covent Garden BRITISH

With so many pricey traditional restaurants in London, the Earl of Bradford took a gamble that the city had room for reasonably priced, well-prepared British cuisine. His instinct was correct and Porters has become popular with people looking for the tastes they remember from boarding school and old-fashioned family dinners. The meat pies and puddings are particularly good; try the unusually flavored lamb and apricot pie with mint and Lady Bradford's famous banana and ginger steamed pudding.

17 Henrietta Street (half a block off the Covent Garden square). ☎ *020-7836-6466. Internet:* www.porters.uk.co. *Reservations highly recommended. Tube: Covent Garden. Main courses: £7.95–£10.95 ($13.25–$18.25); fixed-price menu £16.95 ($28.25) each for two people only. AE, DC, MC, V. Open: Lunch and dinner daily.*

Rules
$$$$ Covent Garden BRITISH

In a clubby, nineteenth-century setting, Rules is the oldest restaurant in London, established in 1798. The restaurant serves up game from its own preserve and some of the most staunchly British food in town, beloved of everyone from Charles Dickens to Graham Greene. You can't go wrong with the venison or wild fowl, or try the sea trout, mussels, or a delicious pie — just make sure you cap the meal off with one of Rules's famous puddings. This truly is a special place, well worth a splurge.

35 Maiden Lane (one block off the Strand). ☎ *020-7836-5314. Reservations required. Tube: Charing Cross or Covent Garden. Main courses: £14.95–£17.95 ($24.90–$29.90); pretheater set-price dinner Mon–Fri £18.95 ($31.60). AE, DC, MC, V. Open: Lunch and dinner daily. Closed Dec 24–27.*

London's runner-up restaurants

London is chock-a-block with restaurants, but perhaps the neighborhood with the densest concentration of inexpensive eateries (Indian, Italian, Asian, and more) is in no-longer-so-seedy Soho. Leicester Square/Piccadilly is the easiest place to grab a Döner kebab (a pita wrap with spiced lamb and a picante sauce) or other vaguely Middle Eastern street food from a hole-in-the-wall joint. Some of the cheapest (but still excellent) Indian and Asian restaurants now cluster just south of the British Museum in the south end of Bloomsbury (around, though usually not on, New Oxford Street).

Several of London's museums and sights have extremely good cafeterias or restaurants on the premises, so that you don't have to leave them at lunchtime. You may want to plan on a meal in the Tate, National Gallery, or St. Martin-in-the-Fields church (where you get to eat in the crypt atop tomb slabs).

The most discriminating diners shop for their picnic delicacies in the gourmet food departments of **Harrods** at 87-135 Brompton Road or Fortnum and Mason at 181 Piccadilly. **Marks and Spencer,** at 458 Oxford Street, has a cheaper grocery department for less fancy staples.

Chor Bizarre

$$$ This eatery is still one of my favorite pan-Indian places, but its recently climbing prices have knocked it out of the top choices. Come to see the unusual, fun decor — an assortment of items picked up at Indian bazaars — and the maharaja thali, a sampler feast of specialties from across the subcontinent. Seeing a show? Their four-course, pretheater dinner at £25 ($41.65) includes a car ride to the theater. Kids eat free Saturday lunch. *16 Albemarle Street between Piccadilly and Grafton Street (☎ 020-7629-9802; Tube: Green Park or Piccadilly Circus).*

The Cow

$$$ The Cow is a fashionable Notting Hill address for high quality pub grub of the new school of British cooking. *89 Westbourne Park Road (☎ 020-7221-0021; Tube: Westbourne Grove).*

The Eagle

$$ The Eagle pioneered the concept of a pub actually serving edible food, specializing in Mediterranean-style dishes. *159 Farringdon Road (☎ 020-7837-1353; Tube: Farringdon).*

The Enterprise

$$ Try this place for tasty pub grub. *35 Walton Street (☎ 020-7584-3148; Tube: South Kensington).*

The Ivy

$$$ Dine on well-prepared international and French dishes while hob-nobbing with the stars of the London theatre scene after (or before) the show, as well as business moguls, London movers and shakers, and any mere mortal lucky enough to get a reservation. *1 West Street, just off Cambridge Circus (☎ 020-7836-4751; Tube: Covent Garden or Leicester Square).*

North Sea Fish Bar

$$ A beloved London institution serving some of the best chippies in town. *7-8 Leigh Street (☎ 020-7387-5892; Tube: Russell Square).*

Pollo

$ A Soho legend for laughably cheap, enormous portions of Italian home-cooking in a convivial, crowded, no-frills atmosphere. *20 Old Compton Street, two blocks north of Shaftesbury Avenue (☎ 020-7734-5917; Tube: Leicester Square).*

The Rock and Sole Plaice

$ London's oldest fish 'n' chips joint, founded in 1871. *47 Endell Street (☎ 020-7836-5785; Tube: Covent Garden).*

Wagamama

$ A popular, and hectic, basement Japanese noodle house; a perfect break from the British Museum. *4 Streatham Street, off Coptic Street, around the corner from the British Museum (☎ 020-7323-9223; Tube: Tottenham Court Road).*

Exploring London

The history of London is so vast, it's easy to measure time by events of grand destruction. The Great Fire of 1666 destroyed nearly every last inch of the medieval city. As architectural luck would have it, a Renaissance genius named Christopher Wren was on hand to assist in rebuilding the city, raising over 50 churches and countless other buildings. With World War II came the Blitz, when German warplanes nearly destroyed the city during saturation bombing raids. Today, the end result is that the City of London is an odd architectural mix of medieval houses, Renaissance churches, Victorian public buildings, and post-modern bank headquarters.

London's top sights

The British Museum

The Brits have quite possibly the world's greatest archaeological collection. You can spend several days exploring this intriguing museum, although you can also do the highlights in two to three hours. My advice: Spend a couple of half-days here.

The British Museum has treasures that span history as well as the globe, from the Rosetta Stone — the key that cracked the code of Egyptian hieroglyphics — to the towering winged bull/men that guarded the gates to Assyrian palaces in 880 b.c. You can also see the 2,000-year-old Lindow Man, who was ritually strangled and drowned in a peat bog that preserved his shriveled body, and the famous Elgin Marbles, the grandest of the carved reliefs that once decorated Athens' Parthenon. Kids seem fascinated by room after room of Royal Egyptian mummies.

The museum is under construction for the next year, so you may have to excuse some of the dust. The museum is turning the central courtyard into a high-tech visitor's center and exhibition space. Guided tours of the museum's highlights costs £6 ($10) per person, but specialized "Eye Openers" tours of themed parts of the collections are free.

Great Russell Street (a block off of Oxford Street). ☎ *020-7636-1555; Internet:* www.british-museum.ac.uk. *Tube: Holborn, Tottenham Court Road, or Russell Square; from Tottenham Court Road, take exit 3 out of the station, and then take the first right outside of the station. Open: Mon–Sat 10:00 a.m.–5:00 p.m., Sun 2:30 p.m.–6:00 p.m. Admission: Free, but donations greatly appreciated.*

The National Gallery

A huge, neoclassical edifice houses some of the finest works the thirteenth to twentieth centuries have to offer (start with the oldest paintings, in the modern Sainsbury wing way off to the left of the main entrance). Give your tour about two to three hours. The works include da Vinci's *Virgin of the Rocks,* one-third of Uccello's *Battle of San Romano,* Botticelli's erotic *Venus and Mars,* and Michelangelo's unfinished *Entombment.* El Greco's *Agony in the Garden* hangs alongside works by other Spanish greats Goya and Velázquez. Rubens, Vermeer, and a pair of Rembrandt self-portraits represent the northern European Renaissance.

The nineteenth-century British artists are well-represented with Gainsborough, Constable, and Turner, but are outshined by impressionist masters Monet, Degas, Renoir, Seurat, and Cézanne. My favorite hidden treasures are da Vinci's huge drawing of the *Virgin and Child,* in an antechamber off the first room, and Hoogstraten's masterful optical illusion *Peepshow.* Free guided tours are available, but to set your own pace, donate £3 ($5) and carry along the informative digital audio tour. The onsite Brasserie restaurant is surprisingly excellent for museum chow.

Trafalgar Square (at the top of the square; you can't miss it). ☎ *020-7747-2885. Tube: Charing Cross. Open: Daily 10:00 a.m.–6:00 p.m. (Wed until 9:00 p.m.). Admission: Free.*

Westminster Abbey

This grandiose early English Gothic abbey is one of Europe's major churches and the burial ground of many famous Brits — one of the country's greatest honors is to be buried in this hallowed hall. A tour only takes about 30 to 45 minutes, though history buffs may want to linger longer over their heroes. Every English monarch from William the Conqueror in 1066 to Elizabeth II in 1953 was crowned here (save Edwards V and VIII), and most of them (up to 1760) are buried here as well, some in fantastic tombs. Many of the early sixteenth-century royal tombs were carved by Pietro Torrigiani, a Florentine who studied sculpture with — and bullied — the young Michelangelo.

The right transept is known as Poet's Corner, with memorials to Britain's greatest writers and creative types, plus the graves of Chaucer, Robert Browning, Rudyard Kipling, D. H. Lawrence, Dylan Thomas, Noel Coward, and Sir Laurence Olivier. Other notables who rest in peace inside the abbey include Sir Isaac Newton, Charles Darwin, Lord Baden-Powell (founder of the Boy Scouts), and composers Benjamin Britten and Handel. You can take an audio tour for an additional £2 ($3.30) or sign up for a £7 ($11.65) guided Super Tour. Although the Royal Chapels are closed on Sundays, you can explore the rest of the abbey unless a service is in progress. For information on times of services, call the Chapter Office (☎ 020-7222-5152).

Broad Sanctuary. ☎ 020-7222-7110. Tube: Westminster or St. James Park; enter through the north transept. Open: Nave: Mon–Sat 8:00 a.m.–6:00 p.m. (7:45 p.m. on Wed); Royal Chapels: Mon–Fri 9:00 a.m.–4:00 p.m. (and 6:00–7:45 p.m. Wed), Sat 9:00 a.m.–1:45 p.m. Closed Sun, but you can attend services. Admission: £5 ($8.35) adults, £3 ($5) students and seniors, £2 ($3.35) children 11–16.

Parliament and Big Ben

The many debates of British Parliament ensue inside this series of neo-Gothic 1840 buildings — a complex most famous for its 336-foot Victoria Tower, which is home to the world's most famous timepiece (still wound by hand) and is often referred to by the name of its chime's biggest bell, the 13.5-ton Big Ben. You are welcome to watch debates in either the House of Lords, which is more formal, or the House of Commons, which is much more lively and controversial — you're likely to eavesdrop on shouting matches of often witty personal attacks and learned obscenities. Sessions can last until 11:00 p.m., though you may want to stick around only for an hour or so.

Bridge Street and Parliament Square (the line to get inside forms at the St. Stephen's entrance). ☎ 020-7219-4272; House of Lords 020-7219-3107. Tube: Westminster; Parliament is right across the street. Open: Mid-Oct–July. House of Commons: Wed 9:30 a.m.–1:30 p.m., Mon–Wed 2:30 p.m.–10:30 p.m.; Thurs 11:30 a.m.–7:30 p.m.; and Fri 9:30 a.m.–3:00 p.m.; House of Lords: Mon–Thurs 9:30 a.m.–1:00 p.m. (last entry at noon). Admission: Free.

Tower of London

You best come early to beat the long lines at London's best medieval attraction, a site of intrigue, murder, and executions galore. The hour-long tours guided by Beefeater guards are highly entertaining and informative (every half hour, 9:35 a.m. to 2:30 p.m., until 3:30 p.m. in summer). You want to explore more on your own, too, so count on at least another full hour to investigate the Crown Jewels, the Armory, and such. The Beefeaters take you past the Bloody Tower where Sir Walter Raleigh awaited execution for 13 years and where King Edward IV's two young sons were murdered. You walk through the 900-year-old White Tower (undergoing renovations, but still housing an armory of swords and plate mail, as well as a gruesome collection of torture instruments), and into Tower Green, where Thomas Moore, Lady Jane Grey, and two of Henry VIII's wives (Anne Boleyn and Catherine Howard) were beheaded.

All the gore should be enough trade-off for the kids when you have to wait in line to be whisked past the Crown Jewels on a moving sidewalk.

As you're whisked by the jewels, be sure to drool over the world's largest cut diamond, the 530-carat Star of Africa (set in the Sovereign's Sceptre), and to stare aghast at Queen Victoria's Imperial State Crown (still worn on occasion), studded with over 3,000 jewels. Say hello to the resident ravens, who are rather pampered because legend holds that the Tower will stand so long as they remain.

Tower Hill. ☎ *020-7709-0765. Tube: Tower Hill; head across Tower Hill Road to the Tower of London. Open: Mar–Oct, Mon–Sat 9:00 a.m.–6:00 p.m., Sun 10:00 a.m.–6:00 p.m.; Nov–Feb, Tues–Sat 9:00 a.m.–5:00 p.m., Sun–Mon 10:00 a.m.–5:00 p.m. Admission: £10.50 ($17.50) adults, £6.90 ($11.50) kids.*

Victoria & Albert Museum

While discussing London and all it has to offer, I know you must wonder if the only descriptive adjectives in my vocabulary are "greatest," "wonderful," and "fascinating." But the Victoria & Albert Museum truly is the greatest museum of decorative arts in the world. If your interest is mild, 90 minutes will suffice; 2½ hours or more if you're into it. While interior decorating aficionados are perusing a quite amazing collection of fourteenth-century embroidery, Chinese vases, Indian furnishings, and historic British candlesticks — many of them better-preserved examples than what you can find in the original countries — less enthusiastic companions can amuse themselves with the largest collection of Renaissance sculpture outside Italy (featuring Donatello, Rossellino, and Bernini) and the "Fakes and Forgeries" gallery, cataloguing some of the best attempts at knocking off old masters. Chunks of the galleries will be closed on and off for refurbishment until 2001.

Cromwell Road ☎ *020-7938-8500. Internet:* www.vam.ac.uk. *Tube: South Kensington; the museum is directly across Cromwell Road from the station. Open: Daily 10:00 a.m.–5:50 p.m. (in summer, special exhibitions often reopen it Wed evenings 6:30 p.m.–9:30 p.m.). Admission: £5 ($8.35) adults, £3 ($5) seniors, free for students and under 18.*

Tate Britain/Tate Modern

The Tate has two main collections. The official "national collections of British art" (fifteenth century to today) means room after room filled by Gainsborough, Reynolds, Stubbs, Blake, Constable, and especially Hogarth and J. M. W. Turner. This collection has expanded to fill the entirety of the museum's traditional seat in a neoclassical building on Millbank.

The famed international modern art collection has moved to a huge renovated former power station on Bankside. The modern half of the collection includes art from the Impressionists on — from Rodin's *The Kiss* and dozens of pieces by Picasso, Matisse, and van Gogh to Dalí, Giacometti, and Modigliani, and later works by Mark Rothko, Jasper Johns, Henry Moore, Julian Schnabel, Frank Stella, Anselm Keifer, and a host of other contemporary-era artists.

Judging how long you should spend in the expanded Tate is hard; count on at least an hour in the modern art wing, perhaps only 30 minutes communing with the British artists (unless you're a big fan). The Tate's original building also has an excellent cafe.

Tate Britain: Millbank. ☎ *020-7887-8000; 020-7420-0055 for advance tickets. Tube: Pimlico, and then walk to Vauxhall Bridge Road and turn right (walking toward the river). Make a left onto John Islip Street. The Tate Gallery is on your right. Open: Daily 10:00 a.m.–6:00 p.m. Admission: Free (it does charge for the frequent and excellent special exhibitions).Tate Modern: Bankside.* ☎ *020/7887-8888. Tube: Southwark. Open: Sun–Thurs 10:00 a.m.–6:00 p.m., Fri–Sat 10:00 a.m.–10:00 p.m. Admission: Free (it does charge for exhibitions).*

St. Paul's Cathedral

Christopher Wren's architectural Renaissance masterpiece, St. Paul's Cathedral, was one of the few structures to withstand the Nazi air raids of World War II. Captured on newsreel footage, the image of the grand church's survival became a rallying point for Britain's pride and indomitable spirit during the darkest days of the war. This embodiment of stiff British upper lip continues into the crypt, where national heroes such as the Duke of Wellington (who defeated Napoleon at Waterloo) and Lord Nelson are buried, alongside architect Wren, painters Constable and Turner, and adventurer/hero T. E. Lawrence (also known as Lawrence of Arabia).

Less patriotic visitors can enjoy climbing the 365-foot-high dome that glitters with mosaics — or rather, they can enjoy the acoustic effects of the whispering gallery halfway up (murmur against the wall and someone 158 feet away on the opposite side can hear you) and the 360° panorama of London from the top (after 426 steps). Half-hour guided tours of the church (Monday at 11:30 a.m. or Thursday at 2:30 p.m.) cost £10 ($17) — including church admission — and get you into bits normally closed to the public. Merely eyeballing the church is a 20-minute deal; give yourself at least 45 more minutes to climb the dome.

St. Paul's Churchyard. ☎ *020-7246-8348. Tube: St. Paul's, then walk down New Change Street toward the large golden dome. Open: Mon–Sat 8:30 a.m.–4:00 p.m. (galleries open at 9:30 a.m.). Admission: Cathedral, £4 ($6.65) adults, £2 ($3.35) kids 6-16; Galleries £3.50 ($5.85) adults, £1 ($1.65) kids.*

More cool things to see and do in London

From tea sipping to beer guzzling, from Shakespeare to those cheesy wax dummies, you'll never be at a loss for something to do in London.

✔ **From Kumquats to Wedgewood: Strolling Portobello Road Market.** Antique collectors, bargain hunters, and a lot of tourists are what you'll find at London's most popular market street. Vendors set up by 5:30 a.m.; the outdoor fruit and veggie market runs all week (except Sunday), but on Saturday the market balloons into an enormous flea and antiques mart. About 90 antique shops line the roads around this section of London, so that even during the week you can browse their dusty treasures (serious shoppers pick up the Saturday Antique Market guide). To get to the market, take the Tube to Notting Hill Gate.

✔ **Embarking on a London Pub Crawl.** Theater aside, the real traditional London evening out starts around 5:30 p.m. at your favorite pub. Among the most historic and atmospheric ale houses are the sawdust-floored and rambling **Ye Olde Cheshire Cheese** at Wine Office Court (off 145 Fleet Street; ☎ **020-7353-6170**); Dryden's old haunt the **Lamb and Flag,** known as "Bucket of Blood" from its rowdier days (33 Rose Street; (☎ **020-7497-9504**); the Art Nouveau **Blackfriar** (174 Queen Victoria Street; ☎ **020-7236-5650**); and **The Anchor,** where the present pub dates from 1757—but a pub has been at this location for 800 years, with Dickens and Shakespeare as past patrons (34 Park Street; ☎ **020-7407-1577**). Make sure you order some true English bitters, hand-pumped and served at room temperature. Try Wadworth, Tetley's, Flowers, and the London-brewed Young's and Fuller's. Most pubs are open Monday through Saturday from 11:00 a.m. to 11:00 p.m. and on Sunday from noon to 10:30 p.m.

✔ **Making a Shopping Pilgrimage to Harrods.** Posh and a bit snobbish (no shorts, no backpacks), Harrods (87-135 Brompton Road; ☎ **020-7730-1234**) is the only store in the world that offers you any item you can possibly want and backs up its word. Legend has it that a customer jokingly asked if the Harrods staff could procure him an elephant — then he got the bill. With 1,200,000 square feet and 300 departments, it carries just about everything. Its fabulous food halls are still the highlight of a visit — 500 varieties of cheese, anyone?

✔ **Raising Your Pinkies at a Proper Afternoon Tea.** Possibly the best British culinary invention was deciding to slip a refined, refreshing extra meal into the day, between 3:00 p.m. and 5:30 p.m. — a steaming pot of tea accompanied by a tiered platter of delicious finger sandwiches, slices of cake, and scones with jam and clotted cream. A full tea serving can run anywhere from £5 ($8.35) to £21 ($35). One of London's classiest (and most expensive) afternoon teas is at the ultra-traditional **Brown's Hotel,** 29-34 Albemarle Street (☎ **020-7493-6020;** Tube: Green Park). Less pricey but just as good are the teas at two of London's legendary department stores: the inimitable **Harrods Georgian Restaurant,** on the fourth floor at 87-135 Brompton Road (☎ **020-7730-1234**; Tube: Knightsbridge); and at **Fortnum and Mason's,** 181 Piccadilly (☎ **020-7734-8040;** Tube: Piccadilly Circus or Green Park), either in the refined **St. James's Restaurant** (if you're just doing this once, go for the St. James's) or the more work-a-day **Fountain Restaurant.**

✔ **The Changing of the Guard at Buckingham Palace.** (☎ **020-7839-1377** or 09068-505-452) The Queen's London home is one of Europe's most overrated attractions, but I include it here for its fame alone. Watching the guard change is like sitting through a bad halftime show by an overdrilled marching band. Come to the palace to make faces at the stoically unresponsive (and long-suffering) Beefeater guards if you must, but skip the 11:30 a.m. changing of the guard (daily April to August 7, and then every second day). In August and September, you can take a spin through the palace if the Queen's not in (if the flag's a-waving, she's home).

✔ **Romeo, Oh Romeo — Shakespeare at the Globe Theater.** If you saw *Shakespeare in Love,* you know what the rebuilt Globe Theater looks like. Shakespeare was once part owner of, as well as performer in and main playwright for, a theater called *The Globe* at the Thames Bankside. Shakespeare's Globe Theatre is a recently built replica of the O-shaped building, with an open center and projecting stage, so that the first time since the Great Fire of 1666 burned all the old theaters down, you can listen to a Shakespearean-era performance in the sort of playhouse for which it was written. Performances are May to October; tickets for seats run ₤5 to ₤20 ($8.35 to $33.35). For only ₤5 ($8.35), you can be a groundling, standing in the open space right in front of the stage (not so easy on your feet — or your head, if it rains). Call ☎ **020-7401-9919** for the box office. Even if you don't stop for a show, make some time during the day to come for a tour (☎ **020-7902-1400;** Internet: www.shakespeares-globe.org).

✔ **Club Hopping.** The city that gave the world punk, new wave, techno, and electronica still has one of the world's most trend-setting clublands. The nature of the art means that any place I pen in this book will be out before the guide is, so do yourself a favor and pick up *Time Out* magazine to find out what's hottest this week. A few perennial favorites (sure to be full of tourists) include the once-fab-now-touristy-but-still-gloriously-tacky-in-neon **Hippodrome** (☎ **020-7437-4311**) at Charing Cross Road and Cranbourne Street; the formerly massively hip, and still massively loud, garage and house beats of the **Ministry of Sound** (☎ **020-7378-6528**), 103 Gaunt Street; and the joyful sacrilege of dancing to house tunes in a converted church at **Limelight** (☎ **020-7434-0572**), 136 Shaftesbury Avenue.

✔ **The Play's the Thing — An Evening at the Theater.** London rivals New York for the biggest, most diverse theater scene. The West End has dozens of playhouses, but there are many other venues as well. The *Time Out* and *What's On* magazines list and often review the week's offerings, and the weekly pamphlet "Official London Theatre Guide" is stacked up virtually everywhere. You are best off going directly to the box office to get your tickets, which can cost anywhere from ₤15 to ₤50 ($25 to $83), though you can also buy them from **Global Tickets** (☎ **800-223-6108** in the United States; 020-7734-4555 in the U.K.; Internet: www.globaltickets.com), which also has a desk in the main tourist office on Regent Street. If you want to try to get last-minute tickets at a discount, the *only* official spot is **Leicester Square's half-price ticket booth,** a funny-looking faux half-timbered shed on the south side of the square. The tickets there are half-price (plus a ₤2/$3.35 service fee) and sold on the day of the performance only. The seats are usually up in the rafters, and the service doesn't carry the big productions, such as *Phantom of the Opera*.

✔ **Madame Tussaud's (☎ 020-7935-6861)** is something between a still-life amusement ride and a serious gallery of historical likenesses. It's more than a wax museum, but less than the must-see attraction it's made out to be. Madame herself took death masks from the likes of Marie Antoinette (which was easy, what with her head already detached and all); Ben Franklin (while very much alive) personally sat for her to mold a portrait. Some of the historical dioramas are interesting — although whether they're £9.50 ($15.85) worth of interesting I leave up to you to decide. The museum is open daily from 9:00 a.m. to 5:30 p.m.

✔ **Setting Your Watch: A Day in Greenwich.** London may set its watches by Big Ben, but Ben looks to the **Old Royal Observatory** at Greenwich for the time of day (☎ **020-8858-4422;** £9.50/$15.85 combined ticket gets you into the Maritime Museum, below). This Thames port and shipping village keeps Greenwich Mean Time, by which the world winds its clock. Come to the observatory to straddle the Prime Meridian (0° longitude mark) and have one foot in each hemisphere, board that most famous of clipper ships the **Cutty Sark (☎ 020-8858-3445,** admission £3.50/$5.85), and, at the **National Maritime Museum (☎ 020-8858-4422;** combination ticket with Old Royal Observatory, above), immerse yourself in the history of the proud Navy that won and maintained the British Empire for centuries. All these sights are open daily 10:00 a.m. to 5:00 p.m. Greenwich is also home to the massive **Millennium Dome (☎ 020-8305-3456),** a sort of multimedia combo entertainment/educational/theme park that occupies 130 acres under the world's largest dome. The **Tourist Centre (☎ 020-8858-6376),** at 46 Greenwich Church Street, can give you more information. To get here, take the Jubilee Tube line to North Greenwich, the train from Charing Cross Station or the Docklands Light Railway from the Tower Hill Tube stop. But the classic route to Greenwich is an hour's float down the Thames in a ferry from Westminster or Charing Cross Piers.

And on Your Left, Big Ben: Seeing London by Guided Tour

You can get an excellent overview of the city's layout, and see many of the architectural sights at a snappy pace, from the top of a double-decker bus on **The Original London Sightseeing Tour** (☎ **020-7877-1722;** Internet: www.TheOriginalTour.com). You can find flyers all over the city outlining the different tours offered by this hop-on/hop-off bus with running live commentary. At £12 ($20), the "Original Tour" is the best all-around, spinning a 90-minute loop of the top sights with 6 minutes (15 in winter) between buses. Tickets are good all day — if bought after 2:00 p.m., all the next day as well.

Of the many walking tour outfits in this city, by far the biggest and best is **London Walks (☎ 020-7624-3978;** Internet: www.walks.com or london.walks.com). I can think of no better London investment for fun, education, and entertainment. Just £5 ($8.35) — £3.50 ($5.85) for

seniors or students under 26, free under 15 with a parent — buys you
two hours with an expert guide on a variety of thematic walks: neighborhood jaunts, museums, pub crawls, or walks in the footsteps of
Shakespeare, Churchill, Christopher Wren, or Jack the Ripper. On my
last visit, I did eight of them (buy four at a time for a discount).

Suggested One-, Two-, and Three-Day Itineraries

If you're the type who'd rather organize your own tours, this section
offers some tips for building your own London itineraries.

If you have one day

London in a day takes full-throttle sightseeing. Be at the Tower of
London before 9:35 a.m. to get on the first tour. After perusing the
Crown Jewels there, take off for the British Museum (grab lunch along
the way) to ogle the Rosetta Stone, Egyptian mummies, and Elgin
Marbles. Be at Westminster Abbey by 3:00 p.m. to pay homage to the
British monarchs, English poets, and other notables entombed therein.
Have an early "pre-theatre" dinner at Rules or The Ivy, and then spend
the evening doing whatever floats your boat: attending a play or a
show, indulging in a pub crawl (an early play may leave you time to
pub-crawl a bit afterward), or just drinking in the street acts and nighttime crowds milling around Leicester Square.

If you have two days

Begin Day One marveling at the spoils of the old empire in the British
Museum. Move along to the stellar collection of Renaissance paintings
in the National Gallery, stopping early on for a sandwich in the excellent
cafeteria. Lunch tides you over until you get to fabled Harrods department store, where you can take a break from the window-shopping to
indulge in an afternoon tea in the Georgian Restaurant. Spend the late
afternoon however you like, but make sure you get tickets ahead of time
for a play or show (whether it's Shakespeare at the Globe or a West End
musical), and book ahead at Rules or The Ivy for a late, post-theatre
dinner (in fact, try to reserve a week or so beforehand).

Start off Day Two at the Tower of London on one of the excellent
Beefeater tours. Spend the late morning climbing the dome of
Christopher Wren's masterpiece, St. Paul's. After a late lunch, be at the
meeting place for the London Walks tour that intrigues you the most
(several leave from near St. Paul's itself). Try to get to Westminster
Abbey early enough to pop into the Royal Chapels before they close at
4:00 p.m.; the rest of the church stays open until 7:00 p.m. Duck out
and head to the neighboring Parliament House to get inside and witness British Government in session.

If you have three days

Spend the morning of Day One in the British Museum, which catalogues human achievement across the world and throughout the ages. During lunch, call the Globe Theatre to see whether a play is on for tomorrow at 2:00 p.m. (if so, book tickets). Try to finish lunch by 2:00 p.m. and then head to the nearest stop on the map for the Original London Sightseeing Tours and take the 90-minute bus loop past the major sights of London. After you're good and oriented, plunge right into the Old Masters of the National Gallery. Have a traditional British dinner at Rules or Porters and try to get to bed early; you need to wake up early the next morning.

Day Two is the day for the London of the Middle Ages and Renaissance. Be at the Tower of London by 9:30 a.m. to get in on the first guided tour of this medieval bastion and its Crown Jewels. Afterward, visit St. Paul's Cathedral and grab some lunch. Then head across the Thames River to tour the newly rebuilt Shakespeare's Globe Theater and experience the open-air setting in which a play by the Bard was meant to be seen. If possible, see a play here (plays start at 2:00 p.m.). The tour itself only takes an hour; a play takes two to four hours.

After a particularly long play, grab a quick dinner; if you just do the tour, you have the late afternoon to spend as you like; perhaps squeeze in a visit to the Tate Gallery to indulge in some of the best art of the nineteenth and twentieth centuries. Either way, finish dinner by 6:30 or 7:00 p.m. so that you can join whichever historic pub walk (or something more kid-oriented, such as the Jack the Ripper walk) London Walks is running that evening (they start at either 7:00 or 7:30 p.m.; the brochure tells you where to meet). After your introduction to British ales and pub life, call it a night.

Yesterday was medieval, but for Day Three you're going to stiffen your upper lip with some Victorian-era British traditions. Start out at 9:00 a.m. by paying your respects to centuries of British heroes, poets, and kings buried at Westminster Abbey. Drop by the Victoria and Albert Museum for miles of the best in decorative arts and sculpture. Have a snack (not lunch) on your way to the world's grandest and most venerable department store, Harrods. After a bit of high-class browsing inside, stop by the fourth floor's Georgian restaurant at 3:00 p.m. sharp for a proper British afternoon tea. Linger and enjoy your tea time.

Head over to Big Ben and the buildings of Parliament around 5:30 p.m. and, if government is in session (October through July), get in line to go inside and watch Parliament at work, vilifying one another in a colorfully entertaining way that makes the U.S. Congress seem like a morgue. Or, if you go ga-ga over musicals (or are itching to see a cutting-edge London play), go see a show. Either way, you'll be getting out late, so make sure you have reserved a restaurant that specializes in late, after-theater meals (Chor Bizarre is a good choice).

Exploring Beyond London

Although you can find enough to do in London to keep you busy for weeks, a day trip into the English countryside is a magnificent way to escape the bustle of the city. My top choices are these three: Bath, with its ruins and stately eighteenth-century mansions; Salisbury, with its imposing Gothic cathedral and Stonehenge nearby; and Oxford, one of the world's greatest college towns.

If planning your own day trips is too much trouble, check out **Green Line** (☎ **020-8668-7261**) in London, which offers guided bus trips. Bath, Stonehenge, the Cotswolds, and Avebury are grouped into a very full day; the cost is £24 ($40) for adults and £18 ($30) for those under age 15 or over 60. Oxford is a half-day trip; the cost is £6 ($10) for adults and £2.40 ($4) for those under 15 or over 60.

Bath: Ancient Rome in Georgian clothing

When Queen Anne relaxed at the natural hot springs here in 1702, she made the village of Bath fashionable again, but she wasn't exactly blazing new territory. The Romans built the first town here in a.d. 75, a small spa village centered around a temple to Sulis Minerva — only those wacky Romans would deify a spa experience, mixing the Latin goddess of knowledge, Minerva, with Sulis, the local Celtic water goddess. When the Georgians were laying out Britain's most unified cityscape in the eighteenth century with the help of architects John Wood Sr. and Jr., they also excavated Britain's best preserved Roman ruins here.

Bath today is a genteel foray into the Georgian world. The highlights include having high tea in the eighteenth-century Pump Room, perusing Roman remains, and admiring the honey-colored stone architecture that drew in its heyday the likes of Dickens, Thackeray, Nelson, Pitt, and Jane Austen. These luminaries enjoyed the fashionable pleasures of a city whose real leader was not a politician but rather the dandy impresario and socialite Beau Nash. Although doable as a day trip from London, Bath's charms really come out after the day-trippers leave, and savvy travelers plan to stay the night and next morning.

Getting there

Trains to Bath leave from London's Paddington Station at least every hour; the trip takes about 1½ hours. The **Tourist Information Centre** (☎ **01225-477-101**) is in the center of town in the Abbey Chambers, on a square off the lower flank of Bath Abbey.

The best introduction to town is to take the free-guided walks that leave from outside the Pump Room Monday through Friday at 10:30 a.m. and 2:00 p.m., Saturday at 10:30 a.m., and Sunday at 10:30 a.m. and 2:30 p.m. From May through September there are also walks at 7:00 p.m. on Tuesday, Friday, and Saturday.

Seeing the sights

Bath's top attractions are clustered together on the main square. A spin through the **Roman Baths Museum** (☎ 01225-477-785) with your digital audio guide in hand gives you an overview of the hot springs from their Celto-Roman inception (the head of Minerva is a highlight) to the seventeenth/eighteenth-century spa built over the hot springs. You can't swim in the classically scenic and steaming main pool anymore, but you can drink a cup of its waters (taste: blech!) upstairs in the elegant **Pump Room** (☎ 01225-444-477). This café-restaurant offers one of England's classic afternoon tea services, but you can also get a good lunch here, all to the musical accompaniment of a live trio or solo pianist. Lunch is served from noon to 2:30 p.m., and tea is served from 2:30 to 4:30 p.m. The museum is open daily, October to March 9:30 a.m. to 5:00 p.m., April to September 9:00 a.m. to 6:00 p.m. (9:30 p.m. in August).

While you're waiting for your seating in the Pump Room, head out to the square to examine **Bath Abbey** (☎ 01225-422-462), the focal point of Bath's medieval incarnation as a religious center. The sixteenth-century church is renowned both for the fantastic, scalloped fan vaulting of its ceilings and the odd, carved Jacob's ladders flanking the facade, which were inspired by a dream of the bishop who rebuilt this church on the site of an earlier one. The Abbey is open April 13 to October 24, Monday to Saturday 9:00 a.m. to 6:00 p.m. (4:30 p.m. in winter), Sunday 1:00 to 2:30 p.m. and 4:30 to 5:30 p.m. Around to the right you can enter the **Heritage Vaults**, whose meager displays trace the history both of the abbey, which in some form dates back to the sixth century, and of the city itself.

Aside from its major attractions, Bath in and of itself is a sight. Visit especially the architectural triumphs of **The Circus** and the **Royal Crescent,** both up on the north end of town. The latter has a highly recommended **Museum of Georgian Life** at No. 1 (☎ 01225-428-126), where the guides can answer all your questions on life during Bath's glory days.

Where to stay

If you can swing the £190-and-up ($316.65) per-double price tag, *the* place to stay in Bath is bang in the middle of one of the city's architectural triumphs at the **Royal Crescent Hotel** (16 Royal Crescent; in the United States ☎ 888-295-4710, in the U.K. toll-free ☎ 0800-980-0987 or 01225-823-333, fax: 01225-339-401). For what are really reasonable prices, you get to live in that restrained Georgian splendor for a few days with a private boat and hot air balloon at your disposal. Otherwise, Georgian **Duke's Hotel** (53-54 Great Pulteney Street; ☎ 01225-463-512, fax: 01225-483-733) has much more elegance than its £65 to £95 ($108.35 to $158.35) price tag per double lets on.

Where to dine

One of Bath's best restaurants is **The Hole in the Wall** (☎ 01225-425-242; closed Sunday), 16 George Street, where the quiet, elegant rooms are reminiscent of a country inn, and the food is a superb variant of Modern British cuisine. With more tourists, but better on a budget is the quaint

Sally Lunn's (☎ 01225-461-634), where the monstrous brioche-like Bath bun was invented in the seventeenth century. You can find it at 4 North Parade Passage, reputedly the oldest house in Bath. Sally Lunn's is closed Monday at dinner.

Gothic Salisbury and mysterious, prehistoric Stonehenge

Many visitors hurrying out to see the famous Stonehenge are surprised to find that they stumble across one of Europe's greatest Gothic cathedrals along the way. Salisbury, gateway to South Wiltshire and its prehistoric remains, is a medieval market town that's a deserved attraction in its own right. Although you can come see the cathedral, scurry out to Stonehenge, and be back in London by nightfall, you'll have to rush to do it.

Getting there

You can find about 18 daily trains making the 90-minute trip from London's Waterloo Station to Salisbury. From here, you can grab a Wilts and Dorset bus for the half-hour leg out to Stonehenge, 12 miles north of the city at the junction of the A303 and A344/A360.

Salisbury's Tourist Information Centre (☎ 01722-334-956) is on Fish Row.

Seeing the sights

The overpowering sight in town is the **Cathedral** (☎ 01722-555-121), whose spire dominates the landscape and whose construction started in 1220 and took a remarkably short 38 years. You can go halfway up the spire for a view of both the church architecture and the surrounding city and then visit the octagonal chapter house for a peek at some medieval manuscripts and one of the four surviving copies of the *Magna Carta*. Don't miss the peaceful cloisters or the brass-rubbing center. The cathedral is open daily 7:00 a.m. to 8:15 p.m. (to 6:15 p.m. October to March); admission is £3 ($5), £2 ($3.35) students and seniors, £1 ($1.65) kids 5 to 18.

History buffs can stop by the **Salisbury and South Wiltshire Museum,** 65 The Close (☎ 01722-332-151), to get information about early humans and the remains of nearby prehistoric sites such as Stonehenge and Old Sarum. The museum is open Monday to Friday 10:00 a.m. to 5:00 p.m. (July and August also Sunday 2:00 p.m. to 5:00 p.m.); admission is £3 ($5) adults, 75p ($1.25) kids.

The tourist office can fill you in on the other Salisbury sights, mostly visitable seventeenth- and eighteenth-century homes, such as the **Mompesson House** (☎ 01722-335-659) on The Close. It's open March 27 to October, Saturday to Wednesday noon to 5:30 p.m.; admission to the house and garden is £3.40 ($5.65) adults, £1.70 ($2.85) children (gardens only, 80p/$1.35 for all).

Stonehenge (☎ **01980-623-108**) itself is, in some ways, a bit of a let-down. Don't get me wrong — Stonehenge is still one of the most incredible sights in Europe, highly conducive to contemplating the earliest dawn of human endeavor and terribly romantic when the sun sets behind it. But keep in mind that a rope barrier keeps you 50 feet away from the concentric circles of enormous standing stones; unfortunately, past visitors were fond of scratching their names into the venerable rocks, which gave rise to the barriers. A new walkway allows you to circle the stones, but seriously mars the beauty of the site.

Although Stonehenge is associated in many people's minds with Druids, that Celtic religious sect was merely using an existing site. Stonehenge was an ancient mystery even to the first century b.c. Druids. Stonehenge was begun by an unknown people before 3,000 b.c. and added to up until 1,500 b.c. All we really know about Stonehenge is that it is a remarkable feat of engineering — some of the stones came from dozens of miles away. Also, the stones act like a huge astronomical calendar, aligned with the summer equinox while still keeping track of the seasons after more than 5,000 years.

The site is open daily, March 16 to May, 9:30 a.m. to 6:00 p.m., June to August, 9:00 a.m. to 7:00 p.m., September to October 15, 9:30 a.m. to 6:00 p.m., October 16 to 23, 9:30 a.m. to 5:00 p.m., October 24 to March 15, 9:30 a.m. to 4:00 p.m.; admission is £3.90 ($6.50) adults, £2.90 ($4.85) students and seniors, £2 ($3.35) children.

Where to stay

Try a £127 ($211.65) double at **White Hart** (☎ **01722-327-476,** fax: 01722-412-761), with a Georgian old wing and a motel-like new one. A less pricey room can be had at **The Kings Arms** (7A-11 St. Johns Street; ☎ **01722-327-629,** fax: 01722-414-246), a Tudor coaching inn where the doubles range from £60 to £78 ($100 to $130) and the pub is warmed by an open fire.

Where to dine

Salisbury's finest dining is on the outskirts of town, but the city center does have **Salisbury Haunch of Venison,** 1 Minster Street (☎ **01722-322-024**), a 1320 chophouse with tasty roasts and grilled meats. **Harper's Restaurant,** 6-9 Ox Row, Market Square (☎ **01722-333-118**), does a good three-course lunch menu of British/International cooking for around £8 ($13.20), though a la carte can get pricey.

Oxford, the original college town

The City of Dreaming Spires, robed dons, budding intellectuals, and punting on the Cherwell is today surrounded by sprawling suburbs and clogged with the bustle of both a university town and a small industrial city. But don't let that keep you from making a pilgrimage to the school that has matriculated the likes of John Donne, Samuel Johnson, Christopher Wren, William Penn, Charles Dodgson (otherwise known as Lewis Carroll), Graham Greene, and Percy Bysshe Shelley. Actually, Shelley never graduated; he was kicked out for helping write a pamphlet on atheism. (Now he has a memorial on Magpie Lane — go figure.)

Getting there

Oxford is a comfortable day trip from London, but of course to really get to know it takes an overnight stay or two (or enrollment at the university). Regular trains from London's Paddington Station take just over an hour; Oxford Citylink buses from Grosvenor Gardens or Victoria Station take about 90 to 100 minutes and cost half as much. The **Tourist Information Centre** (☎ 01865-726-871) is opposite the bus station on Glouchester Green.

Two-hour guided walks leaving from the tourist office give you a good feel for the place and stop at the major colleges and other city sights. If you've only got an hour, head to the train station, where **Guide Friday** (☎ 01865-790-522) sticks you on a bus with a guide who can rattle off commentary as you're whisked around the city.

Seeing the sights

Oxford University's "campus" is the city itself, spread over the town in a series of 36 colleges, each with its own long history and arcane traditions — such as Christ Church College, whose Great Tom bell rings every evening at 9:05 p.m. to signal the closing of the school gates, pealing 101 times in honor of the college's original 101 students.

Many of the colleges incorporate architectural tidbits from their foundings in the thirteenth to sixteenth centuries. Because the primary business here is education, not tourism, fairly strict rules keep visits limited to certain areas at certain times and in small groups (six people maximum). Most colleges, when they are open, allow visitors to poke around discreetly from 2:00 p.m. to 5:00 p.m. (check the notice boards outside each college for specifics). A few charge admission (for example, Christ Church costs £3/$5).

To detail all of Oxford's colleges is impossible, but the top ones include **Christ Church** (☎ 01865-276-492), dating from 1525 with the largest quadrangle in town and that big ol' bell (the top half of the bell tower was designed by Christopher Wren). The college chapel also happens to be the local cathedral, one of the tiniest in England. Try to fit in Merton College, the oldest (1264) with a library whose odd collections include Chaucer's astrolabe; University College, also ancient but whose present architecture is mainly seventeenth century; and perhaps the prettiest overall, Magdalen College, a fifteenth-century gem surrounded by a park and overlooking the Cherwell River.

Of course the campus isn't all that Oxford has to offer. Perhaps your first order of business in town can be to climb the academically unaffiliated **Carfax Tower** (☎ 01865-792-653) in the center of town with an aerial city map in tow. The maps are handed out at the bottom to get a bird's-eye handle on the city layout. The tower is open daily 10:00 a.m. to 5:30 p.m. (to 3:30 p.m. November to March); admission is £1.20 ($2) adults, 60p ($1) children.

If you only visit one museum in town, make it the **Ashmolean Museum** (☎ 01865-278-000), founded in 1683 and one of Britain's best. Beyond the musical instruments, antiquities, and international curios, the painting collection is most impressive, featuring works by Bellini, Raphael, Michelangelo, Rembrandt, and Picasso. The museum is open Tuesday to Saturday 10:00 a.m. to 5:00 p.m., Sunday 2:00 p.m. to 5:00 p.m.; admission is free.

 Also make time to go *punting* on the Cherwell, which is poling a flat-bottomed boat along the placid river (visit **Cherwell Boathouse** at Bardwell Road, ☎ **01865-515-978**).

Where to stay

You can hole up for the night at the **Eastgate Hotel** (23 Merton Street, The High; ☎ **01865-248-244,** fax: 01865-791-681). The hotel is near the river, with modern £110 ($183.35) doubles in a country inn setting.

Where to dine

Oxford's classic eatery is the **Cherwell Boathouse Restaurant** (Bardwell Road; ☎ **01865-552-746**), right on the river with a French cuisine of fresh ingredients and half-priced kids' meals. For pub grub, follow in the footsteps of Thomas Hardy, Elizabeth Taylor, and Bill Clinton (who studied at Oxford), all former regulars of **The Turf Tavern** (4 Bath Place; ☎ **01865-243-235**), a venerable thirteenth-century watering hole at 4 Bath Place.

Chapter 12

Edinburgh and the Best of Scotland

. . . .

In This Chapter

▶ Getting to Edinburgh

▶ Locating what you need while you're in Edinburgh

▶ Exploring Edinburgh by neighborhood or by passion

▶ Discovering Edinburgh's best places to eat and sleep

▶ Heading into the Highlands or wandering west to Glasgow

. . . .

*I*f you believe every Hollywood movie about Scotland, you would think that Highlanders only wear tartan kilts, are all named Heather or Angus, and wear blue face paint while fighting for liberty from the British. Don't forget the bagpipes that play in the background while wooly sheep graze in the glen.

Hollywood aside, the people of Scotland are proud of their heritage, and local political parties are constantly striving for further autonomy from the English. (In fact, the first Scottish Parliament opened while I was in Edinburgh researching this chapter.)

But then again, while visiting Balmoral, Prince Charles is more likely to wear a kilt than the average Scotsman. And whether anyone actually enjoys eating *haggis* — Scotland's answer to "mystery meat" — is unclear. Incidentally, use the word *Scotch* only to describe the whisky, broth, or prevailing northern mist. Calling a person by that word is considered an insult. Refer to the locals here as *Scots* or *Scottish*.

A clearer picture of modern Scotland emerges in the industrial and agricultural center of Glasgow and in Edinburgh, the gateway to the Highlands. Edinburgh is called the "Athens of the North," partly for its renowned university and intellectual life (Sir Walter Scott and Robert Burns lived here, and Robert Louis Stevenson is a native son) and partly because some neoclassical ruins top one of its hills.

Edinburgh is a town of fine arts and shopping, plus some of the most happenin' nightlife in Britain. The city is a cultural capital of Europe and hosts a performing arts blowout every August called the Edinburgh International Festival (see "More cool things to see and do in Edinburgh" later in this chapter). I've toured Edinburgh in a day before, but the town deserves two or three days — more if you can spare it.

Making Your Way to and around Edinburgh

Scotland borders England to the north, so if you're coming to Edinburgh from London, the best choices are a quick one-hour flight or a scenic five-hour train ride that lets you off right in the middle of town.

Getting to Edinburgh by air

Edinburgh Airport (☎ 0131-333-1000) is just eight miles northwest of town and handles flights from all over Great Britain and major cities on the continent (Amsterdam, Brussels, Frankfurt, Paris, and Zurich). You can grab **Airline bus no. 100** (☎ 0131-555-6363) every 15 minutes or so for the 25-minute trip to downtown's Waverly Station; one-way is £3.30 ($2.15). A 20-minute taxi ride from the airport to Edinburgh runs you about £13 ($21.45).

Getting to Edinburgh by train or bus

Nearly every hour, trains from London (a five-hour ride) pull into **Waverley Station,** at the east end of Princes Street. Coaches (buses) from London cost less, but take eight, miserable hours (sleep is impossible) and arrive at a bus depot on St. Andrew Square.

Getting around once you're in Edinburgh

Because historic Edinburgh is not a big area, you can walk most of it easily. But if you plan to travel across town to catch a show or see a sight, consider hopping a bus or hailing a cab.

By bus

City buses are cheap when you need them and offer quick access to the residential districts that surround the city center — where you find the more inexpensive hotels and B&Bs. On Edinburgh buses, you pay by the mile, so you tell the driver where you're getting off and drop exact change in the slot. Rides range from 50p (82 cents) to £1.60 ($2.65).

The **Daysaver Ticket** costs £2.40 ($3.95) for a full day of unlimited rides. The **TouristCard** gets you the same, plus discounts at some sights and restaurants. You can get them for anywhere from 2 days (£4.80/$7.90) to 13 days (£20.20/$33.35). Purchase tickets and passes at the **Waverly Bridge Transport Office** (☎ 0131-554-4494), right above the train station.

By taxi

You can reach Edinburgh's tourist sites easily on foot, but a taxi may be useful if you're traveling longer distances or carrying luggage. Hail a cab or find one at a taxi rank (stand) at Hanover Street, Waverley Station, or Haymarket Station. To call a taxi, dial ☎ **0131-229-2468.** The initial charge is £1.20 ($2) for the first mile and 20p (33 cents) for each mile thereafter. You get a surcharge of 60p ($1) between 6:00 a.m. and 6:00 p.m.

Discovering Edinburgh: What You Need to Know

This section provides information that you need for the basic necessities of getting the most out of your money, as well as what you need in an emergency or if you get stuck.

The local dough

The British unit of currency is the pound sterling (£), divided into 100 pence, called *pee* (p). Roughly, $1 equals 60p, or £1 equals $1.65. British coins include 1p, 2p, 5p, 10p, 20p, 50p, and £1. Bills come in denominations of £5, £10, £20, and £50. Scottish banks can print their own money, so you may find three completely different designs for each note, plus the regular British pounds. All different currency designs are valid.

Where to get info after you arrive

The **Edinburgh and Scotland Information Centre** (☎ 0131-473-3800; Internet: www.edinburgh.org) is in the Waverley Shopping Centre at 3 Princes Street, very near the train station. The Centre is open Monday to Saturday 9:00 a.m. to 7:00 p.m., Sunday 10:00 a.m. to 7:00 p.m., and hands out free copies of the events magazine **What's On in Edinburgh.** However, most other city guides and maps cost £1 ($1.65) or so. The Centre also sells tickets for local tours, some events, and regional coaches. Another information desk is at the airport (☎ **0131-333-2167**).

Where to go in a pinch

Violent crime is rare in Edinburgh, so you should feel safe walking around the city day or night. But keep in mind that the city's drug problem has produced a few related muggings. In case of emergency, keep the following list of references handy:

- ✔ **Consulate:** The U.S. Consulate is at 3 Regent Terrace (☎ **0131-556-8315**).

- ✔ **Doctors/hospitals:** Ask your hotel concierge to recommend a doctor or dentist, or for a hospital, try the **Royal Infirmary,** 1 Lauriston Place (☎ **0131-536-1000**).

- ✔ **Emergency:** Dial ☎ **999** in any emergency.

- ✔ **Transit Info:** Call the **Lothian Region Transport Office** (☎ **0131-554-4494**). For train info, contact **ScotRail** at ☎ **0191-269-0203**; Internet: www.scotrail.co.uk.

- ✔ **Pharmacies:** Edinburgh has no 24-hour pharmacies, but a branch of the drugstore **Boots the Chemist** (48 Shandwick Place; ☎ **0131-225-6757**) is open Monday through Saturday 9:00 a.m. to 9:00 p.m. and Sunday 10:00 a.m. to 5:00 p.m.

Staying in touch

Whether you need to wire home for money or send a virtual postcard from an Internet cafe, Edinburgh offers a variety of ways to keep in touch. Here are a few essential facts and locations for handling your communications needs:

- ✔ **American Express:** Edinburgh's branch is at 139 Princes Street, near Waverley Station (☎ **0131-225-7881**). The office is open Monday to Friday 9:00 a.m. to 5:30 p.m. and Saturday 9:00 a.m. to 4:00 p.m.

- ✔ **Internet Access and Cyber Cafes: Web13** (☎ **0131-229-8883;** Internet: www.web13.co.uk), 13 Bread Street (three blocks southwest of Edinburgh Castle at Lothian Road), is open Monday to Friday 9:00 a.m. to 10:00 p.m, Saturday 9:00 a.m. to 8:00 p.m., and Sunday 11:00 a.m. to 8:00 p.m. The cafe charges ₤1 ($1.65) per 20 minutes. For something a smidge more central, pop into the **International Telecom Centre** (☎ **0131-558-7114;** Internet: www.btinternet. com/~itcl), at 52 High Street on the Royal Mile, open daily 9:00 a.m. to 10:00 p.m. and charging ₤1 ($1.65) for each 15 minutes — pricier, but the coffee is free. Prices in New Town are a bit higher; **Cafe Cyberia** (☎ **0131-220-4403;** Internet: www.cybersurf.co.uk), 88 Hanover Street, is open daily 10:00 a.m. to 10:00 p.m. and charges ₤2.50 ($4.15) per half hour.

- ✔ **Mail:** Edinburgh's main post offices are at 7 Hope Street, off Princes Street (☎ **0131-226 6823**); and 40 Frederick Street, (☎ **0131-226-6937**). Edinburgh post offices are open Monday to Friday 9:00 a.m. to 5:30 p.m., Saturday 9:00 a.m. to 12:30 p.m.

✔ **Telephone:** A local call in Edinburgh costs 10p (16 cents) for the first three minutes. Pay phones accept either coins or phone cards, which are sold at post offices or the tourist board in £1 ($1.65), £2 ($3.30), £4 ($6.60), £10 ($16.50), and £20 ($33) denominations.

The country code for the United Kingdom is **44.** Edinburgh's city code is **0131.** If you're calling Edinburgh from outside the United Kingdom, drop the zero. In other words, to call Edinburgh from the United States, dial **011-44-131** and the number. To call the United States direct from Edinburgh, dial **001** followed by the area code and phone number. To charge a call to your calling card or make a collect call home, dial **AT&T** (☎ **0800-890-011**), **MCI** (☎ **0800-890-222**), or **Sprint** (☎ **0800-890-877** or 0500-890-877).

Touring Edinburgh by Neighborhood

Edinburgh is a port town of sorts; its outskirts rest on the **Firth of Forth,** an inlet of the North Sea. The center of town is an ancient volcanic outcrop atop which glowers **Edinburgh Castle.** Due east of the castle is Waverley train station. Between the two run **Princes Street Gardens** and the sunken train tracks. These gardens effectively divide the city between the **Old Town** to the south and the grid-like **New Town** to the north.

New Town, developed in the eighteenth century, is filled today with hotels and shops. The major east-west streets of New Town are **Princes Street,** bordering the gardens named after it, and **George Street,** which runs parallel to Princes Street two blocks north.

The **Royal Mile,** the main thoroughfare of the **Old Town,** spills off the castle's mount and runs downhill to the east. The Royal Mile is a single road, but it carries several names: Lawnmarket, High Street, Canongate. Farther to the south is the **University District,** one of the hot spots for Edinburgh's famed nightlife.

Staying in Edinburgh

Edinburgh hotels are not cheap. Plus, all the hotels charge three different rates: off-season, high season, and Festival season. If you don't book well in advance for Festival time, you probably won't find a room — at least not anywhere near the city center. Even if you do book in advance, staying near the city center costs more than double the off-season price.

Luckily, Edinburgh has many pleasant suburbs no more than 20 minutes by bus from the center of town — neighborhoods where the rooms cost less year-round and where you can find some of the only free space during the Festival. One such area, around Dalkeith Road between Holyrood Park and The Meadows, is filled with good, inexpensive guest houses that are just a 10-minute bus ride south of the Old Town.

Accommodations, Dining & Attractions in Edinburgh

HOTELS ■
Balmoral Hotel **17**
Crowne Plaza **25**
Dalhousie Castle **34**
George Inter-Continental **15**
Greenside Hotel **28**
Hotel Ibis **19**
Terrace Hotel **29**
Travel Inn **1**

RESTAURANTS ◆
The Atrium **3**
Baked Potato Shop **18**
Cafe Byzantium **8**
Deacon Brodie's Tavern **12**
Indian Cavalry Club **4**
Kebab Mahal **23**
Kelly's Restaurant **24**
Pierre Victoire **7**
Witchery by the Castle **10**

ATTRACTIONS ●
Burns Monument **31**
Calton Old Cemetery **33**
Edinburgh Castle **6**
Georgian House **5**
High Kirk of St. Giles **20**
John Knox's House **26**
Lothian House **2**
Museum of Childhood **27**
National Gallery of Scotland **13**
National Library **21**
National Portrait Gallery **16**
Nelson Monument **30**
Outlook Tower
   and Camera Obscura **9**
Holyroodhouse **32**
Royal Museum of Scotland **22**
Royal Scottish Academy **14**
Scotch Whiskey Heritage Center **11**

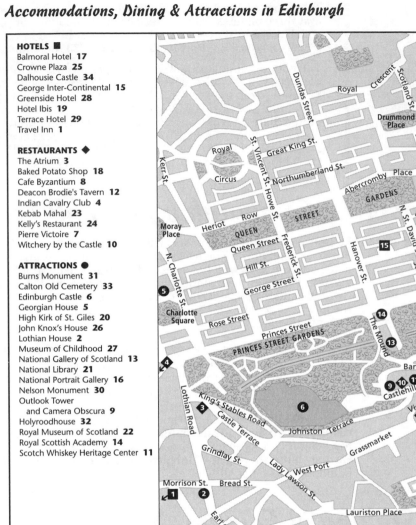

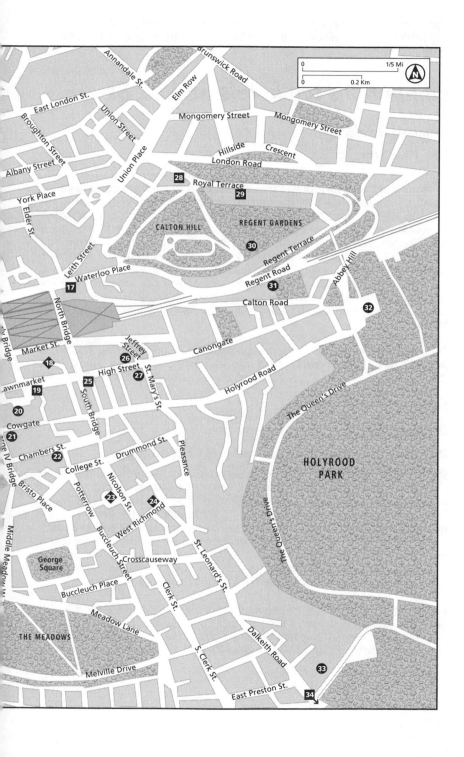

The tourist office has a booklet listing local B&Bs and guest houses, and for £3 ($4.95) the staff can help you find room in one or space in a regular hotel.

Edinburgh's top hotels and B&Bs

Balmoral Hotel

$$$ New Town

Edinburgh's premier luxury hotel perches atop Waverley Station, a 1902 city landmark with its clock tower and kilted doormen welcoming you to a slightly contrived Scottish experience. The RF chain redecorated the hotel in 1998-99, and the large rooms are now outfitted in a Victorian-meets-contemporary-comfort style, discreetly cushy and with full amenities. The refined No. 1 restaurant is highly recommended for international cuisine, as is the modern brasserie-style Hadrian's Restaurant (both overseen by a chef who earned a Michelin star at his last gig). The popular N.B.'s pub has live music on weekends, while the more sedate Lobby Bar specializes in single-malt whiskies. You can take afternoon tea in the Palm Court after a workout in the gym, trip to the spa or sauna, and dip in the indoor pool.

Princes St. (at the east end of the street, practically on top of the train station). ☎ *0131-556-2414. Fax: 0131-557-3747. Internet:* www.rfhotels.com. *Bus: 4, 15, 44 (but if you're arriving by train, you're already there). Rates: £165–£280 ($272.25–$462) double. AE, DC, MC, V.*

Dalhousie Castle

$$$$ Bonnyrigg (eight miles southeast of Edinburgh)

Staying right in charming Edinburgh is convenient, but you can travel just outside the town to find a fifteenth-century castle that offers all the medieval romance that you expect to find in Scotland. Henry IV, Sir Walter Scott, and Queen Victoria all resided at Dalhousie Castle, yet the castle has been renovated to provide luxurious, modern comforts within a castle atmosphere. The castle even has a dungeon restaurant for a unique dining experience. The castle's sylvan setting beside a flowing stream appeals both to romantic and outdoorsy types. The hotel organizes salmon and trout fishing, shooting, and horseback riding expeditions.

Bonnyrigg, Edinburgh (eight miles southeast of the city). ☎ *01875-820-153. Fax: 01875-821-963. Internet:* www.dalhousiecastle.co.uk. *By car: Take the A7 eight miles southeast of Edinburgh toward Carlisle; the castle is just outside the village of Bonnyrigg. Rates: £118–£225 ($194.70–$371.25) double. AE, DC, MC, V.*

Hotel Ibis

$ In Hunter Square, on the Royal Mile

Hotel Ibis is a rare commodity in Edinburgh: an inexpensive hotel with plenty of rooms in a good location. After you see the decor, you may understand why: You wake up thinking you are in Miami. One wouldn't think turquoise and pink can be used together anywhere else. But the rooms are clean and spacious, as are the bathrooms, and some of the rooms look out onto the Royal Mile.

6 Hunter Square Just west of South Bridge on the Royal Mile. ☎ *0131-240-7000. Fax: 0131-240-7007. Bus: 1, 6, 23, 27, 30, 34, 36. Rates: £59.50 double ($98.20). AE, DC, MC, V.*

George Inter-Continental

$$$ New Town

The core of this hotel on tony George Street is a 1755 Georgian house. The refurbished hotel rooms feature all the amenities that modern standards call for. You can enjoy the atmosphere of the original town house in the Scottish restaurant, but the new wing has the best rooms (fourth floor and above), which overlook the street.

19-21 George St. (steps away from St. Andrews Square). ☎ *800-327-0200 from the U.S. or 0131-225-1251. Fax: 0131-226-5644. Internet:* www.interconti.com. *Bus: 4, 15, 44. Rates: £180–£220 ($297–$363) double. AE, DC, MC, V.*

Greenside Hotel

$ New Town

The recently remodeled Greenside Hotel is a four-floor Georgian house, which dates back to 1786. Antiques are situated throughout the hotel, which blend perfectly. All rooms come with private bath and open onto views of a private garden or the Firth of Forth. Drinks are served in the bar.

9 Royal Terrace. ☎ *0131-557-0121. Fax: 0131-557-0022. Bus: 4, 15, or 44. Rates: £60–£80 ($99–$132) double. AE, DC, MC, V.*

Edinburgh's runner-up accommodations

Crowne Plaza

$$$$ Crowne Plaza looks older than its nine years due to Edinburgh's strict zoning rules for the Royal Mile. It has smallish rooms but a stellar location, plus a health club, pool, and restaurant (appetizing international cuisine in a dull subterranean environment). *80 High Street, on the Royal Mile just east of South Bridge.* ☎ *0131-557-9797; Fax: 0131-557-9789; Internet:* www.crowneplazaed.co.uk.

Terrace Hotel

$$ Terrace Hotel offers elegance — and 14-foot ceilings — at a reasonable price in a historic Georgian home. *37 Royal Terrace, on the north side of Calton Hill near Regent Gardens.* ☎ *0131-556-3423; Fax: 0131-556-2520.*

Travel Inn

$ Travel Inn is a massive chain hotel: zippo atmosphere, but some 278 institutional rooms at dirt-cheap rates (plus a full Scottish breakfast for under 10 bucks). *1 Morrison Link, a 10-minute walk west of Edinburgh Castle.* ☎ *0131-228-9819; Fax: 0131-228-9836.*

Dining in Edinburgh

Traditionally, the Scots have started out their day with a bowl of delicious porridge. Canned soup doesn't hold a candle to genuine scotch broth soup (barley in a mutton-flavored stock). Angus beef makes both great steaks and roast beef; Scottish lamb is excellent, as are the many game dishes (rabbit, woodcock, red deer, and grouse).

When it comes to fish, this country excels at preparing haddock, whitefish, herring (usually kippered and eaten for breakfast), and the mighty river salmon. At a Scottish high tea, you can sample freshly baked scones alongside some of the best fresh jams (especially raspberry), heather honeys, and marmalades in Europe. Also excellent are Scottish cheeses — look for cheddars, the creamy, oatmeal-coated Caboc, and cottage cheeses in particular.

Scotland's national "dish" is the infamous haggis, a fat, cantaloupe-size sausage made from sheep lungs, liver, and hearts mixed with spices, suet, oatmeal, and onions. Haggis smells horrible, and you have to wonder whether the Scots themselves ever touch the stuff. Whether haggis is actually a national practical joke played on unsuspecting visitors or an earnest patriotic meal, you do have a cultural obligation to try it — if only once. **Charles MacSween and Son,** Dryden Road (☎ **0131-440-2555**), will be happy to inflict one upon you.

Edinburgh's top restaurants

The Atrium

$$$ **New Town   CONTEMPORARY MEDITERRANEAN**

The stylish and upscale Atrium opened to acclaim in 1993. The restaurant atmosphere consists of oil lamps and rusted metal while located in the atrium of an office building. The menu changes with the trends and the chef's inspiration, but the dishes are always tasty and primarily of

Mediterranean ingredients, such as sun-dried tomatoes, couscous, and arugula. The well-presented dinners may center on anything from seared scallops to roast duck.

10 Cambridge St. (off Lothian Rd., beneath Saltire Court). ☎ 0131-228-8882. Reservations highly recommended. Bus: 10, 11, 15, 16, 17. Main courses: £16 ($26.40) at lunch for two courses, £9.50–£16.50 ($15.70–$27.25) at dinner. AE, MC, V, DC. Open: Lunch and dinner Mon–Sat. Closed Christmas week.

Deacon Brodie's Tavern

$$ Old Town   SCOTTISH/PUB GRUB

This tavern, established in 1806, is a favorite among the locals and tourists who are drawn to the old pub atmosphere, the good food, and the unusual story of its namesake: the real-life model for one of Edinburgh's most famous fictions. A responsible, respectable city councilor and inventor by day, Brodie was by night a thief and murderer. In 1788, his dark side caught up with him, and after a trial, he was hanged on a gibbet he himself helped perfect. The story inspired R. L. Stevenson to write *The Strange Case of Dr. Jekyll and Mr. Hyde.* Morbid history aside, the tavern serves decent pub food on the ground floor, but head upstairs to the wood-lined restaurant, where you may want a second helping of the beef steak pie (a variant on shepherd's pie).

435 Lawnmarket (the western spur of the Royal Mile, near St. Giles's Church). ☎ 0131-225-6531. Reservations suggested. Bus: 1, 6, 23, 27, 30, 34, 36. Main courses: £6.50–£11.95 ($10.75–$19.70). Open: Lunch and dinner daily.

Indian Cavalry Club

$$ New Town   INDIAN

This restaurant is the best of Edinburgh's Indian fare. Nepalese and Burmese dishes join the tandoori and other classic Indian cuisine found in Britain. The restaurant décor has a different theme for each room, much like the era when Britain's imperial flag flew over India. No one in town does curry better, and you can't go wrong with the fixed-price, five-course dinner that gives you a taste of the kitchen's best.

3 Atholl Place (between Shandwick Place and Haymarket train station). ☎ 0131-228-2974. Reservations required. Bus: 3, 21, 23, 26. Main courses: £6.95–£13.85 ($11.45–$22.85); five-course dinner £19 ($31.35); lunch buffet £6.95 ($11.45). AE, DC, MC, V. Open: Lunch and dinner daily.

Kelly's Restaurant

$ Old Town   SCOTTISH

South of Old Town is the small, friendly Kelly's, run by Chef Andrew Ramage. The cuisine is Scottish, influenced primarily by the French. The beef and herb sausages are excellent, as is the roast chicken, and the desserts are some of the finest Scottish sweets in town.

46 W. Richmond St. (take South Bridge, which becomes Nicholson, and turn left on Richmond). ☎ 0131-668-3847. Meals: £5 ($8.25) at lunch, dinners start around £6 ($9.90). Reservations highly recommended. MC, V. Open: Lunch and dinner daily.

Pierre Victoire

$ Old Town   FRENCH

This crowded French bistro has become so popular for its great food at reasonable prices that four branches have sprung up across town. The original restaurant is still the best, though, so stop by for roast pheasant, grilled mussels in garlic, salmon with ginger, and other interesting riffs on French cuisine. A relaxed (if sometimes noisy) atmosphere, a crowd of local devotees, and a good selection of French wines add to the attraction.

10 Victoria St. (just off Grassmarket). ☎ 0131-225-1721. Reservations required. Bus: 1, 6, 34, 35. Main courses: £5.80–£8.90 ($9.60–$14.70); fixed-price lunch £4.90 ($8.10). MC, V. Open: Lunch and dinner Mon–Sat (also Sun during the Festival).

Edinburgh's runner-up restaurants

Baked Potato Shop

$ Baked Potato Shop is a health-conscious and environmentally aware purveyor of scrumptious stuffed potatoes, Indian bhajias (curried dumplings), and (of all things) vegetarian haggis. The single table seats only six. *56 Cockburn St. ☎ 0131-225-7572.*

Cafe Byzantium

$ Cafe Byzantium is an Indian buffet above an antiques market with Victorian vaulted ceilings and beefy portions of everything from sandwiches and crisps (potato chips) to curries and other Indian delicacies. *9 Victoria St. No phone.*

Kebab Mahal

$ Kebab Mahal is the perfect spot to partake in a tasty donner kebab (spicy lamb sandwich) and other Middle-Eastern takeout. *7 Nicholson Square. ☎ 0131-667-5214.*

Witchery by the Castle

$$$$ Witchery by the Castle is a bit of a tourist magnet, but still a lot of fun. The restaurant advertises itself as being the oldest in town. (This building is where the Hellfire Club met in the Middle Ages and where witches were once burned; one witch still reportedly haunts the place). The restaurant boasts an impressive wine list, plus 40 malt whiskies. *Castlehill, at the west end of the Mile, very near the Castle. ☎ 0131-225-5613.*

Exploring Edinburgh

With the exception of the National Gallery, you'll find most of Edinburgh's most popular sights concentrated in Old Town, the rocky outcropping that overlooks the rest of the city.

Edinburgh's top sights

Edinburgh Castle

The castle, a huge part of this city's history, ascends over Edinburgh. The center of the castle protects the twelfth-century, Norman-style St. Margaret's Chapel from an earlier castle. In the Royal Apartments, you can see the bedroom of Mary, Queen of Scots — the very place she gave birth to James VI (later James I of England).

The best feature is the Crown Chamber, where you learn all about the Scottish Honours (the crown jewels) and more than you ever wanted to know about the investiture of the Scottish king. But my favorite part of the tour is being in the prison cells to see the drawings etched into the walls by early nineteenth-century prisoners of the Napoleonic wars. You can whip through in 45 minutes or spend two hours taking all the tours and exploring the nooks and crannies.

Castlehill. ☎ *0131-225-9846. Bus: 1, 6. Open: Nov–Apr, daily 9:30 a.m.–5:00 p.m.; May–Oct, daily 9:30 a.m.–6:00 p.m. Admission: £6.50 ($10.75) adults, £2 ($3.30) kids under 15.*

National Gallery of Scotland

This honey-colored neoclassical temple houses one of the best midsized art museums in Europe, hung with a well-chosen selection of old masters and impressionist masterpieces. Spend a morning (or at least half of one) here in the company of Rembrandt, Rubens, Andrea del Sarto, Raphael, Titian, Velázquez, El Greco, Monet, Degas, Gainsborough, and van Gogh. You may find yourself pleasantly surprised by the many works of largely unknown Scottish artists.

2 The Mound (in the center of Princes Street Gardens, behind the train station). ☎ *0131-556-8921. Bus: 3, 21, 26. Open: Mon–Sat 10:00 a.m.–5:00 p.m., Sun 2:00–5:00 p.m. (during the Festival, Mon–Sat 10:00 a.m.–6:00 p.m., Sun 11:00 a.m.–6:00 p.m.). Admission: Free.*

Our Dynamic Earth

Although the opening was delayed past press time, Edinburgh's first high-tech multimedia museum is highly anticipated. It purports to take one on a journey through time, to witness the creation of Earth and everything the planet has done since.

On Holyrood Rd., in between South Bridge and Holyrood Park. ☎ 0131-550-7800. Bus: 1, 6. Open: Apr–Oct daily 10:00 a.m.–6:00 p.m.; Nov–Mar Wed–Sat 10:00 a.m.–5:00 p.m. Admission: £5.95 ($9.80) adults, £3.50 ($5.80) children and seniors.

The Royal Mile

Walking down the Royal Mile — the main drag of the Old Town that changes names from Lawnmarket to High Street to Canongate — takes you from Edinburgh Castle on the west end downhill to the Palace of Holyroodhouse on the east. The various small museums of the Royal Mile tend to be open Monday through Saturday, 10:00 a.m. to 5:00 p.m. (a few stay open until 6:00 p.m. in summer and are open on Sunday afternoons during the Festival).

Most museums along the Royal Mile are free, but some (Whisky Centre, Camera Obscura, John Knox House, Gladstone's Land) charge a small admission of £1.95 to £4.25 ($3.20 to $7). Simply strolling the Mile from one end to the other takes 20 to 30 minutes. Add in another 20 to 30 minutes for each sight you stop in.

Begin your mile tour at the **Scottish Whisky Heritage Centre,** 354 Castlehill (☎ 0131-220-0441) where you find out all that you could possibly know about the making of single malts; the tour is somewhat cheesy, but you get to swig a few free samples at the end.

Across the street is the **Outlook Tower and Camera Obscura** (☎ 0131-226-3709), the top of which has retained the live image of Edinburgh-out-the-peephole, projected onto a white tabletop that made it famous 150 years ago. The exhibits are updated to include modern advances in optics, such as laser holography.

At 477B Lawnmarket, **Gladstone's Land** (☎ 0131-226-5856) is a restored seventeenth-century home inside and out (open April to October only). A nearby alley leads to **Lady Stair's House** (☎ 0131-225-2425 extension **6593**), which celebrates the lives and works of Scotland's three great writers: Burns, Scott, and Stevenson.

Because it was (twice) briefly a cathedral, that honorary title is sometimes given to the **High Kirk of St. Giles** (☎ 0131-225-8442). It's changed so much over the ages that today the main draw is the **Thistle Chapel,** built onto the church's corner in 1911. The church's minister from 1559 to 1572 was the fiery John Knox, leader of the Scottish Reformation and perpetual antagonist to Mary, Queen of Scots.

Supposedly Knox lived a few doors down at 43-45 High Street, although no actual historical evidence supports this theory. The **John Knox House** (☎ 0131-556-9579) is the only sixteenth-century building still existing on the Royal Mile with projecting upper floors.

Across the street at No. 42 is the **Museum of Childhood** (☎ 0131-529-4142), a museum full of toys from Victorian to recent times. Patrick Murray founded The Museum of Childhood even though he was a confirmed bachelor who insisted he was opening a museum of social science, not a romper room for kids — whom he reportedly detested.

As the Royal Mile becomes Canongate, you pass at no. 142 **Huntly House** (☎ 0131-629-4143), another restored sixteenth-century house filled with period rooms. Across the street is the clock-faced 1591 **Canongate Tollbooth,** a one-time council room, law court, and prison, now housing the **People's Story,** an exhibit on working life in Edinburgh from the eighteenth century to today.

Palace of Holyroodhouse

The royal palace of Scotland was originally the guest house of a twelfth-century abbey, where only ruins are now left. Of James V's sixteenth-century palace, only the north tower — rich with memories of his daughter, the political pawn Mary, Queen of Scots — remains. You can see a plaque where Mary's court secretary Riccio was murdered by her dissolute husband and his cronies, and some of the queen's needlework is on display. Most of the palace was built in the late seventeenth century. Although Prince Charles held his roving court here at one time, the palace was only recently restored after years of neglect. A quick spin takes about 45 minutes.

Canongate (east end of the Royal Mile). ☎ 0131-556-1096. Bus: 1, 6. Open: Mon–Sat 9:30 a.m.–5:15 p.m., Sun 10:30 a.m.–4:40 p.m. Closed last two weeks in May, three weeks in late June/early July, and whenever the royal family is in residence. Admission: £5.50 ($9.10) adults, £4 ($6.60) seniors, £2.70 ($4.45) kids under 17.

Calton Hill

Off Regent Road in eastern Edinburgh rises this odd Romantic paean to classical architecture. Besides a great view of the city and Edinburgh Castle (and behind you, to the Firth of Forth), the hill is scattered with a collection of nineteenth-century "instant ruins." A half-finished Parthenon, started in 1822 to honor Scottish soldiers killed in the Napoleonic wars, is probably the most famous. The Parthenon ended up being no more than a colonnade after funding ran out by 1829 (the unfinished temple was eventually dubbed "Scotland's Shame"). At the summit stands the 100-foot Nelson Monument.

Entrance off of Regent Rd. No phone. Bus: 26, 85, 86. Open: Nelson Monument: Apr–Sept, Mon 1:00 p.m.–6:00 p.m., Tues–Sat 10:00 a.m.–6:00 p.m.; Oct–Mar, Mon–Sat 10:00 a.m.–3:00 p.m. Admission: £2 ($3.30).

More cool things to see and do in Edinburgh

From pints of ale to pint-sized penguins to hikes and kilts and moonlight tours of the city's most haunted sites, Edinburgh offers much more to keep you entertained.

✔ **Scaling Arthur's Seat.** At 820 feet, Arthur's Seat is the result of past volcanic action with the end result being a hill in Holyrood Park. The hill feels more like a mountain after you make the 30-minute climb. After reaching the summit, your efforts are rewarded with a grand view that sweeps across the city below and, in the distance, the Firth of Forth.

✔ **Men in Skirts.** Thinking of sizing yourself for a kilt? The Highlander's dress used to be a 16-foot-long plaid scarf wrapped around and around to make a skirt, with the excess thrown across the chest and up over the shoulder. After an eighteenth-century ban on the wearing of such traditional clan tartans, kilts became a fierce symbol of Scottish pride, and an industry was born. Today, a handmade kilt with all its accessories can run you upward of £500 ($825), but even if a tartan scarf or tie is more your stripe, **Tartan Gift Shops,** 54 High St. (☎ 0131-558-3187), can help you identify your clan (or one close enough) and match you to one of its traditional tartans.

✔ **Visiting a Few Old Edinburgh Haunts.** Although **Robin's Tours** are the best walking tours for hidden Edinburgh and history buffs (call ☎ 0131-225-6593 for times and meeting spots), the most entertaining walks around the city are led after dark by the dead-beats working for **Witchery Tours** (☎ 0131-225-6745). Each dead guide wears a costume to represent an officially deceased Edinburgher whose ghost haunts this city. Your spirit guide leads you on a sometimes spooky, often goofy, and occasionally educational 90-minute tiptoe around the city's key historical and legendary spots in "Ghosts and Gore and Murder and Mayhem." Reserve a spot in advance for this tour.

✔ **Experiencing a Penguin Parade at the Edinburgh Zoo.** From April to September, at 2:00 p.m. daily, the zoo (☎ 0131-334-9171) herds the largest penguin colony in Europe out of its enclosure to run a few laps around a grassy park. Don't miss the gorillas, either (or the great view that stretches to the Firth of Forth). The zoo's at 134 Corstorphine Rd; take bus 2, 26, 69, 85, or 86.

✔ **Sampling the City's Pubs and Nightlife.** Edinburgh is an unsung nightlife capital, with a lively performing arts and theater scene year-round. More nighttime fun can be had at discos, such as the always-trendy Buster Browns, at 25 Market Street, and the enormous Century 2000, at 31 Lothian Road. The city is saturated with pubs and bars, especially in the Old Town around Grassmarket (**Black Bull**, no. 12), Candlemaker Row (**Greyfriars Bobby's Bar,** no. 34), Cowgate (**The Green Tree,** no. 182), and other University-area streets. In New Town, the slightly rundown Rose Street has a good row of pubs (try **Kenilworth** at no. 152). So toss back a pint of bitter or set up your own tasting marathon of wee drams of single-malt Scotch whisky — the night is yours.

For a more archetypal Scottish evening, you can either go with the hokey or the traditional. A bagpipe-playing, kilt-swirling "Scottish Folk Evening" is staged at big hotels such as the Carlton Highland or King James. A less forced *ceilidh* (pronounced *kay*-lee, a folk music jam session) happens nightly at the Tron Tavern on South Bridge or at any of the musical pubs listed in *The Gig* (available at newsstands and in pubs).

✔ **The Edinburgh International Festival.** Since 1947, Scotland's capital celebrates two to three weeks of theater, opera, arts, dance, music, poetry, prose, and even traditional culture (the bagpiping "Military Tattoo" parade uses the floodlit castle as a backdrop) to the city in August.

The festival has also spawned multiple minifestivals, including the famous Fringe Festival (also held in August, with many more acts, a lot more amateurs) and celebrations that center around jazz, film, television, and books. The main festival's headquarters (☎ **0131-473-2000** or 0131-473-2001) are at The Hub on the Royal Mile on Castlehill; those of the Fringe Festival (☎ **0131-226-5257;** Internet: www.edfringe.com) are at 180 High Street.

And on Your Left, Edinburgh Castle: Seeing Edinburgh by Guided Tour

The LRT **Classic Tour Bus** runs circles around the major Edinburgh sights, and a full-day ticket lets you hop on and off at any of its 15 stops. Buses run about 15 minutes apart on the two-hour circuit and have guided commentary along the way; the upper deck of the bus is open in summer. You can get tickets for the tour bus — £6.50 ($10.75) adults, £2.50 ($4.15) kids — at the starting point, Waverley Station.

But perhaps the best way to see Edinburgh with a guide is to join one of the walking tours described under "Visiting a Few Old Edinburgh Haunts" in "More Cool Things to See and Do in Edinburgh," in the previous section.

Suggested One-, Two-, and Three-Day Itineraries

If you're the type who'd rather organize your own tours, this section offers some tips for building your own Edinburgh itineraries.

If you have one day

Start your early morning admiring Old Masters and Scottish Impressionists in the **National Gallery of Scotland.** Cross The Mound and climb Lawnmarket/Castlehill to glowering **Edinburgh Castle.** Tour the bits you like, and then start making your way down the **Royal Mile,** popping into the sights and shops that catch your fancy and stopping for a late Scottish lunch at Witchery by the Castle or, if your purse strings are tighter, Deacon Brodie's Tavern. Finish up with the Royal Mile in time to meet the **Witchery Tours** guide for 90 minutes of "Ghosts and Gore and Murder and Mayhem." Spend the evening hopping from pub to pub, with a pause to dine at Pierre Victoire or the Indian Calvary Club.

If you have two days

Begin Day One exploring Edinburgh's single greatest sight: **Edinburgh Castle.** After you have your fill of medieval battlements and royal history, head to the **National Gallery of Scotland** for a spell of art appreciation. Window-shop your way through New Town en route to **Calton Hill** for a late afternoon panorama over the city.

Take Day Two to take in the bustle, shopping, atmosphere, and some dozen modest attractions that line the **Royal Mile.** Start from the top end at Edinburgh Castle and work your way down to the sixteenth-century royal palace of **Holyroodhouse** anchoring the other end. Pop into **Our Dynamic Earth** on your way to **Holyrood Park,** where you can clamber up Arthur's Seat for the sunset. Finish the day off with a pub crawl though the Old City and the University district.

If you have three days

Spend the first two days as I discuss previously and take Day Three to get out of town, either to track down the Loch Ness Monster or get funky in Glasgow. (Both excursions are described in the next section.)

Traveling Beyond Edinburgh

If you've got a day or so to spare, consider heading out of town. I recommend either traveling north to the Highlands, where you'll witness some spectacular scenery (and perhaps catch a glimpse of that fabled sea monster); or go west to Glasgow, recently reinvented as a splendid museum and shopping town.

On Nessie's trail: Inverness and Loch Ness

Many first-time visitors to the Highlands on a tight schedule view Inverness — ancient seat of the Pictish kings who once ruled northern Scotland — merely as a stepping stone. Their quest is for that elusive glimpse of the monster said to inhabit the deep waters of Loch Ness, which stretches its long finger of water along a fault line southwest from Inverness. The largest volume of water in Scotland, the loch is more enormous than it looks — only a mile wide and 24 miles long, but at its murkiest depths, it plunges 700 to 800 feet to the bottom.

In truth, the Highlands hold more beautiful and rewarding spots, but no one can deny the draw of Loch Ness and its creature. Doing the Loch in a single day from Edinburgh is tough, but it can be done. Take the early train to Inverness, do the Loch in the late morning and early afternoon, and then bus back to Inverness to spend an afternoon seeing a few sights and grabbing an early dinner before jumping a late train back to Edinburgh or the overnight train to London.

Getting There

Seven trains daily connect the two cities, and the trip is 3 ½ hours long. From Inverness, buses run hourly down the Loch to Drumnadrochit (a 30-minute trip; exiting the Inverness train station, turn right and then right again on Strothers Lane to find the bus station).

Inverness's tourist office (☎ **01463-234-353,** fax: 01463-710-609), at Castle Wynd off Bridge Street, is more than used to teaching visitors the basics of Nessie-stalking and other Loch activities from lake cruises to monster-seeking trips below the surface in tiny yellow minisubs (a rather obsessive £100/$165 splurge).

If you just want a quick spin to Nessie's lair, **Lothian Regional Transport** (☎ **0131-554-4494**), 27 Hanover St. in Edinburgh, offers an April to November bus tour of "Loch Ness and the Grampian Mountains" for £25 ($41.25) adults, £17 ($28.05) for children. (You have to provide your own suspension of disbelief.)

In Inverness, **Inverness Traction,** 6 Burnett Rd. (☎ **01463-239-292**), and **Jacobite Coaches and Cruises,** Tomnahurich Bridge on Glenurquhart Rd. (take a taxi or bus 3, 3A, 4, or 4A from Church Road, one block straight ahead from the train station; ☎ **01463-233-999;** Internet: www.cali.co.uk/jacobite), both run half- and full-day tours of the Loch. You can tour by coach (£9.50/$15.70 each way to Castle Urquhart), cruise (£9/$14.85 roundtrip, which means you don't get to get off but must admire the castle from the boat), or coach-and-boat (£12.50/$20.65; bus to Drumnadrochit, cruise the loch a bit, and bus back). Traction runs year-round; Jacobite April to October only.

In Drumnadrochit, **Loch Ness Cruises,** behind The Original Loch Ness Visitor Centre (☎ **01456-450-395;** Internet: www.lochness-centre.com), runs hourly Nessie-hunting cruises on the loch for £8 ($13.20) Easter to October, weather permitting.

Seeing the sights

Despite being one of the older towns in Scotland, **Inverness** looks rather modern. After burnings and other usual destructions over time, Inverness was rebuilt over the last 150 years or so. So although the Castle is impressive enough, it only dates from 1834 to 1847.

A short distance to the east of Inverness, on Auld Castlehill of the Craig Phadrig, is the most ancient area in town. This rise was the original site of the city castle, one of several Scottish contenders for the title of the infamous spot where Macbeth murdered King Duncan in 1040. (Shakespeare lifted many of his best plots straight from history.)

Next to the modern castle sits the free **Inverness Museum and Art Gallery** (☎ 01463-237-114), which gives you the lowdown on the life, history, and culture of the Highlands. You can reach the museum by walking up Castle Wynd from Bridge Street. You can also learn about Gaelic language and culture from the **Highlands Association,** headquartered in the sixteenth-century Abertaff House on Church Street.

Across the river are the Victorian **St. Andrew's Cathedral** on Ardoss Street (check out the Russian icons inside) and the excellent **Balnain House** at 40 Huntly Street (☎ 0463-715-757), whose exhibition of Highland music displays include instruments you can play and a great CD and gift shop. They also sponsor fantastic jam sessions Thursday nights year-round (plus Tuesdays in summer).

The **Loch Ness Show,** (☎ 01463-222-781) just across Ness Bridge on Huntly Street, offers a basic introduction to the Loch, its monster lore, and — what the heck — kilt-making. Farther west lies **Tomnahurich,** or the "hill of the fairies," with a cemetery and panoramic views.

For tooling around the lake, you have to make a choice: the main A82 along the north shore, passing such monster haunts as Drumnadrochit and Urquhart castle, or the more scenic southern shore route of natural attractions — pretty woodlands and the Foyers waterfalls. On a quick trip, the A82 gives you more to remember.

About halfway (14 miles) down the A82 from Inverness is the hamlet of **Dumnadrochit,** unofficial headquarters of Nessie lore. You find two museums here devoted to Nessie. The spanking new **Official Loch Ness 2000 Exhibition Centre,** in the massive stone building (☎ 01456-450-573; Internet: www.lochness.co.uk), is a surprisingly sophisticated and untouristy look at the history of the Loch (geological as well as mythological) and its famously elusive resident. The show takes a strict scientific view of the whole business of Nessie-hunting, really doing more to dispel and discredit the legends and sightings than to fan the flames of speculation.

The older, considerably more homespun **Original Loch Ness Monster Exhibition** (☎ 01456-450-573), is more of a believers' haunt, running down the legend of the monster with a hackneyed old film, a lot of photographs, accounts of Nessie sightings (along with other mythological creatures throughout the world, such as unicorns and Bigfoot), and a big ol' gift shop.

Almost two miles farther down the road (a half-hour walk), **Urquhart Castle** (☎ 01456-450-551) sits in near ruins on a piece of jutting land into the lake. This castle holds the record for the most Nessie sightings. For the history buffs, the 1509 ramparts encompass what was once one of the largest fortresses in Scotland, blown up in 1692 to prevent it from falling into Jacobite hands. When not packed with summer tourists, the grassy ruins can be quite romantic, and the tower keep offers fine Loch views.

Nessie, the monster of the Loch

The legend started in the sixth century after St. Colomba sent a monk swimming across the loch and a giant creature attacked. But after a harsh scolding from the saint, the monster withdrew. The legend, however, lives on.

Is Nessie the Loch Ness Monster that surfaced from the dark waters in the sixteenth century coming to shore while knocking down trees and crushing three men with her tail? Or is she *Nessitera rhombopteryx,* a vestigial survivor from the age of the dinosaurs (her basic description sounds somewhat like that of a plesiosaur — then again, it also kind of matches some species of sea snake).

One definite fact is that the monster sightings have increased in number after the A82 road was built by blasting lakeshore rock back in 1933. Shortly thereafter, innkeeps Mr. and Mrs. Spicer thought they saw something break the surface of the waters one night. The incident was reported on a slow news day in the local paper, and the rumor spread like wildfire.

In the end, the monster may be no more than the collective effect of faked photographs, water surface mirages brought on by too much whisky, a few unexplained lake phenomenon, and a string of Lochside villages whose economies are based on spinning tall tales to visitors. Sonar soundings and a host of keen-eyed watchers have not yet managed to prove, or disprove, Nessie's existence, and that is more than enough reason for 200,000 visitors annually to come, cameras and binoculars in hand, to search for the monster of Loch Ness.

The town of **Invermoriston** sits at the start of Glenmoriston, one of the prettiest valleys in the region, ideal for a short hike. At the head (southwest end) of Loch Ness stands the impressive **Fort Augustus,** an eighteenth-century fortress converted into a present-day Benedictine Abbey. From this "gateway to the Western Highlands" you can cruise Loch Ness or the 60 miles of the Caledonian Canal running from here to Fort William and the sea (22 miles are man-made locks, the rest are natural lochs).

Where to stay and dine

One of the nicest, yet inexpensive, places to stay in Inverness is the **Glen Mhor Hotel** (☎ **01463-234-308,** fax: 01463-713-170), on the River Ness with great views for £59 to £94 ($97.35 to $155.10) per small double and excellent Scottish cuisine in its restaurants. Cheaper fare (steaks, seafood, or pizza) can be had at the modern, laid-back Irish music pub **Johnny Foxes** (☎ **01463-236-577**), on Bank Street at Bridge Street. If you want to stay immersed in monster tales, shack up in Drumnadrochit at the **Polmaily House** Hotel (☎ **01456-450-343,** fax: 01456-450-813) for £46 to £105 ($75.90 to $173.25) per double, depending on the season.

Glasgow

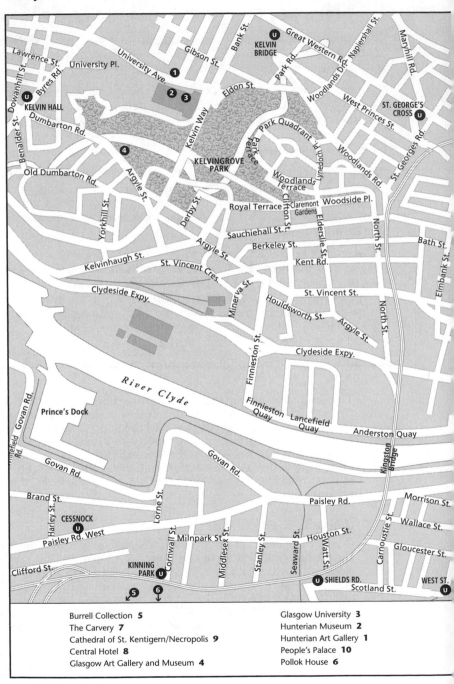

Burrell Collection **5**	Glasgow University **3**
The Carvery **7**	Hunterian Museum **2**
Cathedral of St. Kentigern/Necropolis **9**	Hunterian Art Gallery **1**
Central Hotel **8**	People's Palace **10**
Glasgow Art Gallery and Museum **4**	Pollok House **6**

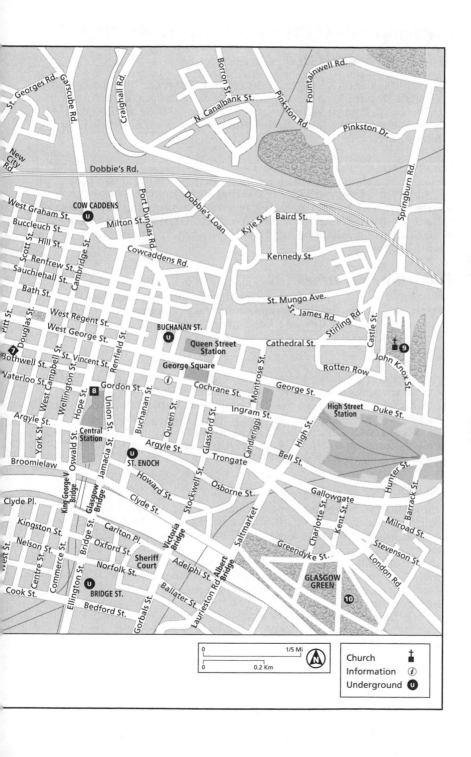

St. Georges Rd.
Garscube Rd.
Craighall Rd.
Borron St.
N. Canalbank St.
Pinkston Rd.
Fountainwell Rd.
Pinkston Dr.
Springburn Rd.
New City Rd.
Dobbie's Rd.
West Graham St.
COW CADDENS
Milton St.
Port Dundas Rd.
Dobbie's Loan
Kyle St.
Baird St.
Buccleuch St.
Scott St.
Hill St.
Cambridge St.
Cowcaddens Rd.
Kennedy St.
Renfrew St.
Sauchiehall St.
Bath St.
St. Mungo Ave.
St. James Rd.
West Regent St.
BUCHANAN ST.
Cathedral St.
Stirling Rd.
Castle St.
Pitt St.
Douglas St.
West George St.
Renfield St.
Queen Street Station
John Knox St.
Bothwell St.
St. Vincent St.
George Square
George St.
Rotten Row
Waterloo St.
West Campbell St.
Gordon St.
Cochrane St.
Montrose St.
High Street Station
Duke St.
Wellington St.
Hope St.
Union St.
Buchanan St.
Queen St.
Ingram St.
Glassford St.
Candleriggs
High St.
Argyle St.
Central Station
Bell St.
York St.
Oswald St.
Jamacia St.
Argyle St.
Trongate
Hunter St.
Broomielaw
ST. ENOCH
Howard St.
Stockwell St.
Osborne St.
Gallowgate
Barrack St.
Clyde Pl.
King George V Bridge
Glasgow Bridge
Clyde St.
Charlotte St.
Kent St.
Milroad St.
Kingston St.
Bridge St.
Carlton Pl.
Victoria Bridge
Saltmarket
Greendyke St.
Stevenson St.
London Rd.
Nelson St.
Commerce St.
Oxford St.
Sheriff Court
Adelphi St.
Albert Bridge
GLASGOW GREEN
Cook St.
Centre St.
Ellington St.
BRIDGE ST.
Norfolk St.
Ballater St.
Laurieston Rd.
Bedford St.
Gorbals St.

0   1/5 Mi
0   0.2 Km
N

Church
Information
Underground

Glasgow: A Victorian industrial city discovers culture

Glasgow was an Industrial Revolution powerhouse, the "second city of the British Empire" from the nineteenth to early twentieth centuries. With its wealth came a Victorian building boom, whose architecture is only beginning to be appreciated as the city comes off a decade-long publicity blitz.

This civic and mental makeover of the 1980s has turned Glasgow from the depressed slum it had been for much of this century into a real contender for Edinburgh's title of cultural and tourist center of Scotland. With friendlier people, more exclusive shopping than the capital, and a remarkable array of art museums, Glasgow has made a name for itself. Spend at least one night, two if you can, to drink in its renewed splendors.

Getting there and around

Half-hourly trains arrive in 50 minutes from Edinburgh, and the eight daily trains (four on Sunday) from London take almost six hours to arrive in Glasgow. The helpful tourist board's office (☎ 0141-204-4400; Internet: www.seeglasgow.com or www.glasgow1999.co.uk) is at 11 George Square.

The old section of Glasgow centers around the cathedral and train station. The shopping zone of **Merchant's City** is west of High Street. Glasgow grew westward, so that the finest Victorian area of the city is the grid of streets known as the **West End.** All of these areas are north of the River Clyde. The city has a good bus system and an underground (subway) that swoops from the southwest in an arc back to the northwest. Rides on either are 65p ($1.10).

Seeing the sights

As far as sightseeing goes, Glasgow offers art, art, and yet more art. Luckily, admission to almost all of Glasgow's attractions is, ahem, scot-free. Make sure you fit in at least the **Glasgow Art Gallery and Museum** (☎ 0141-287-2699), strong on Italian and Dutch old masters, such as Botticelli, Bellini, and Rembrandt, as well as the moderns — Monet, Picasso, van Gogh, Degas, Matisse, Whistler, and Ben Johnson. A whole horde of Scottish artists are represented, too, with works dating from the seventeenth century to the present. Take your time perusing the good collections of sculpture, ethnological artifacts, arms and armor, natural history, decorative arts, and relics of Scotland's Bronze Age.

The other great gallery of Glasgow is the **Burrell Collection** (☎ 0141-649-7151), about four miles southwest of the city center in Pollok Country Park. The huge assortment of art and artifacts was once a private collection. The collection is global and spans from the Neolithic era to the modern day, with special attention to ancient Rome and Greece as well as paintings by Cézanne, Delacroix, and Cranach the

Elder. Also in the park is the eighteenth-century mansion **Pollok House** (☎ 0141-616-6410), with a fine series of Spanish paintings by El Greco, Goya, Velázquez, and others.

Another gallery to visit is the **Hunterian Art Gallery** (☎ 0141-330-5431) at University Avenue, which controls the estate of the great artist James McNeill Whistler (born American, but proud to be of Scottish blood). Art nouveau innovator Charles Rennie Mackintosh designed and built his own home, and though this architectural treasure was demolished in the 1960s, most of it has been painstakingly reconstructed here to house the gallery.

Across the street from the Hunterian Art Gallery is the **Hunterian Museum** (☎ 0141-330-4221), which has a unique archaeological collection, such as Roman and Viking artifacts, to paleontology and geology with dinosaur fossils. You can see an exhibit on the exploits of Captain Cook — in short, enough relics to give naturalists and the kids a welcome break from all those paintings.

The kids — and certainly history buffs — may also get a kick out of the **People's Palace** (☎ 0141-554-0223) on Glasgow Green (Britain's first public park). Beyond a lush greenhouse filled with palms and a tea room, the museum contains a few drips and drabs of artifacts from the Middle Ages and Mary, Queen of Scots, but the main collections bring to light the life of an average Victorian Glasgowian.

After you see enough museums to last for awhile, take a breather in the pews of the **Cathedral of St. Kentigern,** an austerely but gorgeously Gothic thirteenth-century church with a twelfth-century under-church of great pointy arches and web-like vaulting. Below the cathedral is the **Necropolis,** filled with fantastically diverse tombs in a jumble of architectural styles.

Where to stay

The huge **Central Hotel** (☎ 0141-221-9680, fax: 0141-226-3948), at 99 Gordon Street near the central station, has tatty turn-of-the-century charm for just £70 ($115.50) per double; the tourist office can help you book a room.

Where to dine

Although revitalized Glasgow has plenty of refined international eateries these days, beating the value of **The Carvery's** (☎ 0141-248-2656) hearty buffet of British specialties is hard. It's in the Forte Crest Hotel, on Bothwell Street.

Chapter 13

Dublin and the Best of Ireland

· ·

In This Chapter

▶ Getting to and around Dublin

▶ Exploring Dublin's neighborhoods

▶ Reviewing Dublin's top restaurants, hotels, and attractions

▶ Heading into the Irish countryside for excursions and overnight trips

· ·

*I*reland is called The Emerald Isle with good reason — it's a lush, green land with a deep history and unique inhabitants. Ancient ruins and medieval monasteries dot the countryside, structures once inhabited by Celts, Vikings, Normans, and the English. Ireland is the renowned home to literary giants, Irish whiskey, and astounding music.

Although Ireland is part of the British Isles, Ireland is *not* part of the United Kingdom. The Irish fiercely fought for their independence from the British crown (some 750 years) and have been an independent Republic since 1921. However, a few counties in the northern region of Ireland did not agree to become independent and are still part of the United Kingdom.

Unfortunately, Northern Ireland has been faced with "The Troubles" ever since the decision to stay with the United Kingdom. The Troubles consist of a long-standing political and paramilitary conflict between the Protestant minority, which supports British rule, and the Catholic majority, which favors independence from Britain. Terrorist attacks plagued Belfast and London in the 1980s and 1990s as each side sought to subvert the other's legitimacy. While both sides continue to work toward a peaceful resolution, for now Ireland remains a land divided.

The city of Dublin has exquisite museums and a thriving nightlife. But even more appealing is the beautiful, rural landscape and friendly townspeople who await you. I say give Dublin a day or two at most and then take off to the Irish countryside. Renting a car in Ireland to explore the landscape is a great idea.

Making Your Way to and around Dublin

Dublin is a quick one-hour flight from London, making that by far the most convenient way to get to town. (Especially in light of the plodding train-to-overnight-ferry-to-commuter-rail alternative.)

Getting to Dublin by air or land

Dublin International Airport lies about 8 miles (30 minutes) north of the city. Express Airport Coach 747 runs two to three times hourly to Heuston Station for $3 ($4.35). The 41 or 41A city bus will drop you off at Eden Quay on the River Liffey for $1.10 ($1.60); travel time is about 45 minutes. Taxis line up outside the terminal for a quick, easy trip into town; fares average $12 ($17.40) to $15 ($21.75).

Most trains (from the west, south, and southwest) arrive at **Heuston Station,** on the west end of town. Those from the north pull into the more central **Connolly Station. Buses** arrive at the **Busaras Central Bus Station** on Store Street near Connolly Station. For information on train schedules, call **Irish Rail (☎ 01/836-6222).**

Getting around once you're in Dublin

If you prefer to ride a lot, or are staying outside the center of town, the $3.30 ($4.80) one-day bus pass or $10 ($14.50) four-day bus-and-rail pass (good on the DART) is worth your while. You can purchase either one at the bus depot at 59 Upper O'Connell Street.

By bus

Dublin's green double-decker buses can transport you all over the city and suburbs, but keep in mind that Dublin's core is very easily walked. To take a bus, hop on, say where you'll be getting off, and pay the driver (nothing bigger than a $5 note), who charges you according to the number of stops. Up to about five stops is 60p (85 cents); the most you can ever be charged is $1.25 ($1.80) — except at night when the rate is a flat $2.50 ($3.60) fare.

By DART (light rail)

The speedy electric train DART system is really for commuters, with only five stops you may need to worry about: three in the city center (Connolly, Tara Street, and Pearse), the Lansdowne Road station in Ballsbridge, and the Dun Laoghaire station at the ferry docks. DART tickets cost 80p ($1.15). If you're arriving in Ireland by ferry, you can take DART into town (trains run from 7:00 a.m. to midnight). In the event your ferry arrives in the dawn hours, bus 46A runs from the ferry docks to St. Stephens Green from 6:00 a.m. to 11:30 p.m.

By taxi

Do not try to hail a taxi as it whizzes by you on the street. Instead, line up at at one of the city's many *ranks* (stands), where taxis wait for their fares. You find ranks outside all the major hotels and transportation centers as well as on the busier streets, such as Upper O'Connell Street, College Green, and the north side of St. Stephen's Green.

You can also call a taxi. Try **Access Taxis** (☎ **01-668-3333**), **Blue Cabs** (☎ **01-676-1111**), or **Co-op Taxis** (☎ **01-676-6666**). The minimum charge for one passenger is £1.80 ($2.50) for the first mile or the first nine minutes. After that the charge is 80p ($1.15) per mile. Each additional passenger or suitcase is 40p (55 cents). Between 8:00 p.m. and 8:00 a.m. and all day Sunday, you have an extra charge of 40p (55 cents).

Discovering Dublin: What You Need to Know

This section provides information that you'll need for the basic necessities of getting the most out of your money, as well as what you'll need in an emergency or if you get stuck.

The local dough

The Irish unit of currency is the Irish punt (often called pound and, like the British pound, denoted with a £), which is divided into 100 pence, called *pee* (p). Roughly, $1 equals 70p, or £1 equals $1.40. Irish coins include 1p, 5p, 10p, 20p, 50p, and £1. Bills come in denominations of £5, £10, £20, £50, and £100.

Where to get info after you arrive

The main **Dublin Tourism** office is in St. Andrew's Church (☎ **01-605-7700**; Internet: www.visitdublin.com), at Suffolk Street, a block west of Grafton Street. The office is open June to September, Monday to Saturday 9:00 a.m. to 8.30 p.m., Sunday 11:00 a.m. to 5.30 p.m.; winter Monday to Saturday 9:00 a.m. (9.30 a.m. Tuesday) to 5.30 p.m. Smaller branches are at Baggot Street Bridge (near Fitzwilliam Square), the airport, at The Square Towncentre on Tallaght, in Exclusively Irish on O'Connell Street, and Dun Laoghaire's ferry terminal.

The **Temple Bar** neighborhood has its own info center at 18 Eustace Street (☎ **01-671-5717**; Internet: www.temple-bar.ie). Newsstands carry the events magazine *In Dublin*.

Where to go in a pinch

Violent crime is not the norm in Dublin, but with increased drug traffic, crime has risen. As with any place else, don't let yourself become careless. In case of emergency, keep the following list of references handy:

- **Doctors/hospitals:** In an emergency, ask your hotel to call a doctor for you. Otherwise, call the **Eastern Health Board Headquarters,** Dr. Steevens Hospital (☎ 01-679-0700) or the **Irish Medical Organization,** 10 Fitzwilliam Place (☎ 01-676-7273). For an emergency room, go to the **Mater Misericordiae Hospital,** 7 Eccles Street (☎ 01-830-1122).

- **Embassy:** The U.S. Embassy (☎ 01-668-8777) is at 42 Elgin Road.

- **Emergency:** Dial ☎ 999 in any emergency.

- **Pharmacies: Leonard's Corner Pharmacy,** 106 S. Circular Road (☎ 01-453-4282) is open daily 9:00 a.m. to 10:00 p.m. **Crowley's Pharmacy,** on Kilbarrack Road, is open late at night. Call ☎ 01-832-5332 for hours.

- **Transit Info:** The **Dublin Bus** number is ☎ 01-873-4222. The number for **Dublin Area Rapid Transit (DART)** is ☎ 01-703-3504. For **Bus Eireann** (coaches throughout Ireland), call ☎ 01-836-6111.

Staying in touch

Need to wire home for more beer money? Want to get online to check your e-mail? The following information will help keep you in touch while you're touring Dublin.

- **American Express:** The office is at 116 Grafton St. (☎ 01-677-2874), opposite Trinity College. The office is open Monday to Saturday 9:00 a.m. to 5:00 p.m.

- **Internet Access and Cyber Cafes: Central Cyber Cafe** (☎ 01-677-8298; Internet: www.centralcafe.ie), 6 Grafton Street, is open in the heart of town Monday to Friday 8:00 a.m. to 11:00 p.m., Saturday 9:00 a.m. to 11:00 p.m., Sunday 10:00 a.m. to 10:00 p.m. and charges £5 ($7) per hour, with a 20 percent discount for students. **Cyberia Cafe,** in Temple Bar Arthouse, Curved Street (☎ 01-679- 7607), serves food along with e-mail access, which costs £5 ($7) per hour.

  The Pembroke, 31 Lower Pembroke Street, just off Baggot Street in the Pembroke lounge bar (☎ 01-676-2780; Internet: www.pembroke.ie), may charge £6 ($8.40) per hour, but the bar has cable modem connections, is open daily 7:30 a.m. to midnight, and you get access to the bar's full food and drink menu.

- **Mail:** Dublin's main post office is on O'Connell Street (☎ 01-705-7000), open Monday to Saturday 8:00 a.m. to 8:00 p.m., Sunday 10:30 a.m. to 6:30 p.m.

✔ **Telephone:** A local call in Dublin costs 20p (30 cents). Pay phones accept both coins and phone cards, which you can buy at post offices. Ireland's country code is **353.** Dublin's city code is **01.** If you're calling from outside Ireland, drop the initial zero. To call Dublin from the United States, dial **011-353-1** followed by the number.

To call the United States from Ireland directly, dial **001** followed by the area code and phone number. To charge a call to your calling card, or make a collect call home, dial **AT&T** (☎ **1-800-550-000**), **MCI** (☎ **1-800-551-001**), or **Sprint** (☎ **1-800-552-001**).

Touring Dublin by Neighborhood

The city of Dublin is sprawling but most of its sights are concentrated along the **River Liffey** — a nice area for a walk. A lot of the sights that may interest you lie south of the Liffey, except some literary sights to the north around **Parnell Square.**

North of the Liffey, the main thoroughfare is called **O'Connell Street.** O'Connell Street crosses a bridge of the same name to the south side, where it becomes a large traffic circle in front of **Trinity College.** The street then narrows again into the pedestrian **Grafton Street.** Grafton Street continues south to spill into **St. Stephen's Green,** which is something between a square and a gorgeous city park. Off the northeast corner of this square is a complex of huge buildings that house the government and various national museums and libraries. To the east of the square lie several more verdant city spaces, such as **Merrion Square** and **Fitzwilliam Square.** Farther to the southeast is the fashionable embassy and hotel-filled neighborhood of **Ballsbridge.**

Back at that traffic circle in front of Trinity College, College Green leads due west past the impressive Bank of Ireland building and becomes **Dame Street. Temple Bar,** Dublin's always trendy, always fun, pub-, club-, and restaurant-filled district lies between Dame Street and the Liffey. (Temple Bar is connected to the north side of the Liffey by the slim, picturesque span of the **Ha'penny Bridge.**) Dame Street changes names regularly as it moves west, passing Dublin Castle before reaching **Christ Church Cathedral** on the edge of the city center.

Staying in Dublin

You can find a lot of nice, if expensive, hotels in central Dublin, but you can also find some great values if you look hard enough. Most of the larger hotels in Dublin are the huge, uniform chains that are fine for a good night's sleep, but lack much in the way of charm. My advice is to seek out one of the number of hotels converted from historic Victorian and Georgian buildings. One of the nicest (and safest) neighborhoods is east of the city center in the embassy-filled residential zone of **Ballsbridge,** a short DART ride from downtown.

In addition to the hotels listed in the previous and next section, Dublin has a surplus of B&Bs, which generally offer inexpensive lodging in a friendly, small inn atmosphere. **Dublin Tourism** (☎ **01-605-7777,** fax: 01-605-7787) can help you find a B&B room for a £3 ($4.25) fee; the agency books rooms in traditional hotels as well. Another place to check is the **Central Reservation Service** at 1 Clarinda Park North in Dun Laoghaire, south of the city (☎ **01-284-1765,** fax: 01-284-1751).

Dublin's top hotels

Ariel House
$$$ **Ballsbridge**

Ariel House is a family-run hotel located in a stylish, residential suburb just a block from the speedy DART train into town. Ariel House offers modern comfort in a Victorian style with unchanging hospitality to a few fortunate travelers. Reserve early to assure yourself accommodations. The attention to refined detail is evident from the Waterford chandelier and carved cornices in the drawing room, to the period furniture, fine paintings, and Irish linens in the comfy rooms. Rates include a full Irish breakfast.

52 Lansdowne Road (east of the city center, beyond Merrion Square; from the DART station, turn left down Lansdowne Road). ☎ *01-668-5512. Fax: 01-668-5845. DART: Lansdowne Road Bus: 5, 7A, 8, 46, 63, 84. Rates: £80–£160 ($112–$224) double. MC, V.*

Jurys Christ Church Inn
$ **Old City**

One of Dublin's great central bargains, Jurys has rooms large enough to hold a family of four, but the price stays at just £66 ($92.40). The rates are great and the location superior, near Dublin's top sights, but Jurys isn't dripping with charm. Still, it is very clean and furnished with contemporary good taste and all your basic amenities.

Christ Church Place (across from Christ Church, where Werburgh Street, Lord Edward Street, and High Street meet). ☎ *800-448-8355 in the United States (though for some reason that number quotes rates at £100-$140 per night), or 01-454-0000 in Ireland; Internet:* www.jurys.com. *Fax: 01-454-0012. Bus: 21A, 50, 50A, 78, 78A, 78B. Rates: £66 ($92.40) double. AE, DC, MC, V.*

Shelbourne
$$$$ **St. Stephen's Green**

An imposing red-and-white facade on Dublin's most stately square of greenery announces this historic hotel. Built in 1824, the Shelbourne has been host to actors, writers, and the signing of Ireland's constitution. Crackling fires and Waterford chandeliers greet you in the clubby entrance lounges, while guest rooms play out their varied-size comforts with modern conveniences and antique furnishings. Take afternoon tea in the Lord Mayor's Lounge.

27 St. Stephen's Green (right in the center of town, on the north side of the Green).
☎ *800-543-4300 in the United States or 01-676-6471 in Ireland. Fax: 01-661-6006.*
Internet: www.shelbourne.ie. *DART: Pearse Station. Bus: 10, 11A, 11B, 13, 20B.*
Rates: £195–£255 ($273–$357) double. AE, DC, MC, V.

Stauntons on the Green

$$ St. Stephen's Green

Stauntons is a new hotel in a Georgian townhouse on Dublin's central square, but it has a historic feel. The windows are tall, ceilings high, furnishings traditional, and fireplaces blazing in the public rooms. You find green every way you look, because the back rooms open onto Iveagh Gardens. The rates include breakfast.

83 St. Stephen's Green (on the south side of the Green). ☎ *01-478-2300. Fax: 01-478-2263. DART: Pearse Station. Bus: 14A, 62. Rates: £120–£160 ($168–$224) double. AE, DC, MC, V.*

Temple Bar Hotel

$$$ Temple Bar

You find yourself in the midst of all the action at the Temple Bar. Built in 1993, this trendy hotel with the Victorian façade has over 100 rooms decorated in a traditional style with modern facilities. A full Irish breakfast is included in the price, plus a good pub, acceptable restaurant, and Dublin's liveliest neighborhood right out the front door.

Fleet Street (off Westmoreland Street, a block from the Liffey). ☎ *800-448-8355 in the United States or 01-677-3333 in Ireland. Fax: 01-677-3088. DART: Tara Street Bus: 78A, 78B. Rates: £135 ($189) double. AE, DC, MC, V.*

Dublin's runner-up accommodations

Blooms

$$$ A large, amenitied, modern hotel wedged strategically between Trinity College and Temple Bar. *Anglesea Street off Dame Street (*☎ *800-44-UTEL in the United States, 01-671-5622 in Ireland; Fax: 01-671-5997).*

Harding Hotel

$ Harding Hotel was built in 1996 for traveling students and other budgeteers (though the hotel is open to, and patronized, by all types — this is not a hostel). The hotel offers comfortable, if uninspiring, rooms complete with coffeemaker; all this on the edge of trendy Temple Bar with the cheapest rates in central Dublin. *Copper Alley, Fishamble Street, Christchurch off High Street (*☎ *01-679-6500; Fax: 01-679-6504; Internet:* www.iol.ie-usitaccm*).*

Accommodations, Dining & Attractions in Dublin

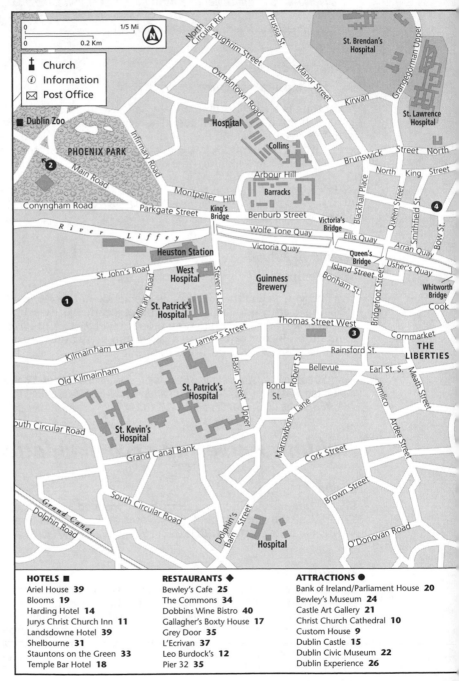

HOTELS ■
Ariel House **39**
Blooms **19**
Harding Hotel **14**
Jurys Christ Church Inn **11**
Landsdowne Hotel **39**
Shelbourne **31**
Stauntons on the Green **33**
Temple Bar Hotel **18**

RESTAURANTS ◆
Bewley's Cafe **25**
The Commons **34**
Dobbins Wine Bistro **40**
Gallagher's Boxty House **17**
Grey Door **35**
L'Ecrivan **37**
Leo Burdock's **12**
Pier 32 **35**

ATTRACTIONS ●
Bank of Ireland/Parliament House **20**
Bewley's Museum **24**
Castle Art Gallery **21**
Christ Church Cathedral **10**
Custom House **9**
Dublin Castle **15**
Dublin Civic Museum **22**
Dublin Experience **26**

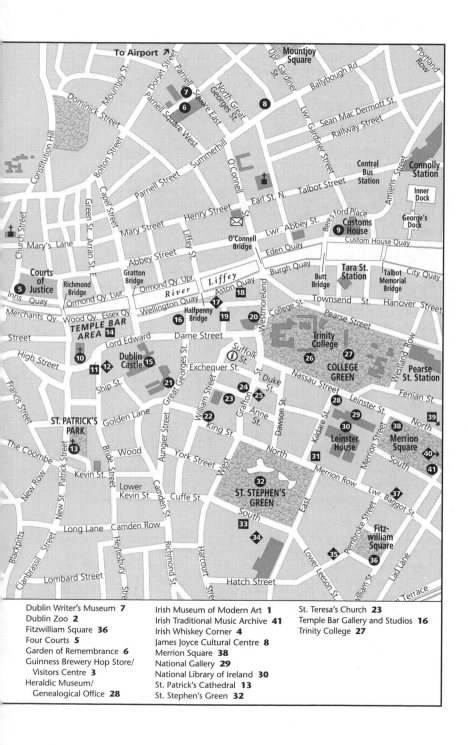

Landsdowne Hotel

$$ Landsdowne Hotel is a Ballsbridge inn of large rooms not far from the Rugby Grounds; the neighborhood's packed with Georgian architecture and shopping. *27 Pembroke Road (☎ 01-668-2522; Fax: 01-668-5585).*

Dining in Dublin

Ireland has surpassed even Britain in the reinventing-your-national-cuisine department. Irish grub is no longer limited to blackened meats and overcooked veggies. The chefs of Ireland have studied both California cooking and French nouvelle to put a new spin on traditional dishes. Plus, in cosmopolitan Dublin, you can find plenty of continental, French, Italian, and other ethnic restaurants to satisfy any hunger craving.

The Irish have a reputation, not entirely undeserved, of being a meat-and-potatoes — and nothing else — sort of people. This reputation isn't really true, but even if it were, Irish lamb and mutton (you're in sheep country now) are quite excellent. So is the steak, especially the beef from central Ireland around Mullingar. As for those potatoes, the Irish have managed to cultivate them from a poor man's food almost into an art form; some varieties of potatoes are so buttery and soft that they need no condiments or accompaniment.

People tend to forget that Ireland is an island, and as such has excellent seafood, too. The wild salmon caught in the Shannon River is a tasty treat, as are the Dublin Bay prawns.

Other Irish foods that may grace your table are roast chicken, *boxty* (potato pancakes wrapped around meaty fillings), *coddle* (boiled bacon, sausages, onions, and potatoes), and lamb stew. Alongside almost every meal, you find slabs of incredible, dense Irish breads, the best being brown bread and the dry soda bread. The most common pub snack is a toasted ham and cheese sandwich, which is just as basic as it sounds.

A traditional, hearty Irish breakfast is a feast you should partake in if only once, even if you're watching your cholesterol. A bowl of deliciously lumpy porridge, eggs, country bacon, scones with marvelous jams and marmalades, black and white puddings (scrumptious, especially if you don't think about the innards and other unknown bits that are in them), and a slice of tomato are all fried up — well, except for the scones and porridge — and served on a plate.

You can't discuss Irish cuisine and not mention beer, the mainstay of any meal. The Irish say that drinking Guinness from a can or bottle as compared to having a fresh pint drawn straight from the tap is like the difference between eating canned peaches as opposed to a ripened peach fresh off the tree. Some beer purists adamantly patronize only the pub at the brewery itself (see "Dublin's top restaurants" for more brewery information) in order to guzzle the rich, black, creamy, yeasty elixir straight from the proverbial vat. Guinness's lager is called *Harp,* and don't miss out on the Guinness rival from Cork, the dark *Murphy's.* Kilkenny's Smithwicks is the best when it comes to ales. For a break from the brew, quality hard cider is also on tap.

The Irish invented whiskey, where the legend pins it on a sixth-century monk. Old Bushmills (established in 1608) is the oldest distillery in the world. The "e" isn't the only difference between Irish whiskey and Scotch or English *whisky;* the unique Irish distillation process gives the stuff a cleaner, less smoky flavor. Other brands to sample include John Jameson, Powers, Paddy's, Tullamore Dew, Murphy, and Dunphy. The Irish drink their whiskey neat — straight out of the bottle at room temperature. A few decades ago, they started dumping Irish whiskey into coffee, mixing in sugar, topping it off with whipped cream, and serving it to arrivals at Shannon airport, hence Irish Coffee. This concoction may be touristy, but very, very tasty.

Dublin's top restaurants

Bewley's Cafe

$ **Near St. Stephen's Green IRISH**

This huge, old-fashioned, high-ceilinged tea room on Dublin's main shopping walkway has been a preferred tea room of Dubliners since 1840. You can get well-prepared light foods, cafeteria-style, but Bewley's is most famous for its teas with scones and jams. You can find other branches at 11-12 Westmoreland Street and 13 S. Great George Street.

78-79 Grafton Street (on the main strolling path in town). ☎ *01-677-6761. Reservations not required. Bus: 15A, 15B, 15C, 46, 55, 63, 83. All foods: £1.65–£5 ($2.35–$7.15). AE, DC, MC, V. Open: Lunch and dinner daily (until 1:00 a.m. Sun–Thurs, until 2:00 a.m. Fri–Sat).*

The Commons

$$$$ **St. Stephen's Green MODERN EUROPEAN**

Michelin has awarded one of its coveted stars to this refined eatery installed in a pair of eighteenth-century town houses. The Commons continues to win praises for its Georgian décor, with modern art mixed in, and its ever-changing and eclectic contemporary menu. The chef often features creations such as confit of duck on a beetroot boxty pancake or grilled shark with peppered carrot. In summer before dinner, enjoy a cocktail in the pretty stone-walled garden.

85-86 St. Stephen's Green (on the south side of the square). ☎ *01-475-2597. Reservations required. Bus: 11, 13, 10, 46A. Fixed-price lunch: £18 ($25.70); fixed-price dinner £32 or £42 ($45.70 or $60). AE, DC, MC, V. Open: Lunch Mon–Fri, dinner Mon–Sat.*

Dobbins Wine Bistro

$$$ Near Merrion Square   IRISH-CONTINENTAL

A perfect spot for intimate dining for Dobbins has seating in a cozy, country interior or on a tropical patio. The chef uses many traditional Irish ingredients in his inventive dishes. The menu changes often, but may include roast herbed lamb; black sole stuffed with salmon, crab, and prawn; or duckling with orange and port sauce.

15 Stephen's Lane (between Upper and Lower Mount Streets, a block east of Merrion Square). ☎ *01-676-4679 or 01-676-4670. Reservations required. Bus: 5, 7A, 8, 46, 84. Main courses: £12.95–£19.95 ($18.50–$28.50); fixed-price lunch £14.95 ($21.35). AE, DC, MC, V. Open: Lunch Mon–Fri, dinner Tues–Sat.*

Gallagher's Boxty House

$$ Temple Bar   TRADITIONAL IRISH

Welcoming, homey Gallagher's is a fixture both of Temple Bar and of traditional Irish cooking. Gallagher's specialties are the grilled potato pancakes called boxty, rolled around fillings of beef, lamb, chicken, or fish. Its open-faced lunchtime sandwiches are excellent, as is its salmon. The clientele is a mix of tourists seeking real Irish cooking and locals doing the same, trying to recapture that old "dinner at Grandma's" feeling.

20-21 Temple Bar (between Essex and Fleet Streets). ☎ *01-677-2762. Reservations recommended, but not always accepted. Bus: 21A, 46A, 46B, 51B, 51C, 68, 69, 86. Main courses: at lunch £2.95–£4.50 ($4.20–$6.45); at dinner £5.95–£12.95 ($8.50–$18.50). AE, MC, V. Open: Lunch and dinner daily.*

Grey Door

$$$ Near St. Stephen's Green   RUSSIAN-SCANDINAVIAN

The upper dining rooms in this Georgian town house are more elegant than the basement Pier 32 restaurant, which is reviewed under "Dublin's runner-up restaurants" in the next section. Here you can dine on quality northeastern European cuisine, such as Kotley Kiev (chicken Kiev stuffed with vodka butter) and Galupsti Maskova (cabbage stuffed with minced lamb).

23 Upper Pembroke Street (off Lower Lesson Street between St. Stephen's Green and Fitzwilliam Square). ☎ *01-676-3286. Reservations required. Bus: 46A, 46B, 86. Main courses: £20–£25 ($28.60–$35.70); fixed-price lunch £15 ($21.45). AE, DC, MC, V. Open: Lunch Mon–Fri, dinner Mon–Sat.*

Dublin's runner-up restaurants

L'Ecrivan

$$$ A traditional Irish restaurant that puts on a bit of French flair (in the kitchen and in the refined dining rooms) to add to the class. Book a table on the garden terrace in warm weather. *109 Lower Baggot Street (*☎ *01-661-1919).*

Leo Burdock's

$ An absolute shrine of the fish and chip crowd, where you get some of the British Isles' greatest chips (french fries) along with your light and flaky fried cod or whiting fish. *2 Werbaugh Street just around the corner from Christ Church Cathedral (☎ 01-454-0306).*

Pier 32

$$$ Pier 32 serves seafood (great cups of seafood chowder) and traditional Irish fare (angus steaks are excellent) amid bare bricks, beams, and fireplaces. The homemade soda bread is beyond compare. *23 Upper Pembroke Street, in the basement of The Grey Door, which is reviewed in the previous section, (☎ 01-676-1494).*

Exploring Dublin

With the exception of the Dublin Writer's Museum, the top sights in town are concentrated south of the River Liffey.

Dublin's top sights

Trinity College and the Book of Kells

In the center of Dublin is a refuge where students bustle with their books. Most visitors to the eighteenth- and nineteenth-century buildings of Trinity College — among whose illustrious graduates are counted Jonathan Swift, Thomas Moore, Oscar Wilde, Bram Stoker, and Samuel Beckett — go directly to the library. Here, in about an hour, you can examine a fine display on the medieval art of manuscript illumination — a craft at which Irish monks excelled.

The library is home to a precious trinity of illuminated manuscripts, including one of Ireland's most richly decorated, the eighth-century *Book of Kells.* Stolen from its monastery in 1007, the book was miraculously recovered from a bog three months later. The book's gold-rich cover was missing, but the near disastrous experience did little harm to the vibrant colors and remarkable detail in what is perhaps the most beautiful, important, and cherished illuminated manuscript in the world.

College Green (enter where Dame Street runs into Grafton Street). ☎ 01-677-2941. DART: Tara Street Station. Bus: 5, 7A, 8, 15A, 15B, 15C, 46, 55, 62, 63, 83, 84. Open: Mon–Sat 9:30 a.m.–5:00 p.m., Sun noon–4:30 p.m. Admission: £3.50 ($5.10) adults, £3 ($4.35) students and seniors, kids under 11 free.

National Museum

Celtic civilization or antiquites buffs should head straightaway to Ireland's foremost archeological collection, which spans prehistory to the Middle Ages. Among the National Museum's treasures are the eighth-century Tara Brooch, an intricately designed jewel of white bronze, and the famed Ardagh Chalice (also eighth century), a cup of beaten silver embellished with engravings, embossing, enamels, and gold filigree.

You can also see row after row of golden torcs, those thick yoke-shaped necklaces that were a symbol of royalty among Celtic peoples (and the only article of clothing Celtic warriors wore into battle according to Roman historians). Antiquities afficionados will want to spend 90 minutes or more; the mildly curious can be out in half an hour.

Kildare Street and Merrion Row. ☎ *01-677-7444. DART: Pearse Station. Bus: 7, 7A, 8, 10, 11, 13. Open: Tues–Sat 10:00 a.m.–5:00 p.m., Sun 2:00–5:00 p.m. Admission: Free.*

Christ Church Cathedral

The remaining bits of the twelfth-century Norman-style church erected here by Strongbow and his followers represent the oldest stone building in Dublin, a 30-minute medieval diversion.

Strongbow himself, who helped conquer Ireland for the Normans, supposedly rests in peace inside. Purists insist the sarcophagus was made about 170 years after Strongbow's death, and that the grave effigy is modeled after the Earl of Drogheda. Still others argue that no matter who built the tomb, Strongbow's entrails at least are interred within, and a few people think that the curious, small half-figure tomb right *next* to the main tomb is Strongbow's. (Myth followers believe that this smaller tomb is that of Strongbow's son, who was sliced in half by his father when Strongbow suspected that junior lacked in the bravery department.)

Since the church was rebuilt in the 1870s, the design is mostly Gothic. The church was once used as an indoor market and you can check out the huge crypt underneath, which was once full of taverns.

Christ Church Place (off Lord Ebury Street). ☎ *01-677-8099. DART: Pearse Station. Bus: 7, 7A, 8, 10, 11, 13. Open: Daily 10:00 a.m.–5:30 p.m. Admission: £2 ($2.85) adults, £1 ($1.40) student.*

St. Patrick's Cathedral

Why does the city have two cathedrals? Primarily because a falling out with Christ Church's clergyman led Dublin's archbishop to name St. Patrick's a cathedral. This Gothic cathedral is believed to be founded on the same site where St. Patrick baptized converts in a.d. 450. The cathedral was raised in 1190 and then rebuilt in the fourteenth century. You can easily tour the cathedral in ten minutes; the main attraction is the floor tomb of Jonathan Swift, of *Gulliver's Travels* fame.

Patrick's Close (off Patrick Street). ☎ *01-475-4817. Bus: 50, 50A, 54A, 56A. Open: Mon–Fri 9:00 a.m.–5:00 p.m., Sun 10:00 a.m.–4:30 p.m. Admission: £1.50 ($2.50).*

National Gallery

In the realm of Europe's art galleries, the National Gallery in Dublin is not superior, yet it has a few important works by major old masters that make a 30-minute tour a requisite for appreciators of art. The highlights are Caravaggio's tumultuous 1602 *Arrest of Christ,* Paolo Uccello's oddball 1440 *Virgin and Child,* and Vermeer's richly lit 1665 *Woman Writing a Letter.* The collections are fleshed out with works by Titian, van Dyck, Goya, Velazquez, Gainsborough, El Greco, and Degas.

Merrion Square W. ☎ *01-661-5133. DART: Pearse Station. Bus: 5, 7, 7A, 8, 10, 11, 44, 47, 48A, 62. Open: Mon–Wed and Fri–Sat 10:00 a.m.–5:30 p.m., Thurs 10:00 a.m.– 8:30 p.m., Sun 2:00–5:00 p.m. Admission: Free.*

Dublin Castle

Dublin Castle sounds nice and medievally Irish, and indeed this was the site of the first earthen fort established by the Vikings. But the castle today, which you can easily tour in 30 to 45 minutes, is mainly seventeenth- and eighteenth-century state apartments and assembly rooms that served the ruling British government for 700 years. Of more ancient lineage, you do get to see the thirteenth-century Record Tower (Norman era) and, in the undercroft, the foundations of that Viking bunker and bits of medieval city wall.

Palace Street (off Dame Street). ☎ *01-679-3713. Bus: 54, 50, 50A, 56A, 77, 77A, 77B. Open: Mon–Fri 10:00 a.m.–5:00 p.m., Sat–Sun 2:00–5:00 p.m. Required 45-minute guided tours every 20-25 minutes. Admission: £3 ($4.30) adults, £2 ($2.85) students and seniors, £1 ($1.40) kids under 11.*

Dublin Writers Museum

Ireland has a multitude of great writers — the short list includes Jonathan Swift, Oscar Wilde, James Joyce, Thomas Mann, Roddy Doyle, and Nobelists George Bernard Shaw, W.B. Yeats, and Samuel Beckett. This eighteenth-century house commemorates Ireland's famed scribes with first editions, letters, busts, and photos. The museum could definitely be more entertaining, but the audio tour enhances the tour a bit (and stretches a visit to about 30 minutes). Only true literary-types need apply.

18-19 Parnell Square N. ☎ *01-872-2077. DART: Conolly Station. Bus: 10, 11, 11A, 11B, 12, 13, 14, 16, 19, 19A, 22, 22A, 36. Open: Daily 10:00 a.m.–5:00 p.m. Closed Mon Sept–May. Admission: £3 ($4.30) adults, £2.35 ($3.40) students and seniors, £1.40 ($2) kids under 12.*

Guinness Brewery Hop Store

Alec Guinness refined his rich, black variant on stout in 1759, and by the mid-eighteenth century his brewery was the biggest in the world. You can't get into the plant itself anymore, but an entertaining audio-visual display is in the little Hop Store museum, with features on Guinness's long and clever advertising history and the lost art of the cooper (barrel-maker). The highlight, of course, is the pub, where you get a free half-pint of the famed brew. A purely academic visit only takes about half an hour; a more in-depth survey of Guinness's velvety pleasures at the pub can go on until last call in the pub.

Guinness — such as any other beer — is best "pulled" from a tapped keg. If you see the bartender fluidly cranking down the tap arm over and over, he's pulling a proper pint. After ordering Guinness, don't grab the glass after the barkeep first puts it down because he's letting the foam settle and will top it off after a minute or two. The famously thick head on a Guinness should stay intact until you get to the bottom of the glass. The old trick is to carve your initials, or a hokey shamrock, into the froth with a knife blade and watch as it remains undisturbed and intact all the way to the bottom.

Crane Street (off Thomas Street). ☎ *01-453-6700 ext. 5155. Bus: 21A, 78, 78A. Open: Mon–Fri 10:00 a.m.–4:00 p.m. Admission: £5 ($7.15) adults, £4 ($5.70) students and seniors, £1 ($1.40) kids under 12.*

More cool things to see and do in Dublin

Atmospheric pubs, great music, and great duty-free shopping are just a few more of the things to keep you busy in Dublin.

✔ **Spending an Evening in the Pubs and Clubs of Temple Bar.** The eclectic, hopping **Temple Bar** area is most people's favorite district of Dublin. This area, a few streets along the Liffey, is packed with pubs, shops, bars, cafes, galleries, entertainment venues, and fun. The neighborhood even has its own tourist office, which publishes the worthwhile *Temple Bar Guide.*

Strolling about is the best way to visit Temple Bar, but proper pub hopping here includes **Flannery's** (48 Temple Bar), **The Norseman** (Essex Street East), **Oliver St. John Gogarty** (57 Fleet Street), and its catercorner neighbor **Auld Dubliner** (Temple Bar and Anglesea Streets.). Clubbers can dress up to wait in line for **Club M** (in Blooms Hotel at Anglesea Street) or **The Kitchen** (6-8 Wellington Quay), a hip, new joint partly owned by U2. (Dublin's hottest disco, though, is **POD,** far from Temple Bar on Harcourt Street.) No need to pub hop just to Temple Bar, though. Make sure you also hit Dublin's oldest and greatest pub, the **Brazen Head** (west of Temple Bar at 20 Lower Bridge Street), as well as the Victorian **Doheny and Nesbitt** (5 Lower Baggot Street), the literary **Davy Byrnes** (21 Duke Street), and two musical bars **Kitty O'Shea's** (23-25 Upper Grand Canal Street) and **O'Donoghue's** (15 Merrion Row).

✔ **Exploring Georgian Dublin.** All over Dublin, you find posters of colorful doorways surrounded by white columns and topped with a half-moon window. These are the **Georgian Doorways of Dublin,** part of an eighteenth-century neoclassical architectural style practiced across Britain during the reigns of Georges I to III. Dublin's great squares are lined with Georgian town houses, especially St. Stephen's Green and Merrion Square. On the latter, at **No. 29 Lower Fitzwilliam Street,** is a restored home you can enter and tour. You can get a self-guided walking tour map of Georgian Dublin from the tourist office.

✔ **Tapping Your Feet on a Musical Pub Crawl.** An interesting tour for anyone who enjoys traditional Irish music or even the New Age music of Enya or Clannad, the **Musical Pub Crawl** is an entertaining guided walk of four Dublin pubs with musicians as tour guides. They introduce you to several traditional instruments and styles, teach you a couple of songs, and give you plenty of time to introduce yourself to Ireland's beer as you go. After this beginner's lesson, you are ready to check out pubs on your own to enjoy *sessions* or impromptu jamming by local musicians. The tour begins in the upstairs room at **Oliver St. John Gogarty's pub** at the corner of Fleet and Anglesea Streets in Temple Bar. Show up at 7:30 p.m. Saturday through Thursday (from May through October).

✔ **Succumbing to a Hokey Audio-Visual "History o'Dublin" Experience.** For a Disneylike tour of Dublin, check out the audio-visual tours that attempt to bring different past eras of Dublin back to life. Trinity College has a 45-minute **Dublin Experience** video (☎ **01-677-2941**) that looks more like a tourist promo than a historical chronicle; it's in the Davis Theater on Nassau Street. The most corny version is **Dublinia** (☎ **01-679-4611**), at Christ Church Place off High Street, which tries to evoke medieval Dublin from the Norman era through the 1530s.

Most fun is the imaginative **Dublin's Viking Adventure** (☎ **01-679-6040**), in Temple Bar off Essex Street, which gives you a simulated ride on a Viking ship and then a tour through a colonial Vikingsburg village peopled with costumed Dubliners. If you reserve ahead, you can top it all off (for £33.50-$48.60) with the "Viking Feast" at 7:30 p.m. Thursday through Sunday.

✔ **Researching Your Irish Roots.** If you're like me — and approximately 40 million other Americans out there — you've got some Irish in ya. Hundreds of Americans come to Ireland every year to seek out their ancestors here, and the Irish are much obliged to help (for a modest fee). Many agencies specialize in lineage tracing, but your first stop should be the **Heraldic Museum-Genealogical Office** (☎ **01-661-8811**) at 2 Kildare Street Checking out at the museum's heraldry exhibit is free, but you pay £20 ($29) to access its consultation service and start tracking down the Gaelic branch of your family tree.

✔ **Discovering Literary Dublin.** If the Writers Museum (discussed in the previous section) isn't enough, immerse yourself in literary Dublin by checking out the definitive **James Joyce Cultural Centre** (☎ **01-878-8547**) at 35 N. Great George's Street and the **Abbey Theatre** (☎ **01-878-7222**), founded at Lower Abbey Street by W.B. Yeats and Lady Gregory in 1904 (plays are put on Monday through Saturday at 8:00 p.m.).

One of the most fun ways to visit the Dublin of books is to take the **Literary Pub Crawl,** a popular guided walking tour that meets at the Bailey Pub on Duke Street at noon and 7:30 p.m. on Sundays year round and daily at 7:30 p.m. May through September (also at 3:00 p.m. June through August). Or try the **James Joyce Dublin Walking Tour,** a special treat you must book in advance through the Joyce Centre, because it is run by the Centre's curator — and Joyce's nephew — Ken Monaghan.

✔ **Shopping, Finally!** This is the country that invented duty-free, so that you would be remiss to not partake in the items of local craft and tradition, from tweeds and tin whistles to Waterford crystal, woolen sweaters, and whiskey. Dublin has several "anything and everything Irish" stores, which are like department store-sized gift shops that cater exclusively to tourists, often by the busload. A few, though, have high quality control and are great if you're on a tight time schedule (all but one of the following are across from the south flank of Trinity College). Head for **House of Ireland** (☎ 01-671-4543), at 37-38 Nassau Street, or **The Kilkenny Shop** (☎ 01-677-7066), nearby at 6-10 Nassau Street You don't have to go all the way to the Arran Islands to pick up thick Irish woolen sweaters. Try the **Blarney Woolen Mills** (☎ 01-671-0068) at 21-23 Nassau Street or, even better, **Monaghan's** (☎ 01-677-0823) at 15-17 Grafton Arcade.

And on Your Left, the Guinness Brewery: Seeing Dublin by Guided Tour

You have the choice of two double-decker bus tours in Dublin, which are both very good for basic orientation and sweeping the sights with some commentary. The more formal, guided bus tour is **Dublin Tour,** which starts at the Dublin Bus office at 59 Upper O'Connell Street Tickets are £8 ($11.60) for adults and £4 ($5.80) for kids under 16; tours leave daily at 10:15 a.m. and 2:15 p.m. For more flexibility, grab a £5 ($7.25) ticket (£2-$2.90 for kids under 16) for all-day access to the hop-on-hop-off **Dublin City Tour** buses, which run in circles from 9:30 a.m. to 4:30 p.m. (April through September) and stop at all the major sights.

The tourist office has several map kits for self-guided walking tours on themes such as Old City, Cultural Heritage, or Rock 'n' Stroll (after all, Ireland is the homeland of great musical artists, such as Van Morrison, U2, the Cranberries, Sinead O'Connor, and the Pogues, among many others).

For a guided hike that includes the basic sights, try **Historical Walking Tours of Dublin** (☎ 01-878-0227). This trek leaves from Trinity

College's front gate Monday through Saturday in June through September. The tours start at 11:00 a.m., noon, and 3:00 p.m.; on Sunday, they start at 11:00 a.m., noon, 2:00 p.m., and 3:00 p.m. From October through May, tours take place on Saturday and Sunday at noon only. You can also join several thematic pub crawls, discussed in the previous section "More cool things to see and do in Dublin."

Suggested One-, Two-, and Three-Day Itineraries

If you're the type who'd rather organize your own tours, this section offers some tips for building your own Dublin itineraries.

If you have one day

Begin with **Trinity College** and its library, which is preserving perhaps the world's greatest illuminated manuscript, the *Book of Kells*. Stay in a historical mood with a visit to the treasures of the **National Museum** before heading over to pedestrianized Grafton Street to grab lunch at **Bewley's Cafe.**

After lunch, you're off to **Christ Church Cathedral** (the moody medieval church built by Strongbow) and its rival **St. Patrick's Cathedral** (Jonathan Swift's old haunt). After a good dose of religion, hie thee to tour the **Guinness Brewery** — for many, the highlight of any trip to Dublin. Continue the beery fun with a **pub crawl through Temple Bar,** stopping for dinner at **Gallagher's Boxty House.**

If you have two days

Start Day One back in school at **Trinity College** to marvel at the *Book of Kells*. Head south to indulge in Dublin's two top museums, the **National Museum** of history, archaeology, and Celtic and Viking culture, and then to the **National Gallery** of paintings. After lunch and a stroll down the banks of the Liffey and across **Ha'penny Bridge,** pop into some stores for some Irish souvenirs (those bulky wool sweaters are truly a worthwhile splurge). Stop by your hotel to drop off your shopping bags so that you can be ready to embark on whichever guided walk tickles your Irish fancy: a musical or a literary pub crawl. Round out the night amid the pubs and bustle of trendy **Temple Bar.**

After the pub crawling excesses of yesterday, begin Day Two at church, visiting Dublin's competing cathedrals, **Christ Church and St. Patrick's.** Tour **Dublin Castle** and, if it seems like fun, the **Dublin Viking Experience** before heading off to the true cathedral of Ireland: the **Guinness Brewery.** Take the evening to sample some of Dublin's historic pubs outside the Temple Bar district.

If you have three days

Spend Days One and Two as above, and take Day Three to tour either the prehistoric **mound tombs north of Dublin** or the **Wicklow Mountains and Glendalough** to the south (both covered in the next section "Traveling the Irish Countryside").

Traveling the Irish Countryside

Lovely as Dublin is, you really shouldn't come to Ireland without seeing a bit of its famed countryside. Scenic drives abound; and the excursions below take you past ruined churches and impressive mansions, along rocky shorelines, and stunning, verdant landscapes.

County Kerry

North of Dublin to passage tombs and ruined medieval abbeys

Several sights just north of Dublin around the Boyne River Valley characterize two of the greatest attractions of Ireland — prehistoric sites and ruined abbeys — both easily done in a day trip.

Getting there

The most convenient base for the region is the town of Drogheda, which has regular rail and bus links with Dublin. Unfortunately, the **tourist office** (☎ 041-37-070) here is open June through August only, so for information you may have to visit the **regional office** (☎ 042-35-484) on Jocelyn Street in the city of Dundalk, farther up the road.

Seeing the sights

Top honors for sightseeing go to **Newgrange** (☎ 041-24-488), Ireland's most famous and most accessible passage tomb. This 36-foot-high mound of stones — some weighing up to 16 tons — was fitted together into a watertight engineering triumph well over 5,000 years ago, before Stonehenge or the Pyramids were even contemplated. You can take part in a guided visit down the 60-foot passage to the center of the tomb. Tours are given daily 10:00 a.m. through 4:30 p.m. from November through February, with evening hours lengthening as the season wears on (by June through September, the tour stays open until 7:00 p.m.). While waiting for your tour, you can walk around the tomb and examine the occasional carved Celtic swirl or decoration.

For more Neolithic fun just a mile from Newgrange, visit the ongoing excavations at the much less-visited collection of grassy mound tombs known as **Knowth** (☎ 041-24-824), a site inhabited from roughly 3000 b.c. to a.d. 1200. The hours are similar to those of Newgrange.

Located six miles northwest of Drogheda are the remains of the monastery **Monasterboice,** now represented mainly by its quiet, monumental cemetery. This graveyard is filled with Celtic high crosses, including the best preserved in Ireland, **Muiredeach's High Cross,** a 17-foot-tall example from a.d. 922 (look at the beautifully preserved "Taking of Christ" panel just above the base). Nearby are the ruins of **Mellifont Abbey,** a twelfth-century religious community of which little remains other than a stretch of colonnade and part of a pretty octagonal lavabo (ca. 1200).

Where to stay and dine

You can stay in Drogheda at the modern **Westcourt Hotel** (☎ 041-30-965,** fax: 041-309-7041) on West Street for £75 ($107) per double. For food, check out the pub at **Weavers** (☎ 041-32-816) on Dominick Street; to sit down for a more complete meal, try the pricey French cuisine at the **Buttergate Restaurant** (☎ 041-37-407) on Millimount Square.

South of Dublin: Mansions and monasteries in County Wicklow

Just an easy 15-minute drive south of downtown Dublin gets you to the gardens of County Wicklow. The sights south of Dublin can easily be visited on a day trip where you can be back in town for dinner.

Getting there

Dublin's tourist office has information on County Wicklow; otherwise, you'd have to drive all the way through the region to Wicklow Town and the area **tourism office** (☎ 0404-69-117) on Fitzwilliam Square. You can see the best of this area by car, but if you're not renting a car, **Gray Line Tours** (☎ 01-661-9666) takes busloads of tourists from Dublin to the major sights from May to September.

Seeing the Sights

A few miles south of Dublin on the N11, just past the town of Enniskerry, lie **Powerscourt Gardens** (☎ 01-286-7676), a thousand acres of late eighteenth-century gardens, grottoes, and fountains that make up one of the prime examples of "civilized naturalism" in Europe. In 1974, the massive manor house was nearly destroyed by fire, but renovations have been taking place. About four miles on is the 400-foot **Powerscourt Waterfall,** tallest in Ireland, but I don't recommend walking the narrow road unless you're very surefooted.

The old Military Road (R115) slices through the wildest heights of the **Wicklow Mountains.** This eerie peatscape covered with heather and reddish scrub looks as if it belongs somewhere on Mars, with only the Sally Gap pass and Glenmacnass waterfalls breaking up the moody boglands.

At Laragh, detour west to visit one of the most magical of Ireland's ruined monastic sites, **Glendalough** (☎ 0404-45-325), filled with high crosses, round towers, pretty lakes, and medieval stone buildings. During the summer, the tour buses can be frequent. All the sights listed here are open daily from about 9:30 a.m. to dusk.

Driving rings around County Kerry

To partake in Celtic culture at its best, check out County Kerry. Ancient Irish traditions flourish here, from music and storytelling to good pub *craic,* or conversation, and some of the country's few remaining Gaelic-speaking pockets. The 110-mile **Ring of Kerry,** a scenic route circling the Inveragh Peninsula, is Ireland's most famous — and most tour bus-engulfed — drive.

Because this area is heavy with tour buses, most visitors take the Ring counterclockwise from Killarney, to make the heavy traffic easier to contend with. The only thing less fun than driving on the left side of a twisty, narrow, two-lane road along a cliff and sharing it with a constant stream of giant buses much too wide for their lane is doing the same thing with all those buses *coming directly at you.*

You can easily visit the Ring in a day, but I'd give the area two or three days in order to spend time in **Killarney,** tour the less-visited **Dingle Peninsula,** and see some of the other less-frequented sights off the Ring.

Getting there

Frequent daily train service arrives from Ireland's big cities into Killarney, the region's main town and tourist center. Killarney also houses the region's main **tourist office (☎ 064-31-633)** in the Town Hall off Main Street.

Seeing the sights

Driving the Ring in Country Kerry, a stretch of route N70 with plenty of sign designations, is a must-do, such as being in San Francisco and driving down Lombard Street. While driving the Ring, you can visit coastal villages, take pictures of inland lakes, and stare in wonder at the mountainous heights of the Inveragh Peninsula along the way. Highlights include the **Kerry Bog Village** at Glenbeigh (thatched cottages re-created for us tourists), **Cahirciveen** (the main town), **Staigue Fort** (a well-preserved, Iron Age, drystone fortress), and the towns of **Sneem** (cottages in festive colors) and **Kenmare** (known for its hand-made lace).

About halfway around the Ring, you can detour onto **Valentia Island,** connected to the mainland by a bridge and home to the **Skellig Island Experience.** This video and display center introduces you to the endangered natural habitats and medieval monastery of the dramatic Skellig Islands off the coast. You cannot get any closer to the interiors of these islets, because boats from Valencia out to the Skelligs themselves can only circle the islands. In order to preserve that precarious nature, no docking is allowed.

You can avoid the crowds by driving a similar, much less visited, and (in my opinion) even more scenic circle around the **Dingle Peninsula,** one inlet to the north of the Inveragh. Dingle is the main town, from which you can hire a boat to take you out to meet Fungi, the resident dolphin of Dingle Bay, if he's in a playful mood.

Relax from all the nerve-racking driving on the Ring in the touristy city of **Killarney,** gateway to a beautiful National Park full of lakes, waterfalls, castles, woodlands, bogs, and the manor house, gardens, and romantically ruined abbey of **Muckross.**

Where to stay and dine

Three miles west of Killarney, near Fossa and right on the Lower Lake, sits the picturesque Victorian-era **Hotel Europe (☎ 800-221-1074** in the United States, in Ireland 064-31-900; fax: 064-32-118), with doubles running £114 to £146 ($139.30 to $178.60). **Foley's (☎ 064-31-217),** in Killarney at 23 High Street, serves excellent Irish food and seafood from Dingle Bay in a Georgian atmosphere.

Part IV
Central Europe

The 5th Wave   By Rich Tennant

LITTLE KNOWN LANDMARKS of EUROPE

The Not-So-Great Wall of Liechtenstein

The Magnificent Fence of Switzerland

The Noble Banister of Marseilles

The Ominous Bulkheads of Prague

In this part . . .

Welcome to Central Europe, the home of sophisticated Paris — fine food, high fashion, and great
art — and dreamy Prague, the showcase city of Eastern
Europe. You will cruise the seventeenth-century canals
of Amsterdam to discover the Rembrandts and van Goghs,
the Red Light District, and Anne Frank's hiding place from
the Nazis. You'll hoist a beer stein in Munich and discover
a city that hosts the oompah-band cheeriness of Bavaria
and the refinement of a cultural center financed by a
progressive industrial sector. In genteel Vienna of the
Hapsburgs, you will explore the city that taught Paris a
thing or two about cafes and the world a lesson in how
to build an opera house. In the Berner Oberland of
Switzerland, you will scale the Alps on thrilling gondola
rides; visit ice palaces carved into glaciers; and witness
sky-scraping vistas from Europe's snowy summit.

Chapter 14

Paris and Environs

• •

In This Chapter

▶ Getting to Paris

▶ Finding what you need once you're in Paris

▶ Exploring the neighborhoods of Paris

▶ The best places to sleep and eat in Paris

▶ Suggested itineraries and side trips

• •

*P*aris is the City of Light — the world capital of romance, birthplace of bohemians and impressionists, muse to Hemingway and the Lost Generation, and the high temple of haute cuisine. You can over-dose on art at the **Louvre,** cruise past eighteenth-century palaces on the Seine, write poetry at a sidewalk cafe table, dance in the colored glow of **Notre-Dame's** stained glass, dine stupendously in a tiny bistro, or steal long kisses atop the **Eiffel Tower.**

It's easy to romanticize this city — and just as easy to belittle it. No doubt you've heard that the people are rude, the museums are crowded, the traffic is horrendous, the **Champs-Elysées** has become a commercialized strip mall, and everything is far, far too expensive.

You shouldn't let these obstacles keep you from having a good time. So not everyone may be as welcoming as folks in the Sicilian country-side — don't expect them to be warm and welcoming, you won't be dis-appointed. Go early to beat the museum crowds. To avoid traffic, take the **Métro** (subway) — there's no reason for you to drive. The Métro is convenient and accessible all around Paris.

Sure, McDonald's and movie multiplexes now dominate the **Champs-Elysées,** but you can find plenty of elegant, authentic Paris elsewhere. And although it's possible to spend all your dough in Paris, I also know of no city more chockablock with great values on everything from meals and hotels to shopping and museums. You have to be willing to search them out, and I'm here to help you do just that.

Finally, although those positives and negatives exist, they are by no means the sum of the city. Paris strikes a lively balance between the vibrant, modern metropolis of the twenty-first century and the majestic, historic city of the Napoleon and Hemingway. It's a city of hip nightclubs, cutting-edge cuisine, and the highest fashion, as well as one of venerable museums, cafe legends, and sweeping eighteenth- and nineteenth-century grandeur. This balance keeps Paris intriguing, keeps it attractive, and keeps visitors and faithful admirers coming back year after year.

Making Your Way to and around Paris

Getting to the center of Paris is easy whether you're arriving by plane or train; as soon as you're there, getting around the city is a breeze, thanks to the efficient Métro subway system.

Getting to Paris by air

Most international flights land at **Charles de Gaulle Airport** (☎ **01-48-62-22-80**), also known as Roissy, 14 miles northeast of the city. A RER (commuter train) line runs into the center for 48F ($8), or you can take a taxi for around 250F ($31.25). Some charter flights, as well as many national flights, land 8.5 miles south of town at **Orly Airport** (☎ **01-49-75-15-15**), from which RER trains to the city center cost 57F ($9.50), a taxi around 150F ($25).

Getting to Paris by rail

Paris has many rail stations, but most international trains arrive at one of the following three. The **Gare du Nord** serves the Netherlands, Belgium, Denmark, northern Germany, and trains from London — the destination for both the *Eurostar* direct train that comes through the **Channel Tunnel** (a dozen trains daily for a three-hour trip — four hours with the time change), as well as trains arriving on the last leg of the old-fashioned (and highly *not* recommended) route: London to Dover by train; Dover to Calais by ferry; and Calais to Paris by train (four trains daily; 10.5 long hours for the trip). **Gare de Lyon** serves the south (Italy and parts of Switzerland), while **Gare de l'Est** handles trains from Switzerland, southern Germany, and Austria.

Getting around once you're in Paris

Paris transport tickets are good on the Métro, bus, and RER lines. Individual tickets cost 8F ($1.35), but a *carnet* (pack of 10) costs only 52F ($8.65). The *Paris Visite* card gets you unlimited travel on all forms of public transportation. The regular pass should be all you need, because it covers zones 1 through 3 (all of central Paris and many of its suburbs). It costs 55F ($9.15) for one day; 90F ($15) for two days, 120F ($20) for three days, and 175F ($29.15) for five days. Kids ages 4 to 11 pay half price.

More comprehensive passes covering zones 1 through 5 (all the 'burbs, including Disneyland Paris) cost twice as much, and passes for zones 1 through 8 (the entire Ile-de-France region) cost three times as much. If you have a spare passport-sized photo (or snap one at one of the booths at major trains and metro stations), you could also get the weekly pass *Carte Orange Hebdomadaire,* which costs 80F ($13.35) for zones 1 and 2, 106F ($17.65) zones 1 to 3. You can buy tickets and passes at most Métro stations and tourist offices.

By Métro (Subway) & RER

The Paris Métro is one of the best subways in Europe, a clean, efficient, and well-interconnected system. Using a Métro map, find which numbered line you want to take and the name of the last station in the direction you want to take it. In the Métro tunnels, follow signs for that line and that last station to get on the train going the right way.

You may have to transfer to another line to get to your destination (though usually not more than once per trip). When transferring, follow the signs labeled *correspondance* to the next line. Don't follow a *sortie* sign, unless you want to exit. You can make unlimited transfers on one ticket so long as you don't exit the system — although you may often find yourself walking long distances in the tunnels that connect some transfer stations.

Most of the lines are numbered and others seem to be assigned letters. The lettered lines (A, B, C, and D) are technically not the Métro, but are part of the overlapping RER network. This high-speed commuter light-rail system services only major stops within the city, and extends much farther out into the suburbs. It uses the same tickets as the Métro (except when you're traveling way out into the 'burbs, for which you'll have to buy a separate ticket), and you can transfer freely between the two systems.

Some RER lines are particularly useful; the C line, for instance, follows the left bank of the Seine closely (no Métro line does this) and also heads out to Versailles. Both ends of all RER lines split off like the frayed ends of a rope as they leave the city, so make sure the train you board is heading out to the numbered fork you want (for example, the C line has seven different end destinations, C1 through C7). Maps on the platforms show you the routes of each fork, and TV displays tell you when the next half dozen trains will be arriving and which number each one is.

By bus

In all my trips to the City of Light, I've never needed to use the bus system, because I find that the Métro works well and is faster than plodding through above-ground traffic. Although buses use the same tickets as the Métro, a single ticket is only good for two *sections* to reach your destination, which can make bus trips expensive. If you're traveling through three or more sections, you need to punch two tickets.

You can find separate maps for each bus route posted at bus stops, and each map has a blue-and-red bar running along the bottom. The stops that appear directly above the blue section of this bar are within that stop's two-section limit. For stops appearing above the red section(s) of the bar, you need to use two tickets. When the number of a bus route is written in black on a white circle, it means that the bus stops there daily; when it's written in white on a black circle, it means the bus doesn't stop there on Sundays or holidays.

By taxi

Because cabs in Paris are scarce, it may be easier to hire one at a stand than hail one in the street. Be careful to check the meter when you board to be sure you're not also paying the previous passenger's fare, and if your taxi lacks a meter, make sure to settle the cost of the trip before setting out. It's more expensive to have a cab pick you up because the meter starts running when the cab receives the call. Try ☎ **01-45-85-85-85,** 01-42-03-50-50, or 01-49-36-10-10 to get a cab.

The initial fare for up to three passengers is 13F ($2.15) and 3.53F (60 cents) per kilometer. Between 7:00 p.m. and 7:00 a.m. the per-kilometer charge rises to 5.83F (95 cents). No surcharges apply if you have several small bags inside the taxi, but stowing larger bags in the trunk costs you 6 to 10F ($1 to $1.65) per bag, plus you pay 5F (85 cents) if you catch your taxi from a major train station.

Discovering Paris: What You Need to Know

Once you're in Paris, you need to know some basic information about money, using the telephone system, and helpful information in case of emergencies.

The local dough

The French unit of currency is the French **franc** (F), which is divided into 100 centimes. Roughly, $1 equals 6F, or 1F equals 17 cents. French coins include 5, 10, 20, and 50 centimes and 1, 2, 5, and 10 francs. Bills come in denominations of 20, 50, 100, 200, 500, and 1,000 francs.

Where to get info after you arrive

The main tourist information office (☎ **08-36-68-31-12** — the charge is 2.23F/38 cents per minute, fax 01-49-52-53-00; Internet: www.paris-touristoffice.com) is at 127 Champs-Elysées, 8e, near the **Arc de Triomph** end. It's open daily 9:00 a.m. to 8:00 p.m. (low season Sundays, 11:00 a.m. to 6:00 p.m.).

There are also offices in all the train stations (except **Gare St-Lazare**) and at every terminal of both **Charles de Gaulle** and **Orly** airports. The tourist office hands out *Paris Selection*, a monthly events magazine, but *Pariscope* (www.pariscope.fr) available at any newsstand, is much better and more in-depth. To reserve tickets for shows and exhibitions, dial ☎ **01-49-52-53-53.**

Where to go in a pinch

Paris is a relatively safe city with little violent crime, but there is plenty of petty theft. Around popular tourist sites, on the Métro, and in the station corridors lurk pickpockets — often children — who aren't afraid to gang up on you, distract you by holding or waving an item near your face, and then make off with your wallet. It only takes seconds, so hold on to your wallet or purse and yell at or push away your attackers — don't hold back because they're just children. Look out for thieves around the **Eiffel Tower,** the **Louvre, Notre-Dame, Montmartre,** and other popular tourist sites. In case of emergency, keep the following list of references handy.

- ✔ **Consulate:** The U.S. consulate is at 2 rue Saint-Florentin (☎ **01-43-12-23-47**).

- ✔ **Doctors/hospitals:** SOS Médicins (☎ **01-47-07-77-77**) recommends physicians. SOS Dentaire (☎ **01-43-37-51-00**) will locate a dentist for you. The U.S. embassy also provides a list of doctors. Both the **American Hospital of Paris,** 63 bd. Victor-Hugo in **Neuilly-sur-Seine** (☎ **01-46-41-25-25**; Métro: Porte Maillot); and the **Franco-British Hospital,** 3 rue Barbes in **Levallois-Perret,** (☎ **01-46-39-22-22**; Métro: Anatole France), staff English-speaking physicians.

- ✔ **Emergency:** Dial ☎ **17** for the police. To report a fire, call ☎ **18.** If you need an ambulance, call the paramedics at the *Sapeurs-Pompiers* (fire department) at ☎ **18,** or ☎ **15** for SAMU (Service d'Aide Medicale d'Urgence), a private ambulance company.

- ✔ **Pharmacies:** One pharmacy in each neighborhood remains open all night. One to try is the 24-hour **Pharmacie Dhéry,** 84 av. des Champs-Elysées, 8e (☎ **01-45-62-02-41**), in the Galerie des Champs-Elysées shopping center. Or check the door of the nearest pharmacy; it will list the pharmacies open at night.

Staying in touch

Need to wire home for more money? Want to get online to check your e-mail? The following information will help keep you in touch while you're touring Paris.

- ✔ **American Express:** The full service office at 11 rue Scribe (☎ **01-47-77-78-75**) is open Monday to Friday 9:00 a.m. to 6:30 p.m. The currency desk only is open Saturday 9:00 a.m. to 6:30 p.m.

- ✔ **Internet Access & Cyber Cafes:** Perhaps the most central is **Cybercafe de Paris** 11 and 15 rue des Halles (☎ **01-42-21-11-11**; Internet: www.cybercafedeparis.com; Métro: Chatelet les Halles) open daily 11:00 a.m. to 11:00 p.m. and charging 1F (15 cents) per minute, or 48F ($8) per hour. Sephora, 70 Champs-Elysées (no phone), is actually a cosmetics store that has eight computers in the back where internet access is free (long lines, though).

C@fe CARI TELEMATION: 72-74 passage de Choiseul, off rue du Quattre Septembre (no phone; Internet: www.cari.com/internet/cybercafe.htm; Métro: Quattre Septembre), is open Monday to Friday 10:00 a.m. to 8:00 p.m., Saturday 1:00 p.m. to 8:00 p.m., and charges 36F ($6) per hour **Clickside,** 14, rue Domat, right off boulevard Saint-Germain at rue Saint-Jacques (☎ **01-56-81-03-00;** Internet: www.clickside.com; Métro: Cluny or Maubert), is open Monday to Saturday 10:00 a.m. to midnight, Sunday 1:00 to 11:00 p.m., and charges 10F ($1.65) per 10 minutes, or 45F ($7.50) per hour.

✔ **Mail:** The most central post office is at the **Louvre,** 52 rue du Louvre (☎ **01-40-28-20-00**) is actually open 24 hours daily (all other Paris post offices open Monday to Friday 8:00 a.m. to 7:00 p.m., Saturday 9:00 a.m. to noon).

✔ **Telephone:** The minimum charge for a local call is 2F (35 cents). Coin-operated phones take 1F, 2F, and 5F coins, but you're more likely to use a phone that requires a *télécarte* (phone card) sold at post offices and tabacs (newsstands/tobacco shops) for 40F ($6.65) or 96F ($16). Just insert the télécarte and dial. For directory assistance, dial ☎ **12.**

France's country code is **33.** Calling anywhere within the country's borders requires dialing a 10-digit phone number (it already includes the city code) even if you are calling another number from within Paris. To call Paris from the United States, dial **011-33,** and then drop the initial zero of the French number and just dial the remaining nine digits. To charge your call to a calling card or call collect, dial AT&T at ☎ **0-800-99-0011;** MCI at ☎ **0-800-99-0019;** or Sprint at ☎ **0-800-99-0087.** To call the United States direct from Paris, dial **00** (wait for the dial tone), and then dial **1** followed by the area code and number.

✔ **Transit Info:** For RATP Métro and bus information (in French), call ☎ **08-36-68-41-14** or check out the Web site at www.ratp.fr. For SNCF French train information, call ☎ **08-36-35-35-35.**

Touring Paris by Neighborhood

The Seine River divides Paris between the Right Bank (*Rive Droite*) to the north and the Left Bank (*Rive Gauche*) to the south. Paris began on the **Ile de la Cité,** an island in the Seine that is still the center of the city and home to **Notre-Dame Cathedral.** It's also connected to the nearby posh residential island of **Ile de Saint-Louis.** Traditionally, people consider the Right Bank to be more upscale with Paris's main boulevards such as **Champs-Elysées** and museums such as the **Louvre.** The old bohemian half of Paris is on the Left Bank with the **Latin Quarter** around the university.

Twenty districts called *arrondissements* divide Paris. These districts start with the first arrondissement (which includes the **Louvre** neighborhood and the tip of the **Ile de la Cité**) and then spiral out from there. At the end of each address in this chapter, you'll see a number followed by an "e" (or in the case of 1, an "er"), such as 8e or 5e. That number refers to the arrondissement. A Parisian address, spoken or written, isn't complete unless the neighborhood name or arrondissement is included. The last two digits of a zip code are the arrondissement, so an address listed as "Paris 75003" would be in the third arrondissement. (Most of these districts also correspond with traditional, named neighborhoods.)

Among the major arrondissements (for tourism) on the Right Bank is the 3e. Called **Le Marais,** this up-and-coming neighborhood manages to remain genuinely Parisian amid the swirl of tourism in the city center. The 4e includes most of the **Ile de la Cité, Ile St-Louis,** the **Beaubourg pedestrian zone,** and the **Pompidou modern art center.**

The 8e — a natural extension westward of the 1er — is Paris's most posh area, consisting of ritzy hotels, fashion boutiques, fine restaurants, and upscale town houses. It centers along the grandest boulevard in a city famous for them: the **Champs-Elysées.** The sidewalks of this historic shopping promenade were recently cleaned up and widened. No more than a string of international chain stores and movie theaters, the Champs-Elysées has become merely a shadow of its former elegant self.

From the **Place de la Concorde** — an oval plaza at the western end of the **Louvre complex** where French royalty met the business end of a guillotine during the Revolution — the Champs-Elysées beelines east-west to the **Arc de Triomphe.** The Arc is one of the world's greatest triumphal arches, a monument to France's unknown soldier and to the gods of car-insurance premiums (surrounding the Arc is a five-lane traffic circle where, it seems, anything goes).

Still echoing with the ghosts of Bohemian Paris, in the northerly reaches of the Right Bank lies **Montemarte,** topped by the fairy-tale gleaming white basilica of **Sacré-Coeur,** and tramped by tourists. The neighborhood is so distinct and (despite the tour buses) charming it gets its own write-up under "More cool things to see and do in Paris" later in this chapter.

Left Bank arrondissements include the 5e, the famous old **Latin Quarter,** named for the language spoken by the university students who gave it its once colorful, bohemian atmosphere. These days, it's another sad Parisian shadow of former glory, its bohemia replaced by gyro stands, souvenir shops, and hordes of tourists wondering why the Latin Quarter was ever famous.

The adjacent 6e retains some of its counterculture charm. The students of **Paris's Fine Arts School** help liven up things here, especially in the now highly fashionable but still somewhat artsy **St-Germain-des-Prés** neighborhood of cafes, brasseries, and restaurants. Tucked into a wide arc of the Seine, the 7e intrudes a bit on the **St-Germain** neighborhood, but its major features are the **Musée d'Orsay,** the **Eiffel Tower,** and the **Rodin Museum.**

Paris Neighborhoods

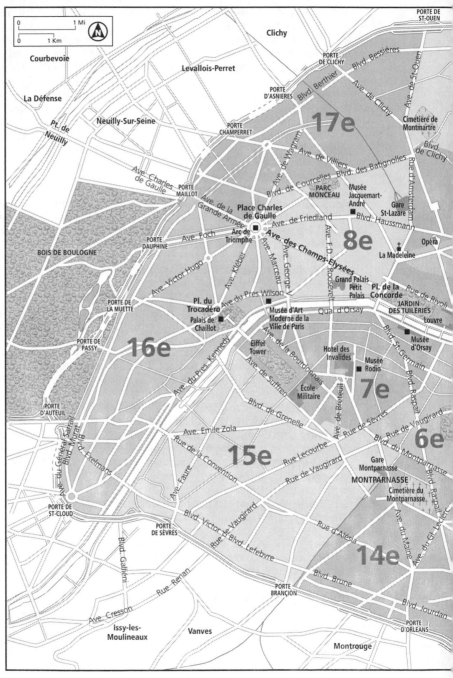

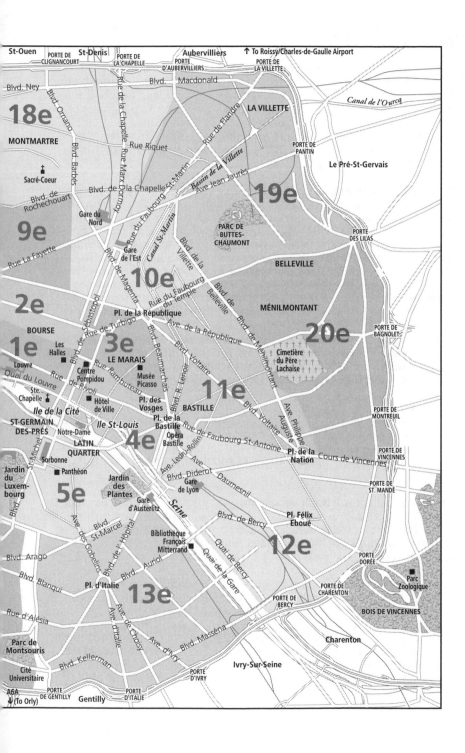

St-Ouen   PORTE DE   St-Denis   PORTE DE   Aubervilliers   ↑ To Roissy/Charles-de-Gaulle Airport
           CLIGNANCOURT   LA CHAPELLE   PORTE   PORTE DE
                                                D'AUBERVILLIERS   LA VILLETTE

Blvd. Ney   Blvd. Macdonald

                                                        LA VILLETTE   Canal de l'Ourcq

18e   PORTE DE
                                    Rue Riquet   PANTIN   Le Pré-St-Gervais
MONTMARTRE

  ✝   Blvd. de la Chapelle·St-Martin
Sacré-Coeur   Ave. Jean Jaurès   **19e**
              Blvd. de
              Rochechouart   Blvd. de la Chapelle·St-Martin

                            Gare du   PARC DE   PORTE
                            Nord   BUTTES-   DES LILAS
9e   CHAUMONT
                            Gare
Rue La Fayette   de l'Est   BELLEVILLE

                                    10e
2e   MÉNILMONTANT
                            Pl. de la République
  BOURSE   Blvd. de Turbigo   Ave. de la République   PORTE DE
1e   Les   BAGNOLET
         Halles   **3e**   **20e**
Louvre   Rue Rambuteau   Cimetière
Quai du Louvre   Centre   du Père   PORTE DE
Ste.-   Pompidou   Musée   Lachaise   MONTREUIL
Chapelle   Hôtel   Picasso
Île de la Cité   de Ville   Pl. des   **11e**
ST-GERMAIN   Île St-Louis   Vosges   BASTILLE
DES-PRÉS   Notre-Dame   Pl. de la   PORTE DE
          LATIN   Bastille   VINCENNES
Jardin   QUARTER   **4e** Opéra   Pl. de la
du   Sorbonne   Bastille   Nation   Cours de Vincennes
Luxem-   ■ Panthéon   Rue de Faubourg St-Antoine   PORTE DE
bourg   Ave.-Ledru-Rollin   ST. MANDÉ
          5e   Jardin   Ave.   Blvd. Diderot
                    des   Gare
                    Plantes de Lyon   Pl. Félix
                    Gare   Eboué
                    d'Austerlitz   Blvd. de Bercy
                                                            12e
                    Bibliothèque
Blvd. Arago   François
                    Mitterrand   PORTE
Blvd. Blanqui   DORÉE   Parc
          Pl. d'Italie   **13e**   Zoologique
Rue d'Alésia   PORTE DE
                                          CHARENTON
Parc de   PORTE DE   BOIS DE VINCENNES
Montsouris   BERCY
Cité   Charenton
Universitaire
A6A   PORTE   PORTE
↓(To Orly) DE GENTILLY Gentilly D'ITALIE   Ivry-Sur-Seine
                      PORTE
                      D'IVRY

Staying in Paris

Paris has some 73,000 hotel rooms, so you're sure to find a bed. The tricky part is finding a quality room in a desirable location and in your price bracket. This city is full of overblown, overpriced hotels and flea-bag dives even the scruffiest backpackers would turn up a nose at. Stick with me, though, and I can help you find something that meets your needs, including some budget hideaways. I've had some of my best stays in Paris in small, fourth-floor walk-ups with unforgettable views across the rooftops.

The general assumption, still holding true (but tenuously) these days, is that the Right Bank has more upscale hotels, while the bohemian Left Bank boasts more inexpensive options. On your first visit, you may want to stay pretty close to the center of town, but don't fret if the only room you can find is out in *les boondocks*. It only takes you a few minutes longer to get to the **Louvre** from the 16e than from the **Latin Quarter** by the Métro. Besides, most repeat visitors find themselves drawn away from the tourist center in favor of a more authentic Parisian neighborhood. For a price you can find that authenticity as close by as the **Marais** or **St-Germain-des-Prés,** but usually at a price.

In addition to the November-to-February low season, July and August are also slow in Paris. You can bargain for good rates at hotels because many of them shut down. Multiple trade fairs during May, June, September, and October tend to book up the city's four-star and luxury hotels.

The visitors tax of 3F to 7F per night (depending on the class of hotel) may or may not be included in the quoted room rates. Proprietors in Paris are notorious for charging varying rates for their rooms, so ask about cheaper digs if you feel the first room they show you is too pricey.

The tourist office will book a room for you for a fee ranging from 20F to 50F ($3.35 to $8.35), depending on the cost of the hotel, but only on the same day you plan to take it. They also broker last-minute rooms that upper-class hotels are having a hard time moving, so you may luck into a deep discount on a posh pad.

Though Paris B&Bs vary greatly in style and room decor, they're usually cheaper than hotels (prices typically range anywhere from $50 to $130), and you can guarantee a certain level of quality by booking a government-approved bed and breakfast through a private reservation agency: **Absolutely B&Bs & More** (☎ 800-380-7420 in the United States; Internet: www.athomeabroad.com), **Bed & Breakfast France** (☎ 800-454-8704 in the United States; **34-68-83-15** in France; Internet: www.bedbreak.com), or **Paris Bed & Breakfast** (☎ 800-872-2632 in the United States; Internet: www.parisbandb.com).

Paris's top hotels

Grande Hôtel Jeanne d'Arc

$ The Marais (3e)

This place sort of reminds me of Grandma's comfortable guest room, with Sears & Roebuck furnishings, fresh carpeting, and fabric on the walls. Its rooms are larger — and certainly cleaner — than your standard French budget pension, and there are amenities galore, such as satellite TV. It's right in the heart of the charming **Marais** district and often booked up to two months ahead of time by regulars, so be sure to make reservations.

3 rue de Jarente (between rue de Sévigné and rue de Turenne, off rue St-Antoine). ☎ *01-48-87-62-11. Fax: 01-48-87-37-31. Internet:* www.parishotels.com. *Métro: St-Paul. Rates: 435F–500F ($72.50–$83.35) double.*

Hôtel d'Angleterre

$$$ Saint-Germain (6e)

The high-beamed ceilings of this eighteenth-century Breton-style inn offer a slice of U.S. history — when this was the British Embassy in 1783, the English finally signed the papers here recognizing American independence. Some rooms have exposed stone walls and four-poster canopy beds, and all boast period furnishings, carved wood closet doors, and silk wall hangings. The "apartments," with two bedrooms, are ideal for families. The homey common lounge has a piano, and there's a small lush courtyard where you can breakfast in summer.

44 rue Jacob (off rue Bonaparte). ☎ *01-42-60-34-72. Fax: 01-42-60-16-93. Métro: St-Germain-des-Prés. Rates: 762F–1,312F ($127–$218.70) doubles. AE, DC, MC, V.*

Hôtel de la Bretonnerie

$$ The Marais (4e)

The Sagots keep a cozy, friendly hotel where each room is done in a classic French style but with a unique decor, from Empire divans or Louis XIII chairs to Napoleon III tables. The nicest are the so-called "chambres de caractère," some with canopy beds, or country-style with heavy beams and floral-print walls. "Classique" rooms are smaller, but still have nice touches, like the occasional four-poster. The cozy duplexes are defined by beamed ceilings and huge curtained windows.

22 rue Saint-Croix-de-la-Bretonnerie (between rue des Archives and rue Vieille-du-Temple). ☎ *01-48-87-77-63. Fax: 01-42-77-26-78. Internet:* www.parishotels.com. *Métro: Hôtel de Ville. Rates: 660F–830F ($110–$138.35). MC, V.*

Hôtel de L'Elysee

$$$ Champs-Elysées (8e)

This small, exceeding friendly inn has been overhauled in Restoration style, with wallpaper of stamped eighteenth-century etchings, built-in closets, half-testers over many beds, and stuccoed ceilings in a few suites. Smallish mansard suite no. 60 features wood beams criss-crossing the space, a bed coving, and skylights set into the low, sloping ceilings that provide peek-a-boo vistas of Parisian rooftops, including a perfectly framed view of the **Eiffel Tower.** All fifth and sixth floor rooms enjoy at least rooftop views, the former from small balconies (nos. 50-53 even glimpse the Eiffel).

12 rue des Saussaies (off rue Faubourg St-Honoré at place Beauvau, two blocks north of Champs-Elysées). ☎ *01-42-65-29-25. Fax: 01-42-65-64-28. Internet:* www.paris-hotel.com/elysee. *Métro: Champs-Elysées-Clemenceau or Miromesnil. Rates: 660F–1,280F ($110–$213.35) doubles. AE, DC, MC, V.*

Hôtel de Lutèce

$$ Ile Saint-Louis (4e)

The Lutèce occupies a converted seventeenth-century house accented with rustic details, such as wood-beam ceilings and terra-cotta floors. It's a refined hotel in a chic neighborhood with comfy rooms that are large for such a central location, even if a few bathtubs could use curtains. It's on a street lined with restaurants and shops, just a five-minute stroll from **Notre-Dame. Des Deux-Iles,** a sibling hotel, is a few doors down; between the two of them, there's a pretty good chance you can get a room.

59 rue Saint-Louis-en-l'Ile (on the main drag of the island). ☎ *01-43-26-23-52. Fax: 01-43-29-60-25. Métro: Pont-Marie. Rates: 902F ($150.35) double. AE, MC, V.*

Hôtel du Jeu de Paume

$$$$ Ile Saint-Louis (4e)

Built in 1634 as a *Jeu de Paume* court (a precursor of tennis), this hotel is a successful marriage of seventeenth-century wood beams and plaster with twentieth-century burnished steel and glass. The impressive, airy, three-story, ancient wood skeleton inside incorporates public lounges, an indoor breakfast terrace, a hanging corridor, and a glass elevator. Most accommodations are on the cozy side of medium, but the simplicity of the stylishly modern decor under hewn beams keeps them from feeling cramped. The three standard duplexes with spiral stairs are roomier (and don't cost any more than a double), but for true bliss check into the suite, a duplex with a lounge below and bedroom above, two baths, and a private terrace overlooking the small stone garden rimmed with flowers where guests can breakfast in nice weather.

54 rue Saint-Louis-en-L'Ile. ☎ *01-43-26-14-28. Fax: 01-40-46-02-76. Internet:* www.JeudePaumehotel.com. *Métro: Pont-Marie. Rates: 950F–1,625F ($158.35–$270.85) doubles. AE, DC, MC, V.*

Port-Royal Hotel

$ Latin Quarter (5e)

Although this hotel is on the far edge of the Latin Quarter, the Métro stop down the block keeps you only minutes from the city's center. These incredible rates come with surprisingly nice, if often smallish, rooms. There's a TV in the breakfast room. Showers cost 15F for five minutes, but they're modern and don't run out of hot water. In short, it's a decent hotel at hostel prices.

8 bd. Port-Royal (near av. des Gobelins). ☎ *01-43-31-70-06. Fax: 01-43-31-33-67. Métro: Gobelins. Rates: 245F–434F ($40.85–$72.35) double. No credit cards.*

Le Relais Christine

$$$$ Saint-Germain-des-Pres (6e)

Passing through the cobbled courtyard to enter this early seventeenth-century building you feel less like you're checking into a hotel and more like the baron and baroness arriving at your own country manor house. Most of the largish rooms are done in a contemporary relaxed style, but a few splash out with grand, repro-Louis XIII decor. Most suites are duplexed, with sitting areas downstairs, marble bathrooms sporting double sinks, and a lofted bedchamber. The basement breakfast/dining room is installed under the low rough vaulting of a thirteenth-century abbey founded by Saint Louis himself.

3 rue Christine (off rue Dauphine, between bv. Saint-Germain and the Pont Neuf). ☎ *800-447-7462 in the United States, 01-40-51-60-80 in Paris. Fax: 01-40-51-60-81. E-mail:* relaisch@club-internet.fr. *Métro: Odéon or St-Michel. Rates: 1,900F–2,350F ($316.15–$391.70) double. AE, DC, MC, V.*

Paris's runner-up accommodations

Caron de Beaumarchais

$ The Marais (4e) Caron de Beaumarchais is a boutique hotel at budget rates, with a small antique-style salon in place of a reception and rooms outfitted as befits an eighteenth-century Marais town house — wood ceilings and a touch of gold about the carved filigree on curving chair backs and mirror frames. Rooms on the front are largest. *12 rue Vieille-du-Temple (off rue de Rivoli)* ☎ *01-42-72-34-12. Fax: 01-42-72-34-63. Métro: Hôtel de Ville.*

Accommodations, Dining & Attractions in Paris

HOTELS ■
Caron de Beaumarchais **36**
Grande Hôtel Jeanne d'Arc **37**
Hôtel d'Angleterre **21**
Hôtel de la Bretonnerie **35**
Hôtel de L'Elysee **6**
Hôtel du Jeu de Paume **41**
Hôtel de Lutèce **43**
Hôtel Keppler **3**
L'Hôtel **23**
Le Relais Christine **28**
Montalembert **20**

Port-Royal Hotel **27**
Quai Voltaire **19**
Timhôtel Louvre **17**

RESTAURANTS ◆
Alain Ducasse **4**
Au Bascou **32**
Bofinger **38**
Brasserie Balzar **47**
Brasserie Lipp **25**
Buddha Bar **7**
Campagne et Provence **45**
Chantairelle **48**

L'Epi Dupin **12**
Les Bookinistes **29**
Man Ray **5**
Restaurant des Beaux-Arts **22**
Restaurant Perraudin **46**
Taillevent **2**
La Taverne du
  Sergent Recruteur **42**

0   1/2 Mi
0   0.5 Km

MONTMARTRE

Moulin Rouge
Bd. de Clichy
Place
Pigalle
Bd. de Rochechouart
Av. Trudaine
Rue de
Rue Condorcet
Casino
de Paris
Ste-Trinité
Musée
Gustave
Moreau
Lazare
Notre-Dame
de Lorette
Folies
Bergère
Bd. Haussmann
Opéra
Garnier
Bd. des
Italiens
Place
de
l'Opéra
Rue St-Augustin
Bibliothèque
Nationale
N.D. des
Victoires
Rue des Petits-Champs
St-Roch
Palais
Royal
Banque
de France
St-Eustache
14 Place
Vendôme
15
TUILERIES
Musée des Arts
Décoratifs
Place du
Carrousel
Musée
du Louvre
Palais
du Louvre
Bourse du
Commerce
Forum
des Halles
16
17
31
18
Ecole Nationale
des Beaux-Arts
Université
Paris V
St-Germain-
des-Prés
Rue du Four
St-Sulpice
Odéon
Sorbonne
Université
Paris VI
Palais du
Luxembourg
26
JARDIN DU
LUXEMBOURG
Université
Paris V
Bd. du Montparnasse
27
St-Médard
Panthéon
St-Etienne
du Mont
Arènes
de Lutèce
20
21
22
23
24
28
29
30
St-Germain
St-Séverin
Notre-Dame
St-Julien
le Pauvre
44
46
47
43
42
41
45
48
LATIN QUARTER
Université
Paris VI
Université
Paris VII
JARDIN DES PLANTES
Museum National
d'Histoire Naturelle
Mosquée
Gare
d'Austerlitz
Gare
de Lyon
ILE DE LA CITÉ
ILE ST-LOUIS
St-Louis
St-Paul
St-Gervais
Hôtel
de Ville
Théâtre de
la Ville
Tour
St-Jacques
St-Merry
Théâtre
du Châtelet
St-Germain
33 Centre
Pompidou
34
35
36
37
38
39
40
Musée
de la
Chasse
Archives
Nationales
St-Denis
Musée
Carnavalet
Place des
Vosges
Place
de la
Bastille
Opéra
Bastille
Théâtre
de la Bastille
LE
MARAIS
St-Ambroise
Conservatoire
des Arts
et Métiers
Place
de la
République
Avenue de la République
32
St-Joseph
St-Laurent
St-Vincent
de Paul
Gare
de l'Est
Gare
du Nord
Bd. de la Chapelle
13
St-Joseph
St-Georges
Place
du Colonel
Fabien
PARC DES
BUTTES
CHAUMONT
Seine
Seine

Information
Church

ATTRACTIONS ●
Arc de Triomphe **1**
Centre Pompidou **33**
Cimetière du Père-Lachaise **39**
Forum des Halles **31**
Jardin des Tuileries **15**
Jardin du Luxembourg **26**

Musée d'Orsay **9**
Musée du Louvre **18**
Musée Picasso **34**
Musée Rodin **11**
Notre-Dame **44**
Opèra Bastille **40**
Palais du Luxembourg **26**

Palais Royal **16**
Place de la Concorde **8**
Place Vendôme **14**
Sacrè-Coeur **13**
Sainte-Chapelle **30**
St-Germain-des-Près **24**
Tour Eiffel **10**

Hôtel Keppler

$ Trocadéro (16e) This older hotel could stand to replace the aging carpets and knockabout pine veneer modular furnishings, but it is clean, resides in a quiet, bourgeois neighborhood just a few blocks away from the Champs-Elysées, and offers killer rates. *12 rue Kepler (between av. Marceau and av. d'Iéna, south of the Arc de Triomphe)* ☎ *01-47-20-65-05; Fax: 01-47-23-02-29. E-mail:* hotel.keppler@wanadoo.fr. *Métro: Georges-V.*

L'Hôtel

$$$$ (or $$-$$$ off-season) St-Germain-des-Prés (6e) This hotel is no longer the flop house where Oscar Wilde died in 1900. Today it's a kind of velvet and pink marble, funky monument to curves, with smallish rooms and furnishings from Louis XV and Empire styles to art nouveau. *13 rue des Beaux-Arts (between rue Bonaparte and rue de Seine, one block from the Quai Malaquais)* ☎ *01-44-41-99-00; Fax: 01-43-25-64-81. Métro: St-Germain-des-Prés.*

Montalembert

$$$$ St-Germain-des-Prés (7e) Montalembert is one of Paris' top hotels, with a unique meld of contemporary design, art deco fashion, and French tradition (and amenities like in-room VCRs, faxes, and modem lines). "Traditionelle" bedrooms are Louis-Phillipe style with heavily lacquered chestnut and gold art deco furnishings; "moderne" rooms incorporate dark sycamore and hand-crafted leather molded along clean, simple, elegant lines. *3 rue de Montelembert (off rue de Bac, behind the church of St Thomas d'Aquin)* ☎ *800-447-7462 in the United States or 01-45-49-68-68 in Paris. Fax: 01-45-49-68-49. Internet:* www.montalembert.com; *Métro: rue de Bac.*

Timhôtel Louvre

$$ Louvre (1e) Timhôtel Louvre is two blocks from the Louvre, once a writers' and artists' crash pad, but now relentlessly renovated into cookie-cutter blandness by a chain selling itself to the business set. Good value, though. *4 rue Croix-des-Petits-Champs (off rue St-Honoré, 2 blocks east of the Palais Royal)* ☎ *01-42-60-34-86; Fax: 01-42-60-10-39. Internet:* www.timhotel.fr. *Métro: Châtelet les Halles or Palais-Royal.*

Quai Voltaire

$$ St-Germain-des-Prés (7e) The Quai Voltaire has midsized rooms with a dreamy Parisian view: overlooking the Seine to the Louvre across the way. That view comes with a price though: traffic noise from the quai that even the double glazed windows don't quite drown out. *19 quai Voltaire.* ☎ *01-42-61-50-91. Fax: 01-42-61-62-26. Métro: rue du Bac or Saint-Germain-des-Prés.*

Dining in Paris

For the French, food is close to a religion, and they gladly worship at the altars of their award-winning celebrity chefs. Traditional haute cuisine — a delicate balance of flavors, sauces, and ingredients blended with a studied technique — includes such classics as *blanquette de veau* (veal in an eggy cream sauce), *pot-au-feu* (an excellent stew of fatty beef and vegetables), *coq au vin* (chicken braised in red wine with onions and mushrooms), *bouillabaisse* (seafood soup), and that hearty staple *boeuf bourguignon* (beef stew with red wine).

But when people started thinking healthy a few decades back, buttery, creamy, saucy French cuisine quickly found itself on the "out." So the French invented *nouvelle cuisine,* which gave chefs an excuse to concoct new dishes — still French, mind you, but less fattening because they use fewer heavy creams and less butter and served only smaller portions.

When the nouvelle trend lost steam, people began spinning off more healthful and/or more creative cooking styles. Add to these styles the mix of French regional restaurants and the many ethnic dining rooms, and you'll never want for variety.

 It's cheaper to eat dinner in Paris these days. France's economic crisis has forced many restaurants to lower their prices, and some top chefs have opened up "baby bistros," where they serve up culinary creations at relatively low prices.

French cheese is justifiably famous, with softies Brie and Camembert and blue-veined Roquefort topping the list. There's no way I can go fully into French wines here, but your waiter or the restaurant's wine steward should be able to pair your meal with an appropriate vintage. Better yet, check out *Wine For Dummies,* published by IDG Books Worldwide, Inc. Ordering wine by the bottle can jack up the cost of your meal in no time, so be careful. Table wine by the liter carafe or *demi* (half a liter) is always cheaper. The top reds are produced in Bordeaux, Burgundy, Beaujolais, and the Loire and Rhone valleys (*Red Wine For Dummies* is a great reference). Great whites hail from Alsace, the Loire, Burgundy, and Bordeaux (consult *White Wine For Dummies* for more information). And don't forget that sparkling white wine from the vineyards east of Paris called Champagne; for more, check out *Champagne For Dummies.*

Some people may be intimidated by the idea of sitting down to what many consider the most refined food on the planet. Don't sweat it. The only people with a need to impress anyone are the chef and kitchen staff. Have your waiter suggest some dishes; then just sit back and enjoy the flavors.

If you're looking for a meal in a hurry, Paris's greatest street food is crêpes, sold at sidewalk stands and from store windows. They're best when cooked fresh on the spot for you, but in touristy areas, crêpe stands often make up stacks in advance and merely reheat them on the griddle when you approach. The cheapest, and in my opinion best, is *au beurre et sucre* (with butter and sugar), although you may prefer Nutella (a hazelnut-chocolate spread) and banana, or ham and cheese.

You can visit a supermarket or gourmet store for your picnic supplies, but it's more fun and Parisian to shop at the little local food stores and street markets. Pick up a baguette at the *boulangerie* (bakery), cured meats and the like at a *charcuterie,* and other groceries at an *épicerie.* Top it all off with some fruit, pastries from a *pâtisserie,* a bottle of wine, and you're set.

Paris's top restaurants

Alain Ducasse

$$$$ Étoile (8e) FRENCH

Alain Ducasse is one of the few chefs ever to garner six Michelin stars at once (spread across two restaurants), so he doesn't need to bother giving any other name to his ludicrously expensive but excellent Paris dining room in an early-twentieth-century town house decorated with a subdued art nouveau clubby elegance. You may avoid permanently spraining your credit card by going for lunch, when the fixed-price menu is at least within the upper range of mere mortals. The cooking is remarkable.

59 av. Raymond Poincaré (between place Victor Hugo and place du Trocadero). ☎ *01-47-27-12-27. Internet:* www.alain-ducasse.com. *Reservations required. Métro: Victor-Hugo. Main courses: 320F–405F ($53.35–$67.50); fixed-price menus start at 950F ($158.35). AE, DC, MC, V. Open: Lunch and dinner Mon–Fri.*

Au Bascou

$ Le Marais (3e) BASQUE

In a simple and softly lit, rustic interior, Jean-Guy Loustau serves up perhaps the best Basque dishes in Paris Consider starting with a *piperade basquaise* (a light terrine of eggs, tomatoes, and spices) before moving on to roast wild duck or rabbit in a red wine sauce. The light, flavorful Basque wines are a perfect accompaniment. Service is snappy, so you may want to save this place for a night when you don't want to linger over dinner.

38 rue Réaumur (between rue du Temple and rue de Turbigo). ☎ *01-42-72-69-25. Reservations recommended. Métro: Artes et Metiers. Main courses: 85F ($14.15). AE, MC, V. Open: Lunch and dinner Mon–Fri, dinner Sat. Closed Dec 25–Jan 1; Aug.*

Bofinger

$$$ Marais (4e)   ALSATIAN

A brasserie is somewhere between a cafe and a restaurant, with great low prices and a cuisine usually based on the Franco-Germanic cooking of the Alsace region — lots of *choucroute* (sauerkraut, usually served with sausages or salamis). They're also good for off-hours dining, tending to stay open continuously from noon to 1:00 a.m. The first, and still the best, is Bofinger, opened in 1864 and sporting a restored 1919 art deco decor. Service can be whirlwind.

5-7 rue de la Bastille (just off place de la Bastille). ☎ *01-42-72-87-82. Reservations recommended. Métro: Bastille. Main courses: 75F–196F ($12.50–$32.65). AE, DC, MC, V. Open: Lunch and dinner daily.*

Campagne et Provence

$$ Latin Quarter (5e)   PROVENÇAL

The Provençal smells emanating from the kitchen are enticing to the few customers lucky enough to secure a table in this small but ever-popular spot. The chef excels at both seafood and game dishes. The wines are worthy, and, for cooking this classy, the price is a bargain.

25 quai de la Tournelle (across from the Ile-St-Louis). ☎ *01-43-54-05-17. Reservations highly recommended (the day before, if possible). Métro: Maubert-Mutualité. Main courses: 115F ($19.15). Lunch menu: 125F ($20.85) Dinner menus: 190F–225F ($31.65–$37.50). MC, V. Open: Lunch Tues–Fri, dinner Mon–Sat. Closed Aug (usually).*

Les Bookinistes

$$ St-Germain-des-Prés (6e)   FRENCH

About a decade ago, a tired *haute* scene and French recession teamed up to inspire top chefs to branch out into what have become known as baby bistros: small, relaxed eateries whose menus are designed by the biggest names in the business but the prices are up to 75 percent below what you'd pay in these chefs' flagship restaurants. Renowned chef Guy Savoy spun off several successful little spots, the best of which is this Seine-side contemporary dining room with a constantly changing menu that hints at a Mediterranean touch.

53 quai des Grands-Augustins (at rue des Grands-Augustins). ☎ *01-43-25-45-94. Reservations required. Métro: Saint-Michel. Main courses: 97F–125F ($16.15–$20.85). Fixed-price lunch menu: 140F–160F ($23.35–$26.65). AE, MC, V. Open: Lunch Mon–Fri, dinner daily.*

L'Epi Dupin

$ St-Germain-des-Prés (7e) FRENCH

Seeing the success of such baby bistros, many young and up-and-coming chefs decided to forgo the fancy restaurant part and start right off with a small, informal, relatively inexpensive trendy bistro. L'Epi Dupin is perhaps the best, with fine modern bistro cuisine in an antique French setting of hewn beams and stone walls. The food runs to ultra-traditional rural French, with lighter, modern alternatives like salmon carpaccio or spit-roasted grouse. Service, while friendly, can be seriously unattentive.

11 rue de Dupin (between rue de Sévres and rue du Cherche Midi). ☎ *01-42-22-64-56. Reservations recommended. Métro: Sèvers Babylone. Fixed-price menus: 110F ($18.35) at lunch, 165F ($27.50) at dinner. AE, MC, V. Open: Lunch and dinner Mon–Fri.*

Taillevent

$$$$ Champs-Elysées (8e) FRENCH

For tradition and a cuisine so scrupulously haute it belongs in a museum, you can do no better than Jean-Claude Vrinat's restaurant named after France's first great chef and cookbook author (a fourteenth-century alchemist). The refined atmosphere is unobtrusive, so you can devote all your attentions to the creations of Jean-Claude Vrinat, who runs one of the foremost kitchens in town and is constantly incorporating the best of new trends into his art. Monsieur Vrinat was the restaurant's sommelier when his father was chef, and Taillevent's wine list is perhaps the best in Paris.

15 rue Lamennais (Four blocks form the Arc de Triomphe off av. de Friedland). ☎ *01-44-95-15-01. Reservations required weeks in advance, months if you can swing it. Métro: George-V. Main courses: 295F–500F ($49.15–$83.35). AE, DC, MC, V. Open: Lunch and dinner Mon–Fri. Closed Aug.*

La Taverne du Sergent Recruteur

$$$ Ile St-Louis (4e) FRENCH

Supposedly, unscrupulous army sergeants would get potential young recruits drunk at this popular seventeenth-century eatery, and the saps would wake up in the barracks the next day as conscripts. These days the only danger is overeating because the fixed price menu gets you all you can eat from a huge basket of veggies and cured meats, bottomless glasses of wine, a selection of basic main dishes, and a cheese board.

41 rue St-Louis-en-l'Isle (on the main drag of the Ile St-Louis, just off rue des Deux Ponts). ☎ *01-43-54-75-42. Reservations recommended. Métro: Pont-Marie. Set-price Menu: 188F ($31.35, with wine). AE, MC, V. Open: Lunch Sun, dinner daily.*

Paris's runner-up restaurants

Brasserie Balzar

$$ Latin Quarter (5e) Brasserie Balzar is the place to go for French comfort food at reasonable prices in the same worn, century-old environment enjoyed by the likes of Sartre, Camus, and James Thurber. *49 rue des Ecoles (at rue d'Ulm)* ☎ *01-43-54-13-67. Métro: Odeon or Cluny-La Sorbonne.*

Brassiere Lipp

$$ St-Germain-des-Prés (6e) Brassiere Lipp is Paris's most famous brassiere, opened in 1880 and a haven for intellectuals, artists, writers, politicos, and American expatriates who try to relive the times Hemingway sat at Lipp's dreaming up stories. It's very popular with Parisian businesspeople at lunch, so come around noon to secure a table. *151 Bd. St-Germain (near the corner with rue de Rennes)* ☎ *01-45-48-53-91. Internet:* www.brasserie-lipp.fr. *Métro: St-Germain-des-Prés.*

Buddha Bar

$$$$ Champs-Elysées (8e) This was last year's hottest ticket and still a prime see-and-be-seen joint and funky place to spot movie stars while dining on French–Pacific Rim fusion cuisine. *8 rue Boissy d'Anglais* ☎ *01-53-05-90-00. Métro: Concorde.*

Chantairelle

$$ Latin Quarter (5e) The Chantairelle is a quirky spot to sample the cooking of the wild Auvergne region, with piped-in bird song and boutique of regional products; book ahead for a table on the pretty little flagstone garden out back. *17 rue Laplace* ☎ *01-46-33-18-59. Métro: Cardinale Lemoine or RER: Luxembourg.*

Man Ray

$$$$ Champs-Elysées (8e) The Man Ray is one of Paris's trendiest restaurants of the moment, co-owned by a Paris nightclub impresario, Sean Penn, and Johnny Depp, with a varied menu that borrows heavily from Asian and Mediterranean kitchens. *34 rue Marbeuf* ☎ *01-56-88-36-36. Métro: Roosevelt.*

Restaurant des Beaux-Arts

$ St-Germain-des-Prés (6e) This restaurant is a bastion of budget dining and hearty portions beloved by travelers and students from the School of Fine Arts across the street alike for its 95F ($15.85) fixed-price menu. *11 rue Bonaparte (at the corner with rue des Beaux Arts — one block from the Seine's Quai Malaquais)* ☎ *01-43-26-92-64. Métro: St-Germain-des-Prés.*

Restaurant Perraudin

$ Latin Quarter (5e) Hungry travelers and locals fill this restaurant up early after the inexpensive classic bistro fare in a convivial, wood-beamed atmosphere. *157 rue St-Jacques* ☎ *01-46-33-15-75. Métro: Cluny; RER: Luxembourg.*

Exploring Paris

By far Paris's best buy is the Carte Musées et Monuments, a pass that lets you into most Parisian sights free (well, 70 of them; the only notable exceptions are the **Eiffel** and **Montparnasse towers** and the **Marmottan** museum). It costs 80F ($13.35) for a one-day pass — if you use it just for the **Louvre** and **Musée d'Orsay**, you save 10 francs. You can also get three-day, 160F ($26.65), or five-day, 240F ($40), versions. The biggest benefit is that you don't have to wait in line! You just saunter up to a separate window, and they wave you through. You can buy the pass at any train station, tourist office, main Metro stations, or participating sights. For more info, visit the InterMusées Web site at www.intermusees.com.

Paris's top sights

The Louvre

The Grand Louvre — a former royal palace opened to the public as an art gallery when the French Revolution struck — has 195,000 square feet of galleries, five million visitors annually, and over 30,000 works on display spanning three millennia. Besides one of the world's top painting galleries, the Louvre also houses a remarkable collection of antiquities from Greece, Etruria, Rome, Egypt, and the Orient; a sculpture section that boasts two of Michelangelo's *Slaves;* and a fine decorative arts division.

A massive reorganization has opened up even more display space than ever before. It would take about three days to properly scratch the surface of all seven departments. Heck, it takes at least half a day merely to walk through the halls to see da Vinci's enigmatically smiling *Mona Lisa,* that armless beauty *Venus de Milo,* and the dramatic *Winged Victory of Samothrace* — just the three most famous of many instantly recognizable artistic icons that call the Louvre home.

The floor plans and information desks on site can help you get a handle on the basic layout and plan your visit. The Louvre's problem is that there are just too many masterpieces. On a first visit you will probably have to ignore most of the works you're passing — pieces that may have been the pride of a lesser museum — in order to devote your art appreciation energies to the greatest hits.

These include an incredible five more da Vinci paintings (the *Virgin of the Rocks* is stupendous), fragments from the Parthenon, Ingres's *The Turkish Bath,* Veronese's enormous *Wedding Feast at Cana,* Vermeer's delicate *Lacemaker,* self-portraits by Dürer and Rembrandt, Uccello's odd *Battle of San Romano,* Géricault's dramatic *Raft of the Medusa,* and David's ceremonious *Coronation of Napoléon I.* If you have the time, try to take in the Louvre over several visits.

You enter the Louvre through the glass pyramid in the Cour Napoléon courtyard, between the qaui du Louvre and rue de Rivoli. ☎ *01-40-20-50-50. Internet:* www.louvre.fr. *Métro: Palais-Royal-Musée du Louvre. Open: Thurs–Sun 9:00 a.m.–6:00 p.m.; Wednesday 9:00 a.m.–9:45 p.m.; Mon 9:00 a.m.–6:00 p.m., plus main galleries until 9:45 p.m. The entrance/entresol, with its information desks, medieval Louvre exhibit, cafes, post office, and shops, stays open daily until 9:45 p.m. Admission: 45F ($7.50) before 3:00 p.m., 26F ($4.35) after 3:00 p.m. and on Sun. Free for those under 18. Free for everyone the first Sun of each month (but crowded).*

Notre-Dame Cathedral

"Our Lady of Paris" is the heart and soul of the city, a monument to Paris's past slung in the cradle of its origins. The twelfth- to fourteenth-century cathedral is a study in gothic beauty and gargoyles, at once solid with squat, square facade towers and graceful with flying buttresses around the sides. It's been remodeled, embellished, ransacked, and restored so often that it's a wonder it still has any architectural integrity at all (during the Revolution, it was even stripped of its religion and rechristened the Temple of Reason).

Notre-Dame is a good hour to 90 minutes out of your day. The lines are long to get in, but at least while you wait you have time to admire the Bible stories played out in intricate stone relief around the three great portals on the facade. Much of the facade was (poorly) restored once in the eighteenth century and then again (as well as could be done) in the nineteenth. If you're keen to see some medieval originals, the upper tier of the central portal is ancient, and much of the sculpture on the right-hand portal has also survived from 1165 to 1175.

The main draw, though, are the three enormous rose windows, especially the 69-foot diameter north window (left transept), which has retained almost all of its original thirteenth-century stained glass. Save Notre-Dame for a sunny day and the best light effects.

No visit to Notre-Dame is complete without tackling the 387 steps up the north tower (give it at least 45 minutes) to examine those grotesque, amusing, or sometimes downright frightening gargoyles. One last thing you shouldn't forget to do is to walk around the building. Those famous flying buttresses at the very back, holding up the apse with 50-foot spans of stone strength, are particularly impressive. Cross the Seine to admire the entire effect from the quay on the Left Bank. There are free (donation appreciated) guided tours in English, Wednesday and Thursday at noon, and Saturday at 2:30 p.m.

At the opposite end of the square from the cathedral, a flight of steps leads down to the Archeological Crypt (☎ **01-43-29-83-51**), a 260-foot gallery extending under Notre-Dame's square. This excavation includes the jumbled foundations, streets, and walls of a series of Parises, including the medieval and Roman cities. There's even a house from *Lutèce* — the town built by the Celtic *Parisii* tribe that flourished on the Ile de la Cité over 2,000 years ago. it's open daily 9:30 a.m. to 6:30 p.m. (10:00 a.m. to 5:00 p.m. in winter); admission is 32F ($5.35).

Place du Parvis de Notre-Dame. ☎ *01-42-34-56-10. Métro: Cité. Open: Cathedral, Mon–Fri 8:00 a.m.–6:45 p.m., Sat–Sun 8:00 a.m.–7:45 p.m. (Sun, open for Mass only 9:30 a.m.–2:00 p.m.). Treasury, Mon–Sat 9:30–11:30 a.m. and 1–5:45 p.m. Towers, Apr–Sept 9:30 a.m.–7:30 p.m., Oct–Mar 10:00 a.m.–5:00 p.m.. Crypt, Apr–Sept 10:00 a.m.–6:00 p.m., Oct–Mar 10:00 a.m.–4:30 p.m.. Admission: Cathedral is free; towers are 27F ($4.50) adults, 18F ($3) ages 18–24 and over 60, 15F ($2.50) ages 12–17; the crypt is the same rates as the towers.*

Eiffel Tower

Looking like two sets of train tracks that crashed into each other, Gustave Alexandre Eiffel's tower rises 1,056 feet above the banks of the Seine. The man who gave the **Statue of Liberty** a backbone designed this quintessential Parisian symbol merely as a temporary exhibit for the Exhibition of 1899 and managed to rivet together all 7,000 tons of it (with 2.5 million rivets) in under two years. Fortunately for the French postcard industry, the tower's usefulness as a transmitter of telegraph — and later, radio and TV — signals saved it from demolition.

Critics of the day assailed its aesthetics, but no one could deny the feat of engineering. It remained the tallest man-made structure in the world until the Chrysler Building stole the title in 1930, and it paved the way for the soaring skyscraper architecture of the twentieth century. The restaurants and bars on the first level are pricey, but not bad. The view from the second level is an intimate bird's-eye view of Paris; from the fourth level, you can see the entire city spread out below and, on a good day, as far out as 42 miles. Visibility is usually best near sunset; pausing for vistas at all levels takes about 90 minutes.

Champs-de-Mars, 7e. ☎ *01-44-11-23-23. Internet:* www.eiffel-tower.com. *Métro: Trocadéro, Ecole-Militaire, Bir-Hakeim. RER: Champ-de-Mars–Tour Eiffel. Open: July–Aug, daily 9:00–midnight; Sept–June, daily 9:30 a.m.–11:00 p.m. (in winter, stairs only open until 6:30 p.m.). Admission: First landing, 20F ($3.35); second landing, 42F ($7); third landing, 59F ($9.85); stairs to second floor, 14F ($2.35).*

Musée d'Orsay

In 1986, Paris consolidated most of its collections of French art from 1848 to World War I in the most unlikely of spots: an old converted train station. Although the Orsay has earlier works by the likes of Ingres and Delacroix, its biggest draw is undoubtedly those crowd-pleasing impressionists.

Many of the works are so widely reproduced that you may wander through with an eerie feeling of déjà vu. Degas' ballet dancers and *l'Absinthe;* Monet's women in a poppy field, his *Rouen Cathedral* painted under five different lighting conditions, and his giant *Blue Waterlilies;* van Gogh's *Restaurant de la Siréne,* self-portraits, peasants napping against a haystack, and his *Bedroom at Arles; Whistler's Mother;* Manet's groundbreaking *Picnic on the Grass* and *Olympia,* which together helped throw off the shackles of artistic conservatism and gave impressionism room to take root.

Add in a generous helping of Cézanne, Gauguin, Rodin, Toulouse-Lautrec, Pissaro, and Seurat, and you could easily spend a full day exploring this museum, though a *quick* run through the highlights would only take around two hours.

1 rue Bellechasse or 62 rue de Lille. ☎ *01-40-49-48-14. Internet:* www. musee-orsay.fr. *Métro: Solférino. RER: Musée-d'Orsay. Open: Tues–Wed and Fri–Sat 10:00 a.m.–6:00 p.m., Thurs 10:00 a.m.–9:45 p.m., Sun 9:00 a.m.–6:00 p.m. June 20–Sept 20, it opens at 9:00 a.m. Admission: 40F ($6.65) adults, 30F ($5) ages 18–24 and over 60 (and Sun for everyone).*

Centre Georges Pompidou

The Pompidou is Paris's homage to twentieth-century creativity. Aside from the gallery of modern art there are exhibits on industrial design, music research, photography, and the history of film. The cafeteria on the top floor has some fantastic views.

Even if you don't want to spend an hour or two with the exhibits inside, come by to shake your head at the wildly colorful and controversial transparent inside-out architecture — which was outrageously avant-garde in the '70s but by 1998 had deteriorated so badly they had to shut it down for 18 months of repairs — and to enjoy Paris's best street performers on the sloping square out front.

Place Georges Pompidou. ☎ *01-44-78-12-33. Internet:* www.cnac-gp.fr. *Métro: Rambuteaux. Open: Mon and Wed–Fri noon–10:00 p.m., Sat–Sun 10:00 a.m.–10:00 p.m. Admission: Entire center, 70F ($11.65) adults, 45F ($7.50) ages 16–25 and 60+, free under 16; Museum of Modern Art only, 35F ($5.85) adults, 24F ($4) ages 16–24.*

Sainte-Chapelle

The interior of this tiny Gothic chapel, almost entirely hidden by the bulk of the Palace of Justice surrounding it, is a sculpture of light and color. The thin bits of stone that hold the tall stained-glass windows and brace the roof seem to dissolve in the diffuse and dappled brightness glowing through the thirteenth-century windows. It's the most ethereal 20 minutes you can spend in Paris. The chapel was built in 1246 to house the Crown of Thorns.

4 bd. du Palais, 1er (in the Palais de Justice on the Ile de la Cité). ☎ **01-53-73-58-50.** *Métro: Cité. Open: Apr–Sept, daily 9:30 a.m.–6:30 p.m.; Oct–Mar, daily 10:00 a.m.–5:00 p.m.. Admission: 35F ($5.85) adults, 23F ($3.85) ages 12–17.*

Rodin Museum

After the critics stopped assailing Rodin's art, they realized he had been the greatest sculptor since Michelangelo, and the studio where Rodin worked from 1908 until his death in 1917 was opened as a museum to house some of the artist's greatest works. In the rose gardens you find *The Thinker, The Gate of Hell, The Burghers of Calais,* and *Balzac.* Inside are collected many famed sculptures — *The Kiss, The Three Shades, The Hand of God, Iris* — along with some of Rodin's drawings and works by his friends and contemporaries. You can do it in 45 minutes.

77 rue de Varenne, 7e (in the Hôtel Biron). ☎ **01-44-18-61-10.** *Métro: Varenne. Open: Tues–Sun, 9:30 a.m.–5:45 p.m. (Oct–Mar to 4:45 p.m.). Admission: 28F ($4.65) adults, 18F ($3) ages 18–26 and over 60. Free on Sun.*

Musée Picasso

Picasso left some $50 million in French inheritance taxes when he died. The state accepted instead 203 paintings, 177 sculptures, and thousands of sketches and engravings. The good news is that this is one of the most representative collections of Picasso's works in the world, spanning his entire career. The bad news is that the space is much smaller than the collection (hence only a 30- to 45-minute diversion), and with the constant rotation of works, you never know whether you'll get to see masterpieces such as *Le Baiser, Pan Flute, Two Women Running Along the Beach, The Crucifixion,* or *Nude in a Red Armchair.*

5 rue de Thorigny, 3e (in the Hôtel Salé). ☎ **01-42-71-25-21.** *Métro: St-Paul or Filles du Calvaire. Open: Wed–Mon 9:30 a.m.–6 p.m. (Oct–Mar to 5:30 p.m.). Admission: 30F ($5) adults, 20F ($3.35) ages 18–25. Sun, 20F ($3.35) for everyone.*

More cool things to see and do in Paris

The attractions reviewed earlier don't even scratch the surface of all Paris has to offer. Find time in your schedule to wander a neighborhood, visit a cemetery, or simply hang out in a cafe, and you'll experience yet another facet of this unforgettable city.

✔ **Squander the Day Away in a Cafe.** Many European cultures have a third place, between home and work, where citizens play out their lives. In Paris, it is the cafe, a sort of public extension of the living room. In the cafe, you can sit all day over a single cup of coffee or order a light meal or a flute of champagne. Ensconce yourself indoors or stand at the bar, but most people choose to sit outside — in a glassed-in porch in winter or on the sidewalk in summer — because one of the cafe's biggest attractions is the people-watching.

Here are some classic cafes. **Les Deux Magots** (☎ 01-45-48-55-25) 6 place St-Germain-des-Prés, established in 1885, was the haunt of Picasso, Hemingway, and Sartre. Sartre wrote a whole trilogy holed up at a table in **Café de Flore** (☎ 01-45-48-55-26), 172 bd. St-Germain-des-Pres, a Left Bank cafe frequented by Camus and Picasso and featured in Gore Vidal novels. The Champs-Elysées may no longer be Paris's hot spot, but **Fouquet's** (☎ 01-47-23-70-60) at no. 99 is still going strong based on its reputation, good food, and favorable reviews by Chaplin, Churchill, FDR, and Jackie Onassis.

Henry Miller had his morning porridge at **La Couple** (☎ 01-43-20-14-20), 102 bd. du Montparnasse, a brasserie that also hosted the likes of Josephine Baker, John Dos Passos, Dalí, and F. Scott Fitzgerald. Finally, you can make a pilgrimage to the art nouveau interiors of the new **La Rotonde** (☎ 01-43-26-68-84), 105 bd. du Montparnasse, risen like a phoenix from the ashes of its namesake that once stood here. In *The Sun Also Rises,* Hemingway writes of the original, "No matter what cafe in Montparnasse you ask a taxi driver to bring you to . . . they always take you to the Rotonde."

✔ **Pay Homage to the Cultural Giants at Père-Lachaise Cemetery.** Chopin, Gertrude Stein, Delacroix, Proust, Rossini, Oscar Wilde, Georges Bizet, Ingres, Isadora Duncan, Pissaro, Molière, Edith Piaf, Modigliani, and the Doors' Jim Morrison — you couldn't imagine most of these people getting together in life, but they fit well together in death. Pick up the map of the graves and spend a morning under the trees of this vast and romantic cemetery of rolling hills and historic tombs. To get there, take the Métro to Père-Lachaise.

✔ **Stroll through Montmartre, the Original Bohemian 'Hood.** Although inundated by tourists these days, Montmartre, an old artists' neighborhood crowning a hill at Paris's northern edge (the 18e), still has an intriguing village flavor. The Abbesses Métro stop is in Montmartre itself, but get off one stop early at Pigalle.

Here you're on the northwest edge of Paris's red light district centered on the sex shop–lined boulevard de Clichy, which features hangers-on like the **Moulin Rouge** at no. 87 (☎ 01-53-09-82-82; Internet: www.moulinrouge.com) with its can-can shows, and the surprisingly quasitasteful **Museum of the Erotic** at no. 72 (☎ 08-36-69-19-18; Internet: www.erotic-museum.com), which is open 10:00 a.m. to 2:00 a.m.

Work your way uphill to the **Basilique du Sacré-Coeur**, a frosty white neo-Byzantine basilica built from 1876 to 1919 and towering over the city. Climb the dome for a vista that on clear days extends 35 miles.

Some of Montmartre's quirkiest sights include a pair of windmills, visible from rue Lepic and rue Girardon, and Paris's only vineyard, on rue des Saules. Next door to the latter, at rue Saint-Vincent 12, is the **Montemartre Museum** (☎ 01-46-06-61-11), dedicated to the neighborhood in a house that was at times occupied by van Gogh, Renoir, and Utrillo.

Pay your respects to the writers Stendhal and Dumas, the composers Offenbach and Berlioz, and the painter Degas at their graves in the **Cimitère de Montemartre** on avenue Rachel. Finish the evening at 22 rue des Saules in Au Lapin Agile (☎ 01-46-06-85-87) — in Picasso and Utrillo's day called **Café des Assassins.** The cover, including first drink, is a steep 130F ($21.70).

✔ **Window-shop with the Best of Them.** Paris is a world shopping capital. On boulevard Haussmann rise Paris's two flagships of shopping, the department stores **Au Printemps** and **Galeries Lafayette.** Au Printemps is a bit more modern and American-styled, and Galeries Lafayette is more Old World French, but both are very upscale and carry the ready-to-wear collections of all the major French designers and labels.

If you prefer to shop boutiques, the best concentrations of stores are in the adjoining 1er and 8e. No single street offers more shops than the long rue du Faubourg St-Honoré/rue St-Honoré and its tributaries. Even if you can't afford the prices, it's fun to have a look. Big fashion houses like **Hermès** (no. 24) hawk ties and scarves; **Au Nain Blue** (no. 406) has one of the fanciest toy emporiums in the world; and the prices at **La Maison du Chocolat** (no. 225) are as rich as the confections.

Window shop for leather at **Didler Lamarthe** (no. 219) or **Longchamp** (no. 390) or for cutting-edge fashion at **Hervé Léger** (no. 29) and **Lolita Lempicka** (no. 14). Just off the rue du Faubourg St-Honoré, at 35 av. Matignon, 8e, women can find **Anna Lowe** for runway samples and slightly worn creations of the big names at a discount. **Réciproque**, 89-123 rue de la Pompe, 16e, has slight bargains on a remarkably wide range of the big labels and top designers.

Some of the best food shopping is concentrated on place de la Madeleine, 8e, home to **Fauchon,** Paris's homage to the finest edibles money can buy (though it faces serious competition from neighbor **Hediard**). Don't forget your Paris outlet for caviar, truffles, foie gras, and other pâtés: **Maison de la Truffe.** Jewels glitter on place **Vendôme,** 1er, at **Cartier** (no. 7), **Chaumet** (no. 12), and **Van Cleef & Arpels** (no. 22). Stink like the best of them with discounts on French perfumes at **Parfumerie de la Madeleine,** 9 place de la Madeleine, 8e, or **Michel Swiss,** upstairs at 16 rue de la Paix, 2e.

✔ **Have a Flea Market Fling.** If the prices at **Cartier, Hermès,** and the like set your head to spinning, you may have more luck at the **Marché aux Puces de Saint-Ouen/Clignancourt,** the city's most famous flea market (open Saturday to Monday). It's a group of several markets comprising almost 3,000 stalls, all along avenue de la Porte de Clignancourt.

Usually Monday is the best day to get a bargain, because the crowds are fewer and vendors are anxious for the dough. Keep in mind, though, that you can get a better price if you speak French and show that you are serious about and respectful of the merchandise.

Hours vary with the weather and the crowds, but stalls are usually up and running between 7:30 a.m. to 6:00 p.m. Take the Métro to Porte de Clignancourt; from there, turn left and cross boulevard Ney, and then walk north on avenue de la Porte de Clignancourt.

✔ **Cruise the Seine.** Is there anything more romantic than slipping down the current of one of the world's great rivers past eighteenth-century palaces? Well, perhaps killing the canned P.A. sightseeing commentary and getting rid of all the other camera-clicking tourists would help the romantic mood, but if it's mood you're after you can always do it as a more refined dinner cruise.

The classic *Bateaux-Mouches* float down the Seine is offered by several companies, the biggest being **Bateaux Parisiens** (☎ 01-44-11-33-44), which departs from quai Montebello or from pont d'Iena at the foot of the Eiffel Tower; and **Les Vedette du Pont-Neuf** (☎ 01-46-33-98-38), which leaves from Pont Neuf on the Ile de la Cité. Vessels depart every half hour (fewer in winter). Regular 90-minute trips with multilingual commentary cost 50F ($8.35).

After dark, the boats sweep both banks with mega-powered floodlights — illuminating everything very well, but sort of spoiling the romance. These tend to be touristy too, unless you opt for a more refined and romantic luncheon or dinner cruises, which are more expensive — 350 to 560F ($58.35 to $93.35) for jacket-and-tie dinners, and the food is only so-so. The setting, however, can't be beat.

A cheaper, and less-contrived, alternative to the daytime tour is the **Batobus** (☎ 01-44-11-33-99), a kind of water taxi (no piped-in commentary) that stops every 25 minutes at five major points of interest: **Hôtel de Ville, Notre-Dame,** the **Louvre,** the **Eiffel Tower,** the **Musée d'Orsay,** and **St-Germain-des-Prés.** A day ticket costs 60F ($10); tickets between stops cost 12F ($2) each. Batobus runs April to November from 10:00 a.m. to 7:00 p.m.

✔ **Pay a Visit to Le Mickey.** Contrary to popular belief, **Disneyland Paris** (☎ 407-934-7639 in the United States, 01-60-30-60-53 in Paris; Internet: www.disneylandparis.com) has been a fantastic success. It gets more visitors than the **Louvre.** The theme park, a slightly Europeanized version of California's Disneyland with both familiar and new versions of rides and those contrived cultural areas, has been inundated with guests since the day it opened. It just ran into financial troubles when more people than expected stayed in Paris rather than in the Disney hotels.

Open hours vary constantly over the season, but generally run daily 10:00 a.m. to 6:00 p.m., 9:00 a.m. to 8:00 p.m. weekends and April to mid-July, and 9:00 a.m. to 11:00 p.m. mid-July to August. Admission January 4 to March 25 is 160F ($26.65) adults, 130F ($21.65) ages 3 through 11; March 26 to November 1 it's 220F ($36.65) adults, 170F ($28.35) children. To get there, take the A line RER to Marne-la-Vallée/Chessy, which is within walking distance of the park. Fare is 85F ($14.15), and the trip takes about 45 minutes.

And on Your Left, the Eiffel Tower: Seeing Paris by Guided Tour

The top tour bus company in town is **Cityrama** (☎ **800-320-0417** in the United States, or 01-44-55-60-01 in France; Internet: www.cityrama.com), which does a two-hour, top sights tour daily at 9:30 a.m., 10:30 a.m., 1:30 p.m., and 2:30 p.m.; it costs 150F ($25).

It also offers a 3½ hour "Paris Artistic" tour of **Notre Dame** and the **Louvre**, plus a drive through the **Marais** and the **Latin Quarter,** for 300F ($50; Monday, Wednesday, Friday, and Saturday at 9:45 a.m.). The "Seinorama" tour lasts 4½ hours, costs 265F ($44.15), and includes a drive up the **Champs-Élysées,** a one-hour Seine cruise, and a hot drink on the second floor restaurant of the **Eiffel Tower** (daily at 2:00 p.m.). You can combine the "Paris Artistic" and the "Seinorama" tours for 480F ($80) and 8½ hours of essential Paris on the "Full Day" tour.

It also does a variety of "Paris by Night" tours (bus around illuminated Paris, or include a Seine Cruise; many throw in a show at the **Moulin Rouge** or dinner in the **Eiffel Tower**). Cityrama offers free pickup from some of the top hotels in town, or meet at their office at 4 place des Pyramids, between rue Saint-Honoré and rue de Rivoli (across from the **Louvre**).

If you prefer a more romantic tour of the city, try a cruise along the Seine.

Finally, **Paris Walking Tours** (☎ **01-48-09-21-40;** Internet: www.pariswalkingtours.com) offers two-hour guided walks along such mouthwatering themes as Paris of the impressionists, Historic **Marais,** Hemingway's Paris, the **Village of montmartre,** Revolution on the **Right Bank,** the **Catacombs,** the **Latin Quarter** to the Sorbonne, or Masterpieces of the **Musée d'Orsay.** Consult *Time Out* for the tours being offered this week and where and when to meet — usually at a Métro station entrance at 10:00 a.m. or 10:30 a.m., and again at 2:30 or 3:00 p.m. They cost 60F ($10) adults, 40F ($6.70) students under 25, and 30F ($5) children. They also do weekend jaunts to places like **Fontainebleau** or **Monet's Garden** at Giverny.

Suggested One-, Two-, and Three-Day Itineraries

If you'd rather organize your own tour and you have a limited amount of time to sample the sights of Paris, try my recommendations for hitting the highlights.

If you have one day

Paris in a day? Better start out as early as possible: be at **Notre-Dame** when it opens at 8:00 a.m. Spend an hour poking around inside and climbing its tower before hustling across the river to do the **Louvre** at a dead trot. You only have time for the top stuff here; pay your respects to *Mona Lisa* and the *Venus de Milo* and have lunch in the cafeteria. Cross the Seine again to pop into the **Musée d'Orsay** and spend two hours or so admiring its horde of impressionists and other French greats. As the sun sets over your full day in Paris, head to the **Eiffel Tower** to toast the City of Light from its heights. Descend and treat yourself to a first-class dinner to celebrate your day in one of the world capitals of cuisine.

If you have two days

Plunge right in on the morning of Day One with the **Louvre**, which is French for "ridiculously huge museum." Lunch in the cafeteria, and by midafternoon, give up on trying to see it all and hustle on over to the **Eiffel Tower** before sunset to get your requisite picture and drink in the panorama of Paris. Have a classy dinner in a fine Parisian restaurant, or dine intimate at a tiny bistro.

Be at the cathedral of **Notre-Dame** early (8:00 a.m.) on Day Two to beat the crowds, and then clamber up the cathedral towers once they open to examine the famed gargoyles up close. Notre-Dame affords a much more intimate view across Paris than the Eiffel gets you. When you get back to ground level, cross the square in front of the cathedral and descend into the **Archaeological Crypt** to puzzle out Paris's earliest origins.

Continue to the far end of the square for the jewelbox chapel of **Sainte-Chapelle**, hidden amidst the government buildings. Grab some lunch on your way to the **Picasso Museum**. Don't stay too long with the works of this twentieth-century master (leave by no later than 2:30 p.m.) because one of Paris's biggies lies ahead: the impressionist treasure trove of the **Musée d'Orsay**. Stay in there as long as they'll let you before heading off to dinner.

If you have three days

Spend Days One and Two as I describe earlier. Day Three is day trip time. Catch the RER out to **Versailles** to spend a day exploring the palace to end all palaces, where a string of kings Louis held court in the powdered-wig exuberance of the eighteenth century. Take at least one guided tour, and save time to wander the acres of gardens.

Return to Paris by late afternoon so you can take the Métro out to the original Bohemian quarter of **Montmartre** and watch the sun set from the steps of **Sacré-Coeur.** Wander the streets, peek at windmills and vineyards, or people-watch and write postcards at a classic Parisian cafe, where you can rustle up some dinner.

Traveling Beyond Paris

Paris is a city where the day trips are as impressive as the in-town attractions. Among the many nearby destinations, following are two that exhibit the France of old in royal and religious splendor — the palaces at **Versailles** and the marvelous cathedral at **Chartres.**

The palace at Versailles

Versailles, with its extravagant seventeenth-century palace and gardens, is Paris's best and easiest day trip. Versailles takes up at least a whole morning, and in summer is packed by 10:00 a.m. Either go seriously early (the grounds open at 9:00 a.m.), or go late — after 3:30 p.m. you pay a reduced fare, and the tour buses have cleared out. In summer especially, this strategy gives you plenty of time to tour the emptying palace and, because the grounds are open until sunset, the extensive gardens as well.

Getting there

You can zip out here in half an hour on the C RER line (you want the C5 heading to Versailles–Rive Gauche station). The ride costs 35F ($5.85), but is free if you have a Eurail pass. It's a 15-minute stroll to the palace from the train station, or you can take a shuttle bus.

Across avenue de Gal de Gaulle from the station and to the right a smidgen is a sunken shopping center with a branch of the tourist information office on the right-hand side (no. 10). The main tourist office (☎ **01-39-50-36-22;** Internet: www.chateauversailles.com) is a five-minute walk to the right of the palace's main entrance at 7 rue des Réservoirs.

Seeing the sights

What started in 1624 as a hunting lodge for Louis XIII was turned by Louis XIV into a palace of truly monumental proportions and appointments over his 72-year reign (1643–1715). The Sun King made himself into an absolute monarch, the likes of which hadn't been seen since the Caesars, and he created a palace befitting his stature.

You can wander the **State Apartments**, **Hall of Mirrors** (where the Treaty of Versailles ending World War I was signed), and **Royal Chapel** on your own (or with an audio tour), but it's much more informative to take one of the guided tours, which gets you into many parts of the palace not open to the casual visitor. These tours are popular and fill up fast, so your first order of business should be to head to the tour reservations office and sign up for one. There's a good chance that you'll have to wait an hour or more, so book an even later tour and use the intervening time to explore the magnificent gardens.

Le Nôtre (who designed London's Greenwich Park and the Vatican Gardens in Rome) laid out the hundreds of acres of palace grounds in the most exacting seventeenth-century standards of decorative garden-ing. The highlights are the **Grand Canal,** two-thirds of a mile long and once plied by a small warship and Venetian gondolas; the **Grand Trianon,** a sort of palace away from home for when the king wanted a break from the main chateau; and the **Petit Trianon,** a jewel of a man-sion done in fine neoclassical style.

Nearby is Marie Antoinette's fairy-tale **Hameau,** or hamlet, created so Her Majesty could enjoy a cleaned-up version of peasant life. Here the Queen fished, milked the occasional cow, and watched hired peasants lightly toil at the everyday tasks she imagined they did in the country — she even had a little "house in the faux country" built here, sort of a thatched mansion.

Versailles has complicated hours and admissions. The various palaces are only open Tuesday to Sunday; the park and gardens open daily (except during bad weather and the occasional official ceremony). May 2 to September, the **Château** is open 9:00 a.m. to 6:30 p.m., the **Grand Trianon** and **Petit Trianon** are open from 10:00 a.m. to 6:30 p.m. October to April, the Château is open 9:00 a.m. to 5:30 p.m., and the Grand Trianon and Petit Trianon are open Tuesday to Friday 10:00 a.m. to 12:30 p.m. and 2:00 p.m. to 5:30 p.m. and Saturday to Sunday 10:00 a.m. to 5:30 p.m. The gardens are open year-round from 7:00 a.m. to sunset, which varies from 5:30 p.m. to 9:30 p.m.

The basic admission to the Château (☎ **01-30-84-76-18**) is free with the Paris museum pass or is as follows: 45F ($7.50) adults, 35F ($5.85) ages 18 to 25, free under 18. After 3:30 p.m. and all day Sunday, the cost is 35F ($5.85) for everyone over age 18. Use entrance A (A2 with the museum pass). The audio guide for the **King's Chamber** lasts one hour and costs 25F ($4.15) for adults and 17F ($2.85) for ages 7 to 17. Use entrance C.

There are five to nine guided visits offered (a few are in French only and the tour of the garden's groves runs only in summer). Ninety-minute tours cost 37F ($6.15) for adults, 26F ($4.35) for ages 7 to 17; two-hour tours cost 50F ($8.35) for adults, 24F ($4) for ages 7 to 17. Use entrance D. The park is free. The **Grand Trianon** is 25F ($4.15) for adults, 15F ($2.50) for ages 18 to 25, and free for children under 18. The **Petit Trianon** is 15F ($2.50) for adults, 10F ($1.65) for ages 18 to 25, and free for children under 18. A combined ticket to both is 30F ($5) for adults and 20F ($3.35) for ages 18 to 25.

For the most part, there is no cost to see the Gardens all year. On Sundays in May to October, however, there is a weekly fountain water show accompanied by classical music that costs 23F ($3.85) to attend. Also in summer, there are special nighttime displays (usually Saturdays) of fireworks and illuminated fountains, for which tickets run from 70F to 185F ($11.65 to $30.85), depending on where you sit. Call ☎ **01-39-50-36-22** for more information on both summertime spectacles.

Chartres Cathedral

The French sculptor Rodin dubbed the building "The Acropolis of France." "Chartres is no place for an atheist," declared Napoléon upon laying eyes on this greatest of High Gothic cathedrals (still the fourth largest church in the world). Perhaps the would-be emperor had been moved by the ethereal world of colored light that fills the cathedral on a sunny day, streaming through an awe-inspiring 3,000 square yards of twelfth- and thirteenth-century stained glass, turning the church walls into quasi-mystical portals to heaven. Budget three-quarters of a day for Chartres, returning to Paris for dinner.

Getting there

You can see all this for a 71F ($11.85) train ticket from Paris's Gare Montparnasse and less than an hour's ride. The tourism office (☎ 02-37-21-50-00) is right on the place de la Cathédral.

Seeing the sights

The first cathedral was built in the fourth century atop a Roman temple. Many historians hold that the site was religious even before the Romans invaded Gaul (Celtic France), and there's evidence that Druids worshipped in a sacred grove here centuries before Christ.

You can spend hours just scrutinizing the charismatic twelfth-century sculptures adorning the main **Royal Portal,** and their thirteenth-century cousins around to the north and south sides of the church as well. That Royal Portal is part of the west facade, which, along with the base of the south tower, is the only part of the Romanesque church to survive an 1194 fire.

The cathedral was quickly rebuilt in the thirteenth century, and the rest remains an inspiring tribute to High Gothic architecture. Tear your eyes from the stained glass inside for at least long enough to admire the sixteenth- to eighteenth-century choir screen, whose niches are filled with statuettes playing out the Life of the Virgin.

You can take an excellent guided tour in English for 40F ($6.65) Monday to Saturday at noon or at 2:45 p.m. with Malcolm Miller, whose been doing this for over 40 years. Meet just inside the cathedral on the left side.

You can climb the tower for gargoyle close-ups May 2 to August from 9:00 a.m. to 6:00 p.m., September to October and March to April from 10:00 a.m. to 11:30 a.m. and 2:00 p.m. to 5:00 p.m., and November 2 to February from 10:00 a.m. to 11:30 a.m. and 2:00 p.m. to 4:00 p.m. (year-round, the tower opens at 2:00 p.m. on Sundays); admission 25F ($4.15), 15F ($2.50) ages 12 to 25.

Make time to explore the cobbled medieval streets in the *Vieux Quartiers* (old town) and visit the sixteenth- to nineteenth-century paintings in the Musée des Beaux-Arts de Chartres (☎ **02-37-36-41-39**) at 29 Cloître Notre-Dame.

Where to stay and dine

When hunger strikes, head to the second floor of 10 rue au Lait for the tasty bistro food of **Le Buisson Ardent** (☎ **02-37-34-04-66**). If you decide to make a night of it, rest your weary head for 420 to 490F ($70 to $81.65) per double at the **Hôtel Châtlet** (☎ **02-37-21-78-00**, fax: 02-37-36-23-01), 6-8 **Jehan-de-Beauce**, where many of the antique-styled rooms have panoramic views of the cathedral.

Chapter 15

Amsterdam and Environs

● ●

In This Chapter

▶ Finding your way to and around Amsterdam

▶ Visiting Amsterdam's best hotels, restaurants, and signts

▶ Exploring the neighborhoods of Amsterdam

▶ Planning your trip to Amsterdam one day at a time

● ●

Considering all of the great European cities, Amsterdam is rather young. Founded in 1200 as a fishing village at the mouth of the Amstel River, it rapidly grew into the western world's trading powerhouse. The seventeenth century ushered in the Dutch Golden Age, marked by a vast trade network and the American colony of Nieuw Amsterdam (later New York), that filled its coffers while painters such as Rembrandt colored its cultural life.

Elegant, seventeenth-century row houses that often look impossibly tall and skinny line the canals of Amsterdam, a city of 7,000 gables. For many years, property was taxed on the width of the frontage, so people built their houses as narrowly as possible. To get maximum square footage out of such skinny property, Amsterdammers extended their structures high and deep.

Following a bout with strict Protestant laws, Amsterdam became an exceedingly tolerant city within a continent of prejudice. This made it attractive to religious and other dissidents from Europe, such as the Jews and the English Puritan Pilgrims, a stuffy, devoted bunch that eventually sailed from here to Massachusetts. Wealthy, seventeenth-century Amsterdam dug a slew of new canals, built stacks of town-houses, and welcomed the artists with its beckoning atmosphere of tolerance and cultural interest.

The traditions of encouraging high art and tolerance while discouraging prudish morality laws have endowed the city with some of its greatest attractions. Amsterdam has some of the world's most famous museums; besides Rembrandt, the Dutch arts claim native masters such as Frans Hals, Jan Vermeer, Jan Steen, Vincent van Gogh, and Piet Mondrian. Its cityscape is one of the most beautiful and cohesive anywhere, with 250-year-old town houses lining well-planned and scrupulously manicured canals.

The Dutch leniency toward drugs and prostitution has grown into a huge tourism industry that lures students and other hip, mellow types to the city's "smoking coffeehouses" and visitors of all stripes who giggle and gawk at the legal brothels in the (in)famous Red Light District.

Nazi occupation during World War II threw the bright light of Dutch tolerance into sharp, shadowed relief with its anti-Semitism. Despite the best efforts of many locals, thousands of Amsterdam Jews were seized and deported. Among them was Anne Frank, a teenager whose hiding place still stands and whose diary remains one of the most powerful and enduring pieces of Holocaust literature.

No other city has such an eclectic mix of sights, from the basest of pleasures to the most somber reflections on human cruelty. Spanning from the Renaissance to the modern period, the Dutch presence and strength in the fine arts is an obvious tourist draw. Visitors also come to shop for diamonds, to drink Amsterdam beers such as Heineken and Amstel in brown cafes (so-called because the best of them are stained brown from decades, if not centuries, of smoke), or to go see the tulip fields and the windmills. To really appreciate Amsterdam, you should plan on spending at least two full days there — for many, the museums alone will take at least that long.

Making Your Way to and around Amsterdam

Thanks to Amsterdam's continuing popularity with visitors who are eager to sample its free-for-all lifestyle, getting to Amsterdam by air or rail couldn't be easier.

Getting to Amsterdam by air

Amsterdam's ultra-modern Schiphol Airport (☎ **900-0141,** costs Dfl1/50 cents per minute) is serviced by KLM, the national Dutch carrier, as well as many other international airlines.

Regular trains provide a connection from Schiphol Airport to the Centraal train station in about 20 minutes for Dfl7.50 ($3.75). Or, ask your hotel if it's part of the consortium that is serviced by the KLM shuttle bus that can whisk you straight to your hotel — for three times the cost of the train. If convenience is your priority, the easiest way to transport yourself and your luggage from the airport to your hotel is to hail a taxi for a steep Dfl70 to Dfl80 ($35–$40).

Getting to Amsterdam by train

Trains from Brussels, Paris, several German cities, Italy, Switzerland, and Eastern Europe arrive in Amsterdam at **Centraal Station,** built on an artificial island in the Ij River bounding the city's north edge. The square in front of the station has the city's main tourist office and tram terminal. You can take a tram to your hotel, or a pick up a taxi from the taxi stand outside of the station.

Getting around once you're in Amsterdam

Amsterdam's efficient trains, trams, and buses make getting around the city exceedingly simple.

By bus

The tickets in Amsterdam work differently from the ticket systems of most other cities. You can buy a single trip from the bus driver (board at the front) that costs Dfl3 to Dfl7.50 ($1.50 to $3.75), depending on how many zones you'll be passing through.

It's more economical — if more confusing — to buy a long, skinny Dfl11.50 ($5.75) *strippenkaart,* which has nothing to do with the Red Light District attractions. This **multiple-use ticket** has 15 strips on it, each good for one zone (it's actually a seminational ticket, good in Amsterdam, Rotterdam, or Utrecht). They are available for sale at the newsstands, post offices, or the GVB ticket booth outside Centraal Station.

When you board the bus, ask the driver how many zones to your stop (in central Amsterdam, usually only one or two), fold back that many "strips" plus one, and stamp it in the machine on the bus. It's the "plus one" rule that gets most visitors. In other words, if you're going three zones, skip the first three strips and fold back the ticket so that the fourth strip is at the end and then stamp that fourth strip; if you're going just one zone, stamp the second strip. You can transfer as often as you like for the next hour, provided you stay within the number of zones you've stamped.

If all this stripping drives you batty, and you plan to ride a lot, just buy a **day ticket** *(dagkaart)* from the driver or any ticket dispenser. This ticket gives you unlimited travel all day for Dfl10 ($5). Two- to nine-day passes are also available. The doors on trams and buses don't open automatically; you have to punch the *deur open* button. All the lines operate as explained here, except lines 4 and 13, where you board the back of the bus and deal with the conductor, not the driver; and line 5, where you have to get a ticket from a machine ahead of time. If all else fails, keep in mind that Amsterdam, with all its canals, is a city made for walking.

By taxi

The best way to see Amsterdam is to travel on foot, by tram, or on a bicycle. However, upon your arrival and your departure, getting yourself and your bags to and from the airport is easiest by taxi. Taxis are easy to find at the stands in front of most major hotels or at

Leidseplein, Rembrandtplein, or Centraal Station. To call for a taxi, dial ☎ 020-6777-7777. Initially, the charge is Dfl5.60 ($2.80) and then Dfl2.80 ($1.40) for each additional kilometer.

By tram

Ten of Amsterdam's 16 trolley, or tram, lines begin and end at Centraal Station. Dam Square, Muntplein, and Museumplein are the other main tram connection points. This is also true for buses.

Discovering Amsterdam: What You Need to Know

This section provides information that you'll need for the basic necessities, including maximizing your money and helpful resources in case of emergency.

The local dough

The guilder is the Dutch unit of currency. It is somewhat confusingly abbreviated Dfl because once upon a time they were called florins). It is divided into 100 cents. Conveniently, $1 equals roughly Dfl2; or Dfl1 equals 50¢. Dutch coins include 5, 10, and 25 cents and 1, 2.50, and 5 guilder. Bills are in denominations of 10, 25, 50, 100, and 250 guilder.

Where to get info after you arrive

In the Netherlands tourist offices are indicated by VVV (usually in a blue-and-white triangle). Amsterdam's most comprehensive VVV office is just outside the Centraal train station at Stationsplein 10. There's also a small desk in the station itself, a branch in the heart of town at Leidseplein 1, and another at the corner of Stadionplein and Van Tuyll van Serooskerkenweg.

The only phone number to call is ☎ 900-400-4040 or 06-3403-4066, which costs Dfl1 (50 cents) and delivers a recorded message (in Dutch). Hang on and you can speak with a live, English-speaking person (Monday to Friday 9:00 a.m. to 5:00 p.m.). The Web site www.visitamsterdam.nl, is free. You can find an information desk covering all of the Netherlands in Schiphol Plaza at the airport.

Where to go in a pinch

Although violent crime is rare, the Dutch tolerance of drugs invites and brings with it drug-related crime. Protect yourself against pickpockets in all tourist areas; on public transportation; and around **Damrak, Dam Square,** and the **Red Light District.** The Red Light District becomes less than savory after dark, particularly as the evening wears on and tourists have returned to their hotels. It is best to avoid this area late at night; I do not recommend that you wander the District alone or call attention to yourself. If you simply must walk through this area late at night, at least make sure you are in a group of people. If you should find yourself in an emergency situation, here are a few contacts to keep handy:

- **Doctors/hospitals:** Call ☎ **06-3503-2042** for a listing of doctors and dentists. For emergency care, try Academisch Medisch Centrum, Meibergdreef 9 (☎ **020-566-3333**) or Onze Lieve Vrouwe Gashuis, Eerste Oosterpark-straat 179 1e (☎ **020-599-9111**).

- **Emergency:** Dial ☎ **0611** for an ambulance or to report a fire. Call ☎ **622-2222** for the police.

- **Pharmacies:** An **apotheek** is a pharmacy that fills prescriptions; a **drogerji** sells toiletries. For a list of pharmacies that fill prescriptions at night or on weekends, call ☎ **06-3503-2042** or check the door of any apotheek; a sign will direct you to the nearest late-night pharmacy.

Staying in touch

Low on cash? Can't wait to check your e-mail? The following information will help keep you in touch while you're touring Amsterdam.

- **American Express:** This one particular branch of American Express, Damrak 66 (☎ **020-520-7777**), boasts an ATM. The other office is at Van Baerlestraat 39 (☎ **020-671-4141**). Monday to Friday 9:00 a.m. to 5:00 p.m. and Saturday 9:00 a.m. to noon are the operating hours for both.

- **Consulates:** The United States Consulate (☎ **020-664-5661**) is at Museumplein 19.

- **Internet Access & Cyber Cafes:** Located at Bloemgracht 82 (☎ **020-421-1482;** Internet: www.madprocessor.com), this cyber cafe is open Tuesday to Sunday 2:00 p.m. to midnight and charges Dfl6 ($3) per hour.

- **Mail:** The main post office is at Singel 250 (☎ **020-556-3311**), open Monday to Wednesday and Friday 9:00 a.m. to 6:00 p.m., Thursday 9:00 a.m. to 8:00 p.m., Saturday 10:00 a.m. to 1:30 p.m. There's also one at Centraal Station, Oosterdokskade 3-5 (☎ **020-622-8272**), open Monday to Friday 9:00 a.m. to 9:00 p.m., Saturday 9:00 a.m. to noon.

- **Telephone:** A local call in Amsterdam costs Dfl.50 (25 cents) for three minutes. Almost all pay phones in the Netherlands accept only **phone cards,** which are sold at newsstands, post offices, tobacconists, and train stations for Dfl10 ($5), Dfl25 ($12.50), and Dfl50 ($25). Coin phones take Dfl.25, Dfl1, Dfl2.50, or Dfl5. On both coin and card phones, watch the digital reading: It tracks your decreasing deposit, so you'll know when to add more coins or another card. For directory assistance, call ☎ **06-8008.**

✔ The country code for the Netherlands is **31.** Amsterdam's city code is **020,** but drop the initial zero if you're calling from outside the Netherlands. To call Amsterdam from the United States, dial **011- 31-20,** then the number. To charge a call to your calling card, dial **AT&T** (☎ **06-022-9111**), **MCI** (☎ **06-022-9122**), or **Sprint** (☎ **06-022- 9119**). To call the United States from the Netherlands direct, dial 001 followed by the area code and number.

✔ **Transit Info:** For transportation information, call ☎ **06-9292.**

Touring Amsterdam by Neighborhood

Infiltrated by canals of water, Amsterdam is like Venice. On a map, it looks like half of a spider web, with the canals as the threads radiating out from the center in tight, concentric arcs. Here, you must think in terms of the canals and six major squares as opposed to addresses, compass directions, and streets.

There are a few street names you should remember, starting with Damrak. Think of the Damrak as the backbone of the **City Center.** It runs from the Centraal Station at the north end of town straight down to **Dam Square,** the heart of the city and where the first dam was built across the Amstel River (hence the name *Amstelledamme,* later to become Amsterdam).

Out the other end of Dam Square, the name of Damrak changes to **Rokin,** which curves down to the square and transportation hub of Muntplein. East of Muntplein, on the City Center's southeast corner, is **Waterlooplein,** home to one of the city's premier music halls and a flea market.

On the other side of the Canal Zone southwest of Muntplein is **Leidseplein,** the bustling, throbbing center of Amsterdam's liveliest quarter of restaurants, nightclubs, and theaters. The Museumplein is farther south, ground zero for art lovers and museum hounds. Nearby is **P. C. Hoofstraat,** Amsterdam's most fashionable shopping area.

You'll also want to stroll the streets of the city and immerse yourself in the architecture and atmosphere of the neighborhoods. The City Center is a few straight canals and a tangle of medieval streets. The arc of the Singel Canal/Amstel River/Oude Schans surrounds it and runs from the Centraal Station south to Muntplein, with Dam Square in the middle. This is where you can find the **Red Light District.**

Next is the **Canal Zone,** wrapped around the City Center in a big arc. It's a series of six concentric canals laid out with seventeenth-century regularity. The irregular canal Singelgracht bounds this neighborhood. To the south lies The **Museumplein,** where you'll find the city's greatest art museums, the finest shopping, and some of the best small hotels.

The most upscale residential district (of interest to upwardly mobile Amsterdammers but not to visitors) is **Amsterdam South,** which is further south. The Jordaan, a grid of small streets between two canals at the northeastern end of the Canal Zone, is a neighborhood that is grow-ing increasingly fashionable with several good restaurants. **Amsterdam East,** east of the City Center, is the fairly pleasant, residential, working class and immigrant neighborhood with attractions such as the zoo and the tropical museum.

Staying in Amsterdam

There are beds in Amsterdam outside of the Red Light District, but the hotel crunch can get tight in July and August — especially in the budget places, which fill up with students eager to test Amsterdam's legendary lenient drug policy.

Many of those picturesquely tall, gabled houses lining canals and his-toric streets have been converted into inns, but be forewarned: Dutch staircases give new meaning to the word "steep." The older the build-ing, the more difficult it is for a hotel to get permission for installing an elevator, so be sure to ask before booking if stairs present a problem.

A room with a canal view costs more, but it's often worth it for the atmosphere; plus, they're often better outfitted and are sometimes larger than the rooms without views. The following choices listed are all in pleasant, safe neighborhoods.

For help finding accommodations anywhere in the Netherlands, con-tact the free Netherlands Reservations Centre (☎ **070-320-2500**, fax: 070-320-2611). The VVV tourist office will also reserve a room for you on the spot for a Dfl5 ($2.50) fee and a deposit.

Amsterdam's top hotels and B&Bs

Avenue Hotel

$$ City Center

The Avenue has all the bland, standardized charm of any international chain. But for solid, reliable comfort (if smallish rooms), American-style amenities at a great price, and a safe location near the rail station, you can do no better. The full Dutch breakfast adds local color.

Nieuwezijds Voorburgwal 27 (one street east of Spuistraat, just a few minutes from the Centraal Station). ☎ *020-623-8307. Fax: 020-638-3946. Internet:* www. embhotels.nl. *Tram: 1, 2, 5, 11, 13, 17. Rates: Dfl200–Dfl275 ($100–$137.50) double, including breakfast. AE, DC, MC, V.*

Hotel Acro

$ Near the Museumplein

One of Amsterdam's not-so-secret bargains, although it is recently rising in price, the Acro has bright, clean, and well-kept small rooms close to the city's major museums and P. C. Hooftstraat's shops. With a shower in every room, a full Dutch breakfast included in the rates, and the hopping Leidseplein restaurant quarter just across the canal, what more could you ask for?

Jan Luykenstraat 44 (near the corner with Honthorststraat). ☎ *020-662-0526. Fax: 020-675-0811. Tram: 2, 5, 6, 7, 10 to Rijksmuseum. Rates: Dfl175 ($87.50) double. AE, DC, MC, V.*

Hotel Jan Luyken

$$$$ Near the Museumplein

Nestled in a trio of nineteenth-century buildings between the city's top museums and P. C. Hooftstraat's shops, this hotel, boasting refined amenities and personalized service, is a good splurge option. It offers you the best of both worlds: an intimate inn with comfortably furnished bedrooms and complimentary afternoon tea in the lounge — and a pricey hotel with business services; modern baths; and several bars, patios, and dining spaces for relaxing.

Jan Luykenstraat 54-58 (between Va de Veldestraat and Van Baerlestraat). ☎ *020-573-0730. Fax: 020-676-3841. Internet: www.janluyken.nl. Tram: 2, 5, 20, 3, 12. Rates: Dfl370–Dfl540 ($185–$270) double, including breakfast. Children 4–12 half price. AE, DC, MC, V.*

Hotel Toren

$$$ Canal Zone

The Toren has medium-sized rooms in two buildings on a posh stretch of canal and is one of the best values in canalside accommodations. The furnishings are worn, but the staff is helpful, and there's even a cute (read: floral prints) small guest house available for extra privacy. Insist on a room overlooking the canal; some of the cramped rooms in the center of the hotel don't even have windows.

Keizersgracht 164 (near Raadhuisstraat, close to the Westerkerk and Anne Frank House). ☎ *020-622-6352. Fax: 020-626-9705. Internet: www.toren.nl. Tram: 13, 14, 17, 20. Rates: Dfl235–350 ($117.50–$175) double. AE, DC, MC, V.*

RHO Hotel

$ City Center

Recently renovated, this hotel in a former gold company building is one of the most conveniently located in Amsterdam. It's on a quiet side street off Dam Square, with an art nouveau lobby that hints at its origins as a turn-of-the-century theater. Unfortunately, the rooms are thoroughly modern and functional. The hotel provides all the amenities and is an excellent price for this level of comfort.

Nes 11-13 (just off the southeast corner of Dam Square). ☎ *020-620-7371. Fax: 020-620-7826. Tram: 1, 2, 4, 5, 9, 14, 16, 24, 25 to Dam Square. Rates: Dfl190–Dfl230 ($95–$115) double, including breakfast. AE, MC, V.*

Rembrandt Residence

$$$ Canal Zone

In the center of canal land, the Rembrandt Karena has many canalside rooms. Whether you stay in the main eighteenth-century house or one of the small sixteenth-century homes lining the Singel out back, you have a good chance of getting a canal view. The rooms are more modern than their settings: They have a full complement of amenities, almost all are of a generous size, and the odd wood beam or fireplace is a reminder of the buildings' history.

Herengracht 255 (above Raadhuisstraat). ☎ *020-623-6638. Fax: 020-625-0630. Internet:* www.bookings.nl/hotels/rembrandt. *Tram: 13, 14, 17 to Magna Plaza. Rates: Dfl190–Dfl350 ($95–$175) double, with the lowest rates available via the Website. Children under 14 stay free in parents' room. AE, DC, MC, V.*

Amsterdam's runner-up accommodations

Ambassade Hotel

$$$ This hotel fills out ten seventeenth-century canal houses for a bit of fashionable charm at relatively affordable prices. Almost all rooms look through floor-to-ceiling windows over the canal. *Herengracht 335-353.* ☎ *020-626-2333; Fax: 020-624-5321; Internet:* www.ambassade-hotel.nl.

Amstel Botel

$ Amstel Botel is nothing if not unique and cheap: a huge houseboat with 176 bare-bones cabins. It's moored in front of a Le Corbusier-designed post office on the Amsterdam harbor (the best cabins feature water views). *Oosterdokskade 2-4 just east of Centraal Station.* ☎ *020-626-4247; Fax: 020-639-1952.*

Bridge Hotel

$$ This place has huge rooms and modern amenities overlooking the skinniest bridge over the Amstel River. *Amstel 107-111, near Magere Brug.* ☎ *020-623-7068; Fax: 020-624-1565; Internet:* www.thebridgehotel.demon.nl.

Grand Hotel Krasnapolsky

$$$$ This hotel faces the Royal Palace with its modern, posh rooms and Victorian feel emanating from its antique and famed genteel restaurant. You pay for the style and central location, though. *Dam 9.* ☎ *020-554-9111; Fax: 020-622-8607; Internet:* www.krasnapolsky.nl.

Owl Hotel

$ The Owl is a neat little hotel on the Vondelpark just a few short blocks from the Museumplein. *Roemer Visscherstraat 1 of Eerste Constantijn Huygensstraat.* ☎ *020-618-9484; Fax:* 020-618-9441; *E-mail:* manager @owl-hotel.demon.nl.

Accommodations, Dining & Attractions in Central Amsterdam

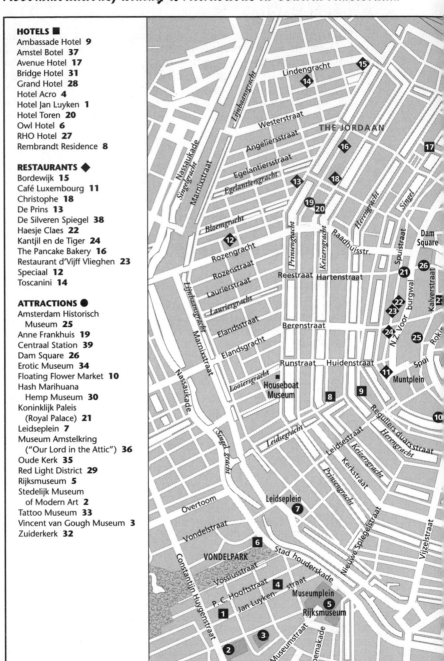

HOTELS ■
Ambassade Hotel **9**
Amstel Botel **37**
Avenue Hotel **17**
Bridge Hotel **31**
Grand Hotel **28**
Hotel Acro **4**
Hotel Jan Luyken **1**
Hotel Toren **20**
Owl Hotel **6**
RHO Hotel **27**
Rembrandt Residence **8**

RESTAURANTS ◆
Bordewijk **15**
Café Luxembourg **11**
Christophe **18**
De Prins **13**
De Silveren Spiegel **38**
Haesje Claes **22**
Kantjil en de Tiger **24**
The Pancake Bakery **16**
Restaurant d'Vijff Vlieghen **23**
Speciaal **12**
Toscanini **14**

ATTRACTIONS ●
Amsterdam Historisch
  Museum **25**
Anne Frankhuis **19**
Centraal Station **39**
Dam Square **26**
Erotic Museum **34**
Floating Flower Market **10**
Hash Marihuana
  Hemp Museum **30**
Koninklijk Paleis
  (Royal Palace) **21**
Leidseplein **7**
Museum Amstelkring
  ("Our Lord in the Attic") **36**
Oude Kerk **35**
Red Light District **29**
Rijksmuseum **5**
Stedelijk Museum
  of Modern Art **2**
Tattoo Museum **33**
Vincent van Gough Museum **3**
Zuiderkerk **32**

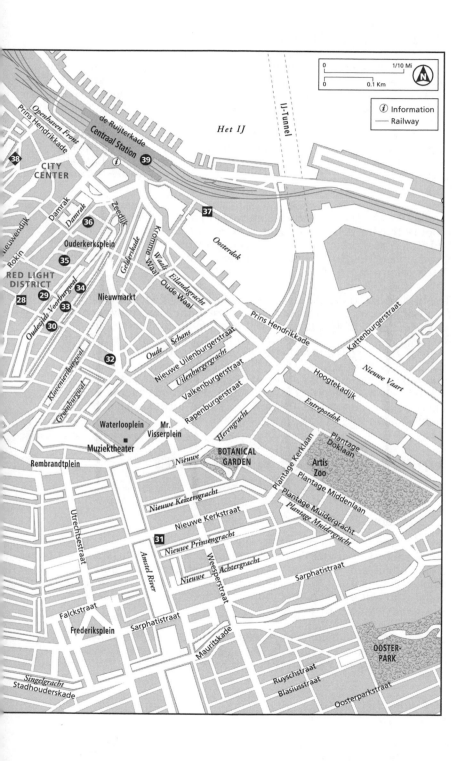

0   1/10 Mi
0   0.1 Km

i Information
— Railway

Het IJ

IJ-Tunnel

de Ruijterkade

Openhaven Front

Prins Hendrikkade

Centraal Station 39

i

38

CITY
CENTER

37

Oosterdok

Nieuwendijk

Damrak

Damrak

Zeedijk

36

Ouderkerksplein

Geldersekade

Kromme Waal

Waals

Eilandsgracht

Oude Waal

Rokin

35

RED LIGHT
DISTRICT

34

Nieuwmarkt

28   29

Oudezijds Voorburgwal

33

30

Oude Schans

Kloveniersburgwal

Groenburgwal

32

Nieuwe Uilenburgerstraat

Uilenburgergracht

Valkenburgerstraat

Rapenburgerstraat

Prins Hendrikkade

Kattenburgerstraat

Nieuwe Vaart

Hoogtekadijk

Entrepotdok

Herengracht

Waterlooplein

Mr.
Visserplein

Muziektheater

Nieuwe

BOTANICAL
GARDEN

Plantage Kerklaan

Plantage
Doklaan

Rembrandtplein

Artis
Zoo

Plantage Middenlaan

Plantage Muidergracht

Utrechtsestraat

Nieuwe Keizersgracht

Plantage Muidergracht

Nieuwe Kerkstraat

31

Amstel River

Nieuwe Prinsengracht

Weesperstraat

Nieuwe Achtergracht

Sarphatistraat

Falckstraat

Frederiksplein

Sarphatistraat

Mauritskade

OOSTER-
PARK

Singelgracht

Stadhouderskade

Ruyschstraat

Blasiusstraat

Oosterparkstraat

Dining in Amsterdam

As the capital of a trading nation and former imperial power in the Near and Far East, Amsterdam has a good selection of restaurants serving all sorts of cuisines, from Dutch to Indonesian. Traditional Dutch cuisine tends to be hearty and rather uninventive, but it's still good and filling.

Specialties include *Hutspot* (beef rib stew) and *pannekoeken,* massive pancakes that can be eaten topped with sugar or fruit as a dessert or with meats and cheeses as a main course. Consider a Dutch beer such as Heineken, Grolsch, Amstel (all light *pils* brews), or a dark Belgian beer to compliment your main dish.

Famous for its excellent Indonesian restaurants, *the* dish to try in town is not Dutch, but rather the Indonesian feast called *rijsttafel.* This "rice table" smorgasbord of Southeast Asian specialties consists of 17 to 30 tiny dishes, offering you a taste of some of the best food the former Dutch colony has to offer.

The traditional snack of Amsterdam are small sandwiches called *brood-jes,* available everywhere, but the best are at the specialty *brood-jeswinkel* Eetsalon Van Dobben, at Korte Reguliersdwarsstraat 5-9 (off Rembrandtsplein), or Broodje van Kootje, on the Leidseplein. For the unusual, try some seafood on the go, fresh from the counter of Vishandel de Kreft at Vijzelstraat 3, near the Muntplein. You can buy ultra-fresh picnic supplies at the market on Albert Cuypstraat, at the health-foody Boerenmarkt Farmer's Market at Noodermarkt, or in Albert Heijn supermarkets (there's one at the corner of Leidstraat and Koningsplein).

Amsterdam's top restaurants

Bordewijk

$$ Jordaan   FRENCH

Against a starkly modern setting, the food is richly textured and taste-fully French, with modern accents and Italian and Asian twists. The food is accompanied by attentive but not overbearing service, and the menu changes constantly. It may include rib roast in a Bordelais sauce or red mullet with wild spinach. An outdoor terrace on the canal makes dining al fresco even more attractive.

Noordermarkt 7 (at the north end of Prinsengracht). ☎ *020-624-3899. Reservations highly recommended. Tram: 3, 10, 13, 14, 17. 3-course fixed-price dinner: Dfl56 ($28). AE, MC, V. Open: Dinner Tues–Sun.*

De Prins

$$ Canal Zone   DUTCH/FRENCH

One of the best deals in the city, this tiny neighborhood place is so pop-ular for its inexpensive brown cafe-style food that the limited tables fill up fast, so call ahead. In a seventeenth-century canal side house, Dutch and French dishes are expertly prepared at remarkably low prices. This is one of your best bets for an opportunity to mix with the locals. It's also open late, until 1:00 a.m. during the week and until 2:00 a.m. on Friday and Saturday.

Prinsengracht 124 (near the Anne Frank House). ☎ *020-624-9382. Reservations not accepted. Tram: 13, 14, 17. Main courses: Dfl19.80–Dfl27.50 ($9.90–$13.75). AE, DC, MC, V. Open: Lunch and dinner daily.*

Kantjil en de Tiger
$$$ Canal Zone   JAVANESE/INDONESIAN

This large and popular restaurant features a good *rijsttafel* for two and a tasty *nasi goreng Kantjil* (fried rice with pork kebabs and stewed beef). Southeast Asian specialties such as shrimp in coconut dressing complete the menu. The multilayered cinnamon cake is worth saving room for.

Spuistraat 291 (below Raadhuisstraat). ☎ *020-620-0994. Reservations recommended. Tram: 1, 2, 5. Main courses: Df5–Dfl46 ($2.50–$23). AE, DC, MC, V. Open: Dinner daily.*

The Pancake Bakery
$ Canal Zone   DUTCH/PANCAKES

The name says it all: This canal side joint does one thing only — *pannekoeken* — and it does it great. One of these disks topped with Cajun chicken or curried turkey and pineapple may be your dinner. For dessert, fruit compotes, syrups, and ice cream are typical pancake stuffings. Its decor is simple and slightly rustic, but in summer join the crowds (and the syrup-seeking bees) at the long tables outside with a canal view.

Prinsengracht 191 (one block from the Anne Frank House). ☎ *020-625-1333. Reservations suggested. Tram: 13, 14, 17. Main courses: Dfl8–Dfl19 ($4–$9.50). AE, MC, V. Open: Lunch and dinner daily.*

Restaurant d'Vijff Vlieghen
$$$$ Canal Zone   DUTCH

An Amsterdam institution for 350 years, "The Five Fliers" resides in a string of five canal-front buildings. It offers a variety of historic decors and an excellent cuisine prepared by a chef determined to prove that traditional recipes can be exquisite. Try the wild boar with stuffed apples or smoked turkey fillet with cranberry. If gin is your drink of choice, its list of Dutch gins offers more than 40 selections. Often there is outdoor seating in summer.

Spuistraat 294-302 (below Raadhuisstraat). ☎ *020-624-8369. Reservations recommended. Tram: 1, 2, 5, 11. Main courses: Dfl47–Dfl60 ($23.50–$30). DC, MC, V. Open: Dinner daily.*

Speciaal

$$$$ Jordaan INDONESIAN

This crowded little place is one of Amsterdam's premier Indonesian restaurants and is the best place to loosen your belt and dig into a full *rijsttafel*, including *rendang* (beef), *ayam* (chicken), *ikan* (fish), and *telor* (eggs). Also try the *spekkoek*, a rich layered cake that is the house specialty.

Nieuwe Leliestraat 140-142 (just above Bloemgracht). ☎ *020-624-9706. Reservations highly recommended. Tram: 3, 10. Main courses: Rijsttafel costs Dfl45.50–Dfl60 ($22.75–$30). AE, MC, V. Open: Dinner daily.*

Amsterdam's runner-up restaurants

Café Luxembourg

$-$$ This large, stylish cafe draws an international crowd and serves huge portions of everything from soup and sandwiches to dim sum. *Spuistraat 24, near Spui.* ☎ *020-620-6264.*

Christophe

$$$$ Amsterdam's Michelin-star restaurant is a bastion of elegance and classic French cuisine with a Mediterranean twist, courtesy of French-Algerian chef Jean Christophe. Dress up for this one. *Leliegracht 46, between Prinsengracht and Keizersgracht.* ☎ *020-625-0807.*

De Silveren Spiegel

$$$-$$$$ Another old school Dutch eatery, serves refined versions of Holland staples in an old merchant's house from 1614; there's a small garden out back. *Kattengat 4-6, off Singel.* ☎ *020-624-6589.*

Haesje Claes

$$$ Dutch to the core, from the Delftware and hanging lamps to the hutspot and Ijsselmeer paling (eel). *Spuistraat 273-275, near Spui.* ☎ *020-624-9998.*

Toscanini

$$-$$$ Toscanini does excellent southern Italian cooking in a simple, laid-back (read: for long dinners only) atmosphere. *Lindengracht 75, off Brouwersgracht.* ☎ *020-623-2813.*

Exploring Amsterdam

The **Museum Card,** Dfl55 ($27.50) adults, Dfl25 ($12.50) under age 24, Dfl45 ($22.50) over age 55, gets you into most Amsterdam museums, including all listed here save the Anne Frank House. You can buy it at participating museums or the tourist office; bring a passport-sized photo.

Amsterdam's top sights

Rijksmuseum

Although it doesn't get as much publicity as the Louvre or the Uffizi, Amsterdam's Rijksmuseum is one of the top museums in Europe. Not surprisingly, it has the largest collection of Dutch masters in the world. Rembrandt is the star of the show, with a couple of self-portraits, the gruesome *Anatomy Lesson,* the racy *The Jewish Bride,* and his master-piece, *The Night Watch,* which is the defining work for the Golden Age of Dutch painting.

Frans Hals is well represented, with *The Merry Drinker* being one of his best portraits. There are party scenes courtesy of Jan Steen, de Hooch's intimate interiors, still-lifes by Bollengier, and four Vermeer paintings, including the famed *Woman Reading a Letter* and *The Kitchen Maid.* One of my favorites from among the lesser-known pieces is Avercamp's *Winter Landscape with Ice Skaters,* a scene that sums up the Netherlands I had always pictured from storybooks growing up. You could easily spend all day here, and many art lovers do, but if necessary, you can get away with just a long morning.

Stadhouderskade 42 (at Museumplein). ☎ ***020-673-2121.*** *Tram: 2, 5, 6, 7, 10. Bus: 26, 65, 66. Open: Daily 10:00 a.m.–5:00 p.m. Admission: Dfl15 ($7.50) adults, Dfl7.50 ($3.75) kids 6–18.*

Anne Frankhuis (Anne Frank House)

As 13-year-old Anne Frank began her diary in July 1942, she dealt with the usual problems of adolescence, including feelings about her family and the boy next door. She also included the defining fact of her life: She was Jewish and had just moved into a hidden attic apartment with seven other people, comprising two families, as the Nazis occupied Amsterdam. Anne lived here for two years, with only a crack in the window and some pictures of movie stars on the wall to remind her of the outside world.

The Franks and their companions were betrayed eventually, and they all were deported to concentration camps. Anne went first to Auschwitz, and then was moved to Bergen-Belsen when the Nazis retreated. She died of typhus just weeks before the camp was liberated. Of the eight people who lived in the attic, only her father, Otto, survived. His model of the rooms as they looked in those years of concealment and Anne's photos on the walls are all that adorn the small apartment hidden behind a swinging bookcase. A photograph downstairs details the Holocaust in Amsterdam, and the bookshop carries copies of Anne's remarkable diary in dozens of languages. Half a million people come to pay their respects here every year, so expect crowds and arrive early.

To dig deeper into the history of Amsterdam's Jewish population, visit the **Joods Historisch Museum** (☎ **020-626-9945;** Internet: www.jhm.nl), Jonas Dani'l Meijerplein 2-4. Located near Waterlooplein, which was the heart of the Jewish district, this vast museum chronicles the 350 years of Jewish history and culture in the city. Open daily from 11:00 a.m. to

5:00 p.m., admission is Dfl8 ($4) for adults and Dfl2 ($1) for ages 10 to 16. Ever a tolerant country, the Netherlands welcomed hundreds of mainly Sephardic Jews fleeing persecution in Spain and Portugal in the fifteenth and sixteenth centuries.

The Portuguese Synagogue at Mr. Visserplein 3, built in 1665, is the only still-functioning temple to survive from that period. Although at first restricted to certain trades such as diamond-cutting, by 1796 Jews in Amsterdam were granted full civil rights, unheard of in that era in Europe, a position they enjoyed until the Nazi occupation.

Prinsengracht 263 (just below Westermarkt). ☎ *020-556-7100. Internet:* www.annefrank.nl. *Tram: 13, 14, 17. Open: Apr–Sept daily 9:00 a.m.–9:00 p.m., Oct–Mar daily 9:00 a.m.–7:00 p.m. Admission: Dfl10 ($5) adults, Dfl5 ($2.50) children 10–17.*

Vincent van Gogh Museum

The most famous modern artist of the Netherlands died an under-appreciated, tormented genius who sold only one painting in his lifetime — to his brother. Bouts of depression landed him at an asylum at one point and at another to hack off his own ear after an argument with the painter Gauguin. Yet even while the artistic establishment was virtually ignoring him, van Gogh managed to carry the freedom of impressionism to new heights, and he created an intensely expressive style all his own.

This monument to the artist offers a chronological progression of his works, including 200 paintings and 500 drawings, alongside letters and personal effects (some of which feature in the paintings on display). A few of his more famous canvases here include *The Potato Eaters, Sunflowers, The Bedroom at Arles, Gauguin's Chair, Self Portrait with a Straw Hat,* and *The Garden of Daubigny.* At the end of the exhibit hangs the powerful *Crows over the Cornfield,* one of the last paintings the troubled master completed in 1890 prior to committing suicide at the age of 37.

Paulus Potterstraat 7 (at Museumplein). ☎ *020-570-5200. Internet:* www.vangoghmuseum.nl. *Tram: 2, 5, 16. Bus: 26, 65, 66. Open: Daily 10:00 a.m.–6:00 p.m. Admission: Dfl12.50 ($6.25) adults, Dfl5 ($2.50) ages 3–18.*

Stedelijk Museum of Modern Art

For modern art from impressionism to the present, spend a morning at the Stedelijk. The permanent collections and regularly staged exhibitions highlight many movements and styles of the past century. Picasso, Chagall, Cézanne, Monet, Calder, Oldenburg, Warhol, Jasper Johns, and Man Ray are featured artists. Of particular interest are Gerrit Rietveld's *Red Blue Chair* and paintings by Mondrian — two major forces in the Dutch abstract De Stijl movement, which prefaced the Bauhaus and modernist schools. There is also a large collection by the Russian Kazimir Malevich, who experimented with supersaturated color in a style he called Suprematism. The recently restored building itself is a stylish 1895 example of the northern neo-Renaissance.

Paulus Potterstraat 13 (at Museumplein). ☎ ***020-573-2737.*** *Tram: 2, 5, 16. Bus: 26, 65, 66. Open: Apr–Sept, daily 10:00 a.m.–6:00 p.m.; Oct–Mar daily 11:00 a.m.–5:00 p.m. Admission: Dfl9 ($4.50) adults, Dfl4.50 ($2.25) kids 7–16.*

Red Light District

Dutch pragmatism and tolerance has led to the establishment of the best-known, safest, and cleanest prostitute zone of any Western city. It has become one of Amsterdam's major sightseeing attractions for its sheer openness. Amsterdam never presumed to have the capability to stop the world's oldest profession, so it decided to regulate it and confine the licensed brothels to the old city streets surrounding the Oude Kirk, or Old Church.

These houses of ill repute display their wares behind plate-glass windows. The storefronts of some of the prettiest seventeenth-century homes in Amsterdam are occupied by women half-naked or wrapped in leather watching TV, darning socks, reading books, and otherwise occupying themselves until a customer comes along. At such time they either close the blinds or abandon the window for the privacy of an inner room.

Prostitutes pay their taxes, and the state ensures that they have regular medical checkups and health coverage. However, this didn't stop 60 percent of them from contracting HIV in the days before the spread of the disease was understood.

The district is mostly frequented by five types of people. Three are harmless: lots of tourists — giggling, blushing, gawking, considering, or shaking their heads in disbelief — as well as darty-eyed career guys in suits and the age-old sailors. Two other types can be scary and tragic: unlicensed prostitutes strung out on heroin and trolling the streets, and packs of shifty, seedy men who look like all they do is indulge in drugs and brothels.

Come prepared to be provoked or saddened by the sight of scantily clad women behind glass, who manage to look bored and provocative at the same time — and be even more careful and aware than usual. Don't take any pictures — they don't want their faces recorded by anyone, and you could find your Nikon being pitched into one of the canals. I've always felt pretty safe here during the day, but by night I'd either steer clear entirely or stick only to the main streets — and leave my valuables at the hotel.

The Red Light District fills the streets around the canals Oudezijds Achterburgwal and Oudezijds Voorburgwal. Tram: 4, 9, 16, 24, 25 to Dam Square, and then duck behind the Grand Hotel Krasnapolsky.

Museum Amstelkring ("Our Lord in the Attic")

The giant **Gothic Oude Kirk** (Old Church) is just down the block, and this tiny, well-preserved baroque church is much more interesting. In the heart of the Red Light District, it's spread across the connected third floors of three seventeenth-century homes. Now Amsterdam is famed for its tolerance, but in the sixteenth and seventeenth centuries, the practice of any religion except for the official Dutch Reformed Calvinism was forbidden. To worship, Jews, Mennonites, Lutherans, and in this instance, Catholics, had to go underground — or aboveground, as the case may be — and hold services in secret. One of the houses below the church has been restored for visitors — it's the oldest house in Amsterdam open to the public.

Oudezijds Voorburgwal 40 (about 3 blocks from Centraal Station, on the far side of the Damrak's canal). ☎ *020-624-6604. Tram: 1, 2, 4, 5, 9, 11, 13, 16, 17, 24, 25 (any to Dam Square). Admission: Dfl7.50 ($3.75) adults, Dfl6 ($3) seniors, students, and children. Open: Mon–Sat 11:00 a.m.–5:00 p.m., Sun 1:00 p.m. –5:00 p.m. Closed Jan 1.*

More cool things to see and do in Amsterdam

From romantic canal cruises to beer-swilling in a brown cafe, Amsterdam offers plenty of ways to indulge yourself.

✔ **Cruise the Canals.** Amsterdam has 160 canals spanned by more than 1,200 bridges, so your trip won't be complete until you take a canal cruise on a glass-roofed boat with multilingual commentary (recorded or live). This is the best way to get a feel for the city and see its gabled houses, lithe bridges, busy harbor, and some unforgettable sights. Some of these sights include the unlikely **Cat Boat,** home to about 150 of the furry felines who are *supposed* to detest being anywhere near water. Most tours depart from the Damrak or near the Rijksmuseum or Muntplein and last an hour. They run every 15 to 30 minutes in summer (9:00 a.m. to 9:30 pm), every 45 minutes in winter (10:00 a.m. to 4:00 p.m.), and cost around Dfl10 to 15 ($5 to $7.50) adults, Dfl8 to 10 ($4 to $5) children.

Similar tours are operated by more companies than you could shake an oar at, so here are just a few contact numbers: **Amsterdam Canal Cruises (**☎ **020-626-5636), Holland International (**☎ **020-622-7788), and Meyers Rondvaarten (**☎ **020-623-4208).** For romantics, there is a two-hour night cruise with wine and cheese or a three-hour dinner. The former run nightly year-round for Dfl45 ($22.50); dinner cruises run nightly April through November, Tuesday and Friday only in winter for Dfl145 ($72.50). Reservations are required, so contact Holland International (☎ **020-622-7788)** or Keytours (☎ **020-624-7304).**

✔ **Only in Amsterdam: Sex Museums.** These places are as squeaky clean as their subject matter allows and are full of tourists giggling, not dirty old men. **The Amsterdam Sex Museum (**☎ **020-622-8376),** Damrak 18, has more of a carnival-like atmosphere of the two, with a section of antique porn photographs that border on being of historical interest and a room of everything you don't want to know about deviant sexual practices. (Open daily 10:00 a.m. to 11:30 p.m.)

The **Erotic Museum (☎ 020-624-7303)**, Oudezijds Achterburgwal 54. is more clinical and adds some mock-ups of an S&M "playroom" and a re-created alley from the Red Light District in the good old days. Hours are noon to midnight daily.

✔ **Drink Beer in a Brown Cafe, Gin in a Proflokaal.** When the Dutch want to go to the proverbial place where everybody knows their name, they head to the neighborhood brown cafe. This is the best place to try Dutch beer, where glasses drawn extra frothy from the tap are beheaded by a knife-wielding bartender. Hundreds of these cafes are in the city, but a few of the best include the **1642 Café Chris,** Bloemstraat 42, plays opera music on Sunday nights; **Gollem,** Raamsteeg 4, has over 200 beers to offer; **Hoppe,** Spuistraat 18-20, is an always-crowded classic from 1670; **Reijnders,** has some great people-watching on the Leidseplein at no. 6; and **De Vergulde Gaper,** Prinsengracht 30, another good place for people-watching with coveted terrace tables and an atmospheric interior.

After you've become familiar with the local beer, try the hard liquor the Dutch made famous. Visit a gin-tasting house, or a *proflokaal,* which looks like a brown cafe, but is usually owned by the distillery itself. It's customary to take the first sip no-hands, slurping it from the brim-filled shot glass as you lean over it. Try **Brouwerij 't IJ,** Funenkade 7, in a now defunct windmill near the harbor (good beers, too); **Café de Doktor,** Rozen-boomsteeg near Spui Square, has lots of antiques and tasty fruit brandies; or the **1679 Wijnand Fockink,** Pijlsteeg 31, where they've already heard all the English jokes about their name. There's a series of liqueur bottles painted with portraits of all the city's mayors since 1591.

✔ **Smoke 'Em if You Got 'Em.** We officially can't condone this, but we also can't write about Amsterdam without mentioning the special class of "coffeehouses" in town where the drug of choice isn't the caffeine. The European Union is exerting increasing pressure, and the Netherlands is cracking down on drugs, but the country is still lenient with marijuana. Contrary to popular belief, weed *is* illegal here, though the police unofficially tolerate possession of a small amount for personal use — less than 5 grams (it used to be 30). These venerable establishments are allowed to sell small amounts of grass and hash — they even have marijuana menus! They can also sell joints (rolled with tobacco) and various hash products, coffee, tea, and juice, but no food. The most famous smoking coffee shop is **Bulldog,** whose main branch is at Leidseplein 15 (☎ 020-627-1908).

✔ **Is It Hot in Here? Spend an Afternoon in the Tropics**. Maybe because the Dutch winters are so cold and icy or because the Dutch Empire once had footholds in many of the world's warmest climes, this ethnographic museum focuses on life in the tropical corners of the globe. The **Tropenmuseum (☎ 020-568-8215)** investigates the indigenous cultures of the country's former colonies in India, Indonesia, and the Caribbean.

The best exhibits are set up as typical villages you can wander through. They are so realistic that you almost wonder where all the inhabitants went. This place may be a good bet when the kids' (or your own) interest in Dutch old masters starts flagging and something more casual is desired for a change of pace. It's in East Amsterdam on Linnaesstraat 2 at Mauritskade; take tram 9. It's open Monday through Friday 10:00 a.m. to 5:00 p.m., Saturday and Sunday noon to 5:00 p.m.; Admission is Dfl12.50 ($6.25) for adults, Dfl7.50 ($3.75) for children 17 and under.

✔ **Cycle around Amsterdam on Two Wheels.** The Dutch are some of the most avid bicyclists, probably because their country is so flat and bikable. There are 15 million in this country . . . and 12 million bikes. The streets are divided into lanes for cars, lanes for pedestrians, and lanes for bikes (each even has its own stoplights). Renting a bike is one of the best ways to explore Amsterdam away from the tram routes and major sights (quiet Sundays are best). The only hills will be the humps of the bridges over scenic canals. For rentals, try **Take a Bike,** Stationsplein 12-33 (☎ **020-624-8391**). Prices are Dfl8 ($4) per day, Dfl32 ($16) per week.

And on Your Left, the Cat Boat: Seeing Amsterdam by Guided Tour

Circle Tram 20 is a city-run hop-on/hop-off service with 30 stops and trams every 10 minutes from 9:00 a.m. to 7:00 p.m. Grab it at major junctures such as Centraal Station, the Damrack, Dam Square, Waterloopleine, Rembrandtplein, Leidseplein, Museumplein, and Westermarkt. You can use it with any regular public transport ticket, available at the tourist office or from the conductor at the back of the tram.

For a quick overview of town, take a three-hour bus tour for about Dfl45 ($22.50) from **Key Tours** (☎ **020-624-7304**), Dam 19; or **Holland International Excursions** (☎ **020-551-2800**), Dam 6. Even better, take a cruise on the canals.

Munich's Mike's Bike Tours, (☎ **020-622-7970;** Internet: www.mikesbiketours.com/amsterdam.html), has recently expanded to Amsterdam, with half-day tours that include a tool around the canals in town, and a ride outside the city to see windmills and a cheese farm and clog factory (touristy, but fun). The price is just 32DM ($17.80). Meet daily at 11:30 a.m. or 4:00 p.m. near the west entrance to the Rijksmuseum

And don't forget about touring Amsterdam from the canals' point of view; see "Cruising the Canals" under "More cool things to see & do in Amsterdam" above. Amsterdam's most innovative tour has to be the municipal Museumboot, **Prins Hendrikkade** (☎ **020-622-2181**), a boat that stops near 16 of the city's museums, including all of those mentioned in this chapter. The full-day fare — Dfl22 ($11) for adults, Dfl18

($9) under age 13 — includes discounts on admissions for some museums. It leaves every half an hour (every 45 minutes in winter).

Suggested One-, Two-, and Three-Day Itineraries

If you're pressed for time and prefer to organize your own tour, this section offers tips for building your own Amsterdam itinerary.

If you have one day

Start off the day early with a canal cruise at 9:00 a.m. Get to the **Rijksmuseum** when it opens at 10:00 a.m. and spend about 90 minutes enjoying the Rembrandts and Vermeers. Then pop down the block for another 45 minutes in the company of Holland's towering master modernist at the **Vincent van Gogh Museum.** Head to the **Pancake Bakery** for a quick canalside lunch then stroll up the street to pay your respects at the **Anne Frank House.**

Because Amsterdam attracts all types, I'll leave the late afternoon up to you: tour a few diamond factories, titillate at one of the sex museums, stroll the canals, or make the rounds of the brown cafes (or of the other kind of cafe). In the early evening take the requisite shocked spin through the Red Light district — before sunset if you can manage it; i.e.: before the seedy night elements come out, but while the ladies are putting their best, er, foot forward for the businessmen who stop by on their way home. Cap the day off with an Indonesian feast at **Kantjil en de Tiger.**

If you have two days

Start off Day One with the ol' canal cruise — the best intro to the charming side of Amsterdam money can buy. Head to the masterpieces in the Rijksmuseum next and spend two hours or so perusing the Old Masters. After lunch, pay homage to more modern masters at the nearby **Vincent van Gogh Museum and Stedelijk Museum of Modern Art.** In the early evening, do the **Red Light District** and follow it with a thoroughly Dutch dinner at **Restaurant d'Vijff Vlieghen.**

Begin Day Two indulging in a favorite Dutch pastime: Rent a bike and tool around on your own, or take one of Mike's excellent guided bike tours. Lunch at the **Pancake Bakery** before seeing the **Anne Frank House,** and then head across to the old part of town to see the Oude Kirk and the bizarre **Museum Amstelkring,** also known as "Our Lord in the Attic." Spend the early evening hopping between brown and gin cafes, then poke around the Leidseplein district for the best little Indonesian restaurant you can find for dinner.

If you have three days

Spend Days One and Two as outlined above and take Day Three to do either the recreated folk village of **Zaanse Schans** in the morning and **Haarlem** in the afternoon, or — especially if you're in town for the spring flower season — Haarlem in the morning followed by a drive, bike ride, or train trip through the flower-bedecked **Bloembollenstreek.** All are covered in the next section, "Traveling Beyond Amsterdam."

Traveling Beyond Amsterdam

Several interesting destinations are an easy day trip from Amsterdam — among them the tulip region near Haarlem, the traditional village of **Zaanse Schans,** and **the Vincent van Gogh Museum** in **Hoge Veluwe national park.**

The other Haarlem

Haarlem makes perhaps the most pleasant day trip from Amsterdam, offering a much more laid-back and less hectic version of a tidy Dutch city. Some great museums are there too.

Getting there

Every half hour or so a train makes the 20-minute jaunt from Amsterdam. The local **VVV tourist office** (☎ **023-616-1600;** Internet: www.noord-holland-toernis.nl) is just outside the station at Stationplein 1.

Seeing the sights

The town's pretty central square, Grote Markt, is anchored by the late Gothic church St. Bavokerk, better known as the **Grote Kerk.** Inside are artist Frans Hals's tombstone and a cannonball embedded in the wall during the Spanish siege of 1572 to 1573. It also houses one of the world's great organs, a 68-stop 5,068-pipe beauty built by Christian Müller from 1735 to 1738 — both Handel and a 10-year-old Mozart once came to play it. Mid-May to mid-October there are free organ recitals Tuesdays from 8:15 to 9:15 p.m. (also on Thursdays in July and August). Seventeenth-century shops and houses are nestled together like barnacles on the church's south side. These were built so they could be rented for additional income to help with the church's upkeep.

Haarlem's biggest attraction is the **Frans Hals Museum** (☎ **023-511-5775**), Groot Heiligeland 62, set up in the pensioner's home where the painter spent his last days in 1666. Frans Hals's works make up the bulk of the collections, but many Dutch painters from the sixteenth century to the present are represented as well. The works are all displayed in seventeenth- century-style rooms that often bear a striking resemblance to the settings in the works themselves. Open Monday through Saturday 11:00 a.m. to 5:00 p.m. and Sunday from 1:00 to 5:00 p.m., the admission is Dfl8 ($4) adults and Dfl3.50 ($1.75) for ages 10 to 17.

Where to stay and dine

The Hotel Carillon (☎ 023-531-0591) has clean Dfl130 ($65) doubles in the heart of town at Grote Markt 27. The boisterous, tavern—such as **Stadscafe** (☎ 023-532-5202) at Zijlstraat 57—has hearty Dutch food at great prices.

Touring the tulips

Tulips aren't even Dutch! They came to the Netherlands from Turkey in the 1590s and quickly became popular. By 1620, tulips gained popularity and growers couldn't keep up with the demand. By the year 1636, rare tulip bulbs were being sold for their weight in gold. Soon after, though, the floral market bottomed out in the Great Tulip Crash. Bulbs have come down in price a wee bit since then, and the Netherlands is still one of the world's largest producers of flowers.

The **Bloembollenstreek** is Amsterdam's bulb belt, home of the tulip. It's located between Haarlem and Leiden and stretches across a 19-mile strip of land. These lowlands along the North Sea are fields of gladioli, hyacinths, lilies, narcissi, daffodils, crocuses, irises, dahlias, and the mighty tulip for miles as far as the eye can see. January is when the earliest blooms burst into color, and the floral show doesn't slow down until the late-blooming lilies make their exit near the end of May. Mid-April, though, is the Time of the Tulip.

Getting there

Haarlem is just a quick 15-minute ride by train from Amsterdam. Buses run between Haarlem and Leiden to service the region.

Bus 172 heads to Aalsmeer from Amsterdam's Centraal train station.

Seeing the sights

While you're driving or biking through the countryside, which is rewarding in itself, there are a few stop-offs you'll want to make as well. **The Frans Roozen Nursery** (☎ 023-584-7245) in Vogelenzang is one of the first sights as you head south from Haarlem on the N206. Established in 1789, the free guided tours will give you an excellent introduction to the fine art of tulip husbandry. Open from 8:00 a.m. to 6:00 p.m. daily.

If you're here from March 26 to May 24, rush to the **Keukenhof Gardens** in Lisse (☎ 0252-465-555; Internet: www.keukenhof.nl), to see their 7,000,000-plus bulbs in full bloom over 80 acres. These are perhaps the top floral gardens on Earth. Open daily from 8 a.m. to 7:30 p.m., there are cafeterias on-site so you don't have to miss any of the surrounding chromatic spectacle. Take bus 54 from Leiden.

One of the bulb-field region's chief attractions is just six miles south of Amsterdam at the **flower auction** in Aalsmeer (☎ 0297-392-185). Seventeen million cut flowers daily (and 2 million other plants) are auctioned at a speedy pace (cut flowers especially are extremely perishable and must be moved quickly). As you watch from the visitors gallery, giant dials tick down rapidly from 100 to 1 — as the numbers count down, the price drops — and the first bidder to buzz in on that lot stops the clock at that price and gets the bouquet. Because there's only one bid, it's like a huge game of chicken. The auction runs Monday through Friday from 7:30 a.m. to 11:00 a.m. (try to show up before 9:00 a.m. for the best action).

Tilting at windmills

Luckily, progress doesn't mean loss of history. When the Dutch pave the way for progress, they also set aside space for preservation. As industrialization of the countryside north of Amsterdam started during the first half of the twentieth century, people realized that a way of life and mode of architecture was rapidly disappearing. In the late 1950s, dozens of local farms, houses, and windmills dating from that ever-popular seventeenth century were broken down, carted off, and reassembled into a kind of archetypal "traditional" village called Zaanse Schans, where the Dutch seventeenth century lives on.

Getting there

Zaanse Schans is about 10 miles northwest of Amsterdam, just above the town of Zaandam, to which there are numerous daily trains from Amsterdam (a 12-minute ride). The **Zaandam tourist office** (☎ 075-616- 2221) has information about the village.

Seeing the sights

Although **Zaanse Schans** (☎ 073-616-8218) is a little bit of a tourist trap, it's not just a sightseeing attraction — people actually live in most of the cottages and houses, doing their daily tasks in as much an early eighteenth-century way as possible. The grocery stores and the like are truly from a different era, and a few of the buildings are museums for the public, including the four working windmills. Short cruises on the river Zaan are also popular. The parts of the village for visitors are open April through October 10:00 a.m. to 5:00 p.m. daily (some exhibits are open in winter as well).

If you'd like to see some more impressive windmills, head 66 miles south of Amsterdam to the **Kinderdijk** region (it's below Rotterdam). Nineteen functioning, old-fashioned windmills built from 1722 to 1761 dot the landscape like sailboats, turning their 42-foot-long sails slowly in the wind on Saturdays from 1:30 p.m. to 5:30 p.m. in July and August. For the rest of the year, they just sit there looking picturesque. The visitor's mill is open to the public April through September, Monday through Saturday, 9:30 a.m. to 5:30 p.m. Take the train from Amsterdam's Centraal Station to Rotterdam, and then the metro to Zuidplein, and then bus 154.

Biking Hoge Veluwe and taking the number 12 to the Kröller Müller Museum

One of the Netherlands' top modern art museums and Europe's largest sculpture garden is the **Kröller Müller Museum.** It's set in the middle of **Hoge Veluwe,** a 13,750-acre national park of heath, woods, and sand dunes. This is my favorite Dutch excursion and can easily be done as a day trip from Amsterdam if you are an avid art lover.

Getting there

Trains scheduled twice hourly run from Amsterdam to Arnhem in 65 minutes. From Arnhem's station, hop on the no. 12 bus. It stops in the park both at the museum and at the visitors' center/cafeteria (☎ **0318-591-627**), where you can pick up maps of the park.

Before taking that bus in Arnhem, do some advance reconnoitering by popping into the city's **VVV tourist office** (☎ **0900-202-4075** or 026-442-6767) at Stationsplein 45 outside the station to pick up park info and maps.

Seeing the sights

Biking is the primary form of transportation in Hoge Veluwe park; grab a free white bike by any entrance or at the visitors' center — just drop it off before you leave. Under the visitor's center lies the **Museonder,** a series of displays and tunnels dedicated to underground ecology. As you bike through the calm, lush greenery of the park, you might catch glimpses of red deer, foxes, wild boar, or badgers, which is one reason that visitors flock to the modern **Kröller Müller Museum.** Many of its rooms have paintings from radically different artists and eras all side by side like wallpaper. There isn't enough wall space to display all 278 (!) van Gogh works, so they're rotated. Other featured artists include Picasso, Mondrian, Seurat, Monet, and Braque.

Works by Rodin, Oldenburg, Henry Moore, Barbara Hepworth, Mark di Suvero, and Lipchitz are featured in the 27-acre sculpture garden behind the museum. It's a great setting for sculpture. My favorite is Jean Dubuffet's enormous *Jardin d'Emaille,* an interactive artscape of the sculptor's patented white-with-black-lines raised above ground level, so you have to climb a set of stairs. This enables you to wander around on the art (which, when I was 11 years old, I thought was just a fantastic concept).

The museum is open Tuesday through Sunday 10:00 a.m. to 5:00 p.m. The park itself is open daily as follows: November through March 9:00 a.m. to 5:00 p.m., April 8:00 a.m. to 8:00 p.m., May 8:00 a.m. to 9:00 p.m., June through August 8:00 a.m. to 10:00 p.m., September 9:00 a.m. to 8:00 p.m., and October 9:00 a.m. to 7:00 p.m. Once you pay your admission to the park — Dfl8 ($4) for adults, Dfl4 ($2) for children ages 6 to 12 — the museum is free. Call the museum (☎ **0318-591-627**) for admission times, though the sculpture garden is closed November to March.

Chapter 16

Munich and Bavaria

*M*unich is Germany's center of intellect and industry, a lively European arts and culture hub, and the world capital of beer and classy cars (but don't mix those last two). Munich is also the gateway to the rustic, folklore-saturated Bavarian region. It is equally comfortable as a vibrant university town where the Nobel Prize–winning author Thomas Mann and Albert Einstein rank among the famed intelligentsia, and as an economic powerhouse, with cutting-edge industry surrounding it.

Each autumn, Munich is home to beer and food bashes, oompah bands, and old-fashioned good times during a month-long celebration called Oktoberfest. Munich's cultural events, theaters, and museums are sure to keep you busy for several days. (Don't try to it in one day, because you'll miss out on so much.)

Making Your Way to and around Munich

With one of the most modern airports in the world and one of the largest train stations in Europe, Munich's status as a major travel hub means that you'll have no trouble finding your way there.

Getting to Munich by air

The ultra-modern **Franz Joseph Strauss Airport** (☎ **089-9752-1313**) is 18 miles northeast of Munich. You can catch the S8 S-Bahn (light-rail train), which leaves the airport every 20 minutes, for the 40-minute trip to Munich (14.40DM/$8).

Getting to Munich by rail

Trains to Munich arrive at the high-tech **Hauptbahnhof train station** on the city's western edge. From here, the S-Bahn runs into the center of town.

For help or tickets, skip the lines and head to the private **EurAide** agency (www.euraide.de), staffed by English-speakers and geared toward helping railpass holders, selling tickets and supplements, and helping you plan rail journeys from Munich (Room 3 next to track 11). It's open June to October 3, daily 7:45 a.m. to noon and 1:00 to 6:00 p.m.; in winter, the hours are Monday to Friday 7:45 a.m. to noon and 1:00 to 4:45 p.m.

Getting around once you're in Munich

Munich was one of the first cities to close many of the streets in its Altstadt (old center) to cars, making getting around the inner city by foot both enjoyable and a necessity (not even trams are allowed). But buses, trams, and two light-rail systems (the **U-Bahn** and **S-Bahn**) are available to help you get around Greater Munich.

Buses, trams, S-Bahns, and U-Bahns all use the same **tickets,** which you buy at machines in S-Bahn/U-Bahn stations. The longer your trip, the more zones you'll cross, and the more you'll pay. One zone covers about two S-Bahn or U-Bahn stops or four bus or tram stops. If you have a Eurail pass, you can use it on the S-Bahn, so don't buy a separate ticket.

You'll may more for a **single ticket,** so always check the chart of stops posted on the machine and press the button for the number of zones it says you'll be riding. Brief trips (two train stops or four bus/tram stops) cost 1.80DM ($1); each full zone costs 3.60DM ($2).

You can save money by purchasing a **Streifenkarte (strip card),** which gives you ten strips to use over several rides for 15DM ($8.35). Fold over the ticket to the number of strips your journey "costs." Brief trips cost one strip, but each full zone costs two strips. Each time you stamp a set of strips, those are good for three hours and unlimited transfers, as long as you are headed in the same direction (in other words, it doesn't cover your return trip). You can also use it for multiple passengers — for two people to ride two zones, simply stamp four strips.

The **Tageskarte (day ticket)** is an even better deal. For 9DM ($5) you have unlimited access within the central zone for a full day (22DM/$12.20 for three days). For 18 DM/$10, you can have access to all of Greater Munich — a 50-mile radius. If you're traveling with your family, the **Day Partner Ticket** lets two adults and up to three kids ride for 13DM/$7.20 (33DM/$18.35 for three days).

By U-Bahn and S-Bahn (subway and light rail)

The **S-Bahn** is a state-run commuter train line that covers a wider area than the U-Bahn (and is often aboveground); the U-Bahn runs mostly underground as a city subway. In the center of Munich, they're both subways. The most important difference between the S-Bahn and the U-Bahn is that you can use your rail pass on the S-Bahn, but not on the U-Bahn. The major junctures of multiple lines are Hauptbahnhof, Karlsplatz, Marienplatz, Sendlingertor, and Odeonsplatz.

Most S-Bahn lines discussed in this chapter (S1 through S8) run the same east-west route through the city, and stop at Hauptbahnhof, Karlsplatz, Marienplatz, and Isartorplatz. The most useful of the U-Bahn lines (**U3** and **U6**) run north-south through the city center, and stop at Sendlingertor, Marienplatz, and Odeonsplatz before going to Schwabing.

By tram and bus

Trams and buses are great for getting to a few areas within the Altstadt and for traveling in Greater Munich, but they are less effective at getting you where you want to go in the center of town. The 19 tram runs along Maximilianstrasse and the northern part of the Altstadt before heading to Hauptbahnhof. The 52 and 56 buses putter around the Altstadt's southeastern corner.

By taxi

With Munich's efficient public transportation system, you shouldn't need to take a taxi — and at their steep prices, you probably won't want to. The initial charge is 5DM ($2.80) and then 2.20DM ($1.20) for each additional kilometer. You'll be charged an extra 1DM (55 cents) per bag for luggage. You can call a taxi to pick you up by dialing ☎ **089-21-610** or 089-19-410, but that'll cost you 2DM ($1.10) more for the convenience.

Discovering Munich: What You Need to Know

This section provides information that you'll need for the basic necessities of maximizing your money, as well as what you'll need in case of emergency.

The local dough

The German unit of currency is the Deutsch Mark (DM), divided into 100Pfennig. Roughly, $1 equals 1.80DM; or 1DM equals 55 cents. German coins include 1, 2, 5, 10, and 50Pfennig. Bills come in denominations of 5, 10, 20, 50, 100, 200, 500, and 1,000DM.

Where to get info after you arrive

Munich's main **tourist office** (☎ **089-2333-0300,** fax: 089-2333-0233; Internet: www.munich-tourist.de) is at Hauptbahnhof (the main train station) in a storefront to the left of the main entrance. The hours are Monday to Saturday, 10:00 a.m. to 8:00 p.m. and Sunday 10:00 a.m. to 6:00 p.m. You'll find getting in touch with someone easiest from Monday to Thursday 10:00 a.m. to 3:00 p.m. and Friday 10:00 a.m. to 12:30 p.m. You can also find a tourist office branch at the airport and an office downtown in the Rathaus at Marienplatz 2, open Monday to Friday 10:00 a.m. to 8:00 p.m. and Saturday 10:00 a.m. to 4:00 p.m.

Where to go in a pinch

While visiting Munich, you may be targeted for petty crimes such as purse-snatching and pickpocketing. You probably don't have to worry about falling victim to violent crimes, but you should be careful in pop- ular areas such as the Marienplatz and around the Hauptbahnhof, espe- cially at night.

In case of emergency, keep the following list of references handy:

✔ **Emergency:** Dial ☎ **110** to call the police. For an ambulance, dial ☎ **089-19-222** or 089-557-755. Call ☎ **112** to report a fire.

✔ **Doctors/Hospitals:** For a list of English-speaking physicians and dentists, contact the U.S. Consulate or ask an international phar- macy (*apotheke*) for recommendations. If you have a medical emergency on a weekend or in the evenings 8:00 p.m. to 1:00 a.m., you can call ☎ **089-551-771** for **Notfallpraxis, Elisenstrasse 3,** which staffs doctors of varied specialties.

✔ **Pharmacies: Apotheke** in Munich rotate the duty of staying open nights and weekends. For the location of the nearest 24-hour pharmacy, check the sign in the window of any pharmacy or call ☎ **089-594-475. The International Ludwigs-Apotheke,** Neuhauser Strasse 11 (☎ **089-260-3021**), is open Monday to Friday 9:00 a.m. to 8:00 p.m. and Saturday 9:00 a.m. to 4:00 p.m.

Staying in touch

Need to wire home for more beer money? Can't continue without checking your e-mail? The following information will help keep you in touch while you're touring Munich.

✔ **American Express:** You'll find American Express offices at Promenadeplatz 6 (☎ **089-2280-1465** or 089-290-9000), and Kaufingerstrasse 24 (☎ **089-2280-1387**). They are open Monday to Friday 9:00 a.m. to 5:30 p.m. and Saturday 9:30 a.m. to 12:30 p.m.

✔ **Consulate:** You may contact the U.S. Consulate at Königstrasse 5 (☎ **089-28-880**).

✔ **Internet Access and Cyber Cafes: The Internet-Cafe** (www.icafe. spacenet.de) is a cafe/pizzeria with two locations, Nymphenburger Str. 145 next to Rotkreuzplatz (☎ **089-129-1120;** U-Bahn: U1), and **Altheimer Eck 12,** between Marienplatz and Karlsplatz-Stachus (☎ **089-260-7815**). Their tack is a bit different: After you order something to eat or drink, Web surfing is free. Sodas run 6DM ($3.35); both of the places listed here are open 11:00 a.m. to 4:00 a.m.

✔ **Mail:** A large post office is on Bahnhofplatz, across from the train station, and is open Monday to Friday 7:00 a.m. to 8:00 p.m., Saturday 8:00 a.m. to 4:00 p.m., and Sunday 9:00 a.m. to 3:00 p.m.

✔ **Telephone:** Germany's country code is **49.** The city code for Munich is **089.** If you're calling Munich from outside Germany, you can drop the city code's initial zero. In other words, to call Munich from the United States, dial **011-49-89** and the number.

A local call in Munich costs 30Pfennig (15 cents) for the first three minutes. If you're calling from a pay phone, just deposit more coins as needed. Some phones in Germany accept only phone cards, which are available from newsstands in 12DM ($6.65) and 50DM ($27.80) denominations. To charge your call to a **calling card,** you can call **AT&T** (☎ **0800-225-5288**), **MCI** (☎ **0800-888-8000**), or **Sprint** (☎ **0800-888-0013**). To call the United States direct, dial **001** followed by the area code and phone number.

✔ **Transit Info:** For public transportation information, call ☎ **089-210-330** or visit www.mvv-muenchen.de. For S-Bahn information, call ☎ **089-557-575.** For train info, call ☎ **089-19-419.**

Touring Munich by Neighborhood

Munich's sights are not confined to its **Altstadt,** or old center — as in many European cities. Munich's cultural attractions are spread across town. The tangled streets of the Altstadt are at the core of the city, bearing a combination of medieval and contemporary structures that have been restored or replaced after World War II bombing.

Marienplatz is the heart of the city, with its bustling square and a light-rail juncture underneath. **Neuhauserstrasse** is one of the city's main east-west routes and begins at **Karlsplatz** (a few blocks east of **Hauptbahnhof** station). This street changes names to **Kaufingerstrasse** and beyond Marienplatz, it becomes **Im Tal.** This street leads east into **Isartorplatz,** on the Altstadt's eastern edge. Just a few blocks away is the **Isar River,** which borders the eastern edge of the city.

Maximilianstrasse is the other main east-west route and is filled with art galleries and designer boutiques. This fashionable street runs from the Isar River west into the Altstadt and ends at **Max Joseph Platz —**

the location of the **Residenz** royal palace — just a few blocks north of Marienplatz (see "Munich's top sights," later). **Residenzstrasse** runs from Max Joseph Platz to **Odeonsplatz.** Odeonsplatz is an elegant, if heavily trafficked, square surrounded by neo-Renaissance buildings that marks the Altstadt's northern edge.

From Odeonsplatz, **Ludwigstrasse/Leopoldstrasse** heads due north toward the University district and **Schwabing,** a trendy quarter filled with restaurants and cafes. **Prinzregentenstrasse** runs east-west just north of the city center. It passes along the southern border of the **Englischer Garten** park and is lined with several museums (including the Bavarian National Museum). An area of neoclassical buildings houses more museums (including both the **Neue and Alte Pinakotheks**) to the northwest corner of the Altstadt. You can reach this area via **Briennerstrasse,** which heads west out of Odeonsplatz.

Staying in Munich

Munich has a healthy supply of hotel rooms that serve a large tourist trade, as well as a commercial and industrial trade. Unfortunately, year-round demand keeps prices high.

Rates in Munich rise when a trade fair is in town, during the summer tourist season, and during Oktoberfest. You'll want to book a room well in advance for the city's big keg party, or you'll pay high prices or end up a long way from the center — or both.

If you arrive in town without a hotel, the tourist offices at the train station and at the airport will land you a room. However, you must show up in person; neither will book a room over the phone.

Munich's top hotels

An der Oper
$$ Near the Residenz

An der Oper is a great value right in the heart of town, near major sights, shopping, theater, and the Hofbräuhaus. Rooms are modern and basic, with sitting areas and little touches like mini-chandeliers instead of bed-side lamps. Most rooms are midsized to large. The restaurant serves a mix of Bavarian and French cuisine.

Falkenturmstrasse 11 (just off Maximilianstrasse, near the Residenz end). ☎ *089-290-0270. Fax: 089-2900-2729. Tram: 19. Rates: 270–340DM ($150–188.90) double. AE, MC, V.*

Hotel Am Markt

$ Near Marienplatz

You may have to hunt to find this budget favorite — it's near Munich's outdoor market. The owner keeps the place spotless, welcoming all sorts of visitors from families to students to stars of stage and opera. Rooms are spare but functional, small but comfortable; the price reflects the plumbing, not the season. (This is one place that doesn't raise prices for Oktoberfest.)

Heiliggeiststrasse 6 (a tiny alley between the Tal and the Viktualienmarkt). ☎ *089-225-014. Fax: 089-224-017. U-Bahn or S-Bahn: Marienplatz. Walk under the arches of the Altes Rathaus; the hotel is down the first right turn off the Tal. Rates: 150–170DM ($83.35–94.45) double with bathroom, 110–116DM ($61.10–64.45) double without bathroom. No credit cards.*

Kempinski Hotel Vier Jahreszeiten

$$$$ Near the Residenz

You may have to splurge at this grand old hotel, built in 1858 for Maximilian II to accommodate the overflow of guests from his nearby Residenz. But the extra cash is worth it if you appreciate discreet service, constantly renovated rooms, a rooftop pool, a bevy of fine restaurants, boutique shops, posh accommodations, and the proximity of shopping, theater, and galleries. The least expensive rooms are in the uninteresting 1972 wing; if you're splurging anyway, go for the modern rooms in the original building.

Maximilianstrasse 17 (three blocks from the Residenz and hard to miss). ☎ *800-426-3135 in the United States; 089-21-250 in Germany. Fax: 089-2125-2000. E-mail: reservation.* hvj@kempinksi.com. *Tram: 19. Rates: 520–820DM ($288.90–455.55) double. AE, DC, MC, V.*

Platzl

$$$ Between Marienplatz and the Residenz

You're just steps away from all the sights of the Altstadt when you stay at this hotel. Rooms are midsized but cozy, outfitted with rich fabrics and new furnishings. The hotel is owned by a brewery, and the legendary Hofbräuhaus is across the street. You can just stumble home after a night of carousing. A folk theater is next door for your sober entertainment.

Sparkassenstrasse 10 (at the corner with Munzstrasse). ☎ *089-237-030. Fax: 089-2370-3800. Internet:* www.platzl.de. *U-Bahn: U3 or U6 to Marienplatz. Rates: 320–440DM ($177.80–244.45) double. AE, DC, MC, V.*

Accommodations, Dining & Attractions in Munich

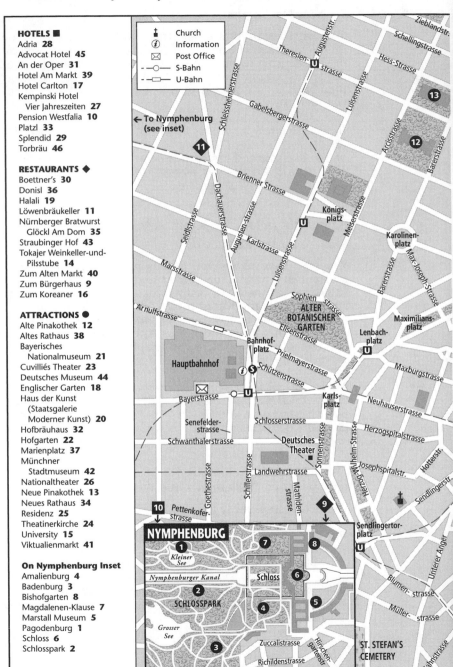

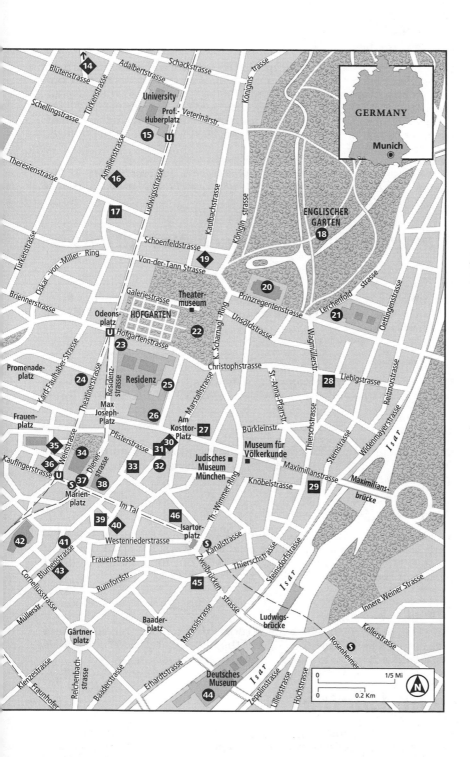

Splendid

$$ Near the Isar

You'll find a great value here in an Old World hotel with Oriental carpets, chandeliers, and antiques in the public rooms and bedrooms that are out-fitted in neo-Bavarian baroque country style. Splendid is located just out-side of the Altstadt (with free parking, no less), near the river, and close to several museums. You can get an inexpensive room without a bath (there's one just down the hall), and breakfast is served on the trellised patio in summer.

Maximilianstrasse 54 (1 block before the Maximilian Bridge over the Isar). ☎ *089-296-606. Fax: 089-291-3176. U-Bahn: U4, U5. Tram: 19, 20. Rates: 210–320DM ($116.65–177.80) double. AE, DC, MC, V.*

Munich's runner-up accommodations

Adria

$$ Adria is a stylishly modern place triangulated between the Isar River, the Englisher Garten, and the old center. *Liebigstrasse 8a.* ☎ *089- 293-081. Fax: 089-227-015.*

Advocat Hotel

$$ This minimalist contemporary hotel sits comfortably between Isartorplatz and the river. Baaderstrasse 1. ☎ *089-216-310. Fax: 089-216-3190.*

Hotel Carlton

$$ You'll enjoy the neo-baroque comfort of this hotel on the edge of trendy Schwabing, very near Munich's art museums. Fürstenstrasse 12. ☎ *089-282-061. Fax: 089-284-391.*

Pension Westfalia

$ This cozy little guesthouse is tucked away overlooking the Englisher Garten. It's a bit of a walk from the Altstadt, but you'll find it a wonderful escape (and inexpensive, especially if you opt for a bathless room). Mozartstrasse 23. ☎ *089-530-3777. Fax: 089-543-9120.*

Torbräu

$$$ This place has basic, modern rooms with a fifteenth-century pedi-gree, and it's just inside the edge of the Altstadt. Tal 41. ☎ *089-225-016. Fax: 089-225-019.*

Dining in Munich

The primary food groups in Munich are sausage, beer, salted white radishes, and pretzels, so don't even think about dieting while you're here. Sausages (or *wurstel,* to the natives) come in many shapes, sizes, and stuffings. Look for these items on any menu: bratwurst (finger-sized seasoned pork), frankfurter (the forerunner of hot dogs, but more appetizing), blütwurst (blood sausage), leberwurst (liver), and, Munich's specialty, weisswurst (veal, calf brains, and spleen, spiced to mild deliciousness and boiled). The proper way to eat weisswurst is to cut it in half, dip the cut end in mustard, and suck the filling out of the casing in one fell slurp.

Another word you'll see on menus is *knödel,* which means dumpling. Knödel may be made of *semmel* (bread), *leber* (liver), or *kartoffel* (potato). You can usually get these specialties in a beer hall tavern, where people sit communally at big tables. The outdoor *biergarten* is a wonderful Munich tradition. For more information on both, see "More cool things to see and do in Munich."

Now about that beer. Munich is one of the world's beer capitals, and you'll want to raise toast after toast of light beer (light refers to the color, not the calories). You can get light beer in a giant liter-sized mug called *ein Mass.* At Oktoberfest tents, if you order *ein Bier,* you'll usually get a half-liter; if you want the giant one, you'll need to order it by name.

Munich beer types include: *weissbier* (made with wheat); *pils* (ale); *dunklesbier, bock,* or *dopplebock* (all dark beers); and the beer-and-lemonade spritzer called *radlermass.* All beers are made under the strictest quality guidelines and almost never contain preservatives. (Germans drink it so quickly, there's no need for preservatives.) *Helles* means light-colored beer; *dunkles* is dark beer.

Munich's top restaurants

Donisl

$ On Marienplatz   BAVARIAN/INTERNATIONAL

Munich's oldest beer hall has summer tables outside and skylit, pine-panelled galleries inside. The Bavarian cuisine menu features the traditional weisswurst; but the restaurant also serves specials that draw from many culinary traditions (when the chef offers duck, dive for it). An accordion player makes it feel that much more Bavarian.

Weinstrasse 1 (just above Marienplatz). ☎ *089-220-184. Reservations recommended. U-Bahn or S-Bahn: Marienplatz. Main courses: 11.95DM ($6.65). AE, DC, MC, V. Open: Lunch and dinner daily.*

Halali

$$$ North of the Residenz   FINA BAVARIAN

Refined, but still traditionally Bavarian, Halali features a candlelit dining room with a few dozen trophy antlers. It serves traditional Bavarian dishes — blütwurst, venison, and other game — but with delicate flavors and attractive presentations. Red wine, not beer, is the beverage of choice in this upscale eatery.

Schönfeldstrasse 22 (three long blocks north of Odeonsplatz). ☎ 089-285-909. Reservations required. U-Bahn: Odeonsplatz. Main courses: 29–39DM ($16.10–21.65). Fixed-price menus: Lunch 37DM ($20.55); dinner 85DM ($47.20). AE, MC, V. Open: Lunch and dinner Mon–Fri, dinner Sat.

Nürnberger Bratwurst Glöckl Am Dom
$$ Near Marienplatz   BAVARIAN

This place is my choice for best traditional Munich beer-hall grub. You can't get any more Bavarian than rustic dark wood tables and carved chairs and tin plates full of wurstel. Since 1893, this place has served up the finger-sized sausage specialty of nearby Nürnburg. Get the 21.50DM ($11.95) assortment platter for a sampling of several wursts. The platter, a pretzel, and a tankard of Augustiner Bollbier or Tucher Weissbier make the perfect meal.

Frauenplatz 9 (off the back end of the cathedral). ☎ 089-295-264. Reservations suggested. U-Bahn or S-Bahn: Marienplatz. Main courses: 10.20–34.50DM ($5.65–19.15). No credit cards. Open: Lunch and dinner daily.

Zum Alten Markt
$$$$ Near Marienplatz   BAVARIAN/INTERNATIONAL

It's a hole-in-the-wall, but the atmosphere and the incredible menu are worth the trip. Try the chef's specialty of black truffle tortellini in a cream sauce or the *tafelspitz,* an Austro-Bavaria's boiled beef dish that was the favorite of Emperor Franz Josef.

Am Viktualienmarkt, Dreifaltigkeitsplatz 3 (on the city market square). ☎ 089-299-995. Reservations recommended. U-Bahn or S-Bahn: Marienplatz. Bus: 52. Main courses: 23.50–33.50DM ($13.05–18.60). Fixed-price menu: 69DM ($38.35). No credit cards. Open: Lunch and dinner Mon–Sat.

Zum Bürgerhaus
$$$ South of Hauptbahnhof   ALPINE

One of the few Munich restaurants to survive World War II bombings, this place retains a cozy, wood-panelled countryside charm. The cuisine is uniquely pan-Alpine, with specialties that include venison in red wine, noodles in a herbed cream/mushroom sauce, lamb with rosemary, and *Burgerhaus Pfanne,* a pan-fried mix of turkey, veal, and pork.

Pettenkoferstrasse 1 (just outside the southwest edge of the Altstadt). ☎ 089-597-909. Reservations recommended. U-Bahn or S-Bahn: Sendlinger Tor Platz. Bus: 18, 20, 21, 27, 31, 56. Main courses: 18.50–31.50DM ($10.30–17.50). AE, MC, V. Open: Lunch and dinner Mon–Fri, dinner Sat.

Munich's runner-up restaurants

Boettner's

$$$$ This place serves inspired international cuisine and is the still the hottest restaurant in town, despite its recent move (well, it did take the woody interior and refined service with it). *Boettnerstrasse 9, off Platzl square just north of the Hofbräuhaus.* ☎ *089-221-210.*

Löwenbräukeller

$ This fine beer hall is far enough from the center to keep away most of the tourists (which means the locals still patronize it in droves). The beer garden along the side is perfect on a warm day. *Nymphenburgerstrasse 2.* ☎ *089-526-021.*

Straubinger Hof

$$-$$$ This Paulaner-brand brew hall serves up platters of würstel, cheese, and even a mean Tafelspitz. *Blumenstrasse 5.* ☎ *089-260-8444.*

Tokajer Weinkeller-und-Pilsstube

$$ This place serves scrumptious, inexpensive Hungarian dishes heavily laden with pepper and paprika, and Hungarian ex-pats are more likely to drink a Danube red wine than beer. *Belgradestrasse 61.* ☎ *089-308-6825.*

Zum Koreaner

$ You'll find this excellent and devastatingly cheap Korean spot in a residential neighborhood just a few blocks north of Odeonsplatz. *Amalienstrasse 46.* ☎ *089-283-115.*

Exploring Munich

The **Munich Welcome Card** costs 12DM ($6.65) for one day, 29DM ($16.10) for three days (or 42DM/$23.35 for a Partner Card for two), and allows you free transportation on train, bus, and tram routes within the city center, plus small discounts (around 30 percent) on some sights, including the Residenz Museum and Schatzkammer, the Deutschesmuseum, St. Peter's Tower, and Schloss Nymphemburg. You can buy it at tourist offices or most hotels.

You can get a two-day **combined ticket** for 12DM ($6.65) adults, 8DM ($4.45) students and seniors, that gets you into both the **Alte and Neue Pinakotek,** as well as the **Staatsgalerie** of twentieth-century art (Prinzregentenstrasse 1; ☎ 089-2112-7137) and the **Shack-Galerie** of nineteenth-century German painting (Prinzregentenstrasse 9; ☎ 089-2380-5224).

Munich's top sights

Marienplatz

In the center of Munich is the lively, cafe-lined Marienplatz, home to street performers and the daily bustle of the city. This city square is bounded along its long north side by the pinnacles and tracery of the nineteenth-century Neues Rathaus, done in neo-gothic style. The clock on this town hall is equipped with a bi-level glockenspiel, the fourth largest in Europe, whose mechanical jousting show plays out daily at 11:00 a.m. and noon (and at 5:00 p.m. in summer).

St. Peter's Church is on the southeast corner of the square, with a 300-foot tower that you can climb for a small fee. You'll be rewarded with excellent city views that reach the Alps on clear days.

Residenz Palace

The official residence of Bavarian royalty is a rambling palace that was started in 1385 and added on to until World War I. A medieval merchant family, the Wittlesbachs, rose to power in Bavaria in 1180 and didn't relinquish power until revolutionaries came banging at the Residenz front door in 1918 — making them, by a long shot, Europe's longest-lasting dynasty.

You'll want to see the Residenz Museum, the Treasure House, and the Cuvilliés Theater. To see all the details, you have to take both a morning and an afternoon tour, but you can enjoy the ornate splendors on your own in just a couple of hours.

In the Residenz Museum, 120 rooms of Wittlesbach history and furnishings, you'll want to see the Ancestor's Gallery (1728–1730), a royal photo album of oil portraits set into the gilded stucco walls of a long hallway; and the huge Renaissance Hall of Antiquities, covered with sixteenth- and seventeenth-century frescoes. Don't miss Maximilian I's Reiche Kappelle, a closet-sized chapel featuring inlaid marble, gilding, and ivory carvings. The Residenz is so big that they open separate sets of rooms in the morning (10:00 a.m. to 2:30 p.m. for Circular Tour I) and the afternoon (12:30 to 4:00 p.m. for Circular Tour II).

The Bavarian crown jewels, some dating back to a.d. 1000, are kept in the Schatzkammer (Treasure House), but the greatest treasure is the gold St. George Slaying the Dragon (1590). It's a wonder the saint, encumbered by all those diamonds, rubies, sapphires, and other gems, ever managed to slay the emerald beast.

Around the corner is the beautiful Cuvilliés Theater (☎ **089-2185-1940**). It was named after its architect, a former court jester who overcame eighteenth-century prejudices at his dwarfism, won the patronage of the Wittlesbachs, and became one of southern Germany's most important architects. Summer concerts and opera help you enjoy the setting, which premiered Mozart's *Idomeneo* in 1781.

Max Joseph Platz 3. ☎ 089-290-671. U-Bahn: U3, U5, U6 to Odeonsplatz. Open: Museum and Treasure House, Tues–Sun 10:00 a.m.–4:30 p.m.; Cuvilliés-Theater, Mon–Sat 2:00–5:00 p.m., Sun 10:00–5:00 p.m. (except when rehearsing or setting stage for a production). Admission: Museum and Treasure House, each 7DM ($3.90) adults, 5DM ($2.80) students and seniors, or a combined ticket to both for 12DM ($6.65) adults, 8DM ($4.45) students and seniors; Cuvilliés Theater, 3DM ($1.65) adults, 2DM ($1.10) students and seniors. Kids under 15 are free at both.

Alte Pinakothek (Old Art Museum)

Reopened in 1998 after a long renovation, the Alte Pinakothek is no Louvre or Uffizi, but its rich collection of fourteenth- to nineteenth-century works is well worth an hour or three of your time. You'll find paintings by Italian Renaissance artists Giotto, Filippo Lippi, Botticelli, Perugino, Signorelli, Leonardo da Vinci *(Madonna and Child),* Raphael *(Holy Family* and a couple of versions of *Madonna and Child),* Titian *(Christ with the Crown of Thorns* is one of his most mature works), and Tintoretto. It also has several works by Rubens and some Spanish pieces by El Greco, Ribera, Velasquez, and Murillo.

As you might expect, the Dutch and Germans are very well-represented. Roger van de Weyden's works are numerous, including the huge *St. Colombia Altarpiece;* loads of Rembrandts and Van Dycks grace the walls; and a host of good Germanic altarpiece paintings by maestros of the mid-fifteenth to mid-sixteenth centuries.

Albrecht Dürer's *Self Portrait* (circa 1500) is the centerpiece of the collection. Many artists in the past had painted themselves into the background or crowds in large works as a kind of signature, but Dürer was the first to make himself, the artist, the star of the show. Full frontal portraiture had been used only to portray Christ prior to this self-portrait.

Barerstrasse 27 (off Theresienstrasse, several long blocks northwest of city center). ☎ 089-2380-5216. U-Bahn: U2 to Königsplatz. Tram: 27. Bus: 53. Open: Wed and Fri–Sun 10:00 a.m.–5:00 p.m., Tues and Thurs 10:00 a.m.–8:00 p.m. Admission: 7DM ($3.90) adults, 4DM ($2.20) students and seniors. Sun free.

Neue Pinakothek (New Art Museum)

Across from the Altes Pinakothek, the Neue Pinakothek covers the late eighteenth to mid-twentieth centuries with the likes of Gainsborough, Goya, Delacroix, Manet, Monet, Degas, Cézanne, van Gogh, Gustav Klimt, Max Beckmann, and Edvard Munch. An amusing section displays works by the "Nazarenes," a group of early nineteenth-century German artists trying their darndest to paint like fifteenth-century Italian artists. You can have fun with this collection, but the older set of paintings is a better choice if you're on a tight schedule. Visit the Alte Pinakothek first, and then see if you have an hour or so left for these galleries.

Barerstrasse 29 (off Theresienstrasse, several long blocks northwest of city center). ☎ 089-2380-5195. U-Bahn: U2 to Königsplatz. Tram: 27. Bus: 53. Open: Tues and Thurs–Sun 10:00 a.m.–5:00 p.m., Wed 10:00 a.m.– 8:00 p.m. Admission: 7DM ($3.90) adults, 4DM ($2.20) students and seniors. Sun free.

Bayerisches Nationalmuseum (Bavarian National Museum)

The National Museum has an impressive collection of medieval church art, including statuary, altarpieces, and carved ivories (look for the a.d. 400 Munich Ivory showing the Lamentation and Christ ascending into Heaven). The Bavarian sculptor Tilman Riemenschneider carved in the early sixteenth century and often managed to fashion the most eloquent, expressive figures out of plain, unpainted wood.

This museum's hodgepodge collection features armor from the sixteenth to eighteenth centuries, baroque porcelain confections, delicate stained-glass panels, and elaborate Christmas crèches from Germany, Austria, Italy, and Moravia. The Weaver's Guild Room is painted with stories from the Bible and the life of Alexander the Great.

Prinzregentenstrasse 3 (off the southeast corner of the Englischer Garten, north-east of the city center). ☎ *089-211-241. U-Bahn: U4, U5 to Lehel. Tram: 20. Bus: 53. Open: Tues–Sun 9:30 a.m.–5:00 p.m. Admission: 3DM ($1.65) adults, 1.50DM (80¢) students and seniors. Sun free.*

Deutsches Museum (German Museum of Science and Technology)

If you have kids, you don't want to miss this fantastic see-and-touch science museum. The placards are in German and English, and the rooms cover industrial machinery, the digging of tunnels, astronautics, computers and microelectronics, textiles, mining, and electricity in wonderful detail.

You'll especially enjoy the High Voltage demonstrations (11:00 a.m., 2:00 p.m., and 4:00 p.m. daily) — they actually produce lightning. A hangar filled with historic aircraft and a collection of venerable cars, including the very first automobile (an 1886 Benz), are not to be missed if you're interested in transportation. You'll also find the first diesel engine (1897), the first electric dynamo (1866), and the lab bench at which Hahn and Strassmann first split the atom (1938).

The Deutsches Museum is one of the few museums in Munich that is open on Monday.

Museuminsel 1 (on an island in the Isar river). ☎ *089-21-791. Internet: www.deutsches-museum.de. U-Bahn: U1, U2 to Fraunhoferstrasse. S-Bahn: Isartorplatz. Tram: 18. Open: Daily 9:00 a.m.–5:00 p.m. Admission: 10DM ($5.55) adults, 4DM ($2.20) students; 6DM ($3.30) seniors; kids under 6 free.*

Schloss Nymphenburg

The Wittelsbachs spent summers in a sophisticated countryside palace, Schloss Nymphenburg, named after the nymphs frescoed in its main entrance hall (concerts are presented here in summer). This place started as a modest Italianate villa in 1664 and was changed radically over the next 150 years, including a change of face to French baroque.

A network of pavilions at the palace provides interesting architecture and artwork. The south pavilion (where Queen Caroline resides) features Ludwig I's Gallery of Beauties — an arrangement of portraits commissioned by the king of the 36 most beautiful women in the realm. In the Mastrallmuseum, you find a collection of royal coaches including King Ludwig II's wedding coach, entirely gilded and encrusted with rococo stucco swirls.

Nymphenburg has a park of more than 500 acres of grassy lawns, English-style gardens, canals, and pavilions. Visit Electress Amalia's Amalienburg pavilion, which features extravagant rococo inside, and the Badenburg on the lake, with its frescoed-ceilinged bath in the basement. The pseudo-Chinese Pagodenburg and the religious retreat Magdalenenklause also offer an enjoyable visit.

Schloss Nymphenburg 1 (three miles west of the city center). ☎ 089-179-080. U-Bahn: U1 to Rotkreuzplatz, then tram 12 toward Amalienburgstrasse. Bus: 41. Open: Hours are very complicated, so give or take an hour for the following: Apr–Sept, Tues–Sun 9:00 a.m.–12:30 p.m. and 1:30–5 p.m. (Oct–Mar, it closes at 4 p.m.) Admission: Full admission 11DM ($6.10) adults, 8DM ($4.45) students and seniors; limited admission (Schloss, Amalienburg, Marstallmuseum) 8DM ($4.45) adults, 6DM ($3.35) students and seniors; Amalienburg and Badenburg only, 3DM ($1.65) adults, 2DM ($1.10) students and seniors; Schloss only, 5DM ($2.80) adults, 4DM ($2.20) students and seniors.

More cool things to see and do in Munich

You'll find plenty of ways to enjoy beer, the great outdoors, and more beer in Munich.

- ✔ **Eat lunch at a biergarten.** Bring your own food, and order huge mugs of beer. Biergartens are generally open 10:00 a.m. to 10:00 p.m. or midnight. They usually offer simple sandwiches as well, and pretzels and other snacks are always available. Try these biergartens: the **Biergarten Chinesischer Turm** (☎ 089-95-028) in the heart of the Englischer Garten Park under the shade of a Chinese pagoda; the **Augustinerkeller** (☎ 089-594-393) at Arnulfstrasse 52, several long blocks past Hauptbahnhof; and the **Hirschgarten** (☎ 089-172-591), in the middle of Nymphenburg Park, the world's largest beer garden (it can seat 8,000).

- ✔ **Watch an entire city drink itself into a stupor at Oktoberfest.** For the better part of a month, tens of thousands of people do nothing but party medieval-style, listening to oompah bands, roasting whole oxen on spits, and drinking more than 5 million liters of beer. Oktoberfest (www.munich-tourist.de/english/o.htm) is the world's ultimate keg party. It started with the celebrations for Prince Ludwig's marriage to Princess Therese in 1810, and the locals enjoyed themselves so much that they made it an annual event.

The name is a bit misleading, because the first weekend in October is the end of the festivities — the fun starts about two weeks before the end of September. If you're feeling the effect of too much partying, you can lie on a cushion in a "recovery tent" and rest to zither music. The action centers on the Theresienwiese park fairgrounds, southwest of Hauptbahnhof, but the whole city has a distinct party air (just follow the smell of the beer). You must reserve a hotel room months in advance; call the tourist office to determine the exact dates of this year's festival.

✔ **Spend an afternoon in the Englischer Garten.** Munich's Englischer Garten (named after a British ex-pat who first devised the park) stretches for three miles along the west bank of the Isar River. Here, you can enjoy a beer under a faux Chinese pagoda or just enjoy the shady trees.

The park features beer gardens, trees, grassy lawns, bicycle paths, and streams and lakes where you can swim. Around the Eisbach, some people (mostly men) sunbathe in the nude, and near the park's southern entrance, just behind the Haus der Kunst on Prinzregentenstrasse, you'll see a Japanese teahouse in the middle of a small lake. Traditional Japanese tea service is available the second and fourth weekends of each month from April to October at 3:00 p.m., 4:00 p.m., and 5:00 p.m. (Sunday also at 2:00 p.m.).

And On Your Left, More Beer: Seeing Munich by Guided Tour

You've got two choices for orientation bus tours. The **Stadtrundfahrt Blue Bus** is a straightforward affair — just hop on in front of Hauptbahnhof and buy your 17DM ($9.45) ticket onboard. The hour-long tour is delivered in eight languages; departures are at 10:00 a.m., 11:00 a.m., noon, 1:00 p.m., 2:00 p.m., 3:00 p.m., and 4:00 p.m. daily.

Panorama Tours (% 089-5502-8995), Arnulfstraase 8, with tours leaving from Bahnhofplatz, at Herties Department Store, also offers an hour-long city highlights bus tour for 17DM ($9.45), daily at 10:00 a.m., 11:00 a.m., 11:30 a.m., noon, 1:00 p.m., 2:30 p.m., 3:00 p.m., and 4:00 p.m. This tour company also offers 2½-hour, 30DM ($16.65) tours that, in addition to the city orientation tour, spend some time exploring a single site. One visits the Olympic Area where you can climb its 960-foot Olympic Tower (10:00 a.m. and 2:30 p.m.); another spends time in the Alte Pinakothek (10:00 a.m.); and a third heads to the Schloss Nymphenburg (2:30 p.m.).

But perhaps the most popular way to see town is with the native English-speaking ex-pats at **Mike's Bike Tours** (☎ 089-651-4275 or 0172-852-0660; Internet: www.bavaria.com/mike). Mike's offers four-hour, 33DM ($18.35) spins around the sights of central Munich (including 45 minutes in a beer garden) between 11:30 a.m. and 4:00 p.m. daily (September 19 to October, at 12:30 p.m. only). From June to August 16, they also run extended, six-hour, 43DM ($23.90) tours daily at 12:30 p.m. that go to Schloss Nyphenburg and the Olympic Park. All tours meet under the tower of the Altes Rathaus on Marienplatz.

Suggested One-, Two-, and Three-Day Itineraries

If you have one day

Start the day off with a tour of the Residenz, the most impressive downtown palace in Europe. Take in the Old Masters paintings in the Alte Pinakothek before moseying on down to Marienplatz around noon to take in the clock tower show and grab a late lunch in a beer hall or (if it's summer) the biergarten in the middle of the Viktualienmarkt.

Enjoy the displays in the Bayerisches Nationalmuseum after lunch, and then set off for what everyone really comes to Munich for: drinking enormous tankards of beer. Have dinner downstairs in Nürnberger Bratwurst Glöckl Am Dom — or just nibble on würstel as you crawl from beer hall to beer hall.

If you have two days

Spend Day One as above, and then on the morning of Day Two, head out to Schloss Nymphenburg for more royal splendor. In the late afternoon, stroll the Englischer Garten (look for the modern art galleries that ring its southern edge), or investigate the scientific wonders of the Deutsches Museum.

If you have three days

Spend Days One and Two as above. On the morning of Day Three, head out of town for another excursion, either to the somber concentration camp museum at Dachau, or to the picturesque Alpine town of Innsbruck. Depending on what time you get back into town, wind down with one last stein of beer at one of the biergartens mentioned earlier in this chapter.

Exploring Beyond Munich

The Bavarian Alps is a region of spectacular scenery; any trip from Munich into the surrounding countryside is bound to be unforgettable. In addition to the excursions mentioned here, Munich is just two to three hours away from **Innsbruck** by train. Innsbruck is covered as excursions from Vienna, Austria, in Chapter 17.

Mad King Ludwig's fairy-tale castle: Neuschwanstein

Ever wonder where Walt Disney got the idea for that precious Cinderella castle at his theme parks? He drew direct inspiration, and even some architectural blueprints, right from Bavaria's storybook castle, Neuschwanstein.

King Ludwig II — in many ways the epitome of a nineteenth-century romantic — built or renovated many a castle for himself. But the only thing that would completely satisfy him would be to create a castle that looked like something from a story by the Brothers Grimm.

Neuschwanstein was the result and is still a stunning, dreamlike sight, perched halfway up a forested mountain near a waterfall. It features slender towers, ramparts, and pointy turrets done in pale gray. Sadly, the castle was never quite finished, and the king got to live in his half-completed fantasy for only 170 days before his death.

You can take a bus or make a strenuous 25-minute downhill walk from Neuschwanstein to Hohenschwangau, to find the much more practical castle created by Ludwig II's father. Between these two fortresses and Munich, off a side road, hides the pilgrimage church of Wieskirche, one of the most glorious examples of the late baroque period in Germany.

Getting there

Although you can do all this in a day, you may find it more relaxing to stay a night in Füssen and trek to Neuschwanstein from there. Take a late train into Füssen and spend the night so you can be up early and get to Neuschwanstein with the first wave of crowds. (It's crowded early in the day, too but the lines haven't backed up yet.)

You really need a car for this trip, but you can use public transportation from Munich in a pinch. Take one of the nearly hourly trains to Füssen (a two-hour trip), from which hourly buses make the ten-minute trip to the castle parking lot. The sister castles of Neuschwanstein and Hoheschwangau are usually referred to collectively on road signs as *Königsschlösser* (king's castles).

When driving into this castle complex, you'll have your choice of parking lots in Schwangau, that little tourist center by the lake. Park in Lot D for the quickest (but steepest) walk up to **Neuschwanstein** (20 to 30 minutes). Go farther down the road to the big lot on the right if you want to take the longer (but less steep) paved road up (30 to 45 minutes). It's a fairly strenuous hike either way. Horse-drawn carriages (8DM/$4.45 uphill, 4DM/$2.20 downhill) will take you as far as the ticket office, which is two-thirds of the way up.

For the easiest route, take the shuttle bus that leaves from near Hotel Lisl, overshoots the castle, and stops at Marienbrücke, a bridge across the gorge above Neuschwanstein (3.50DM/$1.95 uphill, 2DM/$1.10 downhill). This lets you walk (steeply) back downhill in 10 minutes to the castle, and gives you a great view of the castle with Alpsee Lake and its valley in the background.

Panorama Tours (☎ 089-5490-7560), Arnulfstrasse 8, leaves from the Bahnhofplatz at Herties Department Store to do the Royal Castles Neuschwanstein/Linderhof (78DM/$43.35, not including the 21DM/$11.65 for admission). The tour takes 10½ hours and leaves daily (8:30 a.m.) from April to October and Tuesday, Thursday, Saturday, and Sunday from November to March.

You can get information on Neuschwanstein at the tourist offices in Munich and Füssen. The local **tourist office** (☎ 08362-81-980; Internet: www.schwangau.de) in the tiny village/parking lot of Schwangau is closed mid-November to mid-December.

Seeing the sights

The tour of **Neuschwanstein** shows you some of the weirdest and most theatrical details, including the king's bedroom — almost every inch covered in intricately carved wood — his near-finished neo–Byzantine-Romanesque Throne Room, and the huge Singers Hall, covered with paintings that refer to the work of composer Richard Wagner.

The king was positively enthralled by Wagner's music; he supposedly convulsed and writhed in such bliss to the strains of the composer's operas that his aides feared he was having an epileptic fit. Ludwig bailed Wagner out of debt and poured money into whatever project the composer desired. He often neglected his state duties while supporting Wagner.

This was the sort of thing that earned Ludwig II the moniker "Mad King Ludwig," but the monarch probably wasn't certifiable. Although beloved by his subjects as a genial and well-meaning ruler, Ludwig's withdrawal into his fantasies caused him to lose touch with his court and the political machinations in Munich. In 1886, he was deposed in absentia, and a few days later his body was found drowned, under suspicious circumstances, in a few feet of water at the edge of a lake.

You can visit the interior of Neuschwanstein by guided tour only, May to October daily from 8:30 a.m. to 5:30 p.m., in winter daily from 10:00 a.m. to 4:00 p.m. Admission is 12DM ($6.65) adults, 9DM ($5) students and seniors, free for those under 15. As Bavaria's biggest tourist draw, Neuschwanstein is packed by 9:00 a.m., and the crowd doesn't thin out until 4:00 p.m. or so. You can wait hours just to take the 35-minute tour (in English).

At the bottom of Neuschwanstein's hill is the tiny village/parking lot of Schwangau, which serves as a lunch stop for tour-bus crowds. Across the road and up a short hill is **Hohenschwangau** (☎ 08362-81-127), a sandy-colored castle restored in neo-gothic style by Ludwig's father (Maximilian II). By comparison, it's almost ordinary, but tours (usually in German, unless enough English speakers show up) can prove interesting.

Ludwig made his home in this castle for 17 years (and hosted his buddy Wagner). Try to picture yourself moving in here — even if the Hall of the Swan Knight, with its dramatic wall paintings of the

Germanic myths, might be a little too fancy except for special occasions. It's open daily, May to October 8:30 to 5:30 p.m., in winter 10:00 a.m. to 4:00 p.m. Admission is 12DM ($6.65) adults, 9DM ($5) students and seniors, free under age 15.

The Nazi concentration camp at Dachau

In 1933, in a little town outside Munich called Dachau, SS leader Heinrich Himmler set up Nazi Germany's first concentration camp. Between 1933 and 1945, 206,000 prisoners were officially registered here, and countless thousands more were interned without record.

Getting there

To spend an hour or two here remembering the darkest days of modern history, take the S2 **S-Bahn train** from Marienplatz here in 20 minutes. From Dachau station, bus 724 or 726 takes you to the camp (☎ **08131-84-566** or 08131-1741).

Panorama Tours (☎ **089-5490-7560**), Arnulfstrasse 8, leaves from the Bahnhofplatz at Herties Department Store to tour Dachau (40DM/$22.20) in 4½ hours from May 15 to October on Saturday (1:30 p.m.).

Seeing the sights

The taunting Nazi slogan *Arbeit Macht Frei* (Work Brings Freedom) is inscribed on the gate where you enter. Allied troops razed the 32 prisoners' barracks to the ground when they liberated the camp in 1945, but two have been reconstructed to illustrate the squalid living conditions. Each barrack was built to house 208 people; by 1936, they accommodated up to 1,600 each.

The former kitchen is now a museum with photographs documenting the rise of the Nazis and the persecution of Jews, communists, gypsies, homosexuals, and other "undesirables." You can watch a short documentary film (the English version usually shows at 11:30 a.m. and 3:30 p.m.).

The ovens of the crematorium and a gas chamber disguised as showers are at the back of the camp. No prisoners were gassed at Dachau (however, more than 3,000 Dachau inmates were sent to an Austrian camp to be executed in this manner); this room was used for beatings and cruel interrogations. Although Dachau, unlike other camps such as Auschwitz in Poland, was primarily for political prisoners and not expressly a death camp, more than 32,000 people died here, and thousands more were executed. The camp is scattered with Jewish, Catholic, and Protestant memorials.

The camp is open Tuesday to Sunday 9:00 a.m. to 5:00 p.m.; admission is free, and free tours are conducted in English June to August at 12:30 p.m.

Chapter 17

Vienna and the Best of Austria

● ●

In This Chapter

▶ Getting to Vienna

▶ Finding what you need after you're in Vienna

▶ Exploring the neighborhoods of Vienna

▶ Discovering Vienna's best places to sleep, eat, and hang out

▶ Planning side trips to charming Austrian towns

● ●

*M*ore than any other European city, Vienna maintains a link with the past. In attitude, architecture, and interior décor, Vienna still reverberates with the stately elegance of the Hapsburg dynasty, which ruled the Austro-Hungarian Empire in the eighteenth and nineteenth centuries. The city on the Danube is pure refinement: Its imperial palaces and art museums delight, its rococo churches and surprisingly ornate beer taverns excite, and its charming cafes and awe-inspiring concert halls thrill.

Vienna lays claim to one of Europe's richest and most varied musical heritages, including the birthplace of the waltz and home to the likes of Mozart, Haydn, Beethoven, Schubert, the Strauss family, Brahms, Mahler, and the Vienna Boys Choir (not to mention the late pop star Falco, the one-hit wonder behind *Rock Me Amadeus*). Plan for at least two or three days in Vienna — a slightly longer stay can help not only take in all the sights, but also because it will give you time to just walk, sample more delectable pastry, and people-watch in a fantastic European capital.

Making Your Way to and around Vienna

Vienna is a relatively brief five-hour train ride from both Munich and Prague, making it a convenient destination to reach by either air or rail. Once there, you'll find most tourist sights concentrated in a small part of the city center.

Getting to Vienna by air

Wien Schwechat airport (☎ **01/7007-2233;** Internet: www.vienna
airport.com) is 12 miles southeast of the city. Buses leave every
20 minutes (☎ **01/5800-2300**) a 25-minute ride to Wien Mitte/Land-
strasse (70AS/$5.60); other buses to Südbahnhof and Westbahnhof
stations are also available. Trains leave the airport at least twice an
hour for the half-hour ride to the city's center, stopping at Wien-Mitte/
Landstrasse station then Wien-Nord, for 38AS ($3.05).

Getting to Vienna by rail

By train, you arrive in Vienna at **Westbahnhof** (trains from northern
and central Europe) or **Südbahnhof** (southern and parts of central
Europe). Trains from Prague and Berlin occasionally arrive at the
northerly **Franz-Josef Bahnhof,** and if you're coming from Prague or
the airport, you may disembark at **Wien Mitte/Landstrasse** on the eastern edge of the city.

The **U-Bahn** (subway) and tram system will run you between any of
these stations and the center of town — except Südbahnhof, from
which you can catch the D tram downtown (you need to look for it in a
terminal on the station's eastern side, not right out in front where the
other trams stop).

Getting around once you're in Vienna

You use the same ticket for all Viennese public transportation. Tickets
are available at *Tabak-Trafiks* (tobacco/newsstands), automated
machines at major stops and U-Bahn stations (note: they only accept
coins and 100AS bills here), and on trams. Tickets cost 19AS ($1.50), or
22AS ($1.75) when purchased on the tram. Or, you may prefer **passes,**
which you can buy for one day (50AS/$4), three days (130AS/$10.40), or
eight days (265AS/$21.20) of travel. After 10 p.m., you end up paying an
extra night fare onboard buses. A cost-saving option is the **Vienna
Card,** which I describe in "Vienna's top sights."

By U-Bahn (subway)

Although inner-city Vienna is great for hoofing it, you'll need public
transportation for some of the longer hauls. To get where you want to
go as quickly as possible, I recommend the *U-Bahn* (subway). The U3
heads from Westbahnhof station through the center of town, stopping
at Stephansplatz, and then proceeds on to Wien Mitte/Landstrasse station. The U1 cuts through the center of town north-south, stopping at
Karlsplatz, Stephansplatz, Swedenplatz (near the Danube Canal), and
Praterstern/Wien Nord (at the Prater city park). The U2 curves around
the Ring's west side to Karlsplatz, where it ends, and the U4 continues
circling around the Ring's eastern half before heading off north to the
Friedensbrücke stop (the closest to Franz-Josef Bahnhof).

By tram

For a more scenic way to get about town, try the tram. Lines include: 18 (Südbahnhof to Westbahnhof), D (hedging around much of the Ring before veering off to Südbahnhof), and 1 and 2 (circling along the Ring, with stops at major sights).

You can also take buses that crisscross the center of town (1A, 2A, and 3A) or head out to the burbs.

By taxi

While you can see most of the touristy sites in Vienna on foot, you may prefer the comforts of a taxi for trips from the airport or train station to your hotel. Expect to pay around 350AS ($28) for the taxi ride between airport and downtown. Be aware that taxis won't cruise the streets of Vienna looking for you. Instead, you need to hire taxis at stands located throughout the city, or call ☎ **31-300,** 60-160, or 81-400.

The initial taxi fare for one passenger is 27AS ($2.15) and 14AS ($1.10) per kilometer. You pay a 16AS ($1.30) surcharge for luggage, and a 10AS (80 cents) surcharge at special times, including after 11:00 p.m., Sundays, and holidays. Of course, additional passengers cost more (16AS/$1.30), as does calling a taxi by phone (16AS/$1.30). Rides to the airport cost an extra 130AS ($10.40).

Discovering Vienna: What You Need to Know

This section provides information that you'll need for the basic necessities of getting the most out of your money, as well as what you'll need in an emergency or if you get stuck.

The local dough

The unit of currency in Austria is the schilling (AS), which is worth 100 groschen. Roughly, $1 equals 12.5AS; or 10AS equals 80 cents. Austrian coins come in 2, 5, 10, and 50 groschen, and 1, 5, 10, and 20 schillings. Bills are in 20, 50, 100, 500, 1,000, and 5,000 schillings denominations.

Where to get info after you arrive

The helpful **Vienna Tourist Board** office is behind the Staatsoper, at Kärntnerstrasse 38. (☎ **01/2111-4444,** fax: 01/216-8492. Internet: www. vienna-tourism.at or info.wien.at.) Open daily 9:00 a.m. to 7:00 p.m. The office has a series of informative pamphlets on a variety of Viennese tourist activities (the Spanish Riding School, restaurants, *Heurige,* cafes, and so on), as well as free copies of the events rag *Wien Monatsprogramm. Vienna A to Z,* a pocket guide of the city, is available for 40AS ($3.20).

Where to go in a pinch

Vienna has its share of purse-snatchers and pickpockets, so be especially cautious in crowded, touristy areas, especially Kärntnerstrasse between Stephansplatz and Karlsplatz. Be careful when taking out your wallet or opening your purse in public areas — many pitiable children who beg for money are accompanied by adult thieves who snatch wallets and run. The only central area that can become somewhat scary after dark is Karlsplatz, which is frequented by heroin addicts. In case of emergency, keep the following list of references handy:

- ✔ **American Express:** Vienna's American Express office is located at Kärntnerstrasse 21-23 (☎ **01/51-540**) and is open Monday to Friday, 9:00 a.m. to 5:30 p.m. and Saturday 9:00 a.m. to noon.

- ✔ **Doctors/hospitals:** If you have an emergency at night, call ☎ **141** (7:00 p.m. to 7:00 a.m. daily) for a list of doctors. For a list of English-speaking physicians, call the **Doctor's Association** at ☎ **1771,** or try the U.S. Embassy. For emergency medical care, go to the **Neue Allgemeine Krankenhaus** at Währinger Gürtel 18-20 (☎ **01/40-400** or 01/404-000).

- ✔ **Embassy:** The U.S. Embassy (☎ **01/31-339**) is located at Boltzmanngasse 16.

- ✔ **Emergency:** Dial ☎ **144** for an ambulance; call the police at ☎ **133;** or report a fire by calling ☎ **122.**

- ✔ **Pharmacies:** Vienna's pharmacies are generally open Monday to Friday 8:00 a.m. to noon and 2:00 to 6:00 p.m., Saturday 8:00 a.m. to noon. Look for signs outside each pharmacy that lists which drugstores are open during the off hours, or call ☎ **1550.**

- ✔ **Transit Info:** For transportation information, call ☎ **01/587-3186.**

Staying in touch

Whether you need to wire home for money or send a virtual postcard from an Internet cafe, here are a few essential facts and locations for handling your communications needs while in Vienna:

- ✔ **Internet Access & Cyber Cafes: Mediencafe im Amadeus,** Kärntnerstrasse 19, on the 5th floor of Steffl (☎ **01/5131-45017;** Internet: www.amadeusbuch.co.at), offers free Web surfing Monday to Friday 9:30 a.m. to 7:00 p.m., Saturday 9:30 a.m. to 5:30 p.m.

  Cafe Einstein: Located at Rathausplatz 4 (☎ **01/405-2626;** Internet: www.einstein.at/engl), Cafe Einstein is a cool cafe with a historic-looking pub, lots of atmosphere, and surf stations that charge you by the second (0.03AS/0.2 cents)— which comes out to 54AS ($4.30) per 30 minutes. Open Monday to Friday 7:00 a.m. to 2:00 a.m., Saturday 10:00 a.m. to 2:00 a.m., Sunday 10:00 a.m. to midnight.

- **Cafe Stein:** Located at Wahringerstrasse 6-8 (☎ 01/3197-2419; Internet: `www.cafe-stein.com`), and open daily 10:00 a.m. to 11:00 p.m., this cafe provides Internet access for 65AS ($5.20) for 30 minutes.

- **Mail:** The main post office is at Fleischmarkt 19 (☎ 01/515-510), open Monday to Friday 8:00 a.m. to 5:00 p.m.

- **Telephone:** A local call in Vienna is only 2AS (16 cents). All public phones take coins, and phones return unused shillings at the end of calls. Some phones take pre-paid phone cards called *Wertkarte,* which you can purchase from post offices (many of which are open 24 hours a day), newsstands, and tobacconists. Phone cards are available in 50AS ($4), 100AS ($8), and 200AS ($16) denominations.

  Austria's country code is **43**; Vienna's city code is **01**. Drop the zero if calling from outside Austria. To call Vienna from the United States, dial **011-43-1** followed by the phone number; to call Vienna from another Austrian city, dial **01** and then the number.

  To charge a call to your calling card or credit card, insert 2AS into the pay phone and dial **903-011** for **AT&T,** ☎ **903-012** for **MCI,** or ☎ **903-014** for **Sprint.** To call the United States direct from Austria, dial **001** and then the area code and phone number. For an **international operator,** dial **09.** For Austria **directory assistance,** dial ☎ **11811;** for international directory assistance, call ☎ **11813.**

Touring Vienna by Neighborhood

Vienna's inner city is the oldest part of town and home to the most spectacular sights and almost all the hotels and restaurants recommended in this chapter.

The **Ringstrasse,** or Ring Road, encircles the inner city with an elegant, tree-lined thoroughfare. This tram-routed boulevard follows the outline of the medieval city walls of yesteryear. The road is studded with many of Vienna's most prized gems: churches, palaces, and museums. Although the Ring is a continuous stretch of road, its name changes often. Just remember this: Any road whose name ends in *-ring* (such as Opernring or Kärntner Ring) is part of this avenue.

Forming the northeast border of the old city is the **Danube Canal** (the actual famed river, which isn't any shade of blue, is farther northeast). The northward-running shopping boulevard **Kärntnerstrasse** begins where Kärntner Ring becomes Opernring at the Staatsoper opera house. This avenue bisects the inner city to **Stephansplatz,** the epicenter of town and home of St. Stephan's cathedral.

The only place you're likely to venture outside of Vienna's Ring is the refined neighborhood of **Karlsplatz** (just southeast of the Staatsoper) with its namesake church, history museum, and major U-Bahn (subway) junction. You may also head west of the Ring a bit to the **Naschmarkt** fresh produce market and maybe a touch further beyond that to **Mariahilferstrasse,** the wide shopping street that runs from the Opernring to **Westbahnhof** train station.

Accommodations, Dining & Attractions in Vienna

HOTELS ■
Hotel Am Stephanplatz **22**
Hotel Astoria **14**
Hotel Austria **33**
Hotel Kärntnerhof **31**
Hotel Neuer Markt **17**
Hotel Post **34**
Hotel Royal **24**
Hotel Schneider **1**
Hotel Wandl **21**
Pension Nossek **20**
Pension Pertschy **18**

RESTAURANTS ◆
A Tavola **26**
Augustinerkeller **16**
Buffet Trzesniewski **19**
Drei Husaren **25**
Figimüller **30**
Firenze Enoteca **27**
Griechenbeisl **32**
Gulaschmuseum **29**
Kardos **36**
Plachutta **35**
Rathauskeller **4**

ATTRACTIONS ●
Augustinerkirche **12**
Die Burgkapelle
   (Vienna Boys' Choir) **8**
Freud Museum **5**
Gemäldegalerie Akademie
   der Bildenen Künste
   (Academy of Fine Arts) **2**
Hofburg Palace Complex **7**
Kaiserappartements
   (Imperial Apartments) **10**
Kaisergruft
   (Imperial Crypt) **15**
Kunsthistorisches Museum
   (Museum of Art History) **3**
Mozart-Wohnung Figarohaus
   (Mozart Memorial) **28**
Neue Burg **6**
Schatzkammer
   (Imperial Treasury) **9**
Spanische Reitschule
   (Spanish Riding School) **11**
Staatsoper (Opera House) **13**
Stephansdom
   (St. Stephan's Cathedral) **23**

Church †
Post Office ✉
Subway ●

When you're trying to figure out a **Viennese address,** remember that the building number comes *after* the street name. A number before the name, especially a Roman numeral, indicates the *bezirk* (city district) that address is in. (The inner city, the stuff within the Ring, is *bezirk* I.)

Staying in Vienna

If you're on a shoestring, you can find a concentration of cheap, plain hotels around Westbahnhof, a short tram ride from the center of town. This area is usually safe at night, except as you near Karlsplatz, a pretty plaza that junkies claim after dark. Vienna's popularity booms in late spring and late summer, and rooms can get scarce, so reserve ahead or resign yourself to staying in the suburbs.

The **tourist office** (☎ 01/2111-4444, fax: 01/2111-4445; E-mail: rooms@ info.wien.at) can help you find lodging in a hotel room or private home.

Vienna's top hotels

Hotel Astoria

$$$$ Near the Staatsoper

Recapturing the twilight days of the Austro-Hungarian Empire, this classic hotel has a frayed but cared-for elegance. Its location is prime for shopping and visiting the opera house and the cathedral. Avoid the dark and cramped interior rooms, and try your luck at getting one of the front rooms (outside, Kärntnerstrasse is pedestrian-only, so you won't be disturbed much at night). While hard to snag, the large, light-filled "superior" corner rooms feature lovely marble fireplaces, stucco wall decorations, and nineteenth century furnishings are definitely worth asking about (however as the staff laments, "we only have so many corners."). Also, check out the *Jugendstil* (art nouveau) restaurant for wonderful Austrian cuisine.

Kärntnerstrasse 32-34 (entrance actually on side road Führichgasse, four blocks north of Kärtnerring). ☎ *01/515-770. Fax: 01/515-7782. Internet:* www.austria-trend.at. *U-Bahn: Stephansplatz. Rates: 2,050–3,000AS ($164–$240) double. AE, DC, MC, V.*

Hotel Kärntnerhof

$ North of Stephansdom

Take just a few minutes' walk north of the cathedral to find this comfortable hotel, modest but not spare, with pricing right for any bracket (especially if you choose one of the cheapest rooms that share a bath). Near-modern accommodations are a bit worn and frayed at the edges (an overhaul of some of the older baths would be a welcome addition) but the facilities are sparkling clean. If you're traveling with a group or family, ask about the three roomier apartments, which each have two bedrooms joined by a short hall.

Grashofgasse 4 (near the corner of Kollnerhof and Fleischmarkt). ☎ *01/512-1923. Fax: 01/513-222-833. Internet:* www.karntnerhof.com. *U-Bahn: Stephansplatz. Rates: 920–1,790AS ($73.60–$143.20) double; 20 percent lower Nov–Mar 15. AE, DC, MC, V.*

Hotel Royal

$$$$ Near Stephansdom

Situated at the intersection of two prestigious streets on a corner of the cathedral square, this hotel offers good value at a great location. Don't miss the piano in the antique-filled lobby — it was once owned by Wagner. However, don't stay at the Royal for history; it was built in 1960. For the best accommodations the hotel has to offer, choose one of the corner rooms with their spacious foyers and balconies that overlook the Stephansdom.

Singerstrasse 3 (at the corner with Kärntnerstrasse). ☎ *01/515-680. Fax: 01/513-9698. Internet:* www.kremslehner.hotels.or.at/royal. *U-Bahn: Stephansplatz. Rates: 1,650–2,000AS ($132–$160) double. AE, DC, MC, V.*

Hotel Schneider

$$$$ Just southeast of the Ringstrasse

A favorite of entertainers, this modern hotel is redone with contemporary modular furnishings every few years. Although not located within the Ringstrasse's border, art lovers will be thrilled with its location behind the Academy of Fine Arts and near the Kunsthistoriches Museum. The Schneider's comfortable apartments, which feature small kitchenettes (a nearby produce market can help you take care of the details), are great for families and groups. The main street is noisy, so light sleepers should request a room on the back, and only a few rooms have A/C, so be sure to ask for it.

Getreidemarkt 5. ☎ *01/588-380. Fax: 01/5883-8212. U-Bahn: Karlsplatz. Rates: 1,720–2,200AS ($137.60–$176) double. AE, DC, MC, V.*

Hotel Wandl

$$$ Near Stephansdom

Halfway between the cathedral and the Hofburg, this good-value inn has been run by the same family for generations. Pleasant, nice-sized rooms feature functional furniture. Be sure to ask for a room with a view of St. Stephan's steeple.

Petersplatz 9. ☎ *01/534-550. Fax: 01/534-5577. Internet:* www.hotel-wandl.com. *U-Bahn: Stephansplatz. Rates: 1,450–2,200AS ($116–$176) double with bathroom; 1,200–1,350AS ($96–$108) double without bathroom. AE, DC, MC, V.*

Pension Pertschy

$$ Near Stephansdom

One of Vienna's most atmospheric hotels — and a bargain to boot. Located smack-dab in the middle of town, this family-owned and operated hotel is situated in a gorgeous baroque building (dating back to 1723). Rooms are decorated in old-fashioned Biedermeir style and include lovely chandeliers (a few even have 200-year-old ceramic heaters). Take advantage of one of the hotel's larger, homey rooms, which have sofas or easy chairs.

Habsburgergasse 5 (just off the Graben). ☎ **01/534-490.** *Fax: 01/534-4949. Internet:* www.pertschy.com. *U-Bahn: Stephansplatz. Rates: 1,240–1,560AS ($99.20–$124.80) double. DC, MC, V.*

Vienna's runner-up accommodations

Hotel Am Stephanplatz

$$$$ This hotel may be modern for the most part (though some rooms have rococo stylings), but its location, right on the cathedral square, can't be beat. *Stephansplatz 9 (*☎ **01/534-050;** *Fax: 01/5340-5711).*

Hotel Austria

$-$$ Hotel Austria lies in all its functional glory just a few blocks north of the cathedral, in a quiet residential neighborhood still but a few minutes' stroll from the tourist sights. The cheapest rooms come without a private bath. *Am Fleischmarkt 20 (*☎ **01/51-523;** *Fax: 01/5152-3506).*

Hotel Neuer Markt

$-$$ Hotel Neuer Markt occupies a baroque building on a fountain-blessed square, in the perfect location, halfway between the cathedral and the opera house. *Seilergasse 9 (*☎ **01/512-2316;** *Fax: 01/513-9105).*

Pension Nossek

$ Pension Nossek was once home to Mozart and has been a simple, sensible inn on the main shopping drag near the royal palace since 1909. *Graben 17 (*☎ **01/5337-0410;** *Fax: 01/535-2646).*

Hotel Post

$-$$ Hotel Post is another ancient hotel that once hosted the likes of Mozart and Hayden; today, below the comfy, modern bedrooms, a cafe/wine bar still pipes in their music. Rooms without bath are the true bargain. *Fleischmarkt 24 (*☎ **01/515-830;** *Fax: 01/5158-3808).*

Dining in Vienna

Viennese cooking is varied and palate-pleasing — with German, Swiss, and Italian influences, as well as more eastern-tinged Turkish, Hungarian, and Balkan flavors. Far and away, Vienna is most famous for being the birthplace of *wiener schnitzel,* a simple and steam-roller-flat cutlet of pork or veal breaded and fried (traditionally in lard), which is then tucked into a roll as a sandwich or served on a plate that can barely contain the cutlet.

Tafelspitz is another delicious (and dyed-in-the-wool) Viennese dinner-time domain. This boiled beef dish served with applesauce topped with horseradish shavings has been popular for centuries, — in fact, Emperor Franz Joseph was noted for eating it daily. From Hungary (the other half of the Austro-Hungarian Empire), the Viennese pantry has several spicy influences; look for paprika popping up in a variety of dishes, especially in the flavorful pork or beef stew called *gulasch.*

The Ottoman Turks besieged Vienna frequently throughout the sixteenth and seventeenth centuries and in the process introduced the city to a beverage that would eventually become one of Vienna's passions — an exotic drink called kaffee (coffee). (For the skinny on the best Viennese cafes, head to the section "More cool things to see and do in Vienna.") And of course, mouth-watering pastries are a necessity with any cup of kaffee — and just try to order only one! Vienna's world-renowned baked goods include *strudel,* which comes with numerous tempting fillings (*apfelstrudel* with apple is still the reigning pastry king). Other irresistible choices include cream-filled horns called *gugelhupf* and the cakes *rehrucken* (chocolate cake encrusted with almonds).

Ready to overload on chocolate? Set your sights on sampling some sachertorte, the original chocolate lover's delight (with a unique touch of apricot jam). The **Hotel Sacher** (Philharmonikerstrasse 4; ☎ 01/51-456) was the birthplace of this tempting creation in 1832, but found itself engaged in a long legal battle with **Café Demel** (Kohlmarkt 14; ☎ 01/533-5516) during the 1960s over the right to call its dessert delight the "Original Sachertorte." Although the Hotel Sacher won, your taste buds will be hard-pressed to tell the difference, so sample the sweets at both places! Either can push a choco-holic into palate ecstasy.

Top Austrian beers include lighter fare such as Gold Fassl, Kaiser, and Weizengold (a wheat beer). Or, if you prefer richer brews, try Gösser Spezial and Eggenberger Urbock (the latter dates back to the seventeenth century and is considered one of the world's most powerful beers).

When it comes to enjoying the best of Austria's wines, you'll find that whites dominate. While the pinnacle white is the fruity Grüner Veltiner, the country's dry Rieslings are also quite celebrated, along with several fine Chardonnays and Pinot Blancs. Also, keep your palate open to sample some Eiswein, a special Austrian dessert wine made from grapes that are allowed to ripen on the vine until after the first frost hits. This unusual growing process freezes water in the grapes and concentrates the fruit's alcohol level and taste. And don't forget about schnapps, delightfully flavored liqueurs that the Austrians distill from unusual fruits like rowan berries, quinces, juniper, or apricots.

Vienna's top restaurants

Augustinerkeller
$ Near the Staatsoper   AUSTRIAN

Serving simple meals such as schnitzel, spit-roasted chicken, and *tafelspitz* since 1954, this vaulted brick cellar under the Hofburg palace features long communal tables and a nice selection of Viennese beer and wine. While more touristy elements — including wandering accordion players in the evenings, starting at 6:30 p.m. — tend to drive away the locals, it's still a fun dining experience with ample and palette-pleasing food.

Augustinerstrasse 1 (a little ways off Albertinaplatz, across from Augustinia church). ☎ *01/533-1026. Reservations not necessary. U-Bahn: Stephansplatz. Main courses: 94–219AS ($7.50–$17.50). AE, DC, MC, V. Open: Lunch and dinner daily.*

Drei Husaren

$$$$ Near Stephansdom   VIENNESE/INTERNATIONAL

Decorated with Gobelin tapestries and antiques, this fine establishment has been regarded as Vienna's top eatery since World War I. You can sample both traditional and more inventive Viennese cuisine, including an hors d'oeuvres table filled to the brim with more than 35 goodies, *kalbsbrücken Metternich* (the chef's specialty veal dish), and cheese-filled crêpes topped with chocolate topping.

Weihburggasse 4 (off Kärtnerstrasse, two blocks south of Stephansplatz). ☎ *01/512-1092. Reservations required. U-Bahn: Stephansplatz. Main courses: 270–425AS ($21.60–$34). Tastings menus: 940–1,005AS ($75.20–$80.40); fixed-price lunch 440AS ($35.20). AE, DC, MC, V. Open: Lunch and dinner daily. Closed mid-July to mid-Aug.*

Figimüller
$$ Near Stephansdom   VIENNESE

This perennially popular Viennese *beisel* (tavern) is home to wiener schnitzel so colossal it overflows the plate it's served on. The dining room (dating back over 500 years) has an aged glow from thousands of delighted diners who've settled down to generous helpings of salads, sausages, *tafelspitz,* and goblets of exceptional wine.

Wollzelle 5 (go one block north on Rotenturmstrasse from Stephansplatz and turn right; it's up an alley half a block down on the left). ☎ *01/512-6177. Internet: www. figlmueller.at. Reservations recommended. U-Bahn: Stephansplatz. Main courses: 105–185AS ($8.40–$14.80). No credit cards. Open: Lunch and dinner daily. Closed Aug.*

Firenze Enoteca

$$$ Near Stephansdom   TUSCAN/ITALIAN

If you're experiencing schnitzel overdose, head on over to the premier Italian eatery in Vienna. The delightful decor with reproduced frescoes recalls the Italian Renaissance, while the cuisine highlights central Italian staples like spaghetti with seafood, penne with salmon, and veal cutlets. Also, say good-bye to beer for a meal, and get yourself a bottle of smooth Chianti to enjoy with your meal.

Singerstrasse 3 (one short block south of Stephansplatz, Singerstrasse branches off to the left/east; the restaurant is 2 blocks down). ☎ *01/513-4374. Reservations recommended. U-Bahn: Stephansplatz. Main courses: 98–360AS ($7.85–$28.80). Lunch menu: 200–250AS ($16–$20). AE, DC, MC, V. Open: Lunch and dinner daily.*

Griechenbeisl

$$$ North of Stephansdom   AUSTRIAN

Beethoven and Mark Twain (among other fans) certainly can't be wrong! This 550-year-old restaurant with its iron chandeliers and low vaulted ceilings has been a favorite for centuries. Your taste buds will thrill to more hearty dishes including venison steak, Hungarian goulash, and an excellently prepared *tafelspitz*. Plus, the accordion and zither music will get your feet tapping.

Fleischmarkt 11 (From Swedenplatz, take Laurenzerberg away from the Canalto Fleischmarkt and turn right). ☎ *01/533-1977 or 01/533-1941. Reservations suggested. U-Bahn: Swedenplatz. Tram: N, Z. Main courses: 148–270AS ($11.85–$21.60). AE, DC, MC, V. Open: Lunch and dinner daily.*

Kardos

$$$ East of Stephansdom   HUNGARIAN/BALKAN

Huge portions and elements of Vienna's eastern heritage await you at Kardos. From its Gypsy-rustic accents and deep wooden booths to its exotic fare that includes such tasty treats as *grammel* rolls stuffed with spiced pork, Balkan fish soup, and grilled meats, Kardos highlights the days when Austria's influence extended far and wide. Be sure to get the ball rolling with the Hungarian apricot aperitif *barack*.

Dominikaner Bastei 8 (Take Wollzeile several long blocks east of Stephansdom and turn left up Stuben Bastei, which becomes Dominikaner Bastei). ☎ *01/512-6949. Reservations recommended. U-Bahn: Schwedenplatz. Main courses: 125–215AS ($10–$17.20). AE, MC, V. Open: Lunch and dinner Mon–Sat.*

Vienna's runner-up restaurants

A Tavola

$ A decent — and remarkably cheap — Tuscan (really, a bit pan-Italian) restaurant in the heart of the Austrian capital. *Weihburggasse 3-5* (☎ *01/512-7955).*

Buffet Trzesniewski

$ This was neighbor Franz Kafka's favorite spot for a wide selection of scrumptious finger sandwiches and beer. *Dorotheergasse 1 (☎ 01/512-3291).*

Gulaschmuseum

$ A laid-back beisel with a few tables on the sidewalk and 16 types of goulash on the menu, along with grills and other paprika-inspired Hungarian dishes. *Schulerstrasse 20 (☎ 01/512-1017).*

Plachutta

$$$$ Plachutta is famed for its some dozen different preparations of tafelspitz in a halfway rustic, halfway refined ambience. *Wollzeile 10 (☎ 01/512-1577).*

Rathauskeller

$$ Vienna's 100-years-plus beer hall-style restaurant under the town hall (common to most German and Austrian towns), with vaulted ceilings and a killer Rathauskellerplatte (an assorted platter of meat dishes made for two). *Rathausplatz 1 (☎ 01/4051-2190).*

Exploring Vienna

If you're going to be in town for few days, consider picking up the **Vienna Card,** which gives you three days unlimited public transportation plus discounts at 30 city sights and museums. The card runs 210AS ($16.80) and is available at the tourist office, hotel desks, or U-Bahn stations. Note that the card costs 80AS ($6.40) more than a regular three-day transport-only ticket, so be sure to flip through the brochure and make sure that you can get the full use of the card.

Vienna's top sights

Stephansdom (St. Stephan's Cathedral)

The heart of Vienna lies in this visual and cultural landmark from the twelfth to fourteenth century. (Fun fact: Mozart's 1791 pauper funeral was held here.) Visit the fanciful tombs, an impressive fifteenth-century carved wooden altar, and a crypt filled with urns containing the entrails of the Hapsburgs. See the quintessential Viennese vista with its colorful pattern of mosaic-like tiling from atop the 450-foot, 343-stepped **Steffl** (south tower). The unfinished north tower (named for its *Pummerin* bell) offers a less impressive view, but you can catch a glimpse of the Danube.

Stephansplatz 1. ☎ 01/51-552. U-Bahn: Stephansplatz. Open: church, Mon–Sat 6:00 a.m.–10:00 p.m., Sun 7:00 a.m.–10:00 p.m.; north tower, daily 9:00 a.m.–6:00 p.m. (8:30 a.m.–5:00 p.m. in winter); south tower, daily 9:00 a.m.–5:30 p.m. Church tours, Mon–Sat 10:30 a.m. and 3:00 p.m., Sun 3:00 p.m.; catacomb tours, Mon–Sat at 10:00, 11:00, and 11:30 a.m. and daily at 1:30, 2:00, 2:30, 3:30, 4:00, and 4:30 p.m. Admission: The church is free, but the south tower costs 30AS ($2.40) adults, 10AS (80¢) kids under 15. The church tour, catacombs tour, and north tower each cost 40AS ($3.20) *adults, 15AS ($1.20) for children under 15. A special 7:00 p.m. evening tour includ-ing a spin around the roof costs 130AS ($10.40).*

Hofburg Palace

A wonder of connective architecture, the palace of Hofburg (actually the Hapsburgs' winter home) is a jumpled complex that was added on to from 1279 to 1913. Although spread out over several blocks and featuring numerous entrances, the main entrance on Michaelerplatz ushers you into the majestic courtyard of **In der Burgm,** which leads to the **Kaiserappartments,** or Imperial Apartments (**☎ 01/533-7570**). The **Silberkammer** next door displays the silver and porcelain collected from eighteenth- and nineteenth-century Hapsburg table settings.

The **Schatzkammer** (Imperial Treasury) (**☎ 01/533-7931**) is another must-see attraction at the Hofburg. Head left from the In der Burg court-yard and enter through the Swiss Court. The Treasury, Europe's great-est, houses a collection of historic gems and jewelry guaranteed to impress even the most jaded of tourists.

The **Neue Burg,** or New Castle (**☎ 01/521-770**) is yet another section of the palatial estate worth taking in. Constructed in the early twentieth century, the building's elegantly curving exterior houses several collec-tions (all viewable with the purchase of a single ticket). Collections include (in descending order of interest): historical musical instruments (many used by famous composers; try the audio tour even though it's in German — it features wonderful snippets of period music); arms and armor (crossbows, pistols, and more); and classical statues (mainly from the Greco-Turkish site of Ephesus). An entrance next door (closer to the Ringstrasse) leads to the **ethnography museum,** featuring the only intact Aztec feather headdresses in the world.

The palace takes up many square city blocks, but the main entrance is on Michaelerplatz. Each section has its own phone number, which is listed in the pre-ceding description. U-Bahn: Herrengasse or Stephansplatz (walk down Graben, then left onto Kohlmarkt). Tram: 1, 2, D, J. Open: Kaiserappartments/Silberkammer, Mon–Sat 8:30 a.m.–4:30 p.m., Sun 8:30 a.m.–1:00 p.m.; Schatzkammer and Neue Burg, Wed–Mon 10:00 a.m.–6:00 p.m.; ethnography museum Wed–Mon 10:00 a.m.–4:00 p.m. Admission: Kaiserappartments or Silberkammer, 80AS ($6.40) each, 60AS ($4.80) stu-dents, 40AS ($3.20) under 15; or 95AS ($7.60), 75AS ($6) students, 50AS ($4) under 15, combined. Schatzkammer, 100AS ($8) adults, 70AS ($5.60) students, children, and sen-iors; Neue Burg, 60AS ($4.80) adults, 40AS ($3.20) children; ethnography museum 50AS ($4) adults, 25AS ($2) students and seniors, free under 10.

Staatsoper (State Opera House)

One of the world's greatest opera meccas, the regal Staatsoper has a mar-velous musical heritage dating all the way back to its 1869 opening with a performance of Mozart's *Don Giovanni.* Mahler and Strauss — among other classical musical titans — have served as its musical directors. Take a short 35-minute tour during the day, or even better, catch a thrilling performance there at night (see "More cool things to see and do in Vienna" later in this chapter).

Opernring 2. ☎ 01/514-442-959. Internet: www.wiener-staastoper.at. *U-Bahn: Oper or Karlsplatz. Tram: 1, 2, D, J, 62, 65. Open: The ever-changing schedule of tours (2–5 daily in English, starting as early as 11:00 a.m. and usually the last no later than 3:00 p.m.) is posted at an entrance around on the right (east) side. Admission: Tours cost 60AS ($4.80) adults, 45AS ($3.60) seniors, 30AS ($2.40) students, or 20AS ($1.60) kids.*

Kunsthistoriches Museum

An amazingly diverse and deep art collection awaits you in this 100-room museum. Start with ancient Egyptian and Greco-Roman art and work your way through the Renaissance and then on to the Flemish, Dutch, and German masters like Memling, Van Dyck, Rembrandt, and especially Breughel the Elder (the majority of his known works are here).

Must-see pieces include Dürer's *Blue Madonna,* Vermeer's *The Artist's Studio,* and works by Italian masters Titian, Raphael, Veronese, Caravaggio, and Giorgione. Top ancient works consist of a Roman onyx cameo of the *Gemma Augustea,* a roly-poly blue hippopotamus from 2000 b.c. Egypt (which also serves as the museum's mascot). Also check out Archimboldo's idiosyncratic and allegorical still lifes–cum-portraits, cobbling together everyday objects to look like a face from afar. Craggy, wooden-faced *Winter* is really Francis I of France and flame-haired *Fire* just may be Emperor Maximillian II himself.

The museum is in a massive nineteenth-century building on Maria Theresien Platz (across the Burgring from the Neue Burg). ☎ 01/5252-4489. U-Bahn: Babenburgerstrasse. Tram: 1, 2, D, J. Open: Tues–Sun 10:00 a.m.–6:00 p.m. Admission: 100AS ($8) adults, 70AS ($5.60) students and seniors, free for children under 11. Guided tours (in English at 11:00 a.m. and 3:00 p.m.) 30AS ($2.40).

Akademie der Bildenden Kunste-Gemaldegalerie
(Academy of Fine Arts)

If time permits, try to make at least a quick stop at this small but choice gallery with a fine painting collection that covers the fifteenth to seventeenth centuries. It features a 1504 *Last Judgment* by Hieronymus Bosch (a major influence to the surrealists), as well as a teenage *Self Portrait* by Van Dyck and other works by Rubens, Guardi, Rembrandt, and Cranach the Elder.

Schillerplatz 3 (just south of the Staatsoper). ☎ 01/58-816. U-Bahn: Karlsplatz. Tram: 1, 2, D, J, 62, 65. Open: Tues–Sun 10:00 a.m.–4:00 p.m. Admission: 50AS ($4), 20AS ($1.60) students.

Scloss Schönbrunn

You have to travel about four miles from Vienna's center to experience the city's last great sight — but it's definitely worth the effort. Scloss Schönbrunn was the baroque playground of Empress Maria Theresa and served as the Hapsburgs' summer palace after its completion in the mid-eighteenth century. Like Hofburg, this palace sprawls, but only 40 of its 1,441 rooms are open to visitors.

Two different tours lead the way through the state apartments that brim with gorgeous chandeliers and old-world detail. The basic "Imperial Tour" guides you through 22 rooms and costs 90AS ($7.20) adults, 80AS ($6.40) students, or 45AS ($3.60) under 15; but for just 30AS ($2.40) more, the "Grand Tour" gives you all 40 viewable rooms. Play your cards right, and you can also enjoy a guided Grand Tour for 25AS ($2) more. (Be sure to call ahead for tour costs and times; summertime tours leave as frequently as every 30 minutes.)

Your visit is not compete without a jaunt through the extravagant roccoco gardens, complete with faux "Roman ruins" and a baroque Gloriette coffeehouse that overlooks the gardens (a fantastic photo op). Open daily 9:00 a.m. to 5:00 p.m.; 20AS/$1.60 adults, 10AS/80 cents ages 6 to 15. And if imperial coaches are your thing, don't miss the Wagenburg carriage museum.

Schönbrunner Schlossstrasse. ☎ *01/8111-3239. Internet:* www.schoennbrunn.at. *U-Bahn: U4. Open: Palace, daily Apr–Oct 8:30a.m.–5:00 p.m., Nov–Mar 9:00 a.m.– 4:30 p.m.; Gardens, daily until sunset. Admission: See tours above.*

More cool things to see and do in Vienna

Eat, drink, and watch some horse ballet. From Ferris wheels to wine-bar crawls, there's plenty to keep you busy in Vienna both day and night.

> ✔ **Spending a Night at the Opera.** Vienna's **Staatsoper** is a truly world-class theatrical venue, and you don't want to miss experiencing a performance, even if you don't consider yourself an opera aficionado. The season runs September to June, and you can get tickets at a variety of prices (140AS/$11.20 to 2,450AS/$196) at the box office one month in advance by calling ☎ 01/514-442-960 or the day after the season opens by calling ☎ 01/513-1513, or on the Web at www.culturall.com (programs on-line at www.oebthv.gv.at).

> Or, save a few bucks and try your luck by purchasing last-minute tickets the day before the performance at the box office for a flat 400AS ($32). Standing room *Praterrestehplatz* tickets at the Staastoper are an amazing bargain — a mere 30AS ($2.40; balcony or gallery) to 50AS ($4; parterre) on the day of a performance. Be sure to show up at least three hours before the performance to get in line for a space. Bring a scarf and tie it around the railing at your standing spot — that's all you need to do to save your place. Then, wander through the glitter rooms and circulate among the black-tie crowd until the performance begins.
>
> When the summer heat chases the company out of the State Opera House, you can still get your opera fix. Check out **open-air Mozart operas** at Schloss Schönbrunn (☎ 01/512-0100, or at the box office on performance days ☎ 01/877-4566; Internet: www.wwtn.co.at). The Schloss also stages musical concerts year-round; call for info ☎ 01/8125-0040; Internet: www.imagevienna.com).

✔ **Drinking java, eating strudel, and people-watching at a Kaffeehaus.** Legend has it that Vienna's first coffeehouse was established in 1683 — and certainly, coffeehouses have been a vibrant part of Viennese culture ever since. One of the grander is an old haunt that was a fav of Freud, the chandeliered **Café Landtmann** at Dr. Karl Lueger Ring 4 (☎ **01/532-0621**).

Of course, the granddaddy of all Viennese cafes is **Café Demel** (☎ **01/535-1717;** Internet: www.demel.at), which moved to Kohlmarkt 14 in 1888 and hasn't changed its ornate decor since. You can enjoy your kaffee in a variety of ways, the most popular being *schwarzer* (black), *melange* (mixed with hot milk), or *mit schlagobers* (topped with whipped cream).

✔ **Seeing the Vienna Boys Choir.** Dating all the way back to 1498, this Viennese institution has been the training ground for talented musicians, including Joseph Hayden and Franz Schubert. Catch a sonorous Sunday or holiday Mass on (September to June only) at 9:15 a.m. in the **Hofburg's Burgkapelle,** with accompanying members of the Staatsoper chorus and orchestra. You can pick up tickets at the box office the preceding Friday from 5 to 6 p.m. Get in line early — this is one of the few times you'll find people shelling out $6 to $27 to go to church. Of course, standing room is free, but you still need a ticket. Also, you can try reserving tickets up to eight weeks in advance by writing to: Hofmusikkapelle, Hofburg, A-1010 Vienna, Austria (☎ **01/533-992-775** or 01/533-9927).

✔ **Riding the Riesenrad in Prater Park.** Courtesy of Johann Strauss, Sr. in 1820, this former imperial hunting ground on the Danube Canal is the true birthplace of the waltz. Aside from the lovely grounds, visit the park to experience its year-round amusement park/fair that's bursting with restaurants, food stands, a beer garden. Also, take a spin on the Riesenrad — at 220 feet and 100 years, one of the world's oldest (and slowest) operating Ferris wheels.

✔ **Watching the Horse Ballet at the Spanish Riding School.** You don't have to attend a show to see the world-famous Lippizaner horses strut their stuff. The Hofburg's Spanish Riding School teaches complicated baroque horse choreography, based on sixteenth-century battle maneuvers. The horses and riders practice regularly (Tuesday to Saturday mornings 10:00 a.m. to noon: April to June 25, August 30 to October 8, and November 16 to December 18). You can purchase training session tickets from your travel agent or at the door for 100AS ($8).

However, if only the full, 1 hour 20 minute show will do (April through June and September through December, at 10:45 a.m. and 7:00 p.m.), reserve a ticket as far in advance as possible by faxing 01/535-0186 or e-mailing office@srs.at; tickets run 250AS ($20) to 900AS ($72), with 200AS ($16) standing-room spots. Hour-long dressage training sessions to classical music take place during the show season at 10:00 a.m. some mornings, and you can observe for 250AS ($20).

✔ **Taking a Heuriger crawl in Grinzig.** *Heurige* is the name of both Viennese new wines and the country taverns that serve them. Most *heuriger* are centered around the fringes of the famous Vienna Woods, just a 15-minute tram ride northeast of the city center. The tradition's capital is the former village, now suburb, of Grinzing, home to about 20 taverns (take tram 38 from the underground station at Schottentor, a stop on the U2 U-Bahn and trams 1, 2, and D).

Due to the rising popularity of *Heuriger* crawling, the village works hard to maintain its medieval look. Stroll down Cobenzigasse, sample the wine at *heurige* along the way while you enjoy the sounds of accordion and zither music.

And on Your Left, the Opera House: Seeing Vienna by Guided Tour

There are plenty of **city orientation tours,** but why pay $20 when a tram ticket gets you the same thing minus the stilted commentary? Armed with a good map, the cheapest and most fun tour is self-guided. Buy an all-day ticket, step onto the no. **1** or **2 tram,** and ride it all the way around the Ring, hopping on and off at sights where you want to spend time. The whole ride only takes half an hour if you don't get off. After you're oriented, you can abandon the tram to visit the sights off the Ring, such as the Hofburg Palace and Stephansdom. The tourist office has a brochure called **Walks in Vienna** that can fill you in on other, more organized guided tours.

Suggested One-, Two-, and Three-Day Itineraries

If you're the type who'd rather organize your own tours, this section offers some tips for building your own Vienna itineraries.

If you have one day

Be at the **Hofburg** and in the Imperial Apartments at 9:15 a.m. to admire the excesses of the Hapsburgs, and in the **Schatzkammer** around 10:00 a.m. for its impressive medieval crown jewels and other royal artifacts.

Exit the Hofburg by the main Michaelerplatz entrance and start strolling up Kohlmarkt, pausing to indulge in a coffee and snack/early lunch amid the nineteenth-century elegance of **Cafe Demel.** Turn right on the Graben to arrive at **Stephansdom.** Tour the cathedral, climb its south tower for a city panorama, and then start waltzing your way down the main pedestrian drag Kärntnerstrasse. Settle into the ground floor cafe of the **Hotel Sacher** for a sinfully delicious Sachertorte.

Continue to the end of Kärtnerstrasse where it hits the Ring. Admire the **Staatsoper** exterior and, unless you'll be doing standing-room-only (for which you'll return here shortly) stop into the box office to pick up discounted day-of-performance tickets for tonight's opera. Then hop tram 1, 2, or D heading west/clockwise (left) around the Ring one stop and get off at Burgring for the **Kunsthistorishes Museum** and 90 to 120 minutes of exquisite Old Masters and ancient statues.

For those who buy regular seats for the opera, let the evening unfold thusly: Get right back on the no. 1 or 2 tram and ride it clockwise halfway around the Ring road, past the greatest glories of Viennese architecture. Get off at Schwedenplatz and transfer to the U1; go two stops north, getting off at Praterstern. Enjoy the city park–cum-carnival of Prater by taking a late afternoon spin on the **Reisenrad** (Ferris wheel) and tossing back a few tall cold ones in the **Biergarten** before returning to the **Staatsoper** half an hour before the performance begins. You can also stop for dinner along the way, or just have some schnitzel in the Prater. If you have plenty of time to make it to the opera at your leisure, get off the U1 at Schwedenplatz again and simply get back on the no. 1 or 2 tram to continue all the way around the Ring to the opera house. If you dallied too long in the Prater, stay on the U1 all the way to Karlsplatz, two blocks south of the Staatsoper. If you're still hungry after the proverbial fat lady sings, nearby Augustinerkeller stays open until midnight.

Fans of standing-room-only tickets need to plan their evening like so: Depending on how late it is when you get out of the museum, you either have time (half an hour) to ride the no. 1 or 2 tram clockwise almost all the way around the Ring Road (getting off back at the Staastoper), or you can just mosey the two long blocks back (counterclockwise) to the opera house. You will need to have picked up a snack to eat while waiting in line at the opera house — be there by 5:00 p.m. for the best spots. Have dinner late at **Augustinerkeller,** after the performance is over.

If you have two days

Spend Day One as outlined in the preceding section. That's a pretty packed day, so take Day Two to relax at Vienna's suburban sights. Head out in the morning to **Scloss Schönbrunn** for even more imperial excess than you saw at the Hofburg. After marveling at Hapsburgian opulence and taking a spin through the gardens, return downtown on the U4, transferring at Karlsplatz to the U2 toward Schottenring. Get off at the Schottentor stop and hop tram 38 out to Grinzing for an afternoon of *heuriger* crawling, snacking and drinking your way through Vienna's specialty foods and white wines. If you're in town during the season (and booked tickets long before you left on this trip), get back to town by 6:30 p.m. so you can take in the 7:00 p.m. show of the Lippizaner horses at the famed **Spanish Riding School.**

If you have three days

Days One and Two in the preceding sections give you all the best Vienna has to offer. Take Day Three for a big day trip out to the lovely Austrian village of **Innsbruck,** which I cover in "Traveling beyond Vienna."

Traveling Beyond Vienna: Innsbruck

Although Innsbruck is technically in Austria, you'll find traveling there from Munich, Germany (which I also cover in the book) much faster and convenient. This section provides directions from both Munich and Vienna, and it's a perfect excursion to do en route between the two.

Innsbruck, famous for hosting the Winter Olympics as well as the imperial family of the Austro-Hungarian Empire, is a sleepy little gem of a town, bordered by the stupendous Alps and a milky white river. The village is also a great starting point for fabulous hiking, skiing, and scenic driving.

Getting there

Ten daily trains arrive at Hauptbahnhof from Vienna (5 hours away), passing through Salzburg (2 hours away). 14 trains arrive from Munich daily (1½ to 2 hours away).

The **tourist office** is at no. 3 Burggraben, a road which rings the Altstadt at the end of Maria Theresien Strasse. (☎ **0512/59-850,** fax: 0512/598-507; Internet: www.tiscover.com/innsbruck.)

Purchase the **Innsbruck Card** to get free access to all city sights and free public transportation. The tourist office sells 24-hour cards for 230AS ($18.40), 300AS ($24) for two days, or 370AS ($29.60) for three days.

Seeing the sights

Walking the Maria Theresien Strasse, you pass through a triumphal arch and reach the rustic, souvenir shop-lined **Herzog Friedrich Strasse. Stadtturm** tower is at the end of the street, offering gorgeous views of the surrounding Alps. Open daily 10:00 a.m. to 5:00 p.m. (6:00 p.m. July and August; 4:00 p.m. November to February). Admission is 22AS ($1.75 adults), 11AS (90 cents) kids.

The street ends in a wide spot, which the **Goldenes Dachl** overlooks. The structure is basically an overblown imperial balcony erected and gilded for Emperor Maximillian I in the sixteenth century as a box seat for the festivities on the square below. Admiring it from below is enough, though its Maximillian-oriented museum is open daily May to September 10:00 a.m. to 6:00 p.m., Tuesday to Sunday in winter 10:00 a.m. to 12:30 p.m. and 2:00 to 5:00 p.m. Admission is 60AS ($4.80) adults, 20AS ($1.60) kids.

Turn right on Universitätsstrasse then left on Rennweg for a half-hour tour of the exuberant, curving, baroque stylings of Maria Theresa's **Hofburg** palace (☎ **0512/587-186**), open daily 9:00 a.m. to 5:00 p.m.; admission 55AS ($4.40) adults, 10AS (80 cents) kids.

Next door is the equally rococo **Dom** (cathedral), its altar decorated by Cranach the Elder's Maria Hilf. Across from the Hofburg at no. 2 Universitätsstrasse is the **Hofkirche,** containing a massive, statue-ridden monument to Maximillian I. It's open Monday to Saturday 9:00 a.m. to 5:00 p.m. Admission is 20AS ($1.60) adults, 10AS (80 cents) kids. Its neighbor is the **Tiroler Volkskunst-Museum** (☎ 0512/584-302), a folk museum celebrating everyday life in the history of the Tyrol district. It's open Monday to Saturday 9:00 a.m. to 5:00 p.m., Sunday 9:00 a.m. to noon; admission is 40AS ($3.20) adults, 15AS ($1.20) kids.

Outside the Alstadt is the **Alpenzoo** (☎ 0512/292-323) at Weiherburggasse 37, which virtually clings to the Alpine cliffs and features regional wildlife. It's open daily 9:00 a.m. to 6:00 p.m. (5:00 p.m. in winter). Admission is 70AS ($5.60) adults, 35AS ($2.80) kids. From the center, cross the Inn river, turn right, and follow the signs a long way; you can also take bus N, D, E, or 4 from the Altes Landhaus on Maria-Theresien Strasse.

The zoo sits at the base of the **Hungerburg plateau,** which offers magnificent city views (funicular from Rennweg 41: 8:00 a.m. to after 5:00 p.m.; 54AS/$4.30 adults, 22AS/$1.75 kids). From here, the Nordkette cable car (similar hours; 200AS/$16 adults, 100AS/$8 kids) journeys into the mountain wilderness to Hafelekar, a 7,702-foot vista and starting point for hiking the Alps. Visit the Innsbruck's tourist office for info on glacier ski packages (running year-round) that include both lift tickets and rentals for as low as 550AS ($44).

Where to stay and dine

Please your palate at the inexpensive **Restaurant Ottoburg** (☎ 0512/574-652) at Herzog Friedrich Strasse 1, an Austrian tradition since 1745. The **City-Hotel Goldene Krone** (☎ 0512/586-160, fax: 0512/580-1896; Internet: www.touringhotels.at) at Maria Theresien Strasse 46, features modern comforts and baroque touches, in a lovely house just outside the Altstadt. Doubles run 650 to 1,350AS ($52 to $108).

Chapter 18

Bern and the Swiss Alps

. . . .

In This Chapter

▶ Finding your way to Bern and the Swiss Alps

▶ Locating what you need once you're in Bern and the Berner Oberland

▶ Exploring in and around Bern

▶ Discovering the best places to sleep and eat in Bern and the Berner Oberland

▶ Heading into the Alpine countryside

. . . .

*A*lthough the Swiss capital of **Bern** is a fine place to visit — and, unlike Switzerland's larger cities, still has an almost medieval, Swiss village feel — the real attractions of this country are those mighty, snow-covered Swiss Alps. Therefore, I cover Bern fully, but as a gateway city. Then, halfway through these pages, you may notice the chapter sort of starts over again with the **Berner Oberland** south of Bern, a region that encompasses the legendary 13,642-foot peak of the Jungfrau, Queen of the Alps.

Making Your Way to and around Bern

Bern has direct rail connections to the surrounding countries. This includes service via a high-speeed rail line from France, making the train a quick, and quite scenic, option. The city itself is compact enough that once you're there, navigating it is a breeze.

Getting to Bern by air

The tiny **Berne-Belp Airport** (☎ 031-960-2111), 9km (5.6 miles) south of the city, receives flights from several major European cities. A shuttle bus runs from the airport to the city's train station, where you can find the tourist office. The 20-minute trip costs 14SF ($9). A taxi from the airport to the city costs 38SF ($25). Most European and transatlantic passengers fly into **Zurich's Kloten Airport,** from which an hourly train (48SF/$32) makes the 90-minute trip to Bern.

Accommodations, Dining & Attractions in Bern

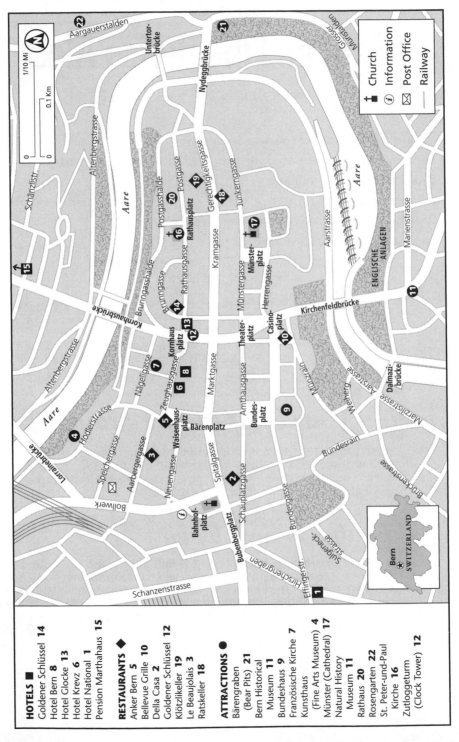

1/10 Mi

0.1 Km

Church
Information
Post Office
Railway

Aargauerstalden
Unterfor-brücke
Nydeggbrücke
Altenbergstrasse
Schänzlistr.
Aare
Grosser Muristalden
Aare
Aarstrasse
Marienstrasse
ENGLISCHE ANLAGEN
Postgasse
Postgasshalde
Gerechtigkeitsgasse
Junkerngasse
Rathausplatz
Rathausgasse
Kramgasse
Münstergasse
Münster-platz
Herrengasse
Kornhausbrücke
Brunngasshalde
Brunngasse
Nägeligasse
Kornhaus platz
Zeughausgasse
Waisenhaus platz
Bärenplatz
Marktgasse
Theater-platz
Amthausgasse
Bundes-platz
Münzrain
Casino-platz
Kirchenfeldbrücke
Aarstrasse
Marzillistrasse
Dalmazi-brücke
Welherg.
Bundesrain
Bundesgasse
Bruckenstrasse
Speichergasse
Hodlerstrasse
Altenbergstrasse
Aare
Lorrainbrücke
Aarbergergasse
Neuengasse
Spitalgasse
Schauplatzgasse
Bollwerk
Bahnhof-platz
Bubenbergplatz
Schanzenstrasse
Sulgeneck strasse
Hirschengraben
Effingerstr.

Bern
SWITZERLAND

HOTELS ■
Goldener Schlüssel **14**
Hotel Bern **8**
Hotel Glocke **13**
Hotel Krevz **6**
Hotel National **1**
Pension Marthahaus **15**

RESTAURANTS ◆
Anker Bern **5**
Bellevue Grille **10**
Della Casa **2**
Coldener Schlüssel **12**
Klötzlikeller **19**
Le Beaujolais **3**
Ratskeller **18**

ATTRACTIONS ●
Bärengraben
(Bear Pits) **21**
Bern Historical
Museum **11**
Bundeshaus **9**
Französische Kirche **7**
Kunsthaus
(Fine Arts Museum) **4**
Münster (Cathedral) **17**
Natural History
Museum **11**
Rathaus **20**
Rosengarten **22**
St. Peter-und-Paul
Kirche **16**
Zutloggeturm
(Clock Tower) **12**

Getting to Bern by rail

Bern's **Hauptbahnhof train station** (☎ 031-328-1212) is at the west end of the **Altstadt (Old Town).** Ticketing, track access, and lockers are in the basement. Luggage storage and train and tourist info are on the ground floor. For national rail information, hit the Web site www.sbb.ch, call ☎ **0900-300-300** (1.19SF/79 cents per minute), or use the computers in the **SBB train info office** (across from the tourist office) to look up and print out your itinerary.

If you leave the train station from the most obvious exit, at the tourist office, you'll be facing south; turn left to head into the **Altstadt.**

Getting around after you're in Bern

You can buy two types of public-transit tickets (good for both buses and trams): the 1.50SF ($1) version good to travel up to six stops (valid for 45 min.), and the 2.40SF ($1.60) version for longer rides (over six stops, up to 90 min.). Nothing in this chapter is more than six stops away, so always get the cheaper ticket. Buy your ticket from the machine at each stop. There's a daily ticket for 7.50SF ($5), but you'd have to make more than four trips a day to save any money.

By tram and bus

Bern's **bus and tram system** (☎ 031-321-8888) is extensive, but the Altsadt's small enough to cover on foot. However, if you're visiting the **Bear Pits,** you may want to take bus no. 12 on the way back uphill toward the city center and station. Most buses and trams begin and end their routes around the **Hauptbahnhof,** and many on **Bubenbergplatz** just to the station's south.

"Moonliner" night buses run Fridays and Saturdays at 12:45 a.m., 2:00 a.m., and 3:15 a.m. and cost 5SF ($3.35); the no. M3 runs from the train station through the Altstadt and returns via the casino.

By taxi

If you are only sightseeing in Altstadt, you can see it all on foot. If, however, you want to taxi to your hotel, cabs congregate at the train station, Casinoplatz, and Waisenhausplatz; or you can call ☎ **031-371-1111**, 031-311-1818, or 031-301-5353. The fare is 6.50SF ($4.35) plus a hefty 2.70SF ($1.80) per kilometer, or 3SF ($2) per km from 8:00 p.m. to 6:00 a.m., and on Sundays and holidays.

Discovering Bern: What You Need to Know

This section provides information that you'll need for the basic necessities of getting the most out of your money, as well as what you'll need in an emergency or if you get stuck.

The local dough

The Swiss unit of currency is the Swiss franc (SF), divided into 100 centimes. Roughly, $1 equals 1.5SF; or 1SF equals 66 cents. Swiss coins include 5, 10, 20, and 50 centimes and 1, 2, and 5 francs. Bills come in denominations of 10, 20, 50, 100, 500, and 1,000 francs.

Where to get info after you arrive

The **Bern Tourist Office** (☎ **031-328-1212,** fax: 031-312-1233; Internet: www.bernetourism.ch) is in the Hauptbahnhof (train station). Summer hours are daily 9:00 a.m. to 8:30 p.m.; October to May, it's open Monday to 9:00 a.m. to 6:30 p.m. and Sunday 10:00 a.m. to 5:00 p.m. There's a smaller info station inside the building at the **Bear Pits** (offering a free 20-minute multimedia show on "Bern Past and Present"). June to September, it's open daily 9:00 a.m. to 5:00 p.m.; October and March to May, hours are daily 10:00 a.m. to 4:00 p.m.; and November to February, it's open Friday to Sunday 10:00 a.m. to 4:00 p.m. The local paper, *Berner Zeitung,* maintains an excellent Website full of events and Bern info at www.bernerzeitung.ch (**sorry, German**).

Where to go in a pinch

With the exception of the park that surrounds **Parliament,** where heroin addicts roam after dark, you should feel comfortable on the streets of central Bern day or night. But don't let your sense of safety lull you into carelessness; take the usual precautions to protect yourself against crime. In case of emergency keep the following information handy:

- ✔ **Doctors/Hospitals:** For a list of doctors and dentists, dial ☎ **031-311-2211,** or the national English-speaking tourist hotline ☎ **157-5014** (1.40SF/93 cents per minute). For emergency care, go to **Insel Hospital,** Freiburgstr. (☎ **031-632-2111**). For an ambulance, dial ☎ **144.**

- ✔ **Emergencies:** Dial ☎ **117** for the police; ☎ **144** for an ambulance; ☎ **118** to report a fire; and ☎ **140** (not a free call) for car breakdown.

- ✔ **Pharmacies: Central-Apotheke Volz & Co.,** Zeitglockenlaub 2 (☎ **031-311-1094**), staffs English-speaking attendants. Located near the **Clock Tower,** it's open Monday 9:00 a.m. to 6:30 p.m.,

Tuesday to Friday 7:45 a.m. to 6:30 p.m., and Saturday 7:45 a.m. to 4:00 p.m. To find out which drugstore's turn it is to stay open 24 hours or on Sunday, dial ☎ **031-311-2211.**

Staying in touch

Whether you're sending home "wish you were here" postcards or looking to call a local ski-rental shop, the following information will help you keep in touch while in Bern:

- **American Express:** Bern no longer has a full American Express representative, so you have to change your traveler's checks at a bank. However, AMEX travel and mail services are handled by the local travel agency **7-Seas Travel,** Kramgasse 83, 3000 Bern 7, Switzerland (☎ **031-327-7777**). AMEX cardholders can have their post sent to "Your Name/AMEX Cardholder" at the above address and 7-Seas will hold it for you at no charge.

- **Embassies:** The U.S. embassy is at Jubiläumsstr. 93 (☎ **031-357-7011**). The U.K. embassy is at Thunstr. 50 (☎ **031-359-7700**). The Canadian embassy is at Kirchenfeldstr. 88 (☎ **031-357-3200**). Australia only offers Visa information at ☎ **157-560-005.**

- **Internet Access and Cyber Cafes:** The traveler's best bud in Bern is the **BZ Café,** Zeughausstrasse 14 (no phone). It's run by *Berner Zeitung,* the local daily paper, and lets you use the half-dozen computers with lightning ISDN access for free (yes, it's popular, but they even have some Sega game systems for you to play while you wait).

  If they're too busy, you can log on at the **Jäggi bookstore,** Spitalgasse 47–51 (☎ **031-320-2020**), for 5SF ($3.35) per half hour, or at the **Stauffacher bookstore,** Neuengasse 25 (☎ **031-311-2411**), for 12SF ($8) per hour.

- **Mail:** Bern's main post office (☎ **031-386-4111;** Tram/Bus: 5, 9, 10, 12, 13, 14, 16, 19) is at Schanzenpost 1 (behind the train station), open Monday through Friday from 7:30 a.m. to 6:30 p.m. and Saturday 8:00 a.m. to 11:00 a.m. There are several branches throughout the Altstadt.

- **Telephone:** A local call in Bern costs 60 rappen (40 cents). Switzerland's phone system is highly advanced — most booths contain digital, multilingual phone books — and few phones accept coins anymore. You can use your major credit card in most pay phones, or buy a *Taxcard* (prepaid phonecard) in denominations of 5SF ($3.35), 10SF ($6.65), and 20SF ($13.35) from the train station, any newsstand, gas station, or post office. For direct dialing internationally, you may want the *Value Card* versions for 20SF ($13.35) or 50SF ($33.35). Dial ☎ **111** (not free) for directory assistance.

  Switzerland's country code is **41.** Bern's city code is **031.** If you're calling Bern from beyond Switzerland's borders, drop the city code's initial zero. To call Bern from the United States, dial ☎ **011-41-31** followed by the phone number.

The rumor in Switzerland is that they will soon follow the examples of France, Italy, Spain, and parts of the United States by incorporating its city codes into the numbers themselves — meaning you will have to dial the codes even when calling another number within a city, and must start adding that initial zero when dialing from abroad. A timetable has not yet been set for the change, but if you're having trouble dialing, try that trick.

To charge your call to a calling card, dial the appropriate number: **AT&T** (☎ **0800-890-011**), **MCI** (☎ **0800-890-222**), or **Sprint** (☎ **0800-899-777**). To call direct from Bern abroad, dial **00** followed by the country code (**1** for the United States), the area code, and the number.

✔ **Transit Info:** For rail information call ☎ **031-157-3333.** For bus information call ☎ **031-386-6565** or 031-321-8621.

Touring Bern by Neighborhood

Bern's most interesting section, the **Altstadt** (Old City), is very small and easily navigable on foot. Tucked into a sharp, U-shaped bend of the **Aare River,** it's basically made up of five long, arcaded streets (whose names change at every block), two large squares (**Bärenplatz** Waisenhausplatz/Bundesplatz and **Kornhausplatz**/ Casinoplatz), and a dozen cross streets. There are also lots of shop-lined passageways not shown on most maps that cut through buildings from one main drag to another.

Imagine this bend of the Aare as a sideways "U." At the open (western) end of the U is the **Hauptbahnhof** train station. From there, you can follow the **Spitalgasse** east into the heart of the Altstadt. The street's name soon changes to **Marktgasse,** the main road of the Old City. Just south of the Altstadt, across the Aare, are several museums and the embassy district (take the Kirchenfeldbrücke Bridge to get there).

Staying in Bern

Bern is small for a national capital, and conventions and international meetings overbook it regularly. For this reason, I choose some of town's larger hotels to try to maximize your chances of finding a room. Make reservations far in advance whenever you plan to visit.

Bern has no real high season. **Interlaken** has a high season in the summer (the rates go way up at most hotels, but not at the ones I've listed in this section). After you're up into the Alps, high season is all year *except* during a brief period in midsummer, when ski conditions aren't great.

The folks at the Bern tourist office (☎ **031-328-1212,** fax: 031-312-1233; Internet: www.bernetourism.ch) will book you a room for free, or use the big hotel board and free phone just outside the tourist office (at the top of the escalators down to the train tracks).

Bern's top hotels

Hotel Bern

$$$$ Bern, Altstadt

This massive hotel is popular with diplomats and business travelers who are drawn to its modern rooms and large selection of in-house restaurants. Rooms facing the streets are bigger and brighter than those opening onto the small inner courtyard. The cheaper rates apply during weekends and holidays. Children under 16 stay free in parents' room (or at 20 percent discount in a separate one).

Zeughausgasse 9 (just off Kornhausplatz). ☎ *031-329-2222. Fax: 031-329-2299. Internet:* www.hotelbern.ch. *Bus/Tram: 5, 9, 10, 12. Rates: 210–280SF ($140–$186.65) double. AE, DC, MC, V.*

Hotel Goldener Schlüssel

$$ Bern, Altstadt

Jost Troxler runs his hotel and restaurant (I recommend it later) with care, and keeps the prices low for an inn just "99 steps" from the **clock tower.** The modular furnishings are beginning to show wear, but remain sturdy. Rooms on the back overlook a medieval Bern sweep of rooftops and are the quietest (except for the charming hourly chimes of the nearby bell tower). Though at the moment the eight top-floor accommodations share two toilets and one shower, they'll soon be converted into fewer but larger rooms, each with a private bathroom.

Rathausgasse 72 (just off Kornhausplatz). ☎ *031-311-5688. Fax: 031-311-0216. Internet:* www.goldener-schluessel.ch. *Bus/Tram: 5, 9, 10, 12. Rates: 114SF ($76) double without bathroom, 145SF ($96.65) double with bathroom. AE, MC, V.*

Hotel National

$$ Bern, near Hauptbahnhof

The prices are low at this imposing 1908 castle-in-the-city, but it's a bit lifeless. The elevator doesn't make it up to the fifth floor, where the bathrooms and furnishings are newer and the modern double-glazed windows more efficient at blocking traffic noise from the boulevard below. Accommodations are larger than most in Bern, with patterned rugs atop the carpet and a hodgepodge of faux antique and modular furnishings. The hotel incorporates the popular South American–themed Shakira bar.

Hirschengraben 24 (just south of the train station) ☎ *031-381-1988. Fax: 031-381-6878. Internet:* www.nationalbern.ch. *Bus: 9, 10, 16. Rates: 100–120SF ($66.65–$80) double without bathroom, 120–150SF ($80–$100) double with bathroom. AE, DC, MC, V.*

Bern's runner-up accommodations

Hotel Glocke

$$–$$$ This hotel is pretty cheap and right on the main square in town — a bit noisy, but located perfectly. Management seems far more concerned with running the restaurant and the ground-floor Quasimodo disco bar (cheap grub) than attending to its hotel guests. *Rathausgasse 75.* ☎ *031-311-3771; Fax: 031-311-1008. Rooms without a bathroom save you about $15 a night.*

Hotel Kreuz

$$$ The Hotel Kreuz is another large, amenitied, business-oriented hotel like its neighbor the Bern. Many rooms hide foldaway beds for families. *Zeughausgasse 39–41.* ☎ *031-329-9595; Fax: 031-329-9596; Internet:* hotelkreuz@ swissonline.ch.

Pension Marthahaus

$ The Marthahaus is Bern's only pension, with cheap rates and rooms a bit larger than those of the central hotels — plus the lady who runs it is a sweetheart. Rooms with private bathrooms ($17 more) also come with TVs and phones and have slightly nicer furnishings. *Wyttenbachstrasse 22a, (north of the Aare River).* ☎ *031-332-4135; Fax: 031-333-3386.*

Dining in Bern

Switzerland has taken culinary influences from the surrounding countries of Germany, France, and Italy, giving Swiss cooking a very international flavor. Cheese is a holey Swiss ingredient. There are about 100 varieties besides the sour, hole-riddled Emmentaler we generically refer to as "Swiss cheese." Emmentaler and Gruyère, along with white wine, garlic, and lemon, often get thrown together in a melting crock, carried to your table, and called fondue, one of the country's specialties.

Another national specialty is raclette, created when half a wheel of cheese is held over an open fire; when the exposed surface begins to melt, it is rushed over to you, and a melted layer is scraped off on your plate. This dish, too, is meant to be eaten with hunks of brown bread.

To go with your cheese, the Swiss offer the omnipresent rösti (a sort of delicious hash brown), lake fish, or sausages. Another typical Bernese dish is the Bernerplatte, a plate of sauerkraut or beans, piled with sausages, ham, pigs' feet, bacon, or pork chops.

An excellent way to wash it all down is with one of Switzerland's fine white or light red wines or a hand-crafted local beer. Swiss chocolates are some of the world's finest (Nestlé is a Swiss company). Though some locals eat it at breakfast, many Americans find that a bit too rich so early in the morning.

Cheap cafes and restaurants line Bern's two main squares, **Bärenplatz and Kornhausplatz**. The arcaded streets of the city are filled with kiosks selling *donner kebab* (pita stuffed with spicy lamb and a hot sauce), various Asian nibblers, pizzas, pretzel sandwiches, and *Gschnätzltes,* a Bern specialty of fried veal, beef, or pork (order *sur chabis* sauerkraut to go with it).

For a variety of quick-bite options, the indoor marketplace **Markthalle,** Bundesplatz 11, has lots of small food booths hawking prepared specialty foods to take away or to enjoy at a small table. It's open Monday through Friday 8:00 a.m. to 7:00 p.m. (9:00 p.m. Thursday), Saturday 8:00 a.m. to 4:00 p.m.

The supermarkets **Migros** (Marktgasse 46/Zeughausgasse 31), and **Coop** (in the Ryfflihof department store on Neuengasse) can provide fresh picnic ingredients, and both have inexpensive cafeterias where meals generally weigh in at under 20SF ($13.35). They are open weekdays 8:00 a.m. to 6:30 p.m. (opening 9:00 a.m. Monday and closing 9:00 p.m. Thursday), Saturday 7:00 a.m. to 4:00 p.m.

Bern's top restaurants

Della Casa
$$$$ Altstadt SWISS

This creaky local legend is pushing 110 in a building from the 1500s. The low-ceilinged, wood-paneled rooms are slathered with off-green paint, and the service is friendly and furious. The staff weaves expertly among the large crowded tables to bring the abundant portions of ravioli and *lamm-médaillons* (tender lamb medaillons in a rich sauce sided with rice and green beans) with Swiss efficiency. If you feel like loosening your wallet straps (and your belt), splurge on the local specialty *Bernerplatte,* an enormous platter of grilled meats served over beans and kraut — it'll cost 40SF ($27) but probably tide you over for two meals. Most regulars prefer the jovial tavern atmosphere on the ground floor to the fancier, more sedate dining room upstairs.

Schauplatzgasse 16. ☎ 031-311-2142. Reservations recommended. Bus: 9, 10, 12, 16. Main courses: 19.50–40SF ($13–$27). Quick lunch menu: 19.50SF ($13); full meal menu 23SF ($15). AE, MC, V. Open: Lunch Mon–Sat, dinner Mon–Fri.

Goldener Schlüssel

$$$ Altstadt   SWISS

You can tuck into hearty Swiss peasant cooking such as *Bauern Bratwirst erlebnis* (a 200-gram sausage under an onion sauce with rösti), or one of several vegetarian dishes of Indian or Mexican inspiration in this converted stone and wood 16th-century stable. Wash it all down with a half-liter bottle of a local Bern brew, *Mutzenbügler.*

Rathausgasse 72 (in the center of town). ☎ *031-311-5688. Reservations recommended. Bus/Tram: 9, 10, 12. Main courses: 19–33.50SF ($12–$21). Open: Lunch and dinner daily.*

Ratskeller

$$ Altstadt   SWISS

The starched-tablecloth restaurant is a bit pricey (the laid-back, brick vaulted keller underneath is cheaper), but for professional service and excellent meat dishes, this is one of the best splurge deals in town for a quiet, understated dinner. The *Oberlander rösti* are a house specialty, the cheesy rösti layered with bacon and topped by a fried egg.

Gerechtigkeitsgasse 81. ☎ *031-311-1771. Reservations recommended. Bus: 12. Main courses: 17.50–32.50SF ($11.65–$21.65). Fixed-price lunch menu: 19.80SF ($13.20). AE, DC, MC, V. Open: Lunch and dinner daily (cellar open only at lunch).*

Bern's runner-up restaurants

Anker Bern

$ The Anker Bern ain't fine dining, but this dark-wood locals' tavern does offer low-cost hearty meals — 15 types of pizzas, nine of rösti — in a convivial atmosphere. *Kornhausplatz/Zeughausgasse 1* ☎ *031-311-1113; Internet:* www.roeschti.ch.

Klötzlikeller

$$ Since 1635 Klötzlikeller has been the best and most authentic of Bern's old-fashioned brick-vaulted keller (cellar joints), serving big glasses of wine and beer alongside a limited menu of excellent Swiss specialties and hosting live music some evenings. *Gerectigkeitsgasse 62.* ☎ *031-311-7456.*

Le Beaujolais

$$$ Le Beaujolais is a candlelit-yet-comfy French bistro with refined food at reasonable prices. *Aarbergergasse 50–52.* ☎ *031-311-4886.*

Exploring Bern

Bern's historic center is comfortably scenic and walkable, with low-key sights like a dozen statue-topped fountains dating back to the 1500s and the **Zytgloggeturm (Clock Tower)**, on Kramgasse at the corner with Bärenplatz, which for over 460 years has treated Bern to a simple mechanical puppet show four minutes before every hour. May to October, there's a 45-minute tour of the clock's inner workings daily at 4:30 p.m.; it costs 6SF ($4) adults and 3SF ($2) children.

Bern's top sights

Kunstmuseum (Fine Arts Museum)

This museum preserves the world's largest collection of paintings and drawings by Bern native Paul Klee, offering a unique insight into this early-twentieth-century master's skill with color and expression. Though it also has a smattering of Old Masters like Fra' Angelico, Duccio, and Delacroix, the museum's particular strength is late-nineteenth- and early-twentieth-century art: a few works each by the best impressionists and surrealists along with paintings by Kandinsky, Modigliani, Matisse, Picasso, Léger, Pollock, and Rothko.

Hodlerstrasse 12. ☎ 031-311-0944. Open: Tues 10am–9pm, Wed–Sun 10:00 a.m.–5:00 p.m. Bus: 20, 21 (or 5-min. walk from train station). Admission: 6SF ($4) adults, 4SF ($2.65) students.

Bernisches Historisches Museum (Bern Historical Museum)

Switzerland's second-largest historical museum is housed in a fanciful faux-medieval castle from 1894 and contains a rich collection of artifacts. There's a bit of everything, from Burgundian suits of armor, furnishings and decorative arts, and Flemish tapestries to the original fifteenth-century carvings from the cathedral's *Last Judgment* portal and dioramas of everyday life in Bern over the past three centuries. Don't miss the Oriental collection (mostly Islamic), rendered all the more fascinating by its post-industrial display cases.

Helvetiaplatz 5. ☎ 031-350-7711. Open: Tues–Sun 10:00 a.m.–5:00 p.m. Tram: 3, 5. Admission: 5SF ($3.35) adults, 3SF ($2) students/seniors. Free Sat.

Münster (Cathedral)

On Münsterplatz, with its sixteenth-century Moses fountain, is Bern's Gothic cathedral from 1421, with enormous stained-glass windows and an elaborate *Last Judgment* carved over the main door (most of its reproduction; the originals are in the Bernisches Historisches Museum). The biggest draw of the cathedral is its 300-foot belfry, the highest in Switzerland, which offers a great panorama across Bern and its river with the Alps in the distance.

More Bern museums

Bern's only truly great museum is the **Kunstmuseum** (I list it earlier in the chapter), though the **Historical Museum** (also listed earlier) is worth a visit as well. All save the Kunstmuseum are on or near **Helvetiaplatz**, just over **Kirchenfeld Bridge**.

The best of the rest is the **Schweizerisches Alpines Museum (Swiss Alpine Museum)**, Helvetiaplatz 4 (☎ **031-351-0434**), explaining all you ever wanted to know about the Alps via maps, do-it-yourself slide shows, and a whole passel of scale relief models of Alpine regions, some dating from 1800. Admission is 5SF ($3.35) adults, 3SF ($2) students/seniors; it's open Monday 2:00 p.m.–5:00 p.m. and Tuesday–Sunday 10:00 a.m.–5:00 p.m. (mid-October–May closed noon–2:00 p.m.).

Others that may pique your interest are the **Naturhistoriches Museum (Natural History Museum)**, Bernastrasse 15 (☎ **031-350-7111**), not the best of its kind, but you can pay your respects to Barry (1800–14), the most famous of the old rescue St. Bernards (he saved over 40 people before retiring to Bern at age 12); and the **Museum fur Kommunikation (Museum of Communication)**, Helvetiastrasse 16 (☎ **031-357-5555**), spanning everything from stamps to cell phones. Admission at either is 5SF ($3.35) adults and 3SF ($2) students. Both keep hours roughly Tue–Sun 10:00 a.m.–5:00 p.m.; the Natural History Museum is also open Monday 2:00 p.m.–5:00 p.m.

Münsterplatz. No phone. Open: Easter Sunday–Oct, the cathedral is open Tue–Sat 10:00 a.m.–5:00 p.m. and Sun 11:30 a.m.–5:00 p.m.; Nov–Easter, hours are Tue–Fri 10:00 a.m.–noon and 2:00 p.m.–4:00 p.m., Saturday 11:00 a.m.–noon and 2:00 p.m.– 5:00 p.m., and Sun 11:30 a.m.–2:00 p.m.. Admission: Cathedral, free; belfry 3SF ($2), 1SF (65 cents) ages 7 to 16.

Einstein Haus

A young German dreamer named Albert Einstein was working as a third-class technical expert in the Bern patent office in 1905 when he came up with $E = mc^2$. It was while living at this house that he devised his famous "Special Theory of Relativity," revolutionizing twentieth-century science. The modest museum consists mainly of photos and photocopied letters, most translated into English.

Kramgasse 49. ☎ 031-312-0091. Open: Tues–Fri 10:00 a.m.–5:00 p.m., Sat 10:00 a.m.– 4:00 p.m. (Nov and Feb, Tues–Fri 1:00 p.m.–5:00 p.m., Sat noon–4:00 p.m.). Admission: 3SF ($2) adults, 2SF ($1.35) students/children; free under 6.

More cool things to see and do in Bern

Bears, chocolate, and a refreshing dip in the river are just a few of the additional treats this Alpine town has to offer.

✔ **Floating down the Aare.** Unlike most capital cities, Bern has a river so unpolluted the locals actually swim in it regularly. In warm weather, join the Bernese for a short hike up the river and then a leisurely float down the Aare to a free public beach just below the Altstadt (make sure you get out at the beach, as a dam/waterfall is the river's next stop).

✔ **Feeding the Bears.** Bern's most unique sight has to be the **Bärengraben (Bear Pits)**, just on the other side of Nydeggbrücke bridge from the Altstadt. Here you'll find up to 12 very well-fed live examples of Bern's civic symbol roaming around. Bern has had bear pits since at least 1441 — formerly on the square still named Bärenplatz, here since 1875. The bears are out daily 9:00 a.m.– 4:00 p.m. (to 6:00 p.m. in summer); the keeper sells 3SF ($2) bag-gies of fruit to feed them — these hairy fellows will ham it up to get you to drop them a piece of apple or carrot. Remember they're strict vegetarians. To the Bear Pits' left, a long path leads up the hillside to a ridge planted with Bern's fragrant **Rosengarten (Rose Garden),** with killer views over medieval Bern.

✔ **Observing how a federal government can operate on just $5 per citizen per year.** Switzerland began as a confederation of three forest cantons in 1291. Today's 23 cantons retain a remarkable degree of autonomy and governmental powers, making this one of the West's least centralized democracies. The federal chambers meet only four times a year for three-week sessions to debate legislative issues and foreign treaties. If you're curious for a glimpse into such a lean federal machine, you can tour the 1902 **Bundeshaus (Parliament),** Bundesplatz (☎ **031-322-8522;** Internet: www.parliament.ch), whose dome was modeled loosely on that of Florence's cathedral. The free tours are given Monday through Friday at 9:00 a.m., 10:00 a.m., and 11:00 a.m. and 2:00 p.m., 3:00 p.m., and 4:00 p.m. as well as Sunday at 10:00 a.m. and 11:00 a.m. and 2:00 p.m. and 3:00 p.m. (except when Parliament is in session, at which time you can observe from the galleries).

✔ **Shopping till you Drop: Chocolates, Watches, and Swiss Army Knives.** Bern has 3.7 miles of virtually continuous shopping arcade running down its three parallel main streets, with even more shops crowding the alleys and corridors connecting them.

Switzerland is home to **Nestlé, Lindt,** and those triangular **Toblerone** chocolates. You can get these famous factory-made chockies at **Merkur,** Spitalgasse 2 (☎ **031-311-0425**). If you want handmade sweets from a traditional confectioner, head to **Confisserie Abegglen,** Spitalgasse 36 (☎ **031-311-2111**), or **Confisserie Tschirren,** Kramgasse 73 (☎ **031-311-1717**) and in the Markthalle on Bubenbergplatz 9.

If you're in the market for a fine watch, the shop with the most reasonable prices is **Columna,** Spitalgasse 4 (☎ **031-311-0975**). If you're using this guide mainly to save enough to afford that 3,000SF ($2,143) Rolex (that's the cheapest model), put on your best and head to the burnished wood shrine of **Bucherer,** Marktgasse 38 (☎ **031-328-9090**).

The **Hullinger Swiss Knife Shop,** Aarbergergasse 11 (☎ 031-311-1992), carries cutlery in addition to Swiss Army knives, but you'll get the best prices from the locksmith's shop **Schlüssel Bern,** Neuengasse 5 (☎ 031-312-1315). You can also find knives, watches, cuckoo clocks, and a little bit of everything Swiss (or imagined to be Swiss) at general souvenir shops like **Swiss Plaza,** Kramgasse 75 (no phone); **Edelweiss,** Gerechtigkeitgasse 21 (no phone); or **Boutique Regina,** Gerechtigkeitgasse 75 (☎ 031-311-5616).

And on Your Left, Da' Bears: Seeing Bern by Guided Tour

The tourist office sponsors a bus tour of the center and major sights with a multilingual guide, costing 23SF ($15) adults and 12SF ($9) children. It runs 2:00 p.m. to 4:00 p.m. June through September daily; April, May, and October, Monday through Saturday; and November through March on Saturday only.

A two-hour walking tour of the **Altstadt** costs 12SF ($9) and leaves at 11:00 a.m. daily June through September. May through October, you can also see the city from below via a 90-minute raft tour daily at 5:00 p.m. (30SF/$20 adults, 20SF/$13 children) — this is a genuine rubber raft deal, not a cruise-type river boat, meaning you help paddle and need to bring a swimsuit.

Suggested One-, Two-, and Three-Day Itineraries

If you're the type who'd rather organize your own tours, this section offers some tips for building your own Bern-centered itineraries.

If you have one day

You can do the best of Bern easily in a day. First thing, head to the **Kunstmuseum** to commune with the works of Paul Klee and other old and modern masters. At 11:00 a.m., take a tour of **Parliament.** Then just head up to **Marktgasse** and start strolling downhill toward the far end of the **Altstadt,** taking in the ambiance of the city, its soft gray stone buildings with their coats of arms and red-tiled roofs and the cobbled streets with their statue-topped fountains. If you're a fan of genius, pop into the **Einstein Haus** before having lunch at **Klötzlikeller.**

After lunch, mosey across the river to visit the **Bear Pits** and climb up to the **Rose Gardens** for their beautiful vista across Bern. Head back into the Altstadt and detour left up Junkerngasse to visit the **Münster** (cathedral) after it reopens at 2:00 p.m. and climb its tower for another great cityscape. If you have time left, cross the river to the south to check out the **Bern Historical Museum** before it closes at 5:00 p.m. End with a traditional Swiss dinner at **Della Casa** and a drink at the **Pery Bar.**

If you have two days

Spend Day One as the one-day itenerary, only save the **Bern Historical Museum** for the morning of the seond day. After the historical museum and before lunch, check out the **Swiss Alpine Museum,** plus any of the others that catch your fancy. After lunch, head up to Bern's mini-mountain, the **Gurtenkulm,** or spend the afternoon shopping downtown. If you have only two days for all Switzerland, forget all that and spend Day Two in the Alps.

If you have three days

There's nothing left in Bern to see, so if you have a third day, get up early and splurge 204SF ($136) on a round-trip to the **Jungfraujoch,** Europe's highest train station slung 11,333 feet up between two of the mightiest Alps (see "Exploring the Berner Oberland" later in this chapter).

Exploring Beyond Bern

Because I'm spending the remainder of this chapter in the countryside, the excursions from Bern I recommend are more urban — the banking captial of Zurich, and Basel, a college town with an amazing repository of art.

Zurich: Swiss counterculture meets high finance

Switzerland's largest city and banking capital, Zurich is the prettiest of the country's big cities. Its oldest quarter is spread over the steep banks on either side of the swan-filled **Limmat River** as it flows out of the Zürichsee (Lake Zurich).

Zurich has always been a hotbed of radicalism and liberal thought. The Swiss Protestant Reformation started here in the sixteenth century, and the twentieth century has drawn the likes of Carl Jung, Lenin (who spent

World War I here, planning his revolution), Thomas Mann, and James Joyce, who worked on *Ulysses* in Zurich and returned a month before his death in 1941. Joyce's grave in **Friedhof Fluntern cemetery** (take tram 2) is near those of Nobelist Elias Canetti and *Heidi* author Joanna Spyri.

I recommend spending a relaxing 48 hours in Zurich, but you still can get a surprisingly good feel for the city in just a day.

Getting there

Zurich is well connected with Europe's major cities and is only 75 to 120 minutes from Bern by train (50 daily). Trains arrive at **Hauptbahnhof** (main train station) on the riverbank at the north end of town. The tourist office (☎ **01-215-4000,** fax: 01-215-4044; Internet: www.zurichtourism.ch) is at the station, Bahnhofplatz 15.

From the station, the tree-shaded shopping street of **Bahnhofstrasse** runs south, paralleling the **Limmat** a few blocks away, all the way to the shores of the **Zürichsee.** Running off to the left of this street are a series of medieval alleys that lead down to the river. Several bridges cross the river to the wide Limmatquai Street. Narrow side streets lined with shops lead to the other half of the old city.

You'll need to hop a **tram or bus** for some of the outlying sights and hotels, even though you can get to most of central Zurich on foot. The cost is 1.90SF ($1.25) for rides up to five stops, 3.20SF ($2.10) for longer trips, and 6.40SF ($4.25) for a *Tageskarte* 24-hour ticket.

Seeing the sights

The thirteenth-century **St. Peter's Church** at St. Petershofstaat 6 has the largest clock face in Europe — 28.5 feet across with a 12-foot minute hand. Nearby is one of Zurich's top sights, the Gothic **Fraumünster** church, with five 1970 stained-glass windows by artist Marc Chagall.

From here, cross the Münsterbrücke over the Limmat River to reach Zurich's cathedral, the twin-towered **Grossmünster.** Founded on a site said to be chosen by Charlemagne's horse (he bowed his head on the spot where a trio of third-century martyrs were buried), its construction ran from 1090 through the fourteenth century. The stained glass was designed by Swiss artist Alberto Giacometti in 1933. Climb the tower (2SF/$1.35) May to October for a great city view.

A long walk up Kirchgasse from the church and a left on Seiler Granben/Zeltweg takes you to Heimplatz and the **Kunsthaus** (☎ **01-251-6765**), Zurich's fine arts museum. The main collection starts with the impressionists of the late nineteenth century and runs to contemporary times, featuring works by Monet, Degas, Cézanne, Chagall, Rodin, Picasso, Mondrian, Marini, and especially the Swiss-born Giacometti. Admission is 5SF ($3.35) for adults, 2.50SF ($1.65) for children, and it's closed Monday (you can also take tram 3 here).

Zurich's cheapest sight is the park lining the mouth of the Zürichsee. You can stroll the west bank of the lake up and down the **General Guisan quai** (at the end of Bahnhof-strasse), which leads to an arboretum. Also at the base of Bahnhofstrasse are the piers from which dozens of steamers embark for tours of the lake. Most boat trips fall into two categories. The four-hour journey all the way to the opposite end of the lake and back (add in more time to get off and explore en route) runs about 26SF ($17.35). A 90-minute jaunt just around the northern end of the lake costs about 10SF ($6.65).

Before boarding the train out of town, pop into the free **Landesmuseum (Swiss National Museum)** just behind the station at Museumstrasse 2 (☎ 01-218-6511).

Where to stay and dine

Zur Oepfelchammer (☎ 01-251-2336), Rindermarkt 12 (just off the Limmat), serves up reasonably priced Swiss and French cuisine in a friendly, atmospheric ambiance. Although a bit pricey at 400 to 500SF ($266.65 to $333.35) a double, the romantic **Hotel Zum Storchen** (☎ 01-227-2727, fax: 01-227-2700; Internet: www.storchen.ch), Am Weinplatz 2, is the best bet in town — an 640-year-old inn right on the river in the center of Zurich's Altstadt. The tourist office can help you find someplace cheaper or other rooms if you can't find a room here.

Three, three, three countries in one! A visit to Basel

The Swiss answer to Four Corners, USA is Basel, a university city that features a pylon on the **Rhine River** where you can walk in a circle and move from Switzerland into Germany, then France, and back into Switzerland (the spot's called **Dreiländereck**). Basel's number of museums (27) makes it an art capital of Switzerland, and it claims Hans Holbein the Younger (along with thinker Friedrich Nietzsche) among its famous past residents. Non-art lovers needn't bother visiting, but if you have a thing for paintings, give the city at least a day or two if you're a fan of modern and contemporary art.

Getting there

Half-hourly trains make the 60- to 75-minute trip from **Bern** and arrive at **SBB Hauptbahnhof.** There's a small branch of the tourist office in the train station, but the main office (☎ 061-268-6868, fax: 061-268-6870; Internet: www.baseltourismus.ch) is on the Rhine at Schifflände 5, just past the Mittlere Bridge (take tram 1). Basel's compact, historic center lies mainly on the south bank of the Rhine River.

Seeing the sights

Although it has an impressive fourteenth-century **Münster** (cathedral), whose elaborately carved facade is the pride of Basel, this city is really about museums. Top honors go to the eclectic collections of the **Kunstmuseum** (☎ 061-271-0828; Internet: www.kunstmuseumbasel.ch), at St. Alban Graben 16. It has everything from Holbein the Younger and Konrad Witz to van Gogh, Picasso, Klee, Chagall, Rodin, and Alexander Calder.

Next-door is the **Museum für Gegenwartskunst** (☎ 061-272-8183), with contemporary art ranging from the 1960s to the present day by the likes of Bruce Nauman, Joseph Beuys, and Donald Judd. Nearby you can also find the **Kunsthalle** (☎ 061-272-4833), at Steinenberg 7, whose changing installations by contemporary artists are advertised on banners throughout town. Most museums are closed on Monday. There's also a world-renowned zoo (☎ 061-295-3535), at Binningerstrasse 40, a seven-minute stroll from the train station, with 600 species represented.

Where to stay and dine

The restaurant **Zum Goldenen Sternen** (☎ 061-272-1666), St. Alban-rheinweg 70 (at the Rhine's edge), has served up a good, inexpensive medley of French-accented Swiss and continental dishes since 1421. Art aficionados with shallow pockets will want to stay just across the river from the main part of town at the **Hotel Krafft am Rhein** (☎ 061-690-9130, fax: 061-690-9131), overlooking the Rhine at Rheingasse 12. The setting is nineteenth century, and the rooms are modern and comfy. Rates are 194 to 295SF ($129.35 to $196.65) for doubles.

Exploring the Berner Oberland

The triple peaks of the **Eiger** (13,025 feet), **Mönch** (13,450 feet), and **Jungfrau** (13,642 feet) dominate the Jungfrau region. A trip through the area can be a thrilling, scenic ride on trains that hug (or punch through) cliffsides and ski-lift gondolas that dangle high above mountain glaciers.

The gateway to the Berner Oberland is **Interlaken,** a bustling resort town in the foothills of the Alps that is flanked by a pair of lakes and is just a one-hour train ride from Bern. Interlaken itself doesn't have too much to hold your interest, but it makes an optimal base for forays into the Berner Oberland.

The Alps are scattered with tiny villages and quaint resort towns. One of the most visitor-friendly of these is **Mürren,** where you may notice that I recommend a few restaurants and hotels. Although I think you should visit the region at least three or four days, on the tightest of schedules you could take an overnight train to Interlaken, switch for a train up to **Jungfraujoch** to spend the day, and make it back to Interlaken by evening for another overnight train out — but that's pushing it.

Getting to the Berner Oberland

There are two trains an hour between Bern and Interlaken (a 50- to 60-minute ride), some requiring a change in Spiez. Get off at Interlaken's **Westbahnhof station** for the main part of town; at **Ostbahnhof station** to transfer to trains into the Jungfrau region.

The Berner Oberland

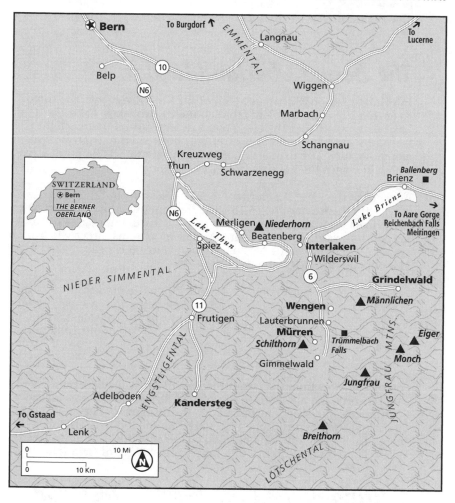

Where to get info after you arrive

For information on the Berner Oberland and the Alps, the **Tourist Office of Interlaken** (☎ **033-822-2121,** fax: 033-822-5221; Internet: www. interlakentourism.ch) is the unofficial central information bureau, with maps and advice on getting around the region. It's a seven-minute walk from Westbahnhof train station, in the Hotel Metropole at Höheweg 37. The tourist office is open Monday through Friday from 8:00 a.m. to noon and 2:00 p.m. to 6:00 p.m., Saturday 8:00 a.m. to noon; in summer, it stays open 30 minutes later on weekdays, until 5:00 p.m. Saturday, and also is open Sunday 5:00 p.m. to 7:00 p.m. **Mürren's Tourist Office** is in the Sportszentrum (☎ **033-856-8686,** fax: 033-856-8696; Internet: www.muerren.ch).

If you understand German, you can find good ski info at www.
berneroberland.com. General info on the Berner Oberland,
plus timetables for the major trains and cable cars, is supplied at
www.jungfraubahn.ch.

The Berner Oberland layout

Interlaken lies on the brief stretch of the Aare River (yes, the same
river that runs through Bern) that connects two lakes, **Lake Thun** and
Lake Brienz — hence the city's name, which means "between the
lakes." Its busiest tourist area stretches between the two train stations
along the Aare. The road that connects the stations is Bahnhof Strasse,
which becomes the parklike Höheweg.

Now about the **Alps;** the Berner Oberland is large, but this chapter
stays with the western half — it's the most popular and the easiest to
reach from Interlaken. Imagine you're standing in Interlaken and looking south toward the Alps. There are low mountains directly in front of
you. Behind them, to the east, is a trio of enormous peaks called **Eiger,**
Mönch, and, the most famous, **Jungfrau.**

Farther off to the west (right) is the slightly more modest peak of the
Schilthorn. Running south from Interlaken between the Jungfrau and
Schilthorn is a wide valley called the **Lauterbrunnen;** this is where the
area's main train line leads to various Alpine destinations (halfway up
the valley in the town of Lauterbrunnen is a station where you'll transfer trains frequently).

Scattered throughout the upper reaches of this valley are many
small resorts and alpine towns, such as **Mürren** (at the base of the
Schilthorn), and **Wengen** (halfway to the **Jungfrau**). Between
Interlaken and Lauterbrunnen town, the Alpine foothills are inter-
rupted by a valley that branches off to the east from Lauterbrunnen
Valley. Train tracks lead through here to the village of **Grindelwald.**

Getting around the Berner Oberland

Unfortunately, the various scenic and private rail lines — not to mention funiculars, ski lifts, and cable cars — that connect the peaks and
towns are ridiculously expensive. Rail passes such as Swissrail or
Eurail only get you a 25 percent discount at most. Always ask about
discounts for children, seniors, students, and so on. For each of the
sights in this chapter, I give directions and some idea of the frequency
of trains and connections.

Traveling around the Berner Oberland means plenty of train changes,
but this usually turns out to be kind of fun (if pricey). The wait between
connections is usually anywhere from five to ten minutes. Because the
schedule is consistent, and trains tend to run hourly, it's fairly easy to
hop off at any station, go see whatever town you're in, and pick up the
transfer an hour or two later.

The tourist office in Interlaken has Berner Oberland transportation maps (get one if you plan to explore) and schedules of the whole system. The staff is usually very good at helping you work out an itinerary. There is a summer Berner Oberland Regional Pass that gets you 7 days of travel (3 days for free, 4 at 50 percent off) for 150SF ($100), or 15 days (5 days free, 10 at 50 percent off) for 190SF ($126.65), but again it gets you only a discount on the **Jungfraujoch** and **Schilthorn rides.** More likely to work to your advantage is the Family Card. For around 20SF ($13.33), this card lets children under 16 ride free and unmarried young adults ages 16 to 25 get half off the regular price.

Staying in the Berner Oberland

At Interlaken and Berner Oberland resorts, you receive a "guest card" from your hotel for significant discounts on everything from the **Jungfrau train** to adventure outfitters. If it doesn't give it to you, be sure to ask for it.

Interlaken certainly doesn't lack hotels, but it also doesn't lack visitors to fill them. If you're having trouble finding a room, there's a hotel billboard with a phone outside each train station, or visit the tourist office, which can book you a room for free (heck, the office is located in the town's most modern hotel). The tourist offices of **Mürren** and other Berner Oberlander towns can help you find rooms as well, but these burgs are so small that you can do just as well following one of the many hotel signs as you exit the station.

The Berner Oberland's top hotels

Alpenruh
$$$ Mürren

One of Mürren's top choices is this Alpine-cozy but fully amenitied hotel next to the cable-car station with an excellent restaurant and private sauna. Best of all, it'll give you a *free* voucher for a morning ride up to the Schilthorn where you can breakfast in style — already a 44SF ($29.35) per person savings. The hotel stays open year-round, though the excellent restaurant closes in November.

Mürren. ☎ *033-856-8800. Fax: 033-856-8888. Internet:* www.schilthorn.ch. *Rates: 200–250SF ($133.35–$166.65) doubles. AE, DC, MC, V.*

Hotel Weisses Kreuz
$$ Interlaken

On the classiest drag in town, which is basically a city park, this year-round hotel has functionally spartan rooms. The comfort is good, the price is right, and the people-watching from its terrace is unparalleled.

Höheweg (at the corner with Jungfraustrasse). ☎ *033-822-5951. Fax: 033-823-3555. Internet:* www.weisseskreuz.ch. *Rates: 160–220SF ($106.65–$146.65) double. AE, DC, MC, V.*

Victoria-Jungfrau Grand Hotel

$$$$ Interlaken

If you can swing the price tag, this massive 1865 landmark of over-the-top Alpine architecture is *the* place to check in, joining a long list of dignitaries and royalty over the years. Antiques fill the rooms, the most expensive of which overlook the park of **Höheweg** and the **Alps** beyond.

Höheweg 41 (several blocks from Interlaken West station). ☎ *800-874-4002 in the United States; 033-828-2828. Fax: 033-828-2880. Internet:* www.victoria-jungfrau.ch. *Rates: 420–640SF ($280–$426.65) double. AE, DC, MC, V.*

The Berner Oberland's runner-up accommodations

Splendid

$$ The Splendid is a nondescript modern hotel with comfy rooms, all the amenities, glimpses of the mountains, and a popular corner pub featuring Interlaken's only Internet access. Rooms without bath are cheaper. *Höheweg 33 (in the center of Interlaken)* ☎ *033-822-7612; Fax: 033-822-7679.*

Chalet-Hotel Oberland

$$ The Chalet-Hotel Oberland is another modernish hotel offering somewhat nicer, newer, and roomier accommodations at the same price as the Splendid (no views, though). *(Just off Interlaken's main drag.)* ☎ *033-827-8787; Fax: 033-827-8770; Internet:* www.chalet-oberland.ch.

Alpina

$ The Alpina offers lower prices than the Alpenruh and great clifftop vistas across the Lauterbrunnen Valley. *(In Mürren.)* ☎ *033-855-1361; Fax: 033-855-1049; Internet:* www.muerren.ch/alpina.

Dining in the Berner Oberland

Most hotels in Berner Oberland resort towns either require or offer some meals in their own restaurants — and, in fact, there are few enough nonhotel restaurants to go around in these towns. This is not a hardship, really, for the food is usually quite good, especially in the hotels that I recommend here. However, I'd rarely opt for full board; that way, at least one meal a day you can take to try out the *other* hotel dining rooms in town!

For a primer on Swiss foods, see "Dining in Bern" earlier in this chapter.

In **Interlaken,** there's a **Migros supermarket** just to the right of the Westbahnhof to fill your daypack for picnics and hikes, and a huge new Co-op supermarket center across from the Ostbahnhof. There's also a Co-op market in **Mürren.**

The Berner Oberland's top restaurants

Hirschen
$$$ Interlaken SWISS

There has been a Gasthaus Hirschen here since 1666, an oasis of old-fashioned flavors and Alpine hospitality in touristy Interlaken. The low wood-paneled ceilings and overdressed tables strike an odd balance somewhere between rustic and fussy, but you'll be glad the fussiness spreads to their exacting standards in the kitchen — this is by far the best Swiss dining in town. Try the *Hirschen Platte* for two, a platter of grilled meats with *rösti* and a salad.

Hauptstrasse 11 (in Matten, the southerly neighborhood of Interlaken). ☎ *033-822-1545. Reservations recommended. Main courses: 9.50–49SF ($6.35–$32.65). AE, DC, MC, V. Open: Dinner Mon and Wed–Fri, lunch and dinner Sat and Sun.*

Restaurant im Gruebi
$$$ Mürren SWISS

Located in the **Hotel Jungfrau,** this restaurant excels in both mountain views (from its outdoor terrace or the glassed-in hexagonal dining room) and local cuisine, from herb-flavored rack of lamb for two to fondue bourguignonne.

In the Hotel Jungfrau (follow signs from the station). ☎ *033-855-4545. Reservations recommended. Main courses: 12–42SF ($8–$28). Fixed-price menus: 37–39SF ($24.65–$26). AE, DC, MC, V. Open for lunch and dinner daily.*

Restaurant Piz Gloria
$$ Schilthorn SWISS

To cap off an idyllic trip to the Swiss Alps, dine in Europe's most stratospheric restaurant — it slowly rotates atop a 9,804-foot mountain. If you can tear your eyes away from the view for a moment, sample the hearty Hungarian goulash or sirloin steak. This place is also a good place to have a high-altitude breakfast if you catch the first cable car up.

*Atop **Schilthorn** mountain, above Mürren. ☎ **033-855-2141**. Reservations suggested, but not required. Cable car: Half-hourly cable cars from Mürren will get you here in 20 min. (58.20SF/$38.80 round-trip, or 44SF/$29.35 "early bird" rate before 7:30 a.m.; discounts for various rail- and ski-pass holders); the last car down leaves at 6:00 p.m. (5:00 p.m. in winter). Main courses: 20–42SF ($13.35–$28). AE, DC, MC, V. Open: Daily from the first cable car's arrival until the last one's departure. Closed Nov 15–Dec 15, one week in May, and during blizzards.*

The Berner Oberland's runner-up restaurants

Il Bellini

$$$$ Il Bellini is one of the best Italian restaurants in Switzerland and a worthy splurge. Even on a budget, though, you can ride the skyscraping Metropole's elevator to the 18th floor and the **Top o' Met** cafe, where just 3.50SF ($2.35) will buy you a hot cocoa against a backdrop of Interlaken's best Alpine panorama. *Höheweg 37 in Interlaken's Hotel Metropole.* ☎ *033-828-6666.*

Stügerstübli

$ Stügerstübli is a rough-and-ready locals' joint in the center of Mürren offering the cheapest nonhotel eats in town. ☎ *033-855-1316.*

Goldener Anker

$ The Goldener Anker serves cheap, hearty, and surprisingly good food in an unassuming modern tavern atmosphere. *In Interlaken at Marktgasse 57 (between the train tracks and the river).* ☎ *033-822-1672; Internet:* www.anker.ch

Exploring the Berner Oberland

Prepare for the unique climate of the skyscraping Alps before you get on that train to the top of the world. A warm sunny day in Interlaken may still be sunny atop the Jungfrau, but the wind can bring temperatures deep into negative territory, so bring a heavy jacket. The sun reflects strongly off all that snow and UV rays are more concentrated, so be sure to wear sunglasses and sunscreen. The highest peaks poke into a very thin atmosphere (about 30 percent less oxygen than at sea level), so it's easy to overexert yourself into dizziness and hyperventilation.

Check the weather conditions and forecasts before you set off into the mountains. An overcast day can make an excursion to the panoramic terraces of Jungfrau or Schilthorn a moot point, and avalanche warnings may crimp your skiing or hiking plans. Displayed on TVs at train stations, tourist offices, and hotel rooms and live-linked at www.swisspanorama.com is a live video feed that switches from the **Jungfraujoch** to the **Schilthorn** to **Männlichen.** The Web site www.meteotest.ch will fax or e-mail you a personalized weather forecast, or you can check in with the local tourist office. Real-time forecasts are available at ☎ 033-855-1022 for the Jungfraujoch, ☎ 033-856-2655 for the Mürren/Schilthorn area, ☎ 033-855-4433 for the Männlichen/Kleine Scheidegg area, or ☎ 033-854-5054 for the First ski area above Grindelwald.

The Queen Peak at Jungfraujoch

The most spectacular and rewarding excursion in the region is to **Jungfraujoch,** where at 11,333 feet — the highest rail station in Europe — your breath quickens by the stupendous views and the extremely thin air. An elevator takes you up from the station to the even higher **Sphinx Terrace** viewpoint to look out over Europe's longest glacier, the 25km (15.5-mile) **Great Aletsch,** whose melt-off eventually makes its way to the Mediterranean.

The view goes on seemingly forever — on a clear day, you can even see as far as Germany's **Black Forest.** One of the popular attractions is the **Eispalast (Ice Palace),** a warren of tunnels carved into a living glacier and filled with whimsical ice sculptures, including a family of penguins and a sumo wrestler. There's a mediocre restaurant (22SF/$15 fondue) and a cafeteria up top in case you didn't pack a lunch.

Trains run half hourly from **Interlaken's Ostbahnhof** (2.5 hour.; 159SF/$106 round-trip). You change once in Lauterbrunnen (☎ 033-855-1261), pause in Wengen, and change again in **Kleine Scheidegg** (☎ 033-855-1417) before making the final run to **Jungfraujoch station** (☎ 033-855-2405). Since 1894, this popular route has run like a machine well-oiled with tourist money, so the transfers are smooth.

Four of the last 6 miles of track are in tunnels, but the train pauses a few times to let you peer out through windows in the rock at the glaciated surroundings. On your way back down, you can change trains at Kleine Scheidegg to detour west through **Grindelwald.** For more information, contact the Jungfraubahnen directly at ☎ 033-828-7233 or on the Web at www.jungfraubahn.ch.

A bit of Bond history atop the Schilthorn

A favorite excursion of mine is to take a ride from **Mürren** — home to a fabulous **Sportzentrum** sports complex, with an indoor pool, outdoor skating rink, squash, tennis, curling facilities, and more — up the dizzying cable car to the 9,804-foot peak of the **Schilthorn.** The trip takes you across the Lauterbrunnen Valley with views of the **Big Three peaks**, so you get a great panorama of the Alps' poster children. The summit shares its scenic terrace with the **Piz Gloria** restaurant (recommended earlier).

When the financiers building Europe's most spectacularly sighted restaurant atop the Schilthorn went over budget, James Bond came to the rescue. A film company used the half-finished structure to play the role of "Piz Gloria," headquarters of evil SPECTRE leader Telly Sevalas in *On Her Majesty's Secret Service.* George Lazenby (filling in for 007 between Sean Connery and Roger Moore's gigs), got a real view to his kills as he fought bad guys while hanging from the cable car lines (and on skis and in a bobsled . . .). After shooting wrapped, the film company helped pay for the restaurant's completion and, because the movie provided such great advance publicity, the restaurant decided to take its stage name.

There are half-hourly trains to **Mürren** from **Interlaken's Ostbahnhof**, with a change at Lauterbrunnen (60 minutes; 15.60SF-$10). When the funicular-train line from Lauterbrunnen to Mürren is snowed in, take the hourly Postbus (15 min.; 2.60SF-$1.75) to Stechelberg and the half-hourly **Schilthornbahn cable car** (☎ 033-856-2141; Internet: www.schilthorn.ch) up to Gimmelwald (first stop) and Mürren (10 minutes; 14.40SF/$10). Half-hourly cable cars from Mürren get you to the top of the **Schilthorn** in 20 minutes (58.20SF/$39 round-trip or 44SF/$29 "early-bird" rate before 7:30 a.m.; discounts for various rail- and ski-pass holders). If you're up for a workout, you can hike up in a rather demanding, but exhilarating, 5 hours (a 4,363-foot climb).

Mürren's **Tourist Office** is in the Sportszentrum (☎ 033-856-8686, fax: 033-856-8696; Internet: www.muerren.ch). It's open Monday through Friday 9:00 a.m. to noon and 1:00 p.m. to 6:30 p.m. (to 8:30 p.m. Thursday), Saturday 1:00 p.m. to 6:30 p.m., and Sunday 1:00 p.m. to 5:30 p.m.

Skiing and other outdoorsy stuff

If you came to Switzerland hoping to log a few miles of **Alpine skiing,** there's no better base for it than **Wengen,** a resort under the looming **Jungfrau trio** and near the **Lauterbrunnen Valley** with some 100km (62 miles) of pistes, 23 lifts (from cable car to T-bar), and access to most of the region's major ski areas (Wengen, Männlichen, and Kleine Scheidegg). There are half-hourly trains here from **Interlaken's Ostbahnhof**, with a change in Lauterbrunnen (45 to 55 minutes; 11.80SF/$8). Those arriving by car will have to leave their wheels in the garage down in Lauterbrunnen (☎ 033-855-3244) and take the train up to car-free Wengen.

The tourist office (☎ 033-855-1414, fax: 033-855-3060; Internet: www.wengen.com) can help you make sense of the multitude of trails, some 20 lifts (both cable car and chair), and over 7 miles of cross-country terrain. They can also point you toward rental outfitters and the local branch of the famous **Swiss Ski School** (☎ 033-855-2022). Less intrepid sports enthusiasts can skate or curl in town.

When there isn't much snow, Wengen sports over 500km (310 miles) of hiking trails (most open in summer only, but 50km/31 miles open in winter too). One of the most popular is a fairly flat jaunt along the wide ridge of the Männlichen massif, from the top of the Männlichen cable-car station (☎ **033-855-2660**) to Kleine Scheidegg (1.5 hours; descending gradually about 555 ft.). A bit more of a workout, but wonderfully scenic, is the steady uphill walk (none of it too steep) from **Wengen** to **Kleine Scheidegg**, most of it with a terrific panorama of the **Jungfrau** group before you and the Schilthorn across the valley (2.5 to 3 hours; climb a total of 2,594 feet).

Even more spectacular hikes are available down in **Lauterbrunnen Valley** (Lauterbrunnen town is 15 minutes by train or 90 minutes by foot below Wengen). From Lauterbrunnen, take the hourly postal bus or walk in 45 minutes to **Trümmelbach Falls** (☎ **033-855-3232**), actually 10 stair-stepped waterfalls in one as glacial melt off from the surrounding mountains thunders down the deep crevice of a gorge at 20,000 liters per second. April to November, you can ride an elevator up the inside of the cliff to stroll behind the cascades daily 9:00 a.m. to 5:00 p.m. (July and August, 8:00 a.m. to 6:00 p.m.); bring a raincoat. Admission is 10SF ($7) adults and 4SF ($2.65) children 6 to 16. Also near Lauterbrunnen, **Staubbach Falls** is a 1,000-foot ribbon of water plunging straight down the valley's cliffside at the edge of Lauterbrunnen town.

Hike the hills from Grindelwald

Cars can reach **Grindelwald** (half-hourly trains from **Interlaken's Ostbahnhof** take 36 min. and cost 9.40SF/$6; be sure you're on the right car, as the train splits in half at Lauterbrunnen), so this resorty village in the eastern alpine foothills gets more crowded than its less accessible neighbors. However, it is also one of the best bases for hiking.

The **Tourist Office** (☎ **033-854-1212**, fax: 033-854-1210; Internet: www. grindelwald.ch) has trail maps covering everything from easy scenic rambles to rock climbing up the sheer eastern face of **Mount Eiger**. It's open mid-December through April, Monday through Friday 9:00 a.m. to noon and 2:00 p.m. to 6:00 p.m., Saturday 9:00 a.m. to noon and 2:00 p.m. to 5:00 p.m., and Sunday 10:00 a.m. to noon and 3:00 p.m. to 5:00 p.m.; June through October, Monday through Friday 8:00 a.m. to 7:00 p.m., Saturday 8:00 a.m. to 5:00 p.m., and Sunday 9:00 to 11:00 a.m. and 3:00 to 5:00 p.m.; May and November through mid-December, Monday through Friday 8:00 a.m. to noon and 2:00 to 6:00 p.m. and Saturday 8:00 a.m. to noon. Or, **Bergsteigerzentrum** (☎ **036-535-200**) can organize guided hikes of all degrees of difficulty, from glacier-climbing lessons to an easy, three-hour guided romp along the foot of Mount Eiger.

An hour's hike up to **Milchbach** brings you to the base of the **Obere Gletscher** glacier, whose milky white runoff gives the spot its name. If you continue 45 minutes up the side of the glacier, you're treated to the **Blue Ice Grotte**. Glacial ice turns a deep, resonant blue as you get down into it, and you can take a spin inside a slowly creeping glacier here for 5SF ($3) mid-May to October. A postal bus can run you back down to town in 15 minutes.

One of the region's best picture postcards — the snowcapped Alps rising from behind a flat-glass mini-mountain lake called the **Bachsee** — is a fairly easy hour's uphill hike (only about 232 feet total elevation) from the first cable-car station above Grindelwald.

Castles and cute villages: Around Interlaken's lakes

When you tire of the heights, you can explore the mild weather and resorty feel of Interlaken's lakes. The **Thunersee (Lake Thun)** is the more popular of Interlaken's two lakes (☎ **033-251-0000** or 033-654-7266; Internet: www.thunersee.ch). A four-hour boat tour (☎ **033-334- 5211;** Internet: www.bls.ch) runs year-round (eight times daily in summer, once daily in winter) for 33.20SF ($22).

The lake's main town of **Thun** (tourist info at the train station; ☎ **033-222-2340**) lies at the opposite end of the lake from Interlaken. Thun has long since overgrown its island core — perched where the lake flows out to become the Aare River again. On the Aare's right bank lies Thun's **Hauptgasse,** the arcaded and shop-lined main drag. From the 17th-century town hall on Rathausplatz, you can climb a long stairway up to **Castle Kyburg,** a fortress from the 1100s. This is occasionally open as a museum with military collections, archaeological finds, and a Gobelin tapestry (when open, it keeps hours 9:00 a.m. to 6:00 p.m. June through September 10:00 a.m. to 5:00 p.m. April, May, and October; and 1:00 p.m. to 4:00 p.m. in winter).

You're more certain to find open the **Oberhofen Castle** (☎ **033-243-1235** or 033-431-235), on the lake's north shore. Its rooms are set up just as they appeared in various periods from the sixteenth to the nineteenth century. Mid-May through mid-October, it's open Monday 2:00 p.m. to 5:00 p.m. and Tuesday through Sunday 10:00 a.m. to noon and 2:00 p.m. to 5:00 p.m.

You can also tour **Lake Brienz** (www.brienzersee.ch) out the other end of Interlaken for 26.40SF ($18). The round-trip takes a little under 3 hours; it stops at the lakeside village of **Iseltwald** and at **Geissbach,** whose magnificent waterfalls you can reach via a funicular (May through October; 4.50SF/$3.20) from the boat's final stop, the wood-carving town of **Brienz.**

Near Brienz, outside the village of **Ballenberg,** is the **Swiss Open-Air Museum of Rural Dwellings and Lifestyles** (☎ **033-951-1123**), 2,000 acres laid out roughly as a map of Switzerland with the vernacular architecture of each of the country's regions and cantons re-created using original buildings. Rather than eat at the cafeteria, save your hunger for the freshly made breads, cheeses, and sausages sold at the various working farmhouses and "settlements" that make up the park. This odd but enjoyable museum/park is open April 15 through October, daily 10:00 a.m. to 5:00 p.m.; admission is 14SF ($9) adults, 12SF ($8) students, and 7SF ($5) children. The bus leaves Brienz at 2:26 p.m., returning from Ballenberg at 4:55 p.m. (If ferries don't float your boat,

Chapter 19

Prague and Environs

●●●

In This Chapter

▶ Getting to and around Prague

▶ Covering what you need to know

▶ Exploring Prague by neighborhood

▶ Discovering the best places to sleep and eat

▶ Planning itinerarires and side trips

●●●

*P*rague emerged from behind the Iron Curtain in 1989 to shine once again as a beautiful world-class city. Cobbled streets weave past baroque palaces, lively beer halls, glowering castles, and light-infused cathedrals. Summer is a tourist's delight. For entertainment, some of the best street musicians in Europe play on elegant bridges spanning the swan-filled river.

When the Communist Bloc disintegrated with the Soviet Union's breakup, a group of Czech activist writers and artists led by Vaclav Havel encouraged Czechoslovakia to make a peaceful transition from communism to democracy. The movement, which many called the "Velvet Revolution," also peaceably redrew the ancient dividing line between the Czech and Slovak Republics. Prague became the hot new destination, a "Paris of the '90s" for Gen-Xers imitating Hemingway's ex-pat routine. But because of rapid expansion, the city's magic was doused by skyrocketing prices and tainted by the influx of Western culture (McDonald's, for example).

But Prague has finally revived itself. In summer, backpackers and bus tour groups flock to the city, drawn to prices lower than most of Western Europe. If you're looking for a romantic setting, you'll find it here. And you'll probably hear more English than Czech spoken on the streets of the Old Town.

In the fall and winter, the crowds are gone, and Prague is all yours. Look for the magic, and spend several days of your trip here to fully capture the city's dreamy flavor. The skyline is dotted with spires, steeples, and towers, and Prague becomes a fairy-tale place at sunrise and sunset.

With a little practice, you can pronounce tongue-twisting Czech words with ease. Vowels are usually short, but any accent makes them long. Consonants are pronounced more or less as in English, except slightly roll your r's, and c sounds like *ts, čv* sounds like *ch, ch* sounds like *k, j* sounds like *y, řv* sounds like *rsh, šv* sounds like sh, *w* sounds like *v,* and *z* sounds like the slurred *zh* sound in *azure* or *pleasure.* Pronounce consonants followed by an apostrophe (d, n, t) as if there were a *y* following them. For example, *deěkuji* (thank you) is pronounced dyeh-KOO-ee; *chci* (I would like…) is spoken ktsee; and *nàměstì* (square) is pronounced nay-mee-STEE.

Making Your Way to and around Prague

For travel to your hotel, you can pick up a bus or taxi at the airport; train stations are connected to the subway lines. Although subway stations abound in central Prague, the best way to explore the city is on foot.

Getting to Prague by air

From Prague's small **Ruzyně airport**, 12 miles west of the city center, a half-hourly ČEDAZ (☎ **02-2011-4296**) shuttle bus runs in 30 minutes to náměstí Republiky, for 90Kč ($2.80). City bus 119 will take you from the airport to the Dejvická Metro stop in 40 minutes; bus #108 can get you to the Hradčanská Metro stop (both on line A). A taxi from the airport downtown should cost around 400Kč ($12.10). If you don't want to wait in line at the curb, call one of the radio taxi companies listed under "By taxi" later in this chapter to ensure getting a fair deal and a lower rate (though you will have to wait ten minutes or more).

Getting to Prague by rail

Trains arrive in Prague either at the **Hlavní Nádraží (Main Station)** on the east edge of Nové Měvsto; or, from Berlin and other northerly points, at the smaller **Nádraží Holešovice (Holešovice Station)** across the river to the north of the city center.

Both train stations, especially the main one, are seedy and chaotic. Dozens of hoteliers practically assault you the instant you step off the train, trying to sell you a hotel room — very annoying. Just ignore them and push ahead. If you want a reputable accommodation agency in the station, see the section on hotels in this chapter.

Getting around once you're in Prague

You can use the same tickets for all of Prague's public transportation. The 8Kč (25 cents) nepřestupní ("no change") version is good for 15 minutes or 4 metro stops, but you cannot change to another bus/tram (you can transfer within the metro). With the 12Kč (35 cents) přestupní ("change") version, you can make unlimited bus, tram, or metro transfers within the 60-minute time limit (90 minutes from 8:00 p.m. to 5:00 a.m. and on weekends).

You can buy tickets from machines at Metro stations, newsstands marked Tabak or Tafika, and DP ticket kiosks. You can get unlimited-use passes for 1 day at 70Kč ($2.10), 3 days at 180Kč ($5.45), 7 days at 250Kč ($7.60), or 15 days at 280Kč ($8.50).

By Metro (subway)

Prague's Metro (subway) system does a good job of covering the town with only three lines: A, B, and C. Each line intersects the other two only once: A and B at Můstek (the north end of Václavské náměstí), A and C at Muzeum (the south end of Václavské náměstí), B and C at Florenc (a regional bus station).

By tram and bus

The tram system, supplemented by buses, is a more complete network that effectively covers much of central Prague. In winter, the tram seats are heated. Beware of tram 22: many people call it the "pickpocket tram" because of the pickpockets who prey on visitors using the tram. The line passes by the National Theater and heads through the Malá Strana up to Prague Castle. Staré Město has only a few public trams and buses following its boundary roads. Several lines skirt the riverbank (especially tram 17) to hit Staroměstské náměstí, which also has a Metro line A station.

By taxi

You probably don't want to use a taxi unless your hotel is a great distance from Prague's center. The taxi drivers are notorious for ripping off unsuspecting tourists. If you must take a taxi, call a radio cab. In a pinch, hail one on the street, but be careful — you may end up with an unlicensed mafia cab ("mafia" here means that you're likely to be taken for a ride — financially, that is).

Wherever you get the cab, keep an eye on the meter. The display window on the left shows your fare; the window on the right should read 1, 2, 3, or 4, indicating the rate you're being charged. (The higher the number, the higher the rate.) Unless you venture far out from the center of town, the window on the right shouldn't read anything but 1 (although the parking lot of the main railway station is zoned "2"). The initial charge should be 40Kč ($1.20) and then 18Kč (55 cents) per kilometer. If the rate is increasing by more than that, question it.

Don't let a taxi driver cover the meter's displays or change the rate as he changes gears. Let the cabbie see you making a note of the taxi number and any other identifying info as you get into the cab, and sit in the front seat to keep an eye on the driver.

Your chances of getting an honest cabbie are better if you call a radio cab company (most Praguers will tell you *never to* hail a cab, especially ones waiting around tourist sights). Because the trip is logged in an office, it's more difficult for the driver to inflate the fare. Companies with English-speaking dispatchers include **AAA Taxi** (☎ **02-312-2112** or 1080 locally), or **ProfiTaxi** (☎ **1035**).

Discovering Prague: What You Need to Know

Knowing your way around the local currency and having a plan in case of emergency can make the difference between a pleasurable trip and a possible nightmare. This section gives you a sense of what's in store money-wise and directs you to some helpful resources if you need help, either minor or big-time.

The local dough

The Czech unit of currency is called the koruna (Kč) and is divided into 100 hellers. Roughly, $1 equals 33Kč, or 10Kč equals 30 cents. Czech coins include 10, 20, and 50 hellers and 1, 2, 5, 10, 20, and 50 koruna. Bills come in denominations of 20, 50, 100, 200, 500, 1,000, and 5,000 koruna.

Where to get info after you arrive

Although you've planned well for your visit to Prague, you're bound to have a question or three once you set foot on foreign soil. Check out these sources of information:

Prague Information Service, at Na Príkope 20 (☎ **02-264-023;** or 187 or 02-544-444 for general information; Internet: www.prague-info.cz), has become the main information office in town, though what's free is scanty and it charges 20 to 27Kč (60 cents to 80 cents) for most of its booklets. PIS is open 9:00 a.m. to 7:00 p.m. (5:00 p.m. weekends); you'll find other branches in the Old Town Hall at Staroměstské nám 1 (☎ **02-2448-2018**), in the train station (☎ **02-2423-9258**), and (summer only) in the tower over the Mala Strana end of Charles Bridge (no phone).

Čedok, Na Príkopě 18 (☎ **02-2419-7111,** fax: 02-232-1656), was once the state-run visitors bureau, but today specializes more in tourist services (air, rail, bus, theater, and concert tickets, plus room-booking). Another

resource, especially for hotels, is **AVE Ltd.** (☎ **02-2422-3226** or
02-2422-3521, fax: 02-5731-5193; Internet: www.avetravel.cz), found in
the train stations.

If you're gutsy enough, you can sometimes get good information by
waltzing into the priciest hotel you see, acting like a registered guest,
and asking the concierge for information. Newsstands carry an English-
language weekly newspaper, the **Prague Post** (www.praguepost.com),
packed with useful information and events calendars. Also, you can
visit these Web sites: www.ticketpro.cz or pis.eunet.cz.

Where to go in a pinch

In case of emergency, keep the following list of references handy:

- ✔ **Emergency:** Dial ☎ **158** to call the police, or ☎ **150** report a fire.
  For an ambulance, call ☎ **155.**

- ✔ **Embassy:** The U.S. Embassy is located at Tržiště 15
  (☎ **02-5732-0663**).

- ✔ **Doctors/hospitals:** In a medical emergency, call or taxi to the
  Foreigner's Medical Clinic, **Na Homolce Hospital,** Roentgenova 2,
  Praha 5 (☎ **02-5292-2146** or 02-5292-2522 at night). If your condition is not life-threatening, go to one of the branches of the
  First Medical Clinic of Prague, at Vyšehradská 35, Praha 2
  (☎ **02-292-464**) or Na Perštýně 10, Praha 1 (☎ **02-2421-6200**). The
  clinic offers emergency care, house calls, and referrals to specialists. They're open Monday to Saturday, 7:00 a.m. to 7:00 p.m. (with
  a 24-hour emergency service at ☎ **0603-555-006**).

- ✔ **Pharmacies:** A Czech pharmacy is called a *lékárna.* Several pharmacies remain open 24 hours a day, including Palackého 5, Praha
  1 (☎ **02-2494-6982**), and Lekama U Anděla, Štefánikova 6, Praha 5
  (Metro: Anděl; ☎ **02-537-039** or 02-5732-0918).

- ✔ **Safety:** Walking or taking the Metro or trams alone at night is safe,
  but always be on the lookout for pickpockets, especially on
  Charles Bridge, around parts of Old Town, and on public transportation. Wenceslas Square is a little seedy during the day; at
  night it is traveled mainly by prostitutes.

Staying in touch

Need to wire home for more beer money? Want to get online to check
your e-mail? The following information can help keep you in touch
while you're touring Prague.

- ✔ **American Express:** Prague's American Express office, Václavské
  nám 56, Praha 1 (☎ **02-2421-9992**), is open daily 9:00 a.m. to 7:00
  p.m. It provides the following services: currency conversion, sightseeing tours, air tickets, and car rental. It does not sell train tickets.

- **Internet access and cyber cafes:** In the Old Town, **Hermes Internet Cafe,** Nekazanka 10, off Na Prikkopě in the Staré Město (☎ 02-2421-6554; Internet: www.hermescafe.cz), is open 24 hours daily and charges 100Kč ($3.05) per hour. **Internetcafe Prague,** 25 Narodni, at the southern edge of Staré Město (☎ 02-2108-5286; Internet: www.highland.cz), is open Monday to Friday 9:00 a.m. to 9:00 p.m. and charges 60Kč ($1.80) for 30 minutes.

  In the New Town, **Café Electra,** Rasinovo nabrezi 62, on the river south of Jiraskuv Bridge in the southerly part of Nové Město (☎ 02-297-038; Internet: www.electra.cz), is open 8:00 a.m. to midnight and charges 80Kč ($2.40) per hour. **Cafe-Com,** Na Porici 36, just north of Nám. Republiky in the northerly part of Nové Město (☎ 02-2481-9435; Internet: www.cafe-com.cz), is open daily 9:00 a.m. to midnight and charges 25Kč (75 cents) for 15 minutes.

  Across the river, **Internet Cafe U Zlate ruze,** Thunovska 21, behind Sternberg Palace in the Malá Strana (☎ 02-5753-3974; Internet: www.internetpoint.cz), is open daily 10:00 a.m. to 8:00 p.m. and charges 3 cents per minute.

- **Mail:** You can find a 24-hour post office at Jindrišská, just off Václavské nam.

- **Telephone:** A local call in Prague costs at least 4Kč (12 cents). Pay phones accept either coins or **phone cards,** sold at post offices, tobacconists, or newsstands in denominations ranging from 150 to 600Kč ($4.55 to $18.20). Coin-operated phones do not make change, so insert money as needed, but use smaller coins. Here's something to confuse you: A Czech dial tone sounds like a busy signal in the United States; the Czech busy signal sounds like a U.S. dial tone. For Czech **directory assistance,** call ☎ 120 or 121; for international directory assistance, dial ☎ 0149.

  The country code for the Czech Republic is **420.** Prague's city code is **02;** drop the initial zero if you're calling from outside the country. In other words, to call Prague from the United States, dial **011-420-2** followed by the number. To charge a call to your calling card, dial AT&T (☎ 00-4200-0101), **MCI** (☎ 00-4200-0112), or **Sprint** (☎ 00-4208-7187). To call the United States direct from Prague, dial **001** followed by the area code and number.

- **Transit info:** Call ☎ 02-2422-4200 or 02-2422-3887 for **train** info. (You can also get information online through Germany's Deustsche Bahn site, Internet: bahn.hafas.de, or the Czech Railways site, Internet: idos.datis.cdrail.cz). For **city-to-city bus** info, call ☎ 1034. And for **flight** info, call ☎ 02-367-814 or 02-2011-3314 (www.csa.cz).

- For Metro info, call the **Muzeum station** (A and C lines) at ☎ 02-2264-0103 or the Můstek station (line B) at ☎ 02-2264-6350. For city **tram and bus** info, call ☎ 02-6731-0176, or check online at www.dp-praha.cz. Prague public transit is also online at www.dp-praha.cz.

Touring Prague by Neighborhood

Central Prague is divided into four main neighborhoods that straddle both sides of the **Vltava River.** This river flows through the city from the south and then curves off to the east. **Staré Město** (Old Town) is tucked into a bend of the river (on the east bank), hemmed in by the Vltava on the north and west and by the continuous arc of streets **Národní/Října/Na příkopé/Revoluční** on the south and east.

Staré Město, which means Old Town, is Prague's center. You'll find meandering streets dating back to the Middle Ages and wide boulevards from more recent centuries. The area was declared a UNESCO World Heritage site in 1993. This area, filled with restaurants, cafes, and gorgeous Gothic and baroque architecture, is a great place to spend most of your time. Within Staré Město is **Josefov,** the famed old Jewish quarter. The focal point of the Old Town is **Staroměstské náměstí,** or Old Town Square.

Surrounding the Old Town on all but the riverside is the **Nové Město** (New Town). New Town is much less interesting than the Old City or the Malá Strana district (described below). It is comprised mostly of office and apartment buildings. Still, you may enjoy the National Theater here, and the hotels are generally less expensive than those in Old Town.

In the center of Nové Město is **Václavské náměstí** (Wenceslas Square), a four-block-long divided boulevard sloping gradually up to the dramatic neo-Renaissance National Museum. The strip down the middle (for pedestrian traffic) is lined on both sides with sausage stands and neoclassical and art nouveau buildings. (This area has been called "New Town" since its 1348 founding; it's just a coincidence that much of that medieval neighborhood was replaced in the nineteenth and twentieth centuries by an even newer New Town.)

You cross a statue-lined **Karlův most** (Charles Bridge) from the Old Town into the **Malá Strana,** the "Little Quarter" on the west bank of the Vltava River. The area around the **Prague Castle,** originally settled by Germans in 1257, became very popular a few centuries ago, leaving a legacy of Renaissance and baroque palaces. Above the Malá Strana is the small **Hradčany,** the "Castle District," which houses the city's major sight, Prague Castle. Over the centuries, many palaces (several now housing museums) and monasteries have gathered around this traditional seat of government.

Beyond Prague's four traditional neighborhoods, the city has sprawled outward in every direction. One outlying neighborhood that you may want to visit is on the eastern edge of New Town. **Vinohrady** was named after the vineyards (owned by the king) that once filled this upscale residential zone. If Prague has a modern trendy district, Vinohrady is it — clean, full of shops and restaurants, and just a short hop from the city center on the Metro line A.

Accommodations, Dining & Attractions in Prague

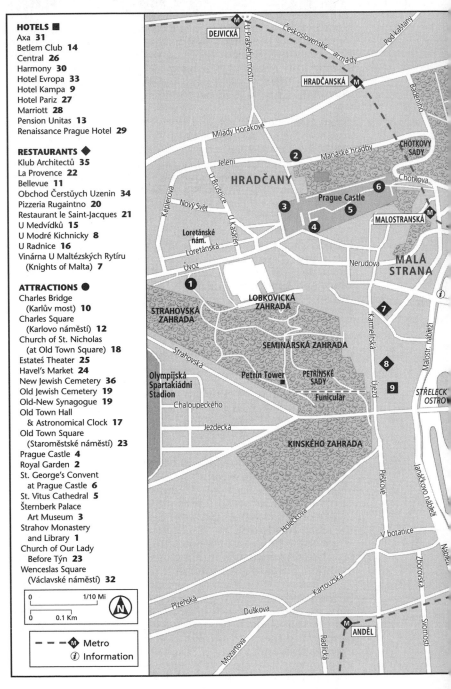

HOTELS ■
Axa **31**
Betlem Club **14**
Central **26**
Harmony **30**
Hotel Evropa **33**
Hotel Kampa **9**
Hotel Pariz **27**
Marriott **28**
Pension Unitas **13**
Renaissance Prague Hotel **29**

RESTAURANTS ◆
Klub Architectů **35**
La Provence **22**
Bellevue **11**
Obchod Čerstých Uzenin **34**
Pizzeria Rugaintno **20**
Restaurant le Saint-Jacques **21**
U Medvídků **15**
U Modré Kichnicky **8**
U Radnice **16**
Vinárna U Maltézských Rytíru
  (Knights of Malta) **7**

ATTRACTIONS ●
Charles Bridge
  (Karlův most) **10**
Charles Square
  (Karlovo náměstí) **12**
Church of St. Nicholas
  (at Old Town Square) **18**
Estateś Theater **25**
Havel's Market **24**
New Jewish Cemetery **36**
Old Jewish Cemetery **19**
Old-New Synagogue **19**
Old Town Hall
  & Astronomical Clock **17**
Old Town Square
  (Staroměstské náměstí) **23**
Prague Castle **4**
Royal Garden **2**
St. George's Convent
  at Prague Castle **6**
St. Vitus Cathedral **5**
Šternberk Palace
  Art Museum **3**
Strahov Monastery
  and Library **1**
Church of Our Lady
  Before Týn **23**
Wenceslas Square
  (Václavské náměstí) **32**

```
0              1/10 Mi
0        0.1 Km
```

- - - - ⓂMetro
ⓘ Information

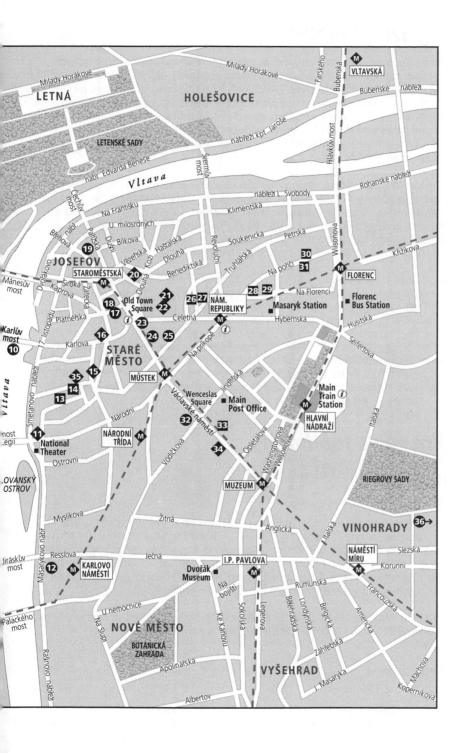

Staying in Prague

Prague is an expensive city, probably the most expensive in eastern Europe, but the rates are nowhere near those of, say, London. Prices soared in the years after the fall of the Iron Curtain, but prices have stabilized and, in some cases, have gone down as the forces of competition temper runaway inflation and development. Prague may not be as cheap as you might hope, but it won't be as expensive as you may fear. The priciest rooms are in the most desirable neighborhoods: Staré Město and Mála Strana.

The rapid capitalist invasion has also led to some dubious business practices. Many hotels charge one price for Czechs and another for foreign tourists. It's annoying, but unavoidable. Hotels won't give you a good exchange rate from koruna to dollars, so try not to pay your bill in dollars or Deutschmarks (though most business-oriented hotels still tie their rates to one of those two stable currencies).

Remember: As soon as you step off the train at the station, you'll be accosted by an army of hotel representatives trying to sell you a good deal on a room. These deals are almost always false. They're either located way out from the center of town and much more of a dump than the "creative" photos suggest, or they're full of hidden extras that pump the price way up. Avoid the guys selling these rooms, and visit a more legitimate accommodations agency. Plenty of these agencies will help you find a hotel room, a pension, or even a full apartment. Among the more reputable ones are the Prague Information Service, AVE Ltd., and Čedok — all mentioned as tourism offices previously.

Prague's top hotels

Betlem Club

$$ Staré Město

The Betlem Club is a pleasant enough hotel in a quiet corner of the Old City across the street from the church where Jan Hus started his protestant revolution. Most of the rooms are done in shades of brown, tan, gray, brass, and the odd orange splash, but they are immaculately kept. They're oddly shaped, but most are of a good size (except for some of the top floor mansard rooms, which can be comically cramped).

Betlémské Námčstí 9. ☎ 02-2222-1574. Fax: 02-2222-0580. Metro: Národní Třída. Rates: 2,600–3,600Kč ($78.80–109.10) doubles. No credit cards.

Hotel Evropa

$$ Nové Město

You'll probably be impressed by the remarkable, statue-topped art nouveau facade (circa 1903–05) and classy sidewalk cafe of Prague's prettiest hotel. Unfortunately, the rooms seem to belong to a different hotel entirely.

They vary widely in size and decor. Most are merely adequate, and some verge on dingy, but many also have a bit of faded low-rent, turn-of-the-twentieth-century style hanging about. But the rooms on the high-ceilinged first two floors make for quite an enjoyable stay.

Václavské nám. 25. ☎ *02-2422-8117. Fax: 02-2422-4544. Metro: Můstek. Rates: doubles 2,600Kč ($78.80) without bath; 3,990Kč ($120.90) with bath. AE, MC, V.*

Hotel Kampa

$$$ Malá Strana

The Kampa inhabits a seventeenth-century armory on a quiet side street across the river, about a five-minute walk from the Charles Bridge. The simple, whitewashed, somewhat large rooms are boringly institutional, but comfy enough, fitted with plain-Jane dark wood furnishings. Try to get one overlooking the river or nearby park.

Všehrdova 16 (just off Újezd). ☎ *02-5732-0404. Fax: 02-5732-0262. Metro: Malostranská. Rates: 3,960–4,380Kč ($120–132.75) double. You get a 5 percent discount if you pay cash. AE, MC, V.*

Hotel Paříž

$$$$ Staré Město

This whimsically fantastic Czech art nouveau behemoth was built in 1904 at the edge of the Old Town. It's hands-down my choice for luxury in town, with far more character than most Prague business hotels. The large rooms were overhauled in 1998 and fitted with a modern interpretation of Deco — soft sofas and chairs in a sitting corner and contemporary prints on the walls. The lobby is flanked by the Café de Paris and the Sarah Bernhardt, serving French and international delicacies, the ceilings feature nouveau chandeliers, and the walls are wrapped with aqua and gold mosaics.

U Obecního domu 1 (off Nam. Republicky). ☎ *800-888-4747 in the United States; 02-2422-2151 in the Czech Republic. Fax: 02-2422-5475. Internet:* www.hotel-pariz.cz. *Metro: Můstek. Rates: 9,180Kč ($270) double. AE, DC, MC, V.*

Pension Unitas

$ Staré Město

This place is as minimalist as you'll find, but it's probably the most central, too. In its history, it was a prison of the Communist-era secret police and then was run by nuns, which should give you some idea about the glamour of the rooms: a bit like crammed college dorms. But they are clean and bright. They've kept the original penitentiary doors on the basement cells — sleeping two to six in bunk-beds (P6 was once President Havel's cell, back when he was a dissident) — but they've been painted a festive pink. In 1996, they added a three-star wing, the **Cloister Inn,** where doubles go for 2,750 to 4,200Kč ($80 to $125) and are larger with varnished pine modular furnishings, a sofa in each room, and modern baths.

Bartolomějská 9 (one block north of, and parallel to, Národní and the Old Town's southern edge). ☎ **02-232-7700.** Fax: 02-232-7709. Internet: www.cloister-inn.cz. Metro: Staroměstská. Rates: 1,200Kč ($36.35) double (higher during holidays). No credit cards.

Prague's runner-up accommodations

Axa

$$ This place is a sort of modern health spa (pool, fitness center, weight rooms, and so on) that happens to rent rooms; it's on one of Prague's main city middle-class shopping boulevards. Na Poříčí 40. ☎ **02-2481-2580.** Fax: 02-232-2172. Internet: www.vol.cz/AXA.

Central

$$ Okay, so it ain't much to look at, but the name is fitting and the rooms are surprisingly reasonable for the location. Rybná 8. ☎ **02-2481-1013.** Fax: 02-232-8404.

Harmony

$$$ This hotel is moderate and modernized. You'll find it across the street from the Axa (described above), but staff refused to show me any rooms, so I can't say much more. Na Poříčí 31. ☎ **02-232-0016.** Fax: 02-231-0009.

Marriott

$$$$ The Renaissance Prague Hotel's brand-new 1999 neighbor and sister hotel has all the bland-but-cushy amenities of a typical Western chain. V. Celnici 7. ☎ **02-2224-4444.** Fax: 02-2224-4445. E-mail: praguemarriott@terminal.cz.

Renaissance Prague Hotel

$$$$ This soullessly modern, cookie-cutter international hotel was built in 1993 — but it has all the comforts of home. V Celnici 7. ☎ **02-2182-2100.** Fax: 02-2182-2200. Internet: www.renaissancehotel.com.

Dining in Prague

Traditional Czech cuisine is usually simple and hearty. Soups are meaty and frequently flavored with garlic. A favorite is hovězí polévka s játrovými knedlíčky (liver dumplings in beef stock). Praguers are fond of dumplings, called knedlíčky, made of bramborové (potatoes) or houskové (bread) and sliced into discs. Dumplings are side dishes to such favorites as svíčková na smetaňe, a beef pot roast sliced and served with a creamy and rich vegetable sauce and a sour cranberry chutney.

Also check out *pečená kachna,* roast duck with bacon dumplings and sauerkraut. Game dishes, such as *zvěřina* (venison), *zajíc* (hare), *bažant* (pheasant), and *hus* (goose), are usually roasted. Popular freshwater fish are *pstruh* (trout) and *kapr* (carp). Hungarian *guláš* (beef goulash) is a good, cheap standby for quick lunches. The best desserts are *ovocné knedlíky* (fruit dumplings), *vdolek* (jam tarts), and chocolate- or fruit-filled *paličinky* (crêpes).

Czech *pivo* (beer) is a great brew. Light-colored beer is *světlé* (svyet-lay); dark beer is *černé* (cher-nay). This is the home of **Pilsner Urquell**, the country's famed lager (the brewery also makes a smooth, for-local-consumption-only beer, **Gambrinus**). If you're a beer-drinker, you might also want to try **Staropramen** (the most common Prague suds), **Velkopopovický** (a wonderful dark beer), and **Kozel** (a spicy, but not bitter, brew).

By far, the most renowned Czech beer is **Budvar,** the original Budweiser — although it's nothing like the watery, mass-produced American beverage. (Budvar and Anheuser-Busch have been fighting for years over the name rights; their provisional settlement over the issue explains why you won't find Budweiser in some European markets and why you can't get Budvar in the United States.)

With the exception of some of the better restaurants and the tourist-trap places nearest the sights, meals in Prague can be very inexpensive. One of the trade-offs is remarkably poor service, a relic of the Communist era, when restaurant patrons received their meals only at the extreme convenience of the server. When service is haughty, ignore it and don't tip; when service is scarce, just chalk it up to economic growing pains. As investors start finer restaurants in Prague, their attention to service and food presentation should trickle down through the rest of the industry.

Watch out for these restaurant rip-offs:

 ✔ Every item brought to your table may be charged to your bill, including bread, bowls of nuts, and so on. Often, these small items turn out to be ridiculously expensive. Make sure that you know the price of everything before you eat it.

 ✔ Examine your bill closely at the end of the meal to make sure it isn't padded with items that you didn't order. Also, some restaurants doctor the amount written on a credit card slip, so you may want to write the total, in words, somewhere on the slip.

These few bad apples shouldn't ruin your *jablkový* (apple) strudel; just be wary.

For quick eats, tasty, tiny, open-faced sandwiches called *chelbíčky* are all the rage at **U Bakaláře** (Celetná 12). Sidewalk stands hawk *klobásy* (grilled sausages) and *párky* (boiled frankfurters) served with bread and *hořčice* (mustard).

Prague's top restaurants

Bellevue (formerly Parnas)
$$$$ Staré Město INTERNATIONAL

Here, you'll find the best food in one of the city's finest restaurants. And you can enjoy it surrounded by live music and, if you scam a window seat, a view of Prague Castle. The international menu varies from spinach tagliatelle in a salmon cream sauce to braised rabbit, always well prepared and presented. But the veggie dishes are less than thrilling. Sunday brunch features live jazz. Incidentally, the restaurant names can get confusing: This was once the location of a famed restaurant called Parnas, which is now located down the street by the National Theater. Stick with Bellevue; the food is far better.

Smetanovo nábřeží 2 (at the foot of Legli Bridge). ☎ *02-2422-7614. Reservations highly recommended. Metro: Staroměstská. Main courses: 360–690Kč ($10.90–20.90). Fixed-price menu: 790–990Kč ($23.93–30). AE, DC, MC, V. Open: Lunch and dinner daily.*

Restaurant Le Saint-Jacques
$$$ Staré Město FRENCH

You can enjoy solid French cuisine in this welcoming, friendly restaurant. Try the tasty French onion soup, light grilled salmon, juicy beef fillet in a green peppercorn sauce, and *tarte Tatine* apple pie for dessert. All are available at good prices. The live piano and violin music some nights can overpower the small rooms, but at least the low light of the candles keeps you from "appreciating" the contemporary art on the walls.

Jakubská 4. ☎ *02-232-2685. Internet:* www.infor.cz/lesant-jaques. *Reservations recommended. Metro: Náměstí Republiky. Main courses: 250–650Kč ($7.60–19.70). AE, MC, V. Open: Lunch Mon– Sat, dinner daily.*

U Modré Kichnicky
$$$$ Mala Strana CZECH/GAME

This very private and relaxing art nouveau–styled space is renowned for its traditional Czech game dishes. The interior contains a series of small dining rooms with vaulted ceilings and playfully frescoed walls. Service is professional and friendly, and the refined cookery manages to rise above most "Bohemian cuisine" in town, while still remaining adamantly Czech — lots of duck and venison alongside salmon, trout, and rabbit (but you can get beef, pork, and chicken as well).

Nebodviská 6 (a small street parallel to Karmelitská, south of the castle). ☎ *02-5732-0308. Reservations recommended. Tram: 12 or 22. Main courses: 320–724Kč ($9.70–21.95). No credit cards. Open: Lunch and dinner daily.*

U Radnice
$ Staré Město   CZECH

This place is truly an original. If you want quality, traditional working-class goulash, come to this steadfast holdout in the heart of the old city. U Radnice also has a pub and bar; the laid-back, beer-and-pretzels atmosphere rubs off on the dining room.

U Radnice 10 (at the back of the west side of Staroměstské náměstí). ☎ *02-2422-8136. Reservations not accepted. Metro: Staroměstská. Main courses: 150–280Kč ($4.55–8.50). No credit cards. Open: Lunch and dinner daily.*

Vinárna U Maltézských Rytířů (Knights of Malta)
$$ Malá Strana   CZECH

This is one of Prague's most beloved eateries, a bastion of Czech food, good flavors, and warm welcomes. Seating is limited (especially in the atmospheric, candlelit basement), so reserve ahead to enjoy duck breast with cranberry sauce and potato gnocchi, a lamb cutlet, or pasta with fresh vegetables. The apple strudel with ice cream and egg nog is a must for dessert.

Prokopská 10 (off Karmelitská). ☎ *02-536-357. Reservations recommended. Metro: Malostranská. Main courses: 325–440Kč ($9.85–13.35). AE, MC. Open: Lunch and dinner daily.*

Prague's runner-up restaurants

Klub Architektů
$$ This little place occupies a series of hot vaulted cellar rooms under Jan Hus' old church; the food can be uneven, but the convivial atmosphere is catching and the prices are low. *Betlémské náměstí 5.* ☎ *02-2440-1214.*

La Provence
$$$ La Provence serves a sometimes uneven Provençal-inspired cooking (though coq au vin and roasted duck are both winners), but it's set below one of the city's trendier bars, so the convivial-leaning-to-noisy atmosphere is guaranteed. *Štupartská 9, one long block off the east side of Staroměstské náměstí.* ☎ *02-232-4801 or 02-9005-4510.*

Obchod Čerstvých Uzenin
$ Here's a great Czech deli that has goulash and other stand-up hot foods available at the back. *Václavské náměstí 36 (no phone).*

Pizzeria Rugaintno

$ You'll find excellent wood-oven pizzas, and a few pasta dishes, in boisterous rooms here. They even have a no-smoking section! *Dušní 4.* ☎ *02-231-8172.*

U Medvídků

$$ This beer hall dates from 1466. The beer on tap is the original Budvar, and the Czech food is hearty and filling. *Na Perštýně.* ☎ *02-2421-1916.*

Exploring Prague

The **Prague Card** is a **combined admissions pass** to some 40 sights, including the Prague Castle sights and Sternberg Palace. The card lasts for three days and costs 480Kč ($14.55) for adults, 380Kč ($11.50) students and children. You can buy the card at American Express, Čedok, or the Metro stations Holšovice or Muzeum.

Prague's top sights

Prague Castle (Prazský Hrad)

The Prague Castle sternly overlooks the entire city and is its own tiny city. Work began in the ninth century and seems to never stop, with the constant renovations taking place. The castle is enclosed by massive fortifications and spills over with churches, palaces, buildings, shops, and alleys that together take a full day to explore properly. (You might be able to make a *quick* run-though in two to three hours.) This is Prague's only truly must-see sight. The massive cathedral is one of Europe's grandest Gothic churches.

Construction on **St. Vitus Cathedral,** the castle's centerpiece, began under Emperor Charles IV in 1344. After a long interruption, it was finished in the nineteenth and twentieth centuries in a neo-Gothic style that tried to follow the original plans closely. The mosaic over the door dates from 1370. The light-filled interior of the cathedral contains the sumptuously decorated **Chapel of St. Wenceslas** (built in the fourteenth to sixteenth centuries). The sarcophagi of Bohemian kings are stored in the crypt.

The **Royal Palace** was the home to kings since the ninth century. The vaulted Vladislav Hall is still used for state occasions such as the inauguration of the Czech president, but the Czechs don't celebrate like they used to. In the Middle Ages, knights on horseback entered through the Rider's Staircase for indoor jousting competitions.

St. George's Basilica was built in the tenth century and is the oldest Romanesque structure in Prague. Its adjacent convent houses a museum of Gothic and baroque Bohemian art (☎ **02-5732-0889,** open Tuesday to Sunday 10:00 a.m. to 6:00 p.m.). The row of tiny houses clinging to the inside base of the castle ramparts was known as **Golden Lane,** because they were once home to goldsmiths and shopkeepers; today the area houses souvenir stands and cafes. Franz Kafka worked, and perhaps lived, for a time at #22. Whether alchemists practiced their craft of trying to turn lead into gold on this "golden" lane is a point of debate. Some say yes, but others point to a similar lane off the left flank of St. Vitus Cathedral as "Alchemy Central."

Main entrance at Hradčanské náměstí. ☎ 02-2437-3368. Internet: www. hrad.cz. *Metro: A to Malostranská or Hradčanská. Tram: 22, 23. Open: Castle grounds, daily 5:00 a.m.–12:00 a.m. (6:00 a.m.–11:00 p.m. Nov–Mar); most castle sights, daily 9:00 a.m.–5:00 p.m. (tower of St. Vitus Cathedral, Apr–Oct only); castle gardens, daily 10:00 a.m.–6:00 p.m. (closed Nov–Mar). Admission: Castle grounds and gardens are free. Combined ticket (good for three days) to St. Vitus Cathedral, Royal Palace, and St. George's Basilica, 120Kč ($3.65) adults, 60Kč ($1.80) students. English guided tours are 60Kč ($1.80) extra.*

National Gallery at Sternberk Palace (Sternberskýpalác)

Prague's main art gallery is housed in a gorgeous late seventeenth-century palace near the Castle. Its works span the fifteenth to twentieth centuries, including paintings by Rembrandt, Brueghel the Elder, Klee, and Munch. The finest piece is Dürer's huge *Feast of the Rosary,* painted in 1506.

Hradčanské náměstí 15 (across from the main entrance to Prague Castle). ☎ 02-2051-4599. Metro: A to Malostranská or Hradčanská. Tram: 22. Open: Tues–Sun 10:00 a.m.–6:00 p.m. Admission: 70Kč ($2.10) adults, 40Kč ($1.20) students and children.

Charles Bridge (Karlův most)

This may be the loveliest and liveliest bridge anywhere in Europe. The statue-lined Charles Bridge is bustling with people throughout the day and evening — tourists, musicians, street performers, caricature artists, and crafts peddlers. The 1,700-foot span was constructed in the four-teenth century, but the majority of statues date from the early eighteenth century. (Actually, what you'll see on the bridge are copies; most of the originals have been moved inside for protection from the weather.)

Two of the earliest statues include the 1629 crucifix near the Old Town end (great effects during sunrise or sunset) and, halfway across, the haloed statue of St. John Nepomuk (1683), which honors the holy man tortured to death by King Wenceslas IV and then tossed off the bridge. A bronze plaque under the statue describes the event; rub the shiny, worn figure of the plummeting saint for good luck.

Climb the towers at either end for great bridge and city spire panoramas. The climb will cost you 30Kč (90 cents) for adults, 20Kč (60 cents) for students under 26 and seniors. The Mala Strana (West) Tower is open daily 10:00 a.m. to 6:00 p.m. (closed November to March); the Old Town (East) Tower is open daily March to October 10:00 a.m. to 6:00 p.m., November to February 10:00 a.m. to 5:00 p.m.

Old Town Square (Staroměstské náměstí)

A massive memorial to the fifteenth-century religious reformer and martyr Jan Hus graces the crossroads of Prague and its most gorgeous baroque square, Staroměstské. Beautiful buildings surround the square, which is perpetually crowded with street performers, tourists, and the general bustle of the city. Sit at an outdoor cafe table, and just watch it all for a while.

You can climb the tower in the **Old Town Hall** (☎ 02-2422-8456) for views across the rooftops, but its most popular feature is the **Astronomical Clock.** Rather than tell the hour, this fifteenth-century timepiece keeps track of moon phases, equinoxes, and various Christian holidays tied to them. On every hour from 8:00 a.m. to 8:00 p.m., it puts on a glockenspiel-style show of marching apostles and dancing embodiments of Evil.

Here's a grisly tale for you: The architect of the clock, Master Hanus, did such a good job that the city council feared he might one day build a better one elsewhere. To ensure that their clock remained superior, they had him blinded. Legend has it that, in despair and revenge, Master Hanus jumped into the clock's mechanism, crushing himself and throwing the works off-kilter for a century.

The **Church of Our Lady Before Týn** stands out with its twin multi-steepled towers. It's mainly Gothic, dating from 1380, and is the seat of Prague's Protestant congregation.

Staroměstské náměstí. Metro: A to Staroměstská. Tram: 17, 18, 51, 54. Bus: 135, 207. Open: Old Town Hall, Tues– Sun 10:00 a.m.–6:00 p.m. (5:00 p.m. Nov–Mar). Admission: Old Town Hall tower 30Kč (90 cents) adults, 20Kč (60 cents) students and children.

Jewish Prague (Josefov)

The Jewish ghetto lies on the north end of the Old Town. Jews lived in Prague before the tenth century, but by the twelfth century, they were confined to a small part of town. At the time, this area was walled off. Ironically, even though 88,000 of the country's 118,000 Jews died during the Holocaust, Nazi occupiers spared this center of Jewish culture. Hitler had been collecting the riches of Judaism as he exterminated Jews across Europe, and he planned to put all the scrolls, torahs, and other artifacts on display in Prague, turning Josefov into a "museum to a vanished race."

Most of those seized items were returned in 1994 to the diaspora from which they had been taken, but more than 39,000 local items (and more than 100,000 books) from Bohemia and Moravia stayed here in Prague as part of the **Jewish Museum,** its collections split among several of the synagogues that survived the ghetto's 1906 "rehabilitation." You can see Josefov's highlights in maybe 45 minutes to an hour, but I recommend spending a full morning here.

Your first stop should be the sixteenth-century **Maisel Synagogue,** on Maiselova, a renovated space that contains an exhibit of historical Jewish objects from the tenth to the eighteenth centuries. Part II of this collection (eighteenth century to present) resides in the gorgeous neo-Renaissance/Iberian-styled 1868 **Spanish Synagogue,** on Dušní, reopened in late 1998 after a decades-long restoration of its lush, Moorish-inspired decorations.

Although that collection covers the religious history of Czech Jews, their fascinating socio-cultural history is the subject of the exhibits that start in the **Klausen Synagogue** (on U Starého Hřbitova) and cover Jewish festivals. The exhibits continue in the nearby **Ceremonial Hall,** the cemetery's former mortuary hall, highlighting the customs and traditions surrounding illness and death, including a fascinating series of small paintings depicting all the steps in funeral ceremonies.

The **Old Jewish Cemetery,** off U Starého Hřbitova, behind a high wall, is one of Prague's most evocative sights. This Jewish burial ground dates back to the fifteenth century — when Jews couldn't bury their dead outside of the ghetto. Within this one-block plot, they had to find final resting places for some 20,000–80,000 deceased (the exact number is unknown). Consequently, they stacked the bodies 12 deep in some places. The shady, overgrown, undulating ground is blanketed with some 12,000 time-worn tombstones lurching and tilting in varying degrees of disrepair. The air is melancholy yet serene. This is one sight in Jewish Prague that you don't want to miss. The somewhat elaborate sarcophagus of the holy man Rabbi Loew (he died in 1609; see sidebar titled "Of myths and monsters") stands out.

Still an active temple and therefore not part of the Jewish Museum group is the **Old-New Synagogue,** Cervaná 2, built in 1270 and the only Gothic temple of its kind remaining. The small interior is beautiful, with high ceilings crisscrossed with five-ribbed fan vaulting. (Gothic church vaulting uses four ribs, but because those ribs represent the cross, the Jews decided five would be a bit more appropriate.)

Of myths and monsters

Jewish Prague's mythology boasts one of the first Frankenstein-type monsters. The legend goes that, in the sixteenth century, Rabbi Loew scraped clay from the riverbed and fashioned it into a giant that he called **Golem.** Loew placed a prayer scroll in the Golem's mouth, and the figure came to life, charged with protecting the Jews from persecution. Eventually, as in all good monster stories, the creature ran amok, and Rabbi Loew summoned all his power to subdue the Golem. As the magical life seeped out of his creation, the rabbi dragged the disintegrating clay body up to the loft of the Old-New Synagogue, where a lifeless mound of clay supposedly remains to this day.

Josefov's most moving sight is the **Pinkas Synagogue,** on Široká, built in the flamboyant high Gothic style of the sixteenth century. From 1950 to 1958, Holocaust survivors painted on the inside walls the names of 77,297 Czech Jews who died under the Nazi regime. The Communist Regime closed the synagogue and, claiming that dampness was leading to the deterioration of the walls, had the place replastered. As soon as communism ended and the synagogue was reopened, the Jews began the meticulous, four-year task of inscribing those names back on the walls. Upstairs are drawings (from a collection of 4,000) made by Jewish children while interned at the nearby Terezín Nazi camp (see "Exploring beyond Prague," later in this chapter). Of the 8,000 children who passed through there on the way to concentration camps, only 242 survived.

The ticket reservation center is at U Starého Hřbitova 3a; the Jewish Museum administrative headquarters are at Jáchymova 3; for individual sights, see the preceding sections. ☎ *02-2481-0099, 02-231-7191 or E-mail:* marek.selnekovic@ ecn.cz *to reserve tickets for the Jewish Museum sights, as well as the Old-New Synagogue. Internet:* www.jewishmuseum.cz. *Metro: A to Staroměstská. Tram: 17, 51, 54. Bus: 135, 207. Open: Jewish Museum and its synagogues, Sun–Fri 6:00 a.m.–6:00 p.m. (9:00 a.m.–4:30 p.m. Nov–Mar); the Old-New Synagogue, Apr–Oct Sun–Fri 9:00 a.m.–6:00 p.m. (5:00 p.m. Fri), Nov–Mar Sun–Fri 9:00 a.m.–4:30 p.m. (2:00 p.m. Fri). Admission: Jewish Museum sights and synagogues, 250Kč ($7.60) adults, 190Kč ($5.75) students; Old-New Synagogue, 200Kč ($6.05) adults, 160Kč ($4.85) students.*

Strahov Monastery (Strahovský Klášter)

Founded in 1140 by the Premonstratensian monks (an order that still lives here), this monastery was rebuilt in the Gothic style of the thirteenth century. It's renowned for its libraries, both the collections — more than 125,000 volumes, many of them priceless illuminated manuscripts — and for the long baroque hall that houses the philosophy and theology books. The ceiling fresco of the *Struggle of Mankind to Know Real Wisdom* is not to be missed. Also check out the baroque Church of Our Lady.

Strahovské nádvoří 132. ☎ *02-2051-6695. Tram: 22. Open: Tues–Sun 9:00 a.m.–noon and 12:30–5:00 p.m. Admission: 35Kč ($1.05).*

More cool things to see and do in Prague

Concerts, boating and beer — Prague has much more to offer visitors, both day and night.

✔ **Go concert-hopping.** As my first visit to Prague ended, I seriously considered abandoning the planned next leg of my journey to stay here. I had seen plenty of sights, but I had truly fallen in love with the dozens of classical concerts offered every evening throughout town — in churches and concert halls, in intimate private chambers and large public halls, under street arches, and in the squares. Many estimate that more musicians per capita live in the Czech Republic than anywhere else. The **Prague Information Service** (see "Where to get info after you arrive" earlier in the chapter) sells tickets at all its offices, or you can contact **Ticketpro** (☎ **02-2481-4020;** Internet: www.ticketpro.cz) or **Bohemia Ticket International** (☎ **02-2421-5031** or 02-2422-7832; Internet: www.ticketsbti.csad.cz).

In the city that gave the world the composers Smetana and Dvořák, and where Mozart wrote *Don Giovanni* and found greater acclaim than in his native Austria, you'll have a smorgasbord of offerings to choose from: an organ concert in the Týn Church, a chamber ensemble in a defunct monastery, or the Czech Philharmonic in the nineteenth-century **Dům umělců (Rudolfinum),** Alšovo nábřeží 12 (☎ **02-2489-3111**).

The *Prague Post* lists most events around town, or you can just wander the Old City, especially around Staroměstské Square, where you'll find the highest concentration of posters proclaiming the week's concerts and venues. If it's playing, attend Mozart's *Don Giovanni* in the venue where it premiered, the restored 1783 **Stavovské divadio (Estate's Theater),** Ovocný thr 1 (☎ **02-2421-5001;** Internet: www.anet.cz/nd). This theater is the only baroque performance space preserved just as it appeared in Mozart's day.

✔ **Make friends in a beer hall.** "Wherever beer is brewed, all is well. Whenever beer is drunk, life is good." So goes the Czech proverb. Praguers love their *pivo* (beer) — they consume 320 pints per year per Czech — and they love their local *hospoda* (pub or beer hall). Beer halls serve as gathering places for almost everyone.

Refer to the restaurant section for information about the different types of Czech beer, but you may need a quick lesson in beer-hall etiquette.

•**Share tables.** Always ask *Je tu volno* ("Is this spot taken?").

•**Put a coaster in front of you if you want beer.** Never wave down the waiter — he'll ignore you entirely.

•**Nod at the waiter and hold up your fingers for how many beers you want.** He'll leave a marked slip of paper at your table with the drinks.

The waiter visits you only twice (at the most), so when he comes around again, order all the beer you'll want for the rest of your stay. Pay him when he drops off your drinks, or you may have to wait for hours.

Check out the famous beer hall, **U Fleků**, Křemencova 11 (☎ 02-2491-5118), a brewery from 1459 (check out the brass band in the courtyard garden). Or go to the 1466 **U Medvídkůo**, na Perštýně 7 (☎ 02-2421-1916), for real Budvar on tap and good Czech pub grub. For a real, albeit famous, Praguer's bar, hit **U Zlatého tygra**, Husova 17 (☎ 02-2422-9020), a smoky haunt of writers and politicians.

✔ **Visit a park along the river.** Letná Park (Letenské sady) is a wide, flat swath of trees and shrubs on the western bank of the Vltava River, north of Malá Strana. You can find plenty of picnic spots, lots of paths winding through the trees and along the river, and even a beer garden in summer on the park's north side. Walk along the river tossing bread to, and making friends with, Prague's famed mute swans. Tram 1, 8, 25, or 26 will get you there.

✔ **Rent a paddle boat.** The Vltava is a beautiful river, filled with graceful swans and spanned by dramatic bridges. Sometimes, you're compelled to become a part of it — but don't. It's so polluted that swimming is out of the question. But from March–September, you can rent paddle boats (30Kč/90 cents per hour) and rowboats (20Kč/60 cents per hour) from **Půojčovna Romana Holana** at the docks of Slovanskýostrov, an island two blocks south of the National Theater.

Next door, **Rent-A-Boat** costs twice as much, but you can rent a rowboat with a lantern at the bow in the evenings (until 11:00 p.m.) and row around the river under the romantic moonlight and floodlit spires of the city. This boat will cost you 80Kč ($2.40) per hour. Rent-A-Boat also stays open until October (November if the weather holds).

And on Your Left, Prague Castle: Seeing Prague by Guided Tour

Plenty of outfits run **bus tours** of the city. Try these for the best reputation and prices:

Martin Tour (☎ 02-2421-2473; Internet: www.martintour.cz) runs a variety of city tours (general, Jewish Prague, historical, river cruises) lasting from 75 minutes to 3½ hours. Tours cost from 250Kč to 670Kč ($7.55 to 20.30). You can hop on at Staroměstské náměstí, Náměstí Republiky, Melantrichova, or Na Příkopě.

Premiant City Tour (☎ 0601-212-625 or 02-2494-8722; Internet: premiant.mujweb.cz) also runs city intro, historical/Jewish Prague, and river cruises lasting 2 to 3½ hours. The cost is 350Kč to 410Kč ($10.60 to 12.40). Tours leave from Na Příkopě 23.

If you're interested in a walking tour, try **Prague Walks** (☎ **02-267-9891** or 0603-841-363). Walking tours run daily. The cost is 250Kč ($7.60), 200Kč ($6.05) students. Tours meet under the Astronomical Clock on Staroměstské náměstí (look for the person with the ID badge and "Prague Walks" poster). Various walks cover introductory Prague (90 minutes; at 10:00 a.m. and noon), Prague Castle (two hours; noon and 2:00 p.m.), Jewish Prague (one hour; 1:00 and 3:00 p.m.), Franz Kafka (one hour; 4:00 p.m.), architecture (75 minutes; 2:00 p.m.), and mysterious Prague (one hour; 4:00 and 6:00 p.m.).

Suggested One-, Two-, and Three-Day Itineraries

If you're the type who'd rather organize your own tours, this section offers some tips for building your own Prague itineraries.

If you have one day

Spend a full morning exploring **Prague Castle** — the **Cathedral, the Royal Palace, St. George's Basilica,** and other sights nearby. Make your way down to the river, grab an eat-as-you-go lunch along the way, and cross the remarkable **Charles Bridge** into the **Staré Město.** Take your first left to walk up into **Josefov,** and spend the afternoon in the museums, synagogues, and cemetery of the Jewish quarter.

When evening falls, make your way to the lovely heartbeat of Prague, the baroque building–lined square **Staroměstské nám,** where dozens of billboards, posters, and ticket hawkers allow you to browse for the best classical concert to suit your tastes happening that evening. Stop by a Prague Information Service (PIS) office when you get to town and book tickets in the morning, or the best ones may be sold out. If it's summer, you could wait until you're crossing the Charles Bridge around lunchtime — a PIS office/ticket booking center is in the base of the tower at the **Malá Strana** end of the bridge.

If you have two days

Spend all of Day One in the **Malá Strana.** Start off at **Prague Castle,** but take a bit more time after seeing the big sights to enjoy some of the temporary exhibits that rotate through its galleries and halls. Pop into **Sternberg Palace** afterward for a dip into Renaissance and baroque art. Then make your way down to **Malostranské nám,** exit it on **Karmelitská** street, and take the first left down **Prokopská,** which becomes **Nebodviská,** to have a filling Czech lunch at **U Modré Kichnicky.**

After lunch, continue down Nebodviská to **Hellichova,** take a right, cross Karmelitská, and wind your way up through the **Seminářská Zahrada** (Seminary Gardens) to the library and frescoes inside the **Strahovský Klášter** (Strahov Monastery) at the western edge of the gardens. Hop on Tram 22 and ride it all the way around to the back side of Prague Castle to **Malostranské nám** again, where you can get off and mosey on down to **Charles Bridge,** crossing back into the **Old Town** to rustle up some dinner and a concert.

Start off Day Two in **Josefov,** exploring the sights, synagogues, and culture of Jewish Prague. If Prague's Jewish history intrigues you, leave early enough (by 1:00 p.m.) to get to Florenc station and grab a bus for the hour's ride outside town to the Nazi internment camp at Terezín (see "Exploring beyond Prague," later in this chapter). If you've had your fill at Josefov, spend your afternoon wandering the **Old Town,** popping into its baroque churches, relaxing with the locals in Staroměstské nám, and browsing for the evening's concert. Dine at **Restaurant Le Saint-Jacques,** or just get some goulash at a pub.

If you have three days

Spend Days One and Two as outlined above, and on Day Three head out to imposing **Karlštejn Castle.** Definitely do **Terezín** on the afternoon of Day Two, because on Day Three, you'll be back in Prague early enough to engage in that rewarding wander around the **Staré Město** in the late afternoon (be sure to catch the sunset over the **Charles Bridge**).

Exploring Beyond Prague

Several fascinating destinations are just a short bus or train ride from the city center. You can explore a fourteenth-century castle and a "model" Nazi internment camp that was designed to mask Hitler's true motives.

Medieval Karlštejn Castle

This highly picturesque, fourteenth-century castle perched scenically above the river is Prague's most popular day trip. (Tour companies love it, and more than 350,000 people visit annually.)

It takes only a few hours to get here, see the castle, and return to Prague, but you can stick around for lunch and enjoy Karlstejn's small-town setting. (But be aware that it's usually quite crowded.)

Getting there

You can get to the castle by **train** in about 45 minutes. The trains leave from Prague's Smíchov Station (take Metro line B to Smichovské nádraží).

Martin Tour (see the section "And on Your Left, Prague Castle: Seeing Prague by Guided Tour," earlier in the chapter) does five-hour trips to Karlštejn Castle for 910Kč ($27.60), leaving at 10:00 a.m. and including lunch; **Premiant** does it in four hours (at 10:00 a.m. and again at 2:15 p.m.) for 690Kč ($20.90) adults, 590Kč ($17.90) students. From April–September, you might want to ride instead with **Central European Adventures** (☎ 02-232-8879, or at Prague Information Service or TicketPro), whose 680Kč ($20.60) price includes transportation from Prague (8:30a.m. at the Astronomical Clock) to the castle, a guide, plus an 18-mile round-trip bike excursion to a nearby cave. (All run Tuesday to Sunday only.)

This is a one-trick town, so you won't find a tourism office; just hike up to the castle and the admissions office for information.

Seeing the castle

The walk uphill to the **castle** (☎ 0311-681-617) from the train station is a rigorous mile. (Unfortunately, no buses are available for those who can't manage the walk.) Charles IV built the fortress (between 1348 and 1357) to protect the crown jewels, which have been moved.

A nineteenth-century restoration stripped the place of later additions and rebuilt it in line with how folks from the Romantic Era thought a medieval castle should look (close to the original, but a bit fanciful in places). You can get inside only by guided tour, which takes you through parts of the South Palace to see the Audience Hall and Imperial Bedroom — both impressive in an austere, medieval way.

Sadly, vandalism and the environmental impact of too many visitors has closed the castle's most spectacular rooms, including the famed Holy Rood Chapel with its ceiling of glass "stars." But the view from the castle across the fertile river valley makes the climb worth it. The tour costs 150Kč ($4.55). It's open daily from 9:00 a.m. to noon and 12:30 to 4:00 p.m. (closing at 7:00 p.m. in July and August; 6:00 p.m. May, June, and September, 5:00 p.m. April and October).

Where to dine

The main road leading up to the castle is littered with souvenir shops and restaurants. The best food is at **Restaurace Blanky z Valois,** a cozy place serving good Czech food with a French twist.

Side Trips from Prague

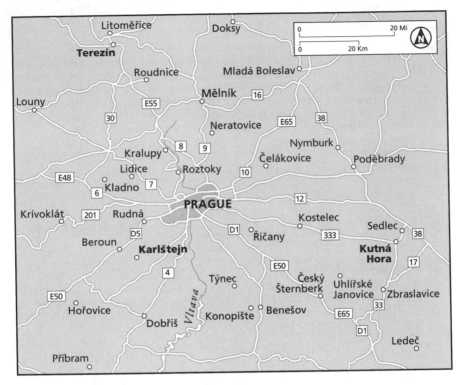

The Nazi camp at Terezín

Terezín was built as a city/fortress in the nineteenth century. The Nazi camp here was not a death camp or concentration lager. It served mainly as a transfer station in the despicable traffic of human cargo — sending Jews, homosexuals, Gypsies, and political dissidents on to other, more deadly destinations. At least half of the 140,000 people who passed through Terezín ended up in the death mills of Auschwitz and Treblinka.

Terezín's infamy is that it was the site of one of the most effective public relations deceptions perpetrated by SS leader Himmler. In 1944, the Nazis allowed three Red Cross workers to visit the camp to see whether the horrible rumors about SS methods were true. Instead, they found a model guarded community, a self-governed modern ghetto with children studying at school, stores stocked with goods, internees apparently healthy — and none of the overcrowding that they had suspected. The Red Cross had no idea that all this was elaborately staged.

Getting there

Terezín is an hour's bus ride from Florenc station. You'll need a full morning to fully explore it. **Martin Tour** (see the section "And on Your Left, Prague Castle: Seeing Prague by Guided Tour," earlier in the chapter) tours Terezín in five hours (9:00 a.m. Wednesday, Friday, and Sunday) and costs 1,100Kč ($33.35); **Premiant's** visit lasts four and a half hours (9:00 a.m. Monday, Wednesday, Friday, and Sunday) and costs 950Kč ($28.80).

You can find an **information office** (☎ 0416-92-369) on the town's main square, Náměstí čs. Armady 84.

Seeing the camp

The **Main Fortress** (Hlavní Pevnsot) houses a **Ghetto Museum** (☎ 0416-782-577), detailing life in this camp and the rise of Nazism; it's open daily from 9:00 a.m. to 6:00 p.m. (5:30 p.m. October to April). The prison barracks, execution grounds, and isolation cells can be found in the **Small Fortress** (☎ 0416-782-225), a 10-minute walk away; it's open daily from 8:00 a.m. to 6:00 p.m. (4:30 p.m. October to April). In front is the **Jewish Cemetery,** where bodies exhumed from Nazi mass graves were properly reburied; it's open Sunday to Friday from 10:00 a.m. to 5:30 p.m. The **Magdeburg Barracks** (☎ 0416-782-948) re-create a Ghetto dormitory. You'll see displays on Ghetto art and music here. It's open daily from 9:00 a.m. to 6:00 p.m. (5:30 p.m. October to April). Admission to the Main Fortress is 50Kč ($1.50). A combined ticket costs 100Kč ($3.05).

Where to dine

As you might expect, Terezín doesn't offer many places to eat. However, in the main parking lot you'll find a small stand where you can buy snacks and drinks. Inside the Main Fortress, near the museum, is a decent, inexpensive restaurant with Czech fare.

Part V
Mediterranean Europe

"Funny—I just assumed it would be Carreras too."

In this part . . .

A h, bright and sunny Mediterranean Europe. An area of winding coastal drives and long, moonlit dinners, of gemlike islands and afternoon siestas, of ripe olives and fine wine. The Mediterranean life runs at a slower pace and is more laid back than that of northern and central Europe.

Come with me and discover the ruins of ancient Greece and Rome. But a few dusty rocks and chipped columns do not make a Western civilization. I guide you through the museums and churches of Rome, Florence, and Venice. These sites are filled with masterpieces by Michelangelo, Raphael, Donatello, da Vinci, Botticelli, and many, many others.

From there we'll head to Spain. Madrid boasts its own share of artistic treasures, but excursions to Toledo and Segovia will give you a taste of the country's stunning landscape. Barcelona awaits with its distinctively whimsical architecture and a vibrant, happening nightlife. And finally, it's off to the warm simplicity and sunshine of Santoríni in the Greek islands.

Chapter 20

Rome and Southern Italy

*A*s the center of the ancient Roman Empire and then the vibrant Christian empire, Rome is appropriately titled the "Eternal City." A hint at Rome's glorious past is highlighted in the city's 2,000-year-old ruins, which include major sights like the Roman Forum, Pantheon, and, of course, the Colosseum. And Rome wasn't just togas and Caesars — the culture also produced sculptures in abundance. View the cream of the crop in the Vatican, Capitoline, and Roman National museums.

Following the Roman Empire, the Christian empire added more than 900 churches to the city. Actually, "church" doesn't begin to fully describe these amazing houses of worship — they're more like magnificent museums filled to the brim with the greatest art from the Renaissance and baroque eras (the greatest of these being St. Peter's basilica). All the artistic masters are represented in Rome: Michelangelo, Raphael, Borromini, Bernini, Botticelli, and Caravaggio in many of their greatest sculptures and paintings.

Although history abounds, modern Rome hasn't sat on its laurels. Between visiting ruins and browsing magnificent museums, try to sample a bit of this bustling city's more simple joys: a morning cappuccino, the hum of motorscooters, deliciously hearty meals. Find time for leisurely evening strolls past Renaissance palaces and fountains or just sitting in one of the many Roman *piazze* (squares).

The saying goes it would take a lifetime to see all of Rome, but that seems a little off to me — I'd wager the figure is more like 100 lifetimes. Rome wasn't built in a day, so you can't expect to experience it in one day either. You can, however, get a good sampling of its wonderful flavors in three or four. Because you can't possibly see everything, before you depart, be sure to toss a coin into the Trevi Fountain — legend has it that if you do, you're destined to return someday.

Making Your Way to and around Rome

Rome is a perennially popular destination, with plenty of flights available on a wide variety of international airlines. Rome is also easily accessible by train from most major European cities.

Getting to Rome by air

Most international flights land at **Leonardo da Vinci International Airport,** also called **Fiumicino** (☎ **06-6595-3640** or 06-65-951; Internet: www.adr.it), 18 miles west of the city. To get downtown, follow the treni signs for hourly nonstop trains to the main rail station, Stazione Termini (30 min.; 16,000L/$9). You can also take a local train every 20 minutes to the Tiburtina station (45 min.; 9,500L/$5) from the same tracks (get off at Ostiense and walk to the Piramide Metro stop to catch the B line to Termini; 1,500L/80 cents).

Many charter and continental flights land at the smaller **Ciampino Airport** (☎ **06-7934-0297** or 06-794-941), nine miles south of the city. Outside the terminal, a COTRAL bus (2,000L/$1.10) leaves about twice an hour for the 20-minute trip to Anagnina, the terminus of Metro line A, where you can grab a subway to Stazione Termini (1,500L/80 cents).

Taxis from either airport cost about 80,000L ($43), plus around 5,000L ($2.70) for each suitcase.

Getting to Rome by rail

The majority of trains headed for Rome stop at **Termini,** the main station on Piazza dei Cinquecento (☎ **800/888-088** or 06-4730-6599, or 1478-88-088; Internet: www.fs-on-line.com). A few long-haul trains may stop only at the Tiburtina station northeast of the center, from which you can hop on the Metro (subway) and head for Termini.

Getting around once you're in Rome

You purchase the same 1,500L (85 cents) *biglietto* (ticket) to ride any public transportation within Rome. Tickets are good for 75 minutes during which you may board the Metro system one time and transfer buses as frequently as you need — all you have to do is get your ticket stamped on the first bus and then the final bus you ride. You can also buy daily (6,000L/$3.35) and weekly (24,000L/$13.35) passes. Look for passes and tickets at *tabacchi* (tobacconist shops indicated by a brown-and-white T sign), Metro stations, newsstands, and machines near major bus stops. Be sure you keep your ticket with you as you travel in order to avoid paying a fine.

By metropolitana or metro (subway)

Because of Rome's rich ancient heritage, its Metro (subway) system is small and not particularly developed (seems that whenever the city attempts adding a new leg to the subway, it encounters ruins that archaeologists must examine). The Metro is essentially two lines, the orange A line and the blue B line, that intersect at Termini. Line A runs from Ottaviano (a dozen blocks from the Vatican — though someday the line is supposed to have a closer stop) through such stops as Flaminia (near Piazza del Popolo), Spagna (Spanish Steps), Termini, and San Giovanni (Rome's cathedral). You'll find the B line great for hitching rides from Termini to popular destinations like Circo Massimo (the Circus Maximus) and the Colosseo (Colosseum).

By bus

Thankfully, Rome has a much more developed bus and tram system, so you can avoid walking for miles. (Visit the tourist office for a freebie map of the city's bus route.) The 64 is a popular line because it runs from Termini to the Vatican (but be careful, the 64 is also fondly referred to as the "Pickpocket Express" for its high number of con artists who prey on travelers). You'll also frequent the 116 and 117, two petite electric buses that scurry the streets of the *centro storico*.

Many bus routes originate out of the large Piazza dei Cinquecento right outside Termini. Additionally, the *centro storico's* three major squares are a major hub for converging and transferring. These include: Largo di Tritone (east of the Trevi Fountain), Largo di Torre Argentina (south of the Pantheon), and Piazza San Silvestro (just off the Corso, between the Spanish Steps and Trevi Fountain).

By taxi

Although Rome is a wonderful town for walking or taking the bus, you may prefer a comfortable taxi ride for your journey from the train station or airport to your hotel. Look for taxi stands in major piazze, including Largo Argentina, Piazza Venezia, at the Pantheon, and in front of Termini.

Or, pick up the phone for a taxi (☎ **3570** or 4994). However, be aware that the meter begins running from the moment the driver answers your call. Taxis charge an initial fee of 4,500L ($2.50), plus 200L (10 cents) per kilometer. You pay extra charges for luggage (2,000L/$1.10 per bag), nighttime travel (5,000L/$2.70), and Sunday rides (2,000L/$1.10).

Discovering Rome: What You Need to Know

You know you have to exchange your money, but what kind of money are you going to exchange it into? You know you want to keep in touch with your family back home, but how? And what if you have an emergency? Who do you call? No, don't call Ghostbusters! You'll find all of this handy — no, *crucial* — information on basic stuff you need or need to know in this section.

The local dough

Lire (L) are the Italian units of currency. Roughly, $1 equals 1,800L; or 1,000L equals 55 cents. Italian coins include 50, 100, 200, and 500 lire. With two types of 50-lire coins and three different 100-lire pieces, you can easily get confused by the abundance of lire (though all coins are clearly marked). You may still encounter 10-lire and 20-lire coins (though they're completely worthless), as well as *gettoni,* old grooved phone tokens (these are worth 200L). Look for a new 1,000L coin soon. Bills come in denominations of 1,000L, 2,000L, 5,000L, 10,000L, 50,000L, and 100,000 lire.

Where to get info after you arrive

The **main tourist office** (☎ **06-4889-9253,** fax: 06-4889-9228; Internet: www.informaroma.it) is at Via Parigi 5, about a five-minute walk straight out from the station and across several piazze and traffic circles. It's open Monday to Saturday 8:15 a.m. to 7:00 p.m. The tiny and frequently jam-packed **tourist information office** at Termini station (☎ **06-4890-6300**) is really only useful on Sundays, when the main office is closed.

You find a numerous helpful **information kiosks** in Rome, including: Largo Goldoni/Via del Corso (☎ **06-6813-6061**); Via Nazionale (☎ **06-4782-4525**); Piazza Tempio della Pace, near the Roman Forum (☎ **06-6992-4307**); Piazza d. Cinque Lune, off Piazza Navona (☎ **06-6880-9240**); Lungotevere Castel Sant'Angelo (☎ **06-6880-9707**); Via del Tritone, at La Rinascente department store (☎ **06-6920-0435**); and Piazza San Giovanni in Laterano (☎ **06-772-3598**).

Visit any newsstand for a copy of *Roma C'è,* which list events (in Italian), or purchase Thursday's *La Reppublica* newspaper and dive into the pullout *Trovaroma* section. For events info in English, look for the monthly *Wanted in Rome.*

Where to go in a pinch

Random violent crime in Rome is very rare, but petty thieves — particularly pickpocketing children— seek out travelers. Most pick-pockets frequent the buses running from Termini to other biggie tourist traps (be extra careful on bus no. 64, the infamous "Pickpocket Express"). Protect your personals at the following top attractions: Termini, Piazza del Popolo, the Forums, the Colosseum, and around the Vatican.

In case of emergency, keep the following references handy:

> ✔ **Doctors/Dentists:** First aid is available 24 hours a day in the emergency room *(pronto soccorso)* of major hospitals; see "Hospitals" later in this listing. Also try the **International Medical Center,** Via Giovanni Amendola 7 (☎ **06-488-2371**). Call the **U.S. Embassy** at ☎ **06-46-741** for a list of English-speaking doctors and dentists.

✔ **Embassy:** The U.S. Embassy is at Via Vittorio Veneto 121 (☎ 06-46-741). For passport and consular services, head to the consulate, left of the Embassy's main gate, open Monday to Friday 8:30 a.m. to 1:00 p.m. and 2:00 to 5:30 p.m.

✔ **Emergencies:** Dial ☎ 113 in any emergency. Or call ☎ 112 for the Carabinieri (the often more useful, military-trained police forces), ☎ 118 or 5100 to summon an ambulance, or ☎ 115 for the fire department. *Pronto Soccorso* is Italian for "first aid," but you can also use the phrase to get to an emergency room. Call ☎ 116 for roadside assistance (not free).

✔ **Hospitals:** English-speaking doctors are always on duty at the **Rome American Hospital,** Via Emilio Longoni 69; (☎ 06-22-551), and at the privately run **Salvator Mundi International Hospital,** Viale delle Mura Gianicolensi 67 (☎ 06/586-041).

✔ **Pharmacies:** So that a pharmacy is always open (including weekends and holidays), *farmacie* have set up on a rotating schedule, which you can find outside each pharmacy. The three always open 24 hours are: **Farmacia Internazionale,** Piazza Barberini 49 (☎ 06-482-5456); Piazza Risorgimento 44 (☎ 06-372-2157); and Via Arenula 73 (☎ 06-6880-3278). The **Station International Pharmacy,** Stazione Termini (☎ 06-488-0019), is open 7:00 a.m. to 10:00 p.m.

Watch out for the thieving children

Thieving children often roam around tourist areas and subway tunnels. They aren't physically dangerous, but whenever they're around, a tourist and his money may soon be parted. They often approach looking pitiful, begging and waving scraps of cardboard, occasionally scrawled with a few words in English. This flurry of cardboard is a distraction beneath which their fingers can quickly relieve your pockets of valuables. If you see a group of kids dressed in colorful but filthy rags headed your way, do your best to give them a wide berth, forcefully yell " *Va via!*" ("Scram!"), or loudly invoke the *polizia.* If they get too close, shove them away — don't hold back just because they're kids.

One popular scam, used primarily by female pickpockets, is to toss a swaddled baby at you (usually it's a doll in blankets, but sometimes they throw the real thing!), and while you rush to catch it, they or their waiting brood fleece you in the blink of an eye.

Women should be aware there's occasional drive-by purse snatchings by young Vespa-riding thieves. Keep your purse on the wall side of the sidewalk, wear the strap diagonally across your chest, and try to keep from walking along the sidewalk's edge. And if your purse has a flap, keep the clasp side facing your body to deter pickpockets. Men should also take precautions: Keep your wallet in your front pocket rather than the rear and your hand on it while riding the bus.

Staying in touch

Need to wire home for more money? The beauty of Rome still can't keep you away from your e-mail? The following information can help keep you in touch while you're touring Rome.

✔ **American Express:** The office is to the right of the Spanish Steps at Piazza di Spagna 38 (☎ 06-67-641). May to September, it's open Monday to Friday 9:00 a.m. to 7:30 p.m. and Saturday 9:00 a.m. to 3:00 p.m.; October to April, hours are Monday to Friday 9:00 a.m. to 5:30 p.m. and Saturday 9:00 a.m. to 12:30 p.m. To report lost or stolen traveler's checks, call ☎ 800/872-000; to report lost or stolen AMEX cards, call ☎ 800/864-046.

✔ **Business Hours:** As in most of Italy, almost all shops and offices, most churches, and many museums observe a siesta-like midafternoon shutdown called *riposo,* roughly noon or 1:00 p.m. to 3:00 or 4:00 p.m. It's a good idea to figure out the few sights in town that remain open during *riposo* so you can save them — and a leisurely lunch — to fill this time. Most shop hours are Monday 3:00 or 4:00 p.m. to 8:00 p.m. and Tuesday to Saturday 8:00 a.m. to noon or 1:00 p.m. and 3:00 or 4:00 p.m. to 8:00 p.m. Food shops are generally also open Monday mornings but closed Thursday afternoons. However, more and more stores are posting *orario continuato* ("no-stop") signs and staying open through *riposo.*

✔ **Internet Access and Cyber Cafes:** You can log on to the Internet in central Rome at **Thenetgate,** with locations at Piazza Firenze 25 (☎ 06-689-3445), open Monday to Saturday 10:30 a.m. to 10:30 p.m.; and Via in Arcione 103 (☎ 06-6992-2320), open Monday to Saturday 10:30 a.m. to 11:30 p.m. and Sunday to 10:30 p.m. A 20-minute visit is 5,000L ($2.80), with 1 hour (including mailbox) at 10,000L ($5.55). Access is free at the Piazza Firenze branch Saturdays 10:30 to 11:00 a.m. and 2:00 to 2:30 p.m., at Via in Arcione Thursday and Sunday 8:30 to 9:00 p.m.

You can kill two birds with one stone with the latest Roman traveler's trend: wired laundromats. Just north of Stazione Termini, **Bolle Blue** (locations at Via Palestro 59 and Via Milazzo 20B) and **Splash** (Via Varese 33) let you log on for 4,000L ($2.20) per half hour while your grubby travel togs get clean.

✔ **Mail:** The Italian mail system is notoriously slow, and friends back home may not receive your postcards for anywhere from one to eight weeks (sometimes longer). The **main post office** is at Piazza San Silvestro 19, 00187 Roma, Italia (off Via del Corso, south of the Spanish Steps). It's open Monday to Friday 9:00 a.m. to 6:00 p.m., Saturday 9:00 a.m. to 2:00 p.m., and Sunday 9:00 a.m. to 6:00 p.m. You can pick up stamps at any *tabacchi* (tobacconists).

If you want your letters to get home before you do, use the **Vatican post office.** It costs the same and is much quicker and more reliable — but you must use Vatican stamps, available only at their post offices. You can visit three different offices: to the left of the basilica steps, just past the information office; behind the right-hand colonnade of Piazza San Pietro (where the alley ends beyond souvenir stands); and in the Vatican Museums.

✔ **Telephone:** Local calls cost 200L (10 cents). Phones accept either coins, a phone card (*carta telefonica*), or both. You can buy phone cards in a variety of denominations — 5,000L ($2.80), 10,000L ($5.55), or 15,000L ($8.35) — at newsstands and *tabbachi* (tobacco shops). To use the card, break off the card's corner, insert the card, and dial. A digital display on the phone tells you how much money you have left on a card. For directory assistance, dial ☎ **12.**

✔ Italy's country code is **39.** To call Rome from the United States, dial **011-39,** followed by the number. (If it's been a while since you were last in Italy, be aware to changes in the phone system; you *must use* "city codes" with each number as well as that initial zero at all times.)

✔ To charge your calls to a calling card, insert 200L (which the phone gives back at the call's end), and contact **AT&T** at ☎ **172-1011, MCI** at ☎ **172-1022,** or **Sprint** at ☎ **172-1877.** You can also call these numbers to place a collect call or dial the **Italcable operator** at ☎ **170** (free). If you must dial the United States directly from Italy, dial ☎ **001** followed by the area code and phone number.

✔ **Transit Info:** ATAC (city buses) ☎ **800-431-784** (Internet: www.atac. roma.it). COTRAL (suburban buses) ☎ **06-591-5551.**

Touring Rome by Neighborhood

The curving **Tevere (Tiber River)** forms an S-shaped dividing line through Rome. East of the Tevere has most of they city's **centro storico (historic center).** Although Rome has numerous official "administrative districts," locals usually orient themselves based on their location relative to such-and-such major monument or so-and-so piazza (square), so this chapter tries to do the same. However, Rome is nearly bursting at its seams with monuments and piazze (which essentially break the city into little neighborhoods). That said, finding your way in Rome can be a tad complicated. Purchase a good map (or use the one included in this chapter), and you should eventually figure out the lay of the land.

If you arrive at **Termini,** Rome's main train station, the first neighborhood you encounter is just east of the city center in the grid of nineteenth-century streets. This part of town offers a few sights and some churches of note, but for the most part, this area is pretty boring. And, even though you can find scads of cheap hotels, it's not the most savory area to stay.

The northern tip of the city center features the oval **Piazza del Popolo,** with three major thoroughfares radiating south from here: Via del Babuino, Via del Corso, and Via di Ripetta. **Via del Corso** (usually just called the **Corso**) cuts the center of town into halves.

From the Corso, head east to reach the popular **Trevi Fountain** and **Spanish Steps.** Rome's ritziest hotels — as well as stylish shopping on boutique-lined **Via dei Condotti** — border these touristy sights.

West of the Corso you find the medieval **Tiber Bend area,** home to many of the great Roman sights, including the **Pantheon,** the vibrant **Piazza Navona,** the market square of **Campo de' Fiori,** and the medieval **Jewish Ghetto** (which continues to be home to Europe's oldest Jewish population, numerous houses of worship churches, and a few small museums). The Tiber Bend area, so lovely for walking and people-watching, offers some of Rome's best restaurants and much of it is pedestrian-only.

The **Piazza Venezia** serves as a rather abrupt ending to the Corso. The famous (and enormous) **Vittorio Emanuele Monument** (nicknamed the Giant Typewriter or Wedding Cake) dominates this major traffic circle and bus juncture. Head west from Piazza Venezia and you reach Via Plebescito, which becomes **Corso Vittorio Emanuele II,** a broad boulevard that chops the Tiber Bend area in half while proceeding on to the river and the Vatican (Piazza Navona and the Pantheon lie to the north of it; Campo de' Fiori and the Jewish Ghetto to the south).

At Piazza Venezia, you can take stairs up to **Capitoline Hill,** the seat of Roman government dating all the way back to before the Empire. From the piazza, the expansive **Via dei Fori Imperiali** beelines to the **Colosseum,** passing two famous forums: the Roman and the Imperial. The monuments in this area are often referred to collectively as **Ancient Rome.** The residential area of **Aventine Hill** lies south of the monuments and beyond that another hill is home to newly trendy dinner and dancing environ known as **Testaccio.**

Although the preceding neighborhoods are the ones you'll frequent, a few others deserve mention. Northwest of the train station (east of the Spanish Steps area) is home to numerous embassies and the famous main drag known as **Via Veneto.** As the center of La Dolce Vita ("the sweet life"), which Federico Fellini made famous in 1960 with a film of the same name, Via Veneto is still brimming with cafe life — although today's version is overpriced and pretty darn touristy. Via Veneto butts up against the southern portion of a large park, **Villa Borghese,** which is located northeast of the *centro storico* and is accessible from Piazza del Popolo.

On the other side of the Tevere, you'll find two other major neighborhoods of interest: **Vatican City and St. Peter's** and **Trastevere.** The Vatican and surrounding areas are tourist magnets, complete with shops, eateries, and lodging to cater to visitors. (Generally, hotels in Vatican City are modestly priced, but bland and modern; to really experience Rome, try staying elsewhere.) South of the Vatican and parklike **Gianicolo** hill, you encounter Trastevere. At one time Bohemian, now fashionable, this medieval district still maintains many authentic restaurants and shops.

Staying in Rome

Break out of the boring hotels that crowd the gridlike streets around Termini train station and try some of Rome's more interesting accommodations in the historic center. Of course, if all the rooms in the historic center are taken, or you just don't have the cash, settle for hotels in the northern area around Termini. (The area south of the station, while making efforts to improve, can be somewhat dicey, and I don't recommend spending a lot of time here at night.)

Rome's top hotels

Albergo Abruzzi

$ Near Piazza Navona

The prime rooms at this popular hotel actually offer views of the Pantheon — and for less than $100! Of course, a deal this good is also quite popular. Book your room as early as possible and be sure to make your deposit in the form of an international money order in order to beat the budget travelers and students at their own game. Of course, not all rooms are created equal here, but they all are sizable, rather spartan, and clean. Okay, so you have to walk down the hall to the bathrooms, and some of the rooms (particularly the ones facing the piazza) can be noisy — but with this view and that location, who can complain?

Piazza della Rotunda 69. ☎ 06-679-2021. No fax. Bus: 116 (or one of the many to Largo Argentina and walk four blocks north). Rates: 120,000–150,000L ($66.65–$83.75) doubles. No credit cards.

Albergo Cesàri

$$$ Near Piazza Navona

Location, location, location — this one has it for sure! Albergo Cesari is just off the Corso, right in the heart of popular attractions such as the Pantheon, the Spanish Steps, the Trevi Fountain, and the Roman Forum. Notable guests during the hotel's two-century-old history include Stendhal (the French author) and Italian statesman Giuseppe Garibaldi. The rooms today are mordern and comfortable, with a few antiques thrown in here or there for effect. To get the rock-bottom rates, plan on sharing a bath.

Via di Pietra 89A (just off the Corso, a block south of Piazza Colonna). ☎ 06-679-2386. Fax: 06-679-0882. Internet: www.italyhotel.com/ roma/cesari. *Bus: 56, 60, 62, 81, 85, 96, 116, 117, 160, 175, 492, 628, 850. Rates: 300,000–340,000L ($166.65–$188.90) doubles. AE, DC, MC, V.*

Casa Kolbe

$ Near the Forum

If you love archaeology but don't need too many amenities, this monastically quiet converted convent may be perfect. It's as hidden as you can get in the heart of Rome, around the corner from the Roman Forum's "back door" on the little-traveled side street hugging the west flank of the Palatine Hill. Most of the large, basic, institutional rooms overlook palm-filled gardens, but those on the second floor street-side enjoy a low panorama of Palatine ruins.

Via S. Teodoro 44 (bordering the east side of the Palatine archaeological zone). ☎ **06-679-4974.** *Fax: 06-6994-1550. Bus: H, 44, 63, 81, 95, 160, 170, 628, 715, 716, 780, 781. Rates: 135,000L ($75) double. AE, MC, V.*

Hotel Campo de' Fiori

$$ Near Campo de' Fiori

A gem for the budget-conscience traveler, the rooms here vary greatly: Some are carpeted and modern while others have rustic touches like beamed ceilings and brickwork. Some are large, while a few are about the size of the beds. The killer room is No. 602 (sorry, no elevator), which offers a choice vista of Rome's domes and rooftops (all visitors can enjoy the view from the roof terrace). Most bathrooms are shared and clean, but private baths are available for a higher price. The hotel also rents four nearby apartments.

Via del Biscione, 6 (just off the northeast corner of Campo de' Fiori). ☎ **06-687-4886** *or 06-6880-6865. Fax: 06-687-6003. Bus: 46, 62, 64, 116. Rates: 200,000–250,000L ($111.10–$166.65) double. MC, V.*

Hotel Columbus

$$$$ Near the Vatican

Michelangelo's patron, Pope Julius II, once owned this lovely fifteenth-century palazzo, and certainly the place feels like a Renaissance castle, complete with oil paintings and tapestries. Most bedrooms are fairly simple yet comfortable, but a few choice rooms have remnants of decorated ceilings and frescoes.

Via della Conciliazione 33 (on the wide boulevard leading to St. Peter's). ☎ **06-686-5435.** *Fax: 06-686-4874. Bus: 23, 34, 62, 64, 982. Rates: 470,000L ($261.10) double. AE, DC, MC, V.*

Hotel Raphael

$$$$ Near Piazza Navona

For plush accomodations look no further than the Raphael. Just pull back the ivy curtains on this elegant hotel located in a distincly medieval setting, and you'll find well-appointed, contemporary rooms and a fantastic view from the roof terrace. With facilities and amenities aplenty (it even has a fitness room), you can kick back in style. But heads up: A couple of the rooms are surprisingly small.

Largo Febo 2 (just off the northwest corner of Piazza Navona). ☎ **06-682-831.** _Fax: 06-687-8993. Internet:_ www.raphaelhotel.com. _Bus: 70, 81, 87, 115, 116, 186, 492, 628. Rates: 660,000L ($366.65) double. AE, DC, MC, V._

Rome's runner-up accommodations

Alimandi

$$$ A standardized, modern, tour group-style hotel, but one of the better ones, with a great location three blocks from Rome's best daily food market and just a staircase from the Vatican Museums. _Via Tunisi 8, at Via Veniero and the base of the steps up to Viale Vaticano_ (☎ **06-3972-3941;** _Fax: 06-3972-3943; Internet:_ www.travel.iol.it/alberghi/alimandi_)._

Astoria Garden

$$$ This hotel has fantastic prices (because it's near Termini) for the comfort and style in a late-nineteenth-century palazzo with private garden. Stuccoed ceilings and dark oils in the lounges conjure an old-world atmosphere. Ask for one of the renovated rooms, done in High Turin-style; some even have Jacuzzis. A/C is 20,000L ($11) extra. _Via V. Bachelet 8, the one-block stretch of Via Varese just before Piazza Indipendenza_ (☎ **06-446-9908;** _Fax 06-445-3329; Internet:_ www.hotelastoriagarden.it_)._

Lydia-Venier

$$ Here you'll find low prices on high-ceilinged spic-and-span rooms on a quiet block of the heart of the city. Enjoy the lavishly frescoed eighteenth-century breakfast room (remnants of this decor spill over into a few guest rooms with the odd fresco or gilded stucco ceiling). _Via Sistina 42, almost a block from the top of the Spanish Steps_ (☎ **06-679-1744;** _Fax: 06-679-7263)._

Navona

$$ The Navona is run by a very friendly family. The first floor has functional or wicker furnishings, terracotta/wood slat ceilings, Valentino bath tiles, and wonderfully firm beds on the top floor (a space once owned by Percy Bysshe Shelley). No elevator, but you can get A/C for 35,000L ($19) extra. If the Navona's full, it might send you to its equally nice and recently renovated **Residence Zanardelli** just off the north end of Piazza Navona. _Via dei Sedari 8, off Corso del Rinascimento, between Piazza Navona and the Pantheon_ (☎ **06-686-4203** _or 06-6821-1391; Fax: 06-6880-3802)._

Scalinata di Spagna

$$$$ Always a top choice and considered a "steal," given all the pricey hotels in its neighborhood. Aside from a few boring rooms, many feature antique furniture and low wood ceilings. Enjoy breakfast and the spectacular view on the rooftop terrace. Reserve early. _Piazza Trinità dei Monti 17, at the top of the Spanish Steps_ (☎ **06-679-3006** _or 06-6994-0896; Fax: 06-6994-0598)._

Accommodations, Dining & Attractions in Rome

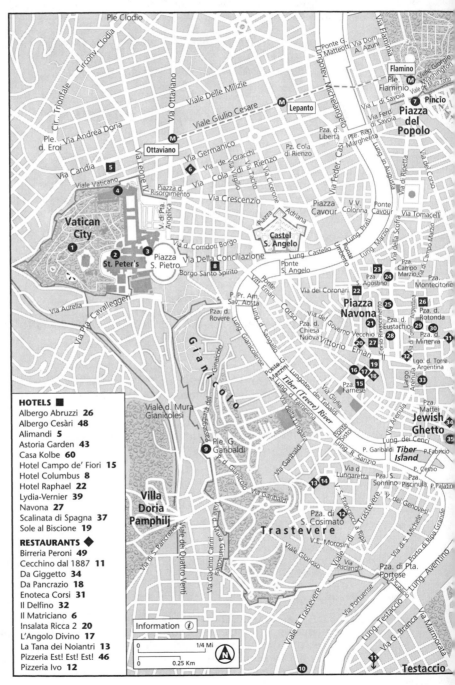

HOTELS ■
Albergo Abruzzi **26**
Albergo Cesàri **48**
Alimandi **5**
Astoria Garden **43**
Casa Kolbe **60**
Hotel Campo de' Fiori **15**
Hotel Columbus **8**
Hotel Raphael **22**
Lydia-Vernier **39**
Navona **27**
Scalinata di Spagna **37**
Sole al Biscione **19**

RESTAURANTS ◆
Birreria Peroni **49**
Cecchino dal 1887 **11**
Da Giggetto **34**
Da Pancrazio **18**
Enoteca Corsi **31**
Il Delfino **32**
Il Matriciano **6**
Insalata Ricca 2 **20**
L'Angolo Divino **17**
La Tana dei Noiantri **13**
Pizzeria Est! Est! Est! **46**
Pizzeria Ivo **12**

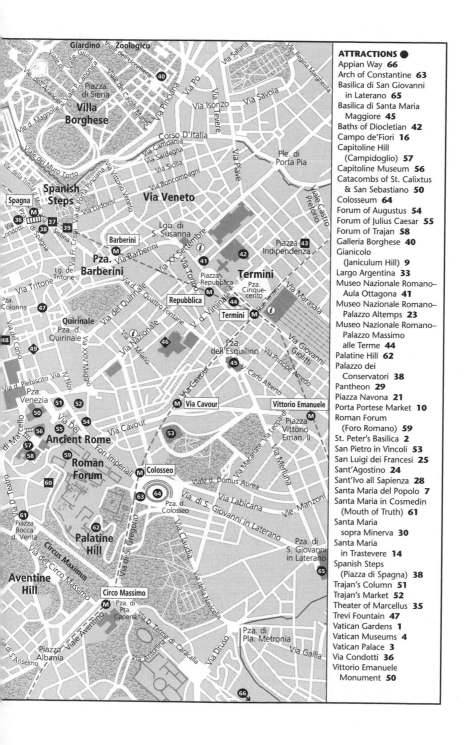

ATTRACTIONS ●

Appian Way **66** ●
Arch of Constantine **63**
Basilica di San Giovanni
  in Laterano **65**
Basilica di Santa Maria
  Maggiore **45**
Baths of Diocletian **42**
Campo de'Fiori **16**
Capitoline Hill
  (Campidoglio) **57**
Capitoline Museum **56**
Catacombs of St. Calixtus
  & San Sebastiano **50**
Colosseum **64**
Forum of Augustus **54**
Forum of Julius Caesar **55**
Forum of Trajan **58**
Galleria Borghese **40**
Gianicolo
  (Janiculum Hill) **9**
Largo Argentina **33**
Museo Nazionale Romano–
  Aula Ottagona **41**
Museo Nazionale Romano–
  Palazzo Altemps **23**
Museo Nazionale Romano–
  Palazzo Massimo
  alle Terme **44**
Palatine Hill **62**
Palazzo dei
  Conservatori **38**
Pantheon **29**
Piazza Navona **21**
Porta Portese Market **10**
Roman Forum
  (Foro Romano) **59**
St. Peter's Basilica **2**
San Pietro in Vincoli **53**
San Luigi dei Francesi **25**
Sant'Agostino **24**
Sant'Ivo all Sapienza **28**
Santa Maria del Popolo **7**
Santa Maria in Cosmedin
  (Mouth of Truth) **61**
Santa Maria
  sopra Minerva **30**
Santa Maria
  in Trastevere **14**
Spanish Steps
  (Piazza di Spagna) **38**
Trajan's Column **51**
Trajan's Market **52**
Theater of Marcellus **35**
Trevi Fountain **47**
Vatican Gardens **1**
Vatican Museums **4**
Vatican Palace **3**
Via Condotti **36**
Vittorio Emanuele
  Monument **50**

Sole al Biscione

$$ Sole al Biscione is Rome's oldest hotel (founded 1462) — and it shows in some corners with peeling linoleum and sway-backed cots. But most rooms are in rather better shape than that, most are sizeable, and those on the fourth floor even get a Roman rooftop view. Great location. *Via del Biscione 76, half a block north of Campo de Fiori (*☎ *06-6880-6873; Fax: 06-689-3787).*

Dining in Rome

Typically, evening meals in Rome are events: gigantic, multicourse affairs that last for hours. While you may suspect that this conga line of courses is just a trick to make you spend more money, Italians actually often eat meals this huge (although in today's faster paced world, less frequently).

Dining out Italian style means ordering at least two courses — preferably stretching out the meal even longer with some tasty wine and spirited conversation. If you're not looking for a mega-meal, just ask for *mezza portions* (half portions) for your selected courses.

Roman taste temptations begin with appetizers, and the best local choice is simple *bruschetta* (peasant bread grilled, rubbed with garlic, drizzled with olive oil, and sprinkled with salt; order it *al pomodoro* and they'll top it with a heap of cubed tomatoes). Another specialty meal starter that is especially popular is *carciofi* (artichokes), done *alla giudea* (lightly fried in olive oil) or otherwise.

The first course (called the *primo*) can go a variety of ways: Try a soup like *stracciatella,* egg-drop and parmesan in broth, or a pasta like *spaghetti all'Amatriciana* (spicy tomato sauce dappled with pancetta bacon), *alla carbonara* (with eggs, *pancetta*, and cracked pepper), or *al pomodoro* (in a regular ol' tomato sauce); *penne all'arrabbiata* ("hopping mad" pasta quills in a spicy tomato sauce); or *gnocchi* (potato-based pasta dumplings).

During the main course (*secondo*), you may choose to get adventurous with some "traditional local cuisine." Popular dishes include *coda alla vaccinara* (braised oxtail with tomatoes) and surprisingly appetizing *pajata* (made with calves' intestines still clotted with mother's milk). Or something a little more familiar, order *pollo* (chicken), *scallopine* (veal cutlets, cooked in various ways), *involtini* (veal rolled with veggies and stewed in its own juices), or *bocconcini di vitello* (nuggets of veal, typically stewed with potatoes and sage). One of the best Roman secondi is *saltimbocca,* or "jumps-in-the-mouth"; it's a veal cutlet cooked until tender in white wine with sage leaves and served with a slice of prosciutto ham draped over it.

For a finale, sample *tiramisù* (espresso-soaked ladyfingers layered with sweetened, creamy mascarpone cheese and dusted with cocoa) or *tartufo* (vanilla and chocolate ice cream, both dusted with cocoa and containing a fudge center).

Although Florence is more famous for its ice-cream, the gelato in Rome is still a savory treat. For the ultimate in sinfully sweet snacking, visit the nineteenth-century **Giolitti** (☎ 06-699-1234), a few long blocks north of the Pantheon at Via Uffici del Vicario 40. Of course, you can find several other find ice-cream parlors about town; just be sure the one you choose has a sign advertising *produzione propria* (homemade).

Roman table wine is most often fruity, light, and white and originates in the hills to the south. Look for **Frascati, Castelli Romane,** and **Orvieto Classico** (an excellent white from a town north of Rome). Most restaurants in town have nicely stocked cellars that feature the best wines Italy has to offer.

Restaurants throughout Italy tack on the unavoidable "bread and cover" charge (*pane e coperto*) that runs anywhere from 1,500L to 10,000L (85 cents to $5.55). Although you can generally eat fairly cheaply in Italy, do keep in mind that most meals include much more than just a first and second course, including water and wine, an appetizer, coffee, dessert, and a digestivo (after-dinner drink) — all of which add to your total bill.

The finest in Roman "fast food" has to be *pizza rustica* or *pizza a taglio,* which you can buy from tiny shops where they cut the pizza of your choice from big, steaming sheets. Prices are by weight; 4,000L ($2.25)-worth is usually plenty for one. Expand your palate with a buffet of *margherita* (tomato sauce, cheese, and basil), *napolitana* (with anchovies), *patate* (with julienned potatoes, but no sauce), *rosso* (just the sauce), or *bianca* (just the dough, brushed with olive oil and salt, sometimes with rosemary).

For picnic supplies, you may stop by a variety of little shops, including *alimentari* (small grocery stores), *forno* (bakery), and *fruttivendolo* (fruit and vegetable stand), or head to a **Standa** department store basement which doubles as a supermarket (Viale Trastevere 60 or Via Cola di Rienzo 173, near the Vatican).

Rome's top restaurants

Cecchino dal 1887

$$$$ In Testaccio (south of Ancient Rome)   ROMAN

Started as a blue-collar wine shop more than a century ago, this establishment is now a Roman temple of refinement and classic cuisine. Savor such local sensations as *pajata* and *coda alla vaccinara,* which evolved because the only ingredients available to slaughterhouse workers a hundred years ago were undesirable feet, tails, and other offal. Cecchino has menu items for the less adventurous, too. And don't miss the wine cellars carved into the "hill" (actually it's a really old pile of discarded jars).

Via di Monte Testaccio 30 (in trendy Testaccio, just south of the Aventine Hill). ☎ **06-574-3816.** *Internet:* www.cecchino-dal-1887.com. *Reservations very highly recommended. Bus: 75. Main courses: 12,000–35,000L ($6.65–$19.45). AE, DC, MC, V. Open: Lunch Tues–Sun, dinner Tues–Sat. Closed Aug, one week around Christmas, and Sun June–Sept.*

Da Giggetto

$$ **Near Campo de' Fiori   ROMAN/JEWISH**

For Roman Jewish cuisine, look no further than this popular eatery in the Jewish Ghetto. Enjoy the house specialty *carciofi alla giudia* (lightly fried artichokes) among the columns of the still standing ruins. Other flavorful fare includes *fiori di zucca* (stuffed zucchini flowers), *fettucine all' amatriciana*, and *saltimbocca*.

Via de Portico d'Ottavia 21-22 (one block up from Lungotevere d. Cenci). ☎ **06-686-1105.** *Reservations recommended. Bus: H, 44, 81, 95, 170, 160, 628, 715, 716, 780, 23, 280. Main courses: 12,000–24,000L ($6.65–$13.35). AE, DC, MC, V. Open: Lunch and dinner Tues–Sun. Closed Aug 1–15.*

Enoteca Corsi

$ **Near Piazza Navona   ROMAN**

This dirt-cheap, old-fashioned enoteca has kept up with the times — but not the prices — so while the wine shop looks every inch the *vini olii* of 1937, behind it and next door are large, fan-cooled rooms with long tables to accommodate the lunchtime crowds of local workers. The chalkboard menu changes daily but may run the mill from *penne all'arrabbiata* to delectable specials like *zucchine ripiene* (baked zucchini flowers stuffed with minced meats).

Via del Gesù 88 (off Via d. Plebescito). ☎ **06-679-0821.** *Reservations not accepted. Bus: 46, 56, 60, 62, 64, 70, 81, 87, 115, 186, 492, 628, 640. Main courses: 12,000L ($6.65). AE, DC, MC, V. Open: Mon–Sat noon–3:30 p.m. Closed Aug.*

Il Matriciano

$$$ **Near the Vatican   ROMAN**

Join the politicians and movie stars at Il Matriciano for a country-style meal that's both refined and relaxed. From a sidewalk table, sample the restaurant's namesake pasta: *bucatini* (thick, hollow spaghetti) *all' amatriciana*. Other typical Roman dishes include *trippa* (tripe) and *abbacchio* (succulent roasted lamb).

Via dei Gracchi 55 (from the north side of Piazza del Risorgimento, head up Via Ottaviano and turn right onto Via dei Gracchi). ☎ **06-321-3040.** *Reservations highly recommended. Metro: Ottaviano. Bus: 32, 81. Main courses: 18,000–26,000L ($10–$14.45). AE, DC, MC, V. Open: Lunch and dinner daily. Closed Aug 6–21, Wed Nov–Apr, and Sat May–Oct.*

La Tana dei Noiantri

$$$ Trastevere   ROMAN/ITALIAN/PIZZA

Everybody comes to this Trastevere spot for the romance of dining out on the cobblestones, under the tent-like umbrellas of a pocket-sized piazza. The interior is more formal, with wood ceilings and painted coats of arms hanging above baronial fireplaces. The crisply bow-tied waiters serve a wonderfully hot *penne all'arrabbiata.* The best among the secondi are *abbacchio arrosto con patate* and *fritto cervello di abbacchio* (fried lambs brains and zucchini).

Via della Paglia 1–3 (the street leading west out of Piazza Santa Maria in Trastevere). ☎ *06-580-6404. Reservations highly recommended. Bus: 23, 280, H, tram 8. Main courses: 15,000–25,000L ($8.35–$13.90). AE, MC, V. Open: Wed–Mon noon–3:00 p.m., 7:30–11:30 p.m.*

Pizzeria Ivo

$ In Trastevere   PIZZA ROMAN

You'll find this beloved pizza parlor packed with equal parts locals and tourists just about any time of day or night. But don't let the crowds scare you off — popularity has kept taste high and prices low. Pizzeria Ivo is a wonderful place to have your first date with genuine, wood-oven Italian pizza. Favorites include the "plain" *margherita* (tomato sauce, mozzarella, and basil), *al prosciutto,* and the *capricciosa* (which can include whatever the chef wishes, but is likely to feature olives, anchovies, prosciutto, and a fried egg).

Via San Francesco a Ripa 158 (from Viale di Trastevere, take a right onto Via Fratte di Trastevere, then left on Via San Francesco a Ripa). ☎ *06-581-7082. Reservations not usually necessary. Bus: H, tram 8, 44, 75. Pasta and pizza: 8,000–16,000L ($4.45–$8.90). Main courses: 9,500–15,000L ($5.30–$8.35). DC, MC, V. Open: Dinner Wed–Mon.*

Rome's runner-up restaurants

Birreria Peroni

$ A German-style beer hall (owned by Italy's leading brewery) serving Italian and Teutonic specialties since 1906. Its buffet is popular at lunch with the local business set, so show up early. *Via San Marcello 10, north of Piazza SS. Apostoli (*☎ *06-679-5310).*

Da Pancrazio

$$$$ Da Pancrazio has fine food and one major selling point: the basement rooms are set into the restored arcades of Pompey's b.c. 55 theater. It's like dining in a museum. *Piazza del Biscione 92, just off the northeast corner of Campo de' Fiori (*☎ *06-686-1246).*

Insalata Ricca 2

$$ The best-located of Rome's popular mini-chain of excellent vegetarian restaurants, offering lighter, low-fat fare, oversized salads, and outdoor tables. *Piazza Pasquino 72, southwest of Piazza Navona (☎ 06-6830-7881).*

Il Delfino

$ Il Delfino offers fast, cheap, and reliable service to visitors determinedly tramping about the heart of the centro storico. Delicious self-service hot foods and pizze and a fantastically convenient location two blocks south of the Pantheon. *Corso Vittorio Emanuele 67, at the corner of Largo Argentina (☎ 06-686-4053).*

L'Angolo Divino

$-$$ One of Rome's modern wine bars, old-fashioned in style (its was converted from the owner's family wine shop) but contemporary in the kitchen, serving platters of cheeses, salamis, and smoked fish alongside vegetable terrines and quiches — and, of course, dozens of wines by the glass. *Via dei Balestrari 12, a block southeast of Campo de' Fiori (☎ 06-686-4413; Internet:* www.angolodivino.it*).*

Pizzeria Est! Est! Est!

$ A 100-year-old pizza joint patronized by local police and shopkeeps at the box canyonlike end of a side street. Order an appetizer of supplì (gooey fried balls of rice and mozzarella) and olive ascolane (green olives stuffed with minced meat, breaded, and fried) before your excellent pizza. *Via Genova 32, off Via Nazionale (☎ 06-488-1107).*

Exploring Rome

You can purchase a new, excellent-value 20,000L ($11.10) **three-day ticket** granting admission to the Colosseum, Palatine, Palazzo Massimo alle Terme, and Palazzo Altemps (separately, those admissions would cost 44,000L/$24.45). Buy it at any of the participating sights.

Rome's top sights

St. Peter's Basilica (Basilica di San Pietro)

St. Peter's is one of the grandest creations of Rome's Renaissance and baroque eras, the pulpit for a parish priest known as the Pope, and the biggest European church. St. Peter's takes at least an hour — not because there's so much to see but because it takes that long to walk from one end to the other and back. (Fun fact: St. Peter's is longer than two football fields.) More comprehensive visits take two to three hours and include a climb up Michelangelo's dome (offering a gorgeous view), a trek into the crypt and papal tombs, and a visit to the treasury to experience a fine collection of silver chalices, embellished robes, and fragments of statuary.

Do be aware of and observe St. Peter's strict dress code — you won't be allowed to enter if you do not come dressed appropriately. Proper dress means no skirts above the knee, no shorts, and no bare shoulders. If your dress isn't quite up to code, gents and ladies alike can purchase big, inexpensive scarves from a nearby souvenir stand and wrap them around their legs as a long skirt or throw them over their shoulders as a shawl.

Approach the church by means of the Bernini's oval colonnade, the string of columns that encase the **Piazza San Pietro.** As you enter, look right and be awe-struck by the church's single greatest sight, **Michelangelo's Pietà,** carved by the artist when he was only in his early 20s. Unfortunately, the scuplture has been guarded behind protective glass since the 1970s (thanks to the efforts of a hammer-wielding lunatic). Under the dome is **Bernini's Baldacchino,** all twists and columns, that serves as the altar canopy.

Piazza San Pietro (there's an information office/bookshop on the the the square to the left of the steps up to the church). ☎ **06-6988-4466** *or 06-6988-3712. Metro: Ottaviano/San Pietro. Bus: tram 19, 23, 32, 34, 46, 46/,49, 51, 62, 64, 81, 98, 492, 881, 907, 982, 990, 991. Open: Church: daily 7:00 a.m.–7:00 p.m. (6:00 p.m. Sept–Mar); Crypt: daily 7:00 a.m.–6:00 p.m. (5:00 p.m. Oct–Mar); Dome: daily 8:00 a.m.–6:00 p.m. (4:30 p.m. Oct–Feb); Treasury: daily 9:00 a.m.–6:30 p.m. (4:00 p.m. Oct–Mar). Admission: The church, sacristy, and crypt are free; the dome is 5,000L ($2.80) adults, 1,000L (55 cents) students, or 6,000L ($3.35) to take the elevator most of the way. The Treasury is 5,000L ($2.80). Ask about the 10,000L ($5.55) guided tour of the subcrypt around St. Peter's tomb at the information office or call the Ufficio Scavi at* ☎ **06-6988-5318.**

Vatican Museums

Not only is the Vatican the center of the Catholic faith, it is also home to one of the greatest museum complexes in the world. With 12 apartments and collections all worth viewing (including the wonderful Raphael Rooms and the amazing Sistine Chapel), you certainly need some help in seeing it all. Luckily, you can choose from four color-coded itineraries that vary in focus and duration. Plan A lasts around 90 minutes (shuttling you through the Sistine and the Raphael Rooms), while plan D takes five hours. Also, be aware that you'll probably need an extra 30 to 45 minutes for waiting in lines for any tour. For the best short visit possible (about 2½ hours), take a quick jaunt through the Picture Gallery (about 20 to 30 minutes) and then move onto plan A.

To avoid waiting in line with busloads of tourists, I recommend arriving at the Vatican super early — in the summer, about 30 minutes before it opens, if possible. After you take in the museums, head on over to St. Peter's, which is immense enough to hold tens of thousands of people, no problem.

Your first stop is most likely the **Pinacoteca (Picture Gallery),** which houses Leonardo da Vinci's unfinished *St. Jerome,* Giotto's *Stefaneschi Triptych,* and Caravaggio's *Deposition from the Cross.* The most famous work here is certainly Raphael's masterpiece, the huge study in colors and light called the *Transfiguration,* which Raphael had not quite completed by the time of his sudden death at the age of 37.

The pinnacle of Renaissance painting fills the ceiling and end wall of the **Sistine Chapel.** Originally, Pope Julius II had hired Michelangelo to create a magnificent burial site for him, but then switched the artist to another job — painting the chapel ceiling. Michelangelo at first balked at the request, saying that he was a sculptor, not a frescoist, but eventually he agreed to work on the ceiling.

After four years of arduous work, the frescoes were unveiled. Michelangelo had transformed the barrel-vaulted ceiling of the chapel into a blueprint for the continuing development of Renaissance art, developing new means of depicting the human form, new methods of arranging frescoes, and new uses of light and color that painters would embrace for generations to come. He covered the Sistine ceiling with nine scenes from Genesis (the fingers-almost-touching **God Creating Adam** is but the most famous) and ringed these with figures of the ancient prophets and sybils and with nudes in contorted positions that show off brilliant attention to human musculature.

The walls of the chapel are covered by wonderful frescoes from earlier Renaissance biggies including Signorelli, Botticelli, Pinturicchio, Perugino, Ghirlandaio — all works that would command attention if they weren't under such a fabulous ceiling. In 1545, at the age of 60, Michelangelo returned to the chapel to paint the entire end wall with a *Last Judgment* — a masterwork of color, despair, and psychology.

If I had to choose the other top sight in the Vatican, it would be the **Pio-Clementino Museum,** which houses ancient Greek and Roman sculpture. Look here for the famed *Laocoön* group (first century b.c.), the *Apollo Belvedere* (ancient Roman copy of a fourth-century b.c. Greek original), and the muscular *Belvedere Torso,* a first-century b.c. fragment of a Hercules statue that served as inspiration to Renaissance artists such as Michelangelo.

And of course, the Vatican has numerous other museums, but you need months to get through all of them. Some the best include: collection of **Egyptian** and **Etruscan** artifacts, a **Modern Religious Art** gallery with robes by Matisse, an **Ethnological Museum** covering 3,000 years of history across all continents (the stuff from China is particularly good), an outstanding **Library,** and a museum devoted to the **History of the Vatican.**

Viale Vaticano (on the north side of the Vatican City walls, between where Via Santamaura and the Via Tunisi staircase hit Viale Vaticano; about a 5–10 minute walk around the walls from St. Peter's). ☎ **06-6988-3333;** *Internet:* www.vatican.va. *Bus: 49 stops in front; or tram 19, 23, 51, 81, 492, 907, 982, 991 to Piazza del Risorgimento. Open: Nov–Feb Mon–Sat 8:45 a.m.–1:45 p.m.; Mar–Oct Mon–Fri 8:45 a.m.–4:45 p.m., Sat 8:45 a.m.–1:45 p.m. Also open the last Sun of each month 8:45 a.m.–1:45 p.m. Last admission is one hr. before closing. Admission: 18,000L ($10) adults, 12,000L ($6.65) students and ages 6–14. Free the last Sun of each month (and crowded like you wouldn't believe).*

Roman Forum and Palatine Hill

The Forum was the birthplace of the Roman Republic, nestled snugly between the Capitoline and Palatine Hills. And the Palatine Hill is where Rome began in the eighth century b.c. as just a wee Latin village. Be sure to bring along your imagination when you visit. With all the dusty arches and crumbling columns, some visitors have a hard time picturing the glory of Ancient Rome, but this archaeological zone is certainly a joy to discover nevertheless.

You can explore the Forum and surrounding areas in about an hour or two, but many visitors choose to pack a lunch and spend four or five hours touring. Do keep in mind that the area gets pretty darn dusty and hot (especially in August), so visit early in the day, bring along some water, and wear a protective hat.

Under republican rule, this patch of drained swamp land became Rome's public "forum" of temples, administrative halls, podiums for speakers, markets, and law courts. The forum today is a collection of columns and debris sprinkled about that designates where important buildings once stood. Their names will mean almost nothing if you're not a fan of ancient history, so the following touches on the more visually stunning sights.

As you enter on the eastern side, you see the triumphal **Arch of Septimius Severus** (a.d. 203), which lists the emperor's military victories in what are today Iran and Iraq. As you stroll east among the ruins, find your way back against the south side of the grounds to explore partially rebuilt **House of the Vestal Virgins** (third to fourth centuries). The building was home to the consecrated young women who tended the sacred flame in the nearby Temple of Vesta. Head back to the Forum's north side and check out the massive brick remains and ceilings of the **Basilica of Constantine and Maxentius** (fourth century), which once served as the public law courts. (Early Christians adopted this architectural style for their houses of worship, which is why so many ancient churches are called basilicas.) Trot back south and east, and discover yet another triumphal arch, this time the **Arch of Titus** (a.d. 81). This arch illustrates scenes from the war that ended with the expulsion of Jews from Judea and thus began the Jewish diaspora throughout Europe.

Next, take a hike up the **Palatine Hill,** home to that original Latin village and later to the dwelling of wealthy families and the the first emperors. The hilltop is overgrown and tree-shaded, and features gardens and fragments of ancient villas. Despite its fine little museum and lovely view, most visitors don't even climb the hill. Use this fact to your advantage and have a romantic, scenic escape from the crowds. Stroll among the passageways of the mansion of ancient Rome's rich and famous. From Palatine Hill's southern portion, you can look out over the long grassy oval that was the **Circus Maximus,** where Ben Hur-types used to race chariots (joggers are the only athletes you find today).

Across Via dei Fori Imperiali from the Roman Forum, you can see many other small forums, collectively known as the **Imperial Forums.** These were partly unearthed in the 1930s, but recently the digging started up again as part of a long-awaited, ambitious project to create a vast archaeological park extending from the Capitoline Hill, across the Roman and Imperial Fori, to the Colosseum. Broad boulevard Via dei Fori Imperiali will be reduced to a raised viaduct for buses and taxis.

Things are changing daily at this exciting new endeavor — you can get an update and view a live video-cam feed at www.capitolum.org — but current visitors enter part of it to explore the wide semi-circle of ancient Rome's multilevel shopping mall, **Trajan's Market,** at Via IV Novembre 94 for 3,750L ($2.10) admission.

At the western foot of the Palatine Hill, on Piazza della Bocca della Verità, sit two small temples from the second century b.c. and the church **Santa Maria in Cosmedin,** with its early twelfth century bell tower and marble inlay floors. Crowds flock to the front porch of this church to stick their hands inside the **Mouth of Truth,** a fourth-century b.c. sewer cover with a gaping maw. Medieval legend says that if you stick in your hand and tell a lie, the Mouth will clamp down on your fingers (apparently, a priest once added some sting to this belief by hiding behind the Mouth with a scorpion, dispensing justice as he saw fit).

Via dei Fori Imperiali (Forum entrance across from where Via Cavour ends). ☎ **06-699-0110;** *Internet:* www.capitolium.org. *Bus: 27, 85, 87, 115, 117, 175, 186, 850. Open: Forum: Mon–Sat 9:00 a.m.–7:00 p.m. (summer, also 9:00 p.m.– midnight for guided tours only at 12,000L/$6.65), Sun 9:00 a.m.–2:00 p.m. Palatine Hill and Museum: Mon–Sat 9:00 a.m.–7:00 p.m. (summer, also 9:00 p.m.–midnight for guided tours only at 12,000L/$6.65), Sun 9:00 a.m.–2:00 p.m. Admission: Forum free; Palatine Hill and Museum 12,000L ($6.65).*

Colosseum

Blood and gore and sport — who could ask for anything more?! The world's most famous sports arena, with its large, stately oval shape and broken-toothed profile is top sight for any visitor and 50,000 others. Started in a.d. 70, this grand amphitheater housed fights between gladiators as well as exotic animals while onlooking emperors decided whether the loser got the thumbs up signal to live or thumbs down to be finished off.

As the empire slipped away, so did the Colosseum. Earthquakes shook its foundations, and folks many years later took its stones and marble to construct other buildings. Truth be told, I find the inside to be a tad disappointing — the original seats and wooden floors are gone. The main area is now a maze of walls, which were once holding pens and corridors for equipment, animals, and gladiators. However, sometime in the year 2000, visitors to the Colosseum will be able to tour the upper levels, and a section of the floor will be reinstalled. Until then, the most impressive aspect of the Colosseum is gazing at it from on horizon, enjoying its unmistakably Roman silhouette.

Colosseo. ☎ **06-700-4261.** *Metro: B to Colosseo. Bus: 13, 27, 30B, 81, 85, 87, 117, 175, 186, 673, 810, 850. Open: Winter daily 9:00 a.m.–3:00 p.m., summer daily 9:00 a.m.–7:00 p.m. Admission: 10,000L ($5.55).*

Museo Nazionale Romano (National Roman Museum)

In 1998, Rome took what was once a single museum — one which languished for decades in a quasi-mythical state inside the eternally closed Baths of Diocletian — and split it up across the city in four incredible "Museo Nazionale Romano" collections, together comprising the best ancient Roman statuary, mosaics, and frescoes you can possibly see, a "where have you been all my life" experience for antiquities buffs.

The Ludovisi, Mattei, and Altemps Collections of Classical statuary are now displayed in the sixteenth- to eighteenth-century **Palazzo Altemps** near piazza Navona (Piazza di Sant'Apollinare 44; ☎ **06-683-3759**), itself a gorgeous space, with a grand central courtyard and many original frescoed and painted wood ceilings.

More statues plus exquisite ancient Roman mosaics, bronzes, incredible frescoes, coins, and jewelry are packed into the **Palazzo Massimo alle Terme** near Termini train station (Largo di Villa Peretti, where Piazza del Cinquecento meets Via Viminale; ☎ **06-4890-3500**).

Bathhouse art and colossal statuary fill the echo-y ancient brick chamber of the **Aula Ottagona,** an original part of Diocletian's baths just off Piazza della Repubblica (Via G. Romita 3; ☎ **06-488-0530**), and they are also putting the finishing touches on a collection installed in the original **Baths of Diocletian** space (Via E. De Nicola 79; call Aula Ottagona for info) with its massive cloisters designed by Michelangelo.

For addresses and phone numbers, see above. Metro: For all but Palazzo Altemps, Repubblica. Bus: For all but Palazzo Altemps, any to Termini; for Palazzo Altemps: 70, 81, 87, 115, 116, 116T, 186, 492, 628. Open: Palazzo Altemps, Tues–Fri 9:00 a.m.–9:00 p.m., Sat 9:00 a.m.–midnight, Sun 9:00 a.m.–8:00 p.m. Palazzo Massimo, Tues–Sat 9:00 a.m.–8:00 p.m. Aula Ottagona, Tues–Sat 9:00 a.m.–2:00 p.m., Sun 9:00 a.m.–1:00 p.m. Admission: On combined ticket (see "Exploring Rome"), or Palazzo Altemps, 10,000L ($5.55); Palazzo Massimo alle Terme and Aula Ottagona combined 12,000L ($6.65).

Musei Capitolini (Capitoline Museums)

On the Piazza del Campidoglio, behind Piazza Venezia's Vittorio Emanuele monument, a reproduction bronze statue of Marcus Aurelius stands proud and almost seems to bless Rome (two of Rome's best museums). To the left of the statue is the **Palazzo Nuovo,** housing ancient sculpture such as busts of philosophers past, the *Dying Gaul,* and the *Mosaic of the Doves.*

If your trip allows you time for just one museum, make your stop the **Palazzo dei Conservatori.** Its entrance courtyard brims with oversized marble bodyparts — a head, hands, foot, arm, and kneecap — from what was once a 40-foot-tall statue of Constantine II. The in-house collection includes the a.d. first-century *Spinario,* a little bronze child plucking a thorn from his foot, and the Etruscan bronze *She-Wolf,* crafted in the late sixth century b.c. (the suckling toddlers were added in the sixteenth century).

But the real gems of the musuem are its paintings — wonderful works by Guercino, Titian, Veronese, Pietro da Cortona, Rubens, and two by Caravaggio: the *Gypsy Fortune Teller* and the surpringly sensual *St. John the Baptist.*

Piazza del Campidoglio. ☎ **06-6710-2071.** *Bus: 44, 56, 60, 70, 75, 81, 87, 95, 160, 170, 628, 640, 715, 716, 780, 810. Open: Tues–Sun 9:00 a.m.–7:00 p.m. Admission: Both museums are on the same 10,000L ($5.55) ticket; they're free (and crowded) the last Sun of the month.*

Pantheon

In the poetic words of Byron, the Pantheon is "simple, erect, severe, austere, sublime..." And, as you'll find, this lovely description doesn't even begin to capture the power and magic that this best-preserved of Rome's ancient buildings holds. Emperor Hadrian designed the Pantheon in the a.d. second century, and his skilled eye was instrumental in creating mathematically exact, almost gravity-defying space inside.

Some amazing factoids await: The 1,800-year-old bronze entrance doors weigh 20 tons each. The circular inside and ceiling is a perfect hemisphere and features an 18-foot *oculus,* or hole, in the center that lets rain and light in. The dome is exactly 140 feet across, and the building is 140 feet high.

This marvel of engineering remained unduplicated until the Renaissance — an only recently have scholars actually figured out all the building's architectural secrets. For starters, the roof is poured concrete (a Roman invention) made of light pumice stone, and the weight of it is distributed by brick arches embedded sideways into the walls and channeled into a ring of tension around the lip of the oculus. (twenty-five-foot thick walls also come in handy here.)

Although the decor is spare, the building houses the tombs the painter Raphael as well as Italy's short-lived nineteenth-century monarchy (two of the total three kings lie here). Fortunately, the Pantheon has survived for centuries because people — barbarians, over-zealous Christians, and other — have recognized its classic beauty and left the building alone for the most part.

Piazza della Rotunda. ☎ **06-6830-0230.** *Bus: 116 stops here, or take 44, 46, 56, 60, 62, 64, 65, 70, 75, 81, 87, 115, 170, 186, 492, or 710 to Largo Argentina, then walk north for three long blocks. Open: Mon–Sat 9:00 a.m.–6:30 p.m., Sun 9:00 a.m.–1:00 p.m.. Admission: Free.*

Galleria Borghese

My choice for the finest small museum in the world goes to this recently reopened and restored collection. Take 45 to 90 minutes and stroll this frescoed early seventeenth-century villa, enjoying the finest marble sculptures the baroque period has to offer. See masterpieces by the rococo genius, Gianlorenzo Bernini, including his *Aeneas and Anchises* (which he finished when he was only 15), *Hades and Persephone, Apollo and Daphne,* and the vibrant *David* — which serves as the baroque response to Michelangelo's Renaissance creation. The Renaissance David is contemplative, all about proportion and philosophy. This baroque *David* all action, with a twisting body about to let a stone fly from his sling. While you're on the ground floor, be sure to see the room with six Caravaggio paintings. The second floor houses the rest of the painting collection, with works by Andrea del Sarto, Titian, Corregio, and a large masterpiece by a young Raphael, *The Deposition.*

In the northeast corner of Villa Borghese Park, off Via Pinciana. ☎ **06-32-810.** *Bus: 95, 490, 495 (to the middle of the park); 52, 53, 910 (to Via Pinciana). Open: Tues–Sat 9:00 a.m.–9:00 p.m., Sun 9:00 a.m.–7:00 p.m.; entry times every two hours. Admission: 10,000L ($5.55), plus 2,000L ($1.10) booking fee. You have to call ahead and reserve an entry time and ticket; in summer they can be fully booked up to two weeks ahead of time.*

The Via Appia Antica and the Catacombs

The Via Appia Antica was built in 312 b.c. but is still a major Roman roadway that is bordered with ancient tombs of Roman families and miles of catacombs chiseled out of the soft tufa stone below. The catacombs, of course, are the famous burial site for thousands of early Christians. Wander in awe through miles of musty, dusty tunnels with tens of thousands of burial niches (which each hold two to three bodies). Most of the niches are still capped with headstones, but many others are open, so skulls and bones are plentiful — macabre, yes, but also quite interesting. Take a tour lead by a priest and monk, but be prepared for a bit of Christian-centric history and a heavy dose of sermonizing. You can spend all day at the catacombs, but a one- to two-hour visit is probably enough if you can get a spot in one of the popular English-language tours.

Although the **Catacombe di San Sebastiano** has tunnels that go on for seven miles and the esteemed bones of Sts. Paul and Peter were once hidden here, the tour is one of shortest and least satisfying of all the catacombs visits. (However, you *do* get to see some well-preserved stuccoes and frescoes in several pagan tombs that were once part of an aboveground cemetery. The **Catacombe di San Domitilla** are the oldest of the catacombs and, hands-down, the winner for most enjoyable catacomb experience. Groups are small, and most guides are genuinely entertaining. There are fewer "sights" than in the other catacombs — although the second-century fresco of the *Last Supper* is impressive.

The **Catacombe di San Callisto** offer a huge parking lot — as well as huge crowds from the tour buses. The tour is the cheesiest of the catabomb tours, full of canned commentary and stilted jokes. Some of the tunnels, however, are phenomenal, 70 feet high and less than 6 feet wide, with elongated tomb niches pigeon-holed all the way up to the top. Of all the catacombs, these are among the oldest and certainly the largest (12 miles of tunnels spread over 33 acres and 5 levels that house the remains of half a million Christians). You also get to ogle some of the earliest Christian frescoes and carvings.

Via Appia Antica 136 (San Sebastiano) and 110 (San Callisto), or Via delle Sette Chiese 283 (San Domitilla). ☎ **06-785-0350** *(San Sebastiano), 06-5130-1580 (San Callisto), 06-511-0342 (San Domitilla). Bus: Metro A to San Giovanni Metro stop, then bus 218 to Largo M.F. Ardeatine, near the gate to San Callisto; from here, walk right on Via d. Sette Chiese to San Domitilla, or left down Via d. Sette Chiese to San Sebastiano. Sun, only bus 760 trundles down Via Appia Antica from the Circo Massimo Metro stop. Open: 8:30 a.m.–noon and 2:30–5:00 p.m.; San Sebastiano closes Sun and Nov, San Callisto closes Mon and Feb, San Domitilla closes Tues and Jan. Admission: Each catacomb charges 8,000L ($4.45) adults, 4,000L ($2.20) ages 6–15.*

More cool things to see and do in Rome

From biking to shopping to just plain hanging out and taking in the city scenery, there's much more of Rome to keep you entertained.

✔ **Sample Cafe Life in Piazza Navona.** Rome is bursting with charming public squares, but the oblong and lively Piazza Navona is one of the premiere hangouts. Okay, so you do pay a pretty penny for food and drink at the cafes that border the piazza (particularly if you order from the cute exterior tables). But don't think of it as buying a $6 cappuccino— think of it as admission for a front row seat to an energetic circus of color, sight, smell, and sound. And for the perfect snack, visit **Tre Scalini** (☎ **06-687-9148**) and check out its legendary tartufo ice cream balls.

✔ **Flex Your Shopping Muscles around the Spanish Steps.** Italy's artistic heritage is not only housed in its museums and churches. Italy, like Paris, is a world center for high fashion and design. Although most of the big-name designers are centered out of Florence and Milan, they all have boutiques in Rome. You can find the most famous shops in a triangle of couture formed by the streets between Piazza del Popolo, the Spanish Steps, and the Corso. On Via de' Condotti experience the fashions of **Gucci** (no. 8), **Valentino** (no. 13), and **Benetton** (no. 18-19); shoes from **Fragiacomo** (no. 35), and **Ferragamo** (no. 73-74); jewelry and silver from **Bulgari** (no. 10) and **Buccellati** (no. 31); and some of the finest men's shirts in the world at **Battistoni** (no. 61A).

Via Frattina is home to **Max Mara** fashions (no. 48), fine lingerie at **Brighenti** (no. 7-8) and the **French Princesse Tam-Tam** (no. 72), and antique and modern silver at **Anatriello del Regalo** (no. 123) and **Fornari** (no. 133). Via Borgognona boasts fashions from **Givenchy** (no. 21), **Fendi** (no. 36A-39), and **Gianfranco Ferré** (no. 42B). Via del Babuino offers the relatively affordable "Emporio" division of fashion giant **Armani** (no. 119), sportswear at **Oliver** (no. 61), historic prints at **Olivi** (no. 136), and paintings of Italian scenes— no Renaissance masterpieces, but good prices and fine quality control— at **Alberto di Castro** (no. 71) and **Fava** (no. 180). A bit farther south, where Via Tritone hits the Corso at no. 189, is **La Rinascente**, Rome's biggest and finest upscale department store.

Truth be told, the big fashion names aren't much cheaper in Rome than they are in the United States. So if you plan to splurge, check out the prices back home before you buy in Rome so you know what kind of deal you're actually getting. Or, if you're like many shop-a-holics, price isn't even an issue — it's just the thrill of purchasing Ferragamo pumps in Italy.

✔ **It's Hip to Be (in a) Square.** Rome is as much about its squares and fountains as it is about museums and monuments. Take the time to visit the lively, oval **Piazza Navona.** Hit the morning flower and veggie market on Campo de' Fiori, Rome's public execution ground in the Middle Ages. The center of **Largo Argentina** sits a good 15 feet below street level (to what was ground level in ancient Roman times). Trees shade the remains of three small temples and (along the west edge) a bit of Pompey's Curia, the building Julius Caesar was leaving when he was assassinated.

The off-center, yet graceful curves of the **Spanish Steps** are covered with bright azaleas in spring and are teeming with visitors year round; they're capped by the twin-towered Trinità dei Monti church and at the bottom by the beloved "Ugly Boat" fountain.

A few blocks to the south sits an even more famous set of waterworks, the huge baroque confection called the **Trevi Fountain,** presided over by a muscular Neptune. Legend (and a host of American movies) holds that if you toss a coin into this fountain, you will one day return to Rome. Some say you should toss it backward over your shoulder. Others insist you use three coins for it to work. City authorities don't want you throwing any coins, because they rust at the bottom and do irreparable damage to the fountain.

✔ **See a Church — Take a Peek.** Stepping into Rome's churches is one of my favorite pastimes. And because Rome has in the region of 914 churches, you can keep yourself entertained for some time. Some of Rome's top houses of worship include the following:

First built in the fourth century, the mammoth cathedral **San Giovanni in Laterano** has been robbed and reworked so often that almost nothing original remains. The great pilgrimage church of **Santa Maria Maggiore** sparkles with scintillating mosaics, many of which date back to the fifth century. **San Luigi dei Francesi** features three paintings on *St. Matthew* by Caravaggio, while his *Adoration of the Shepherds* adorns the nearby church of **Sant'Agostino**.

You can see Michelangelo's muscular *Christ* and frescoes by Filippo Lippi in **Santa Maria Sopra Minerva,** Rome's only Gothic church. **Santa Maria del Popolo** has frescoes by Pinturicchio, two of Caravaggio's most famous paintings (*The Conversion of St. Paul* and *The Crucifixion of St. Peter*), and a Raphael chapel. Join the crowds at **San Pietro in Vincoli** who gather to see Michelangelo's *Moses* statue. Over a millenium old, **Santa Maria** in Trastevere has an elaborate floor of twelfth-century marble inlay and gorgeous medieval mosaics in the apse.

✔ **Get Funky in Trastevere.** Trastevere is equal parts working-class and modern trendiness, which makes it a popular hang out for Brits and Americans. The neighborhood is fairly busting at the seams with eateries (both casual trattorie and sophisticated restaurants). Its web of tight ancient streets and peppy piazze offer fun shopping, bars, clubs, galleries, and even an English language movie house (the Pasquino, just off Piazza Santa Maria in Trastevere).

✔ **Pedal Your Way through the Borghese or the Via Appia Antica.** Hop on a bike and see all that Villa Borghese park has to offer — fountains, monuments, groomed gardens, a nice zoo, and three museums (the Galleria Borghese, plus a big ol' museum of Etruscan antiquities called the *Villa Giulia* and the city's modern art gallery).

Sundays are great for biking because traffic is light and many roads are closed to cars — essentially the city is yours. Bike Via de Fori Imperiali (which heads for the Colosseum, passing the Roman and Imperial Forums) and Via Appia Antica (lined with tombs, picnickers, and early Christian catacombs).

Rent bikes or scooters at **Treno e Scooter** (☎ 06-4890-5823), at track 1 inside Termini station; **I Bike Rome,** Via Veneto 156, in section 3 of the underground parking lot (☎ 06-322-5230); or **Roma Solutions Rent A Scooter,** locations at Via F. Turati 50 near Termini (☎ 06-446-9222) and Corso V. Emanuele II 204 near Piazza Navona (☎ 06-687-6922).

✔ **Bargain and Deal at Rome's Porta Portese Flea Market.** Every Sunday, from 7:00 a.m. to 1:00 p.m., the tranquil streets in the southwest corner of Trastevere come alive with Rome's biggest, most chaotic flea market, **Porta Portese.** The fun, frenetic gathering began as a black market after World War II but now features such varied goodies as second-hand appliances, bootleg pop music, slightly used clothing, antiques, furniture, paintings, car parts, underwear, grilled corn cobs, birds, religious icons, and comic books. Take tram 8 or buses 44 or 75, get off with the crowd halfway down Viale Trastevere, and watch out for pickpockets.

And on Your Left, the Colosseum: Seeing Rome by Guided Tour

The quality of your guided **bus tour** experience in Rome depends on how much you're willing to spend. For 15,000L ($8.35), the city-run **ATAC bus 110 (☎ 06-4695-2252)** offers a three-hour trek in an old-fashioned bus. However, your "guide" on this affordable tour is your information leaflet. It leaves from outside Termini at 10:30 a.m., and 2:00, 3:00, 5:00, and 6:00 p.m.

Green Line Tours (☎ 06-483-787) offers audioguide tours in a variety of languages. You choose when to ride and when to get off and explore. Costs 30,000L ($16.65) for a day ticket (10:00 a.m.-3:00 p.m.).

Live commentary costs a bit more. Plan on shelling out 53,000 to 60,000L ($29.45 to $33.35) to **American Express (☎ 06-6764-2413)**, Piazza di Spagna 38, for its four-hour intro tours, which depart at 9:30 a.m. and/or 2:30 p.m. daily, depending on the season. Choose from your basic overview of all Rome and the Vatican or a tour that focuses mainly on ancient Rome.

Suggested One-, Two-, and Three-Day Itineraries

If you're short on time and you prefer to organize your own tour of Rome, this section offers some recommendations for hitting the highlights.

If you have one day

Rome wasn't built in a day, so don't expect to see it all in one. Spend the early morning at the Vatican Museums (you'll have time only for the highlights: the Pinacoteca, Raphael Rooms, and Sistine Chapel) and St. Peter's, having lunch on the run to see the Roman Forum. After taking a gander at the Colosseum, check out the Pantheon and then wander the churches and piazze of the Tiber Bend area, making sure to stop by the Spanish Steps. After dinner, swing past the Trevi Fountain to toss in a few coins and ensure your return to the Eternal City.

If you have two days

Spend more time at the Vatican Museums and St. Peter's from Day One (which day depends on what days of the week you're in town and therefore when you can best visit various museums), and add to the Day One experience the churches and museums of the Tiber Bend, including the Pantheon, Palazzo Altemps, and Galleria Doria Pamphilij. Have the earliest reservation possible at the Galleria Borghese for the other morning, then see the Palazzo Massimo alle Terme on your way down to the Forum/Colosseum, taking a *passeggiata* past the Spanish Steps at dusk and the Trevi Fountain after dinner.

If you have three days

What should you not miss after you've glimpsed Rome's best-known areas? The Capitoline Museums are tops, followed by the Etruscan Museum and the baroque paintings in the newly renovated Palazzo Barberini. You could also spend more time on the day you do the Forum seeing more of ancient Rome at Trajan's Markets and the Imperial Forums, and hiking beyond the Colosseum to descend through two millennia of history under San Clemente church, leaving all the musuems and churches of the Tiber Bend to the third day.

Exploring Beyond Rome

If you can tear yourself away from Rome, you'll find the splendor of Tivoli and the quiet cobble streets of Ostia Antica, both just a short hop away.

The good life: The villas of Roman emperors, princes, and popes at Tivoli

Since the dawn of Rome, Tivoli (just 19 miles east of Rome) has served as home away from home for the wealthy and powerful. Emperor Hadrian started things in the second century by building a gorgeous vacation home here, and others, including a Renaissance cardinal and nineteenth-century pope, followed suit.

Getting there

Take Rome's B Metro to Ponte Mammolo stop, where you catch the COTRAL bus to Tivoli-Villa d'Este (every 30 minutes) or Tivoli-Villa Adriana (every hour).

American Express (☎ 06-6764-2413), Piazza di Spagna 38, has a five-hour tour of Tivoli for 63,000L ($35).

The best way to see Tivoli is to take a picnic, spend the day, and return to Rome in time for dinner. Tivoli's **tourist office** (☎ 0774/311-249 or 0774/21-249) is on Largo Garibaldi.

Seeing the sights

Hadrian served the ancient Roman empire as a general and later Emperor, traveling much of the known-world during his lifetime. He also tried his hand at being an architect when he designed **Hadrian's Villa (☎ 0774/530-203),** which brims with international influences — Egyptian, Greek, and Asian. Although much of the estate is still being unearthed, look for the Canopus, a sacred Egyptian canal 225 feet long and lined with statues; the Lyceum (the ancient school where Aristotle taught), the Maritime Theatre (a pool featuring an island retreat); and several baths. Plan on two to four hours to fully explore the grounds and perhaps enjoy a picnic lunch under the cypress and olive groves that mingle with the remains of ancient columns. It's open daily 9:00 a.m. to 6:00 p.m. Admission is 8,000L ($4.45) for adults, free for visitors under 17 and over 60.

During the sixteenth century, Cardinal Ippolito d'Este, whose mother was the infamous Lucrezia Borgia, took a thirteenth-century convent and renovated it into the extravagant **Villa d'Este**. However, the real draw here are the spectacular gardens and nearly 100 fountains, including spacious pools, spurting jets, stair-stepping cascades, wall fountains covered with mossy gargoyles, and one that once even played an organ with the force of its water. The fountains are most spectacular when water is pumping through them at full force. To get the best effect, call ahead and check that the fountains will be full blast (sunny weekend days are your safest bet). The villa is open daily 9:00 a.m. to 6:00 p.m. Admission for adults is 5,000L ($2.80) when the fountains are down to a trickle, 8,000L ($4.45) when the waterworks are at their best; free for those under 17 and over 60.

If the fountains aren't pumping at the Villa d'Este's, consider visiting the **Villa Gregoriana,** a nineteenth-century retreat with tranquil gardens and the largest, most delightful water-staircase in town — it's like you're watching water fall in slow motion as it softly trips down to the gardens below. Savor the lovely valley vistas and explore a few intriguing grottoes that are a bit off the beaten path, too. One warning: Following the waterfall to the gardens below is effortless, but climbing back to the top is a surprisingly laborious task. It's open daily 9:00 a.m. until one hour before sunset. Admission is 2,500L ($1.40).

Where to dine

Since the 1950s, **Le Cinque Statue (☎ 0774/335-366),** Via Quintillio Varo 1, has been offering Tivoli visitors honest home cookin', Roman style.

No time for Pompeii? Visit Ostia Antica

The ancient Roman republic constructed Ostia to serve as Rome's port (the Tiber River wasn't deep enough ever to be useful for trade). The city flourished and at one point had nearly 100,000 inhabitants. In the fourth century, the river's mouth began to fill with silt and the shoreline began to slid away. Eventually, the empire fell, disease set in, and Ostia became a marshy bog. The city was rediscovered in the early twentieth century, but has never gained a popular flowing, even though the scenery is gloriously reminiscent of a long lost era so you don't have to fight the crowds. And it gets better: The city is just a fast ride via public transportation from the heart of Rome.

Visit Ostia bright and early in the a.m., explore the site for two to three hours, and trot on back to Rome for lunch (or picnic in the ruins, if you prefer).

Getting there

Take the **Metro line B to Magliana station** and transfer to the Lido train (you'll need another Metro ticket) and ride it 20 minutes to the Ostia Antica stop.

You won't find a **tourist office.** Just beeline to the site's entrance (☎ **06-5635-8099**) for a map and more info.

Seeing the sight

Solitude is usually yours at Ostia. Stroll this ancient town and do a little imagining. What must life have been like? Walk the cobble streets, relax in the plaza, and picture what it must have been like to attend a Greek tragedy in the theater. Roam among the columns of a raised temple or savor a picnic in the company of a solitary, armless, nameless statue, or get an intimate look at the crumbling mosaic floor of what must have been a wealthy citizen's home. Ostia Antica is open daily from 9:00 a.m. to 7:00 p.m. (5:00 p.m. October to March); the small on-site museum closes at 1:30 p.m. Admission is 8,000L ($4.45) for adults, free to visitors under 17 or over 60.

Chapter 21

Florence and the Tuscany Region

● ●

In This Chapter

▶ Getting to and around Florence

▶ Deciding which artistic masterpieces to see

▶ Choosing a restaurant that will please your palate

▶ Finding the best hotels in your price range

▶ Planning trips within and around Florence

● ●

*1*f you are an art or history buff with even a modest interest in the Renaissance, Florence is a must-see destination on your trip to Europe. For more than two centuries beginning in the late 1300s, artists, writers, musicians, philosophers, and scientists sparked a creative movement in Florence that essentially killed the Middle Ages throughout Europe and came to be called the Renaissance, or "rebirth."

The Florentine Renaissance was an era of spirited artistic and intellectual activity, and symbols of it are still very much in evidence there today. Your exploration of the Renaissance in Florence may include Michelangelo's *David,* Giotto's frescoes in Santa Croce, Brunelleschi's ingenious cathedral dome, and the Uffizi Galleries — the world's most esteemed collection of Renaissance artwork, from Da Vinci's *Annunciation* to Botticelli's *Birth of Venus.*

But there's more to Florence than just centuries-old art. You can enjoy a sumptuous Tuscan meal with plenty of Chianti wine from the countryside. Or you can test the durability of embossed plastic at the high-fashion and fine-leather boutiques in the city that brought the world Gucci, Pucci, Ferragamo, and Beltrami.

The Leaning Tower of Pisa and the quaint hill towns of the Tuscany region are all close enough to make easy day trips from Florence. Or you can stay in Florence and let the lush greenery and warm sunshine of the Boboli Gardens inspire you to write or paint your own masterpiece. Spend at least two days here; three if you can swing it.

Making Your Way to and around Florence

Though it is a good-sized city, Florence is by no means the mega-metropolis that many European travelers are used to tackling. This can make getting there a little more difficult — most flights from outside Italy land at an airport that's 60 miles away — but getting around town is comparatively easy.

Getting to Florence by air

Amerigo Vespucci Airport is 3.1 miles northwest of Florence, but most of the flights that land there come from within Italy. From the airport, visitors can take city bus number 62, which departs every 20 minutes for Stazione Santa Maria Novella, Florence's main terminal located on the western edge of the city's historic center. The ride takes about 30 minutes and costs less than a dollar. For around $15, visitors can also take a metered taxi from the airport directly to their hotel. Most flights from elsewhere in Europe land at **Galileo Galilei Airport** in Pisa, 60 miles from Florence. A frequent one-hour train service, which costs $4.35, connects the airport to Stazione Santa Maria Novella.

Getting to Florence by rail

Trains to Florence pull into **Stazione Santa Maria Novella,** which is often abbreviated as S.M.N. The station is on the western edge of the city's compact historic center, and a 10- to 15-minute walk to some hotels and major attractions. If your hotel is not within walking distance, or if you simply don't want to haul your luggage through the streets, you can get a taxi at a stand outside the station in the Piazza Stazione.

Getting around once you're in Florence

Florence's *centro storico* (old center) is much smaller than that of most European travel destinations, and most of it is reserved for pedestrians, so it's extremely easy to get around on foot. Walking from one end of this tourist area to the other only takes about 30 minutes.

By bus

Even though Florence is so pedestrian-friendly, the bus system can help you get your bags from the train station to your hotel or visit the sights farthest outside the central city. Almost all bus routes begin, stop, or end at the train station, and many also pass through Piazza San Marco (near the Accademia, where *David* is housed). Most routes make only three or four stops before heading out of Florence and on the way to the hills. The bus system does not serve the historic center of the city very well, though the new electric minibuses A, B, C, and D do dip into it.

Bus tickets good for 60 minutes cost 1,500L (85 cents), and tickets good for three hours cost 2,500L ($1.40). You can take as many different rides as you want within the time limits; just stamp one end of your ticket in the orange box on the first bus you board. You can also get a 6,000L ($3.35) 24-hour ticket and an 11,000L ($6.10) three-day pass. Tickets are available at newsstands and in *tabacchi* (tobacconists, marked by a white "T" against a brown background).

By taxi

Taxis are not an economical way to get around town. Their rates are not cheap, and the one-way street system forces the drivers to take convoluted routes; you're usually better off on foot. But taxis are useful when you need to get your luggage between your hotel and the train station in the *centro storico,* where a bus is a rare sight. Because the train station is in the *centro storico,* the taxi ride can't be too far from most any hotel and shouldn't cost more than 15,000L ($8.35).

The standard rate for taxis is 1,430L (80 cents) per kilometer, with a 4,400L ($2.45) minimum charge (the minimum is 9,500L/$5.30 from 10:00 p.m. to 6:00 a.m., 7,500L/$4.15 on Sundays), plus 1,000L (55 cents) per bag. You can't hail a cab, but you can find one at a taxi stand in or near a major piazza; otherwise you have to call for one (a Radio Taxi) at ☎ **4242,** 4798, or 4390.

Discovering Florence: What You Need to Know

This section includes a few pointers to make your stay even more enjoyable and to help you find assistance in case of an emergency.

The local dough

The unit of currency in Italy is the *lire* (L). Roughly, $1 equals 1,800L; or 1,000L equals 55 cents. Italian coinage can be confusing because there are two types of 50L coins and three different 100L coins. Other change denominations include 200L and 500L. You may occasionally see old 10L and 20L coins — though they're completely worthless — as well as *gettoni,* old grooved phone tokens that are worth 200L. The government will release a 1,000L coin soon. Bills come in denominations of 1,000L, 2,000L, 5,000L, 10,000L, 50,000L, and 100,000L.

Where to get info after you arrive

The city's largest **Tourist Information Office** (☎ **055-290-832,** fax: 055-276-0383; Internet: www.firenze.turismo.toscana.it) is at Via Cavour 1r, about three blocks north of the Duomo. This office, slightly larger and less harried than one at the train station, offers lots of literature, including details on current museum hours and concert schedules.

From March to October, it's open Monday to Saturday, 8:15 a.m. to 7:15 p.m.; and Sunday, 8:15 a.m. to 1:15 p.m. From November to February, hours are Monday to Saturday, 8:15 a.m. to 1:45 p.m. (Lately the office has been experimenting with staying open to 7:15 p.m. year-round.) There's a tiny **train station info office** with some maps and a hotel booking service (see "Runner-up accommodations") at the head of the tracks. It is open Monday to Saturday, 9:00 a.m. to 9:00 p.m. (to 8:00 p.m. from November to March). The train station's main **Ufficio Informazioni Turistiche** (☎ 055-212-245; Internet: www.firenze.turismo.toscana.it) is outside the station. With your back to the tracks, take the left exit, cross onto the concrete median, and turn right; it's about 100 feet ahead. Ask for a free copy of **Avvenimenti,** a helpful monthly publication, or **Firenze Oggi,** a 2,000L ($1.10) bimonthly. The office is usually open Monday to Saturday, 8:15 a.m. to 7:15 p.m. (to 1:15 p.m. in winter).

Ignore listings for the **information office** just off Piazza della Signoria at Chiasso Baroncelli 17r; it relocated in 1998 to an obscure side street south of Piazza Santa Croce, Borgo Santa Croce 29r (☎ 055-234-0444). It is open Monday to Saturday, 8:15 a.m. to 7:15 p.m.; and Sunday, 8:15 a.m. to 1:45 p.m.

The bilingual *Concierge Information* magazine, free at the front desks of top hotels, contains a monthly calendar of events and details on attractions. *Firenze Spettacolo,* a 3,000L ($1.60) Italian-language monthly sold at most newsstands, is the most detailed and up-to-date listing of nightlife, arts, and entertainment.

Knowing the business hours

In the summer, most businesses and shops are open 9:00 a.m. to 1:00 p.m. and 3:30 to 7:30 p.m. That midday shut-down is a siesta-like naptime called *riposo,* but more and more stores are opting to follow an *orario continuato* (no-stop) schedule. Many shops are closed Monday mornings, the majority close on Sunday, and some also close Saturday afternoons. *Alimentari* (small grocery stores) are open Monday to Saturday but in low season are closed Wednesday afternoons and in high season are closed Saturday afternoons. Standard bank hours are Monday to Friday, 8:20 a.m. to 1:20 p.m. and 2:45 to 3:45 p.m. Restaurants are required to close at least one day per week (their *giorno di riposo*), though the day varies.

Where to go in a pinch

You can feel very safe in all of central Italy, which has practically no random violent crime. Florence, like any city, has plenty of petty thieves looking to pick your pocket, plus a few light-fingered children (especially near the train station), but otherwise there aren't any dangers that are hard to avoid. You should stay out of the Cascine park at night, when you may risk getting mugged, and you probably won't want to hang out with the late-night heroin addicts shooting up on the Arno mudflats below the Lungarno embankments on the edges of town. In case of an emergency, keep these numbers handy.

✔ **Consulate:** The **consulate of the United States** is at Lungarno Amerigo Vespucci 38 (☎ 055-239-8276), near its intersection with Via Palestro; it's open Monday to Friday, 8:30 a.m. to 1:00 p.m. and 2:00 to 5:30 p.m.

✔ **Emergency:** Dial ☎ 113 for the local police or ☎ 112 for the *carabinieri* (the military-trained and more useful of the two police forces). To report a fire, dial ☎ 115. For an ambulance, dial ☎ 118. For roadside vehicle service, call ☎ 116.

✔ **Transit Information:** Call ☎ 055-565-0222.

✔ **Dentists and Doctors:** For a list of English-speaking dentists or doctors, ask at the **United States consulate** (☎ 055-239-8276), or the **British consulate** (☎ 055-284-133). Visitors who need emergency medical care can call **Volunteer Hospital Interpreters** at ☎ 055-234-4567; the interpreters are always on call and offer their services free.

✔ **Pharmacies:** Three places offering English-speaking service and 24-hour schedules are the **Farmacia Communale,** at the head of track 16 in the train station (☎ 055-216-761); **Molteni,** Via dei Calzaiuoli 7r, just north of Piazza della Signoria (☎ 055-289-490); and **All'Insegno del Moro,** at the Duomo square, Piazza San Giovanni 20r (☎ 055-211-343).

Staying in touch

Whether you're calling home or logging on to check your e-mail, Florence offers plenty of ways to stay in touch with the rest of the world.

✔ **American Express:** AMEX is at Via Dante Alighieri 22r (☎ 055-50-981), open Monday to Friday, 9:00 a.m. to 5:30 p.m.; and Saturday, 9:00 a.m. to 12:30 p.m. The office will cash all traveler's checks (not just American Express checks) without a fee.

✔ **Internet Access and Cyber Cafes: Thenetgate** (www.thenetgate.it) has locations at Via Cavour 144r (☎ 055-210-004), Via dei Cimatori 17r (☎ 055-219-491), and Via Sant'Egidio 10r (☎ 055-234-7967). All are open Monday to Saturday, 10:30 a.m. to 10:30 p.m. in summer; daily, 10:40 a.m. to 8:30 p.m. in winter. **Internet Train** has locations at Via dell'Oriuolo 25r (☎ 055-263-8968), Borgo San Jacopo 30r (☎ 055-265-7584), and Via Gulefa 24A (☎ 055-214-794); all locations are open daily, 10:00 a.m. until "very late" (usually between 10:30 p.m. and midnight). Both businesses charge 10,000L ($5) per hour.

✔ **Mail:** Florence's main post office is at Via Pellicceria 3, off the southwest corner of Piazza della Repubblica. You can buy stamps *(francobolli)* and pick up letters sent *Fermo Posta* (Italian for General Delivery) after showing some ID. The post office is open Monday to Friday, 8:15 a.m. to 7:00 p.m.; and Saturday, 8:15 a.m. to 12:30 p.m. All packages heavier than 2 kilos (4½ pounds) must be properly wrapped and brought around to the parcel office at the back of the building (enter at Via dei Sassetti 4, also known as Piazza Davanzati).

✔ **Telephone:** A local call costs 200L (10 cents) in Italy. Pay phones take coins or phone cards (*carta telefonica*), which you can buy from many newsstands and all *tabbachi* (tobacconists) in increments of 5,000L ($2.80), 10,000L ($5.55), and 15,000L ($8.35). Before you insert it, break off the corner of the card. A digital display shows you how much money is left on the card. For directory assistance, call ☎ **12** (remember, though, that it's unlikely the operators will speak English).

Italy's country code is **39.** To call Italy from the United States, dial **011-39,** and then the number. If you want to use a calling card, insert 200L (you'll get it back) and call **AT&T** at ☎ **172-1011, MCI** at ☎ **172-1022,** or **Sprint** at ☎ **172-1877.** You can also call these numbers to make a collect call or dial the **Italcable** operator at ☎ **170** (free). To call the United States directly from Italy, dial **001** followed by the area code and phone number.

Touring Florence by Neighborhood

Two focal points lie at the core of Florence's **centro storico (old center)**: **Piazza San Giovanni/Piazza del Duomo** and, several blocks to the south, **Piazza della Signoria.** The two piazzas (squares) are linked by **Via Calzaiuoli,** a wide, pedestrian-choked promenade, and the center of medieval Florence takes shape in the maze of cobblestone streets between them. The formidable **Palazzo Vecchio** is in the bustling Piazza della Signoria, a statue-filled square lined with cafes. The Uffizi Galleries, Florence's most famous art museum, stretches off the Palazzo Vecchio.

West of this central area and in the middle of **Via Roma** is Florence's primary shopping district, the nineteenth-century **Piazza della Repubblica.** Nearby is the main artery of Florence's high-fashion industry, **Via de' Tournabuoni.** As it heads south, Via Roma changes names — first becoming **Via Calimata,** and then **Via Por Santa Maria.** Farther south along this road you will find **Ponte Vecchio,** a famous bridge over the Arno River lined with goldsmith and silversmith shops. In the middle of the bridge, some extra space between buildings creates a small piazza with wonderful river views. From the Ponte Vecchio, **Via Guicciardini** leads up to **Piazza Pitti** and the appropriately named Pitti Palace.

Northwest of Piazza del Duomo is **Piazza Santa Maria Novella,** which sits in front of a church by the same name and marks the western edge of the historic city. Just north of the church is the train station, which is surrounded by streets full of cheap hotels. Between the station and the Duomo are **Piazza San Lorenzo** and the **Mercato Centrale** (indoor Central Market). The streets around them are filled with the stalls of leather merchants.

Three main streets head north from Piazza del Duomo: **Via de' Martelli/Via Cavour** leads straight up to **Piazza San Marco,** site of the

San Marco monastery; **Via Ricasoli** heads to the Accademia, home of Michelangelo's *David;* and **Via de' Servi** runs into the gorgeous **Piazza SS. Annunziata,** bordered on three sides by porticoes inspired and designed by Brunelleschi. **Borgo de' Greci** wanders east from Piazza della Signoria to **Piazza Santa Croce,** home to a major church, the center of a neighborhood that has many of Florence's best restaurants, and the eastern edge of the visitor's city.

The **Arno River** flows through the southern end of the city; most of Florence is north of the Arno. South of the river is an old artisan's quarter called the **Oltrarno,** which features the famed Pitti Palace and excellent restaurants and shopping. In the middle of the Oltrarno is **Piazza Santo Spirito,** which contains a fine early Renaissance church interior courtesy of Brunelleschi.

Florence uses two different systems for numbering addresses. Shops, businesses, and restaurants have plaques with red numbers, but homes, offices, and hotels have plaques numbered *independently* in black (and sometimes blue). Red addresses show an "r" after the number; black ones may have a "b," but more often have nothing after the number. The two systems overlap, but don't affect each other. So this means that a street with a row of buildings designated shop, restaurant, hotel, shop, and home could have address plaques that read, in order, "1r, 3r, 1, 5r, 3." So if nothing appears to be at the address you wrote down, try looking for a plaque with the same number but in a different color.

Staying in Florence

You can find any kind of sleeping accommodations in Florence, from crash pads for the economically challenged to restored Renaissance palaces for those with money to burn. Florence is so small that staying anywhere in the *centro storico* will put you within easy walking distance of most every attraction.

But keep in mind that the area around the train station (especially to the east) is a boring part of town. Yes, it's packed to the gills with hotels, but these places are more often than not cramped budget joints favored by students. As a last resort, you can almost certainly find a place to sleep just by walking up Via Faenza (the area's main hotel strip) and inquiring at every inn.

If you need help finding a room, the tourism office in the train station will make reservations for you for a fee (3,000 to 10,000L/$1.65 to $5.55) based to the price range of the hotel.

Because Florence's *centro storico* is too small to break up into neighborhoods, I describe the location of the hotels and restaurants in this chapter in relation to the closest landmarks.

Accommodations, Dining & Attractions in Florence

ATTRACTIONS ●
Badia **10**
Baptistery **1**
Bargello **34**
Boboli Gardens **12**
Campanile di Giotto
  (Bell Tower) **3**
Duomo **2**
Galleria Corsini **16**
Galleria dell'
  Accademia **44**
Medici Chapels **20**
Museo dell'Opera
  del Duomo **40**
Museo dell'Opera
  di Santa Croce **30**
Palazzo Pitti **13**
Palazzo Vecchio **25**
Piazzale Michelangelo **28**
Ponte Vecchio **15**
San Lorenzo **41**
San Miniato al Monte **27**
Santa Croce **31**
Santa Maria Novella **18**
Spedale degli Innocenti **45**
Synagogue **38**
Uffizi Galleries **24**

HOTELS ■
Grand Hotel Cavour **9**
Hotel Bellettini **21**
Hotel Brunelleschi **5**
Hotel Firenze **7**
Hotel Medici **4**
Hotel Monna Lisa **39**
Hotel Hermitage **23**
Hotel Pensione Pendini **22**
Hotel Ritz **29**
Hotel Silla **26**

RESTAURANTS ◆
Acqua al 2 **35**
Cibrèo **37**
Da Pennello Ristorante
  Casa di Dante **8**
I' Cche' c'è c'è **32**
I Fratellini **11**
Il Latini **17**
Il Pizzaiolo **36**
Le Mossacce **6**
Trattoria Antellesi **19**
Trattoria Casalinga **14**
Trattoria Zà-Zà **42**
Vivoli **33**

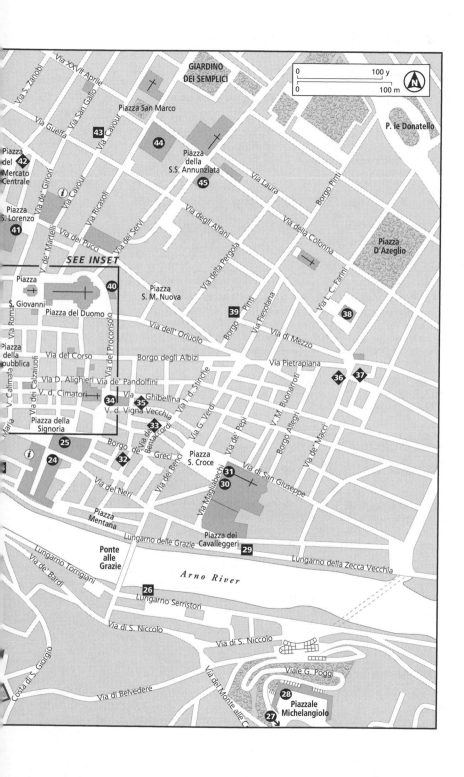

GIARDINO DEI SEMPLICI

Via XXVII Aprile

Via S. Zanobi

Via Guelfa

Via San Gallo

Via Cavour

Piazza San Marco

43

44

Piazza della S.S. Annunziata

45

Via Laura

Borgo Pinti

P. le Donatello

Piazza del Mercato Centrale

42

Via de' Ginori

Via Cavour

Via Ricasoli

Via dei Servi

Via degli Alfani

Via della Colonna

Piazza D'Azeglio

Piazza S. Lorenzo

41

V. de' Martelli

Via dei Pucci

Via della Pergola

Via L. C. Farini

SEE INSET

Piazza

40

Piazza S. M. Nuova

Borgo Pinti

Via Fiesolana

38

S. Giovanni

Piazza del Duomo

Via del Proconsolo

Via dell' Oriuolo

39

Via di Mezzo

Piazza della Repubblica

Via del Corso

Borgo degli Albizi

Via Pietrapiana

Via Roma

Via dei Calzaiuoli

Via D. Alighieri

Via de' Pandolfini

V. d. Cimatori

Via Ghibellina

34

35

V. d. Vigna Vecchia

V. M. Buonarroti

36

37

Via de' Stinche

Via G. Verdi

Via de' Pepi

Borgo Allegri

Via de' Macci

Piazza della Signoria

33

V. Calimala

V. Mara

25

24

32

Borgo de' Greci

Via de' Bentaccordi

Via de' Benci

Piazza S. Croce

Via di San Giuseppe

31

30

Via Magliabechi

Via del Neri

Piazza Mentana

Ponte alle Grazie

Lungarno delle Grazie

Piazza dei Cavalleggeri

29

Lungarno della Zecca Vecchia

Lungarno Torrigiani

Via de' Bardi

Arno River

26

Lungarno Serristori

Costa di S. Giorgio

Via di S. Niccolo

Via di S. Niccolo

Viale G. Poggi

Via del Monte alle C.

Via di Belvedere

28

Piazzale Michelangiolo

27

Florence's top hotels

Hotel Firenze

$ Between the Duomo and Palazzo Vecchio

This establishment is as bare-bones as you'll find, but it's clean and centrally located on a quiet piazza. You can forgive the spartan rooms when, for a rock-bottom price that includes breakfast, you are just a few steps away from Florence's major sights.

Piazza Donati 4 (off Via del Corso). ☎ **055-268-301** *or 055-214-203. Fax: 055-212-370. Bus: 14, 23, 71. Rates: 150,000L ($83.35) double. No credit cards.*

Grand Hotel Cavour

$$$ Near the Bargello

In the 1860s, this comfortable, centrally located hotel was made out of a medieval *palazzo* (palace), and has since been outfitted with modern conveniences and standard comforts, all in contemporary good taste. You can see a breathtaking view of the city's landmarks from the roof terrace, and the front and side rooms look out to the Bargello and Badia towers. The elegant hotel restaurant serves excellent traditional cuisine.

Via del Proconsolo 3 (next to the Badia). ☎ **055-282-461.** *Fax: 055-218-955. Internet:* www.hotelcavour.com. *Bus: 14, 23, 71. Rates: 280,000–320,000L ($155.55–$177.80) double. AE, DC, MC, V.*

Hotel Bellettini

$-$$ Just northwest of the Duomo

Two cordial sisters run this comfortable hotel that sits on a quiet street between the Duomo and the outdoor leather market. The rooms have a mostly modern decor, with a hint of nineteenth-century style and a few antique pieces mixed in. The breakfast spread is ample. The place stays busy all year with many repeat guests.

Via de' Conti 7 (just off Via dei Cerretani). ☎ **055-213-561.** *Fax: 055-283-551. Internet:* www.firenze.net/hotelbellettini. *Bus: 36, 37. Rates: 160,000–180,000L ($88.90–$100) double without bathroom, 200,000–210,000L ($111.10–$116.65) double with bathroom. AE, DC, MC, V.*

Hotel Monna Lisa

$$$$ North of Santa Croce

This eclectic hotel is my splurge choice among Florence's opulent accommodations, most of which look pretty much the same. Set up like the villa of a wealthy Florentine family, this hotel is filled with oil paintings, sculptures, and lush potted plants. Room decor varies widely, in keeping with the private home atmosphere; you may have a coffered wood ceiling, antique furnishings, or a Jacuzzi gracing your room.

Borgo Pinti 27. ☎ *055-247-9751. Fax: 055-247-9755. Internet:* www.monnalisa.it. *Bus: B, 14, 23, 71. Rates: 300,000–570,000L ($166.65–$316.65) double. AE, DC, MC, V.*

Hotel Hermitage

$$$ Very near the Ponte Vecchio and Uffizi

Because it is on a small piazza near the foot of the Ponte Vecchio, rooms at the Hotel Hermitage overlook the Arno River and its famous old bridge. But the roof terrace has the best view; from there, you can see the nearby Palazzo Vecchio. The friendly management serves a filling breakfast, and a 1997 renovation gave most rooms Jacuzzis and wood floors.

Vicolo Marzio 1/Piazza del Pesce (left of the Ponte Vecchio). ☎ *055-287-216. Fax: 055-212-208. Internet:* www.hermitagehotel.com. *Bus: 23, 71. Rates: 370,000L ($205.55) double. MC, V.*

Hotel Pensione Pendini

$$ Between the Duomo and Palazzo Vecchio

For more than 100 years, this classic Italian pension has been a favorite of travelers. The devoted regulars appreciate the mix of antiques and modern conveniences in the usually spacious rooms. The hotel rises above the storefronts and cafes of Piazza della Repubblica, is near the major sights, and is right in the middle of Florence's best shopping area.

Via Strozzi 2 (just through the grand arch of Piazza della Repubblica on the right). ☎ *055-211-170. Fax: 055-281-807. Internet:* www.tiac.net/users/pendini. *Bus: 22, 36, 37. Rates: 190,000–260,000L ($105.55–$144.45) double. AE, DC, MC, V.*

Florence's runner-up accommodations

Hotel Alessandra

$-$$ This hotel has spacious high-ceilinged rooms in a sixteenth-century palazzo near the river and Ponte Vecchio. Air-conditioning is free, but you must request it when you make reservations. *Borgo SS. Apostoli 17, between Via dei Tornabuoni and Via Por Santa Maria (*☎ *055-283-438; Fax: 055-210-619; Internet:* www.hotelalessandra.com*).*

Hotel Casci

$$ Run by the exceedingly helpful Lombardi family and has a frescoed breakfast room (composer Rossini used to live here). Even the double-paned windows can't quite block out the traffic from busy Via Cavour, so ask for a room facing the inner courtyard's magnolia tree. *Via Cavour 13, between Via de' Gori and Via Guelfa (*☎ *055-211-686; Fax: 055-239-6461; Internet:* www.hotelcasci.com*).*

Hotel Silla

$$$ A fifteenth-century palazzo on a shaded riverside piazza just across the Arno. Every room is unique — some rooms have beamed ceilings and parquet floors, others have floral wallpaper and stylish furnishings. *Via dei Renai 5, on Piazza Demidoff, east of Ponte delle Grazie* (☎ *055-234-2888; Fax: 055-234-1437; Internet:* www.hotelsilla.it).

Hotel Brunelleschi

$$$$ A posh property tucked away in the heart of town within the restored remains of a medieval church and a sixth-century Byzantine tower. The rooms are spacious and very comfortable, with large baths, but are disappointingly modern. *Piazza Sant'Elisabetta 3, off Via de' Calzioli* (☎ *055-27-370, 055-290-311, or 055-267-1101; Fax: 055-219-653; Internet:* www.hotelbrunelleschi.it).

Hotel Medici

$-$$ In the heart of the shopping district, with basic accommodations but killer views at budget rates. Secure a room on the fifth or (better yet) sixth floor for a window-filling panorama of the neighboring cathedral. Rooms without a bath are cheaper. *Via de' Medici 6, between Piazza della Repubblica and Via de' Calzaiuoli* (☎ *055-284-818; Fax: 055-216-202*).

Hotel Ritz

$$-$$$ One of the more intimate hotels right on the Arno, with mostly modern mix-and-match furniture and iron-ornamented bed frames. Two rooms on the front have balconies to better enjoy the Arno view, and two on the back (numbers 37 and 38) have small private terraces. The roof terrace has a view of the hilltop village of Fiesole. *Lungarno della Zecca Vecchia 24* (☎ *055-234-0650; Fax: 055-240-863; Internet:* www.tiac.net/users/pendini/ritz).

Dining in Florence

If you're enjoying it as you should, a typical, multiple-course Florentine meal can take a few hours to finish. It begins with an appetizer, traditionally *affettati misti* (assorted salami) and *crostini misti* (round toast and toppings such as liver pâté, mushrooms, tomatoes, and cheese). Your first course (called the *primo*) could be a soup — try the stewlike *ribollita* (vegetables, beans, and bread). You may get one of these pastas as your *primo* instead: *spaghetti alla carrettiera* (in a spicy tomato sauce) or *al pomodoro* (in a plain tomato sauce); *papardelle al cinghiale* (wide noodles in a wild boar sauce); or *crespelle Fiorentine* (pasta layered with cheese and béchamel sauce).

The main course *(secondo)* could be a *pollo* (chicken) dish, *scallopine* (veal cutlets, cooked in one of several ways), *lombatina di vitello* (veal chop), *involtini* (veal rolled with veggies and stewed in its own juices), or *bistecca Fiorentina* (steak grilled and brushed with olive oil and pepper). The waiter will expect you to order a side dish (a *contorno*) to go with this main dish, and *fagioli* — white Tuscan cannellini beans (sometimes served *all'uccelleto*, stewed with sage and tomatoes) — are the tastiest choice.

Your best bets for dessert are *cantucci con vin santo* — tiny, hard almond cookies for dipping in sweet dessert wine — or a *tiramisù*, which are lady fingers soaked in espresso, layered with sweet mascarpone cheese, and topped with cocoa.

Florence makes some of the world's best ice cream, called *gelato*, and no visit is complete without indulging. The city's most renowned purveyor of the cool, creamy snack is **Vivoli** (☎ 055-292-334) at Via Isole delle Stinche 7r, off Via Ghibellina east of Santa Croce. Other ice cream parlors around town are good, too; just look for a sign saying it is *produzione propria* (homemade).

The countryside around Florence is famous across the globe for its wines — especially red Chianti classico, which will probably be the house table wine at a Florentine restaurant. You may also want to try the more complex (and expensive) reds from southern Tuscany: Vino Nobile di Montepulciano and Brunello di Montalcino (perfect to go with steak).

Restaurants in Florence universally add a mandatory "bread and cover" charge (*pane e coperto*) of about 1,500 to 10,000L (85 cents to $5.55) to your bill.

For great take-out food, go to any *tavola calda* (literally "hot table") or *rosticceria* (any *tavola calda* restaurant that also serves spit-roasted chicken), where delicious, preprepared hot meals are sold by weight. Try **Giuliano's** (☎ 055-238-2723) at Via dei Neri 74. For a true Florentine experience, try the boiled tripe sandwich called *lampredotto* at the street stand in front of the American Express office on Piazza de' Cimatori. But don't buy slices of pizza in Florence; you'll get the wrong impression of Italian pizza, which is only good if it comes from Rome or southernmost Italy. For picnic supplies, try any of the *alimentari* (grocery stores) or *forno* (bakeries).

Florence's top restaurants

Acqua al 2

$$ **Just behind the Bargello   TUSCAN/ITALIAN**

Some of the best pasta in Florence is served under the barrel-vaulted ceilings of this popular restaurant. Sample the *assaggio dei primi,* a tasty platter of five flavorful first courses. And if you still have room for a main course, try the poor Tuscan's steak: a perfectly grilled giant portobello mushroom.

Via della Vigna Vecchia 40r. ☎ *055-284-170. Reservations highly recommended. Bus: 14. Main courses: 10,000–25,000L ($5.55–$13.90). AE, MC, V. Open: Dinner daily.*

Cibrèo

$$$$**   (**$ for the *trattoria*)   **North of Santa Croce**   **FLORENTINE**

This is two restaurants in one: a rustically elegant *ristorante* on one side of the kitchen, and a less-expensive *trattoria* on the other (with an abridged selection of the same dishes). This famous haven for food aficionados changes its menu daily, depending on what was freshest that morning at the market next door. The menu does not have any typically Tuscan pastas or grilled meat, but the kitchen's savory creations are still based on traditional Florentine recipes (with an occasional modern touch).

Via A. del Verrocchio 8r (at San Ambrogio Market, off Via de' Macchi). ☎ *055-234-1100. Reservations required for the restaurant, not accepted at the trattoria (come early). Bus: B, 14. Main courses: 45,000L ($25, includes side dish) at restaurant; 16,000L ($8.90, not including 5,000L/$2.80 side dish) at trattoria. AE, DC, MC, V. Open: Lunch and dinner Tues–Sat; closed July 17 through Aug and Dec 24–Jan 1.*

I' Cche' c'è c'è

$$ **Between the Palazzo Vecchio and Santa Croce**   **TUSCAN**

This restaurant's unusual-looking name means "What you see is what you get" in Florentine dialect, and what you get here is quality Tuscan cooking in a simple *trattoria* setting. You can reserve a private table along one of the walls, but I suggest you try sitting at the long, communal table in the middle. Here you can meet locals and travelers who come to fill up on ravioli in a creamy tomato sauce, tagliatelle with mushrooms, and beef rolls stewed in Chianti.

Via Magalotti 11r (just off Via Proconsolo). ☎ *055-216-589. Reservations recommended, but not available for the lunch menu. Bus: 23, 71. Main courses: 15,000–35,000L ($8.35–$19.45); fixed-price menu 20,000L ($11.10); tasting menus 50,000–60,000L ($27.80–$33.35). AE, MC, V. Open: Lunch Wed–Sun, dinner daily.*

Il Latini

$$$ **Near Santa Maria Novella**   **TUSCAN**

This traditional trattoria has managed to keep its food authentic despite becoming a tourist favorite. Join the throng at the door at 7:30 p.m. and wait to be seated at communal tables under wood beams with hanging prosciuttos. The restaurant has a menu, but most people choose the unofficial set meal, where 50,000L ($27.80) buys you a *primo* (soup or pasta), a choice from an overflowing platter of roasted meats for your main course, dessert, and all the house wine you can drink.

Via del Palchetti 6r (off Via d. Vigna Nuova). ☎ *055-210-916. Reservations highly recommended (but still show up early). Bus: C, 6, 11, 36, 37, 68. Main courses: 15,000–25,000L ($8.35–$13.90); fixed-priced meal 50,000L ($27.80). AE, MC, V. Open: Lunch and dinner Tues–Sun; closed 15 days in Aug and Dec 24–Jan 6.*

Le Mossacce

$ Near the Bargello FLORENTINE

The best Italian meals are usually served in simple, small *trattorias* such as this one, where businessmen, farmers, and a few in-the-know tourists line up out the door to take their turn at the hearty Tuscan dishes. Its *ribollita* soup is bested only by the *crespelle*, and its *involtini* are splendid.

Via del Proconsolo 55r (near the Bargello). ☎ *055-294-361. Reservations recommended (but there's always a line, anyway). Bus: 14, 23, 71. Main courses: 9,000–16,000L ($5–$8.90). AE, MC, V. Open: Lunch and dinner Mon– Fri; closed Aug.*

Ristorante Casa di Dante (Da Pennello)

$$ Between the Duomo and Palazzo Vecchio FLORENTINE

This classic Florentine restaurant is descended from a sixteenth-century *osteria* (the term once used for a place with a limited menu of basic fare, most likely simple pastas and wine). One of the keys to Da Pennello's success is its famed antipasto table, a buffet of vegetables, fish, and other delicacies. The rest of the meal here is good, too, with spaghetti in a spicy tomato sauce, grilled sea bass, and the Florentine sponge-cake-and-mousse *zucotto* dessert heading up the list.

Via Dante Alghieri 4r. ☎ *055-294-848. Reservations recommended. Bus: 14. Main courses: 15,000–22,000L ($8.35–$12.20); fixed-price menu 30,000L ($16.65). AE, MC, V. Open: Lunch Tues–Sun, dinner Tues–Sat.*

Runner-up restaurants

I Fratellini

$ A hole-in-the-wall lunch stop from another era, where a glass of wine and a sandwich cost 6,000L ($3.30) and you eat standing on the street. *Via dei Cimatori 38r, just off Via Calzaiuoli.* ☎ *055-239-6096.*

Trattoria Zà-Zà

$$ This Trattoria sits across from the central food market and is patronized by its stall owners, so you know the ingredients are prime. Picture lots of wood benches, Chianti bottles, and thick steaks. *Piazza Mercato Centrale 26r.* ☎ *055-215-411.*

Il Pizzaiolo

$ Florence's only decent pizzeria — probably because the cook is from Naples, where the stuff was invented. Even with a reservation, expect a wait; without one on weekends, forget it: Locals love this place. *Via de' Macci 113r, at the corner of Via Pietrapiana.* ☎ *055-241-171.*

Trattoria Casalinga

$ A bit noisy and service can be surly, but the heaping platters of home cooking are delicious and the prices can't be beat. *Via Michelozzi 9r, between Via Maggio and Piazza Santo Spirito.* ☎ *055-267-9243.*

Trattoria Antellesi

$$ Refined-restaurant style at trattoria prices. It's run by an Italian/American couple, and the menu is a bit more eclectic than at your standard Tuscan joint. *Via Faenza 9r, near the Medici Chapels.* ☎ *055-216-990.*

Exploring Florence

The art and architecture of Florence attracts an overwhelming number of visitors. In summer, you can wait in line for two hours just to buy a ticket to get into the Uffizi Galleries — no joke. I highly recommend that you reserve your ticket ahead of time at ☎ **055-294-883** or on the Web at www.arca.net/uffizi/reservation.htm. This is one thing I always book before I even leave the United States. That number also lets you reserve tickets for the Accademia Gallery (avoiding another interminable line, to see the *David*), as well as the Galleria Palatina in the Pitti Palace and the Bargello (though you don't really need reservations for those last two).

Florence's top sights

The Uffizi Galleries

The Uffizi Galleries are a visual primer on the growth of the Renaissance from the thirteenth to the eighteenth centuries. Although it's not nearly as big as other famous galleries, such as the Louvre or the Vatican, the Uffizi still ranks among the world's best. What it lacks in quantity it easily makes up for in quality, with room after room of recognized masterpieces. You can easily spend all day here, but the super-fast visit will take about three hours.

Your exploration of the Uffizi gets off to a fast start in the first room with a trio of giant *Maestà* paintings tracing the birth of the Renaissance — from the rigid, Byzantine style of Cimabue, through Gothic elements from Sienese great Duccio, to the innovative work by Giotto, who broke painting out of its static mold and gave it life, movement, depth, and emotion. From there, you move through rooms featuring the work of early Sienese masters such as Pietro Lorenzetti and Simone Martini, and then continue on to Florentine and other Tuscan virtuosos such as Fra' Angelico, Masaccio, Piero della Francesca, Paolo Uccello, and Filippo Lippi.

Next you enter a huge room dedicated to Botticelli and focused on his two most famous works, *The Birth of Venus* (the woman rising out of a seashell) and *The Allegory of Spring*. Visitors tend to crowd in front of these for 20 minutes at a time, so you may have to wait to get a good view.

In the meantime, you can enjoy lesser-known works by Boticelli and his contemporary Ghirlandaio, who taught a young Michelangelo how to fresco. After this, you can see works by Signorelli and Perugino; a young Leonardo da Vinci's *Annunciation;* and rooms filled with northern European art from the pre- and early-Renaissance eras (Dürer, Cranach, Hans Holbein the Younger) and Venetian masters such as Correggio, Bellini, and Giorgione.

After you move to the second corridor, Michelangelo's colorful *Holy Family* signals your entry into the High Renaissance. Michelangelo's use of startling colors and his attention to detail in the twisting bodies influenced a generation of artists called mannerists; you'll see them (Rosso Fiorentino, Pontormo, Andrea del Sarto, and Parmigianino) in the next few rooms. These works are mixed in with paintings by some famous artists such as Raphael, Titian, and Caravaggio.

Piazzale degli Uffizi 6 (off Piazza della Signoria). ☎ *055-23-885 or 055-238-8651. Bus: A, B, 23, 71. Open: Summer, Tues–Wed 8:30 a.m.–9:45 p.m., Thurs–Sat 8:30 a.m.–11:15 p.m., Sun 8:30 a.m.–7:15 p.m.; winter, Tues–Sat 8:30 a.m.–9:45 p.m., Sun 8:30 a.m.–7:15 p.m. Ticket window closes 45 minutes before museum. Admission: 12,000L ($6.65), free under 18 and over 60.*

Galleria dell'Accademia (Michelangelo's David)

Many visitors come to Florence with one question on their lips: "Which way to the *David?*" The Accademia contains many magnificent paintings (by Perugino, Botticelli, Pontormo, and others) plus Giambologna's plaster study for the *Rape of the Sabines,* but most people come for one thing only.

In 1501, Michelangelo took an huge piece of marble that a previous sculptor had declared unusable and by 1504 turned it into a Goliath-sized *David,* a masterpiece of the male nude. The sculpture is so realistic — the weight shifted onto one leg, the sling held nonchalantly on the shoulder — that it changed how people thought about sculpting the human body. *David* stood in front of the Palazzo Vecchio for a long time (a replica is there now); inside this gallery room it looks a little oversized, giving it an awkward feel.

The hall leading to the *David* is lined with Michelangelo's *nonfiniti* (unfinished) *Slaves.* Many people find these statues more compelling than the oversized nude in the next room. These *Slaves* are in varying stages of completion and shed light on how Michelangelo approached his craft — fully finishing the abdomen before moving on to rough out limbs and faces. The title of the work is rather fitting because these muscular figures seem to be struggling to emerge from their stony prisons.

At the peak of the summer season, lines start forming early outside the Accademia and can stretch for blocks. If you show up when it first opens and don't have a long wait, you can pop in and admire *David* in about 20 minutes, but it takes at least 45 minutes to wander through the rest of the Accademia's collection. Reserve tickets ahead of time by calling ☎ **055-294-883.**

Via Ricasoli 60. ☎ 055-238-8612. Bus: 1, 6, 7, 10, 11, 17, 20, 25, 31, 32, 33, 67, 68, 70. Open: Tues–Sat 8:30 a.m.–6:50 p.m., Sun 8:30 a.m.–1:50 p.m. Admission: 12,000L ($6.65).

The Duomo (Cathedral), Baptistery, and Giotto's Bell Tower

The Duomo of Florence is decorated in festive white, green, and pink marble, with an extravagant neo-Gothic facade from the eighteenth century, all capped by a huge brick-red dome that extends nobly into the skyline. The cathedral is joined on its bustling square by the Baptistery, Giotto's Bell Tower, and a museum — a group of buildings that together will take you one to three hours to see.

If you're pressed for time and want to see all three buildings in the same visit to the area, go later in the day because the Baptistery is only open in the afternoons. The cathedral closes first, so make that the initial stop. Climbing either Brunelleschi's dome (463 steps) or Giotto's Bell Tower (414 steps) takes about an hour.

Florence's cathedral appears to be inside out — nicely decorated on the outside but rather drab inside. It's best to enjoy it out in front on the little piazza, where visitors gather and musicians and artists display their talents. When you do go inside, there are some interesting early Renaissance frescoes that are colorful but not particularly good. In the crypt, you can see the remains of an earlier church on the same site. Be sure to wander to the back left corner of the cathedral to admire the bronze doors (by Luca della Robbia).

Climb the cathedral's 348-foot-high dome both for its panoramic view and to see Brunelleschi's architectural marvel up close. At the time, experts told him he could never build a dome that big without using scaffolding and supports that would be too costly to build. Brunelleschi proved them wrong by using the secrets of Rome's Pantheon (distributing the weight on embedded stone ribs and building the dome with two shells, which both get thinner nearing the top and center).

To the right of the cathedral is what's known as Giotto's Bell Tower, even though that early Renaissance painter only designed and built the first two levels. Several architects finished it (using their own styles), and the tower became "The Lily of Florence," a 277-foot-high marble pillar with slender windows. If climbing the Duomo's dome didn't tire you out, try clambering up this monument, too — and without the crowds found at the dome. The view's not quite so sweeping, but you get a great close-up of the neighboring dome.

The Baptistery, across from the Duomo, is the oldest building of the group, dating back to between the fourth and seventh centuries. Its bronze doors covered with relief panels are famous; Michelangelo once called them "The Gates of Paradise," and the name stuck. The grandest are the ones facing the Duomo, which were cast by Ghiberti from 1425 to 1453 (though replaced now by replicas). These large panels show the artist's skill in using perspective and composition to tell complicated stories. Inside, the Baptistery is covered with glittering thirteenth-century mosaics, and a cone-shaped ceiling contains a highly detailed *Last Judgment* scene presided over by an enormous Christ.

The Museo dell'Opera Del Duomo (Museum of Cathedral Works) is right behind the cathedral at Piazza del Duomo 9. The museum holds all the statues removed from the outside of the cathedral in order to save them from the elements. The rooms are also filled with early works by Andrea Pisano, Arnolfo di Cambio, and Luca della Robbia, as well as the expressive statues of Donatello, including a wooden *Mary Magdalen* and the leering bald prophet *Habbakuk* (called "Pumpkinhead" by locals). The original panels from Ghiberti's *Gates of Paradise* are gradually being brought out for display as they're cleaned. Michelangelo's *Pietà* group is on the landing between the first and second floors; the figure of Nicodemus in the back is a self-portrait.

Piazza del Duomo/Piazza San Giovanni. ☎ 055-230-2885. Bus: B, 14, 23, 71, 36, 37. Open: Cathedral — Mon–Fri 10:00 a.m.–5:00 p.m.; first Sat of month 10:00 a.m.–3:30 p.m., other Sat 10:00 a.m.–4:45 p.m.; Sun 1:00–5:00 p.m.; free tours every 40 minutes daily, 10:30 a.m.–noon and 3:00 –4:20 p.m. Baptistery — Mon–Sat noon–6:30 p.m., Sun 8:30 a.m.–1:30 p.m. Giotto's Bell Tower — Daily Apr–Oct 8:30 a.m.–6:50 p.m.; Nov–Mar 9:00 a.m.–4:20 p.m. Museo dell'Opera — Mon–Sat 9:00 a.m.–7:00 p.m. Admissions: Cathedral — The church itself is free; Santa Reparata excavations are 3,000L ($1.65); the dome is 10,000L ($5.55), children under 6 free. Baptistery — 5,000L ($2.80), under 6 free. Giotto's Bell Tower — 8,000L ($4.45). Museo dell'Opera — 8,000L ($4.45).

Palazzo Pitti (Pitti Palace)

On the south side of the Arno River, this huge palace, once home to the Medici grand dukes, now houses several museums and an impressive painting gallery. You'd be hard-pressed to visit all six of the museums *and* the Boboli Gardens in one day, but 1½ to 2 hours should be enough for you to run through the main paintings collection, the Galleria Palatina (☎ 055-238-8614; reserve tickets at ☎ 055-294-883). These lavish rooms are appointed to look much the way they did in the 1700s, with works by a mind-boggling list of late-Renaissance and baroque geniuses such as Caravaggio, Rubens, Perugino, Giorgione, Guido Reni, Fra Bartolomeo, Tintoretto, Botticelli, and many more. The selection of works by Raphael, Titian, and Andrea del Sarto is particularly good. Admission is 12,000L ($6.65). From Easter to October, it's open Tuesday to Saturday, 8:30 a.m. to 10:00 p.m.; and Sunday, 8:30 a.m. to 8:00 p.m. In winter, it's open Tuesday to Saturday, 8:30 a.m. to 6:50 p.m.; and Monday, 8:30 a.m. to 1:50 p.m.

If you can only see two parts of the Pitti Palace, make them the Galleria Palatina, described above, and the Boboli Gardens (☎ 055-265-1816), one of the finest Renaissance gardens anywhere. Designed between 1549 and 1656, and located behind the Pitti Palace, the gardens feature statues, fountains, grottoes, a rococo kaffehaus for summer refreshment, and some nice wooded areas to walk in. In 1589, the Medici held a wedding reception in the Boboli Gardens and hired Jacopo Peri and Ottavio Rinuccini to provide musical entertainment. The composers came up with the idea of setting a classical story to music and having actors sing the whole thing. This was the birth of opera. Admission is 4,000L ($2.20) for adults, free under 18 and over 60. The park is open daily from 9:00 a.m. to sunset (it's closed the first and last Monday of each month).

The Italian royal family lived in the Pitti Palace itself during the brief time that Florence was the capital of a newly unified Italy in the 1870s. Although they aren't nearly as nice as those at Versailles or other northern European palaces, the Apartamenti Reali, or Royal Apartments (☎ 055-238-8614), are still a sight to behold with their rich fabrics, frescoes, and oil paintings. From January to May, you can visit the apartments only by guided tour Tuesday and Saturday (and sometimes Thursday) hourly from 9:00 to 11:00 a.m. and 3:00 to 5:00 p.m.

As for other sites in the Pitti Palace, the **Galleria d'Arte Moderna,** or Modern Art Gallery (☎ 055-238-8616), has some good works by the *Macchiaioli* school, the Tuscan version of impressionism. The **Galleria del Costume,** or Costume Gallery (☎ 055-238-8713), has some wonderful dresses that date back to the 1500s. The **Museo degli Argenti,** or Silver Museum (☎ 055-238-8710), is a decorative arts collection that shows off the grand duke's consistently bad taste, but it does have kitsch value. The Galleria d'Arte Moderna and Museo degli Argenti both charge 4,000L ($2.20) admission and are open daily 9:00 a.m. to 2:00 p.m. (closed the first, third, and fifth Mondays and the second and fourth Sundays of each month). The Galleria del Costume costs 8,000L ($4.45) and is open Tuesday to Sunday 9:00 a.m. to 2:00 p.m.

Piazza Pitti (cross the Ponte Vecchio and follow Via Guicciardini). See review in this section for individual phone numbers. Bus: B, C. Open: See review in this section. Admission: See review in this section. In recent years, the Pitti has offered a 20,000L ($11.10) cumulative ticket (15,000L/$8.35 after 4:00 p.m.) that gets you into the Galleria Palatina, Boboli Gardens, Galleria d'Arte Moderna, and Museo degli Argenti.

Bargello (Sculpture Gallery)

What the Uffizi is to Renaissance painting, the Bargello is to sculpture from the same era. You could spend 45 minutes here or, if you get really engrossed, two hours. The collection includes early works by Michelangelo, including a tipsy *Bacchus,* the *Madonna of the Stairs,* and a *Bust of Brutus* that may be a semi-self-portrait. Be sure to see the works by Donatello, the first great sculptor of the Renaissance. A huge second-floor room contains some of his masterpieces, including a mischievous bronze *Cupid* and two versions of a *David* — an early marble work and a bronze that depicts the Biblical hero as a young boy.

Via del Proconsolo 4. ☎ 055-238-8606. Bus: 14. Open: Tues–Sat 8:30 a.m.–1:50 p.m. Also open second and fourth Sun and first, third, and fifth Mon of every month. Admission: 8,000L ($4.45).

Santa Croce

This large Franciscan church on the city's western edge is the Westminster Abbey of the Renaissance. It houses the tombs of several household names: Michelangelo, composer Rossini (*Barber of Seville* and the *William Tell Overture,* more familiarly known as the *Lone Ranger* theme), political thinker/writer Machiavelli, and astronomer and physicist Galileo.

The church also has a monument to poetic giant Dante Alighieri, who was exiled from his beloved Florence on trumped-up charges during a period of political turmoil and whose bones rest in the city of Ravenna, where he died just after completing his masterpiece, the *Divine Comedy* (of which the famed *Inferno* is but one-third).

Inside you can also see two chapels covered by the frescoes of Giotto, an ex-shepherd who became the forefather of the Renaissance in the early fourteenth century. Near the chapels, a corridor leads through the gift shop to the famed leather school (pricey, but very high quality).

Piazza Santa Croce. ☎ *055-244-619. Bus: 23, 71, B, 13. Open: Church — Easter to early Oct, Mon–Sat 8:00 a.m.–6:30 p.m., Sun 3:00–6:00 p.m.; winter, Mon–Sat 8:00 a.m.–12:30 p.m. and 3:00–6:30 p.m., Sun 3:00–6:00 p.m. Museum — Mar–Sept, Thurs–Tues 10:00 a.m.–12:30 p.m. and 2:30–6:30 p.m.; Oct–Feb, Thurs–Tues 10:00 a.m.–12:30 p.m. and 3:00–5:00 p.m. Admission: Church — Free. Museum — 5,000L ($2.80), 2,000L ($1.10) under 10.*

More cool things to see and do in Florence

From shopping at outdoor markets and swanky boutiques to exploring thirteenth-century streets and Roman ruins, Florence has much to occupy the visitor.

✔ **Strike a Bargain at the Outdoor Leather Market.** How are your negotiation skills? Around San Lorenzo church, the streets are filled with stalls peddling imitation Gucci merchandise, souvenir T-shirts, jewelry, wallets, and lots of leather. Many stalls are just extensions of the stores behind them. Every owner seems to speak fluent English, so be ready for the hard sell.

If you are tough and patient, you should be able to get the goods at a reasonable price. But if you can't, at least you get to experience a carnival of colors and noise, and if you are alert for pickpockets, it can be a welcome, down-to-earth break from all that art. The stalls stay open from 8:00 a.m. to 8:00 p.m. (later if business is booming) daily from March to October, and Tuesday to Saturday from November to February.

✔ **Visit Dante's Stomping Grounds.** The labyrinth of narrow, cobbled streets between the Duomo and Piazza della Signoria still looks a lot like it did in the thirteenth century when statesman and poet Dante Alghieri lived in the neighborhood. Dante's house, located appropriately on Via Dante Alghieri, is typical of the era (actually, nobody is sure which building Dante lived in, so a representative one was chosen). Inside is a museum (☎ 055-219-416) that traces the poet's life. Around the corner, at the Badia church, Dante first laid eyes on Beatrice, the woman he loved from afar and the inspiration for his best poems. The museum is open Monday and Wednesday to Saturday from 10:00 a.m. to 6:00 p.m. (4:00 p.m. in winter) and Sunday from 10:00 a.m. to 2:00 p.m. Admission is 5,000L ($2.80), free under age 10.

✔ **Shop on Via de' Tornabuoni.** Florence shares the top spot on the hill of Italian high fashion with Milan. Pucci, Gucci, Beltrami, and Ferragamo all established themselves in Florence, and their flagship stores make for some interesting browsing even if you didn't bring your gold card. Florence has several shopping districts, but the best concentration lies along Via de' Tournabuoni, Florence's Fifth Avenue, and its side streets. On Via de' Tournabuoni itself you can stroll past Ferragamo (16r), Beltrami (48r), and Gucci (73r). Buccellati (71r) specializes in jewelry and silver.

Along nearby Via della Vigna Nuova, you'll find styles from Italy's fashion guru Armani (51r) and Tuscan Enrico Coveri (25r to 29r), as well as stylish women's clothes at Alex (19r). Italy also has more than its share of industrial design gurus. Stop by Controluce (89r) to see some beautifully designed light fixtures.

✔ **Catch the View from Piazzale Michelangiolo.** Buses number 12 and 13 snake up the hills of the artisan's quarter called Oltrarno to Piazzale Michelangiolo, a plateau packed with visitors snapping photos of the Florentine panorama spread before them. Just up the road is a Romanesque church called San Miniato that contains some good medieval art and has a lovely, geometrically precise facade. (Incidentally, this facade made up the original view out the hotel window in E. M. Forster's *A Room with a View.*)

✔ **Spend an Afternoon in Fiesole.** You can experience a bit of Tuscan village life with a ride on Florence's number 7 bus. Older than Florence and overlooking it from above, the hilltop Etruscan village of Fiesole has a few sights, cafes on the main square, and best of all, a cool mountain breeze on even the hottest summer days.

A tourism office (☎ 055-598-720), Piazza Mino 37, is on your right as you step off the bus. Stop by the eleventh-century cathedral, which contains some delicate Mino da Fiesole carvings, and then go up (*way* up) Via San Francesco to the panoramic gardens overlooking a picture-perfect view of Florence down in the valley.

Perhaps the most popular sight in Feisole is the ruins of the Roman theater and baths (☎ 055-59-477), an excavation that has a temple from the fourth century b.c., a theater from the first century b.c. (which now hosts summertime concerts under the stars), and a few arches still standing from some a.d. first century baths.

And on Your Left, the Uffizi: Seeing Florence by Guided Tour

The orientation bus tours offered by **American Express** (☎ 055-50-981) and **SitaSightseeing** (☎ 055-214-721) are fairly similar. Both have morning tours of the top sights and afternoon tours of the secondary sights. Each tour costs 50,000L ($27.80), with museum admissions included. Call for departure times and other specifics.

Suggested One-, Two-, and Three-Day Itineraries

If you don't like tour buses and would prefer to discover Florence and the surrounding region on your own, this section provides some suggested plans of attack.

If you have one day

If you want to see Florence in a day, you'll have no time to pace yourself. It's art-on-the-run time. By 9:00 a.m. (8:30 a.m. if possible), be at the Accademia to see *David*. Spend no more than 30 minutes here so you can be admiring Ghiberti's *Gates of Paradise* in front of the Duomo by 10:00 a.m. Seeing the inside of the Duomo itself takes only 15 minutes, but you might want to give yourself another hour to make it up to the top of Brunelleschi's dome.

After lunch, make your way to Santa Croce to pay your respects to the earthly remains of Michelangelo and Galileo and to see Giotto's frescoes. You might also want to pop into the famous leather school. Exit the piazza on the north end. Take a right on Via Verdi and an immediate left onto Via dei Lavatoi, which will spill out onto Via Isola delle Stinche right above the Vivoli ice cream parlor, with the best gelato in the city. Enjoy your midafternoon snack.

Next, head west to get in line at the Uffizi. Peruse some of the greatest art Italy has to offer until they kick you out just before 7:00 p.m. In the twilight, wander amid the statues of Piazza della Signoria and get an eyeful of the Palazzo Vecchio. Stroll across the Ponte Vecchio before dinner and wander back through the medieval heart of Florence between Piazza della Signoria and the Duomo after a dinner with plenty of good wine.

If you have two days

On Day One, be in line at the Accademia when it opens, spend about 45 minutes there, then move on to San Marco and its Fra' Angelico frescoes, which will gobble up an hour or so. Stop in the Palazzo Medici-Riccardi to see the frescoed Magi Chapel, then visit San Lorenzo and its Medici Tombs by Michelangelo. Now it's time for some lunch, perhaps including some haggling at the outdoor leather stalls in this district. After lunch, head to the Duomo and the Baptistry. Don't spend more than 1½ hours here, including climbing the dome for its spectacular view. Make your way to the Uffizi and spend the rest of the afternoon there until it closes.

On Day Two, start off at Santa Maria Novella and its museum. Next, head over to the Bargello sculpture museum and admire all its Donatello and Michelangelo statues. Have a lunch on the go so you don't miss anything, and spend the *riposo* hours (1:00 to 4:00 p.m.) visiting the tombs of famous Florentines, Giotto frescoes, and leather school in Santa Croce. Next, head across the Ponte Vecchio into the Oltrarno district and make your way to Santa Maria del Carmine to see Masaccio's groundbreaking frescoes in the Brancacci Chapel. Stop by Santo Spirito when it opens at 4:00 p.m., but then hightail it over to the Pitti Palace and get into the painting gallery.

If you have three days

Spend Days One and Two as indicated previously. On the morning of Day Three, take the bus up to Fiesole to enjoy its cool pleasures and Roman ruins. Get back to Florence for lunch, and afterward go back to Palazzo Pitti, this time to stroll amid the Boboli Gardens. Later in the afternoon, take in a few of the churches you've missed — Santa Trínita, Ognissanti, the Badia — or just wander the medieval streets. Shoppers might want to revisit the leather market or hit the fashion strip of Via de' Tornabuoni. Art lovers can head back to the Uffizi.

Exploring Beyond Florence

Several worthwhile sites make easy day trips from Florence. My favorites are Pisa, Siena, and San Gimignano. Each one has its own unique allure.

Pisa: The Leaning Tower and more

When Pisa was one of the maritime commerce centers of the world from the eleventh to the thirteenth centuries, it used its wealth to develop a new religious center for the city. This Campo dei Miracoli, or "Field of Miracles," is a series of simple but beautiful marble buildings with an Eastern-influenced design that became known as Pisan Romanesque. The listing *campanile,* or bell tower, attracts hordes of visitors to Pisa each year to pose for snapshots of them holding up the Leaning Tower.

You can see Pisa's main sights comfortably in two to three hours, which makes it a good half-day trip from Florence (consider picnicking on the grass in front of the Leaning Tower before heading back).

Getting there

Trains leave Florence for Pisa every half-hour; the trip takes 60 to 75 minutes. From the Pisa train station, bus number 1 (or a 15-minute walk) will take you to the Piazza del Duomo (also known as Campo dei Miracoli).

A tiny tourism office sits to the left of the train station exit (☎ **050-42-291**), but the main **tourism office** is just outside the Porta Santa Maria gate on the west end of the Campo dei Miracoli at Via C. Cammeo 2 (☎ **050-560-464** or 050-830-253).

Tuscany

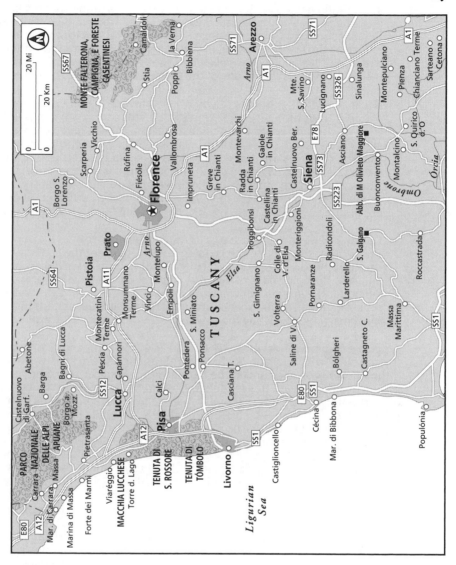

Seeing the sights

The **Campo dei Miracoli** is one of the most picturesque squares in Italy. It is a huge, grassy area studded with gleaming white-and-gray-striped Romanesque and Gothic buildings. The cathedral bell tower, better known as the **Leaning Tower,** is attractive enough to draw attention even if it didn't tilt so curiously. This long cylinder of white marble threaded with colonnade arches is one of the prettiest towers you'll ever see.

Because all that marble is too heavy for the sandy soil to support, the tower started tilting right away in the twelfth century. When builders tried to correct the tilt during construction, they inadvertently gave it a slight banana-like curve. Unfortunately, engineers determined in 1990 that the tower's slant made it too dangerous to hold visitors. Officials closed the tower, wrapped steel bands around it to keep the masonry from falling apart, stacked ugly lead weights on one side, and dug out around it to try to correct the lean by a few feet (it's 15 feet off-center). Sometime after 2001, it should be safe for you to climb again.

Galileo Galilei earned his status as one of the fathers of modern physics in Pisa and, specifically, the Leaning Tower. He spent the sixteenth century watching pendulums, asserting that the Earth revolved around the sun, and dropping balls of differing weights off the tower to prove they would hit the ground at the same time. Many people thought he was nuts, and the Church excommunicated (and nearly executed) him for the blasphemy of suggesting that the universe did not revolve around earth.

Pisa's **Duomo (Cathedral)** (☎ 050-560-547) is a huge Romanesque structure with a facade of stacked colonnades. Make sure you see the medieval bronze doors on the back side of the right transept, facing the Leaning Tower; it was the only set that survived a 1595 fire. The cathedral's interior was rebuilt after the fire, but some items from the earlier era remain — including Cimabue's 1302 mosaic *Christ Pancrator* and one of Giovanni Pisano's greatest carved pulpits (1302 to 1311), a masterpiece of Gothic sculpture. From April to September, the cathedral is open daily from 8:00 a.m. to 8:00 p.m.; in March and October, daily from 9:00 a.m. to 6:00 p.m.; and from November to February, daily from 7:45 a.m. to 1:00 p.m. and 3:00 to 5:00 p.m. (6:00 p.m. Sunday).

If you liked Pisano's pulpit, check out the one in the **Baptistery** sculpted by his dad, Nicola Pisano, from 1255 to 1260. This huge, drum-like building has a Romanesque base, but Nicola and Giovanni Pisano finished it off with a Gothic skullcap of a roof, which contains several small spires and statues. Ask the Baptistery's guard to sing a few notes at the center of the structure so you can hear the outstanding acoustics (when a choir sings, you can hear it for miles).

The north end of the square is bordered by a long wall of Gothic marble that quietly marks the **Camposanto,** a kind of cloister/mausoleum whose halls contain ancient stone coffins and Renaissance tombs. Allied fire-bombs in World War II destroyed most of the dazzling medieval frescoes that covered the walls, but the few that were salvaged — including the macabre *Triumph of Death* — are on display in a side room.

Across the square from the Camposanto, obscured by souvenir stands, is the **Museo delle Sinopie,** which contains the *sinopie*, or preparatory drawings, of the ill-fated frescoes.

Many statues and other works taken off the outside of the Duomo for preservation are in the **Museo dell'Opera del Duomo** (☎ 050-561-820), behind the Leaning Tower. Among them is an eleventh-century Islamic bronze griffin (a beast with an eagle's head and wings and a lion's body). Etchings of the destroyed Camposanto frescoes are on the second floor.

Admission charges for the group of monuments and museums on Campo dei Miracoli are tied together and a bit confusing. The Duomo (cathedral) alone costs 3,000L ($1.65) — but only from March to November, and only after 10:00 a.m., otherwise it's free. The Duomo plus any one other monument is 10,000L ($5.55), as is a ticket good for any two monuments (so if you get the second option plus a separate Duomo ticket, it'll cost just 13,000L/$7.20 for three). A 15,000L ($8.35) ticket gets you into the Baptistry, Camposanto, Museo dell'Opera del Duomo, and Museo delle Sinopie, while an 18,000L ($10) version throws in the Duomo as well. Open hours for all (except the cathedral) are the same: April to September, daily from 8:00 a.m. to 7:20 p.m.; March and October, daily from 9:00 a.m. to 5:20 p.m.; November to February, daily from 9:00 a.m. to 4:20 p.m.

Where to stay and dine

For terrific Pisan cuisine in a traditional *trattoria* setting, head just north of the city walls to **Da Bruno** (☎ 050-560-818), Via Luigi Bianchi. The **Villa Kinzica** (☎ 050-560-419, fax: 050-551-204), Piazza Arcivescovado 2, is not very attractive, but it's just a few steps from the Campo dei Miracoli and has doubles for 150,000L ($83.35). Ask for a room with a view of the Leaning Tower.

Siena, a departure from the Renaissance

Siena is a city of the Gothic Middle Ages rather than the Renaissance. In this overgrown medieval hill town, you'll find brick-and-marble palaces and cafes, not museums and boutiques. It has its own proud artistic tradition, which relies on emotion, elegance of line, and rich color — a shift from Florence's precise, formula-driven, exacting classical painting.

Siena's heavily decorated cathedral is a huge artistic jewel box. But Siena is also a good place to sit back on the sloped Il Campo square, simply enjoying a bottle of Chianti and a good book or taking a nap under the Tuscan sun.

Many people spend only half a day in Siena, but I recommend spending at least one night so you have a good day and a half to absorb its medieval atmosphere and see its scattered sights.

Siena has a plethora of reduced-price ticket combos you can pick up at any of the participating museums or sights. They range from an 8,500L ($4.70) ticket valid for three days that includes the Libreria Piccolomini (inside the Duomo), Museo dell'Opera Metropolitana, and the Baptistery, to the 32,000L ($17.80) one that gets you into just about every major sight in town.

Getting there

Eighteen trains make the 90- to 135-minute trip from Florence daily, but Siena's train station is two miles from town (take bus C to Piazza Gramsci at the north end of town, or a taxi). On a day trip, you'll save time and hassle by taking advantage of these bus companies' offerings: TRA-IN offers an express bus (19 daily; 75-minute trip; ☎ 0577-204-245) and SITA offers a slower bus (18 daily, 1½ to 2 hours; ☎ 055-483-651) directly from Florence to Piazza San Domenico in Siena, a five-minute stroll from the main square.

American Express (☎ 055-50-981) and **SitaSightseeing** (☎ 055-214-721) both run all-day excursions from Florence that include both Siena and San Gimignano, described in the next excursion (73,000L/$40.55).

A **tourism office** (☎ 0577-280-551) is at Piazza del Campo 56.

Seeing the sights

At the center of the city is **Il Campo,** a beautiful, fan-shaped brick area that slopes down to the **Palazzo Pubblico** (1297 to 1310). You can climb the 503 steps of its bell tower, the **Torre di Mangia,** for 7,000L ($3.90) to get an unforgettable view over the city's burnt sienna rooftops out to the green countryside beyond.

Inside the *palazzo* is the **Museo Civico** (☎ 0577-292-226), the best art museum in town. Several paintings done just for this town hall are the museum's most famous. Simone Martini's 1315 *Maestà* — a Mary in majesty surrounded by her court of saints under a canopy — was the artist's first and best work. Across the room is one of his later frescoes, *Guidoriccio da Foligno,* which depicts a gracious knight on horseback with a fabulously checkered cloak.

In the next room is the greatest secular fresco to survive from medieval Europe, the *Allegory of Good and Bad Government and Its Effect on the Town and Countryside.* The length of Ambrogio Lorenzetti's 1338 masterpiece rivals that of its name, wrapping around three walls and depicting the medieval ideal of civic life. On one wall, a badly damaged section shows bad government ruining the town, sending the citizens into hiding, burning the fields, crumbling the buildings, and populating the streets with thieves and armed patrols. On the good-government side, teachers help students, tradesmen sell their goods, women dance in the streets, nobles ride on horseback and go out to hunt, and farmers tend their fields or bring livestock to market.

Admission to the Museo Civico is 8,000L ($4.45) for adults, 4,000L ($2.20) for students and people over 65. The museum's hours are: November to February, Monday to Saturday from 10:00 a.m. to 4:00 p.m., Sunday from 9:30 a.m. to 1:30 p.m.; March to June and September to October, Monday to Saturday from 10:00 a.m. to 6:00 p.m., Sunday from 9:30 a.m. to 1:30 p.m.; July and August, Monday to Saturday from 10:00 a.m. to11:00 p.m., Sunday from 9:30 a.m. to 1:30 p.m. The ticket window closes 45 minutes before the museum does.

Siena's other grand sight, the **Duomo (Cathedral),** is a huge zebra-striped Gothic structure with a facade by Giovanni Pisano and an interior whose floor is a combination of inlaid, carved, and mosaic marble panels (1372 to 1547). At the right transept is the Chigi Chapel, designed by the baroque master Bernini. Nicola Pisano's best pulpit is at the start of the left transept; the intricately carved Gothic panels (which his son, Giovanni, helped create) depict the life of Christ in great detail. Off the left aisle is the entrance to the Libreria Piccolomini, which Umbrian master Pinturicchio filled with frescoed scenes from the life of Pope Pius II. Just outside this room is a large marble altar that holds statuettes of Sts. Peter, Paul, and Gregory carved by a 26-year-old Michelangelo. Admission to the cathedral is free, but the Libreria Piccolomini costs 2,000L ($1.10). From March 16 through October, the cathedral is open daily from 9:00 a.m. to 7:30 p.m.; from November to March 15, it's open daily from 7:30 a.m. to 1:00 p.m. and 2:30 to 5:00 p.m.

If you walk down the steep stairs around the Duomo's right side and turn around at the bottom, you'll see the **Baptistery** — which was built under the cathedral. Inside is a font with bronze panels by some of the early Renaissance's greatest sculptors: Donatello, Ghiberti, and Siena's Jacopo della Quercia. The walls and ceiling are covered with creative frescoes from the fifteenth century (look for the alligator). The Baptistery's hours are similar to the Duomo's, and admission is 3,000L ($1.65).

About 700 years ago, Siena planned an ambitious expansion of its cathedral that would have turned the present Duomo into just a portion of the grand new structure. Builders finished one thick nave wall and started on the new facade wall before the Black Death hit in 1348, killing three-fourths of the town's population. The interior of these walls (enter across from the back right corner of the Duomo's exterior) is now filled with the **Museo dell'Opera Metropolitana** (☎ **0577-283-048**). This museum was set up to hold the sculptures removed from the Duomo for preservation.

Upstairs is Siena's most admired work of art, Duccio's *Maestà*. The style and use of color in this double-sided altarpiece almost single-handedly spawned the Sienese school of painting. Ever since the day in 1311 when it was unveiled and paraded through the streets, critics have regarded it as one of Europe's finest medieval masterpieces.

Later in the museum, you can climb several worn staircases up onto the wall of the unfinished nave for great views across the city. Admission to the museum is 6,000L ($3.35). Its hours are: November though March 15, daily from 9:00 a.m. to 1:30 p.m.; March 16 through

September, daily from 9:00 a.m. to 7:30 p.m.; during October, daily from 9:00 a.m. to 6:00 p.m.

If you're eager for a respite from history and art, visit the **Enoteca Italiana Permanente** (☎ **0577-288-497**), Italy's official wine-tasting bar (774 labels in stock). It fills the echoing brick halls and cellars of the sixteenth century **Fortezza Medicea** fortress in Siena's northwest corner. Glasses range from 2,500 to 5,000L ($1.40 to $2.80), and it's open from noon to 8:00 p.m. Monday and from noon to 1:00 a.m. Tuesday to Saturday.

Where to stay and dine

Good, solid Sienese food is available at **Antica Trattoria Papei** (☎ **0577-280-894**), Piazza del Mercato 6, on a piazza behind the Palazzo Pubblico. For economical sleeping accommodations, try **Cannon d'Oro** (☎ **0577-44-321,** fax: 0577-280-868), Via Montanini 28 (a northerly extension of Via Banchi di Spora). It's only a few minutes from the Campo on the main street in town. Rooms are nowhere near fancy, but they're big and cost only 100,000L to 145,000L ($55.55 to $80.55) per double.

The towers of San Gimignano

Perhaps the most famous of Tuscany's hill towns, San Gimignano bristles with 14 medieval towers that are remnants of the days when tiny city-states such as this were full of feuding families that sometimes went to war right in the middle of town. Although no other city in Italy has saved so many of its towers, what you see today is only a fraction of what used to be there; San Gimignano sported at least 70 towers in the thirteenth and fourteenth centuries. Though this little town is often packed with day-trippers, you won't find any other spot with such a profound Middle Age flavor.

You can see San Gimignano in two to three hours or so, but smart travelers know that all the day-trippers head for their tour buses at dusk, leaving wonderful medieval towns like this virtually untouched. Those who spend the night can absorb the ancient village atmosphere and get to know the locals.

Getting there

The only way to get to San Gimignano is by bus, and you must almost always transfer in the village of Poggibonsi. From Florence, SITA (Via Santa Caterina 17, just west of the train station) sends 26 buses daily on the 50- to 90-minute trip to Poggibonsi, 13 of which meet the connection to San Gimignano with no time to spare. From Siena, Train (Piazza San Domenico) runs about 33 daily buses to Poggibonsi in 35 to 45 minutes. From Poggibonsi, 19 buses make the 20-minute trek to San Gimignano Monday through Saturday, but only two buses run on Sunday (at 7:20 a.m. and 12:55 p.m.).

The **tourism office** (☎ **0577-940-008;** Internet: www.sangimignano. com) is at Piazza del Duomo 1.

Seeing the sights

The small town center consists of two interlocked, irregularly shaped squares, with a thirteenth-century well in the center of one and the **Collegiata** (main church) taking up one end of the other. If you can't resist climbing up one of the looming towers, go to the **Museo Civico/Torre Grossa.** After you admire paintings in the gallery by artists such as Pinturicchio, Gozzoli, and Lippo Memmi (and secular fourteenth century frescoes in an anteroom that show the racier side of medieval courtship), you can climb the tallest remaining tower in town (178 feet). It provides a 360-degree view of the town and the rolling green countryside just outside its walls. From March through October, the place is open daily from 9:30 a.m. to 7:30 p.m.; from November through February, it's open Tuesday to Sunday from 9:30 a.m. to 1:30 p.m. and 2:30 to 5:00 p.m.

Admission to the Museo Civico museum only is 7,000L ($3.90) for adults and 5,000L ($2.80) for children under 18 and students. Admission to the tower only is 8,000L ($4.45) for adults and 6,000L ($3.35) for children under 18 and students. A cumulative ticket (18,000L/$10, 14,000L/$7.80 ages 6 to18) covers admission to the Torre Grossa, the Collegiata, and all the museums in town except the privately run Torture Museum.

The **Collegiata** (☎ **0577-940-316**) has no bishop's seat and therefore technically is no longer a *duomo* (cathedral), but it sure is decorated to look like one. The interior walls are completely covered with a colorful collage of fourteenth- and fifteenth-century frescoes. The ones down the left wall tell Old Testament stories; the right wall features the New Testament. A *St. Sebastian* thick with arrows is against the entrance wall, and near the entrance — high on the interior nave wall — spreads a gruesomely colorful *Last Judgment* scene. Off the right aisle is the tiny **Chapel of St. Fina,** which Ghirlandaio frescoed with two scenes from the young saint's brief life.

Admission to the church is 6,000L ($3.35) for adults, 3,000L ($1.65) for ages 6 to 18. From April to October, the church is open Monday to Friday from 9:30 a.m. to 7:30 p.m., Saturday from 9:30 a.m. to 5:00 p.m., and Sunday from 1:00 to 5:00 p.m.; from November to March, it is open Monday to Saturday from 9:30 a.m. to 12:30 p.m. and 3:00 to 5:00 p.m., and Sunday from 1:00 to 5:00 p.m. The church closes January 27 to February 28.

Where to stay and dine

La Mangiatoia (☎ **0577-941-528**), Via Mainardi 5, has an intimate atmosphere and a hearty Tuscan menu, and its more imaginative dishes are the best. **La Cisterna** (☎ **0577-940-328,** fax: 0577-942-080), Piazza della Cisterna 23-24, is located in the remains of two centrally located towers, with 160,000L to 200,000L ($88.90 to $111.10) doubles and one of the best restaurants in town.

Chapter 22

Venice and Environs

● ●

In This Chapter

▶ Getting to Venice

▶ Finding what you need while you're in Venice

▶ Exploring Venice by neighborhood or by passion

▶ Discovering Venice's best places to sleep and eat

▶ Planning trips out of town

● ●

*V*enice is not just an amazing city — it's also a feat of engineering and determination. Built on water and marshland, Venice's famous canals serve as its main streets, traveled by a variety of boats, including the famous *gondolas.*

Venice's canals and boats hint at the city's seafaring past. During the fifth century, barbarians overran Italy's peninsula, prompting some in the region to flee to where no sane barbarian could attack: the middle of the water. Although the Venetian lagoon was populated with fishing communities, Venice rapidly built up itself as a commercial seafaring powerhouse. Through the power and volume of its shipping and trading, Venice became the Queen of the Adriatic by the sixteenth century, controlling most of the Mediterranean region. Centuries of political stability and wealth allowed Venice to create a rich urban and cultural landscape (including hundreds of churches such as the Basilica de San Marco) and to nurture such great late-Renaissance artists as Titian and Tintoretto.

Modern-day Venice experiences invasions of another sort — every year, up to 1.5 million tourists join the city's 70,000 residents, making the town called *La Serenissima* (the Most Serene) anything but calm. During peak times (June, July, and September), hotels are booked solid, and the crowds can be overwhelming. Venice gets more attention than it wants or can handle; the city government is debating the passage of quota laws to curb the number of tourists. Someday soon, Venice may become the first European city that you'll need a ticket to enter.

Venice can frustrate or enchant. Many people leave feeling like they've been hurried though two days of tourist traps in a canal-side Disneyland. But Venice can also be wonderful — and this chapter shows you how to avoid the crowds and find ways to cut loose from a strict sightseeing agenda. So read on to experience the real Venice.

Making Your Way to and around Venice

Water surrounds Venice, threading its way through every neighborhood — so it's hard to arrive in town without hopping on a boat of some sort. While you're there, your feet are your best means of transportation.

Getting to Venice by air

Flights land at the **Aeroporto Marco Polo**, 8 km (4½ miles) north of the city on the mainland (☎ 041-260-9260 for flight info, 041-260-6111 for the switchboard; Internet: www.veniceairport.it). There are two bus alternatives: The special **ATVO airport shuttle bus** (☎ 041-520-5530) connects with Piazzale Roma not far from Venice's Santa Lucia train station — the closest point to Venice's attractions accessible by land. Buses leave for/from the airport about every hour, cost 5,000L ($2.70), and make the trip in about 20 minutes. The slightly less-expensive, twice-hourly local **public ACTV** bus no. 5 (☎ 041-528-7886) costs 1,500L (80 cents) and takes 30 to 45 minutes. Buy tickets for either at the newsstand just inside the terminal from the signposted bus stop. With either bus, you'll have to walk to/from the final stop at Piazzale Roma to the nearby *vaporetto* stop for the final connection to your hotel. You'll rarely see porters around who help with luggage, so remember to pack light.

A land taxi from the airport to the Piazzale Roma to pick up your *vaporetto* will run about 50,000L ($27).

Getting to Venice by boat

The most fashionable and traditional way to arrive in Piazza San Marco is by sea. For 17,000L ($9), the **Cooperative San Marco/Alilaguna** (☎ 041-523-5775) operates a large *motoscafo* (shuttle boat) service from the airport with two stops at Murano and the Lido before arriving (after about one hour's ride) in Piazza San Marco. Call for the daily schedule of a dozen or so trips from about 6:00 a.m. to midnight, which changes with the season and is coordinated with the principal arrivals/departures of the major airlines (most hotels have the schedule). If your hotel isn't in the Piazza San Marco area, you'll have to make a connection at the *vaporetto* launches (your hotel can help you with the specifics if you've booked before leaving home).

A private **water taxi** (20 to 30 minutes to/from the airport) is convenient but costly — a legal minimum of 87,000L ($47) but usually more around 140,000L ($76) for two passengers with bags. However, it's worth considering if you're pressed for time, have an early flight, have a lot of luggage (a Venice no-no), or can split the cost with a friend or two. A water taxi may be able to drop you off at the front (or side) door of your hotel or as close as it can maneuver given your hotel's location (check with the hotel before arriving). Your taxi captain should be able to tell you before boarding just how close he can get you.

Getting to Venice by rail

Stazione Santa Lucia is the train station in Venice itself. However, don't worry if your ticket is to "Venezia-Mestre" — Mestre is merely a land-lubbing industrial suburb that's one stop short of Venice. Shuttle trains leave Mestre every few minutes for the ten-minute, five-mile ride across the lagoon into Venice proper.

Getting around after you're in Venice

Venice is a walking city. There really isn't any other way to get around. The only time you won't be walking is when you take the *vaporetto* (water bus) between the train station and Piazza San Marco, go on long hauls to outlying islands, or shell out big bucks for a private *taxi acquei* (water taxi).

By vaporetto (water ferry)

The *vaporetto* is Venice's public ferry service that works like the city's bus network. The maps that the tourist office hands out can help you find a route plan. The vaporetto most visitors use is line 82, which chugs regularly from the train station down the Grand Canal, stopping five times (including at the Rialto Bridge and the Accademia) en route to the San Marco stop, which is just off Piazzetta San Marco in the Giardinetti Reali. Line 1 is a commuter line that follows a similar route but takes longer and makes more stops. In summer, lines 3 and 4 also run from the station to S. Zaccaraia, which is just past the Doge's Palace off the other side of Piazzetta San Marco. Line 52 makes the same trip the long way around the Dorsoduro (bypassing the Grand Canal).

A one-way vaporetto *biglietto* (ticket) is a steep 6,000L ($3.25), or 5,000L ($2.70) per person for groups of three or more. A round-trip ticket is 10,000L ($5), while the 24-hour ticket at 18,000L ($10) is a good buy if you're going to make more than three trips in a day. Most lines run every 10 to 15 minutes, 7:00 a.m. to midnight, and then hourly until morning. Most vaporetto docks (the only place you can buy tickets) have timetables posted. Note that not all stations sell tickets after dark; if you haven't bought a pass or extra tickets beforehand, you'll have to settle up with the conductor on board (you'll have to find him — he won't come looking for you) for an extra 1,000L (60 cents) per ticket. If you decide to try for a free ride, you risk a 40,000L ($24) fine, no excuses accepted.

72-hour tickets (35,000L/$19) and 7-day tickets (60,000L/$32) are also available. And there are two special 15,000L ($8) passes: One allows you unlimited travel on the Canal Grande for 12 hours, and the "Laguna Nord" lets you explore the outlying islands for 12 hours. (See "Suggested One-, Two-, and Three-Day Itineraries" in this chapter for more information.)

By traghetto (ferry skiff)

Just three bridges span the Grand Canal. To fill in the gaps, *traghetti* skiffs (oversized gondolas rowed by two standing gondolieri) cross the Grand Canal at eight intermediate points. You can find stations at the end of any street named Calle del Traghetto on your map and indicated by a yellow sign with the black gondola symbol. The fare is 1,000L (55 cents), which you hand to the gondolier when boarding.

By taxi

Taxi acquei (water taxis) charge high prices and aren't for visitors watching their lire. For journeys up to seven minutes (which are highly unlikely), the rate is 27,000L ($15). Add 500L (30 cents) for each 15 seconds thereafter. Each bag over 50cm (19 inches) long costs 2,200L ($1.20), plus there's an additional 8,500L ($4.60) charge for service 10:00 p.m. to 7:00 a.m. and a 9,000L ($4.90) surcharge on Sunday and holidays (these last two can't be applied simultaneously). If the taxi acquei comes to get you, tack on another 8,000L ($4.35). The preceding rates cover up to four passengers; if any more squeeze in, you pay another 3,100L ($1.70) per extra passenger.

Six water-taxi stations serve key points in the city: the **Ferrovia** (☎ 041-716-286), **Piazzale Roma** (☎ 041-716-922), the **Rialto Bridge** (☎ 041-523-0575), **Piazza San Marco** (☎ 041-522-9750), the **Lido** (☎ 041-526-0059), and **Marco Polo Airport** (☎ 041-541-5084). **Radio Taxi** (☎ 041-522-2303 or 041-723-112) can pick you up from any place in the city.

By gondola

What's sleek, black, slightly crooked, and looks like a cross between a coffin and a canoe? It's the gondola, of course, the most popular mode of transportation in Venice until speedboats began roaring down the canals in recent decades. No visit to Venice is complete without taking at least one of these time-honored water taxis for a spin. The average ride lasts about an hour. Before you take any gondola rides, make absolutely certain that you and gondolier agree to the trip's price and duration. To get your money's worth, write down the agreement and time the ride yourself. (Strangely, the gondoliers' watches often run fast).

Officially, gondola rides (if you're using the gondola as a taxi) are 120,000L ($66.65) for the first 50 minutes (for up to six people) and then 60,000L ($33.35) for each 25 minutes after that. (Of course, rides also cost more after 8:00 p.m.) You can find cut-rate, brief trips that follow only the Grand Canal (from the Dogana docks, off Piazza San Marco, to San Toma) for 35,000L ($19.45; ☎ **041-241-9243;** Internet: www.gondolavenice.it). However, a reasonably priced gondola ride is a Venetian rarity. If you encounter a gondolier that even remotely follows the "official" rates, write down his name and tell everyone (including me!) about it.

Discovering Venice: What You Need to Know

As you're planning out the schedule for your visit, keep in mind that standard business hours for shops in Venice are Monday to Saturday 9:00 a.m. to 12:30 p.m. and 3:00 to 7:30 p.m. In winter, shops are closed Monday morning, while in summer they're usually closed Saturday afternoons. Most grocers close Wednesday afternoon throughout the year. Banks are normally open Monday to Friday 8:30 a.m. to 1:30 p.m. and 2:35 to 3:35 p.m. or 3:00 to 4:00 p.m. In Venice and throughout Italy, just about everything is closed Sunday, though tourist shops in the San Marco area are permitted to stay open in high season. Restaurants are required to close at least one day per week *(il giorno di riposo)*, but the particular day varies. Many are open for Sunday lunch but close for Sunday dinner and close Monday when the fish market is closed. Restaurants close one to two weeks for holidays *(chiuso per ferie)* some time in July or August, frequently over Christmas, and sometime in January or February before the Carnevale rush.

The local dough

Lire (L) are the Italian units of currency . Roughly, $1 equals 1,800L; or 1,000L equals 55 cents. Italian coins include 50, 100, 200, and 500 lire. With two types of 50-lire coins and three different 100-lire pieces, you can easily to get confused. You may still encounter 10-lire and 20-lire coins (though they're completely worthless), as well as *gettoni*, old grooved phone tokens (these are worth 200L). Look for a new 1,000L coin soon. Bills come in denominations of 1,000, 2,000, 5,000, 10,000, 50,000, and 100,000 lire.

Where to get info after you arrive

There's a small tourist office in the train station, but you can find a larger and slightly less crowded (but still indifferent) office under the arcade at the west end of Piazza San Marco at no. 71, on the left of the tunnel-like street leading to **Calle dell'Ascensione (☎ 041-529-8711,** fax: 041-523-0399; Internet: www.provincia.venezia.it/aptve). The office is open daily 9:30 a.m. to 6:30 p.m. in summer and Monday to Saturday 9:30 a.m. to 3:30 p.m. in winter.

In summer, the city also opens up a small office at the Palazzina del Santi, also called the **Palazzetto Selva (☎ 041-522-6356),** between the small green park on the Grand Canal called the Giardinetti Reali and the famous Harry's Bar — at the S. Marco *vaporetto* stop. During peak season, a small info booth with erratic hours operates in the Arrivals Hall at the Marco Polo Airport.

If you're a younger traveler (or at least young-at-heart), pick up a **Rolling Venice Card,** which offers discounts on selected hotels (mostly hostel-type accommodations), restaurants, sights, and public transportation. The pass, good for a year, is 5,000L ($2.80), 10,000L ($5.55) if purchased with the special guide geared toward younger visitors. You can buy the card at a booth near the exit of the **train station (☎ 041-524-2852),** or at the **Servizio Politiche Giovanile (☎ 041-274-7650)** at **Corte Contarina,** just west of Piazza San Marco.

Where to go in a pinch

The worst Venetian criminal you'll encounter is the occasional pickpocket. Watch your wallet on crowded streets, near popular tourist sites, and on the vaporetti. One other tip: Don't even think of swimming in the canals. These things are used as sewers. Otherwise, the following is a list of contacts in case you find yourself in a bind.

- **Consulates:** The nearest U.S. Consulate is in Milan at Largo Donegani 1 (☎ 02-290-351), open Monday to Friday 9:00 a.m. to 11:00 a.m. for visas only; from Monday to Friday it's also open for telephone service info 2:00 to 4:00 p.m.

- **Doctors:** For an English-speaking doctor in Venice, call Dott. Sparla (☎ 041-523-0200 in the office or 041-522-7914 at home).

- **Emergency:** In Venice and throughout Italy, dial ☎ 113 to reach the police. Some Italians recommend that you forgo the police and try the military-trained Carabinieri (☎ 112). For an ambulance, phone ☎ 523-0000. To report a fire, dial ☎ 115. For any tourism-related complaint (rip-offs, exceedingly shoddy service, and so on) dial the special agency Venezia No Problem toll-free at ☎ 800-355-920.

- **Pharmacies:** Venice's many drugstores take turns staying open all night. To find out which one is on-call during your visit, ask at your hotel, check the duty rotation signs that appear outside all drugstores, or dial ☎ 041-523-0573.

- **Transit Info:** For flight information, call ☎ 041-260-9206. For rail information, call ☎ 041-715-555. For vaporetto information, call ☎ 041-528-7886.

Staying in touch

Whether you need to wire home for gondola money or send friends and family postcards, there are a variety of ways to stay in touch from Venice. Here are a few essential facts and locations for handling your communications needs:

- **American Express:** American Express is at San Marco 1471, 30124 Venezia, on Salizzada San Moisè just west of Piazza San Marco (☎ 041-520-0844). Summer banking hours are Monday to Saturday 8:00 a.m. to 8:00 p.m. (All other services are available 9:00 a.m. to 5:30 p.m.) Winter hours are Monday to Friday 9:00 a.m. to 5:30 p.m. and Saturday 9:00 a.m. to 12:30 p.m.

- **Internet Access and Cyber Cafes:** To check e-mail, log on at **Venetian Navigator**, Castello 5269 on Calle delle Bande between San Marco and Campo Santa Maria Formosa (☎ 041-522-6084; Internet: www.venetiannavigator.com; Vaporetto: San Marco, Zaccaria, Rialto), daily 10:00 a.m. to 10:00 p.m.

- **Venice's Posta Centrale:** Located at San Marco 5554, 30124 Venezia, on the San Marco side of the Rialto Bridge at Rialto Fontego dei Tedeschi (☎ 041-271-7111; Vaporetto: Rialto), this office sells stamps at Window 12, Monday to Saturday 8:10 a.m. to

7:00 p.m. (for parcels, 8:10 a.m. to 1:30 p.m.). If you're at Piazza San Marco and need postal services, walk through Sottoportego San Geminian, the center portal at the opposite end of the piazza from the basilica on Calle Larga dell'Ascensione. Its usual hours are Monday to Friday 8:15 a.m. to 1:30 p.m. and Saturday 8:15 a.m. to 12:10 p.m. You can buy *francobolli* (stamps) at *tabacchi* (tobacco shops).

✔ **Telephone:** Local calls cost 200L (10 cents). Phones accept either coins, a phone card (*carta telefonica*), or both. You can buy phone cards in a variety of denominations — 5,000L ($2.80), 10,000L ($5.55), or 15,000L ($8.35) — at newsstands and *tabbachi*. To use the card, break off the card's corner, insert the card, and dial. A digital display on the phone tells you how much money you have left on a card. For directory assistance, dial ☎ **12.**

Italy's country code is **39.** To call Venice from the United States, dial **011-39** and then the number. To charge your call to a calling or credit card, dial **AT&T** (☎ **172-1011**), **MCI** (☎ **172-1022**), or **Sprint** (☎ **172-1877**). To call the United States direct from Italy, dial **001,** followed by the area code and phone number.

Touring Venice by Neighborhood

Consider this fair warning: Venice has one of the most confusing, frustrating, and unfathomable layouts of any city. Ever. At first glance, the city seems simple: The palace-lined *Canale Grande* (Grand Canal), a sweeping backward-S curve, wraps around a few big islands while numerous smaller canals snake in and out through the blocks of land. Well, sort of. Being able to actually find anything you're looking for in Venice is much more complicated. Your best defense: Arm yourself with the best map you can buy, take a deep breath, and prepare to get lost repeatedly.

There are two transportation networks in Venice: one of narrow streets; the other of canals. These infrastructures work together occasionally, and sometimes they interfere with each other. Narrow alleyways that run you in circles, dead end, or drop off abruptly into a canal are all common. Often you will find yourself backtracking.

Sometimes, an alleyway that leads you from one place to another will suddenly open up into a large *campo* (square), or cross over a canal on one of Venice's tiny arched marble bridges (the most magnificent of these bridges is the **Rialto Bridge** over the Grand Canal).

If your vision is keen, you can follow the numerous tiny signs that point hither and yon to various major sights. These paths are often convoluted and take three times as long as you might imagine. However, don't fret about being late. Stepping outside your hotel in Venice is always an adventure — simply treat any trek through the city as such, you'll find that getting lost can actually be a truly enjoyable activity.

Centuries ago, someone tried to bring some order to Venice's chaos by dividing the city into six *sestieri,* or districts (which don't include the some 168 outlying islands). The central Venetian district is **San Marco,** filled to the brim with visitors these days. This district features the amazing *Piazza San Marco* (St. Mark's Square) with its cathedral and *Palazzo Ducale* (Doge's Palace). The *Piazzetta San Marco* extends from the Piazza San Marco and runs along the Palazzo Ducale to the Grand Canal. The San Marco is famous for having hundreds of souvenir shops, the ritziest (and most costly) hotels, the world-renowned (and recently burned down, but being reconstructed) La Scala opera house, and many (again, generally expensive) restaurants.

East of San Marco you find the large neighborhood of **Castello,** which offers the *Riva degli Schiavoni,* a classy stretch of lagoon-front property with upscale hotels aplenty. Much of the activity in Castello is centered around the old ship-building sector of the city, the *Arsenale.* This sector with its working navy yard is mostly closed to the tourists.

The northernmost Venetian neighborhood that greets you as you enter Venice by train or car is the **Canareggio.** Canareggio also has the dubious honor of being home to Europe's first incorporated Jewish Ghetto. Cheap lodging exists near the train station, but the neighborhood is largely residential. Unless you're stopping by to see a specific sight, you probably won't spend much of your Venetian adventure in Canareggio.

San Polo (or San Paolo) takes up a huge chunk of the side of city west of the Grand Canal. This commercial district is known for its moderately priced hotels, shopping, and trattorias, as well as some impressive churches that are popular with sightseers. Just a bit north, you find the very untouristy *sestiere* of **Santa Croce,** which is half industrial and half traditional, with a lovely ancient cathedral.

Street smarts: Deciphering Venetian addresses

Venice doesn't label its streets and squares like the rest of Italy does. A *calle, ruga,* or *ramo* is a street; a *rio terrà* is a street made from a filled-in canal; and a *fondamenta* or *riva* is a sidewalk along the edge of a canal. A *canale* or *rio* is a canal. A *campo* or *campiello* is a square (of course there are exceptions here, including Piazza San Marco, Piazzetta San Marco, and Piazzale Roma).

While a street or campo name can be used only once within a Venetian neighborhood, no rule exists against another *sestiere* using the exact same label. As a result, the most popular names (such as Calle della Madonna) are recycled three or four times in Venice, yet refer to streets half a city apart. Because of the confusing naming conventions, save yourself a headache and know the *sestiere* along with any address. (By the way, don't even try to figure out the street-numbering system in Venice — it's devoid of any logic whatsoever.)

On the opposite side of the Grand Canal from San Marco is the trendy southern district of **Dorsoduro.** Although Venice's Carnevale is reputed to rival New Orleans' Mardi Gras, the town's only nightlife is in this neighborhood. The sparsely populated area, with its smattering of bars and cafes, some good trattorie and cheap hotels, and Venice's two great art museums, the Accademia and the Peggy Guggenheim, is popular with younger travelers.

Staying in Venice

Get ready to shell out some clams: Venice is a pricey destination in just about every respect, especially in terms of lodging. As an island, Venetian hotel owners basically have a captive audience and can charge just about any price they please. Summer prices soar astronomically high, and your lodging choices can be pretty slim if you haven't reserved months in advance.

Savvy travelers often take advantage of an easier (and cheaper) stay in Padova, just a half-hour's train ride from Venice (see "Suggested One-, Two-, and Three-Day Itineraries"). As always in Italy, bargaining for a discount doesn't hurt — especially in the slower winter season (just don't get your hopes up for more than 10 to 15 percent off).

If you don't want to hotel-hunt on your own, visit an **AVA hotel association reservations booth** at the train station (☎ **041-715-288**) or in the parking garage at Piazzale Rome (☎ **041-522-8640**). It also offers a "Last-Minute Booking" service, toll-free in Italy at ☎ **167-843-006** or at 041-522-2264. The fee is 1,000L (55 cents), plus a deposit of 20,000 to 75,000L ($11.10 to $41.65; depending on the price of the room), which is credited to your hotel bill.

Venice's top hotels

Boston Hotel
$-$$ San Marco

A frugal favorite, the Boston's cozy rooms filled with their eighteenth-century reproduction Venetian décor is just steps away from Piazza San Marco. The best accommodations feature small balconies that overlook a canal. You can get a TV free upon request. Only 20 rooms have A/C, so request one when booking if you need it.

San Marco, Ponte de Dai 848 (halfway down the north colonnade of Piazza San Marco, a street leads north across a canal; the hotel is just over the bridge on the right). ☎ **041-528-7665**. *Fax: 041-522-6628. Vaporetto: San Marco. Rates: 150,000–330,000L ($83.35–$183.35) double. AE, DC, MC, V. Closed Nov–Feb.*

Accommodations, Dining & Attractions in Venice

HOTELS ■
Albergo al Gambero **19**
Boston Hotel **21**
Hotel Dolomiti **1**
Hotel Gallini **13**
Hotel San Cassiano Ca'Favretto **15**
Hotel San Geremia **2**
Londra Palace **29**
Pensione Accademia **4**
Pensione alla Salute **9**
Pensione la Calcina **7**
Westin Hotel Europa & Regina **10**

RESTAURANTS ◆
Antico Marini **12**
Archimboldo **33**
Bistro de Venise **19**
Brasserie ai Pugni **5**
Da Sandro **14**
Do Forni **20**
Ristorante Corte Sconta **32**
Rosticceria San Bartolomeo **18**
Trattoria Madonna **16**
Trattoria da Remigio **30**
Vino Vino **11**

ATTRACTIONS ●
Accademia **6**
Basilica di San Marco **23**
Bridge of Sighs **24**
Campanile di San Marco **26**
Collezione Peggy Guggenheim **8**
Museo Correr **28**
Palazzo Ducale (Doge's Palace) **25**
Piazza San Marco **27**
Ponte di Rialto **17**
Scuola Grande di San Rocco **3**
Torre dell'Orologio **22**

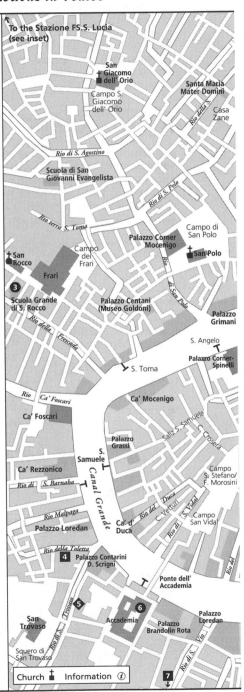

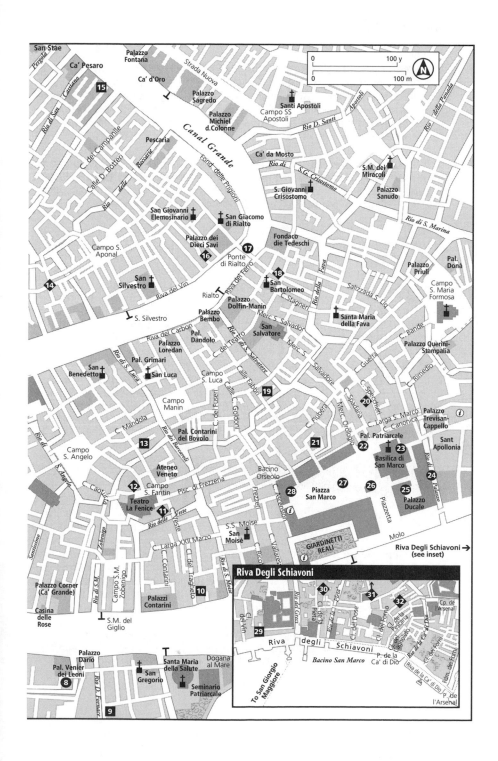

Hotel Gallini

$$ San Marco

If you can't get into the Boston, your next best bet is the Gallini. Run by family, the immaculate Gallini features big, modern rooms with marble and parquet floors and friendly service. Your cheapest bet are rooms that lack baths on the back side of the hotel; more expensive options overlook the charming Rio della Verona canal. Off-season rates are about 10 percent lower.

Calle della Verona (from La Fenice opera house on Campo San Fantin, head up the main street going north, over a bridge, and the hotel is on the right). ☎ *041-520-4515. Fax: 041-520-9103. Internet:* www.veniceinfo.it. *Vaporetto: Sant'Angelo. Rates: 190,000L ($105.55) double without bath, 240,000L ($133.35) double with bath. AE, MC, V.*

Hotel San Cassiano Ca'Favretto

$$$ San Polo

Try this place for moderate splurge. About half the rooms here look across the Grand Canal to the gorgeous Ca d'Oro; most of the others open onto a side canal. This fourteenth-century palace is steeped in dusty Old World elegance, with rooms outfitted with antiques and reproductions. A dining room porch overlooks the Grand Canal.

Calle della Rosa (after you step off the vaporetto, turn left to cross in front of the church, take the bridge over the side canal and turn right. Then turn left, cross another canal and turn right, then left again. Cross yet another canal and turn right, then immediately left and then left again toward the Grand Canal and the hotel). ☎ *041-524-1768. Fax: 041-721-033. Vaporetto: San Stae. Rates: 120,000–450,000L ($66.65–$250) double. AE, DC, MC, V.*

Londra Palace

$$$$ Castello

One of the best values on the prime real estate of the Riva degli Schiavoni. Tchaikovsky wrote his 4th Symphony in room 108 of this nineteenth-century neo-Gothic palace. The cushy accommodations include lacquered furniture and romantic attic rooms. With 100 windows overlooking the San Marco basin, you spend an hour or two just watching people strolling below, as well as distant vistas of the lagoon. Quieter, cheaper rooms look out to the inner courtyard. Its restaurant, Do Leoni, is one of the best hotel dining rooms in town.

Riva degli Schiavoni (on the canal right at the San Zaccaria vaporetto stop). ☎ *041-520-0533. Fax: 041-522-5032. Internet:* www.hotelondra.it. *Vaporetto: San Zaccaria. Rates: 409,000–785,000L ($227.20–$436.10) double. AE, DC, MC, V.*

Pensione Accademia

$$$ Dorsoduro

Venice regulars simply adore this pension. Set up your reservation well in advance to get any room here, let alone one overlooking the breakfast garden, a terrace nestled between two canals. The seventeenth-century villa is fitted with period antiques in the "superior" rooms on the first floor, and the atmosphere is decidedly old-fashioned and elegant. (Fans of the movie *Summertime* will remember that Katherine Hepburn's character lived here.)

Fondamenta Bollani (step off the vaporetto and turn right down Calle Gambara, which doglegs first left and then right. It becomes Calle Corfu, which ends at a side canal; walk left for a few feet to cross over the bridge, and then head to the right back up toward the Grand Canal and the hotel). ☎ *041-523-7846. Fax: 041-523-9152. E-mail:* pensione.accademia@flashnet.it. *Vaporetto: Accademia. Rates: 200,000–345,000L ($111.10–$191.65) double. AE, DC, MC, V.*

Westin Hotel Europa & Regina

$$$$ San Marco

Recently overhauled, this hotel once again ranks among Venice's top hotels. Just a minute or two from Piazza San Marco, down a quaint, hidden side alley, this hotel's Tiepolo and Regina wings sport eclectic turn-of-the-century European furnishings and modern fabrics. The Europa wing is decorated in traditional Venetian style. A cozy bar with tables opens out onto the Grand Canal, and a new open-kitchen restaurant has received good reviews. Room rates vary with season and view (Canale Grande rooms are priciest).

Off Via XXII Marzo (head west out of the southwest corner of Piazza San Marco down Saliz San Mose; cross the bridge to continue straight on Calle Larga XXII Marzo; you'll see hotel signs directing you down the alleyways to the left). ☎ *041-520-0477. Fax: 041-523-1533. Internet:* www.westin.com. *Vaporetto: San Marco. Rates: 655,000–1,155,000L ($363.90–$641.65) double. AE, DC, MC, V.*

Venice's runner-up accommodations

Albergo al Gambero

$-$$ Halfway between San Marco and the Rialto bridge, with 14 canal-side rooms; a three-star hotel at two-star prices. Guests receive a 10 percent discount in the lively ground-floor restaurant, Bistrot de Venise. *San Marco 4687, on Calle dei Fabbri (*☎ *041-522-4384 or 041-520-1420; Fax: 041-520-0431; E-mail:* hotel gambero@tin.it).

Hotel Dolomiti

$ An old-fashioned reliable choice near the train station with large, clean, but ordinary rooms spread over four floors (no elevator). Sergio and Lorenzo and their efficient polylingual staff supply umbrellas, restaurant suggestions, and a big smile after a long day's sightseeing. *Cannaregio 72 to 74, on Calle Priuli ai Cavalletti* (☎ *041-715-113; Fax: 041-716-635; Internet:* www.ciaovenezia.com/dolomiti).

Hotel San Geremia

$ An inn of tastefully renovated rooms, seven of which overlook the little square (better yet, one of two top-floor rooms has a small private terrace). *Cannaregio 290A, on Campo San Geremia* (☎ *041-716-245; Fax: 041-524-2342*).

Pensione alla Salute (Da Cici)

$-$$ One of the best choices in the Guggenheim area, a converted seventeenth-century palazzo with high ceilings and huge windows (ten rooms have canal views; four face the lovely terrace garden). Many are large enough to accommodate families of four or even five at 50,000L ($27.80) per person extra. *Dorsoduro 222, on Fondamenta Cá Balà* (☎ *041-523-5404; Fax: 041-522-2271; E-mail:* hotel.salute.dacici@iol.it).

Pensione La Calcina

$$ This is where John Ruskin holed up in 1876 when penning The Stones of Venice. Half the unfussy but luminous rooms overlook the sunny Zattere and Giudecca Canal toward Palladio's sixteenth-century Redentore. The outdoor floating terrace or the rooftop terrace are glorious places to begin or end any day. *Dorsoduro 780, on Zattere al Gesuati* (☎ *041-520-6466; Fax: 041-522-7045; E-mail:* la.calcina@libero.it).

Dining in Venice

Eating a Venetian meal can take you a few hours to work your way through the numerous courses. This much eating isn't just for tourists; Italians actually eat long, rich meals accompanied by fine wine and lively banter. A Venetian meal begins with an appetizer, usually a seafood dish. The popular *frutti di mare,* or "fruits of the sea," includes a tasty array of shellfish, crustaceans, and tentacled sea creatures.

Another classic starting point is *sarde in saor,* sardines prepared in a sweet-and-sour sauce on slices of grilled *polenta* (cornbread's wetter, more dense cousin). For the first course (called the *primo*), sink your spoon into *zuppa di cozze* (mussels soup) or savor a rice dish such as *risotto alle seppie* (rice stained with squid ink) or *risi e bisi,* a creamy blend of rice and fresh peas, sometimes with bacon. For pasta dishes, sample *spaghetti alle vongole* (with clams) or *al pomodoro* (in a plain tomato sauce).

Many main courses *(secondo)* utilize Venice's coastal setting, so try some fish. Most seafood entrees are priced by weight, grilled or otherwise simply prepared, and served on a bed of bitter red radicchio lettuce. Other popular secondi include *anguille in umido* (eels stewed with tomatoes, garlic, and white wine) and the staple *fegato alla Veneziana* (tender calf's liver cooked with onions). Cap off the perfect meal with your choice of *formaggi* (cheeses) or *tiramisù* (espresso-soaked lady fingers layered with sweetened, creamy mascarpone cheese and dusted with cocoa).

Italy is famed for its wines, and the vineyards around Venice produces some great ones, including the white Soave and reds Bardolino and Valpolicello. The best table wines tend to be whites.

Although dining in Italy is relatively inexpensive, remember that meal costs include much more than just your first and second course. Italian restaurants add an unavoidable "bread and cover" charge (*pane e coperto*) of about 1,500L-10,000L (85 cents-$5.55) to your bill. This *coperto* plus water and wine, an appetizer, coffee, dessert, and a *digestivo* (after-dinner drink) can quickly add up.

Tasty Italian take-out comes in the form of *tavola calda* and *rosticceria,* which sell preprepared hot dishes by weight. Most bars sell *tramezzini,* which are like giant tea sandwiches without crusts that are packed with tuna, ham, tomatoes, mozzarella, and other deli delicacies. For picnic supplies, stop by *alimentari* (grocery stores), *forno* (bakeries), and *fruttivendolo* (fruit and vegetable stands) for everything you need to pack a meal.

Don't waste your time with the take-out pizza slices in Venice; you'll get the wrong impression of Italian pizza, which is only worth eating in Rome and in Rome's southern region.

Venice's top restaurants

Antico Martini

$$$$ San Marco   VENETIAN/INTERNATIONAL

Founded as a simple café in 1720, this eatery is now one of Venice's top restaurants. Since 1921, the Baldi family has maintained the restaurant's airy, clubby atmosphere, especially its outdoor summer dining terrace. Local taste temptations such as *risotto di frutti di mare* and *fegato alla Veneziana* are prepared to perfection. However, the food, partnered with the establishment's reputation and location across from La Fenice opera house, all come at a stiff price.

Campo San Fantin (on the edge of the square occupied by La Fenice opera house). ☎ *041-522-4121. Internet:* www.anticomartini.com. *Reservations required. Vaporetto: San Marco or Santa Maria del Giglio. Main courses: 36,000–68,000L ($20–$37.80); fixed-price menu 78,000–132,0000L ($43.45–$73.35). AE, DC, MC, V. Open: Lunch Thurs–Mon, dinner Wed–Mon.*

Archimboldo

$$$ Castello   VENETIAN/ITALIAN

Archimboldo is always popular and is fast becoming one of Venice's leading restaurants. In the summer, you'll kick yourself for not grabbing an outdoor table to watch action on the canal and sample the restaurant's meticulously prepared Venetian cuisine. And you don't have to stick with Venetian specialties like seafood and liver — enjoy cuisines from the rest of Italy. The ingredients are bought fresh daily, and the wines are heavenly.

Calle dei Furlani (a little street leading east from San Giorgio degli Schiavoni; when you reserve, ask about its boat service from San Marco). ☎ **041-528-6569.** *Reservations recommended. Vaporetto: Arsenale or San Zaccaria. Main courses: 27,000–45,000L ($15–$25); fixed-price lunch 40,000L ($22.20). AE, DC, MC, V. Open: Lunch and dinner Wed–Mon.*

Do Forni

$$$$ San Marco   VENETIAN/INTERNATIONAL

The dining rooms here are like two sides of a coin: One is decorated country style, and the other does its best imitation of an *Orient Express* dining car. Whichever atmosphere you choose, the food remains delicious and purely Venetian. The ample menu features many examples of the sea's bounty, along with a few choice world-cuisine dishes. Do Forni isn't cheap, though, and its bustling energy sometimes detracts from the posh atmosphere.

Calle dei Specchieri (on the street leading north from Piazzetta dei Leoncini, which is around on the left flank of San Marco basilica). ☎ **041-523-2148.** *Reservations required. Vaporetto: San Marco. Main courses: 34,000–48,000L ($18.90–$26.65). AE, DC, MC, V. Open: Lunch and dinner Fri–Wed.*

Ristorante Corte Sconta

$$$ Castello   VENETIAN SEAFOOD

Don't let the spare decor fool you: This trendy, out-of-the-way trattoria has a surprisingly high-quality, all-seafood menu. With an emphasis on freshness (they toss the shrimp live on the grill), seafood fans should make reservations here for their very first night. At this hidden gem you'll hang out with artists, foodies, and writers. In nice weather, you can dine under a canopy of grapevines in the courtyard.

Calle del Pestrin (from San Marco, walk east along Riva degli Schiavoni a ways; you'll pass the church of La Pietà and then over a canal named for it; just after this is a left turn onto Calle del Dose, which leads into Campo Bandiera e Moro; turn right to exit this square on Calle dei Preti; where this road turns right, Calle del Pestrin branches to the left). ☎ **041-522-7024.** *Reservations reccommended. Vaporetto: Arsenale. Main courses: 22,000–35,000L ($12.20–$19.45); fixed-price menu 80,000L ($44.45). DC, MC, V. Open: Lunch and dinner Tues–Sat Closed Jan 7–Feb 7 and July 15–Aug 15.*

Trattoria Madonna

$$ San Paolo   VENETIAN

A veritable seafood mecca that sometimes verges on chaotic. The service here is friendly but occasionally brusque as waiters constantly rush to satisfy diners. You won't be able to linger over your meals here — so only visit if you're looking for fast, delicious, traditional food. If they're offering a mixed fish fry, dig in. Otherwise, check out the Venetian specialties enjoyed by local families, Italian businessmen, and other travelers.

Calle della Madonna (cross the Rialto Bridge and immediately turn left to walk down the Grand Canal's embankment; turn right down the second side street and the restaurant is 100 yards down on the left). ☎ *041-522-3824. Reservations recommended but not always accepted. Vaporetto: Rialto. Main courses: 15,000–25,000L ($8.35–$13.90). AE, MC, V. Open: Lunch and dinner Thurs–Tues Closed Jan 7–Feb 7 and Aug 1–15.*

Vino Vino

$ San Marco   VENETIAN/WINE BAR

The owner of the exclusive, pricey Antico Martini restaurant opened this relaxed, affordable little joint, which specializes in excellent staple dishes coupled with an impressive wine list featuring more than 350 Italian and foreign vintages (all for sale by the bottle as well as by the glass). Order at the counter, and then go find a free seat at the simple tables in one of two cramped rooms. Servers bring your meal out to you as you sit back and enjoy a self-guided wine tasting.

Ponte della Veste (head west out of the southwest corner of Piazza San Marco down Saliz San Mose. Cross the bridge to continue straight on Calle Larga XXII Marzo, from which you'll turn right up Calle delle Veste. The restaurant is at the opposite end of a short bridge, just before La Fenice opera house). ☎ *041-241-7688. Reservations suggested. Vaporetto: San Marco. Main courses: 10,000–15,000L ($5.55–$8.35). No credit cards. Open: Lunch and dinner Wed–Mon.*

Venice's runner-up restaurants

Rosticceria San Bartolomeo

$-$$ A popular tavola calda offering ready-made hot dishes and pizza with no cover charge right in the heart of the action. Short on atmosphere, long on budget value. The dining hall upstairs costs 20 percent more. *San Marco 5424, on Calle della Bissa (☎ 041-522-3569).*

Bistrot de Venise

$$$ An artists' hangout sporting a bistro style and an eclectic menu of Italian, French, and historic fifteenth-century Venetian recipes. Peek in the back room (or check out the Web site) to see what's going on in the evening — art exhibits, live music, poetry readings, and so on. *San Marco 4687, on Calle dei Fabbri below the Albergo al Gambero (☎ 041-523-6651; Internet:* www.bistrotdevenise.com*).*

Brasserie ai Pugni

$ A no-frills canalside pub/bistro with more than 50 interesting sandwiches, some 60 pizza combinations, and no cover charge. It's modern and laid-back, and you know it's all fresh — Venice's last floating produce barge is moored outside the pub. *Dorsoduro 2839, at foot of Ponte dei Pugni* (☎ *041-523-9831*).

Da Sandro

$-$$ A good choice if you're looking for a 12,000L ($6.65) pizza-and-beer meal. Like most pizzerias/trattorias, it offers a dozen varieties of pizza as well as a full trattoria menu of pastas and entrees. *San Polo 1473, on Campiello dei Meloni on the main drag linking the Rialto to Campo San Polo (☎ 041-523-4894).*

Trattoria da Remigio

$$ Famous for its straightforward renditions of Adriatic classics, bucking the current Venetian trends by continuing to offer exquisite food and excellent service at reasonable prices. Locals love it for a night of semi-refinement, so you must book ahead. *Castello 3416, on Calle Bosello near Scuola San Giorgio dei Greci (☎ 041-523-0089).*

Exploring Venice

Even though the city of Venice has been working fiercely on mechanical dams to prevent this, the tides each winter force the Adriatic Sea rushing into Venice's lagoon and the lagoon rushing into the streets. These *acque alte,* or high waters, can raise in-town water levels up to three feet for brief spells (usually one to five hours). When the *acque alte* strike, usually between October and March, low-lying Piazza San Marco is the first area to flood. As the waters rise, you may find yourself having the peculiarly Venetian experience of walking about the packed city street atop long, jerry-rigged bridges of wooden planks.

In addition to the attractions mentioned below, keep in mind that if you come to the city during Carnevale, it's going to be one nonstop party (see Chapter 2 for more information).

Venice's top sights

Piazza San Marco (St. Mark's Square)

A year-round carnival is the best way to describe Piazza San Marco, a gathering place filled to the brim with milling visitors, swarms of hungry pigeons, locals enjoying espresso at outdoor cafes, and couples dancing on the cobblestones to the strains of live piano music. The living room of Venice, San Marco is surrounded on three sides by a sixteenth-century arcade and anchored by one of Italy's most gorgeously mosaic-covered cathedrals (see following entry). You'll find the site mobbed at midday, so try a late night or early morning visit when the space is virtually deserted and has a magical emptiness all its own.

On July 14, 1902, the too-tall **Campanile,** or bell tower (☎ 041-522-4064), crumbled to the ground almost instantly. Because every Italian city feels compelled to have a dome, tower, or some other high edifice for tourists to climb (just kidding!), Venice quickly built a new tower. The new structure resembles the old, but with two major differences: It's now more architecturally sound, and even better, it has an elevator. From atop the tower, take in the many domes and spires of the cathedral's rooftop, along with a sweeping vista of the city and the Grand Canal. Admission is 8,000L ($4.45) for adults and 4,000L ($2.20) for kids; the tower is open daily from 9:30 a.m. to 7:00 p.m. (4:00 p.m. in winter).

The *Torre dell'Orolorgio,* a late fifteenth-century clock tower, enlivens the square and chimes out the hour. The clock tower features two hammer-wielding statues called the Moors of Venice. (Actually, the statues were supposed to represent European shepherds, but time and environmental conditions have darkened the bronze figures to the point where the locals decided they looked more Moorish.)

The core collections of the Museo Civico Correr (☎ 041-522-5625 or 041-522-4951), in the square's southwest corner, take visitors through Venetian painting from the fourteenth to sixteenth centuries, highlighting the works of Tintoretto, Veronese, Carpaccio, and the Bellini family (Jacopo and sons Gentile and Giovanni, the greatest of the three) along the way. But some of the strongest works in the collection are by non-Venetians such as Antonello da Messina and Cosmé Tura. Admission is cumulative with a ticket to the Palazzo Ducale (see the following listing), and it's open the same hours. Piazza San Marco. Vaporetto: San Marco or San Zaccaria.

Basilica di San Marco (St. Mark's Basilica)

No church in Europe is more lavishly decorated, more exquisitely mosaicked, more glittering with gold than Venice's San Marco. Dating back to the eleventh century, the originally Byzantine architecture and decoration now includes Romanesque and Gothic touches, too.

A few basic do's and don'ts here: 1) Dress appropriately — that means no bare shoulders or knees (no shorts, short skirts, or tank tops). 2) Keep silent. 3) No photography is permitted.

Over 40,000 square feet of gold-backed mosaics crafted between the twelfth and seventeenth centuries cover the church's atrium, ceilings, walls, and multiple domes. The oldest were created by Eastern masters, and later ones were based on works by Tintoretto, Veronese, and Titian. The floor carries on a mosaic feel with its wonderfully spiraling marble tiles. The only disappointing aspect of this wonder of architecture? Its immense popularity. Visitors are often pushed through the site like cattle. Still, the 20 to 60 minutes you spend inside (depending on how many of the church's side attractions you visit) will be truly unforgettable.

Don't miss checking out the baptistery alcove, which features a font carved by Sansovino, or taking a peek at the presbytery with its *Pala d'Oro*, a golden trophy studded with gems from Constantinople. The Marciano Museum (also known as *Logia dei Cavalli*) can be entered through an atrium. The Museum offers you a close-up look at some of the building's mosaics as well as houses the original *Triumphal Quadriga* of four horses, life-size bronze sculptures that are truly one of Venice's cultural treasures. Taken in 1204 from Constantinople during the crusades, the sculptures' exact origin is unclear, but they're certainly ancient (the best guess is second century a.d. and either Roman or Hellenistic in origin). The cathedral runs free guided tours in summer, usually around 10:30 a.m. Monday to Saturday (check in the atrium for specifics).

Piazza San Marco. ☎ *041-522-5697 or 041-522-5205. Vaporetto: San Marco or San Zaccaria. Admission: Basilica free; treasury 4,000L ($2.20); presbytery 3,000L ($1.65); Marciano Museum 3,000L ($1.65). Open: Basilica, treasury, and presbytery: Mon–Sat 9:30 a.m.–4:30 p.m., Sun 2:00–4:30 p.m. Marciano Museum: daily 9:30 a.m.–4:30 p.m.*

Palazzo Ducale (Doge's Palace)

One of Italy's grandest and most history-saturated town halls is a confection of Gothic-Renaissance design. Raised in 1309 and rebuilt after a 1577 fire, the palace features public halls with canvases and frescoes by Venice's greatest artists, including lovely works by Veronese and Tintoretto. The guided tour leads you through the palace in about 45 to 100 minutes, depending on your pace.

Even with an informative audio guide and English placards describing the artworks and the civic purpose of each room, you may find wandering the public halls a bit cold and distancing. Your experience may be enhanced by know that the real governing of Venice was never done in these public areas, but rather in a series of low-ceilinged corridors and tiny offices that wrapped around the building like a governmental cocoon (the entrances were hidden behind secret doors set into the gorgeous paintings and carved woodwork in the public rooms).

You can see this inner sanctum — and get a great primer on Venetian politics and intrigue — by taking the 90-minute "Secret Itineraries" tour. Among the stops on the tour are the inquisition room and the "leads," the prison cells in the roof rafters where your guide will recount the tale of Casanova's famous escape. After the tour, you can visit the public palace on your own.

Off the back of the palace, you cross over the famous, enclosed Bridge of Sighs *(Ponte dei Sospiri)*, named by romantic-era writers who imagined condemned prisoners letting out a lament as they crossed it and got their final glimpse of Venice and its lagoon through tiny windows in the center. The cells on the other side preserve the scrawls and graffiti of ancient prisoners.

Piazzetta San Marco, San Marco. ☎ *041-522-4951. Vaporetto: San Marco or San Zaccaria. Admission: 18,000L ($10) adults, 10,000L ($5.55) ages 15–29, 6,000L ($3.35) ages 6–14; the ticket also gets you into the Museo Civico Correr (see description under Piazza San Marco). "Secret Itineraries" tour is an extra 6,000L ($3.35) adults, 4,000L ($2.20) students aged 15–29, 2,000L ($1.10) ages 6–14. Open: Nov–Mar daily 9:00 a.m.–5:00 p.m., Apr.–Oct daily 9:00 a.m.–7:00 p.m. (ticket office closes one hour before museum). "Secret Itineraries" tour in English Thurs–Tues at 10:30 a.m.*

Accademia

If you only have time for one museum in Venice, take in the Accademia. Set aside a good 1½ to 3 hours to peruse the vast collections of masterpieces by Venice's color-loving artists. The museum covers the biggies in Venetian painting, from Paolo Veneziano's fourteenth-century *Coronation of the Virgin* altarpiece to Giorgione's strange *The Tempest* and Giovanni Bellini's numerous *Madonna and Child*s.

Also on display are Carpaccio's intricate *Cycle of St. Ursula,* Titian's late *Pietà,* and Tintoretto's *The Stealing of St. Mark,* commemorating the Venetian merchants who, in 828, spirited the body of the saint away from Alexandria during an era when acquiring bona fide saints was *de rigueur* for relic hunters.

When Paolo Veronese unveiled his *Last Supper,* the puritanical leaders of the Inquisition nearly had a conniption. They threatened him with charges of blasphemy for portraying this feast as a drunken banquet more in keeping with a Roman orgy than the holiest of moments. The painting was unaltered but retitled *Feast in the House of Levi* (certainly a more safely secular title), and the censors let it pass.

Campo della Carità, Dorsoduro. ☎ *041-522-2247. Vaporetto: Accademia. Admission: 15,000L ($8.35). Open: Summer, Tues–Fri 9:00 a.m.–9:00 p.m., Sat 9:00 a.m.–11:00 p.m., Sun 9:00 a.m.–8:00 p.m., Mon 9:00 a.m.–2:00 p.m.; winter, Mon–Sat 9:00 a.m.–7:00 p.m., Sun 9:00 a.m.–2:00 p.m.*

Collezione Peggy Guggenheim

Peggy Guggenheim's former residence in Venice is now one of the world's top modern art museums. The uncompleted (only the first floor was built) eighteenth-century *Palazzo Venier dei Leoni* sits on the Grand Canal and is filled with the late, great art collector's personal favorites. The museum offers a comprehensive survey of avant-garde modern art.

There are works by her short-lived hubby Max Ernst and her discovery Jackson Pollock, as well as pieces by some of her favorites: Picasso (notably, his 1911 *The Poet*), Miró, Mondrian, Brancusi, Duchamp, Kadinsky, Chagall, Dalí, and Giacometti. A racy version of Tuscan sculptor Marino Marini's patented man-on-horseback bronzes stands at attention in the small garden.

Calle San Cristoforo, San Gregorio 701, Dorsoduro. ☎ *041-520-6288. Vaporetto: Accademia. Admission: 12,000L ($6.65) adults, 8,000L ($4.45) students and children. Open: Wed–Mon 11:00 a.m.–6:00 p.m.*

Scuola Grande di San Rocco

A *scuola* was a lay fraternity whose members worked diligently for various charitable causes. Because these private gentleman's clubs were also places to show off, many *scuole* were decorated by commissioned artists. Interestingly, the Scuola di San Rocco held an art competition in 1564 to choose its decorator. Renaissance master Tintoretto outdid his rivals by actually completing an entire painting and secretly installing it in the ceiling of the Sala dell'Albero off the second-floor hall.

The judges were dutifully impressed, and Tintoretto got the job, eventually filling the scuola's two floors with dozens of works over the next quarter century. Be sure to check out the *Rest on the Flight into Egypt* on the ground floor, as well as a huge *Crucifixion* that ranks among the greatest and most moving works in the history of Venetian art. The San Rocco baroque orchestra holds excellent regular chamber concerts in this fantastic setting; for info contact 041-962-999 or www.musicinvenice.com.

Campo San Rocco, San Polo. ☎ *041-523-4864. Internet:* www.sanrocco.it. *Vaporetto: San Tomà. Admission: 9,000L ($5) adults, 6,000L ($3.35) under age 26. Open: Mar 28–Nov 2 daily 9:00 a.m.–5:30 p.m.; Nov 3–Mar 27 Mon–Fri 10:00 a.m.–1:00 p.m., Sat–Sun 10:00 a.m.–4:00 p.m.*

More cool things to see and do in Venice

There's more to Venice than museums and churches. From wandering canalside streets to buying some hand-blown glass, you'll never be at a loss for something fun to do.

- ✔ **Get Lost.** So you've found a great map of Venice? Well, stick it in your traveling bags and forget about it. Hey, if you inevitably get lost in Venice, why not make a day of it! Forget about those "helpful" signposts that dot the cityscape and avoid the crowded squares and attractions. Whenever things start to feel a little too touristy, just walk a block or so away from the action. Doing so enables you to explore Venice's private side — its ancient sounds, its classic energy, its distinctive rhythms.

  Or set aside some time one day and practice the art of Zen walking — simply turn left whenever you feel like it and avoid popular calle and campi all together. Stop for a meal in a little café that seems popular with locals, or purchase some picnic supplies and enjoy a meal at a tiny campo or canalside *riva*. When you're ready to rejoin the world, just wander — you'll quickly find youself in some major square or street, from which you can find your way again.

- ✔ **Cruise the Grand Canal.** Think of the Grand Canal as the watery Champs-Elysées of Venice. The canal is filled to capacity with hundreds of boats of all shapes and sizes: ferries, gondolas, garbage scows, speedboats, and small commercial craft. Buildings and palaces that face the Grand Canal display a variety of styles — from intricate Byzantine-Romanesque to classically proportioned Renaissance and neo-classical.

  Take a relaxing ride on the no. 1 or 82 vaporetto line. Don't get all flustered about which palazzo was built when by whom. Instead, open your eyes (or your camera lens) and explore the rich details of the ride — a mysterious woman clothed in black, workmen tinkering with water-rotted moorings, lazy cats resting precariously on high open windowsills.

✔ **Shop for Fine Glass, Lace, and Carnevale Masks.** This trio of Venetian craft specialties is everywhere about town, in little hole-in-the-wall shops and big, crowded boutiques (it's estimated that there are over 1,000 glass shops in the San Marco district alone).

Be aware of the quality of this items. Many items are machine-produced or crafted elsewhere — sometimes Eastern Europe or Taiwan. Your best guide is to not worry about pedigree and simply purchase things you like. However, if you are looking for the real deal or are buying to build a formal collection, resign yourself to the fact that you'll be charging up your credit card in the process.

The following are some of the top emporia for the most popular crafts. (Every piece on display in these shops is guaranteed hand-crafted by Venetian artisans.):

- •For glass, visit Venini, Piazzetta dei Leoncini (off the left flank of Basilica di San Marco); Pauly & Co, Ponte Consorzi (just behind the Doge's Palace, although they also have boutique shops on Piazza San Marco); or Salviati, on Piazza San Marco.

- •For lace, go to Jesurum, on Mercerie del Capitello.

- •For masks, visit the Laboratorio Artigiano Maschere, at Barbaria delle Tole, in the Castello district.

✔ Incidentally, the most traditional craftsmen of Venetian glass are located on the island of Murano, and the ladies who tat the best lace are on the island of Burano, both described in the section "The islands of the Venetian lagoon."

Or, take the easy route and simply stroll along one of Venice's premier (and priciest) avenues, *Le Mercerie* (head out of Piazza San Marco at the clock tower). This route's fancy boutiques and souvenir shops can give you a wonderful taste of the best of Venice. Note that the avenue is actually a series of different streets with constantly changing names — but don't fret, just realize that all streets begin with the word "mercerie."

And on Your Left, San Marco: Seeing Venice by Guided Tour

Because **American Express** (☎ 041-520-0844) can't run buses in Venice, it is forced to offer guided orientation tours the old-fashioned way — on foot. It offers a morning tour of the major Piazza San Marco sights (40,000L/$22.20) and an afternoon one of palaces and churches in the San Marco and San Polo districts (45,000L/$25). After dark, you can go on one of its "Evening Serenade" gondola tours for 50,000L ($27.80).

Suggested One-, Two-, and Three-Day Itineraries

If you're the type who'd rather organize your own tours, this section offers some tips for building your own Venice itineraries.

If you have one day

The first order of business is wandering through the glittering mosaic wonderland of the **Basilica di San Marco.** Then head next door and take the "Secret Itineraries" tour (in English at 10:30 a.m.) of the **Palazzo Ducale** for an insider's glimpse into the hidden offices, court-rooms, archives, and prisons from which the true Venetian Republic ruled for 900 years.

After a light lunch, tour the **Scuola Grande di San Rocco** for its festival of Tintorettos and the Accademia, Venice's top painting gallery. Spend the evening simply wandering the spellbinding Venetian labyrinth of streets and passages. At some point, either when you arrive or prepare to leave, ride the no. 1 vaporetto line its full length between Piazza San Marco and the Ferrovia — about 45 minutes each way. You'll cruise by the hundreds of proud palazzi lining the principal aquatic boulevard, as postcard perfect early in the morning as late in the afternoon.

If you have two days

Spend the morning of Day One as above, in **San Marco** and touring the **Doge's Palace,** but also take time to ride the elevator to the top of the **Campanile di San Marco** for a terrific panorama across the city. After lunch, head to the **Ca' d'Oro** (north of the Rialto Bridge), Venice's most famous private palace and today a museum providing a look at the interior of one of the great palazzi gracing the Grand Canal as well as a small but fine art collection. Cross the Rialto Bridge into San Polo to see the **Scuola Grande di San Rocco,** and then round off the day with a *bacaro* crawl through the *cichetti* bars around the **Rialto Market.**

Though the city has plenty of official "sights," one of Venice's greatest attractions is the city itself, so spend the morning of Day Two simply lost in the city's back alleyways. For its weathered Oriental beauty, way of life, and Eastern/Western fusion of architecture and wealth of history, Venice has no match. Some of the residential neighborhoods off the beaten track are eastern Castello near the **Arsenale,** the **Ghetto** (once the Jewish quarter) in northern Cannaregio, and the island of **La Giudecca.**

Suitably refreshed and recharged, cross into the **Dorsoduro** neighbor-hood in the afternoon for some hardcore art appreciation. Visit the **Accademia** for a look at the city's Renaissance heritage and the nearby **Collezione Peggy Guggenheim** for one of Europe's best galleries of international twentieth-century works. If you have the time and energy, fit in the **Ca' Rezzonico** as well (like the **Ca d'Oro,** another historic patrician palace restored with a small painting gallery).

If you have three days

On Days 1 and 2, follow the above. Use Day Three to take a circle tour of the best outlying islands in the **Venetian Lagoon:** Murano with its glass factories; Burano with its colorful fishing houses and lace school; and Torcello, a glimpse into what Venice looked like in its early days with a gloriously mosaicked Byzantine church in the middle.

Exploring Beyond Venice

For a change of pace, consider leaving Venice for a day in search of qui-eter (and less touristy) pleasures. A quick boat ride can lead you to various islands in the Venetian lagoon (although low-key, the islands offer some great shopping). Or take a short train ride to Padova, a col-lege town with stunning architecture and art galore.

The islands of the Venetian lagoon

Want to see what Venice looked like before it became a tourist mecca of palazzi and museums? If so, you need go no further the fishing village islands of the northern Venetian lagoon. A mere 1½-mile vaporetto ride takes you to Murano with its rich glass-blowing heritage, **Burano** with its old-fashioned lace works, and **Torcello,** with its remarkable medieval church.

Getting there

Most vaporetto ferries to the islands leave from Fondamenta Nuova in Venice, which is on the far north side of the Castello district. However, you can also ride line 52 to Fondamenta Nuova from San Zaccharia (on Riva degli Schiavoni near Piazzetta San Marco). With luck, the 52 veers off at Fondamenta Nuova to head onto Murano. Otherwise, from Fondamenta Nuova get on line 12 or 13 to Murano. Line 12 takes you from Murano to Burano, and both 12 and 14 go from Burano to Torcello. From Torcello, you can return to Venice on line 12 (to Fondamenta Nuova, where you can catch the 52 back) or take a round-about trek on line 14 (to San Zaccharia).

If you plan to visit the islands of the Venetian lagoon, get up early in the morning and plan to be out-of-town all day (at least five to seven hours). Because the ferries between the islands leave hourly, plan your time on the islands in hour increments. One hour is usually enough for Burano and Torcello; two hours or more for Murano. Additionally, figure the following travel times: 35 minutes for the ride from Venice to Murano, 20 minutes from Murano to Burano, 5 minutes from Burano to Torcello, and 50 minutes from Torcello to Venice.

Seeing the sights

Murano is the largest of the three islands. This active island is home to numerous fishermen and several age-old glass factories. If you're inter-ested in shopping for fine examples of this outstanding craft, head to the island's outlet stores (most stores on Murano take quality seriously). Never pay the sticker price at these stores; instead, bargain for at least 30 percent off the asking price. If you're looking for a one-of-a-kind glass item, talk with any of the glassblowers in the workshops. Most can create original items, especially trinkets, for you on the spot.

If you're interested in the history behind glass craft, stop by the **Museo Vetraio di Murano** (☎ 041-739-586), which offers a large collection of glass objects from ancient Roman times through the nineteenth century as well as displays that explore the history and practice of the craft itself.

For a change of pace, the **church of San Pietro Martire** has unexpected riches in the form of oil paintings by Tintoretto, Veronese, and Giovanni Bellini. For 3,000L ($1.65), you can see sacristy's carved paneling. Also, check out another truly ancient church, **Santa Maria e Donato,** with its gorgeous exterior that features stacked colonnades, dog-tooth molding, and inlaid Byzantine details. Rebuilt in the twelfth century, the current structure features Corinthian columns dating from Roman times, a pulpit from the sixth century, a patterned floor from 1141 that is reminiscent of those in San Marco, and fifteenth-century frescoes.

Note that Murano has five vaporetto docks. You usually land at *Colonna* or *Museo,* but you should continue on to Burano from *Faro.*

Lacemaking is the highlight of your visit to the tiny island of **Burano.** While lace from Burano fetches high prices in Venetian shops, prices on the island can be a bit more reasonable here — beautiful edged hankies are available for around 5,000L ($2.80). Learn a bit about lacemaking's history at the **Scuola di Merletti** (☎ 041-730-034), a shop that keeps this ancient tradition vibrantly alive. Be sure to visit the second floor of the shop, where women still work on extremely delicate and beautiful lace items by hand. Admission is 8,000L ($4.45), and it's usually open Wednesday to Monday from 10:00 a.m. to 5:00 p.m. (The shop often closes during the winter if no tourists appear.) Burano also features a Tiepolo Crucifixion in the parish church of San Martino, streets of brightly painted houses, and a leisurely, seafaring pace that will come as a welcome respite from the frenzy of Venice.

An eleventh-century Byzantine cathedral is the highlight of the grassy, semi-deserted island of **Torcello.** To reach the cathedral from the dock, walk along the island's only canal for about 10 minutes. One wall of the cathedral features a remarkable mosaic of the Last Judgment and the apse has a massive Madonna mosaic. Admission is 5,000L ($2.80), and it's open daily from 10:00 a.m. to 12:30 p.m. and 2:30 to 6:30 p.m. (from November through March, it closes at 5:00 p.m.). Across the square is the tiny **Museo dell'Estuario** (☎ 041-730-761), whose collection includes archaeological fragments and the remains of some ten other churches that once stood on Torcello. Admission is 3,000L ($1.65), and it's open Tuesday through Saturday 10:00 a.m. to 12:30 p.m. and 2:00 to 5:30 p.m., Sunday 10:30 a.m. to 12:30 p.m. (sometimes it closes in winter).

Where to dine

For lunch, consider packing a lunch from Venice (Torcello is great for a relaxed picnic) or sitting down for a hearty meal at the trattorie **Al Corallo** (☎ 041-739-080), Fondamenta dei Vetrai 73 in Murano, or **Trattoria da Romano** (☎ 041-730-030), at Via Baldassare Galuppi 223 in Burano. Or pull out all the stops and splurge on **Locanda Cipriani** (☎ 041-730-150), a refined restaurant in the middle of nowhere on Torcello that was one of Hemingway's favorite dining spots.

The Venetian Islands

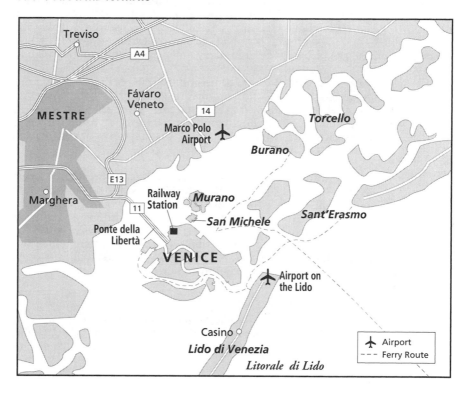

Poking around Padova

For the best day trip (in my opinion) in the Veneto region, make tracks for **Padova** (Padua) — a city of saints and scholars, Giotto frescoes, and arcaded piazze. Right on your way to Bologna, Florence, and Rome via rail, Padova makes a great stop en route to or from Venice. Allow four to five hours (and some hustling) to see the sites, or stay the night and take in the city at a more leisurely pace.

Getting there

Padova is only 32 minutes by half-hourly train from Venice. (For this reason, many savvy travelers choose to stay in Padova during peak tourist season and day-trip to crowded, expensive Venice.)

The **tourist office** (☎ 049-875-2077) is at the train station.

Seeing the sights

The must-see site for Padova is on the northern-most edge of town (take bus 3, 8, 12, or 18 at the Piazza Eremitani off Corso Garibaldi). The **Cappella degli Scrovegni (Arena Chapel)** (☎ 049-820-4550), which Giotto, a master of emotion and artistic technique, adorned with gorgeous frescoes from 1303 to 1306. The chapel as a whole is breathtaking, depicting scenes from the life of Mary and Jesus in 38 panels including the awe-inspiring *Last Judgment,* the insightful *Arrest of Christ,* and the woe-filled *Lamentation of Christ.* Admission (available at the Musei Civici di Eremitani), is 10,000L ($5.55) adults; 7,000L ($3.90) ages 6 to 17. The church is open February to October daily from 9:00 a.m. to 7:00 p.m., November to January daily from 9:00 a.m. to 6:00 p.m.

The nearby **Musei Civici di Eremitani,** Piazza Eremitani 8, houses an archaeological collection on the ground floor, a Giotto *Crucifix,* and minor works by major fourteenth-century Venetian painters (including Giorgione, Jacopo Bellini, Veronese, Tintoretto). Admission is combined with the Scrovegni Chapel. The museum is open the same hours, except it is closed Monday.

Padova's other great sight is the eastern-looking **Basilica di Sant'Antonio** (☎ 049-824-2811), Piazza del Santo 11. Outside, the basilica is all domes and mini-minarets, while altars inside feature Donatello bronzes. Be sure to see the north transept for the tomb of St. Anthony and the south transept for a fourteenth-century fresco of the *Crucifixion.* The church's piazza is dominated by a beautiful bronze sculpture of a man on horseback called *Gattamelata,* also by Donatello. The basilica is open daily 6:30 a.m. to 7:00 p.m. (7:45 p.m. in summer).

Where to stay

If you're looking for value in Paduan hotels, check out the **Leon Bianco** (☎ 049-875-0814), Piazzetta Pedrocchi 12 (at Via Cavour), which offers contemporary doubles in a 100-year-old palazzo for 162,000L ($90).

Where to dine

The extravagantly neoclassical **Caffé Pedrocchi** promises one of Italy's most elegant cafe experiences (☎ 049-876-2576), Piazzetta Pedrocchi 15. Although drinks are pricey, the setting, with its colorful nineteenth-century décor and whimsical references to ancient Rome and Egypt, makes this establishment worth it. In summer, get a table on the stone patio and experience the gentle ebb and flow of Paduan life.

Il Dotto (☎ 049-875-1490), Via Squarcione 23 (off Via Roma), gets my nod for best value in a set-priced menu — for 50,000L ($27.80) you can experience some of the most inventive Paduan cuisine in town.

Chapter 23

Madrid and the Best of Castile

- -

In This Chapter

▶ Getting around in Madrid

▶ Exploring an art-lover's paradise

▶ Finding the best in Spanish cuisine

▶ Seeing the sights outside the city

- -

*M*adrid is the capital city and center of all Spain. It is an art lover's paradise — this is where you'll find works by Picasso, Velázquez, Goya, El Greco, and hundreds of other European artists on display at the Prado Museum. But Madrid is more than just art. It has also gained fame as the home of the evening predinner stroll, called the *paseo*.

Madrid is a round-the-clock city. You can see the royal palace in the morning, an eighteenth-century art gallery in the early afternoon, and bullfights in the late afternoon. After dark, the evening begins with a fashionably late dinner, perhaps followed by a flamenco show or dancing until daybreak at a happenin' nightclub.

Art aficionados can easily spend four to five days in Madrid. If you're not into art, the city is still worth at least two days, plus two more for exploring the surrounding region of Castile on day trips to Toledo and Segovia (see "Traveling Beyond Madrid").

Making Your Way to and around Madrid

Madrid is a long, 13-hour train ride from Paris, the closest non-Spanish city in this book — so unless you're arriving in Madrid from elsewhere in Spain, it's probably a good idea to fly here. When you arrive, you'll find that Madrid's local transportation system is efficient and relatively easy to use.

Getting to Madrid by air

Madrid's airport, **Barajas** (☎ **91-305-8343**), is about 10 miles outside town. The Metro (subway) runs from the airport to downtown (though you have to change to line 4 at Mar de Cristal), or you can take a shuttle bus to Plaza de Colón in the city center for 380 ptas. ($2.55). A taxi into town is at least 2,500 ptas ($16.80), plus airport and baggage-handling surcharges. Plan on 30 to 45 minutes travel time from the airport to downtown.

Getting to Madrid by rail

If you take the train to Madrid, you'll most likely arrive at the city's main station, **Chamartín,** which is the hub for trains coming from eastern Spain and France (international train routes come through the France-Spain border). From Chamartín, which is in the northern suburbs, you can get downtown quickly on Metro line 8.

Madrid has two other train stations. Trains to and from southwest Spain and Portugal come into **Atocha.** (Confusingly, two Metro stops also go by the name Atocha; the one marked Atocha RENFE is the one beneath Atocha train station; the Atocha Metro stop is one stop north of Atocha RENFE.) **Norte,** or Príncipe Pío, serves northwest Spain. **RENFE** is the name of the Spanish national train service; for information, call ☎ **91/328 90 20.**

Getting around once you're in Madrid

Madrid is one of the few European cities where you'll probably want to spend little time strolling around on foot. It has wide boulevards that are great for getting from place to place, but most offer relatively little in the way of character. With a couple of notable exceptions, such as **Plaza Mayor,** you won't miss much by traveling underground on the Metro.

Bus tickets will not work on the Metro, and vice versa, but a single ticket for either is 130 ptas. (85 cents). If you're going to need more than eight bus or Metro tickets, you can save money by buying a ten-ride pass called a *bonos diez viajes* for 680 ptas. ($4.55). After you get on the Metro, you can transfer from one route to another. The bus system, however, does not allow transfers.

By Metro (subway)

Madrid's Metro system has 11 lines, which intersect at the following major junctions: Puerta del Sol, Alonso Martinez, Ópera, and Avienda de América. Although it is slow and crowded at rush hour — name a big-city subway system that isn't — the Metro is otherwise very fast and efficient and is a good way for travelers to cover the hefty distances between Madrid's sights, which are dispersed throughout the city.

By bus

Madrid's bus service is pretty standard for a major-city bus system. But it may in fact be more efficient than most because the buses travel in special lanes and don't have to fight traffic. Still, most conductors don't speak English, so I recommend sticking to the Metro.

By taxi

When you hail a taxi in Madrid, make sure you get a legitimate taxi rather than a *gypsy* cab (which may charge higher fares because it is not metered). The real taxis are black with horizontal red bands or white with diagonal red bands. You can either hail one in the street (a green light on the roof means it's available) or pick one up where they're lined up (usually outside hotels).

Legitimate taxis charge 180 ptas. ($1.20) plus 50 or 75 ptas. (33 cents or 50 cents) per kilometer. The charge for suitcases is 50 ptas. (33 cents) each. A surcharge of 150 ptas. ($1) applies when you take a taxi at night, on Sundays and holidays, or from a train station. The driver adds a surcharge of 350 ptas. ($2.35) on trips to the airport. Drivers are allowed to double the fare on the meter for trips outside the city limits. To call a taxi, dial ☎ **91-447-5180,** 91-547-8200, or 91-371-2191.

Discovering Madrid: What You Need to Know

This section provides information that you'll need for the basic necessities of getting the most out of your money, as well as what you'll need in an emergency or if you get stuck.

The local dough

The peseta (ptas.) is the unit of currency in Spain. Although the exchange rate may vary a little, $1 equals about 150 ptas.; or 100 ptas. is worth about 66 cents. Spanish coins come in denominations of 1, 5, 25, 50, 100, 200, and 500 pesetas. Bills are available in denominations of 500, 1,000, 5,000, and 10,000 pesetas.

Where to get info after you arrive

The **tourism office** in Madrid (☎ **91-366-5477** or 91-540-4010, or 010 within Madrid; Internet: www.munimadrid.es) is at Plaza Mayor 3. The office is open Monday to Friday 10:00 a.m. to 8:00 p.m. and Saturday 10:00 a.m. to noon.

Small tourism offices are also located in **Chamartín** train station (☎ **91-315-9976**) and at the airport (☎ **91-305-8656**).

Enjoy Madrid, a monthly magazine published in English by the tourism office, contains good information, but the office's events guide — *En Madrid* — isn't nearly as complete as the inexpensive *Guia del Ocio,* which you can pick up at newsstands.

Where to go in a pinch

Purse-snatchers and pickpockets are probably the worst criminals you'll find in Madrid, but they are crafty — often working in groups to separate you from your wallet. Even locking your car will not deter an experienced purse-snatcher. So take precautions: Carry only the money you will need until you get back to your hotel, and be alert when riding the Metro. But if something should go wrong and you find yourself in a bind, here are some resources you can turn to:

- ✔ **Embassy:** The U.S. Embassy is located at Calle Serrano 75 (☎ **91-577-4000**).

- ✔ **Emergency:** You can dial ☎ **112** in case of any kind of emergency. To reach the police, call ☎ **091.** Dial ☎ **092** or 91-588-4400 for an ambulance. To report a fire, dial ☎ **080.**

- ✔ **Transit Information:** Call ☎ **91-401-9900** or 91-580-1980 for bus info. You can get train information by calling ☎ **91-328-9020** or logging on to www.renfe.es. Dial ☎ **91-305-8343** for flight information.

- ✔ **Doctors/Hospitals:** You can get a list of English-speaking doctors and dentists from the U.S. Embassy (☎ **91-577-4000**) or by dialing ☎ **061.** For emergency care, there are 24-hour first aid stations in each sector of town, including at Calle Navas de Tolosa (☎ **91-521-0025**). You can also go to the Hospital La Paz, Castellana 261 (☎ **91-734-2600**), or the Hospital 12 de Octubre, Carretera de Andalucía (☎ **91-390-8000**).

- ✔ **Pharmacies:** You should not have any trouble finding a late-night pharmacy. A list of area *farmacias* (pharmacies) that stay open late is posted on every pharmacy. You can also call ☎ **098.**

Staying in touch

Whether you want to keep up with your favorite sports team on the Internet or check in with your friends or co-workers back home, Madrid offers many ways to meet your communication needs.

- ✔ **American Express:** Madrid has two American Express offices. One (☎ **91-322-5500**) is across from the Palace Hotel at Plaza de las Cortés 2. You can find the other office at Calle Francisco Gervás 10 (☎ **91-572-0320**). The offices keep the same hours: Monday to Friday 9:00 a.m. to 5:30 p.m.; and Saturday 9:00 a.m. to noon.

✔ **Internet Access and Cyber Cafes: Cybermad,** C. Atocha 117 (☎ 91-420-0008; Internet: www.geocities.com/cyberlaser1), has ISDN access and is open Monday to Saturday 11:00 a.m. to 11:00 p.m. Prices are 250 ptas. ($1.65) per half hour or 400 ptas. ($2.65) per hour Monday to Thursday, 300 ptas. ($2) per half hour or 500 ptas. ($3.35) per hour Friday and Saturday.

Gopher-Web (www.gopher-web.com) has two locations, at Abdón Terradas 3 (☎ 91-455-0127), and C. Bermudez 66 (☎ 91-399-3439). Both have ISDN access, are open daily 7:30 a.m. to midnight, and charge 700 ptas. ($4.65) per hour.

Vortex Madrid, C. Ave Maria 20 (☎ 91-506-0571; Internet: www.geocities.com/mfbodoque/vortexmadrid.html), is open daily from 10:00 a.m. to midnight, charges 500 ptas. ($3.35) per hour, and puts on shows of local artists.

✔ **Mail:** The main post office is in the stately Palacio de Comunicaciones on Plaza de Cibeles (☎ 91-537-6494). It is open Monday to Friday 8:30 a.m. to 9:30 p.m.; Saturday 9:30 a.m. to 9:30 p.m.; and Sunday 8:30 a.m. to 2:00 p.m.

✔ **Telephone:** Local phone calls cost at least 15 ptas. (10 cents) in Madrid. To use a coin-operated phone, put your coins in the rack at the top of the phone, and they'll roll in as needed to pay for the call. Some phones only accept phone cards, called *tarjeta telefónica,* which you can buy at tobacco shops and post offices. They come in denominations of 1,000 ptas. ($6.65) and 2,000 ptas. ($13.30).

The country code for Spain is **34.** The "91" you see in front of many numbers used to be Madrid's separate city code but is now part of the full number, which means you must always dial it, even if you are calling within the city. If you are calling from the United States, dial **011-34** and then the number.

To use a calling card or call collect, dial **AT&T** (☎ **900-990-011**), **MCI** (☎ **900-990-014**), or **Sprint** (☎ **900-990-013**). To call the United States direct from Spain, dial 07, wait for the dial tone, then dial as you would to place a long-distance call in the States (dial 1, followed by the area code and phone number). Dial ☎ **003** for local directory assistance or ☎ **009** for national directory assistance.

Touring Madrid by Neighborhood

Thanks to Madrid's many major *plazas* (squares) and the splendid boulevards linking them, you can quickly master the city's layout. The most significant plazas are shown on the map in this chapter, but I will describe some of the most important.

Plaza del Sol marks the very center of Madrid (and all of Spain, for that matter; all distances within the country are measured from a 0-kilometer mark in the plaza's southwest corner). The nearby **Plaza**

Accommodations, Dining & Attractions in Madrid

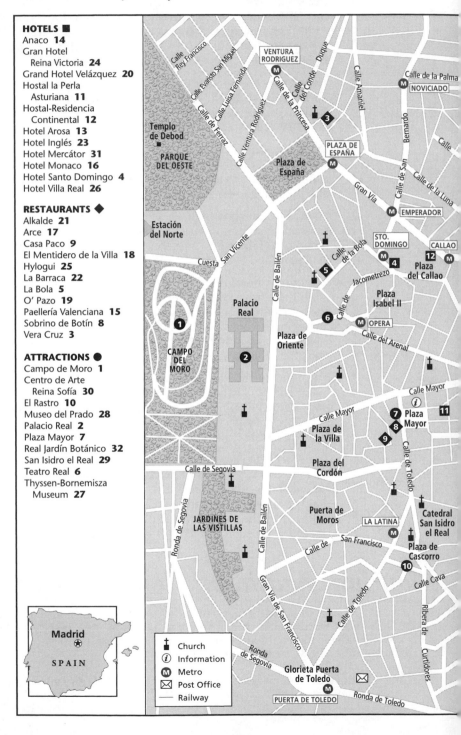

HOTELS ■
Anaco **14**
Gran Hotel
  Reina Victoria **24**
Grand Hotel Velázquez **20**
Hostal la Perla
  Asturiana **11**
Hostal-Residencia
  Continental **12**
Hotel Arosa **13**
Hotel Inglés **23**
Hotel Mercátor **31**
Hotel Monaco **16**
Hotel Santo Domingo **4**
Hotel Villa Real **26**

RESTAURANTS ◆
Alkalde **21**
Arce **17**
Casa Paco **9**
El Mentidero de la Villa **18**
Hylogui **25**
La Barraca **22**
La Bola **5**
O' Pazo **19**
Paellería Valenciana **15**
Sobrino de Botín **8**
Vera Cruz **3**

ATTRACTIONS ●
Campo de Moro **1**
Centro de Arte
  Reina Sofía **30**
El Rastro **10**
Museo del Prado **28**
Palacio Real **2**
Plaza Mayor **7**
Real Jardín Botánico **32**
San Isidro el Real **29**
Teatro Real **6**
Thyssen-Bornemisza
  Museum **27**

Madrid
⊛
SPAIN

✝ Church
ⓘ Information
Ⓜ Metro
✉ Post Office
— Railway

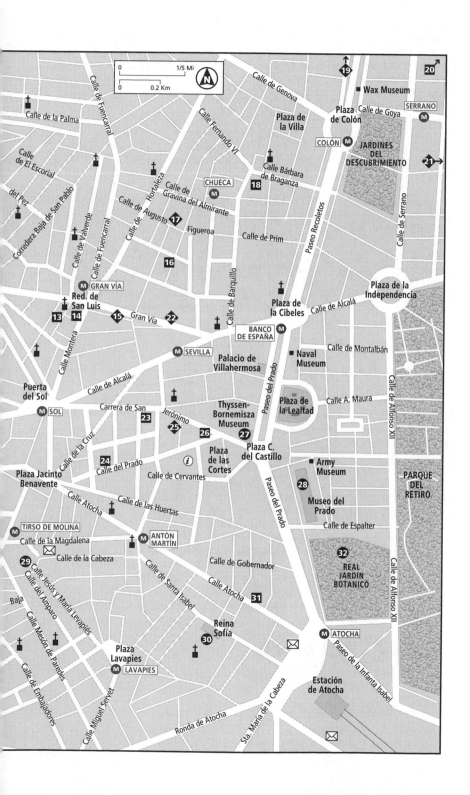

Calle de Genova

0   1/5 Mi
0   0.2 Km
N

Calle de la Palma

Calle de Fuencarral

Calle de El Escorial

del Pez

Corredera Baja de San Pablo

Calle de Valverde

Calle de Fuencarral

M GRAN VÍA

Red. de
San Luis

13 **14**   **15** Gran Vía **22**

Calle Montera

M SOL

Puerta
del Sol

Calle de la Cruz

Carrera de San

Calle de Alcalá

M SEVILLA

23 Jerónimo

25

24 Calle del Prado

Plaza Jacinto
Benavente

Calle de Cervantes

Calle Atocha

Calle de las Huertas

M TIRSO DE MOLINA

Calle de la Magdalena

29 Calle de la Cabeza

Calle Jesús y María

Calle del Amparo

Baja

Calle Mesón de Paredes

Calle de Embajadores

Plaza
Lavapies

M LAVAPIES

Calle Miguel Servet

Calle Fernando VI

Plaza de
la Villa

CHUECA
M

Calle Bárbara
de Braganza

18

Hortaleza

Calle de
Gravina

Calle de Augusto

17

Figueroa

16

Calle del Almirante

Calle de Prim

Calle de Barquillo

Plaza de
la Cibeles

BANCO
DE ESPAÑA M

Palacio de
Villahermosa

Thyssen-
Bornemisza
Museum

26

Plaza
de las
Cortes

(i)

ANTÓN
MARTÍN M

Calle de Gobernador

Calle de Santa Isabel

Calle Atocha

31

Reina
Sofía

30

Paseo Recoletos

Wax Museum

Plaza
de Colón

Calle de Goya

SERRANO
M

COLÓN M

JARDINES
DEL
DESCUBRIMIENTO

Calle de Serrano

Plaza de la
Independencia

Calle de Alcalá

Naval
Museum

Calle de Montalbán

Paseo del Prado

Plaza de
la Lealtad

Calle A. Maura

Plaza C.
del Castillo

27

28

Army
Museum

Museo del
Prado

Calle de Espalter

Paseo del Prado

32

REAL
JARDÍN
BOTÁNICO

Calle de Alfonso XII

M ATOCHA

Paseo de la Infanta Isabel

Estación
de Atocha

Sta. María de la Cabeza

Ronda de Atocha

PARQUE
DEL
RETIRO

19

20

21

Mayor is more scenic, flanked as it is by cafes and colonnades; in the center sits an equestrian statue of Felipe III (by Italian mannerist Giambologna and his student Pietro Tacca). These two plazas constitute the heart of **Old Madrid,** an area filled with authentic Spanish restaurants and nightlife hot spots. Madrid's seventeenth-century district lies south of Plaza del Sol, and you can find pedestrian shopping streets north of the plaza.

The wide, modern **Plaza de España** marks the northwest corner of the city. Calle de Bailén runs south from there, bordering the **Palacio Real** (royal palace) and marking the city's western edge. Madrid's main boulevard, Gran Vía, zigzags from Plaza de España across the northern Old City. Department stores, cafes, movie theaters, and office buildings line the grand boulevard. North of it are the **Malasaña** and **Chueca** districts; they are rundown areas but have nonetheless retained their status as trendy nightlife zones.

Old Madrid's east side is bordered by the tree-planted Paseo del Prado, which runs from north to south from **Plaza de la Cibeles** through **Plaza C. del Castillo** to the Atocha train station square. It's lined with hotels, cafes, and the city's major museums. The vast **Retiro Park,** center of the up-and-coming **Retiro** neighborhood, lies on the east side of the Paseo.

Staying in Madrid

Madrid offers three main types of sleeping accommodations: regular hotels, which can be anything from deluxe, elegant turn-of-the-century establishments to modern, moderately priced inns; *hostales,* bare-bones businesses where travelers usually get good value for their money; and *pensiones,* even simpler, less-expensive boarding houses, often requiring half or full *board* (meals taken on premises).

Many hotels are scattered along the Gran Vía, which is not a good place to be walking after dark, and near Atocha Station. The Old City also has a good selection of accommodations ringing Madrid's central squares, such as Plaza Mayor and Puerta del Sol. These areas attract their share of pickpockets because they are popular travel destinations; but due to their proximity to prime dining and sightseeing, they're also among the most exciting places to be in Madrid.

The tourism office maintains a hotel info Tourist Line at ☎ 901-300-600.

Madrid's top hotels

Anaco

$$ Near the Gran Vía

Located on a tree-shaded plaza near a major crossroads, this budget-friendly hotel features built-in furnishings in its clean, contemporary rooms. The Anaco gets the nod over the Continental (listing follows) because of its air conditioning and nicer rooms. The choicest, largest rooms (with terraces) are on the top floor. But because they're renovating from the ground up, you may prefer the much nicer rooms on the lower levels — which have been overhauled with brand-new furnishings and beds and formidable double-glazed windows (these rooms are church-mouse quiet) and rearranged to open up more space. The renovation had advanced to the third floor in 1999 and should be finished by 2001. The connected *tapas* bar is open until 3:00 a.m.

Tres Cruces 3 (just down from the Metro stop). ☎ *91-522-4604. Fax: 91-531-6484. Metro: Gran Vía. Rates: 9,950–11,880 ptas. ($66.35–$79.20) double. AE, DC, MC, V.*

Gran Hotel Reina Victoria

$$$$ **Near the Puerta del Sol**

The bullfighting stars and discriminating travelers that stay here reveal this historic monument to be one of Madrid's top hotels. An abundance of early twentieth-century flavor is in evidence, and rooms are sound-proofed against the sounds of this bustling neighborhood. And if you want to relax after a busy day, there's even a private plaza.

Plaza Santa Ana 14 (on the Calle del Prado). ☎ *91-531-4500. Fax: 91-522-0307. Metro: Tirso de Molina or Puerta del Sol. Rates: From 30,000 ptas. ($200) double. AE, DC, MC, V.*

Hostal-Residencia Continental

$ **On the Gran Vía**

This *hostal,* in a building brimming with other cheap accommodations, is the finest — clean, updated, and fairly comfy. Remember, basic is still the key word in this price range. Rooms are large, if institutional, and all have a TV, phone, and bath — but no air conditioning. It's right on the busy plaza, though — convenient for the Metro, but the road noise is pretty bad. If you want to save even more, you can try one of the cheaper, less well-kept *hostales* and pensiones at this address.

Gran Vía 44 (just up from the Metro stop). ☎ *91-521-4640. Fax: 91-521-4649. Internet:* www.hostalcontinental.com. *Metro: Callao. Rates: 5,800 ptas. ($38.65) double. AE, MC, V.*

Hotel Inglés

$$ **Near the Puerta del Sol**

If you like to mix food and fun, this may be the place for you. *Tavernas* and *tascas* (see "Dining in Madrid") line the street, and the lobby TV is a magnet for soccer fans. Even though the rooms are boringly contemporary, all are in good condition and many feature sitting areas.

Calle Echegaray 8 (between Carrera de San Jerónimo and Calle del Prado). ☎ *91-429-6551. Fax: 91-420-2423. Metro: Puerta del Sol or Sevilla. Rates: 12,000–15,500 ptas. ($80–$103.35) double. AE, DC, MC, V.*

Hotel Mercátor

$$ Near Atocha Station

This hotel is smack in the middle of an art-lover's paradise, just a short walk to both the Prado and Reina Sofía museums. The furnishings in these modern rooms vary considerably (the best include armchairs and desks), so ask to see several rooms before you sign in. Only seven rooms have air conditioning, so it's best to reserve ahead of time in the summer.

Calle Atocha 123 (one and a half blocks up from Atocha Station). ☎ 91-429-0500. Fax: 91-369-1252. Metro: Atocha or Antón Martín. Rates: 12,700 ptas. ($84.65) double. AE, DC, MC, V.

Hotel Villa Real

$$$$ On Plaza de las Cortés

This almost-10-year-old hotel is one of Madrid's poshest accommodations. It features an unusual mix of neoclassical, modern, and Aztec design, with lots of nice extras — such as satellite TV, modem/fax lines, and built-in mahogany furnishings. Even "standard" rooms, though not large, are split-level with small sitting areas and marble baths with two sinks. The larger rooms feature a small terrace and two bathrooms (one with Jacuzzi). The central location of this comfortably plush hotel is excellent, and the staff is very helpful. Conference rooms are decorated with Greek vases and ancient Roman mosaics (the largest such private collection in world).

Plaza del las Cortés 10 (where the Carrera de San Jerónimo meets Calle del Prado, very near the Paseo del Prado). ☎ 91-420-3767. Fax: 91-420-2547. Internet: www.derbyhotels.es. Metro: Antón Martín. Rates: 22,500–41,600 ptas. ($150–$277.35) double. AE, DC, MC, V.

Madrid's runner-up accommodations

Grand Hotel Velázquez

$$$ A classy Retiro-area hotel with Art Deco charm and largish rooms in a mainly residential neighborhood. *Calle de Velázquez 62 (☎ 91-575-2800; Fax: 91-575-2809).*

Hostal la Perla Asturiana

$ A clean, simple, family-run inn just two blocks from the Puerta del Sol with fantastically low prices. *Plaza de Santa Cruz 3 (☎ 91-366-4600; Fax: 91-366-4608).*

Hotel Arosa

$$$ About as central as you can get, offering standardized comforts and modern art prints on the walls. Try to get one of the trapezoid-shaped corner rooms, where the bed is flanked by a pair of Ionic columns. *Calle Salud 21, at the Gran Via (☎ 91-532-1600; Fax 91-531-3127).*

Hotel Monaco

$$ A fine and proper hotel today, but it retains a bit of the faux luxurious decor that hearkens back to its tenure (from 1890 to the 1950s) as a high-class brothel. Nice digs, plus a good story to put on your postcards home ("Hey, guess where I'm staying . . ."). *Calle Barbieri 5 (☎ 91-522-4630; Fax: 91-521-1601).*

Hotel Santo Domingo

$$ Geared toward business travelers, but its location (just two minutes from Plaza de España), the standardized amenities, and the fifth-floor rooms with balconies overlooking Madrid make it an excellent choice for all — especially at the lower weekend rates. *Plaza Santo Domingo 13 (☎ 91-547-9800; Fax: 91-547-5995).*

Dining in Madrid

The Basque region in the north of Spain is home to the country's best and most innovative cooking, hands down. This ever-changing cuisine is very sophisticated, particularly the Basque codfish recipes and incomparable baby eel dishes. Restaurants in Madrid, however, feature food from all Spain's regions, including two local styles of cuisine called *Madrileños* and *Castillian.* Spain's trademark dish is *paella,* a Mediterranean medley of seafood and rice usually eaten for lunch. On the heartier side of the menu are the roast meats, especially *cordero* (lamb) and *cochinillo* (suckling pig). Spain is the place to be if you like pork; at times it seems like you can't walk into a restaurant without tripping over some *chorizo* sausage and salty *jamón serrano* ham. The king of carnivorous pleasures in Madrid is *cocido madrileño,* a hearty stew of beef, chicken, pig's feet, sausage, garbanzo beans, veggies, pasta, and bread dumplings all cooked together for a long time.

Though Madrid is landlocked, a fleet of trucks and airplanes keeps the capital city well stocked with excellent fresh fish. But ironically, one of Madrid's most popular seafood dishes is *bacalao* — dried salt cod that is softened and served either by itself or *al ajoarriero* (flaked and stewed with tomatoes, potatoes, garlic, and peppers). While you're eating dinner, try to save some room for *flan,* a staple dessert in Spain that many say is even better than a similar French treat, crème caramel. Table wine is usually excellent in and around Madrid, especially the Castillian Valdepeñas and Rioja varieties. My favorite Spanish beverage is *sangria,* a punch made by filling a container with wine, ice, and pieces of fruit. And one of the greatest alcoholic treats in Europe is the sweet, powerful wine from the Spanish city Jerez — we call it sherry in English.

Just thinking about a Spanish breakfast gives me cavities. The traditional morning meal consists of thick hot chocolate and *churros. Churros* are made by forming a bready batter into long sticks, and then deep frying them until a crisp crust forms on the outside. These chewy, hot morsels are then covered with oil and sugar. *Churros* are one of the world's heavenly delights, but your doctor may advise you to stick to coffee or tea and rolls for breakfast.

Madrileños maintain a different eating schedule than the rest of the Continent. They've managed to ward off the infiltration into Europe of the hectic, Americanized daily schedule. Many still find time to eat their biggest meal between 1:00 and 4:00 p.m. After a siesta, at about 5:00 p.m. they go out to *paseo* — an evening stroll to see and be seen and, most importantly, to eat *tapas*.

Tapas are snacks of different kinds eaten in small portions at bars called *tascas*. (The word *tapas* is Spanish for "lid"; the morsels got their name because pieces of bread or slices of ham were once used to keep flies out of wine glasses.) Today, Spaniards turn out by the thousands in the afternoons and evenings to *tapeo* — walk from *tasca* to *tasca*, drink, chat, and chomp up those delicious *tapas*. (I'll mention some of the better *tascas* and describe some typical *tapas* in "More cool things to see and do in Madrid.")

Tasca-hopping is important because it keeps you from getting too hungry before dinnertime, which is about 10:00 p.m. Some restaurants that try to attract travelers serve dinner as early as 8:00 p.m., but few Spaniards would even think of eating that early. Most restaurants — in particular the better and more authentic ones — don't even open their doors until 9:00 or 9:30 p.m. This late supper is usually a light meal.

If you are interested in gathering food for a picnic, visit **Mallorca** (☎ 91-431-9900), at Velázquez 59, for deluxe pickings; **Rodilla** (☎ 91-522-5701), at Preciados 25, for carry-out sandwiches, pastries, and *tapas;* and the **Mercado de San Miguel,** on Plaza San Miguel, for produce.

Madrid's top restaurants

Alkalde

$$$ In Retiro BASQUE/INTERNATIONAL

This place feels less like the fine metropolitan restaurant it is than a Basque country inn, with its stony cellar dining rooms and ham hocks hanging from wood-beamed ceilings upstairs. The combination of incredible cookery and great atmosphere is unbeatable. Be sure to try the *cigalas* (crayfish) and trout Alkalde.

Jorge Juan 10 (off Calle de Serrano, behind the archaeological museum). ☎ 91-567-3359. Reservations required. Metro: Serrano or Retiro. Main courses: 1,650–3,050 ptas. ($11–$20.35); fixed-price menus from 4,700 ptas. ($31.35). AE, DC, MC, V. Open: Lunch and dinner daily. Closed Sat and Sun, July–Aug.

Arce

$$$$ Near the Gran Vía BASQUE

You can find some of Madrid's best, most inventive Basque cuisine here. To make sure that their food is of top quality, the chefs/owners stick to tried-and-true combinations of fresh ingredients. After settling in to the comfy dining room, be sure to try the boletus mushroom casserole or pheasant with seasonal spices.

Augusteo Figueroa 32 (between Calle de Pelayo and Calle de Barbieri). ☎ *91-522-5913. Reservations recommended. Metro: Colón. Main courses: 2,500–3,500 ptas. ($16.65–$23.35); fixed-price menu 6,500 ptas. ($43.35). AE, DC, MC, V. Open: Lunch Mon–Fri, dinner daily. Closed the week before Easter and Aug 15–31.*

Hylogui

$ Near the Puerta del Sol   SPANISH

This is the place for diners who like simplicity and goodness in a restaurant. Hylogui is legendary for serving hearty, tasty, home-style meals in its huge dining rooms at great prices. The house specialty — roast lamb — is delicious, and the potato-*chorizo* stew is a tasty starter. Save room for the *flan;* it is a real treat.

Ventura de la Vega 3 (just off Carrera de San Jerónimo). ☎ *91-429-7357. Reservations recommended. Metro: Sevilla. Main courses: 750–2,750 ptas. ($5–$18.35); fixed-price menu 1,500 ptas. ($10). AE, MC, V. Open: Lunch daily, dinner Mon–Sat.*

La Barraca

$$ Near the Gran Vía   VALENCIAN

This Valencian country inn — just off the bustling Gran Via — has two floors of dining rooms filled with paintings, ceramics, and other Spanish bric-a-brac. The house specialties include *paella à la Barraca* (made here with pork and chicken) and brochette of angler fish and prawns.

Reina 29 (between Calle de Alcalá and Calle Clavel, just off the Gran Vía). ☎ *91-532-7154. Internet:* www.interocio.es/labarraca. *Reservations recommended. Metro: Gran Vía or Sevilla. Main courses: 1,700–3,000 ptas. ($11.35–$20); fixed-price menu 3,500 ptas. ($23.35). AE, DC, MC, V. Open: Lunch and dinner daily.*

La Bola

$$ Between Ópera and Plaza de España   MADRILEÑA

This 1870s tavern offers an escape to Old Madrid — nothing has changed since the days when Ava Gardner and Ernest Hemingway were frequent customers. The lobster cocktail makes a good starter, but the thing to do here is order the delicious *cocido madrileño.*

Calle del la Bola (just north of the Ópera). ☎ *91-547-6930. Reservations required. Metro: Santo Domingo or Ópera. Main courses: 1,400–3,000 ptas. ($9.35–$20); fixed-price menu 2,125 ptas. ($14.15). No credit cards. Open: Lunch Mon–Sat, dinner daily.*

Sobrino de Botín

$$$ Near Plaza Mayor   SEGOVIAN/SPANISH

The Guinness Book of World Records says Botín is the oldest continuously operating restaurant in the world, and it doesn't seem to have changed a bit since it opened in 1725. It has an eighteenth-century tile oven in its open kitchen, as well as hanging copper pots and painted plates on the walls. You can still order roast suckling pig, the house specialty that Hemingway's heroes ate in the final scene of *The Sun Also Rises*. A restaurant doesn't stay in business 275 years without being very popular, so expect the place to be busy.

Calle de Cuchilleros 17 (off Calle de Toledo, a few steps down from Plaza Mayor). ☎ *91-366-4217. Internet:* www.botin.net. *Reservations required. Metro: La Latina or Ópera. Main courses: 880–3,900 ptas. ($5.85–$26). Fixed-price menu: 4,260 ptas. ($28.40). AE, DC, MC, V. Open: Lunch and dinner daily.*

Madrid's runner-up restaurants

Casa Paco

$$-$$$ The Madrid version of a classy barbecue, with mouth-watering steaks and a tapas bar out front to keep you company while you wait for a table. *Plaza Puerta Cerrada 11, just off Plaza Mayor (*☎ *91-366-3166).*

O'Pazo

$$$$ This place may be a bit north of the action, but you won't find Galacian food done any better in Spain's capital — the fish is flown in daily from the country's Galacian coast. Try the zarzuela, a seafood casserole. *Calle Reina Maerceds 20, in Chamartín (*☎ *91-553-2333).*

Paellería Valenciana

$ This restaurant does some of the best Valencian paellas in town, but only at lunch and only if you phone ahead with your order. The set-price menus for 1,250–1,600 ptas. ($8.35–$10.65) come with wine and are an excellent value. *Caballero de Gracia 12 (*☎ *91-531-1785).*

El Mentidero de la Villa

$$ A delicious study in multiculturalism, a sort of Spain-meets-Japan-in-France experience. You never know what the kitchen might turn out, but it's bound to be flavorful and good. *Santo Tomé 6 (*☎ *91-308-1285).*

Vera Cruz

$ Vera Cruz has been satisfying budget-conscious diners with hearty, filling dishes for years. The cocido (stew) is good, and the menú del dia (daily menu) is a steal at 950 ptas. ($6.35). *San Leonardo 5 (*☎ *91-547-1150).*

Exploring Madrid

Madrid is an art-lover's paradise for many reasons, and here's another one: The "Paseo del Arte" combination admission ticket to the Prado, Reina Sofia, and Thyssen-Bornemisza costs 1,275 ptas. ($8.50) — that's a 25 percent savings — and is available at any of the museums.

Madrid's top sights

Museo del Prado

Some experts consider the Prado to be the second-best art museum in Europe (after the Louvre). More than 7,000 works are on display, but don't try to see them all in one day. Pace yourself by spending most of one day and at least half of another day here. Even if you're in Spain just for a day, try to visit for at least three hours.

The lineup of masterpieces ranges from Fra' Angelico's *Annunciation* (1430) and El Greco's eerily lit *Adoration of the Shepherds* (1614) to José de Ribera's *The Martyrdom of St. Philip* (1630) and Rubens' fleshy *Three Graces* (1739). The museum is brimming with many more works by Spanish, Italian, Dutch, Flemish, and French painters. You can buy informative little guides describing nearby paintings from vending machines throughout the museum for 100 ptas. (66 cents).

The supreme masterpiece of Spanish painting, Velázquez's *Las Meninas* (The Ladies-in-Waiting), represents the Prado better than any other work. It depicts a king (Felipe IV) and queen having their picture painted — the painting is not the portrait itself, but rather the royals'-eye view of Velázquez as he's painting their portrait. A mirror in the background reflects the image of the king and queen. Velázquez's masterful perspective is flawless; the scene is so real and the gazes so intense, you get the eerie feeling that their Royal Highnesses must be standing right next to you.

At the Prado you can also see the three-paneled painting *The Garden of Earthly Delights,* painted by Hieronymus Bosch ("El Bosco" to the Spanish) in 1516. It's a strange panorama of tiny nude figures, some half human/half bug, engaging in the oddest of activities. This early surreal vision of heaven and hell rivals anything dreamed up by Salvador Dalí or William Burroughs.

The Prado also displays works by Spanish painter Francisco Jose de Goya, who — after starting out as a tapestry designer — began painting playful, joyful scenes such as *Blind Man's Bluff* in the late eighteenth century. By 1800, he pushed the limits of nudity in art at that time by painting both a *Naked Maja* and a *Clothed Maja*. Goya ended his long career with a very dark expressionistic series called The Black Paintings, the most disturbing and famous of which is *Saturn Devouring One of His Sons* (1823).

Paseo del Prado. ☎ *91-330-2800. Metro: Banco de España or Atocha. Bus: 10, 14, 27, 34, 37, 45. Open: Tues–Sat 9:00 a.m.–7:00 p.m., Sun 9:00 a.m.–2:00 p.m. Admission: 500 ptas. ($3.35) adults, 250 ptas. ($1.65) students, free under 18 and over 65; free to all on Sat after 2:30 p.m. and on Sun.*

Centro de Arte Reina Sofía

This is Madrid's leading modern art museum, and it is filled with works from Spain's twentieth-century greats, such as Picasso, Miró, Dalí, and Gris. Picasso's *Guernica* (1937) overshadows them all; this massive black-and-white commentary on the horrors of war is the most moving, eloquent work in the collection. Picasso's painting is named after a Basque religious center. During Spain's bloody Civil War (1936 to 1939), German bombers working for the forces of fascist dictator Francisco Franco leveled the town, and 1,645 civilians died. The painting is surrounded by studies Picasso made before starting the main work.

Guernica demands your undivided attention, so be sure to allot a solid hour or two in your schedule to visit the gallery.

Calle de Santa Isabel 52 (parallel to Calle Atocha, three blocks from the station). ☎ *91-467-5062. Metro: Atocha. Bus: 6, 10, 14, 18, 19, 26, 27, 32, 34, 36, 37, 41, 45, 46, 55, 57, 59, 68, 86, 119, C. Open: Mon and Wed–Sat 10:00 a.m.–9:00 p.m., Sun 10:00 a.m.–2:30 p.m. Admission: 500 ptas. ($3.35) adults, 250 ptas. ($1.65) students, free under 18 and over 65; free to all on Sat after 2:30 p.m. and on Sun.*

Thyssen-Bornemisza Museum

Straight across the street from the Prado you can find the newest addition to Madrid's art scene. The museum offers a unique survey of European art from the thirteenth century up to the 1960s. It opened in late 1992 to hold a large collection that had outgrown its original home in Switzerland. How large a collection? This list of artists ought to give you some idea: Ghirlandaio, Caravaggio, Ribera, Bernini, Tintoretto, Memling, Rembrandt, Ruben, El Greco, Dürer, Velázquez, Goya, Manet, Monet, Degas, Picasso, Rodin, Homer, Frederick Church, Chagall, O'Keeffe, Hopper, Dalí, Mondrian, de Kooning, and Lucien Freud. You could easily spend one to three hours here.

Paseo del Prado 8. ☎ *91-369-0151. Internet:* www.museotyssen.org. *Metro: Banco de España. Bus: 1, 2, 5, 9, 10, 14, 15, 20, 27, 34, 37, 45, 51, 52, 53, 74, 146, 150. Open: Tues–Sun 10:00 a.m.–7:00 p.m. Admission: 700 ptas. ($4.65) adults, 400 ptas. ($2.65) students and seniors, free under 12.*

Palacio Real (Royal Palace)

Some of the palace's 2,000 rooms are closed to the public because the building is still used for official occasions (even though the royal family now lives outside town).

Construction of the palace began after Madrid's Alcazar fortress-palace burned down in 1734. It's decorated in the baroque and rococo styles preferred by the Bourbon monarchs (especially Carlos II and IV). The palace's lavish air of muted dark blues, burgundies, shiny gold, and gleaming brass surrounds rich marbles, sumptuous tapestries, gilded stuccoes, frescoes, and chandeliers. In the aptly named Porcelain Room, the walls are sheathed in green-and-white ceramics from the royal Buen Retiro factory.

Palace tours last 50 minutes plus a 10- to 20-minute wait, during which you can check out the historical Pharmacy. You can breeze through the building on your own in half an hour. During those rare moments when I reach Museum Overload — when even palatial background art starts getting to me — I like to relax by wandering the gravel paths through the long, green slope of the palace's Campo del Moro gardens, with its fountains and ponds stocked with white and black swans.

Plaza de Oriente, Calle de Bailén 2. ☎ *91-454-8700 or 91-542-0059. Metro: Ópera or Plaza de España. Open: Mon–Sat 9:00 a.m.–6:00 p.m., Sun 9:00 a.m.–3:00 p.m. (Oct–Mar, Mon–Fri 9:30 a.m.–5:00 p.m., Sun 9:00 a.m.–2:00 p.m.). Admission: With guided tour 950 ptas. ($6.35) everyone; without tour 850 ptas. ($5.65), or 350 ptas. ($2.35) students and ages 5–16.*

Museo Lázaro Galdiano

Although the Museo Lázaro Galdiano does not rank among Madrid's elite museums, it is among the best in the second tier of the city's art displays. It is still set up as a private gallery in the nineteenth-century mansion of its founder, Señor Lázaro Galdiano, who collected large amounts of both decorative and fine arts. Of the former, the museum includes crystal and enamels from Limoges, royal daggers and swords, pocket watches (take a look at the cross-shaped timepiece that belonged to Carlos V), medieval armor, and ancient Roman bronzes.

The museum features paintings by El Greco, Velázquez, Goya, Bosch, and Ribera, along with Brits such as Constable, Reynolds, and Gainsborough and Italian rococo master Tiepolo. Unfortunately, you'll have to know your artists pretty well because little more than half the works are labelled. The museum is worth a half hour of your time, unless you detest portraits, which make up the majority of the collection.

Serrano 122. ☎ *91-561-6084. Metro: Núñez de Balboa or Avienda de América. Bus: 9, 16, 19, 51, 89. Open: Tues–Sun 10:00 a.m.–2:00 p.m.; closed Aug. Admission: 500 ptas. ($3.35) adults, 250 ptas. ($1.65) students, free under 16; free to all on Sat.*

Museo de América (Museum of the Americas)

Columbus may have been Italian, but Spain had a lot to do with his voyage to the New World. Spanish Queen Isabella and her husband, Ferdinand, bankrolled his little excursion to find a sea passage to India. Then, when the Spaniards learned that gold, silver, and lots of free land and cheap labor (Indian slaves) were there for the taking in Columbus' New World, explorers, conquistadors, and settlers went over in droves. Ignoring the protests of native inhabitants, they claimed the land for God and for Spain and quickly conquered and colonized most of Central and South America (as well as what is today Florida, Texas, the American Southwest, and California).

Spain's colonial conquests brought vast treasures into royal and private collections. This museum preserves some of what wasn't melted down to make gold bricks and bouillon. It's one of the world's most remarkable collections of Native American artifacts, treasures, textiles, parchments, inscriptions, and jewelry from prehistoric times to the present. Spend an hour or two learning more about the ancient cultures of your own home continent.

Avienda de los Reyes Catolicos 6. ☎ *91-549-2641. Metro: Moncloa. Open: Tues–Sat 10:00 a.m.–3:00 p.m., Sun 10:00 a.m.–2:30 p.m. Admission: 500 ptas. ($3.35) adults, 250 ptas. ($1.65) children; free to all on Sun.*

More cool things to see and do in Madrid

From flea markets to bullfights to tapas bars and flamenco shows, Madrid offers a wealth of diversions to keep you entertained day and night.

✔ **Sift Through the Hidden Treasures of El Rastro's Flea Market.** This busy flea market is one of the biggest and most interesting in Europe. You can find almost anything — antiques, used car parts, paintings, assorted junk, secondhand clothes, and more. Stalls are open Tuesday through Sunday from 9:30 a.m. to 1:30 p.m. and from 5:00 to 8:00 p.m. The best time to go is in the mornings, especially on Sundays. Take the Metro to La Latina; the market fills the streets around Ribera de Curtidores and Plaza Cascorro. Get ready to haggle over prices, and beware of pickpockets.

✔ **See the Spectacle of a Bullfight.** Mixing barbarism with ballet and viewed as something between sport and art form, bullfighting draws the best and brightest young men (and a few women) from all corners of Spain. Bullfighters are the Spanish equivalents of a movie stars or sports heroes, and their fame can be even more fleeting. One misjudgment, one stray into the bull's charge, and their midsections can literally take the bull by the horns.

Their constant proximity to danger explains why matadors take every second in the bullring so seriously. The bullfight is a dance with death that's painstakingly choreographed yet totally unpredictable. If the sight of blood sickens you, please stay away, but the spectacle of the *corridas* (bullfights) offers a uniquely Spanish slice of life.

The main season lasts from early spring to mid-October. **Plaza Monumental de Toros de las Ventas** (☎ **91-356-2200;** Metro: Ventas) is the primary bullring in Madrid (and all of Spain); *corridas* are performed on Sundays and holidays. Seat prices range widely, from 500 to 16,100 ptas. ($3.35 to $107.35), with the cheapest seats being up high and in the sun. Fights start a few hours before sundown, at about 7:00 p.m. in the summer and around 5:00 p.m. in fall and spring.

✔ **Tapeo: Sample Wines and Snacks.** From 5:00 to 8:00 p.m., you can be part of the evening *paseo,* tiding yourself over until your 10:00 p.m. dinner by visiting several tapas bars and snacking on such Spanish specialties as *chorizo* (sausage), *jamón serrano* (salty ham), *tortilla española* (onion and potato omelet wedges), *albondi-gas* (tender meatballs), *calamares fritos* (fried squid), *gambas al la plancha* (grilled shrimp), and *queso manchego* (sheep's cheese). It's cheaper to sit at the bar than to grab a table.

At the **1827 Casa Alberto,** Huertas 18 (☎ 91-429-9356), where the Spanish author Cervantes once lived, snackers are surrounded by bullfighting memorabilia. **Antonio Sanchez,** Mesón de Parades 13 (☎ 91-539-7826), is another *tasca* (tapas bar) loaded with bullring paraphernalia. **Cervecería Alemania,** Plaza de Santa Ana 6 (☎ 91-429-7033), is another Hemingway haunt on a lively little square.

The local minichain jokingly named **Museo del Jamón** (Museum of Ham — slogan: "The tastiest museums in Madrid") serves great tapas, heavy on the pork, in semi-modern crosses between cafes, *tascas,* and butcher shops at Avienda de Córdoba 7 (☎ 91-500-3626), Carrera de San Jerónimo 6 (☎ 91-521-0346), Paseo del Prado 44 (☎ 91-420-2414), Plaza Mayor 7 (☎ 91-531-4550), and Capitán Haya 15 (☎ 91-555-3667).

✔ **Experience the Flamenco Rhythm.** Flamenco is the rhythmic music of suffering, of eroticism, of secret joy. Flamenco evolved from the murky histories of Spain's unwanted classes of Jews and Moors during the Middle Ages, and then was appropriated and interpreted through the gypsy culture of Andalusia. The best fla-menco music and dancing breaks out spontaneously in bars in the wee hours of the morning, when revelers strum guitars, clap their hands, play castanets, and begin moving gracefully to the rhythm.

While lacking in spontaneity, the scheduled flamenco club shows can be just as much of a spectacle. Shows usually start at 10:30 or 11:00 p.m. and last until 2:00 or 3:00 a.m., but many clubs open around 9:00 p.m. to serve dinner before the show. (I suggest eating at a regular restaurant and heading to the club just for the per-formance.) Among the more reliable clubs are **Casa Patas** (☎ 91-369-0496) at Calle Cañizares 10, which costs 1,800 to 2,400 ptas. ($12 to $16) per show, and the slightly less authentic **Café de Chinitas** (☎ 91-547-1502) at Torija 7, which costs about $30 for just the show and a drink.

✔ **Dance the Night Away — Literally.** It may not be the city that never sleeps, but Madrid is the town that parties until sunrise. After a brief *tapeo,* you can dance at a club from about 6:00 to 9:00 p.m. Then you can go eat dinner and return to the clubs around 11:00 p.m. or midnight. The clubs really heat up some-where between 1:00 and 2:00 a.m., and people don't start leaving until the break of dawn. Most clubs have an admission charge of around $10, which includes your first drink.

The most popular nightclubs and discos change faster than a supermodel's wardrobe, but some of the current biggies include **Kathmandu,** Señores de Luzón 3, an Asian fusion disco spinning hip-hop, funk, jungle, and other trendy tunes; the sprawling, any-thing-goes, cross-cultural **Kapital,** Atocha 125; and mainstays the **Art Deco Archy,** Calle Marqués de Riscal 11, and stylish **Joy Madrid,** Arenal 11.

And on Your Left, Palacio Real: Seeing Madrid by Guided Tour

Pullmantours (☎ 91-541-1805), Plaza de Orienta 8, conducts half-day guided bus tours of Madrid. You can get a glimpse of a few major muse-ums on the morning artistic tour, which costs 5,250 ptas. ($35), museum admissions included. Panoramic tours in the morning or after-noon take you past the exteriors of all the sights for 3,000 ptas. ($20). A full-day excursion combining both the artistic and panoramic tours costs 7,400 ptas. ($49.35).

Suggested One-, Two-, and Three-Day Itineraries

If you're the type who'd rather organize your own tours, this section offers some tips for building your own Madrid itineraries.

If you have one day

Begin your day exploring the artistic treasures of the Prado Museum — which should hold you for several hours, at least until lunchtime. Eat a light lunch at the Museo del Jamón on Paseo del Prado before jogging around the corner to pay homage to Picasso's *Guernica* in the Reina Sofia. That and the other modern masters will keep your attention for an hour or more, after which it's time to head back to your hotel for a well-earned *siesta* from all this art.

Make sure you take the time to walk through the Plaza Mayor at the heart of town, perhaps just before setting off on your *tapeo* in the early evening. This stroll through the heart of Old Madrid — from *tapas* bar to *tapas* bar, nibbling and imbibing along the way — should last from around 5:00 to 8:00 p.m. Head back to your hotel to rest up until 9:30 p.m. or so, when you can safely venture out for dinner at Sobrino de Botín.

If you have two days

Spend Day One pretty much as outlined above. Start off Day Two tour-ing the Palacio Royal. Afterward, head to the little Museo Lázaro

Galdiano for a peek at what a private museum once looked like, and then over to the Thyssen-Bornemisza Museum to see what serious money and a penchant for art can grow a private collection into.

If these two days in Madrid represent the full extent of your time in Spain — and if it is the proper season — try to take in a bullfight at 5:00 p.m. If it's not bullfighting season, *tapeo* again this evening. Either way, catch a flamenco show in the later evening (after dinner).

If you will be heading to Spain's Andalusia region at all, skip both the bullfight and the flamenco — you'll find better examples of both down south.

If you have three days

Spend Days One and Two as above, then head off on Day Three for a day trip to Toledo, a commanding large hill town that was once the capital of Spain and also home to that weird Renaissance master El Greco.

Traveling Beyond Madrid

Strange as it may seem, one of the best things to do when you're visiting Madrid is to get out of town. Among the sights in the surrounding area are Toledo, the one-time Spanish capital; the imposing sixteenth-century palace/monastery El Escorial; and Segovia, which features a castle that's like something out of a fairy tale and an incredible cathedral.

Holy Toledo!

Toledo is easily the best day trip from Madrid. The town, and the area surrounding it, is designated as a national landmark, for good reason. Toledo was the capital of Castile until the 1500s, was home to the painter El Greco, and has always been the religious center of Spain — home to the Primate of Spain and one-time host to a thriving Jewish community. You will find Toledo worth the visit for its Gothic cathedral, its Renaissance paintings, and the famous views of the city captured on canvas by many a painter.

If you kick into high gear, you can tour Toledo in just a few hours, making it a long half-day trip from Madrid. You can also spend the whole day there and return to Madrid in the evening. But your best bet is to spend the night in Toledo; that enables you to explore the city at a leisurely pace after the day-tripping crowd left. Don't visit on a Monday, when half the sights are closed.

Getting there

Ten trains make the journey from Madrid's Atocha Station to Toledo every day. The trip takes 60 to 80 minutes one way. When you're in the station just outside Toledo, bus number 5 takes you to Plaza de Zocodover in the heart of the old city (you can find a visitors' information kiosk there).

Pullmantours, in Madrid at Plaza de Orienta 8 (☎ 91-541-1805), runs both half-day (5,650 ptas./$37.65) and full-day (8,700 ptas./$58) jaunts to Toledo. An all-day tour that stops briefly in Toledo before hurrying on to El Escorial and the Valley of the Fallen (a memorial to Spain's Civil War dead) costs 12,000 ptas. ($80).

The Toledo **tourist office** (☎ 925-220-843) is at Puerta de Bisagra, on the north end of town (turn right out of the station, go over the bridge, and walk along the city walls).

Seeing the sights

The **Gothic Cathedral** (☎ 925-222-241) is in the center of Toledo, on Arcos de Palacio. Built from 1226 to 1493, it features a gigantic carved and painted wooden *reredos* (screen) on the high altar, and behind it — illuminated by a skylight — the alabaster and marble baroque Transparente altar. Admission to the church is free, but entry to the treasury — with its 10-foot-high, 500-pound gilded sixteenth-century monstrance (made from gold brought back by Christopher Columbus) — costs 500 ptas. ($3.30). The cathedral is open daily, 10:30 a.m. to 2:00 p.m. and 4:00 to 6:30 p.m.; the treasury is open daily, 10:30 a.m. to 1:00 p.m. and 3:30 to 6:00 p.m.

Although the cathedral contains works by El Greco, fans of his work find that the more important church in town is **Iglesia de Santo Tomé** (☎ 925-210-209), Plaza del Conde 2, Via Santo Tomé. Here the Greek painter's masterpiece, the turbulent *Burial of Count Orgaz* (1586), dominates a tiny chapel. Admission is 150 ptas. ($1), and it's open daily, 10:00 a.m. to 1:45 p.m. and 3:30 to 6:45 p.m. (to 5:45 p.m. in winter).

If you want to see more of El Greco, you can visit his Toledo home, **Casa y Museo de El Greco** (☎ 925-224-046), Calle Samuel Leví. (Actually, his house and studio were probably in the old Jewish quarter, but this is the place set up as an El Greco museum.) Nobody pretends that the works in the museum are his best stuff; the collection is primarily small portrait-style paintings of Christ and the apostles, along with one of his famous views of Toledo. Admission is 400 ptas. ($2.65), and it's open Tuesday to Saturday, 10:00 a.m. to 2:00 p.m. and 4:00 to 6:00 p.m.; and Sunday, 10:00 a.m. to 2:00 p.m.

Some visitors find that the Renaissance-style entrance and stairs of the **Museo de Santa Cruz** (☎ 925-22-1036), Miguel de Cervantes 3, are more impressive than the works inside this former sixteenth-century hospice. Amid fifteenth-century tapestries, jewelry, artifacts, and swords and armor made from Toledo's famous damascene steel (blackened and traced with gold wire), you'll find works by Goya, Ribera, and the omnipresent El Greco — who's represented by the 1613 *Assumption,* one of his last paintings. The artists are great, but these particular works are nothing more than mediocre. Admission is 200 ptas. ($1.30) for adults and free for children. The museum is open Monday to Saturday, 10:00 a.m. to 6:30 p.m.; and Sunday, 10:00 a.m. to 2:00 p.m.

What do you get when a thriving Jewish community is crushed by the Catholic Inquisition and the local diocese takes over the temples? The answer: a synagogue named for the Virgin Mary. The **Sínagoga de Santa María La Blanca** (☎ 925-227-257), Calle Reyes Católicos 2, has been restored to its Hebrew origins, which were heavily influenced by Islamic architecture. Built in the 1100s, it is the oldest of Toledo's eight remaining synagogues and features Moorish horseshoe arches atop the squat columns of the spare interior. Admission is 150 ptas. ($1), and it's open April through September daily from 10:00 a.m. to 2:00 p.m. and 3:30 to 7:00 p.m.; from October to March, daily hours are 10:00 a.m. to 2:00 p.m. and 3:30 to 6:00 p.m.

The fourteenth-century **Sínagoga del Tránsito** (☎ 925-223-665), Calle Samuel Leví, also blends Gothic, Islamic, and traditional Hebrew motifs. This synagogue contains a frieze inscribed with Hebrew script and set with a coffered ceiling. The **Museo Sefardí,** connected to the synagogue, preserves ancient tombs, manuscripts, and sacred objects of Toledo's Sephardic (Spanish Jewish) community. Admission (temple and museum together) is 400 ptas. ($2.65), and it's open Tuesday to Saturday, 10:00 a.m. to 1:45 p.m. and 4:00 to 5:45 p.m.; Sunday, 10:00 a.m. to 1:45 p.m.

The rebuilt **Alcázar** (☎ 925-223-038), Calle General Moscardó 4, which dominates the town's skyline, is not too much to look at now, but this fortress withstood many a siege. In 1936, it held up during 70 days of bombing during Spain's Civil War. A museum inside uses photographs, models, and a walking tour to remember those days of honor and horror. Admission is 125 ptas. (80 cents) for adults and free for those under 10. It's open Tuesday to Sunday, 9:30 a.m. to 1:30 p.m. and 4:00 to 6:30 p.m. (to 5:30 p.m. in winter).

Where to stay and dine

The **Hostal del Cardenal** (☎ 925-224-900, fax 925-222-991), Paseo de Recaredo 24, charges reasonable prices for terrific traditional Spanish cuisine, such as roast suckling pig. It also rents double rooms for 9,115 to 12,150 ptas. ($60.75 to $81). Otherwise, stay at **Hotel Maria Cristina** (☎ 925-213-202, fax 925-212-650), Marqués de Mendigorría 1, which has modern double rooms and a historic setting for 11,600 to 12,200 ptas. ($77.35 to $81.35).

A king-sized monastery: El Escorial

King Felipe II was nothing if not creative — and maybe a bit zealous. When he needed a new royal residence in the late sixteenth century, rather than following in the footsteps of his European peers and building a palace, he built himself a live-in monastery. But not your run-of-the-mill monastery. Fortress-thick walls enclose San Lorenzo de El Escorial, a frescoed and tapestried complex of royal apartments, with a giant basilica, terrific art gallery, opulent library, and Spain's pantheon of royal tombs.

Other than the huge monastery, there's not much else in the town of El Escorial, so allow about two to three hours to tour it.

Getting there

From Madrid, the bus and train trips to El Escorial both take about an hour. Buses from Madrid's Moncha Metro station (you can buy tickets at a kiosk in the station) drop you off right in front of the monastery. About 25 trains leave Madrid's Atocha Station daily for El Escorial; buses meet incoming trains to shuttle visitors the remaining mile to Plaza Virgen de Gracia, a block east of the monastery.

Pullmantours, in Madrid at Plaza de Orienta 8 (☎ 91-541-1805), runs an all-day tour that stops briefly in Toledo before hurrying on to El Escorial and the Valley of the Fallen (a memorial to Spain's Civil War dead). The tour costs 12,000 ptas. ($80).

The **tourist office** (☎ 91-890-1554) is at Floridablanca 10, in the center of El Escorial near Plaza Virgen de Gracia.

Seeing the monastery

Felipe II's royal apartments in the monastery/fortress of San Lorenzo de El Escorial (☎ 91-890-5902) are as austere and monastic as a king could get. He was such a devout Christian that he had his bedroom built to overlook the high altar of the impressive basilica, which has four organs and a dome based on Michelangelo's plans for St. Peter's in Rome. The basilica is also home to Cellini's *Crucifix*. Under the altar is the Royal Pantheon, a mausoleum containing the remains of every Spanish king from Charles I to Alfonso XII. The tapestried apartments of the Bourbon kings, Carlos III and IV, are more elaborate and in keeping with the tastes of most monarchs.

Paintings such as Titian's *Last Supper,* Velázquez's *The Tunic of Joseph,* El Greco's *Martyrdom of St. Maurice,* and works by Dürer, van Dyck, Tintoretto, and Rubens are the source of the New Museum's popularity. The Royal Library houses more than 40,000 antique volumes under a barrel-vaulted ceiling frescoed by Tibaldi in the sixteenth century.

From April to September, El Escorial is open Tuesday through Sunday, 10:00 a.m. to 6:00 p.m.; from October to March it's open Tuesday through Sunday, 10:00 a.m. to 5:00 p.m. Admission is 850 ptas. ($5.65) adults, 350 ptas. ($2.35) children.

Where to dine

Even though El Escorial is an easy half-day trip from Madrid, you'll probably want lunch before you return, so try the heavenly fare at the cave-like **Mesón la Cueva** (☎ 91-890-1516), San Antón 4.

Segovia: A tour through history

Segovia brings to life a cross-section of Spain's history. Still standing here are a Roman aqueduct, a Moorish palace, and a Gothic cathedral. With its medieval streets, Romanesque churches, and fifteenth-century palaces, Segovia is an enjoyable place to stroll and get a sense of what it was like to live in a small Castillian city.

You can easily see Segovia in three to four hours, but if you are in need of a break from the big city, it makes a nice place to hang around for an overnight escape.

Getting there

Trains leave Madrid for Segovia every other hour (they depart Madrid from Atocha Station, but also pause at Chamartín en route). The trip takes two hours. From Segovia's train station, bus number 3 runs to Plaza Mayor in the center of town.

Pullmantours, in Madrid at Plaza de Orienta 8 (☎ 91-541-1805), runs an all-day tour to Segovia and Avila for 7,300 to 10,400 ptas. ($48.65 to $69.35, depending on what sort of lunch you spring for).

The **tourist office** (☎ 921-460-334) is at Plaza Mayor 10.

Seeing the sights

The majestic Roman aqueduct runs 895 yards along the Plaza del Azoguejo on the east side of town. The aqueduct, much of it two tiers high, contains 118 arches and is 96 feet at its highest. It was built in the first century a.d. using stone blocks with no mortar, and it was one of the city's major water sources all the way until the nineteenth century.

The last great Gothic cathedral (☎ 921-462-205) built in Spain is right in the middle of the city. Isabella I (of Ferdinand and Isabella fame) was named queen on this very spot in 1474. The cathedral, built from 1515 to 1558, is all buttresses and pinnacles. It has some beautiful stained-glass windows, which light the carved choir stalls, the sixteenth- and seventeenth-century paintings, and the grille-fronted chapels inside. The attached cloisters were originally part of an earlier church at the same location. Church admission is free, but entry to the cloisters, chapel room, and tiny museum (which holds paintings by Ribera, Flemish tapestries, jewelry, and manuscripts) costs 250 ptas. ($1.65) for adults, 100 ptas. (65 cents) for kids. It's open in spring and summer daily from 9:00 a.m. to 7:00 p.m., fall and winter daily from 9:30 a.m. to 1:00 p.m. and 3:00 to 6:00 p.m.

Segovia's commanding **Alcázar** (☎ 921-460-759), anchors the west end of town. Originally raised between the twelfth and fifteenth centuries, it was largely rebuilt after a disastrous 1862 fire destroyed many of its Moorish embellishments. Behind the formidable exterior are some sumptuous rooms, from the Gothic King's Room to the stuccoed Throne Room. Clamber up the Torre de Juan II, built as a dungeon, for panoramic views. Admission is 400 ptas. ($2.65) for adults, 275 ptas. ($1.85) for kids 8 to 14; it's open daily from 10:00 a.m. to 7:00 p.m. (to 6:00 p.m. from October to March).

Where to stay and dine

The tavern-like **El Bernardino** (☎ 921-433-225), Cervantes 2, offers hearty Castillian specialties, including a huge *paella.* You can get a double room for 7,000 to 8,500 ptas. ($46.65 to $56.65) in the **Gran Hotel la Sirenas** (☎ 921-462-663, fax 921-462-657), Juan Bravo 30. It is a modern hotel on one of Segovia's nicest plazas.

Chapter 24

The Best of Barcelona

*B*arcelona is the capital of the proudly independent region of Catalonia. In the last decade, this Mediterranean city has transformed itself into a vibrant new capital of European commerce and tourism. This triumph is much to the advantage of the tourist anxious to experience local flavor.

A city of beauty and the arts, Barcelona is home to the whimsical architectural style of Antoni Gaudí. Picasso also studied in Barcelona, and the city's Picasso Museum is the best outside of Paris. Painters Salvador Dalí and Joan Miró also spent time here.

So stroll down the shady Las Ramblas promenade, explore the Gothic Quarter around the cathedral, haggle over fruit at the Bouería market, and ride the funicular up to the park on Montjuïc hill, with its museums and re-created Spanish village. Or perhaps just relax with a drink in a tapas bar and watch the world go by for an afternoon.

You may notice that Spanish is spoken a little differently in Barcelona. That's because it isn't Spanish — it's Catalán. As an autonomous region of Spain, Catalonia is slowly reasserting the native traditions that were squashed during Spain's Franco years, including the re-emergence of their native language, a romance tongue closely related to that of the Provence region of France. Evidence of Catalán's comeback coup was visible during the 1992 Olympics, when all the signs and official news reports were printed in Catalán first and Castilian Spanish second.

Barcelona is a great town for just hanging out — the perfect place to schedule extra time to relax without all the usual sightseeing pressures. If you're just passing through, I'd give it at least two full days.

Making Your Way to and around Barcelona

Getting into the city from the airport is fairly simple, and the train station is connected to a subway line. Once in town, getting around by public transportation is also easy.

Getting to Barcelona by air

Trains from Barcelona's **El Prat** airport (☎ **93-478-5000**) run regularly to Estació Sants, or you can board an Aerobús every 15 minutes to Plaça de Catalunya, Passeig de Gracia, or Plaça Espanya.

Getting to Barcelona by train

Most trains bound to Barcelona arrive either at the Estació Sants on the western edge of the Eixample or the Estació de Franca, near the harbor at the base of the Ciutadella park. Both stations are hooked into the Metro network.

Getting around after you're in Barcelona

Tickets for the bus and Metro cost 145ptas. (96 cents). On Sundays, the buses charge 150ptas. ($1). The 795ptas. ($5.30) **T1** pass gets you 10 rides on any city transportion, including bus, Metro, and funicular and is a better buy than the 790ptas. ($5.25) **T2** pass, which doesn't include the bus. A 600ptas ($4) unlimited day pass covers metro, bus, and the local RENFE urban light rail plus night buses. A three-day metro and bus pass costs 1,350ptas. ($9). You can also get free rides on all public transport with the Barcelona Card, described under the sightseeing section that follows.

By public tranportation

Barcelona's Metro system covers the city pretty well. Line 3 runs down Las Ramblas (and to the Sants-Estació train station), and line 4 follows Via Laietana, bordering the eastern edge of the Ciutat Vella. Plaça de Catalunya is one of the main Metro junctions, with nearby Passeig de Gràcia as another main transfer station. You can hoof it from most Metro stations to wherever you're headed, but occasionally you may find it easier to take a bus.

By taxi

Because of the 1992 Olympics, Barcelona's public transportation system has been fully updated, so you probably won't need a taxi except for perhaps travel to and from the airport (though trains and buses run there frequently). In addition to the numerous taxi stands located throughout the city, cabs cruise the streets looking for fares.

Available cars advertise with "Libre" or "Lliure" signs or with an illuminated green sign. If want to call a **taxi,** try ☎ **93-357-7755,** 93-358-1111, or 93-300-3811.

The initial charge is 295ptas. ($1.95) and then 104ptas. (69 cents) for each additional kilometer. After 10 p.m. and on weekends and holidays, the per-kilometer charge is slightly higher. You will be charged an extra 400ptas. ($2.65) for rides to and from the airport plus 300ptas. ($2) per suitcase.

By funicular

Funiculars (cable cars) run up some of the hills around the city, such as Montjuïc; other slopes are fitted with outdoor escalators to ease your way.

Discovering Barcelona: What You Need to Know

This section provides information that you'll need for the basic necessities of getting the most out of your money, as well as what you'll need in an emergency or if you get stuck.

The local dough

The peseta (pronounced *pay*-se-tah and abbreviated pta.) is the Spanish unit of currency. Roughly, $1 equals 150ptas. or 10ptas. equals 6.6 cents. Spanish coins include 1, 5, 25, 50, 100, 200, and 500 pesetas. Bills come in denominations of 500, 1,000, 5,000, and 10,000 pesetas.

Where to get info after you arrive

For tourist information, the main office is underneath **Plaça Catalunya** at the southeast corner of the park (one of those annoying cities that charges for info: ☎ **906-301-282,** within Spain only, costs 65ptas./43 cents per minute; Internet: www.barcelonaturisme.com), with general information, a currency exchange, a hotel reservations desk, a gift shop, and the world's slowest Internet terminals (100ptas/66 cents for 4 minutes, 500ptas/$3.35 for 22 minutes). There's also an info office in City Hall at Plaça Sant Jaume 1. Both are open Monday to Saturday 10:00 a.m. to 8:00 p.m., Sunday 10:00 a.m. to 2:00 p.m. Info desks are installed at Estació Sants and the airport.

Map-dispensing information booths are strategically placed throughout the tourist areas and (late June to late September) 100 multilingual youths in red-and-white jackets offer help and travel tips. You can pick up the local calendar of events, *Guía del Ocio,* at newsstands.

Where to go in a pinch

Petty thieves and pickpockets target tourists, so be particularly alert in the old city when you're in shopping areas and around the popular tourist sights. Be aware of groups or pairs of thieves: One jostles you while another helps you recover—and helps himself to your wallet. Also, the Barri Xinés, while interestingly seedy by day is not an area to loiter in after dark. For reporting a theft and getting new documents, call **Tourist Attention** (☎ 93-301-9060) 24 hours a day. The municipal police staff this organization, and it has English-speaking attendants. Keep the following list of emergency information on hand as you tour Barcelona.

- ✔ **Doctors/hospitals:** Dial ☎ 061 to find a doctor. The U.S. Consulate will provide a list of English-speaking physicians, as will many hotel concierges. If you need a hospital, try the *urgencias* at Hospital Clínic i Provincial, Casanova 143 (☎ 93-454-6000), or Hospital Creu Roja de Barcelona, Dos de Maig 301 (☎ 93-433-1551).

- ✔ **Emergency:** Dial ☎ 092 for the police. For a medical emergency, call ☎ 061 or 93-329-9701 for an ambulance. To report a fire, call ☎ 080.

- ✔ **Pharmacies:** Farmàcias rotate the duty of staying open late. The *farmàcias de guardia* (night pharmacies) are listed in daily newspapers and on the doors of all drugstores, or call ☎ 010.

Staying in touch

Need to wire home for more money? Want to get online to check your e-mail? The following information will help keep you in touch while you're in Barcelona.

- ✔ **American Express:** The American Express office is at Passeig de Gràcia 101 (☎ 93-217-0070). It's open Monday to Friday 9:30 a.m. to 6:00 p.m. and Saturday 10:00 a.m. to noon.

- ✔ **Consulate:** The U.S. Consulate is at Passeig Reina Elisenda 23 (☎ 93-280-2227).

- ✔ **Internet Access & Cyber Cafes:** Avoid the tortoiselike terminals available in the main tourist office (see previous). **El Café de Internet**, Avenida de las Corts Catalanas 656 (☎ 93-412-1915; Internet: www.cafeinternet.es), is open Monday to Saturday 10:00 a.m. to midnight and charges 600ptas. ($4) per half-hour. **Comunicat Ramu**, C. Tigre 22 (☎ 93-412-5053; Internet: www.ramudavala.com), is open 10:00 a.m. to 2:00 p.m. and 3:00 to 9:00 p.m., and charges 700ptas. ($4.65) per hour.

- ✔ **Net-Movil**, Ramblas 140, 2-B (☎ 93-342-4196), is open daily 9:00 a.m. to 10:00 p.m. and charges 800ptas. ($5.35) per hour. Nearby, e-mail from Spain, **Ramblas** 42 (☎ 93-481-7575;

Internet: www.emailfromspain.es), is open Monday to Saturday 10:00 a.m. to 8:00 p.m. and charges 900ptas. ($6) per hour. It offers Spanish lessons, too.

✔ **Mail:** Barcelona's main post office (☎ 93-318-3507) is on Plaça d'Antoni López, where Via Laietana meets Passeig de Colom.

✔ **Telephone:** Local calls cost 25ptas. (16 cents). Pay phones accept coins, Visa or Amex credit cards, and phone cards *(tarjetas),* sold in *estancos* (tobbacconists) or at the post office in increments of 1,000 or 2,000ptas. ($6.65 or $13.35). On some phones, you must put your coins in the rack at the top, then push a button to drop them in.

The country code in Spain is **34.** What was Barcelona's separate city code of **93** is now incorporated as part of the full number, which means you must always dial it (no matter where you are calling from). To call Barcelona from the United States, dial ☎ **011-34** followed by the number.

To charge your call to a calling card or call collect, dial **AT&T** (☎ **900-990-011**), **MCI** (☎ **900-990-014**), or **Sprint** (☎ **900-990-013**). To call the United States direct from Spain, dial 07, wait for the dial tone, then dial 1, the area code, and phone number. Dial ☎ **003** for national directory assistance, or ☎ **025** for international directory assistance.

✔ **Transit Info:** ☎ **010** or Internet: www.tmb.net for city public transport. Call ☎ **93-478-5000** for flight info.

Touring Barcelona by Neighborhood

A split personality of the city is evident in the contrast between the old city and the new city. The **Ciutat Vella** (Old City) is a hexagon of narrow streets nudged up against the harbor. The massive grid of streets that makes up the new city surrounds the old one.

The famed **Las Ramblas** (Les Rambles in Catalan) bisects the Ciutat Vella that runs from the harbor north to Plaça Catalunya. Las Ramblas is a wide, tree-shaded boulevard with street entertainers, flower stalls, cafes, and the bustle of the city. It's a tour in itself. (It runs northwest, but all city maps are oriented with this street pointing straight up and down.) The street degenerated during the fascist Franco era earlier in this century, as did much of old Barcelona but has slowly regained its footing and respectability as new businesses revive the Ciutat Vella.

Barri Gòtic, the medieval heart of town around the cathedral, lies to the east of Las Ramblas. Site of the original Roman city, it's the most fun area for wandering. Lots of shops, museums, and restaurants fill its narrow streets with old buildings. The Barri Gòtic's eastern edge is Via Laietana, and from this wide street over to the Passeig de Picasso stretches the **Barri del la Ribera.** Formerly fallen on bad times as well,

Accommodations, Dining & Attractions in Barcelona

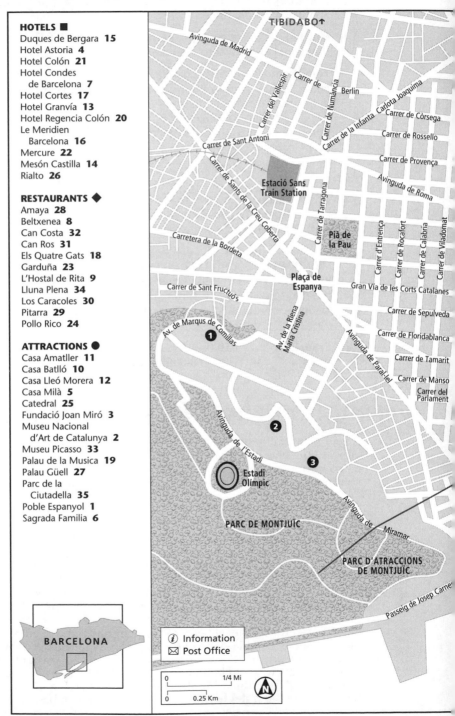

HOTELS ■
Duques de Bergara **15**
Hotel Astoria **4**
Hotel Colón **21**
Hotel Condes
  de Barcelona **7**
Hotel Cortes **17**
Hotel Granvía **13**
Hotel Regencia Colón **20**
Le Meridien
  Barcelona **16**
Mercure **22**
Mesón Castilla **14**
Rialto **26**

RESTAURANTS ◆
Amaya **28**
Beltxenea **8**
Can Costa **32**
Can Ros **31**
Els Quatre Gats **18**
Garduña **23**
L'Hostal de Rita **9**
Lluna Plena **34**
Los Caracoles **30**
Pitarra **29**
Pollo Rico **24**

ATTRACTIONS ●
Casa Amatller **11**
Casa Batlló **10**
Casa Lleó Morera **12**
Casa Milà **5**
Catedral **25**
Fundació Joan Miró **3**
Museu Nacional
  d'Art de Catalunya **2**
Museu Picasso **33**
Palau de la Musica **19**
Palau Güell **27**
Parc de la
  Ciutadella **35**
Poble Espanyol **1**
Sagrada Familia **6**

BARCELONA

ⓘ Information
☒ Post Office

TIBIDABO↑
Avinguda de Madrid
Carrer del Vallespir
Carrer de
Carrer de Numància
Berlin
Carrer de la Infanta Carlota Joaquima
Carrer de Còrsega
Carrer de Rossello
Carrer de Sant Antoni
Carrer de Provença
Carrer de Sans de la Creu Coberta
Avinguda de Roma
Estació Sans
Train Station
Carrer de Tarragona
Pià de
la Pau
Carrer d'Entrença
Carrer de Rocafort
Carrer de Calabria
Carrer de Viladomat
Carretera de la Bordeta
Carrer de Sant Fructuós
Plaça de
Espanya
Gran Via de les Corts Catalanes
Carrer de Sepulveda
Av. de Marqus de Comillas
Av. de la Riena Maria Cristina
Avinguda de Paral·lel
Carrer de Floridablanca
Carrer de Tamarit
Carrer de Manso
Carrer del Parlament
Avinguda de l'Estadi
Estadi
Olímpic
Avinguda de Miramar
PARC DE MONTJUÍC
PARC D'ATRACCIONS
DE MONTJUÍC
Passeig de Josep Carner

0   1/4 Mi
0   0.25 Km

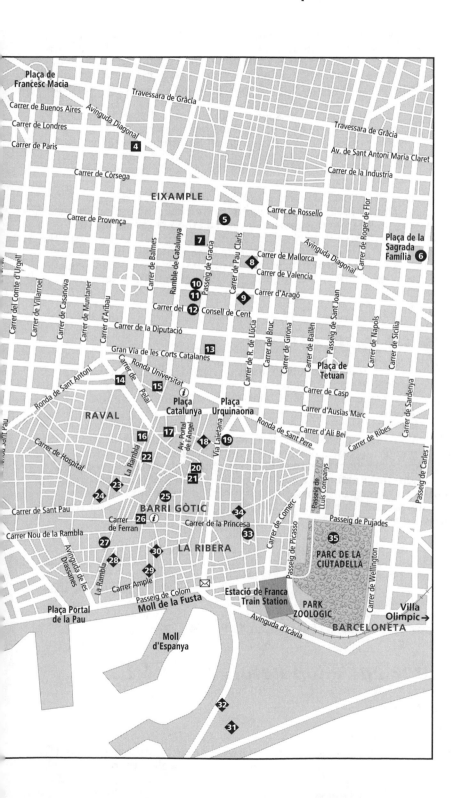

Plaça de
Francesc Macia

Carrer de Buenos Aires

Avinguda Diagonal

Travessara de Gràcia

Carrer de Londres

Carrer de Paris

4

Carrer de Còrsega

Travessara de Gràcia

Av. de Sant Antoni Maria Claret

Carrer de la Industria

EIXAMPLE

Carrer de Provença

5

Carrer de Rossello

Avinguda Diagonal

Carrer de Roger de Flor

Plaça de la
Sagrada
Família **6**

7

Carrer de Balmes

Ramble de Catalunya

Passeig de Gràcia

Carrer de Pau Claris

Carrer de Mallorca **8**

Carrer de Valencia

10

11

9

Carrer d'Aragó

Carrer del **12** Consell de Cent

Carrer de la Diputació

Carrer del Comte d'Urgell

Carrer de Villarroel

Carrer de Casanova

Carrer de Muntaner

Carrer d'Aribau

Carrer de R. de Llúcia

Carrer del Bruc

Carrer de Girona

Carrer de Bailén

Passeig de Sant Joan

Carrer de Napols

Carrer de Sicília

Gran Via de les Corts Catalanes

13

Ronda Universitat

Plaça de
Tetuan

Carrer de Casp

Ronda de Sant Antoni

Carrer de Pelai

14

15

(i)

Plaça
Catalunya

Plaça
Urquinaona

Carrer d'Ausias Marc

Carrer de Sardenya

RAVAL

Carrer de Hospital

Ronda de Sant Pere

Carrer d'Ali Bei

Carrer de Ribes

Passeig de Carles I

16

La Rambla

17

Av Portal de l'Angel

18

Via Laietana

19

22

Passeig de Lluis Companys

20

21

23

24

25

BARRI GÒTIC

Carrer de Sant Pau

Carrer
de Ferran **26** (i)

Carrer de la Princesa

34

Passeig de Comerç

Passeig de Picasso

Passeig de Pujades

35

PARC DE LA
CIUTADELLA

Carrer de Wellington

33

Carrer Nou de la Rambla

27

30

LA RIBERA

Passeig de la Ciutadella

28

La Rambla

29

Carrer Ample

Avinguda de les Drassanes

Passeig de Colom
Moll de la Fusta

✉

Estació de Franca
Train Station

PARK
ZOOLOGIC

Villa
Olimpic →

Plaça Portal
de la Pau

BARCELONETA

Avinguda d'Icàvia

Moll
d'Espanya

32

31

the Barri del la Ribera is now an up-and-coming district of art galleries, bars, clubs, and grand old mansions. South of these two districts is the scenic, lake-spotted **Parc de la Ciutadella.** On a triangular peninsula jutting into the harbor just south of that the former fishing village of **Barceloneta** teems with activity, seafood restaurants, and tapas bars.

The **Barri Xinés,** a historically seedy neighborhood of prostitutes, beggars, and thieves is to the west of Las Ramblas, down near the harbor front. It has improved somewhat and makes an intriguing walk by day, but I wouldn't venture there after dark. Well beyond this, to the city's west, rises the hill of **Montjuïc,** site of the World's Fair and Olympic parks.

The **Plaça de Catalunya** at Las Ramblas' north end is the center of Barcelona and it divides the old city from the new. The grid of streets spreading north from this plaza is known as the **Eixample,** and its grandest avenue is logically named Avinguda Diagonal, as it crosses the grid diagonally. Beyond this, the thoroughly Catalán neighborhood of **Gràcia** expands to the north, where Castilian truly is a foreign language and plenty of colorful, local nightspots add glamour and excitement in the evenings.

Staying in Barcelona

Barcelona's hotels are relatively inexpensive for a big European city. Some guidebooks may disagree with this statement, because the city was dirt cheap until the 1992 Olympics. Now it's merely on the low end of moderate.

The only real concern in Barcelona is safety. Although it's not a seriously dangerous town, pickpockets and other thieves do work the night more brazenly here than in other comparable European cities. Although the situation is rapidly improving, much of the Ciutat Vella still has a slightly unsavory element it picked up earlier in this century. When you're looking for a room, definitely steer clear of the Barri Xinés and anywhere near it.

Most of the Barri Gòtic is pretty safe now, as long as you're watchful of pickpockets, and the part of the Ciutat Vella to the west of Las Ramblas up near the Plaça de Catalunya is just fine (full of hotels). I find the grid of the Eixample a bit boring, but it's certainly a safe neighborhood in which to base yourself, and often you'll find rooms are cheaper there than in the Old City. Additionally, the tourist office will help you find a room; call their special hotel line at ☎ **93-304-3232.**

Barcelona's top hotels and B&Bs

Hotel Astoria

$$ **Sur Diagonal**

Behind an art deco facade and common areas with high ceilings lies a midrange hotel of good service and very well-kept rooms. Older accommodations are done in exposed cedar; more recently renovated ones sport louvered closets, whitewashed walls, and built-in mod units on checkerboard floors.

Carrer de París 201 (at Carrer Granados, one block down from the Diagonal). ☎ *93-209-8311. Fax: 93-202-3008. Internet:* www.derbyhotels.es. *Metro: Diagonal. Rates: 20,200ptas. ($134.65) double. AE, DC, MC, V.*

Hotel Condes de Barcelona

$$$ Eixample

This late-nineteenth century villa is one of Barcelona's finest old-world hotels and is set within one of Barcelona's architectural wonderlands — the Modernisme buildings of the Passeig de Gràcia. The facade is neo-medieval, and the interior is a mix of high-tech and traditional opulence. Rooms come with all the standard amenities, plus marble baths and reproduction Spanish paintings. The art deco piano bar off the lobby is a lovely place to wind down with a drink.

Passeig de Gràcia 73-75 (at Carrer de Mallorca). ☎ *93-467-4786 or 93-467-4780. Fax: 93-467-4785. Internet:* www.condesdebarcelona.com. *Metro: Passeig de Gràcia. Rates: 28,000ptas. ($186.65) double. AE, DC, MC, V.*

Hotel Regencia Colón

$$ Barri Gòtic

Just a few steps from the cathedral on the edge of the Barri Gòtic, the Regencia Colón is one of Barcelona's great central values. The rooms are bland but comfortably worn (though a 1999 overhaul is changing this with new furnishings and parquet floors). Most accommodations are plenty large, though the baths are small, and enjoy amenities from phones and TVs to A/C and minibars. The only drawback is that the hotel is sometimes crowded with tour groups.

Sagristans 13-17 (just north of the cathedral). ☎ *93-318-9858. Fax: 93-317-2822. Internet:* www.hotelregenciacolon.com. *Metro: Jaume 1 or Urquinaona. Rates: 16,500ptas. ($110) double. AE, DC, MC, V.*

Le Meridien Barcelona

$$$$ On Las Ramblas

This Modernisme structure is Barcelona's top hotel, a thoroughly contemporary affair spilling over with amenities, such as heated bathroom floors and in-room VCRs. The location is superb, but even the double glazing can't keep out all the noise of Las Ramblas below. You don't often get such posh comfort so (relatively) cheap.

Ramblas 111. ☎ *800-543-4300 in the United States, 93-318-6200 in Spain. Fax: 93-301-7776. Internet:* www.meridienbarcelona.com. *Metro: Liceu or Plaça de Catalunya. Rates: 42,000–52,000ptas. ($280–$346.65) doubles. AE, DC, MC, V.*

Mesón Castilla

$ Ciutat Vella

A clean budget hotel with lots of amenities (phone, TV, minibar) and a huge breakfast buffet, the Mesón Castilla has a perfect location near Las Ramblas and on the border between the New and Old Cities. Rooms are reliably comfortable, with interesting, ornate headboards; request one of the rooms with a large terrace. Each of the three rooms without bath en suite has a private bath next door.

Valldoncella 5 (a few blocks west of Plaça de Catalunya). ☎ *93-318-2182. Fax: 93-412-4020. Internet:* www.husa.es. *Metro: Universitat or Plaça de Catalunya. Rates: 10,200ptas ($68) double without bath, 11,900–15,000ptas. ($79.35–$100) double with bath. AE, DC, MC, V.*

Mercure (was Hotel Montecarlo)

$$ On Las Ramblas

This is my frugal choice for a hotel in the heart of the action. Although the rooms are functionally modern, the public areas still have the chandeliers, fireplaces, and carved doors that hearken back to the private mansion it was 120 years ago. Rooms are standardized and modern; superior rooms differ mainly by being slightly longer with a small table and chairs and double sinks in the marble baths. You're right on Las Ramblas here, which is wonderful as far as location is concerned, but a bit noisy— request a room overlooking the palms of a quiet interior courtyard.

Rambla dels Estudis 124. ☎ *93-412-0404. Fax: 93-318-7323. E-mail:* montecarlobcn@ i3d.es. *Metro: Plaça de Catalunya. Rates: 16,400–19,500ptas. ($109.35–$130) double. AE, DC, MC, V.*

Barcelona's runner-up accommodations

Duques de Bergara

$$$ This hotel may have been built in 1899, but most of the room decor (especially in the new tower annex) is 1998 conservative-modern, if stylish. Public areas, though, retain the Modernisme touch of architect Emilio Sala i Cortes. *Bergara 11 (*☎ *93-301-5151; Fax: 93-317-3442; Internet:* www.hoteles-catalonia.es*).*

Hotel Cortes

$ The Cortes has comfortable bedrooms, about half of which face a quiet courtyard (the street side isn't too noisy, though). There's also a good, basic restaurant on the ground floor, and even though its merely a block from Plaça de Catalunya and just off the Ramblas, it's the cheapest hotel in this section. *Santa Anna 25 (*☎ *93-317-9112; Fax: 93-302-7870).*

Hotel Colon

$$$$ Under the same management as its neighbor, the Hotel Regencia Colón (reviewed previously), with classier digs — some of which open directly onto the Cathedral façade — at a classier price. *Avienda de la Catedral 7 (*☎ *93-301-1404; Fax: 93-317-2915; Internet:* www.hotelcolon.es*).*

Hotel Granvía

$ Hotel Garnvía has a grand, skylit foyer and high-ceilinged, spacious rooms with antique dressers and worn modern units (the best have rugs scattered on wood floors rather than tired old carpeting). The neighborhood is chic shopping, but still just a few blocks from Las Ramblas in the old quarter of town. *Gran Vía de les Corts Catalanes 642, between Passeig de Gràcia and Carrer Pau Claris (*☎ *93-318-1900; Fax: 93-318-9997).*

Rialto

$ The Rialto has a touch of class to its modernized rooms, and its Barri Gòtic location is hard to beat at these prices. *Ferran 40-42, near Plaça de Saint Jaume (*☎ *93-318-5212; Fax: 93-318-5312).*

Dining in Barcelona

As the capital of Catalonia, Barcelona has plenty of traditional local restaurants that make the excellent casseroles that made this region famous. As a port city, Barcelona has incredible seafood. Make sure you try some of the interesting surf-n-turf combinations, such as the traditional *llagosta i pollastre* (chicken and lobster in a tomato-hazelnut sauce). *Suquet* is made of shellfish stewed with tomatoes, potatoes, saffron, and wine. Unattractive but tasty is *butifarra negra amb mongetes,* a fat, black sausage (pork bellies, blood, and spices) in a plate of white beans.

Nearby Valencia contributes to Barcelona's tables the mighty *paella,* saffron-tinged rice simmered with a medley of seafood, chicken, tomatoes, peppers, beans, pork, hare, and so on.

Don't leave Spain without sampling some Basque cuisine — although Catalonians are no slouches in the kitchen, supremacy for invention and refinement goes to the Basque (see the introduction to Madrid dining in Chapter 23). Spend at least one evening doing a *tapeo,* or tapas bar crawl (see "More cool things to see and do in Barcelona").

For a meal on the run, **L. Simo,** at Passeig de Gràcia 46, makes good sandwiches and salads, and **Las Campanas,** at Mercè 21, specializes in spicy *chorizo* sandwiches, best washed down with ample beer and wine. The best picnic pickings by far are at the excellent La Boquería market on Las Ramblas—it's loaded with produce, meats, fish, and cheeses.

Barcelona's top restaurants

Amaya

$$ On Las Ramblas BASQUE

If you're in the mood to sample some of that famous Basque cuisine and don't want to trek up to Beltxenea (reviewed as follows) — or just want to cut your bill in half — book a table at Amaya. The minimalist decor and subdued lighting remove all distractions so you can pay full attention to both the excellently prepared food and your dinner companion (it's currently a date restaurant of choice for Barcelona couples in their 20s and 30s).

Rambla 20-24 (at Plaça del Theatre, near Las Ramblas' southern end). ☎ *93-318-5085. Reservations recommended. Metro: Drassanes or Liceu. Main courses: 850–2,300ptas. ($5.65–$15.35). AE, MC, V. Open: Lunch and dinner daily.*

Beltxenea

$$$$ Eixample BASQUE

Some of Barcelona's finest Basque chefs hold court in this converted Modernisme apartment building. Splurge for a special occasion here and sample succulent Basque cooking in dishes such as hake garnished with clams or grilled rabbit. In summer, you can dine in the formal garden.

Carrer Mallorca 275 (between Passeig de Gràcia and Carrer de Pau Claris). ☎ *93-215-3024. Reservations recommended. Metro: Passeig de Gràcia. Main courses: 1,650–6,000ptas. ($11–$40). Tasting menu: 6,900ptas. ($46). AE, DC, MC, V. Open: Lunch Mon–Fri, dinner Mon–Sat. Closed Aug.*

Els Quatre Gats

$$ Barri Gòtic CATALÁN

This turn-of-the-century cafe/restaurant was the legendary gathering place of Barcelona's bohemians and Modernisme intellectuals, a place where Picasso once displayed his works. The set-price menu (served until 4:00 p.m.) is one of the city's best values, with dishes based on whatever is most fresh at the market that day. A la carte prices, though, are creeping up, and service can be quite scatterbrained. Some evenings, a live pianist pounds out standards.

Carrer Montsió 3 (just off Av. Portal de l'Angel). ☎ *93-302-4140. Reservations required Sat–Sun. Metro: Plaça de Catalunya. Main courses: 800–2,995ptas. ($5.35–$19.95). Fixed-price menu: 1,500ptas. ($10). AE, MC, V. Open: Lunch and dinner Mon–Sat (cafe open daily).*

Los Caracoles

$$$ Barri Gòtic CATALÁN/SPANISH

This colorful Barcelona institution of good, solid cooking patronized both by artist Salvador Dalí and John Wayne lies near the port. Try the snails (its namesake) or the spit-roasted chicken. Its fame does draw the crowds, but the quality remains uncompromised.

Carrer dels Escudellers 14 (turn east off Las Ramblas at Plaça del Teatre and just follow the curving street). ☎ *93-302-3185. Reservations required. Metro: Drassanes. Main courses: 850–3,700ptas. ($5.65–$24.65). AE, DC, MC, V. Open: Lunch and dinner daily.*

Pitarra

$$$ **Barri Gòtic   CATALÁN**

Named after the famous Catalán poet/playwright who once lived here, Pitarra has stuck to the staples — traditional dishes cooked just like Mama used to do since 1890. The Valencian paella is good, as is the grilled squid, but in winter go for a hearty game dish, such as hare with wild mushrooms.

Carrer de Avinyó 56 (off Carrer de Ferran). ☎ *93-301-1647. Reservations recommended. Metro: Liceu. Main courses: 875–2,800ptas. ($5.85–$18.65). Fixed-price lunch: 1,100ptas. ($7.35). AE, DC, MC, V. Open: Lunch and dinner Mon–Sat.*

Pollo Rico

$ **Ciutat Vella   SPANISH**

Most frugal travelers eventually find their way to Pollo Rico, where you can eat rich with a poor man's purse. On the ground floor, there's scrumptious spit-roasted chicken and *tortillas* (omelettes); you can carry out or sit at the scruffy tables. The comfortable upstairs dining room offers simple fixed-price menus.

Carrer Sant Pau 31 (2 blocks west of Las Ramblas). ☎ *93-441-3184. Reservations suggested. Metro: Liceu. Main courses: 300–1,450ptas. ($2–$9.65). Fixed-price menus: from 900ptas. ($6). No credit cards. Open: Lunch and dinner Thurs–Tues.*

Barcelona's runner-up restaurants

Can Costa

$$$$ One of the best seafood spots in Barcelona's own little contained fishing village of Barceloneta. The baby squid is delectable, as is the paella-like fideuá de peix. *Passeig Joan de Borbó (*☎ *93-221-5903).*

Can Ros

$$-$$$ The place to head for a 1,200 ptas ($8) paella in Barcelonata — if the prices at fancier Can Costa (preceding) put you off your appetite. *Almirall Aixada, of Passeig Joan de Borbó (*☎ *93-221-4579).*

Garduña

$-$$ Garduña might be shut down by one well-timed visit from the health inspector, but this teensy eatery remains the classic restaurant among those that cling around the edges of La Boquería. If not the best food in town, it's certainly among the cheapest. *Morera 17-19 on the south side of La Boquería market, off Rambla de Sant Josep (☎ 93-302-4323).*

L'Hostal de Rita

$-$$ A welcoming, homey little place that does a great rollito de pollo con jamon (chicken rolled with ham) and a fixed-price menu for 1,975 ptas ($13.15). *Carrer d'Aragó 279, at Carrer de Pau Claris, a block off Passeig de Gràcia (☎ 93-487-2376).*

Lluna Plena

$ This place serves hearty Catalán cuisine under a barrel-vaulted, brick ceiling and soft sconce lighting to locals who know you have to book ahead for a table at this popular little spot. *Montcada 2, between Carrer Carders and Carrer de la Princesa (☎ 93-310-5429).*

Exploring Barcelona

The **Barcelona Card,** available at tourist offices, grants you free rides on all public transportation, plus 30 to 50 percent off most sights in town, and 12 to 25 percent off certain shops, tours, and entertainment venues. It costs 2,500ptas. ($16.65) for one day, 3,000ptas. ($20) for two days, and 3,500ptas. ($23.35) for three days.

The other choice is the **ArTicket,** 1,997ptas. ($13.30) gets you admission to six museums, including the Museum of Catalan Art, the Gaudi Museum in *La Pedrera,* as well as the Museum of Contemporary Art, Joan Miró Foundation, Museum of Contemporary Culture, and Antoni Tápies Foundation.

Barcelona's top sights

Cathedral

Behind an elaborate neo-Gothic facade and spire from the nineteenth century lies Madrid's massive Gothic cathedral, a dark, cavernous space with echoes built between 1298 and 1450. There's not much to see inside besides the marvelously carved fifteenth-century choir stalls and ranks of glowing votive candles, but it'll take a good 45 minutes to move through and visit the shady cloisters. This tranquil oasis in the midst of the old city is surrounded by magnolias, palm trees, and ponds with geese.

The little museum adjacent to the cathedral is stuffed with medieval Catalonian art. The Plaça de San Jaume, in front of the cathedral, is a pleasant place to spend time people-watching; at noon on Sundays a troupe performs the complicated folk dance *sardana* here.

Plaça de la Seu. ☎ 93-315-1554 or 93-310-2580. Metro: Jaume I, Liceu. Bus: 14, 17, 19, 22, 24, 40, 45, 51, 59. Open: Church daily 8:00 a.m. to 1:30 p.m. and 4:00 to 7:30 p.m.; museum daily 11:00 a.m. 1:00 p.m. Admission: Church is free; the museum costs 50ptas. (35 cents).

Museu Picasso

Although born in Andalusia, Picasso moved to Barcelona at age 14, and it was here, in the academy where his father taught, that he learned his craft. Barcelona was lucky enough when opening this museum to secure from the master himself many of his earliest works, which his sister had preserved. The very first room disproves the tongue-in-cheek myth that Picasso invented cubism merely because he couldn't draw properly, for here you'll see remarkable drawings and paintings executed with a high degree of realism — all when Picasso was barely a teenager. Of the other 3,000 works in this collection, seek out his *Las Meninas* paintings and drawings, a series of cubist studies made of Velázquez's masterpiece in Madrid's Prado museum (see that entry in Chapter 25). The curious can run through it in half an hour; Picasso fans will want to spend one to two hours.

Montcada 15-19. ☎ *93-319-6310. Metro: Jaume I, Liceu. Bus: 14, 17, 19, 22, 24, 40, 45, 51, 59. Open: Tues through Sat 10:00 a.m. to 8:00 p.m., Sun 10:00 a.m. to 3:00 p.m. Admission: 600ptas. ($4) adults, 250ptas. ($1.65) students, free for those under 17.*

Sagrada Familia

The Sagrada Familia is reminiscent of a giant, drippy sand castle. It's certainly the weirdest-looking church in Europe, an ongoing project that represents the architect Gaudí's creativity at its whimsical, feverish best. Only 8 of what will be 13 spires and the two lesser facades are finished. The Civil War interrupted construction, but it's been picked up again as a slow trickle of donated funds allows work to continue on the nave, remaining towers, and main facade. It may only take an hour or so to tour this work-in-progress, but you could easily spend three just climbing up and down, and across the lithe bridges joining its multitude of spires.

The architectural details are almost Gothic in their intricacy, but with a modern, fluid twist — rosy brown and gray stone is flecked with the colors of Gaudí's signature tile-chip mosaics. You can climb conch-shell spiral stair-cases (or take elevators) up several of the spires to look through the rose windows with no panes. Admire the rounded-off grid of the Eixample around you, and examine up close the funky gargoyles — over here is the Virgin Mary, there a snail creeps up the building's side, and around the corner a stone cypress tree seems to flutter with white stone doves.

In the crypt is a museum that details the ongoing construction and shows, through models and drawings, what Gaudí's original plans were and how the finished building will appear. Gaudí got the Sagrada Familia commission in 1883, and it consumed him. He poured every peseta he had into the project and went begging door to door when funds ran out. He even lived on the site for 16 years. Gaudí died in 1926, after being run over by a trolley, but left behind no master plan for the church. Workers inch toward finishing his masterpiece, but it's unclear exactly what kind of building he ultimately intended. Many (often vocal) critics believe the church should remain unfinished. You can be sure Gaudí's keeping a sharp (albeit posthumous) eye on the proceedings — he is buried in the church crypt.

Carrer de Majorca 401. ☎ **93-455-0247.** *Metro: Sagrada Familia. Bus: 15, 18, 19, 33, 43, 44, 50, 51. Open: daily Nov–Feb 9:00 a.m.–6:00 p.m., Mar and Sept–Oct 9:00 a.m.–7:00 p.m., Apr–Aug 9:00 a.m.–8:00 p.m. Elevator opens at 10:00 a.m. Admission: 800ptas. ($5.35) for entry, plus 200ptas. ($1.35) for the elevator to the top.*

Museu Nacional d'Art de Catalunya

In an enormous 1929 palace atop Montjuïc hill is one of the world's biggest and best collections of Romanesque art, centered around a series of gorgeous twelfth-century frescoes removed from Catalonian churches in the Pyrenees. There's also a good store of Spanish Gothic art and sculpture. Outside the palace is a network of stair-stepping fountains that feature in a sound and light show on summer nights (Thursday through Sunday).

Gaudí or Gaudy? The birth of modernisme architecture

Around the turn of this century, art nouveau arrived in Barcelona in the form of Modernisme, a particularly fluid and idiosyncratic Catalán version of a larger architectural revolution. The high priest of Modernisme, Antoni Gaudí, apprenticed as a blacksmith before taking up architecture. Creative wrought-iron patterns became just one of the many signature details Gaudí incorporated into his flowing, organic structures; he was especially fond of creating colorful mosaics out of chips of ceramic and mirror.

If you see only a handful of Modernisme buildings, make them Gaudí's most famous trio: the Sagrada Familia (see listing); the colorful Casa Battló (Passeig de Gràcia 43) with a roof shaped like a dragon's back and theater-mask balconies; and Casa Milà (Passeig de Gràcia 92), often called *La Pedrera* ("the quarry") for its undulating rocky shape. Here, especially, Gaudí seemed to avoid straight lines at all costs — the place looks like it's melting. There's an exhibition space on Gaudí and Modernisme inside; and for the 500ptas. ($3.35) admission you can also tour the architectural fun park and swirly, ice-cream chimneys. It's open daily 10:00 a.m. to 8:00 p.m. (☎ **93-484-5979** or 93-484-5995).

Two other Modernisme architects of note were Domènech i Montaner and Puig i Cadafalch. To compare them to each other, and to master Gaudí, take a walk down the *Illa de la Discòrdia* ("the block of discord") on Passeig de Gràcia between Carrer del Consell de Cent and Carrer d'Arago. Here, their interpretations of Modernisme compete in the form of apartment buildings. At no. 35 is Montaner's Casa Lleo Morera, at no. 41 is Cadafalch's Casa Amatller, and at no. 43 is Gaudí's Casa Battló. (For these and *La Pedrera,* take the Metro to Passeig de Gracia or Diagonal, which is closer to *La Pedrera.)*

Montaner also designed the gorgeous venue Palau de la Música Catalana, Carrer de Sant Francesc de Paula 2 (☎ **93-268-1000**), now a UNESCO World Heritage Site. Go inside to see the sky-lit stained glass of the inverse dome in the auditorium; 50-minute guided tours Wednesday and weekends every half hour 10:00 a.m. to 3:30 p.m. for 700ptas. ($4.65). One of Cadafalch's other major works is Els Quatre Gats, which I recommended as a restaurant.

Palau Nacional, Parc de Montjuïc. ☎ *93-423-7199. Internet:* www.gencat. es/mnac. *Metro: Espanya. Bus: 61. Open: Tues–Wed and Fri–Sat 10:00 a.m.–7:00 p.m., Thurs 10:00 a.m.–9:00 p.m., Sun 10:00 a.m.–2:30 p.m. Admission: 800ptas. ($5.35).*

Park Güell/Casa-Museu Gaudí

In the northern reaches of the Gràcia district, north of the Eixample, rises one of Gaudí's most colorful creations. It was intended to be an unusual little residential community, but only two houses were built. The city bought the property in 1926 and turned it into a public park with colonnades of crooked columns (they look like tree trunks), narrow gardens, small fountains, and whimsical animals. One sitting area is dominated by a large, spectacular curving bench brightened by a patterned mosaic of tile and mirror; from this spot, you get great views of the city. The entrance is flanked by two mosaicked pavilions designed by Gaudí, but the Casa-Museu Gaudí (☎ **93-284-6446**), where the master lived from 1906–26, was built by Ramón Berenguer. It's filled with Gaudí's models, furnishings, and drawings.

Carrer d'Olot. ☎ *93-284-6446 or 93-219-3811. Metro: Vallcarca. Bus: 24. Open: May–Sept daily 10:00 a.m.–8:00 p.m., Oct–Apr Sun–Fri 10:00 a.m.–2:00 p.m. and 4:00–6:00 p.m. Admission: The park is free; the museum costs 300ptas. ($2).*

More cool things to see and do in Barcelona

From tasty tapas to fiery flamenco, there's much to entertain you in Barcelona, especially at night.

✔ **Tour Spain in a nutshell at the Poble Espanyol.** For the 1929 World's Fair, Barcelona created a simulated Spanish village high on top Montjuïc, where 115 houses and structures reproduce Spanish monuments and buildings from over the last 1,000 years. Many of the replicas are crafts and souvenir shops, but over a dozen have been converted into restaurants that serve cuisines from Spain's various regions. With others housing discos, bars, and a flamenco club, the Poble Espanyol (☎ **93-325-7866**) is an entertaining spot for an evening out. Take the Metro to Espanya then bus 61. Admission is 950ptas. ($6.35), and it's open Monday from 9:00 a.m. to 8:00 p.m., Tuesday to Thursday 9:00 a.m. to 2:00 a.m., Friday and Saturday 9:00 a.m. to 3:00 a.m., Sunday 9:00 a.m. to midnight.

✔ **Enjoy a tapeo.** When in Spain, do like the Spanish — indulge in an early-evening *tapeo* (tapas bar crawl). For more details on this most Spanish of activities (tapas rank somewhere between a snack and a passion), see Madrid's dining section in Chapter 25. One of Barcelona's best *tascas* (tapas bars) is Casa Tejada at Tenor Viñas 3, offering the widest selection in town. Mercè Street in Barceloneta is also renowned for its many tascas. Try Bodega la Plata (no. 28), specializing in deep-fried sardines, and La Jarra (no. 9) — short on refined atmosphere but stupendous in its flavors and authenticity.

✔ **Break out the castanets, it's time for flamenco.** Inspired by the medieval tribulations of Spain's Jews and Moors, and influenced by gypsy rhythms and style, the exotically fluid dance known as the flamenco heats up the night in two of Barcelona's bars. Admittedly, these shows are put on for the tourists — you'll have to head to Madrid or even Andalusia, the birthplace of flamenco, for more authentic versions.

But if Barcelona is your only chance to experience the hand-clapping, guitar-strumming lifebeat of this folk art, try the **Tablao Flamenco Cordobés** (☎ 93-317-6653), at Las Ramblas 35, or **El Tablao de Carmen** (☎ 93-325-6895) in the Poble Espanyol. Call to confirm show times and prices, but there's usually a dinner performance around 8:30 or 9:30 p.m. for 7,500ptas. ($50), and a late show with just drinks around 11:00 p.m. for 4,800ptas. ($32).

✔ **Disco 'til dawn with Barcelona's throbbing nightlife.** Like most of Spain, Barcelona loves late night action, be it bar-hopping, dancing, or just general partying until the wee hours. The most traditional evening can be had in the Modernisme architectural triumph of the **Palau de la Musica Catalán** (☎ 93-268-1000), San Francest de Paula 2, which features year-round classical, jazz, and pop concerts as well as recitals. You can stay passive in your after-dark pleasures at a flamenco bar such as those listed previously or dance your own socks off at clubs **Up and Down** (☎ 93-205-5194), Numància Diagonal 179, the massive **Otto Zutz Club** (☎ 93-238-0722), Carrer Lincoln 15, trendy **Nick Havanna** (☎ 93-215-6591), Roselló 208, or minimalist **Zig-Zag Bar** (☎ 93-201-6207), Platón 13.

And on Your Left, Las Ramblas: Seeing Barcelona by Guided Tour

The public **Bus Turistic** is a hop-on/hop-off service with two different routes: a northerly red route, and a southerly blue one. Although two intersect at Pl. Catalunya, Passeig de Gracia/la Pedrera, and Francesc Macià-Diagonal. With 25 stops and buses every 10 to 30 minutes from 9:00 a.m., it effectively covers all the major points of interest in Barcelona. It costs 1,800ptas. ($12) for one day, 2,300ptas. ($15.35) for two days, and you get an info booklet, and on board is a live info officer who lets you know what's available at each stop. You also get around 10 to 20 percent off at many sights. It runs March 28 to January 6.

Pullmantur (☎ 93-318-0241), Gran Via de les Corts Catalanes 635, offers daily a morning guided bus tour of the old city and Montjuïc, and an afternoon tour of Eixample architectural sights, including Sagrada Familia, the Park Güell, and the Picasso Museum. Either tour costs 4,750ptas. ($31.65), or both (plus lunch) at 12,350ptas. ($82.35).

Suggested One- and Two-Day Itineraries

If you're the type who'd rather organize your own tours, this section offers some tips for building your own Barcelona itineraries. Two full days will give you a good taste of what the city has to offer.

If you have one day

Begin early in the morning at the only grand cathedral of Europe still in the midst of being built, Gaudí's **Sagrada Familia.** Take 90 minutes or so to clamber around its spires and admire the whimsical sculpture adorning it in the oddest hidden corners. Then take the metro to Diagonal for more Modernisme matserpieces in Gaudí's *La Predera* and the famed *Illa de la Discòrdia* along Passeig de Gràcia.

Hop back on the Metro at Passeig de Gràcia stop to tunnel to the Jaume stop so that — after grabbing some lunch on the go — you pop into a museum honoring Barcelona's other artistic giant of the twentieth century, the **Museu Picasso.** Backtrack along Carrer de la Princesa/Carrer de Jaume I to turn right on Carrer de la Dagueria, which becomes Carrer Freneria as it passes some Roman columns and, eventually, spills into the square in front of Barcelona's massive, **Gothic Cathedral.**

As evening draws near, make your way over to the grand promenade of **Las Ramblas** to watch the street performers, the locals out for their *paseo,* and simply stroll one of the greatest pedestrian boulevards in Europe. Cut out by 6:00 p.m. or so to *tapeo* before heading back to your hotel to rest up from your full day before a 10:00 p.m. dinner at **Los Caracoles** or, if you prefer Basque, **Amaya.**

If you have two days

Begin Day One seeing perhaps Barcelona's greatest sight: **Las Ramblas,** that long, wide, pedestrian boulevard that glides right through the heart of the old city, from Plaça de Catalunya to the port. Start at the port end, at the Drassanes metro stop. Stop into **La Boqueria** market to see the string beans stacked perfectly and the dried salt cod piled high. Pause at the twittering, tweeting cages of the tiny portable bird market; toss pasetas to the performers who pose as statues and only move when the clink of change hits their hat. Follow Las Ramblas all the way to Carrer de Portaferrisa and turn right until you get to the **Cathedral.**

For lunch, work your way south through the back streets of the medieval **Barri Gòtic** to Los Caracoles. Then head over to the **Museu Picasso.** Be out of there by 3:30 or 4:00 p.m. so you have plenty of time to get up to **Montjuïc** and the **Museu Nacional d'Art de Catalunya** (it doesn't close until 7:00 p.m.). Afterwards, you can take in a flamenco show and dine in the nearby **Poble Espanyol.**

Day Two is the day for Modernisme. Start it off just as the morning described under "If you have one day," preceding, at **Sagrada Familgia** and among the art nouveau wonderland of **Passeig de Gràcia**. You're in luck that **L'Hostal de Rita** is just a block away from the *Illa de la Discòrdia* for lunch.

Now, because the last day-and-a-half have been pretty packed (and with lots of walking), take the afternoon to relax while still sightseeing. Head up to the Gaudí-designed **Park Güell,** a wonderful place to wander, full of whimsical architectural accents, plus the **Casa-Museu Gaudí,** where the master once lived.

Chapter 25

Athens and the Greek Islands

. . . .

In This Chapter

▶ Getting to Athens and the Greek islands

▶ Finding the most interesting historical sights

▶ Enjoying traditional Greek music and dancing

▶ Locating a hotel with the view for you

▶ Finding the best beaches outside the big city

. . . .

*B*y the fifth century b.c., when the rest of Western civilization was still in its infancy, Athens was already a thriving metropolis, the site of one of the world's first successful democracies. It was home to influential schools of art, architecture, literature, drama, and philosophy that continue to be the touchstones of modern culture.

Three magnificent sights from ancient times are preserved in Athens: the Acropolis Hill, whose Parthenon to Athena is the world's most famous ancient temple; a huge archeological museum; and the Ancient Agora, the civic laboratory in which contemporary democracy was first developed and tested.

Even though Athens has one of the most sacred cultural heritages in Europe, I recommend that visitors see these icons quickly and then venture out into the rest of Greece. Honestly, the rest of the fabled city now leaves much to be desired; it's a tangled, polluted mess of over-development and traffic.

Because Athens is much farther from the heart of Europe than most people realize, first-time visitors to the Continent and those on a whirlwind trip should seriously consider whether to invest the time it takes to visit Greece. They should either fly there from a more central European city (luckily, new no-frills airlines — see Chapter 7 — now make this affordable for many travelers) or be prepared to spend a full six days on a train and ferry just to get from Rome to Athens and back. Don't let me talk you out of seeing Greece if you have your heart set on it. Just remember this: If you try to squeeze it in, you might be sorely disappointed.

If, however, you are able to explore this country and its ancient culture for a while, by all means make the trip. Athens may be congested and dirty, but Greece as a whole is a beautiful, complex, and history-laden country. If you have the time and a willingness to really explore the history, culture, and mythology, you'll find Greece an unforgettable part of your journey.

Making Your Way to and around Athens

In addition to the usual options for getting to a major European city — plane, train, bus, and (for adventuresome travelers) automobile — Athens offers another mode of entry: ferry. But the marine route is not for everyone; schedules are erratic, and the crossing can be quite long. Flying is still the best alternative.

Once you get to Athens, your feet and taxis are likely to be your best transportation bets.

Getting to Athens by air

Hellenikon International Airport (☎ 01-969-4466) is seven miles south of the heart of Athens. A taxi downtown should cost about 2,500Dr ($8.35) and take anywhere from 30 to 90 minutes, depending on traffic. Or you can take city bus number 92 to Sýntagma Square in central Athens near the House of Parliament for 250Dr (85 cents). From the airport's West Terminal, the Olympic Airways shuttle leaves every half hour to take passengers to Sýntagma Square. The fee is 190Dr (65 cents), paid on the bus in exact change only. Express bus number 19 runs from the airport to the ferry port town of Piraeus for 250Dr (85 cents), 500Dr ($1.65) after 11:30 p.m.

Getting to Athens by ferry

Hordes of travelers take the ferry to Greece from Italy, so you'd think ferry operators would have standardized their fares and schedules. You'd be wrong. The most popular crossing is from Brindisi (on the heel of Italy's "boot," a seven-hour train ride from Rome) to the port of Patras in Greece. This boat trip takes 18 to 20 hours; ferries usually leave Brindisi around 10:00 p.m. (but you should be on board at least two hours early). Prices, ranging anywhere from $30 for a deck chair and a restless night outside to $230 for the best cabins, are highest from late June through August. Eurailpass holders get a discount of up to 30 percent.

To get to Athens from Patras, you can catch a bus that leaves every half hour; the trip takes three hours and costs 3,650Dr ($12.15). You can also take one of eight daily trains that makes the trek in 3½–4 hours and costs 1,580–2,980Dr ($5.25–$9.95). You can also catch a bus to Delphi. Make your connections as quickly as possible, because the last train and bus of the day usually pull out very soon after the ferry arrives, stranding unsuspecting travelers in uninspiring Patras overnight.

Remember: Getting from Rome to Athens this way takes about three full days. Many people find that flying is the easiest and least-expensive alternative for getting to Athens (especially after you tally all the rail, ferry, meal, and accommodation costs).

Getting to Athens by rail

Trains from Patras and southern Greece arrive in Athens at **Stathmós Peloponníssou** (Peloponnese Station), about a mile northwest of Omónia Square. Across the tracks is **Larissa Station**, Athens's main train station. This is the arrival spot for trains from the north and, therefore, also from other countries. From this station, you can take trolley number 1 to Sýntagma Square.

Getting to Athens by bus

Regional buses pull into Athens at one of two unimaginatively named bus terminals. **Terminal A** (for buses from Patras; northern, southern, and western Greece; and the Peloponnese) is at 100 Kifíssiou Street (☎ 01-512-4910); from there, city bus number 51 runs to a station near Omónia Square. **Terminal B** (for buses from central Greece, including Delphi, Thebes, and Meteóra) is at 260 Liossíon Street (☎ 01-831-7096); from this terminal, city bus number 24 goes to Amalías Avenue and the National Garden, one block from Sýntagma Square.

Getting around once you're in Athens

I find that the best way to get around town is usually to use my feet and hail the occasional taxi. Except for a few longer excursions to visit museums, you'll probably spend most of your time in or near the pedestrian-friendly Pláka.

Single-ride tickets on both the Metro and the bus/trolley system cost 120Dr (40 cents), but they are not interchangeable. You'll see kiosks for buying bus tickets all over town. For the Metro, you can get tickets at machines and booths inside the stations.

 The traffic in Athens is worse than in any other European city. The horn-honking, erratic driving, pollution, and daily congestion are worse in Athens than even in Rome and Naples. Drivers routinely turn left from the far right lane of a multilane boulevard, or use a string of empty parking spots as their own personal passing lane. I definitely urge you not to drive here.

By Metro (Subway)

Athens' Metro (subway) system is clean and efficient, but not quite finished. Only one line currently exists, connecting Omónia and Monasteráki (nearest the Pláka) and running all the way to the docks at Piraeus (where you catch boats to the Greek islands). Many more stations will eventually serve two other Metro lines, but their completion keeps getting delayed because Athens simply has too many archeological treasures. Construction crews are digging nearly 70 feet below ground, but they still keep running into ancient ruins that need to be excavated before construction can continue.

By bus and trolley

Athens has several overlapping bus and bus-trolley networks. Blue minibuses stop at red signs every two blocks. Minibus route 150 is free and runs from Sýntagma Square up Stadiou St. to Omonia Square before heading to the Monastiraki flea market. Minibuses 100 and 200 both cost, the former following Academias Street and the latter the same general area before dipping into the Kolonaki district.

Green buses 843, 844, and 874 run regularly from downtown Athens to the subway station of Piraeus, Athens' port; from there, bus 905 runs to the ferry docks and trolley 20 goes to the hydrofoil dock.

Unfortunately, Athens changes its bus system and reassigns route numbers on an annoyingly regular basis, so any specific info I've given you here may have changed by the time this book hits the shelves.

By taxi

Taxis are cheaper in Athens than in any major European city — if you pay close attention to avoid getting charged improperly high rates. Taxis are the simplest way to get from doorstep to doorstep, and they occasionally provide the added bonus of a white-knuckle thrill ride.

The charge for taxis is 200Dr (65 cents), plus 60Dr (20 cents) per kilometer. If you leave the city limits, the per-kilometer charge may go up. The fee for luggage is 55Dr (18 cents), and stops at the port of Piraeus or a rail or bus station will bring a 160Dr (55 cents) surcharge. The surcharge is 300Dr ($1) for stops at the airport.

Always use a metered taxi, never a gypsy cab or unmetered car. Make sure the meter rate reads "1" — it should only read "2" if you're going well outside the central city. And don't be shocked if your driver picks up other passengers during your ride. A taxi can carry other customers to destinations that are on the way, but everyone pays separately. Just check the amount on the meter when you climb in, and pay the difference when you get out.

You can hail a taxi on the street or call ☎ **01-993-4812,** 01-921-7942, or 01-801-9000. You will have to pay a 200Dr (65 cents) surcharge when you call a taxi; the surcharge is 300Dr ($1) if you arrange for the taxi to arrive at a specific time.

Discovering Athens: What You Need to Know

In a city as hectic and crowded as Athens, travelers need all the help they can get. This section provides you with some pointers to make your stay in this historic city a little bit easier.

The local dough

The Greek unit of currency is the *drachma* (Dr). Roughly, $1 equals 300Dr, or 100Dr equals 33 cents. Greek coins come in denominations of 1, 2, 5, 10, 20, 50, and 100 drachmas. Paper bills come in denominations of 200, 500, 1,000, and 5,000 drachmas. (You may also see some 50Dr and 100Dr notes; the Greeks are phasing these out. In addition, a 10,000Dr bill was just introduced.)

Where to get info after you arrive

The **Greek Tourist Organization** (EOT) is at 2 Amerikis Street (☎ **01-331-0561** or 01-322-3111, fax 01-322-4148). To get there, go three blocks north from Sýntagma Square on Panepistimou and turn right. The office is open Monday to Friday, 9:00 a.m. to 7:00 p.m.

Another very handy resource for Athens visitors is the **Tourist Police,** 4 Stadiou Street, Office 447 (fourth floor) (☎ **171**). This service offers round-the-clock visitor support in English and is the place to turn if you encounter any problems.

The weekly *Athenscope* magazine lists cultural events in English. You can buy it at news kiosks.

Where to go in a pinch

Greece has the lowest crime rate in Europe, and Athens is the safest major city on the Continent. Visitors who are able to dodge the maniacal Athenian drivers really have only two minor concerns. Women, single women in particular, often get hassled and rudely propositioned by leering shopkeepers (especially in the Pláka). And single men should be aware that unscrupulous bar owners will sometimes try to distract them with beautiful women while the bartender keeps pouring ridiculously expensive drinks. The huge bill comes without any warning of the prices, and the unsuspecting visitor is forced to pay up.

If you should find yourself in a bind, here are some resources to help get you out of trouble:

- ✔ **Embassy:** The U.S. Embassy (☎ **01-721-2951**) is at 91 Vassilíssis Sophías Avenue. If you need emergency help after the embassy is closed, call ☎ **01-779-2301**, the embassy receptionist at ☎ **01-722-3652**, or the embassy duty officer at ☎ **01-729-4301**.

- ✔ **Emergency:** Dial ☎ **100** to reach the police, ☎ **166** for an ambulance, and ☎ **199** to report a fire. If you have car trouble (other than maddening traffic), call ELPA Road Assistance at ☎ **104**; light repairs are free. If you have a run-in with a belligerent hotel, restaurant, or shop owner or taxi driver, call the Tourist Police at ☎ **171**.

- ✔ **Transit Information:** For local bus schedules, dial ☎ **185**; for bus schedules in the rest of Greece, call ☎ **142,** 01-512-4910, or 01-831-7158. For train info, call ☎ **145** (domestic), **147** (international), or 01-362-4402. For flight info, dial ☎ **01-936-9111** (domestic) or 01-969-4466 (international). For domestic ship info, call ☎ **143.** Or for any transportation info, you can always call the Tourist Police at ☎ **171.**

- ✔ **Doctors/Hospitals:** For a list of English-speaking doctors, call SOS Doctor at ☎ **01-331-0310** or the U.S. Embassy (☎ **01-721-2951**). You can find out the location of the nearest hospital from the Tourist Police (☎ **171**), but you usually need a doctor to be admitted. Hospitalinformation is also available by calling ☎ **106.** If you need a doctor between 2:00 p.m. and 7:00 a.m., call ☎ **105.**

- ✔ **Pharmacies:** *Pharmakia* are marked by green crosses. They are usually open from 8:00 a.m. to 2:00 p.m., but if you need one after hours, the location of the nearest 24-hour pharmacy is posted on all pharmacies' doors. You can also find a round-the-clock pharmacy by dialing ☎ **107** or picking up a copy of the *Athens News*. Staying in touch

Staying in touch

No matter where you are in Athens, you're probably just moments away from one means or another of keeping in touch with the rest of the world. Here are a few resources to meet your communication needs:

- ✔ **American Express:** The American Express office is at 2 Ermoú Street (☎ **01-324-4975**), above the McDonald's in Sýntagma Square. It's open Monday to Friday, 8:30 a.m. to 4:00 p.m. On Saturday, only the travel and mail desks are open, 8:30 a.m. to 1:30 p.m.

- ✔ **Internet Access and Cyber Cafes: Skynet Centers**, Odos Voulis 30 and Apollonos 10, in the Pláka (☎ **01-322-7551**; Internet: www.skynet.gr), are open daily from 9:30 a.m. to 8:30 p.m. and charge $5 per hour. **Astor Internet Cafe**, Kapodistriou 22, at Pattision, four blocks north of Omónia Square (☎ **01-523-8546**; Internet: www.astorcafe.gr), is open daily from 10:00 a.m. to 10:00 p.m. and charges $3.50 per hour.

✔ **Mail:** Athens' main post office is on Syntagma Square at Odos Mitropoleos. It is open Monday to Friday, 7:30 a.m. to 8:00 p.m.; Saturday, 7:30 a.m. to 2:00 p.m.; and Sunday, 9:00 a.m. to 1:00 p.m.

✔ **Telephone:** A local call in Athens costs 20Dr (7 cents). Most public pay phones accept only phone cards, which you can buy at newsstands and OTE (the national telephone company) offices for 1,300Dr ($4.35). At other, monitored pay phones, you pay what the meter records; after the call just give your money to the attendant.

The country code for Greece is 30; Athens' city code is 01. You must use the zero before the city code only when you are calling Athens from within Greece; when you call from outside the country, drop the zero. For example, to call Athens from the United States, dial 011-30-1 and the number. To call Athens from within Greece, dial 01 and the number (you're leaving out the 011 and the 30). To use a calling card or to call collect, dial **AT&T** (☎ **00-800-1311**), **MCI** (☎ **00-800-1211**), or **Sprint** (☎ **00-800-1411**). To place a direct call from Greece to the United States, dial 001, the area code, then the telephone number.

For recorded telephone assistance in English, dial ☎ **169.** English-speaking operators are at ☎ **162,** while ☎ **161** gets you the international operator.

Touring Athens by Neighborhood

Athens is a sprawling metropolis with an insatiable appetite for the surrounding countryside, which it continues to devour at a rapid pace. Still, the center of the city preserves the **Acropolis** and many other ancient ruins scattered among Byzantine churches, Turkish buildings, nineteenth-century boulevards, and modern metropolitan gridlock.

The one Athens landmark you have to locate and remember is **Sýntagma Square,** the political, geographical, and traffic center of the city. The **Pláka** stretches to the southwest; this largely pedestrian- and tourist-friendly quarter is one of the most colorful old sections of town. I recommend that you spend the bulk of your visit here.

The southwest corner of the Pláka is bounded by the **Acropolis Hill,** which draws visitors with its majestic **Parthenon** temple and other famous ancient ruins from the time when Athens was the center of Western civilization. The **Monastiráki** neighborhood, which features a flea market and shop-lined street, lies north of the Acropolis and west of the Pláka, next to the **Ancient Agora.**

North of the Pláka and Sýntagma Square, all roads lead to **Omónia Square,** the hub of a district that was the commercial heart of the city at one time. But the neighborhood has recently gotten somewhat rundown. It's still a useful transportation center, but I wouldn't hang out there.

Northeast of Sýntagma Square you'll find the shopping and residential zone called **Kolonáki.** Though no longer the city's trendy hotspot (newer suburbs have stolen that title), it still is a chic, happening spot. Due south of Sýntagma Square is **Mets,** a trendy residential and intellectual quarter.

The relatively undiscovered neighborhood of **Makriyánni** is south of the Acropolis. It is a moderately upscale area, full of good hotels, restaurants, and shopping. Southwest of this neighborhood is an even bigger secret — the **Koukáki** residential zone, with inexpensive hotels and a modest, thoroughly Athenian restaurant scene.

Staying in Athens

Almost all the hotels in Athens are simple and basic. Although you can find some pretty shabby places if you stick to the low end of the price ladder, you can find plenty of clean options if you look around. If you want to stay near the sightseeing and nightlife, the Pláka or Monasteráki are your best bets. The **Koukáki** and **Makriyánni** residential zones have plenty of good, clean hotels, and they are cheaper than the city center. The **Hellenic Chamber of Hotels** (☎ 01-323-7193), 2 Karagiogi Sevias St., Sýntagma Square, can help you book a hotel anywhere in Greece.

You should steer clear of only one area: the downtrodden **Omónia Square** zone. Once a haven for budget inns, it's now too seedy for most people's tastes.

Hotels can add a 10 percent surcharge on stays of fewer than three nights. In the tourism off-season, by all means bargain.

Athens's top hotels

Hotel Acropolis View

$$$ **Makriyánni**

This nice hotel is snuggled into a quiet side street on Philopáppou Hill. It has small, unspectacular, but modern renovated rooms with televisions and air conditioning. A few rooms even live up to the hotel's name. You can get outstanding Acropolis vistas from the roof terrace, especially at sunset.

10 Wemster St. (off Rovértou Gálli, two blocks down from its intersection with Dionysíou Aeropayítou). ☎ *01-921-7303. Fax: 01-923-0705. Rates: 28,500–33,000Dr ($95–$110) double. MC, V.*

Attalos Hotel

$ Monasteráki

Plain-but-nice rooms, cheerful service, and air conditioning keep the Attalos popular among budget-conscious travelers. The roof terrace has a bar for snacks and ice cream and a lovely view to the Acropolis across the city (best when seen at night). This view is also available in 37 of the upper-floor rooms, many with balconies. Streetside rooms have sound-proofed windows (which are pretty effective), and a 1999 renovation upgraded the very clean rooms to include televisions, hair dryers, and in-room safes. The rates quoted here do not include breakfast (an additional 1,500Dr/$5 per person).

29 Athinás St. (1½ blocks from Monasteráki Square). ☎ **01-321-2801.** *Fax: 01-324-3124. Internet:* www.attalos.gr. *Rates: 14,000–16,000Dr ($46.65–$53.35) double. AE, V.*

Elektra Palace

$$$ Pláka

For the price, it's hard to beat this hotel's location — just southwest of Sýntagma Square in the colorful Pláka. The higher the floor, the smaller these clean, contemporarily furnished rooms get (though none are tiny by any stretch). The good news is that the balconies get proportionately larger. The nicest feature is the rooftop pool, with its sweeping Acropolis view, bar, and barbecue service in summer. (About 20 rooms, many of them suites, get the Acropolis view too, but they can't guarantee it when booking.)

18 Nikodímou St. (near Adrianoú St.). ☎ **01-337-0000.** *Fax: 01-324-1875. Rates: 38,800–48,400Dr ($129.35–$161.35) double. AE, DC, MC, V.*

Hotel Acropolis House

$ Pláka

Many original moldings and other classic architectural details adorn this 150-year-old villa. The newer wing of this restored structure is not as charming as the rest, but it has more-modern bathrooms. It's in the pedestrian heart of the Pláka, and you can store your picnic supplies in fridges in the hall. The room price includes a continental breakfast.

6–8 Odós Kodroú St. (the southern extension of Voulís St., after it crosses Nikodímou). ☎ **01-322-2344.** *Fax: 01-324-4143. Rates: 15,300–18,000Dr ($51–$60) double (add 4,670Dr/$15.55 for air conditioning). V.*

Hotel Grande Bretagna

$$$$ Sýntagma Square

This bastion of nineteenth-century luxury has an appropriately neoclassical lobby and 12-foot ceilings in the well-appointed rooms. Accommodations on the busy square have a view (some of the Acropolis), but those on the courtyard are quieter.

Accommodations, Dining & Attractions in Athens

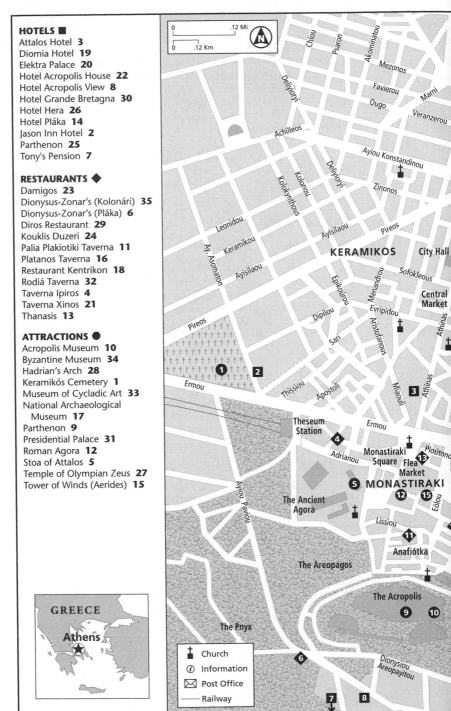

HOTELS ■
Attalos Hotel **3**
Diomia Hotel **19**
Elektra Palace **20**
Hotel Acropolis House **22**
Hotel Acropolis View **8**
Hotel Grande Bretagna **30**
Hotel Hera **26**
Hotel Pláka **14**
Jason Inn Hotel **2**
Parthenon **25**
Tony's Pension **7**

RESTAURANTS ◆
Damigos **23**
Dionysus-Zonar's (Kolonári) **35**
Dionysus-Zonar's (Pláka) **6**
Diros Restaurant **29**
Kouklis Duzeri **24**
Palia Plakiotiki Taverna **11**
Platanos Taverna **16**
Restaurant Kentrikon **18**
Rodiá Taverna **32**
Taverna Ipiros **4**
Taverna Xinos **21**
Thanasis **13**

ATTRACTIONS ●
Acropolis Museum **10**
Byzantine Museum **34**
Hadrian's Arch **28**
Keramikós Cemetery **1**
Museum of Cycladic Art **33**
National Archaeological
  Museum **17**
Parthenon **9**
Presidential Palace **31**
Roman Agora **12**
Stoa of Attalos **5**
Temple of Olympian Zeus **27**
Tower of Winds (Aerides) **15**

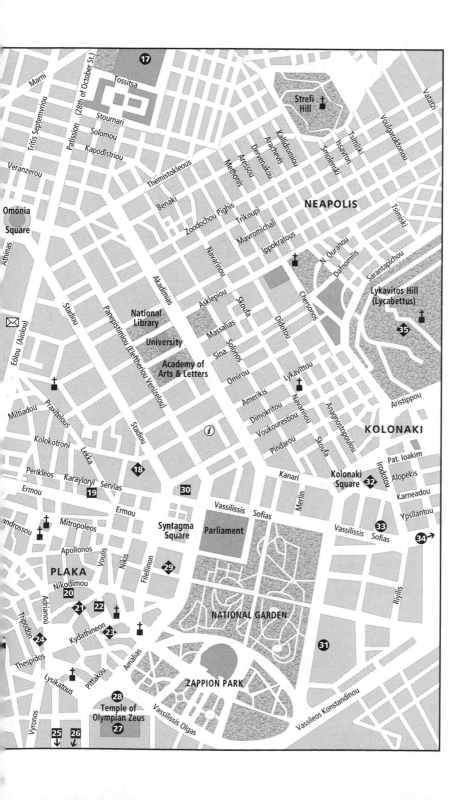

Marni
Tritis Septemvriou
Paitission (28th of October St.)
Tossitsa
Stournari
Solomou
Kapodistriou
Veranzerou
Omónia Square
Athinas
Eólou (Aiolou)
Stadiou
Panepistimiou (Eleftheriou Venizelou)
Miltiadou
Praxitelous
Stadiou
Kolokotroni
Perikleos
Karayloryi
Servias
Ermou
androssou
Mitropoleos
Ermou
Apollonos
Voulis
Nikis
Filellinon
PLAKA
Nikodimou
Adrianoú
Tripodon
Kydathineon
Thespidos
Vyronos
Lysikatous
Pittakou
Amalias

Themistokleous
Benaki
Zoodochou Pighis
Navarinou
Akadimias
National Library
University
Academy of Arts & Letters

Kallidromiou
Arachevis
Dervenakou
Aréssou
Methonis
Trikoupi
Mavromichali
Ippokratous
Asklepiou
Skoufa
Massalias
Sina
Solonos
Omirou
Amerikis
Dimokritou
Voukourestiou
Pindarou
Kanari
Merlin
Syntagma Square
Parliament
Vassilissis Sofias

Smolenski
Tsimiski
Issavron
Strefi Hill
Voulgaroktonou
Valatzi
NEAPOLIS
N. Ourahou
Dafnomilis
Tsimiski
Chersonos
Didotou
Lykavittou
Navarinou
Skoufa
Lykavitos Hill (Lycabettus)
Sarantapichou
Aristippou
KOLONAKI
Anagnostopoulou
Pat. Ioakim
Irodotou
Alopekis
Kolonaki Square
Karneadou
Vassilissis Sofias
Ypsilantou
Riyilis

NATIONAL GARDEN

Vassilissis Olgas
ZAPPION PARK
Temple of Olympian Zeus
Vasileos Konstandinou

105 Sýntagma Square. ☎ *800-325-3589 in the United States or 01-333-0000 in Greece. Fax: 01-322-8034. Internet:* www.HotelGrandeBretagne-ath.gr *or* www.sheraton.com. *Rates: 36,000–132,000Dr ($120–$440) double (rates set in dollars, not drachma, and the lower rates reflect some below-rack rates available through the Web site). AE, DC, MC, V.*

Tony's Pension

$ Koukáki

This one-time hostel is a staple for the budget-minded, but recent renovations have broadened its appeal. It's still a no-frills accommodation, and a bit off the beaten path, but it's run by a very friendly couple and features a small communal kitchen for light cooking.

26 Zacharítsa Street (two blocks from Moussón Street, between Lazéon and Karatza Sts.). ☎ *01-923-0561. Fax: 01-923-6370. Rates: 12,000–13,000Dr ($40–$43.35) double without bath, 12,000–17,000Dr ($40–$56.65) double with bath. MC.*

Athens's runner-up accommodations

Diomia Hotel

$$ A bare-bones hotel on the edge of the Plaka, with decent rates and some rooms (on the top two floors) that glimpse the Acropolis from their window. *Odos Diomias 5, two blocks from Syntagma Square (*☎ *01-323-8034; Fax 01-323-8034).*

Hotel Hera

$$ This hotel really has some of the best Acropolis views in town from the lush rooftop garden. Rooms are boring, but they do have balconies, and this is a quiet part of town. *Odos Falirou 9, between Odos Petmeza and Odos Donta (*☎ *01-923-6682; Fax 01-924-7334).*

Hotel Pláka

$$ This place offers breezy, modern accommodations with comfy amenities and balconies in the heart of the Pláka. Get a room on the fifth or sixth floor on the back side for a great view of the Acropolis (also available from the roof terrace with snack bar). *7 Odos Kapnikareas, at Mitropoleos (*☎ *01-322-2096; Fax 01-322-2412; Internet:* www.tourhotel.gr/plaka*).*

Jason Inn Hotel

$ On the north side of the Agora; a simple, clean, comfortable, relatively quiet, and cheap hotel. What more could you ask for? *12 Odos Asomaton, a block off Ermou (*☎ *01-325-1106; Fax 01-523-4786).*

Parthenon

$ Literally steps from the Acropolis, a modern hotel on the southern edge of the Pláka with cut-rate prices. *Odos Makri 6, just south of Odos Dionissiou Aeropagitou and Hadrian's Arch (*☎ *01-923-4594; Fax 01-644-1084).*

Dining in Athens

Greeks are more concerned about the quality and freshness of the food than the appearance of the restaurant. The old travel adage, "Seek out the place crowded with local families having a good time" definitely holds true in Athens. Lots of eateries look like dives but serve food fit for the gods on Mount Olympus. The dinner hour is rather late, starting anywhere from 9:00 to 11:00 p.m., so be sure to drop by a *taverna* (a Greek café) in the early evening to tide you over.

A key part of the Greek diet are *mezédes,* appetizers served before the meal or on their own (similar to Spain's *tapas*). Greeks eat *mezédes* with wine at a laid-back *taverna* or *ouzo* (a popular anise-flavored hard drink) at an *ouzerie* (a café where you'll find *ouzo*, wine, and *mezédes*). The tastiest are *tzatzíki* (a yogurt, cucumber, garlic, and mint dip), *melitzanosaláta* (eggplant salad), grilled *kalamarákia* (squid), *oktapódi* (octopus), and *loukánika* (sausage).

Other outstanding dishes served either as *mezédes* or as entrees are *dolmádes* (grape leaves stuffed with rice, pine nuts, and currants), *souvlaki* (shish kebabs of pork or lamb), *keftédes* (coriander- and cumin-spiced fried meatballs), *spanokópita* (spinach and feta pie), *moussaká* (an eggplant, potato, and minced meat casserole with a melted cheese crust), and other dishes of *arní* (lamb), *kotópoulo* (chicken), or *choirinó* (pork).

Greek *giaoúrti* (yogurt) is the creamiest and most delicious I've ever tasted. My favorite Greek meal is apple slices dipped in thick, plain yogurt. The ancient Greeks liked *méli* (honey) mixed with nectar so much they called it ambrosia, which means "food of the gods." You may feel the same way after drizzling some over your yogurt for dessert. *Baklavá* is flaky, thin pastry dough called phyllo layered with nuts and soaked in honey. *Sýka Mavrodáfni* is figs baked in red wine and served in a spice, orange-water, and honey sauce.

The quality of the seafood isn't always what you would expect it to be in Athens; overfishing and the resulting restrictions have led to high prices and freshness concerns. The port city of Piraeus boasts the best seafood restaurants in the area.

Wine may have been invented by the Greeks, even though you wouldn't know it from the turpentine-flavored *retsina,* which is flavored with pine resin and has mysteriously become Greece's most famous wine. Un-resined *krasí* may be more palatable to your tastes. Though most Greeks prefer whiskey these days, the national alcoholic beverage is *ouzo,* a clear, anise-flavored liqueur that turns milky white when you add water.

For lunch on the run, gobble a gyro — a pocket of pita bread filled with strips of roasted spiced meat. A good place to get a gyro in the heart of the Pláka is Grill House Pláka (☎ 01-324-6229) at 28 Odos Kidathinéon. But you can find countless other good gyro places all across the city. Otherwise, you can stop by any *taverna* for a nourishing round of *mezédes.*

Athens's top restaurants

Dionysos-Zonar's

$$$$ Kolonáki or Pláka   CONTINENTAL

Two restaurants across town from each other share this name. Both offer an international menu that's a bit on the expensive side for dinner, so come for a lunchtime salad or sandwich instead if you're drachma-conscious. Both locations have outstanding views. The Kolonáki restaurant sits atop Athens' highest hill, with the city on full display below. It's particularly gorgeous at sunset. The Pláka location is on the slope of Philopáppou Hill, around the "back side" of Acropolis Hill, and justifies its high prices with a breathtaking Parthenon view.

Kolonáki branch: Atop Lykavittós Hill; take the cable car from Odos Ploutárchou (above Kolonáki Square). ☎ 01-722-6374. Plaka branch: Dionysíou Aeropayítou Ave. ☎ 01-923-1936. Reservations recommended at both. Main courses at both: 2,500–7,200Dr ($8.35–$24). AE, DC, MC, V. Both open: Lunch and dinner daily. Closed Jan 31–Feb 28.

Diros Restaurant

$$$ Near Sýntagma Square   GREEK

What more could you want? It's not expensive, it's right off Sýntagma Square, it has both an air-conditioned interior and sidewalk tables, and the food couldn't be more satisfying. If you or your little ones need a break from Greek food, this family-friendly joint also serves more familiar dishes such as spaghetti and roast chicken with french fries.

10 Odos Xenofóndos (one block south of Sýntagma Square). ☎ 01-323-2392. Reservations suggested. Main courses: 1,600–4,200Dr ($5.35–$14). Fixed-price menus: 3,800–5,300 ($12.65–$17.65). AE, DC, MC, V. Open: Lunch and dinner daily.

Platanos Taverna

$ Pláka   GREEK

This is a classic Greek *taverna*. It is located on a tree-lined bend in a residential street, and the interior is a simple mix of paintings, photos, and old-fashioned Greek ambiance. Platanos serves hearty mainstays of Greek cuisine cooked simply but with a keen eye for freshness and quality.

4 Odos Dioyénous (near the intersection of Adrianoú and Eólou). ☎ 01-322-0666. Reservations suggested. Main courses: 1,500–2,500Dr ($5–$8.35). No credit cards. Open: Lunch and dinner Mon–Sat.

Restaurant Kentrikon

$$$ Near Sýntagma Square   INTERNATIONAL

Locals find that the excellent food at this huge restaurant is worth the comparatively high prices. The best bets on the menu include the lamb ragoût with spinach, chicken with okra, and the special macaroni. Although everything at this air-conditioned, 1960s joint is quite informal, the service is top-notch.

3 Odos Kolokotróni (one block up from Stadíou). ☎ 01-323-2482. Reservations suggested. Main courses: 1,100–4,600Dr ($3.65–$15.35). MC. Open: Lunch daily.

Rodiá Taverna

$$$ Kolonáki GREEK

The atmosphere at this relatively cheap restaurant is among the best you'll find. The decor includes lacy curtains, dark wood paneling, wine kegs, and a vine-sheltered garden in back. Yet the ambiance cannot steal the show from the superb food; try the octopus in mustard sauce, light *bourékis* (vegetable-filled pastries), or lemon-tinged beef.

44 Odos Aristípou (off Kolonáki Square). ☎ 01-722-9883. Reservations suggested. Main courses: 2,000–3,500Dr ($6.65–$11.65). No credit cards. Open: Dinner Mon–Sat.

Taverna Xinos

$$ Pláka GREEK

Live music and folsky murals give this place an informal feel, but this is one of Athens' best restaurants. For a real cultural treat, arrive after 9 p.m. — that's when the locals and connoisseurs get there — and sit back, relax, and enjoy a liesurely dinner. The *dolmádes, moussaká,* and lamb fricassee are all delicious.

4 Angélou Yéronda (in the heart of the Pláka, between Kidathinéon and Iperídou). ☎ 01-322-1065. Reservations recommended. Main courses: 2,000–2,800Dr ($6.65–$9.35). No credit cards. Open: Dinner daily (sometimes closes Sunday). Closed July or Aug.

Athens's runner-up restaurants

Damigos

$ A cellar taverna specializing in deep-fried codfish and eggplant for almost 150 years. Add in the cheap meats and stews, and you've got one of the best values on the Pláka's main drag. *Odos Kidathineon 41 (☎ 01-322-5084).*

Kouklis Ouzeri

$ The best Pláka joint for mezédes of all shapes and sizes. Pick and choose from the dozen presented on the platter or go all out and splurge on the whole shebang. *Odos Tripodon 14, between Flessa and Thespidos (☎ 01-324-7605).*

Palia Plakiotiki Taverna

$$$ It may look a little contrived — a series of beautiful flowering terraces with a band that appears at one end as the evening wears on to play traditional Greek tunes — but this is the genuine article. It's an ancient taverna where locals still come for good food and a rousing good time singing along with the music. (Prices are a bit high, but think of it as cheap admission for the floor show.) Try to book ahead. *Odos Lissou 26 in the heart of the Plaka (☎ 01-322-8722).*

Taverna Ipiros

$-$$ Filling portions of homey Greek specialties at low, low prices mere steps from the Agora entrance. The best, most genuine choice in an area increasingly poisoned by overpriced tourist joints. *Plateis Ayiou Philippou 15, a few blocks southwest of Monastiraki Square (☎ 01-324-5572).*

Thanasis

$ Thanasis has great souvlaki with a pita for just 330Dr ($1.10), and you can get it to go or sit at an outdoor table amid the throngs at this bustling corner of the Plaka. Good fries, too. *69 Odos Metropóleon, just off Monastiraki Square (☎ 01-324-4705).*

Exploring Athens

The congested, sprawling, and polluted appearance of Athens today can't hide the fact that it was once the center of Western culture. The world-class sights located here are a testament to Athens' history as the seat of European civilization, and they mustn't be missed.

Athens's top sights

The Acropolis and the Parthenon

Located right in the heart of Athens, the Acropolis Hill is where mythology tells us the gods Athena and Poseidon squared off to see who could take better care of the local citizens and thus become the city's guardian and namesake. (Poseidon produced a salt-water spring from the ground; Athena topped him by inventing the versatile olive tree.)

The Acropolis is part of Greece's identity, a landmark that symbolizes the country itself. At the top rests the mighty Parthenon, a temple that rises nobly above Athens, reminding the modern city of its ancient heritage. Allow a good two to three hours to tour the Acropolis and its museum.

You enter by climbing stairs to the Beulé Gate, built by the Roman Emperor Valerian in a.d. 267. The cute little Ionic temple of Athena Nike (built 424 b.c., rebuilt a.d. 1940) is perched on your right as you climb.

The world has bigger and better-preserved ancient shrines, but the Parthenon still remains the poster child of Greek temples. Between 447 and 438 b.c., the Athenians spent lavishly to build this shrine to their patron. A 40-foot statue of Athena (a small Roman copy of it is in the Archeological Museum) once graced this all-marble temple. The structure is perfectly proportioned, and a few architectural tricks make it appear flawless to the naked eye. To compensate for the eye's natural tendency to create illusions, the horizontal surfaces are bowed slightly upward in the middle to appear perfectly level, the columns lean slightly inward to appear parallel, and each is thicker in the middle so it looks like a textbook cylinder to you and me.

The Parthenon remained virtually intact through the Middle Ages. It became an Orthodox church in the sixth century, a Catholic church during the Crusades, and an Islamic mosque when the Turks occupied the region. But its luck ran out when the Venetians attacked the Turkish city in 1687. The Turks stored ammunition in the old temple, and when a Venetian cannonball hit the stockpile, the armaments exploded and blew the Parthenon to pieces.

British Lord Elgin collected almost all the sculpted friezes and pediment pieces from the rubble, destroying many in the process, and shipped them to England from 1801 to 1811. These bits of the original Parthenon remain in the British Museum, even though the Greek government has asked for their return many times. Although the temple was once covered almost entirely with sculptures and ornamental carvings, only a few sculptured spots remain on the Parthenon today.

If you look down the Acropolis' south side, you'll see the half-moon shapes of two theaters. The huge one to the east that is mostly in ruins is the **Theater of Dionysos**, built in 330 b.c. (entrance on Dionyssíous Aeropayítou; ☎ 01-322-4625; admission 500Dr/$1.65). Near the entrance to the Acropolis lies the **Odeum of Heródes Átticus**, which was built in a.d. 174 and restored in recent centuries to stage concerts during the Athens Festival from June to October (for information, call the festival office at ☎ 01-322-1459 or the Odeum at ☎ 01-323-2771).

The Acropolis entrance is on the west side of the hill and can be reached from a path off Dioskoúon and Theorías Streets. ☎ 01-321-0219 (01-323-6665 for the museum). Bus/trolley: 9, 230. Open: In summer, daily 8:00 a.m.–7:00 p.m. (the museum doesn't open until noon on Mondays); in winter, hours vary but are usually shorter, closing at 6:30 p.m. or earlier; the Acropolis is occasionally closed in the early afternoon. Call the Greek National Tourism Organization (☎ 01-331-0437) for details and precise hours for this year. Admission: 2,000Dr ($6.65) adults, 1,000Dr ($3.35) students.

The Ancient Agora (market)

The everyday life of ancient Athenians revolved around the Agora, or marketplace. But like the Forum in Rome, not much is left of the historic market today; it appears as little more than a dusty bowl filled with mangy trees, broken-down pediments among the grass, and rows of broken column stubs marking the borders of temples and buildling from a bygone era. Still, it will take you a good two hours to sift through the rubble and study the reconstructed bits — longer for real students of history.

The Hephaisteion, built between 449 and 444 b.c. (and one of the world's best-preserved Greek temples), and the reconstructed Stoa of Attalos are the two most remarkable remains. A *stoa* was a colonnade (a series of columns spaced evenly apart) supporting a long roof under which shop-keepers set up business, people met, and philosophers held court in the shade. One famous thinker named Zeno held classes under a *stoa* so often that his disciples were known as the Stoics.

The Agora's interesting museum is in the huge Stoa of Attalos, which was built in the second century b.c. and rebuilt in the 1950s. In many ways, it's a museum of modern democracy; the most fascinating artifacts document systems the ancients used to carry out their famous democratic processes. For example, you can see bronze jury ballots — jurors voted with a bronze wheel with a solid axle if they felt the man on trial was inno-cent, with an empty axle if they found the defendant's story as hollow as the rod.

The museum also has a marble *kleroterion* (allotment machine) that looks very much like a modern Lotto machine. Bronze tickets bearing the names of government officials were inserted into slots, and colored balls would fall from a tube and randomly determine who among those names would fulfill various civic duties, such as serving on a committee.

The museum also has a collection of pottery shards called *óstraka,* on which, once a year, Athenians could write the name of any man they thought had gained too much power and thus threatened the democracy. If any person's name appeared on the majority of *óstraka*, he would be *ostracized*, or banished, from Athens for ten years. (And now you know where the term ostracized came from.)

The entrance to the Ancient Agora is on Andrianou Street at Ayiou philippou Square, just east of Monastiráki Square. ☎ *01-321-0185. Open: Tues–Sun 8:30 a.m.–2:30 p.m. Admission: 1,200Dr ($4) adults, 600Dr ($2) students.*

Archeological Museum

This is a testament to all of Greece's eminence and beauty hundreds of years before the rise of Rome and thousands of years before Columbus set sail for the New World. It's truly one of the greatest archeological museums in the world.

You will need three hours for even a perfunctory run-through. Aspiring archeologists will want to stay most of a day and maybe even part of a second. The collections are hard to fully understand and enjoy without plenty of background info, so I recommend you invest in a catalog guide.

Life-sized and oversized bronze statues from Athens' Golden Age (400s b.c.) are the most striking artifacts in the museum. These include Poseidon about to throw his (now missing) trident, a tiny child jockey atop a galloping horse, and the "Marathon Boy" striking a disco pose. Most of these bronzes were found at the bottom of the ocean in shipwrecks by divers in the late nineteenth and twentieth centuries.

Representing the sixth and seventh centuries b.c., the museum presents statues of *kouroi* — attractive young men with cornrow hair, taking one step forward with their arms rigidly at their sides. These figures, adapted from Egyptian models, set the standard in Greek art until the Classical period ushered in more anatomically correct and naturalistic sculpture.

44 Patissíon (October 28 Ave.; several long blocks north of Omónia Square). ☎ *01-821-7717. Internet: www.culture.gr. Bus/trolley: 2, 4, 11, 15, A6, B6, A8, B8, A12, B12, G12, 622, 608, 242, minibus 200. Open: Apr–Oct 15, Mon 12:30 p.m.–7:00 p.m., Tues–Fri 8:00 a.m.–7:00 p.m., Sat–Sun 8:30 a.m.–3 p.m.; Oct 16–Mar, Mon 11:00 a.m.–5:00 p.m., Tues–Fri 8:00 a.m.–5:00 p.m., Sat–Sun 8:30 a.m.–3:00 p.m. Admission: 2,000Dr ($6.65) adults, free for students.*

N. P. Goulandris Foundation Museum of Cycladic Art

If you have another hour to spare, this is the best of all the other museums in town. The Goulandris has wonderfully informative plaques describing each piece in a collection that celebrates the art and simple sculpture of the Cycladic tradition, which began in about 3,000 b.c. Famed twentieth-century artists such as Brancusi, Henry Moore, Modigliani, and Picasso were all inspired by these sculptures. The museum's second floor houses ancient Greek pieces, many from the fifth century b.c.

4 Neophýtou Douká Kolonáki. ☎ *01-722-8321. Internet: www.cycladic-m.gr. Open: Mon, Wed–Fri 10:00 a.m.–4:00 p.m., Sat 10:00 a.m.–3:00 p.m. Admission: 1,000Dr ($3.35), or 500Dr ($1.65) Sat.*

More cool things to see and do in Athens

From seeking out a hidden ruin to taking in a performance of folkloric music and dancing, there's much more in Athens to keep you busy.

✔ **Wander the City in Search of Less Touristy Ruins.** It seems that everyone who visits Athens makes a beeline to the Acropolis, and most also find their way to the Agora and the Archeological Museum, but then many travelers set sail for the islands, leaving the rest of Athens' vast archeological heritage to the few who stay an extra day and explore a bit.

The best of the remaining ancient sites includes **Hadrian's Arch** (on Amalías Avenue, between Vasilissis Olgas and Dionissiou Streets), through which the Roman emperor marched in a.d. 132

to dedicate the gigantic **Temple of the Olympian Zeus** (☎ 01-922-6330). Built a little bit at a time between 515 b.c. and a.d. 132, the temple measures 360 by 143 feet. Fifteen of the original 104 columns are still standing, each an impressive 56 feet high. The sight is open Tuesday to Sunday, 8:00 a.m. to 2:30 p.m.; admission is 500Dr ($1.65).

The octagonal **Tower of the Wind** (where Eolou Avenue ends at Pelopída Street) was built in the first century b.c. and once held a water clock, which measured time by the fall or flow of water. In the eighteenth century, whirling dervishes did their religious spinning dance at the tower.

An ancient cemetery called the **Keramikós** (☎ 01-346-3552), 500 yards from the Agora at 148 Ermoú Street, was outside the walls of the ancient city. You can still see some of the old walls here, as well as the ancient city gates. The cemetery site has roads lined with tombs and includes a section of the Sacred Way. It's open Tuesday to Sunday, 8:00 a.m. to 2:30 p.m.; admission is 500Dr ($1.65)

✔ **See the Changing of the Guard.** Athens' version of this tradition is much more entertaining than its London counterpart. The guards wear shoes with pom-poms on the toes and march in a comical, stiff-legged style. They stand at attention in front of the Parliament building and march back and forth in front of the Tomb of the Unknown Soldier (both are on Sýntagma Square), and the duty-rotation ceremony occurs every Sunday at 10:30 a.m.

✔ **Enjoy Some Greek Music and Dancing.** All over Athens, *bouzoúki* clubs — named after a mandolin-type instrument often played in them — can give you a tase of traditional folk music and dancing. The musical styles include the *rebétika* tunes of the urban lower class or *dimotiká,* upbeat country folk music. Greeks traditionally show their appreciation for the music by smashing plates, but you should check with the staff before you do this because many clubs don't allow this anymore. (Places that still do will charge you or let you buy them before the show.)

As you get farther from the Pláka neighborhood, the clubs get more authentically Greek. Still, most clubs are used to seeing a lot of tourists, and the waiters will teach you some simple dances. Things really get busy at around 11:00 p.m., but if you want a good seat you had better get there early.

For good *rebétika* music, try **Rebétiki Istorís** (☎ 01-642-4937), 181 Odos Ippókratous; **Taximi** (☎ 01-363-9919), 29 Odos Isávron; or **Dioyenis Palace** (☎ 01-942-4267), 259 Syngroú Ave. **Taverna Mostroú** (☎ 01-324-2441), 22 Odos Mnissikléos, is a top-notch *dimotiká* club. More club info is available in *Athenscope* magazine, which you can get at news kiosks.

You can see the most authentic, artistic folk dancing in the open-air shows put on by performers from the **Dora Stratou Folk Dance Theater** (☎ 01-324-4395), May to September nightly at 10:15 p.m. (plus 8:15 p.m. Wednesdays and Sundays) on Philopáppou Hill.

And on Your Left, The Agora: Seeing Athens by Guided Tour

Hop-in sightseeing tours (☎ 01-428-5500; Internet: www.hopin.com) make the rounds of 41 Athenian stops in a two-hour circuit between 9:00 a.m. and 4:00 p.m., and you can get on and off at will (and make use of a free tour guide at the Acropolis; admission is extra). The bus stops at all the major sights in this chapter and on Sýntagma Square.

Tickets cost 8,500Dr ($28.35) and are good for two days; you can get them at travel agents or on the bus. Hop-in also offers variants on the bus tour for 10,000 to 12,000Dr ($33.35 to $40) that include a two-hour guided tour at one of several major sights (Acropolis, Archeology Museum, or Byzantine Museum), including admission fees.

Suggested One-, Two-, and Three-Day Itineraries

If you're the type who'd rather organize your own tours, this section offers some tips for building your own Athens itineraries.

If you have one day

If you see only one sight in Athens, it has to be Acropolis Hill, with its mighty Parthenon, the most famous Greek temple in the world and the symbol of the city itself. Spend the whole morning here admiring the work of the ancients, their temples and theaters, and the sculpture and other artifacts in the on-site museum.

After lunch (grab a *souvlaki* to go and some pita), trolley up to the incredible Archeological Museum, housing one of the richest collections of antiquities in the world.

In the late afternoon, head to the Plaka to explore its alleyways and nightlife. Have dinner under the sycamores of Platanos Taverna, and, if it's between May and September, head to Philopáppou Hill before 10:15 p.m. to take in a performance of the Dora Stratou Folk Dance Theater. In winter, just find a traditional *bouzoúki* club after dinner and clap along.

If you have two days

Spend Day One as described in the previous section. On Day Two, start off at the Ancient Agora, exploring its ruins and visiting the museum inside the famed Stoa of Attalos to see, literally, the machinery of the world's first democracy.

Afterward, delve briefly into the Pláka for an early lunch at one of its sidewalk *tavernas* (Ipiros or Thanasis, reviewed in "Athens's runner-up restaurants," are both excellent). Make sure you get to the Goulandris Museum of Cycladic and Ancient Greek Art by 2:30 p.m. so you can admire its beautiful and highly stylized ancient statues.

Return to the Plaka in the late afternoon to seek out some of the less famous ancient architectural ruins hidden in its back alleys (see "More cool things to see and do in Athens"). Then rustle up some dinner at Palia Plakiotiki Taverna or Taverna Xinos, and find yourself a *bouzoúki* club to plant yourself in for an evening of *retsina, ouzo,* and song.

Or, if you're tired of the Pláka scene, head up to Athens' highest hill and dine with a view at the Kolonáki branch of Dionysos-Zonar's.

If you have three days

If you can manage it, I would definitely give Athens only the two days described previously and spend the third day in Delphi.

The best way to do this, if you're arriving in Greece by ferry, is to take the bus from Patras to Delphi the night you arrive. (I'm not counting this as one of your three days because the boats arrive in the late afternoon.) Stay the night in Delphi, and then spend your first day clambering around the evocative ruins, consulting the oracle (at least in your imagination), and touring the museum before hopping a late afternoon (or evening) bus to Athens. Then you can spend Days Two and Three of your Greek odyssey in Athens.

If you arrive in Greece by plane, spend Days One and Two as previously indicated, but leave Athens on the evening of the second day for Delphi. (See "Exploring Beyond Athens," below, for details.) Spend the night there before exploring the mountainside site the next day, returning to Athens in the evening again for a late dinner.

Exploring Beyond Athens

Most visitors come to Greece to study the remains of an ancient culture or relax on a sun-drenched island. Archeology buffs have a relatively easy choice — it's hard to beat Delphi's interesting artifacts and beautiful mountain setting. But if you're into island-hopping, you've got a dizzying number of choices. Greece has more than 6,000 islands, though fewer than 200 are inhabited. So here's my advice: Visit Santoríni (its Greek name is Thira, but everyone recognizes it by its Venetian moniker). Even though it is the farthest island from Athens, its tourist infrastructure makes the island easy for first-time visitors to negotiate. Santoríni has quite a few interesting ancient sites, as well as quaint seaside villages and hopping nightlife — and let's not forget the beautiful beaches.

Delphi: The center of the ancient world

If I only had time to visit one archeological site in Greece, I would choose Delphi. It's a no-brainer. The ancients couldn't have picked a prettier spot for the place they considered the center of the world. Delphi lies halfway up a mountainside, with the impressive Mount Parnassos surrounding the site and a lush, narrow valley of olive trees stretching down to the Gulf of Corinth.

You can do Delphi in one long day trip from Athens, but you really should stay the night to make the trip less hectic and much more fun. After some time in the manic city, you'll welcome Delphi's small-town beauty and pace.

Getting there

Buses make the 2½hour trip from Athens six times a day (2,900Dr/$9.65). If you're taking the ferry to Greece, I suggest that you bus here right from the ferry terminal in Patras. After spending the next day and night in Delphi, continue on to Athens the following morning.

The **tourism office** (☎ **0265-82-900**) is at 44 Odós Frideríkis. The office of the **Tourist Police** is nearby at 27 Odós Frideríkis (☎ **0265-89-920** or 0265-82-220).

Seeing the sights

Delphi is a two-road town with little side streets connecting the two. The bus will drop you off at the west end of town, and the archeological site is a five- to ten-minute walk from town. (There are few parking spaces at the sight, so if you *must* drive, then head out early.) Many visitors start at the museum, which is along the way to the ruins, but if you want to beat the heat and the crowds, you should rush straight to the outdoor archeological area first thing in the morning. The ruins will put you in the right frame of mind for the more intellectual experience of examining the museum's treasures.

The main ruins area is the **Sanctuary of Apollo** (☎ **0265-82-313**), which extends up the lower slopes of Mount Parnassos. You'll follow the **Sacred Way**, a marble path lined with the ruined treasuries of Greek city-states that tried to outdo each other in their efforts to offer the greatest riches to the sanctuary. The Athenian Treasury, located just past the first bend in the Sacred Way, is a remarkably well-preserved example.

The Sacred Way hits a plateau at what was once the inner sanctum of **the Temple of Apollo.** Pilgrims from all over the Western world came here to seek advice or have their fortunes told by a seer called the Oracle of Delphi, who spoke the wisdom of Apollo in tongues. Earthquakes, looting, and landslides have pretty much destroyed the temple's partially underground chambers.

The fourth century b.c. theater at the top of the sanctuary is the best-preserved of its kind in Greece. (Of course, the Romans helped the preservation process by rebuilding it about 2,000 years ago.) Musicians

and performers competed here in the Pythian Games, which empha-
sized culture more than the Olympic Games because they were held in
honor of Apollo — god of poets and inventor of the lyre. The view of
the whole archeological site is fantastic from the theater, but you can
climb even farther up to the long, tree-lined stadium, which dates to
the sixth century b.c. and was the site of the Pythian Games' athletic
contests.

After you leave the Sanctuary of Apollo, if you keep walking down the
main road, you will see Delphi's most beautiful ruins below you. These
ruins are in the **Marmaria** — so named because later Greeks used the
area as a marble quarry. The most striking sight is the remains of the
small, round temple called **tholos,** built in 380 b.c. In the 1930s, three of
the original 20 columns in the temple's outer shell were re-erected and
a section of the lintel (the horizontal connecting span) was replaced on
top. It's at its most beautiful when the sun sets behind it. Admission to
the ruins as a whole is 1,200Dr ($4) for adults, 900Dr ($3) for seniors,
and 600Dr ($2) for students. The ruins are open daily 8:00 a.m. to 7:00
p.m. (in winter they may close as early as 5:30 p.m., or 3:00 p.m.
Saturday and Sunday).

Delphi's **Archeological Museum** (☎ **0265-82-312**) is nearly as good as
the one in Athens. *Kouri* (stylized statues of youths) from the
seventh century b.c. and gifts that once were part of the Sacred Way's
treasuries are among its artifacts. Don't miss the winged sphinx of the
Naxians or the pride of the museum, a bronze statue of a charioteer
from 474 b.c. that still has a few of the reins that once controlled a
group of horse statues.

The museum also houses the **Omphalós**, or "Navel Stone," a piece of
rock that once marked the spot under the Temple to Apollo that the
Greeks believed was the center of the world. Naturally, the Greeks
relied on myths to settle on this location for the world's belly button.
Zeus was said to have released two eagles at opposite ends of the earth
(which was flat then). Because the birds flew toward each other at
identical speeds, the point where they crashed into each other and fell
to the ground marked the world's central point.

Museum admission rates are the same as for the ruin sites. It is open
Monday, noon to 7:00 p.m.; Tuesday to Sunday, 8:00 a.m. to 7:00 p.m. It
also may close earlier in winter.

Where to stay and dine
The **Taverna Vackchos** (☎ **0265-82-448**), near the bus stop at 31 Odós
Apóllonos, is a simple but delicious and inexpensive restaurant with
great views. Spend the night at the **Hotel Hermes** (☎ **0265-82-318,** fax:
0265-82-639), 27 Odós Frideríkis, where modern doubles cost 11,000Dr
($36.65).

Santoríni

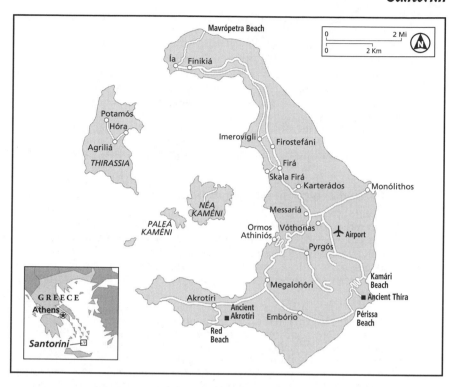

Sunning on Santoríni

Santoríni (Thíra in Greek) is the last island in the Cyclades, a long string of isles in the Aegean Sea littered with ruins and populated by fishermen and sun-worshippers. It is a steep black cliff with streaks of red stone that curves around a caldera (volcanic crater) of green water where newer volcano cones still sometimes hiss and smoke. Black-sand beaches, vineyards, whitewashed villages, and the excavations of ancient cities dot this spit of land.

Santoríni's charms — sunny beaches and the excesses of the "good life" — are not a secret; it is one of the most heavily visited Greek islands. It can get maddeningly crowded and seem like one big disco in July and August, a modern symbol of mythical hedonism. But in the spring and fall, when the visiting hordes diminish, Santoríni shines with the quaint feeling of a small fishing village.

TIP

Some people actually make Santoríni a day trip by plane from Athens. These day-trippers, and the hordes that stop for an afternoon cruise break, make noon the most crowded time on Santoríni. If you stay overnight you can get a friendlier, slightly less-crowded perspective on this crescent-shaped volcanic island. Santoríni is worth a two- to four-day stay if you can swing it, but remember that it virtually shuts down from late October to Easter.

The island that blew its top

Santoríni was a circular volcano until an eruption in the 1600s b.c. blew half the island into the air. This created massive tidal waves, spewed ash all over the region, and sparked earthquakes that swept the Aegean — an event that may have helped destroy the Minoan civilization, which was centered on Crete. A wealthy Minoan city called Akrotíri was on Santoríni, and some historians think that this city's volcanic destruction, just at the dawn of recorded history, fueled the mythology about a "lost continent." In other words, we could be talking about Atlantis.

Getting there and getting around

Several flights make the easy 50-minute trip from Athens each day. Call **Olympic Airways** (15 Filelinon Street, ☎ **01-966-6666** or 01-926-7444), **Air Greece** (20 Nikis Street, ☎ **01-325-5011**), or **Cronus Airlines** (8 Othonos, ☎ **01-331-5510**). Fares start around 38,800Dr ($129.35) round-trip, and — unless you plan on doing other island-hopping along the way — this is generally worth the time you will save over taking the ferry.

Between the various ferry companies there are two to six (in summer) boats daily to Santoríni from Athens' Piraeus port for 5,636Dr ($18.80) in economy, 21,000Dr ($70) in luxury class. For information on the ferry companies and their schedules, visit a travel agent (the Pláka overflows with them) or call the **Port Authority** in Piraeus at ☎ **01-422-6000**. The trip takes 9 to 12 hours, depending on how many stops the ferry makes at other Cycladic islands along the way. There's an interminably long staircase from the ferry port up to Fira, Santoríni's main town, or you can take a cable car that runs every 20 minutes for 800Dr ($2.65).

Buses on the island connect the main town of Fira with the airport, the ruins of Akrotiri, and most villages and popular beaches. Tickets run 230–370Dr (75cents–$1.25), paid on the bus, and most runs leave every 30 to 60 minutes (schedules are posted at the depot in Fira). Taxis from the airport to Fira should cost around 1,500Dr ($5).

Santoríni has no official tourism office, but dozens of private travel agents distribute free info; one of the best is **Kamari Tours** (☎ **0286-31-390**), which is located two blocks south of Fira's main square. It can help you get a hotel or schedule guided tours of the island.

Seeing the sights

If you don't want to take care of making the sightseeing connections yourself, Fira's multitude of travel agents make their living selling half- and full-day bus tours to all the island's villages and sights.

The island's best waterfront is **Kamári Beach,** a 4½-mile-long stretch of black pebbles and sand on the southeast shore of the island (but it's horribly crowded in July and August).

Other popular activities include shopping at the island's overabundance of boutiques and sampling the tasty wine produced with the help of the rich volcanic soil. **Boutari winery** (☎ **0286-81-011**) offers tours that include sampling of several wines. The tours cost 1,200Dr ($4) and run from April to October, Monday to Saturday, 10:00 a.m. to sunset. Ask the driver of the bus from Fira to Akrotiri to let you off at the winery.

But try also to fit in an excursion to Santoríni's two most impressive archeological sites. The ruins of the wealthy Minoan city of **Akrotíri** (☎ **0286-81-366**) lie on the southern tip of the island. Since the 1930s, archeologists have conducted covered excavations of the streets and buildings in this almost-6,000-year-old city (though the parts we can see today are from a settlement from 1500 b.c.). You can wander this emerging ghost town on a plank walkway. Buses run here regularly, and admission is 1,200Dr ($4), 600Dr ($2) students. The site is open Tuesday to Sunday, 8:00 a.m. to 3:00 p.m.; visit early in the morning to beat the crowds and the heat. The nearby Red Beach is a good place to swim and have lunch afterward.

After most of the island was destroyed in a volcanic explosion in the 1600s b.c., a second civilization started around 900 b.c . The capital was **Ancient Thíra**, which lies 1,200 feet above Kamári Beach. The ruins here are not covered, so considerably less is left standing than at Akrotíri. But after searching through the buildings (300 to 145 b.c.), you can have a picnic overlooking the sea and shaded by trees or an ancient portico still supported by Doric columns.

This site has no admission fee, but you'll have to find some way to get there because it's well off the beaten path. You can take the bus to Kamári, which lets you off at the bottom of a difficult and steep 2½-mile hike up to the site. Or you can pay a mule driver at the bus stop 4,000Dr ($13.35) to take you up and around on a half-day tour. Other alternatives are taking a tour offered by one of the island's many travel agents, or paying for a taxi to take you to the site, which should cost about 12,000Dr ($40) round-trip from Fira. The site is open Tuesday to Saturday, 9:00 a.m. to 2:30 p.m.; and Sunday, 9:00 a.m. to 1:00 p.m.

The main town of **Fira** also has a small but outstanding archeological museum (☎ **0286-22-217**), with artifacts from digs on the island as well as early Cycladic figurines. Admission is 800Dr ($2.65) adults, 600Dr ($2) seniors, and 400Dr ($1.30) students; it's open Tuesday to Sunday, 8:30 a.m. to 3:00 p.m.

Where to stay

You will find the most hotels in Fira — but you'll also hear the most noise and run into the most tourists. (Stay in a smaller village if you want to see the true colors of Santoríni.) Try to get a room with a view of the caldera, which is what you'll get in the 24,500–32,500Dr ($81.65–$108.35) doubles at **Loucas Hotel** (☎ **0286-22-480,** fax: 0286-24-882; in winter call 01-577-6232 or fax 01-494-5065).

If you want to stay on the beach at Kamári, try the **Kamári Beach Hotel** (☎ **0286-31-216,** fax: 0286/31-243). The 30,000Dr ($100) doubles all have balconies for enjoying the beach and the sea vistas.

As on most Greek islands, your boat will be greeted by people who want to rent you a room in their house. This is often a pretty good deal in Greece, as long as you ask questions before heading off with the person and don't commit to anything until you see the place. These private rooms can be your only option if you arrive without reservations in July or August. Most rooms cost from 6,000Dr ($20) in the off-season to 15,000Dr ($50) in summer.

Many hotels on Santoríni, including the two mentioned here, are only open April 15 to October 15. In the off-season, the demand for hotel rooms is less than the supply, plus you can negotiate a good deal on a private room.

Where to dine

For light dining in Fira, try **Kástro** (☎ 0286-22-503). It attracts scads of day trippers because it is located across from the cable car terminal, but the snacks, sandwiches, and beautiful views of the volcanic crater are worth the hassle. If you are looking for a more romantic meal, hit **Aris Restaurant** (☎ 0286-22-480), Odós Ayíou Miná; this converted winery serves wonderful *mezédes* and *moussáka*.

If you are at Kamári Beach and want a snack, check out **Alexis Grille** (no phone), located in a pine grove at the beach's north end. For more elegant international fare, try **Camille Stephani** (☎ 0286-31-716), just 500 yards from the bus stop.

Part VI
The Part of Tens

"This is the 5th time down the slope you've claimed a sudden urge to make a snow angel. Why don't you just <u>admit</u> you're falling?"

In this part . . .

The final four chapters are sort of ...*For Dummies* "Top 10" lists, covering in straightforward, brief paragraphs some of Europe's bests, worsts, and little known wonders. I want you to be better prepared than the next guy, who bought one of those densely written guides that lists dozens of hotels (usually without saying anything useful about them) and explains the history of every painting in the museum.

Chapter 26

The Ten Most Overrated Sights and Attractions in Europe

*T*he sights listed in this chapter may not provide what you expect from all the hype you've read. Some of these places still get their own mention again in the destination chapters of this guide. This is because they're too famous not to include and, quite frankly, this is a subjective list of sights that I, and many others, find overrated. You may enjoy the heck out of them, and that's okay, too.

However, several of the sights listed here are so unjustly famous that I simply didn't include them in the book at all. So if you're wondering why the French Riviera is missing, read on and find out.

London's Changing of the Guard at Buckingham Palace

On the yawn scale, I give it about an 8. It features diffident pomp, half-hearted ceremony, and a clearly bored marching band. And it's crowded, too.

London's Madame Tussaud's Wax Museum

Pay $16 to ogle wax portraits (albeit expertly executed) of famous dead people? Kitschy, maybe. A must-see? Never. This place is only famous because it's been franchised around the world — sort of a fast food approach to culture for a museum that's only of marginal historical interest in the first place.

Paris's Champs-Elysées and Rome's Via Veneto

These boulevards were the talk of the town into the 1960s, world-class public living rooms where the rich and famous went to see and be seen sipping coffee at a sidewalk cafe.

Now the Champs-Elysées that Catharine de' Medici first rode her carriage down has become Paris's main drag for fast food chains and movie multiplexes — though it's still monumental. The Via Veneto of Fellini's *La Dolce Vita* (the film that gave up the term *paparazzi*) has gone from glitterati ground-zero to a string of overpriced, internationally affiliated hotels booked only by tour bus companies.

The French Riviera

A disappointment, at least from a beach-going point of view. Americans are used to vast expanses of glittering sand. In Europe, sand is a precious commodity, and the beaches — sand, shingle, pebbles, or outright rocks — are mostly private, crowded, narrow strips of shoreline with tightly packed regiments of umbrellas and changing cabins. Come to the Riviera for the casinos or nightlife, if that's your sort of thing. But don't come for the beaches.

The Leaning Tower of Pisa

Yes, the cathedral bell tower is beautiful to behold and dramatically off-kilter. But, unfortunately, you can't climb it anymore. Due to the stress on the fabric of the building from its poor posture, the tower is closed to the public for the foreseeable future while a series of drastic measures is being undertaken to reduce the lean by a few feet. But if you do go to Pisa, you'll find some stunning examples of Gothic sculpture and Romanesque architecture.

Madrid's Flamenco Shows

The folksy shows given for tourists are often of poor quality and overpriced. In Chapter 25, you'll find my recommendations for the more authentic flamenco shows, but remember that you'll find the real thing (a spontaneous nighttime ritual) in Andalusia.

Athens, Greece

Yes, you'll definitely want to see the Acropolis, Agora, and the Archeological Museum if you visit Athens, but be forewarned that the city itself is dirty, crowded, and boring. And getting there is no easy task — you'll spend three days of your trip traveling by train or ferry if you choose not to fly. Exploring Greece's fascinating interior is a much better choice for spending your time. And then there's always lazing about the islands for loads of fun.

Shopping the "Big Names" in London, Paris, Rome, and Florence

Harrods was an incredible, almost unbelievable institution when it first opened — a block-long, multilevel building packed to the gills with every imaginable item that you might want to buy (and many that you never thought of), all in one place. We have a word for that today: department store. Sure, Harrods is still classier than even top-end chains like Macy's, and it has a nifty food section, but you'll actually find more variety (if not quality) these days at the Mall of America.

Paris's **Rue du Faubourg St-Honoré** is, indeed, lined with remarkable shops and high-end boutiques. But one of the cardinal rules of elite shopping in Europe is that high fashion costs no less in its country of origin (France or Italy) than a New York boutique or upscale factory outlet center in the U.S. This applies to the other streets mentioned in this section, as well as any other street and city in Europe. Yes, there's always the cachet of buying that little black dress in Paris or leather shoes in Florence, but don't make the mistake of thinking that you're coming here for a bargain (those are to be found in stock shops and Europe's outdoor markets).

Via Condotti, the main shopping drag that shoots like an arrow from the base of Rome's Spanish Steps, is now home to a Foot Locker and a Disney Store. The big names of Italian fashion (not to mention the small "Made in Italy" boutiques) have slipped around the corners onto the side streets and parallels of Via Condotti.

Via de' Tornabuoni in Florence has similar problems (though Florence's new Foot Locker and Disney stores are actually located two blocks over on Via de' Calzaiuoli). Aside from Ferragamo's massive medieval palace/flagship anchoring one end, and the original Gucci store in the middle of it, most of the best shops — big name or not — are not on Via de' Tornabuoni. Instead, they reside on tributaries and side streets like Via della Vigna Vecchia.

Fair warning.

Chapter 27

Ten Places in Europe You'll Be Sorry You Didn't See

● ●

In This Chapter

▶ Ireland's charming Dingle Peninsula

▶ Paris's off-the-beaten-track museums

▶ The ruins at Ostia Antica

● ●

*T*his chapter lists some (okay, not quite ten) unforgettable places where you can avoid the tourists and see some cool sights.

Avebury, England

Okay, so it's not entirely unknown, but for all the tour buses that pull over to gape at Stonehenge, nearby Avebury receives perhaps $\frac{1}{20}$ the number of visitors — and in a way, it's more rewarding to visit this stone circle. At Avebury, you can actually wander around amid the stones, and you'll find a small town built into the circle, with a pub, a restaurant, and more (see Chapter 11).

Dingle Peninsula, Ireland

The Dingle is a peninsula to the north of the Ring of Kerry. This spectacular sight is even better because no crowds get in your way (see Chapter 13).

Paris's Lesser-known Museums

Everyone piles into the Louvre and Musée d'Orsay — and they're worth it. But did you know that you can visit the beautiful little Rodin Museum, with all the sculptor's greatest works in his former studio surrounded by a garden in which his *Thinker* ponders amid a bed of roses with the Eiffel Tower in the distance? And you can see the Thermes de Cluny, Paris' museum of the Middle Ages installed in the remains of a Roman-era bath.

You can head to the Marais's Musée Carnavalet, dedicated to the history of Paris, or to the Musée Marmottan on the edge of the Bois de Boulogne woods to see Monet's *Impression, Sol Levant,* the painting that lent the term "impressionism" to the artistic movement. Then you can visit the Picasso Museum, the Dalí Museum, the Orangerie . . . the list goes on and on, and the busloads of tourists don't even know they exist (Chapter 14).

Hoge Veluwe Park, Netherlands

This large park outside Arnhem is little visited by foreign tourists. You can ride its white bikes around the park's many roads and trails for free. Make sure that you stop into the Kröller-Müller Museum, a fantastic and underrated gallery of modern art lost in the middle of the park. The museum features more than 270 works by Van Gogh and a beautiful outdoor sculpture garden (see Chapter 15).

Ostia Antica, Italy

You don't need to go all the way to Pompeii to see an abandoned city. The ghost streets of Rome's ancient port are a short metro ride away and much more romantic (see Chapter 20).

Venetian Islands, Italy

You'll really miss out on seeing the real Venice if you just hang around the touristy areas. A water-bus ride can take you to several small islands in the Venetian lagoon where locals still blow glass, fish, and make lace for a living. You may be the first stranger they've seen in weeks (see Chapter 22).

Arena Chapel, Padova, Italy

Giotto was the father of modern art and many critics feel that he kick-started the Renaissance in the fourteenth century. You can visit his frescoes in Assisi — along with plenty of visitors — but why not try something different. Few people visit this beautiful chapel near Venice, which is covered almost from floor to ceiling with the master's vibrant painting. While the Assisi cycle recovers from 1997's earthquake damage, this is the best place to appreciate Giotto's art (see Chapter 22).

Spain — All of It

Spain spent much of this century under a dictatorship, so it stayed off most tourist itineraries. But this country's rich history and amalgamated heritage of Celtic, Roman, Moorish, and Castillian influences make it one of the most diverse and culturally dense nations in Europe. Madrid is stuffed with museums, and Barcelona is an eminently livable city, but if you have to pick one region to explore, make it the southlands of Andalusia, full of Moorish palaces, Christian cathedrals, bullfighting, whitewashed villages, sherry, and flamenco dancing (see Chapters 23 and 24).

Medieval Hamlets and Hill Towns

If you want to turn back the clock and see villages and small towns where the leisurely pace of life has helped keep the winding stone streets in a time capsule, Europe is the place to go. You'll find places where the only signs of modern civilization are a few cars and telephone wires. Most of these quaint old villages are just a short bus or train ride outside major cities (for example, San Gimigiano, in Tuscany, is merely a hop, skip, and a jump from Florence; and Chartres is just an hour from Paris on the train).

Chapter 28

The Top Ten Gifts for $10 or Less

In This Chapter

▶ European wines

▶ Tulip bulbs

▶ A wheel of French cheese

*T*hese may be gifts for a friend, a loved one, or yourself! Whatever the occasion, you *can* bring home something memorable from Europe without busting your budget.

A Bottle of Wine

You wouldn't know it from the criminal mark-ups in most U.S. restaurants, but the vast majority of even the finer wines in France, Italy, Germany, and elsewhere cost less than $10 a bottle. Sadly, the United States has ridiculously strict Puritanical laws about how much liquor you can bring back without being taxed on it (see Chapter 10), but one bottle is A-OK.

Marbleized Paper from Florence

For over 500 years, Florentines have used sure hands and basins of ink floating on water to marbleize paper (creating colorful, peacock-feather designs or asymmetrical patterns), and they'll paste it onto just about anything, from notebooks to pencils to gift boxes. Or you can just get the paper itself, as gift wrap, and let your friend back home stick it on whatever she or he likes.

Tulip Bulbs from Holland

Gone are the heady seventeenth-century days when some bulbs sold for their weights in gold. However, for your gardening friends back home, what better gift can you find than tulips direct from Holland? Be sure to check with U.S. Customs first (see Chapter 10) about which kinds you're allowed to bring into the United States.

Soviet-era Kitschy Trinkets

Sidewalk vendors in the Czech Republic and around the Brandenburg Gate in Berlin hawk watches, lighters, and the like emblazoned with the hammer and sickle. Prove your party loyalty by coming back to this seething den of capitalism you call America wearing a bona-fide communist souvenir.

A Small Wheel of Cheese from France or Italy

Edible souvenirs! U.S. Customs will let you bring home any cheese so long as it's not liquidy, like a mascarpone or particularly runny brie.

 Note that you *cannot* take home any type of meat — cured, vacuum-packed, or otherwise — no matter what the shopkeep in Europe tells you. For food safety and health reasons, U.S. Customs officials will confiscate your salami if they discover it. (They keep little pâté-loving beagles at Customs check points and baggage claim areas of airports just to sniff this stuff out — I kid you not.) Packaged salmon is okay, though.

A Leather Wallet from Florence's San Lorenzo Street Market

You may have to bargain hard to get one for around $10, but it can be done. And what better gift? It's leather, it's from Florence, and it's genuinely useful.

A Glass Trinket from a Venetian Shop

Venice is famous for its Murano blown glass. Although you can lay out thousands of dollars for a chandelier or hand-crafted set of champagne flutes, many of the souvenir-sized objects crowding the display windows of shops all over Venice can be had for under $10, whether it's a delicate perfume bottle or a teensy, tiny glass gondola.

Religious Objects from Shops around the Vatican

Many items sold in the stores and stands that crowd around the Vatican walls may be considered movingly religious or supremely silly, depending on your ecclesiastical leanings and sense of humor.

Whatever your tastes, a spin through one or two of these shops can prove a worthwhile diversion from a day spent at St. Peter's.

You can find stuff here to make good gifts for faithful and agnostic friends alike. Take a tasteful little gold-plated cross or crucifix on a chain to the Wednesday audience with the Pope so it, too, gets blessed when he does his benediction over the crowd, and then give it to a Catholic friend back home.

The Holy Grail of religious kitsch from Vatican-area souvenir stands (very tough to find) is the Pope-ener: a corkscrew featuring a photographic medallion of His Holiness at the top; you twist his head around, and the "arms" of the corkscrew slowly rise in benediction to bless your wine as the cork is cranked out.

A Tartan Scarf from Scotland

If your friend has Scottish blood, you can get a scarf in the clan pattern. (Shops always have books, posters, or charts on hand to help you figure out which clan various surnames belong to.) You usually have four patterns to choose from: ancient hunting, ancient dress, modern hunting, and modern dress. If you have no clan, you're even luckier; you can just pick the tartan that you like the best.

If your budget can handle more than $10, go "haggis" wild and get the whole kilt-and-caboodle (a nice kilt set will run you well over $500).

A Swiss Army Knife from, You Guessed It, Switzerland

The smallest, simplest knives do, indeed, cost around $10. It's hard to believe that Switzerland's been able to stay neutral this long with an army armed solely with a two-inch blade, corkscrew, and removable tweezers.

Chapter 29

Ten Ways to Break Out of the Tourist Mold

Sometimes it pays to be less touristy when you travel to foreign countries. I always think of Michael Palin in *Around the World in 80 Days;* he cruised the canals of Venice in a garbage scow.

To enjoy the "real" Europe, do something other than what all the other travel books recommend. You'll be rewarded with a unique experience that travelers who stick solely to the major sights miss out on. Here are my suggestions for finding the road less traveled.

Wander a Residential Neighborhood

Meet the locals, drink coffee with them, and play cards or backgammon.

Take a Dip in Bern's Aare River

You may not find many capital cities where the river water is clean enough to swim in, but you'll enjoy this one (see Chapter 18).

Rent an Apartment or Villa

Instead of staying at several hotels in different cities or towns, pick a city or region to explore and rent an apartment or villa. You can almost become a temporary native. Become a "regular" at the cafe on the corner and the little grocery store down the street.

Visit a Small Private Museum

You wouldn't believe the places you can find where wealthy collectors left behind dusty old mansions jumbled with valuable bric-a-brac ranging from Ming vases and Roman reliefs to medieval suits of armor and occasional paintings by a Renaissance master.

Jog with the Locals

Find out where the locals jog, and join them for a morning's (or evening's) run. You'll clear your head, explore a city park, and perhaps make some new friends.

Hike in the Countryside

Leave the crowds of the big city behind, and explore the country on foot. It's nothing like driving around in a car — you'll be glad for the memories when you return home.

Catch a Soccer Match

In Europe, soccer is like packing all the rahs, joys, agonies, and fandom of American baseball, football, basketball, and hockey into one season. Except for a few oddball sports like cricket in England, this is the only sport that most Europeans follow, making it a close runner-up to Christianity as the national religion in each country.

Find out what day the big game is played in town (often Sunday) and where the die-hard fans sit, and then get a seat there and root, root, root for the home team (unless you seem to be seated amidst fans of the opposing team, in which case scream your bloody lungs out for the visitors). Just avoid any obvious hooligans and any sign that a brawl's about to break out.

Help Pick Grapes or Olives

Spend a day picking grapes or olives, and you may even get to pass around the wine bottle with the farmers during breaks. You'll get a hard day's work, but it's a remarkable experience.

Liberate Yourself from Your Guidebook

Yes! I really said it! Stow this and any other guides away once in a while, and check out sights and restaurants without our advice. Wander into a church without even checking to see if it's listed in the book. Try a dish that your menu translator doesn't cover. Enjoy the thrill of discovery. The memories are worth it!

Watch Some Local Television Programs

Watching TV in Europe doesn't make you a couch potato. Tell your friends that you're having a cultural experience!

Appendix A

Toll-Free Numbers and Web Sites

● ●

*I*n this appendix, I deal with the national tourism representatives you can find in your home country and contact before you leave on your trip. You'll also find contact information for the major North American and European national airlines and car rental companies. As for local tourist info offices and their Web sites, look under the "Where to get info after you arrive" section near the beginning of each destination chapter throughout this book.

National Tourist Information Offices

National tourist boards exist to help you plan a trip to their country. If you call, they'll gladly send you a big envelope stuffed with brochures and information packets. Many of them are helpful enough to address specific questions and concerns you may have. Even more useful, now that most of them are online, are the Web sites that are just loaded with country-specific info, as well as links to other sites.

That said, take any mailing from the tourist office with a grain of salt. Most of the material it sends you is promotional and always puts the best spin possible on every aspect of the country — nowhere in the materials will you find a downside. It may send you a brochure of local restaurants, but remember that these places are not the only, or even the best, dining possibilities in town. Most brochures are thinly veiled advertisements written by the properties themselves. The best joint in town may not belong to the promotional consortium that prints the pamphlet. Read between the lines and rely on a quality, impartial third-party guidebook (like this one!) for the real, opinionated scoop on the local scene.

One of the most useful items a National Tourist Office can send you is a list of the local tourist boards in each city and province of the country. Be sure to request one. Local tourist boards have scads more information available, from sightseeing, hotel, and restaurant lists to event calendars, specialized tourism options, walking tour outfits, and so on. Contacting them directly pays off.

Visit the European Travel Commission's site at www.visiteurope.com.

Austrian National Tourist Office

In the United States: P.O. Box 1142, New York, NY 10108-1142 (☎ 212-944-6880); 11601 Wilshire Boulevard, Suite 2480, Los Angeles, CA 90025 (☎ 310-477-2038).

In Canada: 2 Bloor St. E., Suite 3330, Toronto, ON M4W 1A8 (☎ 416-967-3381); 1010 Sherbrooke St. W., Suite 1410, Montréal, PQ H3A 2R7 (☎ 514-849-3708); Suite 1380, Granville Square, 200 Granville St., Vancouver, BC V6C 1S4 (☎ 604-683-5808).

In the United Kingdom: Mail to: P.O. Box 2363, London W1A 2QB. Office at: 14 Cork St., London W1X 1PF (☎ 020-7629-0461).

In Australia: 36 Carrington St., 1st Floor, Sydney NSW 2000 (☎ 02-9299-3621).

Internet: www.anto.com and www.austria-tourism.at

Belgian Tourist Office

In the United States: 780 Third Ave., Suite 1501, New York, NY 10017 (☎ 212-758-8130).

In Canada: P.O. Box 760 NDG, Montréal, PQ H4A 3S2 (☎ 514-484-3594).

In the United Kingdom: 29 Prince St., London W1R 7RG (☎ 020-7629-3777 or 0891-887-799).

Internet: www.visitbelgium.com

British Tourist Authority

In the United States: ☎ 800-462-2748. 551 Fifth Ave., Suite 701, New York, NY 10176 (☎ 212-986-2200); 625 N. Michigan Ave., Suite 1510, Chicago, IL 60611 (☎ 312-787-0464).

In Canada: ☎ 888-VISIT-UK. 5915 Airport Road, Suite 120, Mississauga, Ontario L4V 1T1 (☎ 905-405-1840); for Northern Ireland, 2 Bloor St. West, Suite 1501, Toronto, ON M4W 3E2 (☎ 800-576-8474 or 416-925-6368).

In Australia: Level 16, Gateway, 1 Macquarie Place, Sydney, NSW 2000 (☎ 02-9377-4400).

In New Zealand: 151 Queen St., 17th floor, Auckland 1 (☎ 09-303-1446).

Internet: www.visitbritain.com

Czech Tourist Authority

In the United States: 1109 Madison Ave., New York, NY 10028 (☎ 212-288-0830).

In Canada: P.O. Box 198, Exchange Tower, 130 King St. W, Suite 715, Toronto, ON M5X 1A6 (☎ 416-367-3432).

In the United Kingdom: 95 Great Portland St., London W1M 5RA (☎ 020-7291-9920); 55 Sloane St., London SW1X 9SY (☎ 020-7629-6058).

Internet: www.czech.cz/new_york

French Government Tourist Office

In the United States: 444 Madison Ave., 16th Floor, New York, NY 10022 (☎ 212-838-7800); 676 N. Michigan Ave., Suite 3360, Chicago, IL 60611 (☎ 312-751-7800); 9454 Wilshire Blvd., Suite 715, Beverly Hills, CA 90212 (☎ 310-271-6665). To request information at any of these offices, call ☎ 410-286-8310 or 202-659-7779.

In Canada: Maison de la France/French Government Tourist Office, 1981 av. McGill College, Suite 490, Montréal, PQ H3A 2W9 (☎ 514-288-4264); 30 St. Patrick Street, Suite 700, Toronto, ON M5T 3A3. For general info, fax to 514-845-4868.

In the United Kingdom: Maison de la France/French Government Tourist Office, 178 Piccadilly, London, W1V 0AL (☎ 0891-244-123).

In Australia: French Tourist Bureau, 25 Bligh St., Sydney, NSW 2000 (☎ 02-9231-5244).

Internet: www.francetourism.com

German National Tourist Office

In the United States: 122 E. 42nd St., 52nd Floor, New York, NY 10168 (☎ 212-661-7200); 11766 Wilshire Blvd., Suite 750, Los Angeles, CA 90025 (☎ 310-575-9799).

In Canada: 175 Bloor St. E., North Tower, Suite 604, Toronto, ON M4W 3R8 (☎ 416-968-1570).

In the United Kingdom: Nightingale House, 65 Curzon St., London, W1Y 8NE (☎ 020-7495-3990 or 0891-600-100).

In Australia: Lufthansa House, 143 Macquarie St., 9th Floor, Sydney, NSW 2000 (☎ 02-9267-8148).

Internet: www.germany-tourism.de

Greek National Tourist Organization

In the United States: 645 Fifth Ave., 5th Floor, New York, NY 10022 (☎ 212-421-5777); 168 N. Michigan Ave., Suite 600, Chicago, IL 60601 (☎ 312-782-1084); 611 W. 6th St., Suite 2198, Los Angeles, CA 90017 (☎ 213-626-6696).

In Canada: 1300 Bay St., Upper Level, Toronto, ON M5R 3KB (☎ 416-968-2220); 1233 rue de la Montagne, Suite 101, Montréal, PQ H3G 1Z2 (☎ 514-871-1535).

In the United Kingdom: 4 Conduit St., London W1R D0J (☎ 02-7734-5997).

In Australia: 51-57 Pitt St., Sydney, NWS 2000 (☎ 02-9241-1663).

Internet: www.phantis.com (unofficial, but great) or www.greektourism.com

Hungarian National Tourist Office

In the United States: 150 E. 58th St., New York, NY 10155 (☎ 212-355-0240).

In the United Kingdom: 46 Eaton Place, London, SW1 X8AL (☎ 020-7823-1032).

Internet: www.hungarytourism.hu

Irish Tourist Board

In the United States: 345 Park Ave., New York, NY 10154 (☎ 800-223-6470 or 212-418-0800).

In Canada: 160 Bloor St. E., Suite 1150, Toronto, ON M4W 1B9 (☎ 416-929-2777 or 416-487-3335).

In the United Kingdom: 150 New Bond St., London W1Y OAQ (☎ 020-7493-3201).

In Australia: 36 Carrington St., 5th Level, Sydney, NSW 2000 (☎ 02-9299-6177).

Internet: www.ireland.travel.ie

Italian Government Tourist Board

In the United States: 630 Fifth Ave., Suite 1565, New York, NY 10111 (☎ 212-245-5095 or 212-245-4822); 500 N. Michigan Ave., Suite 2240, Chicago, IL 60611 (☎ 312-644-0996); 12400 Wilshire Blvd., Suite 550, Beverly Hills, CA 90025 (☎ 310-820-2977).

In Canada: 1 place Ville-Marie, Suite 1914, Montréal, PQ H3B 2C3 (☎ 514-866-7667).

In the United Kingdom: 1 Princes St., London W1R 8AY (☎ 020-7408-1254).

In Australia: 44 Market Street, Sidney, NSW 2000 (☎ 02-9262-1666).

Internet: www.enit.it

Monaco Government Tourist Office

In the United States: 565 Fifth Ave., New York, NY 10017 (☎ 800-753-9696 or 212-286-3330); 542 S. Dearborn St., Suite 550, Chicago, IL 60605 (☎ 312-939-7836).

In the United Kingdom: 3-8 Chelsea Garden Market, Chelsea Harbour, London, SW10 0XE (☎ 020-7352-9962).

Internet: www.monaco.mc/usa

Netherlands Board of Tourism

In the United States: ☎ 888-GO-HOLLAND. 355 Lexington Ave., 21st Floor, New York, NY 10017 (☎ 212-370-7360); 225 N. Michigan Ave., Suite 1854, Chicago, IL 60601 (☎ 312-819-1740).

In Canada: 25 Adelaide St. E., Suite 710, Toronto, ON M5C 1Y2 (☎ 416-363-1577).

In the United Kingdom: 18 Buckingham Gate, PO Box 523, London, SW1E 6NT (☎ 020-7828-7900).

Internet: www.goholland.com

Portuguese National Tourist Office

In the United States: ☎ 800-PORTGAL. 590 Fifth Ave., New York, NY 10036 (☎ 212-354-4403).

In Canada: 600 Bloor St. W., Suite 1005, Toronto, ON M4W 3B8 (☎ 416-921-7376).

In the United Kingdom: 22-25A Sackville Street, London W1X 1 DE (☎ 020-7494-1441).

Internet: www.portugal.org

Scandinavian Tourist Boards (in the U.S., all are combined)

In the United States: Mail to: P.O. Box 4649, Grand Central Station, New York, NY 10163. Office at: 655 Third Ave., New York, NY 10017 (☎ 212-885-9700).

In the United Kingdom: Swedish Travel and Tourism Council, 11 Montague Place, London W1H 2AL (☎ 020-7724-5868). **Danish Tourist Board,** 55 Sloane St., London SW1X 9SY (☎ 020-7259-5959). **Finland Tourist Board,** 30-35 Pal Mall, London SW1Y 5LP (☎ 020-7839-4048). **Norway Tourist Board,** Charles House, 5-11 Lower Regent St., London SW1Y 4LR (☎ 020-7839-6255).

Internet: www.goscandinavia.com, www.gosweden.org, www.visitden-mark.com, www.norway.org, **or** www.goiceland.org

Switzerland Tourism

In the United States: 608 Fifth Ave., New York, NY 10020 (☎ 212-757-5944); 150 N. Michigan Ave., Suite 2930, Chicago, IL 60601 (☎ 312-630-5840); 222 N. Sepulveda Blvd., Suite 1570, El Segundo, CA 90245 (☎ 310-335-5980).

In Canada: 926 The East Mall, Etobicoke, Ontario M9B 6K1 (☎ 416-695-2090); 154 University Ave., Suite 610, Toronto, ON M5H 3Y9 (☎ 416-971-9734).

In the United Kingdom: Swiss Centre, Swiss Court, London, W1V 8EE (☎ 020-7734-1921).

Internet: www.switzerlandtourism.com

Tourist Office of Spain

In the United States: ☎ 888-OK-SPAIN. 666 Fifth Ave., 35th Floor, New York, NY 10103 (☎ 212-265-8822); 845 N. Michigan Ave., Suite 915E, Chicago, IL 60611 (☎ 312-642-1992); 8383 Wilshire Blvd., Suite 960, Beverly Hills, CA 90211 (☎ 213-658-7188); 1221 Brickell Ave., Suite 1850, Miami, FL 33131 (☎ 305-358-1992).

In Canada: 2 Bloor St. W., 34th Floor, Toronto, ON M4W 3E2 (☎ 416-961-3131).

In the United Kingdom: 57 St. James's St., London SW1A 1LD (☎ 020-7499-0901).

Internet: www.okspain.org

Airlines and Rental-Car Companies

Check out the following companies for all your traveling needs.

Major North American carriers

Check out www.travelocity.com for the best airfare deals.

Air Canada ☎ 800-776-3000 in the United States, 800-555-1212 in Canada; **Internet:** www.aircanada.ca

American Airlines ☎ 800-433-7300; **Internet:** www.americanair.com

Canadian Airlines ☎ 800-426-7000 in the United States, 800-665-1177 in Canada; **Internet:** www.cdnair.ca

Continental Airlines ☎ 800-231-0856; **Internet:** www.flycontinental.com

Delta Airlines ☎ 800-241-4141; **Internet:** www.delta-air.com

Northwest Airlines ☎ 800-447-4747; **Internet:** www.nwa.com

Tower Air ☎ 800-221-2500; **Internet:** www.towerair.com

TWA ☎ 800-892-4141; **Internet:** www.twa.com

United ☎ 800-241-6522 or 800-538-2929; **Internet:** www.ual.com

U.S. Airways ☎ 800-622-1015; **Internet:** www.usairways.com

European carriers (National and country-affiliated airlines)

Austria: Austrian Airlines. *In the United States and Canada:* ☎ 800-843-0002. *In the United Kingdom:* ☎ 020-7434-7300. *In Australia:* ☎ 02-9241-4277. **Internet:** www.aua.com.

Belgium: Sabena. *In the United States and Canada:* ☎ 800-955-2000. *In the United Kingdom:* ☎ 020-7494-2629. **Internet:** www.sabena.com.

Czech Republic: CSA Czech Airlines. *In the United States and Canada:* ☎ 800-223-2365. *In the United Kingdom:* ☎ 020-7255-1898. *In Australia:* ☎ 02-9247-6196. **Internet:** www.csa.cz.

France: Air France. *In the United States:* ☎ 800-237-2747. *In Canada:* ☎ 514-847-1106. *In the United Kingdom:* ☎ 020-8742-6600. *In Australia:* ☎ 02-9321-1000. *In New Zealand:* ☎ 068-725-8800. **Internet:** www.airfrance.com.

Germany: Lufthansa. *In the United States.:* ☎ 800-645-3880. *In Canada:* ☎ 800-563-5954. *In the United Kingdom:* ☎ 0345-737-747. *In Australia:* ☎ 02-9367-3888. *In New Zealand:* ☎ 09-303-1529. **Internet:** www.lufthansa.com.

Greece: Olympic Airways. *In the United States.:* ☎ 800-223-1226, or 212-735-0200 in New York State. *In Canada:* ☎ 514-878-3891 (Montréal) or 416-920-2452 (Toronto). *In the United Kingdom:* ☎ 020-7409-2400. *In Australia:* ☎ 02-9251-2044. **Internet:** agn.hol.gr.

Hungary: Malev Hungarian Airlines. *In the U.S.:* ☎ 800-262-5380. *In Canada:* ☎ 416-9440-093. *In the United Kingdom:* ☎ 020-7439-0577. *In Australia:* ☎ 02-9321-9111. *In New Zealand:* ☎ 09-379-4455. **Internet:** www.malev.hu/ew/angol.

Iceland: IcelandAir. *In the United States or Canada:* ☎ 800-223-5500. *In the United Kingdom:* ☎ 020-7388-5599. **Internet:** www.icelandair.com.

Ireland: Aer Lingus. *In the United States:* ☎ 800-IRISH-AIR. *In the United Kingdom:* ☎ 020-8899-4747 in London, 0645-737-747 in all other areas. *In Australia:* ☎ 02-9321-9123. *In New Zealand:* ☎ 09-379-4455. **Internet:** www.aerlingus.ie.

Italy: Alitalia. *In the United States:* ☎ 800-223-5730. *In Canada:* ☎ 514-842-8241 (Montréal) or 416-363-1348 (Toronto). *In the United Kingdom:* ☎ 020-8745-8200. *In Australia:* ☎ 02-9247-1307. *In New Zealand:* ☎ 09-379-4457. **Internet:** www.alitalia.com.

The Netherlands: KLM Royal Dutch Airlines. *In the United States:* ☎ 800-374-7747. *In Canada:* ☎ 514-939-4040 (Montréal) or 416-204-5100 (Toronto). *In the United Kingdom:* ☎ 0990-750-9900. *In Australia:* ☎ 02-9231-6333. *In New Zealand:* ☎ 09-309-1782. **Internet:** www.klm.nl.

Portugal: TAP Air Portugal. *In the United States:* ☎ 800-221-7370. *In the United Kingdom:* ☎ 020-7828-0262. **Internet:** www.tap-airportugal.pt.

Scandinavia (Denmark, Norway, Sweden): SAS Scandinavian Airlines. *In the United States:* ☎ 00-221-2350. *In the United Kingdom:* ☎ 020-7734-6777. *In Australia:* ☎ 02-9299-6688. **Internet:** www.flysas.com.

Spain: Iberia. *In the United States:* ☎ 800-772-4642. *In Canada:* ☎ 800-363-4534. *In the United Kingdom:* ☎ 020-7830-0011. *In Australia:* ☎ 02-9283-3660. *In New Zealand:* ☎ 09-379-3076. **Internet:** www.iberia.com.

Switzerland: Swissair. *In the United States and Canada:* ☎ 800-221-4750. *In the United Kingdom:* ☎ 020-7434-7300. *In Australia:* ☎ 02-9232-1744. **Internet:** www.swissair.com.

United Kingdom: (1) British Airways. *In the United States and Canada:* ☎ 800-247-9297. *In the United Kingdom:* ☎ 020-8897-4000 or 034-522-2111. *In Australia:* ☎ 02-9258-3300. *Internet:* www.british-airways.com. (2) Virgin Atlantic Airways. *In the United States and Canada:* ☎ 800-862-8621. *In the United Kingdom:* ☎ 01293-616-161 or 01293-747-747. *In Australia:* ☎ 02-9352-6199. **Internet:** www.fly.virgin.com.

North American car-rental agencies

Avis: ☎ 800-331-1212; **Internet:** www.avis.com

Budget: ☎ 800-527-0700; **Internet:** www.budgetrentacar.com

Dollar (Europcar): ☎ 800-800-6000; **Internet:** www.dollarcar.com

Hertz: ☎ 800-654-3131; **Internet:** www.hertz.com

National: ☎ 800-227-7368; **Internet:** www.nationalcar.com

European car-rental agencies

Auto-Europe: ☎ 800-223-5555; **Internet:** www.autoeurope.com

Europe by Car: ☎ 800-223-1516; 800-252-9401 in California; 212-581-3040 in New York City; **Internet:** www.europebycar.com

Kemwel: ☎ 800-678-0678; **Internet:** www.kemwel.com

Appendix B

Art and Architecture Glossary

• •

*T*his brief glossary only scratches the surface of art history and appreciation in Europe, where the creative tradition spans from the classical sculptures of Greeks and Romans to medieval Byzantine icons, to Renaissance fresco, to impressionist paintings. If you don't have time to get your Ph.D. in art history before your trip, you may want to check out Tom Hoving's *Art For Dummies* book to help you tell your apse from your armbone.

Apse: Usually found behind the altar of a church, this large architectural niche is often shaped as a half-cylinder.

art deco: A kitschy decorative art and architecture style of the 1920s to 1930s that descends from art nouveau but that uses more expensive materials and simpler, somewhat more rectilinear and severe shapes and lines.

art nouveau: This style of architecture, design, and decorative arts characterized by organic asymmetry, inventiveness, and flowing curving lines spanned from the 1880s to 1914. It went by a different name in every country, including Jugendstil (Germany), Liberty Style (Italy), and Modernisme (Spain's Catalán region).

baroque: This general term describes the overwrought art style widely practiced from roughly 1580 to the 1750s; the next big thing after the Renaissance and its mannerist offshoot. It's excessively ornate and self-indulgent, using curving, broken lines in architecture and a myriad of colors, materials, illusory techniques, and large, complex compositions in painting. It concentrated much more strongly than the Renaissance on unified ensembles of painting, architecture, sculpture, decorative arts, and design. Although not of very good quality, it lent itself well to the era of extremely extravagant palace building.

Byzantine: The Eastern-style, iconographic, and ethereal art and architecture of the Byzantine empire (headquartered in Constantinople, which is today Istanbul). Gold mosaics and icons of the Madonna and Child were two influences seen in Western Europe, but it was eventually replaced by the Romanesque and later Gothic movements in Europe between the 900s and 1200s. The Byzantine style (in Western Europe) lasted from the 400s to 1453.

capital (of columns): The top of a column. The three "orders" of classical architecture, though they're applied to many elements, are most often used in the context of discussing what the column capitals look like. The simplest is Doric, with just a plain, square capital, and often the column has no base (the column runs straight into the floor). The Ionic capitals have a pair of big scrolls protruding from each end. The Corinthian capital is carved to look leafy.

caryatid: A column or pillar shaped like a woman.

classical: A general term applied to the art and especially sculpture and architecture of ancient Greece (especially the fifth century b.c. Golden Age) and ancient Rome.

cloister: An inner courtyard of a church, monastery, or convent; a spot for quiet reflection, often containing small gardens and often surrounded on all four sides by an open colonnade.

colonnade: Any row of columns supporting an entablature, roof, or series of arches (in which case, the structure is called an *arcade*). Colonnades often form the open, outer side of a covered walkway.

Corinthian: See capital (of columns).

cubism: An experiment in painting from 1907 to the 1930s, whereby Picasso, Braque, and followers rebuked the concept of trying to create an illusion of strict visual reality in a painting and instead tried to show that subjects could be examined from several different perspectives at once, not just one. Rather than try to create the illusion of depth on the flat plane of a canvas, the artists visually flattened and connected all the planes of an object on a single flat surface. That is to say, cubism shows more than just the side of the object that's facing the artist. Cézanne's theories and African tribal art were strong influences on the cubists.

Doric: See capital (of columns).

flying buttress: A buttress is a structural support, often a stone pillar built in a ramplike slope out from the side of a building to help distribute the gravitational forces pulling on the weighty stone walls of cathedrals. Gothic architecture heavily used the flying buttress, a graceful span of arch connecting the outer, upper walls of a building to a vertical pillar beside it.

fresco: The technique of painting on wet plaster (*fresco* means "fresh" in Italian) so the colors sink below the surface and bond with the wall; also the term for such a painting. This extremely popular way to decorate surfaces lasted from ancient Greek and Roman times through the Renaissance and baroque periods (until the baroque artists popularized oil on canvas).

frieze: The long, horizontal portion of a Classical building that's being supported by all those columns is called an entablature. It's made up of three parts: the architrave (the part that runs right across the tops of the column capitals), the frieze (the wide band in the middle, often decorated with a pattern or a series of carved reliefs), and the cornice (the thin strip at the top, usually projecting out a bit).

Georgian: An elegant eighteenth-century neoclassical architectural style practiced throughout the British Isles during the reigns of Georges I, II, and III (1714 to 1820).

Gothic: This general term describes everything between the Romanesque and Renaissance eras (from the 1000s to the 1500s). More specifically, a late Medieval era in architecture and sculpture. In architecture, that meant churches with lots of stained glass, pointed arches, flying buttresses, and ribbed vaulting. In sculpture, it employed naturalistic figures of flowing lines and expressive faces. In painting, it was called "International Gothic," and it broke away from the stylized rigidity of the Byzantine school with a more naturalistic approach, which facilitated the Renaissance movement. From the late Renaissance on, most people looked back on this era and found it unrefined, vulgar, and uncivilized, and they labeled it all after the name of one of the barbaric peoples who overran the Roman empire, the Goths (even though it more accurately grew out of the styles practiced by the Germanic Franks and Celtic Gauls of modern-day France).

Hellenistic: From *hellas,* the Greek word for Greece. A more flamboyant, experimental, and sometimes unoriginal or absurd version of classicism's main guiding principles (what baroque was to Renaissance, Hellenistic was to Classical). It was the intermingled artistic mainstay of the Mediterranean world from the end of Greece's classical Golden Age until Rome took over (330 to 27 b.c.). It started when Alexander the Great conquered the Middle East and beyond, and then fused Eastern style and sensibility with traditional Western Greek classicism. This style prevailed from fifth century b.c. to 330 b.c.

impressionism: The original *avant-garde* art, whereby artists such as Monet, Renoir, and Degas turned their backs on the realistic art of the establishment and began creating more expressive art with visible brushwork and a concentration on the effect that light has on color and mood, rather than the traditional artistic focus on form and line. Also see the sidebar in Chapter 16. This movement spanned from 1872 to the 1890s.

Ionic: See capital (of columns).

Jugendstil: The German version of art nouveau.

Kouros: A Greek statue of a boy (although female versions also existed) from the seventh to sixth centuries b.c. Very stylized and rigid and heavily influenced by Egyptian models.

Liberty Style: The Italian version of art nouveau.

Mannerism: A sixteenth-century spin-off of the High Renaissance. This artistic movement used increasingly garish colors (in painting), twisting poses (in painting and sculpture), and exaggerations of classicism (in architecture) to stretch Michelangelo's experiments with color, posing, and Renaissance ideals to their logical limits (1530 to 1600).

Modernisme: Catalán version of art nouveau; Gaudí was its most prolific and innovative perpetrator in Barcelona.

Moorish: Anything having to do with the Moors, a Muslim people of Arabic origins who lived in and controlled most of Spain and Portugal (along with the Middle East and North Africa) from a.d. 711 to 1492.

nave: The main aisle of a church, usually containing the main doors, main pews, choir, and/or apse. The altar is usually either at one end of the nave or at the intersection of the nave and transept.

neoclassical: An eighteenth-century revival of interest in the sculpture and architecture of the classical world, caused both by a backlash against the excesses of the baroque and rococo styles and by the fledgling discipline of archaeology, which was uncovering the ancient sites of Greece and Rome. It was more a romanticized rather than accurate version of classical forms, sometimes overemphasizing the mathematical rigidity and austere simplicity of the ancient orders and sometimes softening it up for contemporary tastes. This movement lasted from the 1750s to the mid–nineteenth century.

neo-Gothic: Also called Gothic Revival, a period in which the late-medieval Gothic style became popular again (albeit with some revisions) mainly in England and the United States (whole buildings) and Italy (mostly church facades), roughly at the same time that other tastes were exploring the neoclassical style. This style lasted from the mid–eighteenth to the mid–nineteenth centuries.

pediment: The triangle of space below the roof and above the frieze on the end walls of many classical temples. It's often filled with sculptural groups in low or high relief.

Renaissance: A French word meaning "rebirth," it was later used to refer to a period of intense artistic, literary, and scientific development and change that started in Florence in the fifteenth century when humanist philosophy and a study of classical models led art and architecture to liberate themselves from rigid medieval traditions and explore both the emotional and scientific sides of art. The phenomenon of the Renaissance spread to literature and other arts and from Italy throughout all of Europe by the seventeenth century. This period lasted from 1401 through the 1750s (though in many places it began to devolve into the baroque as early as the late 1500s).

rococo: If baroque was considered over the top, then rococo was garishly, ludicrously lavish. It remains one of the most wildly overdone and exceedingly flamboyant decorative styles ever used, kicked off by the court of Louis XV in France. Good taste went by the wayside. Rococo spaces were covered with expensive marbles, dripping with stuccoes, and otherwise packed with excessive decoration. The artistic community quickly got over this garish style and retreated to the simplicity of the neoclassical. This style lasted roughly from the 1710s to the 1760s.

Romanesque: An early medieval form of architecture (decorated with stylized sculpture, charmingly crude informal frescoes, or Byzantine mosaics) based on ancient Roman models (thus the name) and marked by a heavy construction of thick walls and piers, tiny windows, and low, rounded arches. The English called it the Norman style. This style lasted from a.d. 700s to the 1100s.

surrealism: Before virtual reality, artists such as Dalí and Magritte used a very realistic painting style to create scenes that looked real but were physically impossible (elephants with long, jointed insects' legs, melting clocks, women with drawers instead of breasts, and so on). This style lasted from 1924 to the 1950s, and it wanted to abstain from the traditional metaphors and symbols used by painters and rather to explore the human psyche, which meant that in trying to avoid all symbolism, it quickly ended up simply adopting a new set, becoming rich with the symbolic imagery of psychology (Freudian, usually). The style spread to sculpture, photography, and film as well.

transept: In Latin-cross (crucifix-shaped) churches, it's the shorter cross-arm of the floor plan. In Greek-cross (plus sign-shaped) churches, it's the cross arm of the floor plan that runs perpendicular to the nave.

trompe l'oeil: French for "trick the eye," it's a particularly successful illusory painting technique — painting on a flat wall what appears to be a niche with a statue in it, or making the flat, solid ceiling of a church appear to open up into the heavens through a sky filled with angels, cherubs, and clouds, for example.

Fare Game: Choosing an Airline

Travel Agency:_____ Phone:_____

Agent's Name: _____ Quoted Fare:_____

Departure Schedule & Flight Information

Airline: _____ Airport:_____

Flight #:_____ Date:_____ Time: _____ a.m./p.m.

Arrives in:_____ Time: _____ a.m./p.m.

Connecting Flight (if any)

Amount of time between flights: _____ hours/mins

Airline: _____ Airport:_____

Flight #:_____ Date: _____ Time: _____ a.m./p.m.

Arrives in:_____ Time: _____ a.m./p.m.

Return Trip Schedule & Flight Information

Airline: _____ Airport:_____

Flight #:_____ Date:_____ Time: _____ a.m./p.m.

Arrives in:_____ Time: _____ a.m./p.m.

Connecting Flight (if any)

Amount of time between flights:_____ hours/mins

Airline: _____ Airport:_____

Flight #:_____ Date:_____ Time: _____ a.m./p.m.

Arrives in:_____ Time: _____ a.m./p.m.

Notes

Making Dollars and Sense of It

Expense	Amount
Airfare	
Car Rental	
Lodging	
Parking	
Breakfast	
Lunch	
Dinner	
Babysitting	
Attractions	
Transportation	
Souvenirs	
Tips	
Grand Total	

Notes

Sweet Dreams: Choosing Your Hotel

Enter the hotels where you'd prefer to stay based on location and price. Then use the worksheet below to plan your itinerary.

Hotel	Location	Price per night

Places to Go, People to See, Things to Do

Enter the attractions you most would like to see. Then use the worksheet below to plan your itinerary.

Attractions	Amount of time you expect to spend there	Best day and time to go

Going "My" Way

Itinerary #1

☐ _____
☐ _____
☐ _____
☐ _____

Itinerary #2

☐ _____
☐ _____
☐ _____
☐ _____

Itinerary #3

☐ _____
☐ _____
☐ _____
☐ _____

Itinerary #4

☐ _____
☐ _____
☐ _____
☐ _____

Itinerary #5

☐ _____
☐ _____
☐ _____
☐ _____

Itinerary #6

- ☐ _____
- ☐ _____
- ☐ _____
- ☐ _____

Itinerary #7

- ☐ _____
- ☐ _____
- ☐ _____
- ☐ _____

Itinerary #8

- ☐ _____
- ☐ _____
- ☐ _____
- ☐ _____

Itinerary #9

- ☐ _____
- ☐ _____
- ☐ _____
- ☐ _____

Itinerary #10

- ☐ _____
- ☐ _____
- ☐ _____
- ☐ _____

Menus & Venues

Enter the restaurants where you most would like to dine. Then use the worksheet below to plan your itinerary.

Name	Address/Phone	Cuisine/Price

Notes

Index

• **F** •

Discover Dummies Online!

The Dummies Web Site is your fun and friendly online resource for the latest information about *For Dummies*® books and your favorite topics. The Web site is the place to communicate with us, exchange ideas with other *For Dummies* readers, chat with authors, and have fun!

Ten Fun and Useful Things You Can Do at www.dummies.com

1. Win free *For Dummies* books and more!
2. Register your book and be entered in a prize drawing.
3. Meet your favorite authors through the IDG Books Worldwide Author Chat Series.
4. Exchange helpful information with other *For Dummies* readers.
5. Discover other great *For Dummies* books you must have!
6. Purchase Dummieswear® exclusively from our Web site.
7. Buy *For Dummies* books online.
8. Talk to us. Make comments, ask questions, get answers!
9. Download free software.
10. Find additional useful resources from authors.

Link directly to these ten fun and useful things at
http://www.dummies.com/10useful

For other technology titles from IDG Books Worldwide, go to
www.idgbooks.com

Not on the Web yet? It's easy to get started with *Dummies 101*®: *The Internet For Windows*® *98* or *The Internet For Dummies*® at local retailers everywhere.

Find other *For Dummies* books on these topics:

Business • Career • Databases • Food & Beverage • Games • Gardening • Graphics • Hardware
Health & Fitness • Internet and the World Wide Web • Networking • Office Suites
Operating Systems • Personal Finance • Pets • Programming • Recreation • Sports
Spreadsheets • Teacher Resources • Test Prep • Word Processing

IDG BOOKS WORLDWIDE BOOK REGISTRATION

Register
This Book
and Win!

We want to hear from you!

Visit **http://my2cents.dummies.com** to register this book and tell us how you liked it!

- Get entered in our monthly prize giveaway.

- Give us feedback about this book — tell us what you like best, what you like least, or maybe what you'd like to ask the author and us to change!

- Let us know any other *For Dummies®* topics that interest you.

Your feedback helps us determine what books to publish, tells us what coverage to add as we revise our books, and lets us know whether we're meeting your needs as a *For Dummies* reader. You're our most valuable resource, and what you have to say is important to us!

Not on the Web yet? It's easy to get started with *Dummies 101®: The Internet For Windows® 98* or *The Internet For Dummies®3* at local retailers everywhere.

Or let us know what you think by sending us a letter at the following address:

For Dummies Book Registration
Dummies Press
10475 Crosspoint Blvd.
Indianapolis, IN 46256

BESTSELLING
BOOK SERIES